D.B. Cornish

Faculty of Law.

D1145148

CONSTITUTIONAL LAW

CONSTITUTIONAL LAW

AN OUTLINE OF THE LAW AND PRACTICE OF THE
CONSTITUTION, INCLUDING CENTRAL AND LOCAL
GOVERNMENT AND THE CONSTITUTIONAL RELATIONS OF THE
BRITISH COMMONWEALTH.

BY

E. C. S. WADE
M.A. LL.D. (CAMBRIDGE); HON. D.C.L. (DURHAM)
DOWNING PROFESSOR OF THE LAWS OF ENGLAND IN THE UNIVERSITY OF CAMBRIDGE
FELLOW OF GONVILLE AND CAIUS COLLEGE
OF THE INNER TEMPLE, HONORARY BENCHER AND BARRISTER-AT-LAW

AND

G. GODFREY PHILLIPS
C.B.E., M.A., LL.M.
SOMETIME SCHOLAR OF TRINITY COLLEGE, CAMBRIDGE
OF GRAY'S INN, BARRISTER-AT-LAW

FIFTH EDITION
BY
E. C. S. WADE

1724

LONGMANS, GREEN AND CO
LONDON • NEW YORK • TORONTO

LONGMANS, GREEN AND CO LTD
6 & 7 CLIFFORD STREET LONDON W 1
BOSTON HOUSE STRAND STREET CAPE TOWN
531 LITTLE COLLINS STREET MELBOURNE

LONGMANS, GREEN AND CO INC
55 FIFTH AVENUE NEW YORK 3

LONGMANS, GREEN AND CO
20 CRANFIELD ROAD TORONTO 16

ORIENT LONGMANS PRIVATE LTD
CALCUTTA BOMBAY MADRAS
DELHI VIJAYAWADA DACCA

First Edition	.	.	.	May, 1931
First Edition, Revised		.	.	June, 1933
Second Edition		.	.	May, 1935
Third Edition	.	.	.	January, 1946
Fourth Edition	.		.	November, 1950
Fifth Edition	.	.	.	September, 1955
New Impression		.	.	January, 1957

Permission has been given for this
book to be transcribed into Braille

PRINTED IN GREAT BRITAIN
SPOTTISWOODE, BALLANTYNE & CO. LTD.
LONDON & COLCHESTER

PREFACE TO THE FIFTH EDITION

THE five years which have passed since the last edition have been more eventful in the sphere of foreign relations than in constitutional changes in the United Kingdom. The war in Korea called for an enlargement of the purposes of the Supplies and Services Acts which under a Conservative Administration have remained a feature of current constitutional machinery (Part VIII, Chapter 2). The creation of an Atomic Energy Authority, for which the Lord President is the responsible Minister (Part IV, Chapter 1) and the revival of Civil Defence and the Home Guard (Part IX, Chapter 1) are consequences of the permanent state of international conflict. From the point of view of the constitutional lawyer, the Visiting Forces Act, 1952, which was brought into force by Order in Council in 1954, is a significant enactment in so far as it subjects the members of the armed forces of the North Atlantic Treaty Powers (including those of the United States who have hitherto been excluded) as well as members of the forces of the Commonwealth stationed in the United Kingdom to criminal and civil liability, except when in the case of a crime it is committed on duty or against a member of a visiting force or his property (pp. 406-408).

At Westminster the survival of successive Governments holding office with majorities which in the past would have been dismissed as derisory may well be the most important political feature of the last five years, but for the student of the constitution it merely affords an extreme example of the principle of majority rule. An addition has been made at pp. 99–100 to emphasise the constitutional rôle of Her Majesty's Opposition. The occasions on which claims of breach of privilege have been made in the House of Commons in recent years have been frequent; the claim has seldom succeeded. The chapter on this subject (Part II, Chapter 4) has been recast so as to emphasise that the story of *Stockdale* v. *Hansard* is imperfectly told unless it is linked with the *Sheriff of Middlesex Case* (pp. 122–23). That a member may be found guilty of conduct amounting to contempt of the House of Commons without having infringed any parliamentary privilege is a point upon which there is often confusion (p. 125). The long-drawn-out negotiations on the subject of the political activities of civil servants have now been clarified by Treasury ruling (p. 178).

However important the subject of administrative law may be, it seems out of place to treat it extensively in a text-book which attempts to describe all the main features of the constitution in less than 500 pages. Accordingly Part VII, although enlarged from 66 to 76 pages, remains mainly an introduction to the part played by the courts in deciding disputes with administrative authorities. The rules of natural justice, especially the *audi alteram partem* rule, are now discussed separately from the general topic of excess of powers (pp. 310–16). Comparison with any foreign system of administrative law is purposely avoided lest it might confuse the student who is not yet acquainted with the administrative jurisdiction of his own country. Other additions include a reference to the Lands Tribunal (p. 346) the Judges' Rules (p. 366) the modern procedure of habeas corpus (p. 371) and the Courts-Martial Appeal Court (pp. 417–18).

The policy of the Government towards local government reform is still, at the time of writing, undisclosed. Accordingly it will not be possible to discuss here actual proposals as forecasted in the text. It is perhaps safe to predict that there may be changes in the basis of local finance which will follow the introduction of the new rating valuation in 1956. A redistribution of the powers of county and district councils has been confidently predicted. The status of some densely populated urban areas may well be changed, but not necessarily by the enlargement of the existing category of county boroughs.

Constitutional changes have been numerous in the colonial territories as colony after colony has attained a measure of self-government, but it would enlarge this book out of all proportion to give the details of the many and varied constitutions which have issued from, or with the approval of, the Colonial Office. The constitutional law of colonial territories, like that of Commonwealth States, is a special subject, rather than a part of the constitutional law of the United Kingdom. Part X has, therefore, been revised so as to confine it as far as practicable to a general account of the relationship between the United Kingdom and the other realms and territories of the Commonwealth.

There are two topics which, as in the past, are barely mentioned— the impact of the Welfare State on the relationship between the citizen and his government and the constitutional machinery for adjusting labour relations. Plainly both these matters are of great interest and there is a strong case for including them in a study of the constitution. But there are difficulties in including them in a general text-book. The services of the Welfare State are many and complex, but the settlement of disputes in the insurance and similar courts appears to work as smoothly as the most optimistic reformer could have hoped for ten years ago. This must be the excuse for passing over these courts with a bare mention in Part VII, Chapter 5. It will also be noticed that there is no discussion of the topical subject of legal aid. More disputable is the omission of the machinery for the adjustment of industrial disputes. The status of trade unions remains ambiguous in law; their changing rôle under conditions of full employment is relatively undetermined; disputes between the nationalised boards and their staffs may raise serious constitutional issues. Here, one can only acknowledge the existence of constitutional problems as yet unresolved in the sphere of industrial relations. Merely to describe the mediation services of the Ministry of Labour and National Service would be possible. It would nevertheless be inadequate, as it is the policy of the Minister only to intervene in the last resort when the normal negotiating machinery of trade or industry has broken down.

The size of the book has been kept at under 500 pages, although the actual text is increased by 30 pages. This has only been made possible by (1) passing over the repealed Public Authorities Protection Act, 1893, with a bare mention, (2) omitting any discussion of the negotiations which preceded the Indian Independence Act, 1947, and (3) omitting that part of the Appendix which contained the full documents creating a colonial constitution. The first two topics are now purely of historical interest, while colonial constitutions are so diverse in their contents that to reproduce a typical example would be misleading in the light of recent developments in colonial territories.

For this edition I again accept sole responsibility. I have made a selection of the changes and tendencies of substance, deliberately passing over some matters of topical interest. There will always be differences of opinion as to what is of permanent constitutional importance. In total the changes made in the printed text have been considerable. After five years which have seen the accession of a Queen and the passing of two Parliaments a new edition seemed necessary. My thanks are due to several colleagues who by reason of their interest in topics of public law have given me the benefit of their advice and active help. Particularly am I indebted to Dr. R. B. Cooke, Fellow of Gonville and Caius College, and, as on the last occasion, to Mr. T. C. Thomas, Fellow of Trinity Hall and Mr. H. W. R. Wade, Fellow of Trinity College. With these friends I have had the great advantage of discussing parts of the text. Mr. C. J. Staines has contributed the revised Tables of Statutes and Cases as well as the Index. For this help I am grateful.

E. C. S. WADE.

CAMBRIDGE LAW SCHOOL
6 May 1955

TABLE OF CONTENTS

Table of Contents

PART VII. ADMINISTRATIVE LAW

PART VIII. THE CITIZEN AND THE STATE

PART IX. THE ROYAL FORCES; MILITARY AND MARTIAL LAW

PART X. THE BRITISH COMMONWEALTH

PART XI. CHURCH AND STATE 485

APPENDICES

TABLE OF STATUTES

STATUTES OF OTHER PARLIAMENTS

COMMONWEALTH OF AUSTRALIA

DOMINION OF CANADA

EIRE

NEW SOUTH WALES

NOVA SCOTIA

UNION OF SOUTH AFRICA

TABLE OF CASES.

ABBREVIATIONS

C.B.R.	=	Canadian Bar Review
C.L.J.	=	Cambridge Law Journal.
H.C.	=	House of Commons Paper.
H.E.L.	=	*History of English Law*, by Sir William Holdsworth. (Methuen.)
H.L. or H.C. Deb.	=	House of Lords (or Commons) Debates. (Hansard.)
I.C.L.Q.	=	International and Comparative Law Quarterly.
J. & Y.	=	*Constitutional Laws of the British Empire*, by Sir Ivor Jennings and C. M. Young. 2nd Edition. (Clarendon Press.)
K. & L.	=	*Cases in Constitutional Law*, by Sir David Keir and F. H. Lawson. 4th Edition. (Clarendon Press.)
L.Q.R.	=	Law Quarterly Review.
M.L.R.	=	Modern Law Review
M.P.R.	=	Report of Committee on Ministers Powers, 1932 (Cmd. 4060.)
S.I.	=	Statutory Instrument
S.R. and O.	=	Statutory Rule and Order

PART I.

INTRODUCTION.

Law of the Constitution, pp. 1–35, by A. V. Dicey, 9th ed. (Macmillan).

English Constitutional History, pp. 526–39, by F. W. Maitland (Cambridge University Press).

The Law and the Constitution, by Sir Ivor Jennings, 4th ed. (University of London Press).

CHAPTER 1.

DEFINITION AND SOURCES OF CONSTITUTIONAL LAW.

A.

What is Constitutional Law?

BY a constitution is normally meant a document having a special legal sanctity which sets out the framework and the principal functions of the organs of government of a State and declares the principles governing the operation of those organs. Such a document is implemented by decisions of the particular organ, normally the highest court of the State, which has power to interpret its contents. In addition there are gradually evolved a number of conventional rules and practices which serve to attune the operation of the constitution to changing conditions and thereby to avoid, in the main, alterations to a written document which is designed to be permanent in its operation. It is thus that in 1950 a document framed in 1787 remains in force, with few important amendments, as the constitution of the United States of America.

A constitution does not necessarily or usually contain the detailed rules upon which depend the working of the institutions of government. Legal processes, rules for elections, the mode of implementing services provided by the State, so far as these are matters for enactment, are to be found, not in the constitution, but in ordinary statutes made by the legislature within the limits set by the constitution itself. Such statutes can be altered by the same method as that by which they were originally enacted, whereas changes in the constitution call for a more elaborate process. This is to ensure that it shall not be in the power of those who for the time being can command control

What is a Constitution?

of the legislative organ to vary without special consultations and, may be, direct reference to the electors, the system and principles of government which have been set up with solemn formalities by agreement between all major political interests in the State.

Written Constitutions. A documentary constitution will normally reflect theoretical beliefs. It is, therefore, not surprising that in our own country, where progress has been achieved less by adherence to philosophical concepts than by the process of trial and error, no written formulae have been embodied in a code of rules for government. Hence there is no constitutional document which can form the starting-point of a student's instruction in the constitutional law of the United Kingdom, and it is said that there exists no written constitution. Nevertheless, without abandoning our instinctive dislike of declaring our political philosophy in terms of law, written constitutions have been framed for British communities overseas, whether as colonies or as members of the British Commonwealth, in terms of organs and general rules for their operation. It is noteworthy that such constitutions stop short of attempting to enact fundamental concepts in terms of law. Thus they contain no definition of responsible government; they do not guarantee the primary rights of the subject. In effect they provide little more than the machinery of government. They are, however, helpful to the student as showing that the "unwritten" constitution of the United Kingdom can be reduced, at all events in part, to written, *i.e.* specifically enacted, form.

An important consequence of the absence of a written constitution is that there is no part of the machinery of government, whether organs or functions, which is protected against change by the special requirements for altering a written constitution. This gives Parliament, and in particular, the House of Commons, where the Government normally has an adequate majority, a special responsibility not to use its power of changing the law for the purpose of altering those parts of the machinery of government which have acquired through long usage a special value for preserving the accepted form of political institutions. Equally the power is available for the purpose of achieving constitutional amendment with the minimum of formality where it is desired on all sides, as for example when war conditions demand the sacrifice of a well-established rule for the time being. Such flexibility then has its advantages as well as its dangers. With this explanation we can proceed to discuss the question what is constitutional law, with special reference to our own country.

What is Constitutional Law? There is no hard and fast definition of constitutional law. In the generally accepted use of the term it means the rules which regulate the structure of the principal organs of government and their relationship to each other, and determine their principal functions. These rules consist both of legal rules in the strict sense and of usages, commonly called conventions, which without being enacted are accepted as binding by all who are concerned in government. Many of the rules and practices under which our system of government is worked are not part of the law in the sense that their violation may lead directly to proceedings in a court of law. Though the constitutional lawyer is concerned primarily with the legal aspects of government, there is required for an understanding of constitutional law some knowledge of the chief features of constitutional history and of the working of our political institutions. The constitutional lawyer should also be conversant with the relationship between the citizen and the State, and more particularly with what may be called political relationship rather than economic relationship.

Logically it is difficult to justify the selection of subjects which are normally covered in text-books on constitutional law. Generally speaking the books deal with the functions of the State in relation to the maintenance of order and the defence of the realm rather than with its expanding activities in the social and economic sphere. It is in regard to the latter that the average citizen comes face to face with the official, in the course of day-to-day administration, but his fundamental freedoms, to use a topical expression, are more likely to be infringed in relation to the maintenance of order. It is in this sphere that the courts are likely to be in conflict with the Executive, and it is to the courts rather than to Parliament that the citizen resorts for the redress of his individual grievances. Accordingly the constitutional lawyer has always had a particular interest in the means which the law provides for safeguarding individual liberty, whether of the person or of speech. Included in this category are subjects like freedom from arrest and unlawful imprisonment, freedom of expression of opinion, whether by spoken word or writing, by meetings and processions or by exercising free choice as an elector. Nowadays it is also essential to include something about the impact made on a citizen by the administration of the various public services which are the feature of the welfare State. The lawyer is chiefly concerned with the sources of administrative power and with the adjudication of disputes, particularly when the requirements of a public service, such as housing, or the use of land generally, affect the proprietary rights of the private individual. *Scope of Text-books.*

The exclusion from a work on constitutional law of all but the major features of administrative law [1] is based upon convenience rather than upon principle. Some limit must be placed upon the contents of a text-book concerned with outlines. The constitutional lawyer can cover only part of the vast field of governmental activities. Thus he will discuss the organisation of government departments and the constitutional status of Ministers and civil servants, but not *Constitutional Law and Administrative Law.*

[1] For meaning of administrative law, see Part VII., Chap. 1.

the details of services such as education or housing. He will discuss the office of Secretary of State and the principal functions of the Home Secretary, including the preservation of order, but not the detailed regulations which govern the police forces. Under foreign affairs it is necessary to refer briefly to such topics as the treaty-making power and immunities from court process which are more fully covered by writers on public international law. The structure of the principal organs of government will be described, but only principal functions can be treated in any detail in a work on general principles.

B.

Sources of Constitutional Law.[1]

Meaning of Sources.

Reference has been made to those rules of the constitution which lack the direct force of law. These extra-legal rules complicate the task of stating the sources from which constitutional law is drawn. By sources are meant here—though the term is sometimes used to indicate historical origins—the means whereby force and expression are given to law.

Summary of Sources.

The sources of constitutional law are:

(1) *Rules of Law:*
   (a) *Legislation, i.e.* Acts of Parliament and the enactments of other bodies upon which Parliament has conferred power to legislate.
   (b) *Judicial precedent, i.e.* the decisions of the courts expounding the common law or interpreting statutes.
   (c) *Custom, i.e.* the source of, for example, many of the usages of Parliament.
(2) *Conventional rules, i.e.* rules not having the force of law but which can nevertheless not be disregarded since they are sanctioned by public opinion, and perhaps indirectly by law proper.
(3) *Advisory, i.e.* the opinions of writers of authority.

I.

LEGISLATION.

Meaning of Law.

Rules of law may be defined as "rules of civil conduct recognised by the courts." Such rules may be divided into two categories: (a) those prescribed by legislation, and (b) those to be deduced from the decisions of courts of authority.

[1] For a concise account of the sources of English law, including custom, see Part II. of O. Hood Phillips, *A First Book of English Law*, 2nd ed. (Sweet and Maxwell).

When in the late eighteenth century the constitution of the United States of America was drawn up, definition of the powers of government was regarded as all important and was embodied in a formal document, which was, and is, unalterable save by a process which differs entirely from the method of enacting ordinary legislation. The provision of a constitutional code is a *sine qua non* of every new State, and the principal States of the world have adopted constitutions in the form of definite and comprehensive enactments during the last hundred and sixty years. Great Britain is still without a constitution in this sense. Those statutes which are properly regarded as part of constitutional law are not sections of a code. If a collection were made of all the extant enactments (from the Coronation Charter of Henry I. to the present day) which deal with the form and functions of government, the result would present a most imperfect description of the constitution. Moreover, these enactments can each and all of them be repealed by the simple expedient of an Act of Parliament, unlike formal constitutions, which are expressed to be more or less immutable, contemplate no radical changes and usually can only be varied by processes more elaborate than that of amending ordinary statutes.

Unwritten Constitution of Great Britain.

None the less, although Great Britain has no written constitution, a large part of our constitutional law is based on statutes. The importance of this source of constitutional law can be illustrated by reference to a few statutes of major importance, which, though in law in no different position from any other Acts of Parliament, have always been regarded with peculiar veneration by constitutional lawyers and historians.

Some Principal Statutes.

The importance of the first of them, Magna Carta, 1215, and its numerous confirmations in later years lies not so much in the actual contents, since it preceded the era of representative government, as in the fact that it contained a statement of grievances the settlement of which was brought about by a union of important classes in the community. The Charter set out the rights of the various classes of the mediaeval community according to their different needs. The Church was to be free; London and other cities were to enjoy their liberties and customs; merchants were not to be subject to unjust taxation. The famous clauses which laid it down that no man should be punished except by the judgment of his peers or the law of the land, and that to none should justice be denied, have been described as the origin of trial by jury and the writ of habeas corpus. Trial by jury is, however, to be traced to another source, and the writ of habeas corpus had not yet been devised. But these clauses embody a protest against arbitrary punishment and assert the right to a fair trial and to justice which need not be purchased. The observance of the Charter came to be regarded both by lawyers and politicians as a

Magna Carta.

synonym for constitutional government. It was the first attempt to express in legal terms some of the leading ideas of constitutional government.[1]

Petition of Right.

Another document, enrolled on the statute book as 3 Car 1, c 1., is the Petition of Right, 1628, which contained protests against taxation without consent of Parliament, arbitrary imprisonment, the use of commissions of martial law in time of peace and the billeting of soldiers upon private persons. To these protests the King yielded, though the effect of the concessions was weakened by the view Charles I. held that his prerogative powers were not thereby diminished.

Bill of Rights and Act of Settlement.

It is when we come to the Revolution of 1688 that close attention must be paid to the enactments embodying the terms of the settlement which the Lords and the remnants of Charles II.'s last Parliament arranged with William III. and Mary. The principal provisions of the Bill of Rights, 1689, which laid the foundations of the modern constitution by disposing of most of the more extravagant claims of the Stuarts to rule by prerogative right, were

> That the pretended power of suspending of laws or the execution of laws by regal authority without consent of Parliament is illegal.
>
> That the pretended power of dispensing with laws or the execution of laws by regal authority as it hath been assumed and exercised of late is illegal.
>
> That the commission for erecting the late court of commissioners for ecclesiastical causes and all other commissions and courts of like nature are illegal and pernicious.
>
> That the levying money for or to the use of the crown by pretence of prerogative without grant of Parliament for longer time or in other manner than the same is or shall be granted is illegal.
>
> That it is the right of the subjects to petition the king and all commitments and prosecutions for such petitioning are illegal.
>
> That the raising or keeping of a standing army within the kingdom in time of peace unless it be with consent of Parliament is against law.
>
> That the subjects which are Protestants may have arms for their defence suitable to their conditions and as allowed by law.
>
> That election of members of Parliament ought to be free.
>
> That the freedom of speech and debates or proceedings in Parliament ought not to be impeached or questioned in any court or place out of Parliament.
>
> That excessive bail ought not to be required nor excessive fines imposed nor cruel and unusual punishments inflicted.
>
> That jurors ought to be duly impanelled and returned and jurors which pass upon men in trials for high treason ought to be freeholders.
>
> That all grants and promises of fines and forfeitures of particular persons before conviction are illegal and void.
>
> And that for redress of all grievances and for the amending, strengthening and preserving of the laws Parliament ought to be held frequently.

[1] *H.E.L.*, Vol. III., p. 215.

The Act of Settlement, 1701, not only provided for the succession to the Throne, but added certain important provisions complementary to those contained in the Bill of Rights, especially—

That whosoever shall hereafter come to the possession of this crown shall join in communion with the Church of England as by law established.

That in case the crown and imperial dignity of this realm shall hereafter come to any person, not being a native of this kingdom of England, this nation be not obliged to engage in any war or the defence of any dominions or territories which do not belong to the crown of England, without consent of Parliament.

That no person who has an office or place of profit under the king or receives a pension from the crown shall be capable of serving as a member of the House of Commons.

That after the said limitation shall take effect as aforesaid, judges' commissions be made *quamdiu se bene gesserint*, and their salaries ascertained and established, but upon the address of both Houses of Parliament it may be lawful to remove them.

That no pardon under the great seal of England be pleadable to an impeachment by the Commons in Parliament.

The Bill of Rights and the Act of Settlement mark the victory of Parliament. In the place of Kings who claimed to govern by the prerogative was developed a constitutional monarchy with the result that government is by and through Parliament. It is, however, to be noted that there is nothing in these statutes to secure the responsibility of the King's Ministers to Parliament and indeed the exclusion of all holders of office under the King from membership of the House of Commons quickly proved a stumbling block to the recognition of that responsibility and was modified early in the next reign.

It is not intended to catalogue other principal statutes that form part of constitutional law. To illustrate that statute law is still a vital and important source of constitutional law it is sufficient to mention the Parliament Act, 1911,[1] the Supreme Court of Judicature Act, 1925, the Statute of Westminster, 1931,[2] the Ministers of the Crown Act, 1937,[3] and the Indian Independence Act, 1947.[4]

II.

CASE LAW.

The other source of rules of law are the decisions of courts of authority, *i.e.* the superior courts of record, which are stated in authoritative form in the law reports. Judge-made, or judiciary, law is derived from two sources:

(1) The common law proper. This consists of the laws and customs of the realm which have received judicial recognition in the

---

[1] P. 103, *post.*   [2] Part X., Chap. 3, B.
[3] P. 85, *post.*   [4] Part X., Chap. 3, D.

reasons given from early times by the judges for their decisions in particular cases coming before them. In the reports of these cases governing the particular set of facts before the court are to be found authoritative expositions of the law. In the sphere of constitutional law here are to be found much of the law relating to the prerogatives of the Crown,[1] the ordinary remedies of the subject against illegal acts by public officers,[2] as well as the remedies by way of judicial order of prohibition, certiorari and mandamus [2] and the writ of habeas corpus,[3] which affords protection against unlawful invasion of personal liberty by the Executive.

Examples of judicial decisions are *The Case of Impositions* (1606), 2 St. Tr. 371; K. & L. 48, which defined the scope of the arbitrary power of the Crown to impose duties for the regulation of trade,[4] or the modern case which decided how the discretionary powers of the Crown (the royal prerogative) are limited by a statute conferring similar powers; *Attorney-General* v. *De Keyser's Royal Hotel, Ltd.*, [1920] A.C. 508; K. & L. 86.[5] Again, it is a rule of the common law that the Crown can do no wrong, a rule which long enabled government departments to a large extent to escape legal liability for the wrongful acts of their employees. This rule depended for its validity on the decisions of the courts and it was not until 1947 that the Crown Proceedings Act removed this immunity of the Crown, subject to important limitations where the common law rule still prevails.[6]

(2) Interpretation of statute law. The task of the judge is in theory confined to an exposition of the meaning of the enacted law, and in the case of subordinate legislation (statutory instruments made under the authority of Acts of Parliament) also to an enquiry into the validity of the enactment. In practice, however, judges make law by interpretation. Since most of the powers of government departments and local government authorities are derived from statute, this type of judge-made law is of greater importance in the sphere of public law to-day than the common law. Indeed, generally speaking, as legislation increases in volume—and in the nineteenth and twentieth centuries the output of general legislation has been stupendous—the tendency is to confine the work of the courts more and more to the interpretation of statute law.

III.

CONVENTIONS OF THE CONSTITUTION AS A SOURCE OF LAW.

There are many rules and precepts to be mastered by men and women engaged in public life, as well as by students of constitutional

---

[1] Part IV., Chap. 1, C.   [2] Part VII., Chaps. 2–3.   [3] Part VIII., Chap. 1, A.
[4] P. 34, *post.*   [5] P. 145, *post.*   [6] Part VII., Chap. 4.

law, which are not, at all events directly, part of the law of England in the sense that their validity can be the subject of proceedings in a court of law. In particular, breach of such rules will not result in a civil action or criminal prosecution being directed against the offender. Dicey named these rules conventions of the constitution. Can they properly be called law at all? If the answer is yes, he argues that they are a source of constitutional law. But other writers regard them as no more than practices which experience shows to be necessary for developing, within the law, existing political institutions. As such they are practices which are regarded as binding.

Conventions are numerous and vary in character from a rule which is as invariably observed as if it was enforceable by legal process to a practice which will be abandoned when there is a change in the circumstances from which it arose.

There are many important conventions which govern the exercise of the royal prerogative, and in particular the whole system of cabinet government has been evolved without changes in the rules of law (in the narrow sense) by building up a body of rules of conduct which prescribe within the legal framework what is and is not constitutionally proper.[1] Other examples are to be found in the sphere of political relationship between the members of the British Commonwealth, especially the rules governing the relations between the United Kingdom and the other States. The law and custom of Parliament contains much that is based on precedent alone and has never been the subject of formal promulgation either by Parliament (itself the highest court of law) or by the Supreme Court of Judicature.

The existence of conventions is due to the need for rules to supplement the legal framework of the constitution. Sometimes an Act of Parliament, as did the Statute of Westminster, 1931, and the Ministers of the Crown Act, 1937, may recognise or even reduce to legal form conventional rules. Conventions form a series of rules and practices for the guidance of those who run the machine of government. They are not to be found in the statute book or the law reports. Judges may from time to time recognise their existence, *e.g.* that a Minister of the Crown is answerable to Parliament, but they are not directly required to adjudicate upon their validity or to enforce them by a legal sanction.

The claim of conventions to be considered as part of constitutional law rests largely upon the regularity with which they are in practice followed, and the lawyer must consider the consequences of disregarding them. These consequences are, in the case of Ministers,

---

[1] The terms "constitutional" and "unconstitutional" are not in practice confined to describing obedience to or disregard of conventions as the case may be. The conduct of a Minister is sometimes condemned as being unconstitutional when it involves a breach of law in the narrow sense, *e.g.* acting in excess of authority conferred on him by an Act of Parliament.

loss of office or at least of reputation, and in the last resort fear of revolution. In the sphere of Commonwealth affairs secession is the ultimate sanction. But none of these consequences really explain why the conventional rule is normally followed. The explanation lies in the desire to maintain orderly government. Thus the resolve of Ministers to carry with them the House of Commons, as reflecting public opinion, is the principal factor in securing obedience to those conventions which govern the conduct of Ministers.

Conventions are a mixture of rules based on custom and expediency, but sometimes their source is express agreement. Students must turn to a wealth of material to trace conventions to their source; for example, the letters of Queen Victoria, biographies, such as Sir Harold Nicholson's *George V*, the memoirs of Cabinet Ministers, parliamentary debates, leading articles in the press. Here it will suffice to give three illustrations of conventions as a source of constitutional law.

1. In the sphere of ministerial conduct a Government whose policy in a major matter ceases to command the support of the House of Commons must, through the Prime Minister, either tender its resignation to the Sovereign, or seek to reverse opinion in the House of Commons by advising a dissolution of Parliament and so appeal to the electorate to renew their confidence in the Government.

2. In Commonwealth relations the Sovereign in all matters appertaining to a member State acts on the advice of the Cabinet Ministers in that State, to the exclusion of seeking other advice in particular from the Ministers in the United Kingdom Government.

3. In the parliamentary sphere the House of Commons will not allow any amendment of a financial provision in a Bill to be made by the House of Lords.

It will be seen that there is common to each of these three rules the desire to take the course which ensures that the will of the electorate shall prevail. Such is the nature of responsible government in the democratic way of life.

IV.

TEXT-BOOK WRITERS.

Before leaving the subject of sources, reference must be made to text-book writers. The authority of a legal text-book as a source of law is confined to the extent to which it reproduces the law as enacted by the legislature or decided by the courts. But the lack of interpretation of legislation and the absence of authoritative pronouncements by the courts on matters not covered by legislation are often remedied by the opinions of text-book writers of established reputation; these opinions are not law until accepted as such by the courts. Nevertheless in the field of constitutional law the scope for pronouncement by text-book writers is larger than in any other branch of law with the exception of international law. This is due partly to the existence of conventions which do not require enforcement through the courts, and partly to the fact that many of the problems of constitutional law are not in practice the subject-matter of litigation, even though they relate to law proper. Thus the duty of the Speaker of the House of Commons in regard to the certification of money Bills is defined by the Parliament Act, 1911, but it is probably safe to predict that the courts will never be called upon to interpret these provisions. It is left to text-book writers to pronounce upon their effect. More reliance, then, may be placed upon text-books as a quasi-authoritative source than is the case, for example, with the law of contract. It must, however, be borne in mind that unanimity is not to be expected in the views expressed upon controversial topics. Nevertheless, such works as Erskine May's *Parliamentary Practice* or the critical accounts of the government of the country, such as that given in Bagehot's *The English Constitution*—a masterpiece in its day, and still in many respects not out of date—or Sir Ivor Jennings' *Cabinet Government*—are consulted with a confidence which the practitioner of law cannot afford to give to text-books on branches of private law, where conclusions must be supported by the authority of a statute or a judicial decision.

Writers of text-books on the constitution fall into three classes, namely, historians, political scientists, and lawyers. The historian, to quote Dicey, "is primarily occupied with ascertaining the steps by which a constitution has grown to be what it is." [1] He is mainly concerned with the value of past experience. While it is not to be suggested that the past does not contain many lessons for the present, particularly in an age when respect for tradition is at a discount, it is equally true that, for example, we can find little that is helpful in understanding the position and working of the present House of Commons in an historical account of the Witenagemot or of the Commune Concilium Regni. On the other hand it is essential for an understanding of the constitution to study the development of its organs and, for example, a clear appreciation of the seventeenth-century constitutional struggle is necessary for mastering the subject of the royal prerogative as it exists to-day. — *Historians.*

The political scientist is concerned with the problems of government, as the lawyer is with the rules. The former is naturally attracted by the possibility of deducing abstract principles in relation to the science of government. The task of the student of constitutional law is to master the nature and operations of the existing — *Political Scientists.*

[1] *The Law of the Constitution*, p. 15.

organs of government rather than to attempt generalisations. Nevertheless, the relation between the theory of government and constitutional law is a close one.

Lawyers.   Lawyers who attempt the task of depicting the law of the constitution are handicapped by the unreality of many of the legal terms which they must of necessity employ. For example, it is a correct statement of law to say that the Queen is the fountain of justice, or that the Queen can do no wrong. Yet everybody knows that the Queen does not sit as judge in her own courts, and that illegal acts are sometimes done in the name of the Queen by her servants. The training of the lawyer accustoms him to respect rules of law, irrespective of their political background. He may be impatient with the actions of politicians, but he cannot disregard the activities of the legislature; its processes are of concern to him as affording the means of amending the law. Without his assistance policy could not be transformed into terms of law. Traditionally he is suspicious of executive government with its wide discretionary powers and he watches jealously each attempt to oust the jurisdiction of the courts. The study of constitutional law is vital to an understanding of these matters and it is as well to approach the subject without stressing too much the origins portrayed by the historian or the speculative thinking of the political scientist. So the lawyer may claim to be a guide to the student, provided that he avoids a too legalistic approach to those matters which lie in the field of political conventions.

CHAPTER 2.

THE NATURE OF THE CONSTITUTION.

It has been said that the constitution has no separate existence since it is part of the ordinary law of the land. It is true that there is no special source giving expression to the rules of the constitution in the form of a code which is unalterable save by the act of a special constituent assembly or a specific reference to popular vote. There is, however, a body of law which forms the constitution, partly statutory, partly common law and partly conventional. It would be possible to enact this body of law in the form of a code. Even conventions are capable of enactment. Thus Eire gave statutory authority to the doctrine of ministerial responsibility which in the United Kingdom and most States of the British Commonwealth rests upon convention. Does Constitution Exist?

The British constitution is flexible, not in the sense that it is unstable but in that its principles are alterable and constitutional rules can be changed by the ordinary process of an Act of Parliament or the establishment by general acceptance of a new convention. Despite, or perhaps because of, this flexibility the constitution has so far escaped those radical changes and convulsions which so frequently occur in countries with rigid constitutional codes. Capacity for Development.

For over two hundred years the constitution has been adapting itself to new conditions, usually a little behind the trend of expressed contemporary opinion. In the result there has been a complete change almost imperceptible at any given stage, so gradual has been the evolution from the personal supremacy of the monarch to the collective ascendancy of the political executive—a change which has been marked by the retention of existing forms and organs. Much of the structure is now mere form which is tolerated and indeed venerated because it represents historic continuity. The form is, however, remote from the practical working of the constitution. The framework of the constitution has been empirically constructed in marked contrast both to the carefully devised machinery of continental constitutions and to the provisions of the federal constitutions of the United States, of Canada and of Australia. Process of Evolution.

In the place of kings who governed by the prerogative we have a constitutional monarchy. The Queen is the head of the State and government is carried on in her name, but it is government by an Executive answerable to and dependent for its office upon Parliament. After the Revolution Settlement of 1689 the King could Constitutional Monarchy and Parliamentary Government.

govern only through Ministers who had the confidence of Parliament. This, though it was not at first realised, was the result of the Bill of Rights and Act of Settlement. The prerogative of the Crown came to be exercised by responsible Ministers. Successive extensions of the franchise have made the House of Commons more representative, while social and economic changes have involved widespread development effected by statute in the organisation and functions of government. This process of political evolution has avoided becoming a revolution. But parliamentary government is not to be explained solely in terms of law and convention. To quote from the Report of the Joint Committee of Parliament on Indian Constitutional Reform, 1934:

> Parliamentary government, as it is understood in the United Kingdom, works by the interaction of four essential factors; the principle of majority rule; the willingness of the minority for the time being to accept the decisions of the majority; the existence of great political parties divided by broad issues of policy, rather than by sectional interests; and finally the existence of a mobile body of political opinion, owing no permanent allegiance to any party and therefore able, by its instinctive reaction against extravagant movements on one side or the other, to keep the vessel on an even keel.

Nowadays the concentration of political power in the hands of the Executive, including as it does the direction of the whole economic life of the community, makes it more important than ever to emphasize that majority rule is only tolerable because of the dependence of the rulers upon the last of these factors. Free elections, guaranteed by law to occur at least every five years, and by force of public opinion at a lesser interval, ensure free expression for the mobile body of political opinion whose reactions are watched by every Government, no matter the size of the majority it presently commands in the House of Commons.

Functions of Government. It is customary to divide functions of government into three classes, legislative, executive (or administrative) and judicial. It is not always easy, or indeed possible, to determine under which head an act properly falls, but the organs which mainly perform these functions are distinguishable.

The Legislative Function and the Legislature. The legislative function primarily involves the enactment, after proper scrutiny, of general rules of conduct usually proposed to Parliament by the Executive, but there are types of legislation which determine administrative organisation or procedure rather than prescribe rules of conduct. In the United Kingdom the Legislature consists of the Queen in Parliament, and Parliament sits in two Houses, the House of Lords and the House of Commons. Since the passing of the Parliament Act, 1911,[1] legislative supremacy is in fact exercised

P. 103, *post.*

by the House of Commons. The Queen is an integral member of the Legislature and her assent is required to all Acts of Parliament. As, however, she only acts on the advice of her Cabinet, her assent has been a formality since the development of the principle of ministerial responsibility. A Ministry which has successfully piloted a measure through both Houses of Parliament will never, it may be assumed, advise Her Majesty to withhold her assent to that measure becoming law. The power of the House of Lords to reject measures passed by the House of Commons is limited. There is no power to reject money Bills, and other public Bills, with the exception of a Bill to prolong the duration of Parliament, can only be delayed for a period of one year. Nevertheless, the House of Lords is still an active part of the Legislature. Important Bills which do not involve political controversy are often introduced in that House. As a revising chamber the relief which it affords to a Government which has embarked upon a heavy programme of legislation is considerable, especially when it becomes necessary to limit debate on a Bill in the House of Commons. The amount of time devoted by Parliament to the legislative programme seldom exceeds half the number of days in a session, for the Legislature has other functions to perform. There is the grand inquest of the nation where policy and administration are debated. Indeed the primary function of Parliament is the redress of grievances and thus results its pressure on the Executive. It maintains the Executive in power by endorsing, not without amendment of detail, its legislative programme, and it is ever watchful of administration.

Although some writers attempt to distinguish between the executive and administrative function by confining the first to matters of policy and the second to administration, there is in practice no true distinction. Administration necessarily raises questions of policy, just as policy can only be implemented by administrative action. The Executive Function and the Executive.

The executive function embraces the direction of general policy. This includes the initiation of legislation, the maintenance of order and the promotion of social and economic welfare, and indeed all administration, though some public services are administered not by the departments of the Central Government, but by local authorities [1] and independent statutory bodies.[2] The majority of the powers of the Executive are to-day derived from statutes, though some of the most important are prerogative powers of the Crown [3] based on common law, *e.g.* the conduct of foreign affairs, the summoning and dissolution of Parliament, appointments to the public services, and the control of the armed forces of the Crown. The Sovereign is in law the head of the Executive. The prerogative powers and some statutory powers are vested in the Sovereign or the Sovereign in

---

[1] Part VI., Chap. 2.   [2] Part IV., Chap. 11, A.
[3] Part IV., Chap. 1, C.

Council,[1] but, like those many statutory powers conferred directly upon Ministers, they are in fact exercised by the Government. The Government consists of Ministers who are by convention members of one or other House of Parliament.

The Party System.

The political party having a majority in the House of Commons is entitled to form a ministry. This presents little difficulty when the House of Commons is divided into two parties. The two-party system "has been the normal type to which after occasional interludes we have regularly reverted, for the very reason that it has always centred round the business of maintaining a majority in Parliament for a Government or securing its displacement by another Government." [2] Twice in the present century the substantial representation in the Commons of three political parties has resulted in the leaders of a party holding ministerial office without that party obtaining a clear majority of seats, and, therefore, of supporters in the House of Commons, over the other two parties.[3] The great advantage of the two-party system is to ensure that the Government is vigilantly criticised by an opposition which is waiting to succeed to office and therefore criticises with a sense of responsibility. Under a two-party system minority government is impossible.

Recent Trends.

Of late years the party system has not been working normally. National Governments composed of members of all or more than one of the major political parties have held office on five occasions since 1918. Their formation has been due to grave emergencies in foreign or economic affairs, which caused party differences to be sunk in the interests of national unity. However inevitable and advantageous this form of government has been, it has resulted in depriving the House of Commons of an effective opposition ready to succeed the Government, and this has undoubtedly weakened the control of Parliament over the Executive. In 1945 the Government which was returned to power at the end of the war with Germany commanded so large a majority in the House of Commons that the role of the Opposition was difficult to maintain; as a result of the general election of 1950 this majority declined to a mere handful. In the next year after another election there was a change of government but the Conservatives were only maintained in office by a majority of less than twenty. In theory neither very large nor very small majorities are favourable to the working of the two-party system. The latter in particular militates against the execution of whatever policy the Government thinks is best, while the former

[1] Part IV., Chap. 1, B.

[2] *Thoughts on the Constitution*, by L. S. Amery, 2nd ed., at p. 43 (Oxford University Press).

[3] In the nineteenth century it was not unusual for the Government not to have a majority, *e.g.* Lord John Russell's Ministry in 1846, and Mr. Gladstone's Ministry in 1892–94.

encourages irresponsibility in the Opposition since it has no early prospect of reversing the policy of its opponents in office. "We are the masters now" is not a cry which is appropriate to our constitutional system, no matter how much it may reflect the views of the electorate.

By convention the Queen is advised on all matters by the Cabinet. The acts of the Queen become the acts of her Ministers. The Cabinet consists of the principal Ministers of the Crown, who are invited to sit in the Cabinet by the Prime Minister. A few Cabinet Ministers have no departmental responsibilities, but the majority are entrusted with a particular branch of governmental activity and preside over the government departments which are staffed by civil servants. Thus as members of the Cabinet the principal Ministers advise the Sovereign collectively, while individually they are responsible to the Queen and to Parliament for the conduct of a department. Junior Ministers have departmental duties but are not members of the Cabinet. The Cabinet decides major questions of policy. The departments carry out that policy by administering the law and devising measures to be presented to Parliament for enactment as law. Routine matters are decided in the department without reference to the Cabinet. Inasmuch as the Legislature rarely legislates without the guiding hand of the Government, the Cabinet in practice can prevent any legislation being passed by Parliament which it, or even the Minister chiefly concerned, does not wish to see passed.

The Cabinet System.

In recent years there has been tried the experiment of entrusting a public service to an independent authority set up by Parliament, but not responsible to Parliament through a Minister of the Crown. The National Assistance Board for the administration of supplementary relief is an example of such a body administering a service of a strictly governmental character. Other examples are to be found in the British Broadcasting Corporation and the public corporations which administer the nationalised industries of coal, electricity, gas and transport.[1]

Independent Authorities.

The judicial function is to declare what the law is and to apply the law with a view to its observance. It usually involves also the ascertainment of facts. The judicial function must be invoked by the subject or by the Executive before it can be exercised. The Judges declare the common law and interpret statutes. It is no part of their function to give advice on hypothetical cases, but only to resolve the disputes of litigants. Nor are they concerned with the policy of the legislature, but only to interpret what has been decreed by its enactments.

The Judicial Function and the Judiciary.

Certain legislative and administrative functions are also performed by the Judiciary, *e.g.* the enactment of rules of court and the

[1] Part IV., Chap. 11, A.

administration of the estates of deceased persons. The courts are the Queen's Courts, but the Queen does not exercise justice in person. The final court of appeal in the United Kingdom is the House of Lords. The principal court of first instance with general civil jurisdiction is the High Court of Justice, from which an appeal lies to the Court of Appeal and thence by leave to the House of Lords. From the criminal courts of Assizes and Quarter Sessions, where all serious cases are tried on indictment by judge and jury, an appeal lies to the Court of Criminal Appeal and thence on important points of law only to the House of Lords.[1] The vast majority in number of criminal cases are tried by summary adjudication in the magistrates' courts. Judges of the Superior Courts are independent of the Executive. They are appointed by the Crown, but they hold office during good behaviour, being removable by an address from both Houses of Parliament. While, however, the independence of the higher Judiciary is strictly preserved, many justiciable issues are referred to administrative courts; the composition, procedure and degree of independence of such courts have often been criticised, but they have become an established part of the machinery of justice and in general they operate subject to the supervision of the High Court which can restrain excesses or abuses of jurisdiction, unless such supervision is expressly excluded by statute.

[1] For organisation of the Courts, see Part V., Chap. 1; at County Quarter Sessions a bench of justices presided over by a chairman with legal qualification takes the place of the single judge.

PART II.

GENERAL PRINCIPLES.

Law of the Constitution, by A. V. Dicey, 9th ed. (Macmillan).
    Part I.—The Sovereignty of Parliament.
    Part II.—The Rule of Law, Chaps. IV., XI. and XIII.
    Part III.—The Law and Conventions of the Constitution.
    Introduction by E. C. S. Wade, pp. xxv to CXLVI.

The Law and the Constitution, by Sir Ivor Jennings, 4th ed. (University of London Press).

Thoughts on the Constitution, 2nd ed., by L. S. Amery (Oxford University Press).

History of English Law, by Sir William Holdsworth, Vol. X (Methuen).

INTRODUCTORY.

BEFORE examining more closely the organs of government it will be convenient to study four topics which throw light upon every branch of constitutional law. In Chapter 1 of this Part there will be examined the doctrine of the separation of powers. Convenient though it is to divide the main organs of government into three, the doctrine in its application to modern government does not mean that a rigid threefold classification of their functions is posssible. Its value lies in the emphasis placed upon those checks and balances which are essential to prevent an abuse of the enormous powers which are in the hands of rulers. *(Scope of Part II.)*

In Chapter 2 there will be discussed the supremacy of Parliament, the organ of government which exercises the legislative function; under a system of parliamentary government the House of Commons politically is supreme in that it can in the last resort dismiss the Government which exercises the executive function. Moreover Parliament makes and can repeal the laws which the Judiciary can only interpret. In Chapter 3 there will be discussed the rule of law. We shall observe the effect upon the constitution of the extension of functions of government since 1885 when Dicey first published *The Law of the Constitution* and gave his threefold interpretation of the rule of law as a characteristic of the constitution. In Chapter 4, under the title, Conventions of the Constitution, there will be explained more fully the nature of the constitutional conventions which have already been mentioned as one of the sources of constitutional law.

In Part III. the structure and functions of Parliament will be examined in detail. Similarly in Part IV. there will be examined the *(The Remainder of the Book.)*

structure and some of the functions of the organs of the Central Government, and in Part V. the organisation of the courts and the exercise of the judicial function. Part VI. outlines the structure and functions of the elected councils which administer local government services as general purpose authorities; there are other regional and local authorities responsible for particular services, such as hospitals and river drainage which are not included under the title, local government. In Part VII., Administrative Law, we shall return to those problems (foreshadowed by the study of the separation of powers) which arise from the relationship of one organ of government to another and the exercise by the Executive of legislative and judicial functions. It is here that we shall discuss the chief functions of the Judiciary in relation to administration. In Part VIII. there will be examined the fundamental political rights of the citizen, freedom of person, freedom of discussion and freedom of public meeting. Part IX. deals with the organisation and discipline of the armed forces of the Crown and the topic of martial law; Part X. with the British Commonwealth, the Colonies and Protectorates; Part XI. with religious bodies and the special status of the established Church of England.

CHAPTER 1.

THE DOCTRINE OF SEPARATION OF POWERS.

Meaning of Separation of Powers.

IT has been seen that it is customary to divide the powers of government into three, legislative, executive and judicial. There will now be discussed the doctrine of separation of powers which has played so prominent a part in the theory and practice of constitution making and particularly influenced the framers of the constitution of the United States. To avoid confusion of thought it is important to note that separation of powers may mean three different things: (*a*) that the same persons should not form part of more than one of the three organs of government, *e.g.* that Ministers should not sit in Parliament; (*b*) that one organ of government should not control or interfere with the exercise of its function by another organ, *e.g.* that the Judiciary should be independent of the Executive or that Ministers should not be responsible to Parliament; (*c*) that one organ of government should not exercise the functions of another, *e.g.* that Ministers should not have legislative powers. In considering each of these three aspects of separation of powers we shall consider two quite different questions: (i) How far is there separation of powers in the British constitution to-day? (ii) How far is separation of powers desirable?

The doctrine of the separation of powers was first formulated by the French jurist, Montesquieu,[1] who based his exposition on the British constitution of the first part of the eighteenth century as he understood it. His division of powers did not closely correspond except in name with the classification which has become traditional; for, although he followed the usual meaning of legislative and judicial powers, by executive power he meant only "the power executing matters falling within the law of nations," *i.e.* making war and peace, sending and receiving ambassadors, establishing order, preventing invasion. His statement of the doctrine has been thus interpreted: If the Executive and the Legislature are the same person or body of persons, there must be a danger of the Legislature enacting oppressive laws which the Executive will administer to attain its own ends. Particularly is this true of a personal Executive, not responsible in law to the courts, or politically to a representative assembly. For laws to be enforced by the same body that enacts them results in arbitrary rule and makes the judge a legislator rather than an interpreter of the law. If the one body or person could exercise both executive and judicial powers in the same matter, there would be arbitrary power which would amount to complete tyranny, if legislative powers also were added to the powers of that person or body. Montesquieu did not, it may be surmised, mean that Legislature and Executive ought to have no influence or control over the acts of each other, but only that neither should exercise the whole power of the other.[2]

Though the doctrine was based on a study of the constitution of the United Kingdom, it is in the constitution of the United States rather than our own even in the eighteenth century that its influence can best be seen. Montesquieu, viewing the constitution as a foreign observer, saw the triumph of Parliament in 1689 and its achievement of legislative supremacy with the passing of the Bill of Rights. He saw too that the King still exercised executive power and that the independence of the Judiciary was solemnly declared. A provision of the Act of Settlement which was repealed before it came into force had attempted to exclude Ministers from the House of Commons. Before the eighteenth century was over, however, there had been established in England the Cabinet system under which the King governed only through Ministers who were members of and responsible to Parliament. George III. exercised personal rule, but this took the form of influencing Parliament through the distribution of offices and by the control exercised by the Crown and the Crown's

---

[1] *Esprit des Lois*, Book XI., Chap. 6.

[2] Sir Ivor Jennings, *The Law and the Constitution*, 4th ed., App. 1; Sir Carleton Allen, *Law and Orders*, Chap. 1; "Separation of Powers," by J. Finkelman, 2 *Toronto Law Journal*, p. 313.

supporters over membership of the House of Commons. With the redistribution of seats, including the abolition of rotten boroughs, and the extension of the franchise by the Reform Act of 1832, there began to disappear government by influence and parliamentary government was securely established.

Checks and Balances.

In many continental constitutions separation of powers has meant an unhampered Executive; in England it means little more than an independent Judiciary. It is in the United States that there is a real division of powers between the three organs and strict adherence to the doctrine of separation of powers. The framers of the American Constitution intended that the balance of powers should be attained by checks and balances between separate organs of government. They imitated the form of the English constitution. But by this time in England executive power was passing from Crown to Cabinet. They were influenced too by the form of colonial charters under which separation of executive and legislative functions was a prominent feature.

Executive in U.S.A.

In the United States executive power is vested in the President. The so-called Cabinet consists of the heads of the chief departments (eleven in number), each being personally responsible to the President alone for his own department, but not to Congress (Senate and House of Representatives) or to his colleagues. The President holds office for a fixed term; he is not necessarily of the same political party as the majority in either or both Houses of Congress; he is not removable by an adverse vote; his powers are declared by the Constitution.

Legislature in U.S.A.

Neither the President nor members of his Cabinet can sit or vote in Congress; they have no responsibility for initiating Bills or securing their passage through Congress. The President may recommend legislation in his message to Congress, but he cannot compel it to pay heed to his recommendations. He can, however, veto legislation which has been passed by Congress. Treaties are negotiated by the Executive, but require the approval of a two-thirds majority of the Senate (Upper House). The Senate, though elected, is an undying body since only one-third of its membership falls vacant every two years. The House of Representatives is elected for a fixed term of two years and cannot be dissolved in the interval. As in all countries with federal constitutions, there are in the United States fundamental laws which cannot be altered by a simple vote of the Legislature. The Judiciary is not only independent of the Executive, but acquired at an early date the power to declare laws invalid as being contrary to the constitution. The Federal Supreme Court may declare the actions either of the Executive or the Legislature to be unconstitutional. Despite this rigid demarcation of functions it may be remarked that in practice separation tends to break down.

A clear description of the difference between the Presidential System and the Cabinet system is given in the following extract from the pen of the first Earl of Balfour in Bagehot's *The English Constitution* (Introduction to 1928 edition):

"Under the Presidential system the effective head of the national administration is elected for a fixed term. He is practically irremovable. Even if he is proved to be inefficient, even if he becomes unpopular, even if his policy is unacceptable to his countrymen, he and his methods must be endured until the moment comes for a new election.

"He is aided by Ministers, who, however able and distinguished, have no independent political status, have probably had no congressional (*i.e.* parliamentary) training, and are by law precluded from obtaining any during their term of office.

"Under the Cabinet system everything is different. The head of the administration, commonly called the Prime Minister (though he has no statutory position), is selected for the place on the ground that he is the statesman best qualified to secure a majority in the House of Commons. He retains it only so long as that support is forthcoming; he is the head of his party. He must be a member of one or other of the two Houses of Parliament; and he must be competent to lead the House to which he belongs. While the Cabinet Ministers of a President are merely his officials, the Prime Minister is *primus inter pares* in a Cabinet of which (according to peace-time practice) every member must, like himself, have had some parliamentary experience and gained some parliamentary reputation. The President's powers are defined by the Constitution, and for their exercise within the law he is responsible to no man. The Prime Minister and his Cabinet, on the other hand, are restrained by no written Constitution: but they are faced by critics and rivals whose position, though entirely unofficial, is as constitutional as their own; they are subject to a perpetual stream of unfriendly questions, to which they must make public response, and they may at any moment be dismissed from power by a hostile vote."

Lord Balfour proceeds to emphasise the weakness of the President's position through his narrow prerogatives defined by the constitution. The President is unable to influence legislation or taxation in face of a hostile Legislature which he cannot dissolve.

Enough has been said of the organs of the constitution and the working of the Cabinet system to attempt to answer in relation to the Legislature and the Executive the three questions that may be asked in ascertaining whether there is in the constitution of the United Kingdom a separation of powers:

(*a*) *Do the same persons or bodies form part of both the Legislature and Executive?* The form of the constitution shows the Sovereign as the head of the Executive and also an integral part of the Legislature.[1] More important, however, is the convention so essential to the working of the Cabinet government which secures that Ministers should be members of one or other House of Parliament. Their

[1] P. 15, *ante.*

presence in Parliament makes a reality of their responsibility to Parliament and facilitates co-operation between them and the Legislature, both features which are vital to parliamentary government. Only those who are prepared to abandon the Cabinet system and parliamentary government, as we understand it, will criticise this departure from a strict separation of powers.

Parliamentary Supremacy.

(b) *Does the Legislature control the Executive or the Executive control the Legislature?* Here again there is no separation of powers. The House of Commons ultimately controls the Executive. Strong government has been combined with responsible government by ensuring that Parliament, while leaving the task of governing to the Government, can insist on the dismissal of a Government which does not obtain parliamentary support for its general policy. Even in the eighteenth century Montesquieu's interpretation was inapplicable in practice. Once it had been established that Parliament alone could make laws and vote taxes, it became recognised, gropingly at first in the reigns of William III. and Anne, more clearly under the early Hanoverian Kings, that a Government could only act with strength and speed if it could command the support of Parliament. That support was obtained by entrusting the exercise of the powers of the Crown to Ministers who could command a majority in Parliament. This ensures co-operation between the Government and the Commons.

Influence of Cabinet over Parliament.

To emphasise, however, that Parliament is supreme is not to give the whole picture of the relationship between Legislature and Executive. So long as the Cabinet retains the confidence of Parliament, it exercises a decisive voice in regard to the passage of legislation. Major Acts of the Legislature must in practice originate with the approval, and normally nowadays on the initiative of a Minister of the Crown who acts in important matters of policy with the support and prior approval of the Cabinet. Since the House of Commons is divided into only two main political parties, the leaders of the majority party who form the Cabinet exercise real control over the House. Parliament can dismiss a Ministry, but a political party is unwilling to vote against its leaders. The defeat of a Ministry involves a dissolution of Parliament and the risk that a general election will result in power passing to the opposition party. Thus while Parliament is supreme in that it can make or unmake a Government, a Government once in power tends to control Parliament. In truth there is no separation of powers, but rather a system which can only work if there is co-operation between Legislature and Executive. If the legislative business of a modern State is to be transacted with speed and efficiency, Parliament must accept the lead of the Government and consent to inroads upon the time of private members. Moreover, modern government has become a business for experts. Parliament cannot perform its legislative functions without the assistance of civil servants to whom are available fuller sources of information than to the ordinary public or even to members of Parliament. The officials work out the details of a policy which the Cabinet or a Minister has approved. When concrete proposals have been prepared, the parliamentary machine is employed to put the proposals into the form of law. The speeches of Ministers in Parliament and memoranda published before or contemporaneously with a Bill explain the objects of important measures and the methods by which those objects are to be achieved. The public may have been prepared for important legislative changes by the programme put before the electorate at a general election by the party which subsequently forms the Government. Particularly is the idea of a mandate from the electorate relied upon by Governments in the early sessions after their accession to power. Just as Parliament must accept direction from the Government, so the Government must remember that Parliament represents the electorate. A Government which does not take care that its general policy retains the confidence of the public risks defeat either in Parliament or when it faces the electorate, which it must do at least every five years. But its task is to govern; this is its general mandate and may well justify legislation or other action which was not contemplated at the time of the election.

The ascendancy of the Cabinet over the House of Commons, coupled with the legal and conventional checks upon the suspensory powers of the House of Lords, makes it difficult to maintain that the Legislature in enacting laws exercises a function separate from the Executive. Rather it is the case that the Executive in performing the tasks of governing uses the Legislature as a means of securing those changes in the law which it desires. That there is a risk in the Executive enjoying the power to have enacted any legislation that it wishes is not to be denied. It is one of the outstanding political problems to reach agreement on what safeguards should exist to prevent abuse of this power by the Executive. We may note that a Bill to prolong the life of Parliament beyond the statutory limit of five years is exempted from the provisions of the Parliament Acts, 1911 and 1949,[1] and, therefore, still requires the assent of both Houses and can be rejected by the House of Lords outright. It is not, therefore, possible for the Government to use the House of Commons to postpone a general election by extending the five-year limit, unless, of course, the House of Lords also passes the Bill.

Where there are more than two main political parties, the Government is less sure of its control over Parliament. It may be necessary in order to secure a majority to form a Government which will consist

Three Political Parties.

P. 103, *post*.

of members of more than one political party. There is a tendency for coalitions to separate into their component parts, each bidding for the support of a third party, thus making it more likely that a Government will be defeated by a hostile vote in Parliament. The Cabinet system has been built up on a two-party system. If for any lengthy period there were, as has happened in the past, more than two main political parties with adequate representation in Parliament, there might develop a new relationship between the Government and Parliament, which would inevitably weaken the control of the Government over the Commons.

Delegated Legislation.

(*c*) *Do the Legislature and the Executive exercise each other's functions?* Here we are on debatable ground. The mass of detail involved in modern administration and the extension of the functions of the State to the economic and social sphere has rendered it essential for Parliament to delegate to Ministers the power to make statutory instruments. So long as the main principles of the legislation are laid down in the Act of Parliament, there is little objection in theory to Ministers being given the power to implement those principles by detailed regulations. But it is not easy to decide what is a matter of principle and what is detail which can safely be left to ministerial discretion. Few would deny that delegated legislation [1] is inevitable. It is, however, generally held that, unless it is subject to effective parliamentary scrutiny, there is a real threat to liberty from undue expansion of the power of the Executive. The process of legislation by departmental regulations saves time, can deal with local variations and is more flexible than legislation by Act of Parliament. It can also be used when a Minister requires a wide discretion, to give him freedom to experiment in the administrative field without seeking new powers from Parliament. The power to legislate by statutory instrument is conferred by Parliament and can be taken away by Parliament. Unless, however, the exercise of the power is effectively controlled by Parliament, there is lost that safeguard of liberty which depends upon the law-making power being exercised by the elected representatives of the people who will be affected by the laws that are made. Self-government is endangered when the representatives of the people do not effectively control the making of the laws which the people must obey. This does not, however, mean that Parliament should attempt to supervise every detail of day-to-day administration for which Ministers are responsible. It must, moreover, be borne in mind, when it is said that legislation is the function of Parliament, that the line between legislation and administration is not always easily drawn. The legislative function is the making of general rules. Some Acts of Parliament, especially private and local Acts, decide particular issues, such as authorising the construction of a new length

[1] For a full discussion of this topic, see Part VII., Chap. 6.

of railway, and do not lay down general rules. Here Parliament may claim to be exercising an administrative function using legislative forms.

There must now be examined the relationship between the Judiciary and the other two organs of government. Again the three questions may be asked: Executive and Judiciary.

(*a*) *Do the same persons form part of the Judiciary and the Executive?* The courts are the Queen's Courts, but the Queen only exercises her judicial functions through her judges. The Judicial Committee of the Privy Council,[1] the highest court of appeal from the Colonies and formerly from all the Dominions, is in form a committee of the Privy Council, an executive organ, but in fact it is an independent court of law. The Lord Chancellor, a Cabinet Minister, presides over the Appellate Committee of the House of Lords, which is the final court of appeal from the courts of the United Kingdom. Neither, however, of these apparent exceptions to the separation of powers is of constitutional importance. Only persons with high judicial qualifications in practice can adjudicate on these tribunals.

(*b*) *Does the Executive control or influence the Judiciary or the Judiciary control or influence the Executive?* In this field the separation of powers is strictly observed. Judicial independence is secured by law and by public opinion, and the standard of conduct maintained by both Bench and Bar. The Act of Settlement[2] determined that the judges of the superior courts should have fixed salaries and hold office during good behaviour subject to a power of removal by the Crown exercisable on an address from both Houses of Parliament. It can be stated with confidence that there is no interference by the Executive with the exercise of their judicial functions by the judges of the Supreme Court and the House of Lords. Similarly the courts take no part in the formulation of policy, but simply administer the law as it is, leaving it to the Executive to propose whatever changes in the law may be decided upon if a particular decision of the courts shows the need for such change. That the independence of the Judiciary is desirable no one will deny. An independent Judiciary is the surest protection against abuse of power. Except in so far as it prevents abuse of power and may direct the performance of legal duties, there is no control of the Executive by the Judiciary. It is an essential function of the Judiciary, if application is made to the courts, to check administrative authorities from exceeding their powers and to direct the performance of duties owed by public officials to private citizens.[3] Only an independent Judiciary can impartially perform these tasks. Independence of Judiciary.

---

[1] Part X., Chap. 4.   [2] P. 7, *ante*.
[3] For full discussion of the control of public authorities by the Courts, see Part VII., Chaps. 2 and 3.

Administra-
tive courts.

(c) *Do the Executive and Judiciary exercise each other's functions?*
It is idle to boast of an independent Judiciary if major justiciable
issues are excluded from the jurisdiction of the courts and entrusted
to administrative authorities. Statutes sometimes prescribe that
orders made by Ministers shall not be questioned in the courts.
There is a growing tendency to entrust justiciable issues to administrative courts or even to the decision of individual Ministers as final
arbiters. The reasons for this practice, which will be examined in
Part VII.,[1] are many: the expense of litigation; the belief that judges
are by their training at the Bar and outlook unfitted to decide issues
involving administrative policy; dissatisfaction with the judicial
method of interpreting statutes; the unsuitability of court procedure
for the decision of complicated technical issues. These are powerful
arguments in favour of the reference of many disputes involving
questions of public law to administrative courts. On the other hand,
it is when the citizen has a dispute with the State that he most needs
the protection of an independent tribunal. There is general agreement that except in times of grave emergency disputes involving
freedom of the person and freedom of speech should always be
heard by the ordinary courts. In regard to those administrative
disputes which arise from the entitlement of individuals to statutory
benefits, *e.g.* pensions and all forms of national insurance, the solution has been found in the establishment of administrative courts
which preserve the best features of normal judicial procedure, *i.e.*
publicity, reasonable certainty through adherence to precedent, the
publishing of reasons for decisions, and yet are more appreciative of
the problems of administration and cheaper for the citizen. It is
generally accepted that there should be a right of appeal to an impartial tribunal where an administrative decision rejects a claim to
the payment of benefits or deprives an individual of his property.
There is no agreement as to whether the courts or an *ad hoc* administrative tribunal is to be preferred. The problem is not a simple one.
Moreover it is not easy to decide what is a justiciable issue, the
determination of which should lie, at all events ultimately, with the
ordinary courts of law. Just as it is sometimes difficult to draw a line
between legislation and administration, so it is often difficult to
distinguish between judicial and administrative decisions. Many
decisions given by judges involve the exercise of discretion, *e.g.* the
passing of sentences for crimes or the award of damages. Many
administrative decisions involve the settlement of disputes. Primarily
the judicial function involves the application of settled law to facts,
while an administrative decision is primarily determined by the
discretion of the administration in applying policy, but the line is
often blurred, and frequently the distinction appears one of form

[1] Part VII., Chap. 5.

rather than of substance.[1] Judges of the High Court perform certain purely administrative functions, *e.g.* the administration of the estates of deceased persons and the winding-up of companies. Justices of the peace still have a few administrative duties surviving from the age when the justices in Quarter Sessions were the principal local administrative authority.[2] The exercise of such administrative functions by the Judiciary is, however, simply a matter of organisation and does not involve those questions of principle which arise from the exercise of judicial functions by the Executive which may have a direct interest in securing that the decision does not conflict with the policy of the department.

Finally there must be examined the relationship between the Judiciary and the Legislature:

Judiciary and Legislature.

(*a*) *Do the same persons exercise legislative and judicial functions?* Generally speaking all the higher judicial appointments disqualify for membership of the House of Commons. The House of Lords, the Upper House of Parliament, is the highest court of appeal in the United Kingdom and also exercises original jurisdiction over those impeached by the House of Commons.[3] Formerly it also tried peers accused of treason or felony. The Lord Chancellor presides over the House of Lords sitting in both its legislative and judicial capacities. The Lords of Appeal in Ordinary[4] who sit as judges in the Appellate Committee of the House of Lords occasionally take part also in the legislative business of the House. There is, however, here no substantial infringement in practice of separation of powers. The House of Lords sitting as a court is in substance a court of law with only a historic and formal connection with the House of Lords sitting as a chamber of the Legislature. Lay peers do not take part in the hearing of appeals.[5]

(*b*) *Is there any control by the Legislature over the Judiciary or the Judiciary over the Legislature?* It has been stated that judges of the superior courts may be removed by an address from both Houses of Parliament. Such an address would, however, never be accepted if it interfered with judicial independence. The judges interpret the laws which Parliament enacts, and Parliament can alter the law, should the decisions of the courts in interpreting statutes or in expounding the common law be contrary to the policy of the Legislature. These, however, are the normal functions of both Legislature and Judiciary.

(*c*) *Do the Legislature and Judiciary exercise each other's functions?* The judicial functions of the House of Lords have already been discussed. Each House of Parliament too has the privilege of the High Court of Parliament of enforcing its own privileges and

---

[1] For discussion, see Part VII., Chap. 1.
[2] P. 254, *post.*
[3] P. 239, *post.*
[4] Pp. 75 and 240, *post.*
[5] P. 239, *post.*

punishing those who offend against them.[1] In prescribing rules of court the judges of the High Court, as members of the statutory committee for this purpose, exercise a legislative function, but it is limited to procedural details for the administration of justice. These instances involve no real departure from the separation of powers.

Since the controversies associated with the name of John Wilkes there have been few occasions when Parliament has encroached on the sphere of the courts. Ministers, however, have recently put forward a novel interpretation of ministerial responsibility to Parliament as a justification for the withdrawal from the courts of issues involving civil liberties. Needs of security during the Second World War made it necessary to give to Ministers powers over individual liberties, and in particular a power to detain on suspicion, which could not be questioned in the courts.[2] The grant of such powers was, however, from time to time defended on the ground that it was the duty of Parliament to safeguard liberty and that an individual aggrieved by a ministerial decision should rely upon his Member of Parliament to put forward his grievance. Ministers claimed that being responsible to Parliament they should be judged by Parliament and not by the courts of law. The mere plea of the interests of the State in time of war was reinforced by the plea that the House of Commons was the judge. The danger of this plea lies in the fact that parliamentary criticism of a Minister may and indeed frequently does result in the issue being made one of confidence in the Government. The Minister relies upon the doctrine of collective responsibility to rally the support of his colleagues and the House of Commons hesitates to defeat a Government because of an unjust decision on a point affecting only one individual. It would be a poor day for liberty if Parliament ceased to protect individual freedoms, but an appeal to Parliament cannot take the place of a right to appeal to the courts and an independent Judiciary. This is no mere war-time danger. The arguments used to justify withholding an appeal to the courts from those detained in war time in the interests of the State have been used to withhold an appeal to the courts from those denied permission to sell milk. There are arguments, as has been shown, for the reference of administrative disputes to specially qualified administrative courts, but disputes involving fundamental issues of liberty should be referred to tribunals that are independent of political influence. Access to an independent Judiciary must not be barred on the ground that Ministers are responsible not to the courts but to Parliament.

[1] Part III., Chap. 4.
[2] Part VIII., Chap. 2, B; this power was among the first to be revoked on the cessation of active fighting in Europe in 1945.

There is no separation of powers in the strict sense between Executive and Legislature. Parliamentary supremacy involves ultimate control of the Executive. The practical necessities of parliamentary government make it necessary for Parliament to trust the Government to govern and accept the direction of the Cabinet in regard to the legislative programme, though retaining the right to amend, to criticise, to question and in the last resort to defeat. Practical necessity again demands a large measure of delegation to the Executive of power to legislate by rules, regulations and orders. The independence of the Judiciary has been strictly preserved, but many justiciable issues are referred not to the ordinary courts, but to administrative authorities. Where such reference is expedient, machinery has been devised to secure that reference is made to tribunals which are impartial and, as a general rule, preserve the essential features of a fair trial. *Conclusion.*

No direct answer has been given to the question—how far is separation of powers desirable? Nor is it easy to say dogmatically that a doctrine which has been subject to widely differing interpretations is or is not desirable.[1] It is not difficult to agree with Montesquieu that monopoly of power in any government is dangerous. So far as his exposition failed to admit that the legislature should act as a check on the executive power, *i.e.* in his day the prerogative of the King, his opinion is unacceptable to the modern conception of parliamentary government, even in the field of external affairs. Nor does he take much account of the part played by the common law in moulding constitutional principles and checking real power. His classification has indeed been used to sustain the argument that execution and adjudication are only aspects of the single function of administration. Sir Carleton Allen has pointed out that Montesquieu does not himself use the term, separation, or suggest that the three powers of government should not touch at any point but rather that they should be subject to mutual restraints—the checks and balances which have come since to be recognised as fully developed in our eighteenth-century constitution. If this be so, there is no need to strive to fit separation of powers into the functional organs of our constitution. *How far is separation of powers desirable?*

[1] *Cf.* for example Sir Carleton Allen, *Law and Orders*, chap. 1, and Sir Ivor Jennings, *The Law and the Constitution*, pp. 18 ff. and Appendix I.

CHAPTER 2.
PARLIAMENTARY SUPREMACY.

A.

History of Parliamentary Supremacy.

WE have seen that a system of parliamentary government involves the supremacy of Parliament. Before discussing the legal meaning of legislative supremacy, its practical limitations and how far Parliament in fact exercises its legislative powers, we shall give a brief account of the stages by which Parliament established itself as the sole legislative authority, and how it has come to exercise political supremacy by controlling the Executive. Legislative supremacy was established by the end of the seventeenth century. The responsibility of the Executive to Parliament was not clearly established till after the Representation of the People Act, 1832.

Middle Ages.   It was recognised in the Middle Ages that an Act of Parliament could change the common law. With the Reformation there disappeared the idea that there were certain ecclesiastical rules and doctrines that Parliament could not touch. Henry VIII. and Elizabeth I. made the Crown of England supreme over all persons and causes and used Parliament to attain this end. Even in the seventeenth century it was contended that there were certain natural laws which were immutable,[1] but the common lawyers were the allies of Parliament in the seventeenth-century struggle with the Crown and in order to defeat the Crown's claim to rule by prerogative were forced to concede that the common law could only be changed by Parliament.[2]

The struggle for supremacy.   Legislative supremacy involves not only the right to change the law but also that no one else should have that right. In many spheres the King's prerogative at the beginning of the seventeenth century was undefined and the King exercised through the Council a residue of judicial power which enabled him to enforce his prerogative powers. Acts of Parliament which purpoied to take away any of the inseparable prerogatives of the Crown were held invalid.[3] The struggle for legislative supremacy is closely connected with the royal prerogative to be discussed in Part IV.

[1] K. & L., pp. 1, 2.
[2] Dicey, *op. cit.*, Introduction by E. C. S. Wade, p. lxix.
[3] K. & L., p. 2; "No Act of Parliament can bar a King of his regality."—*The Case of Ship Money* (1637), 3 St. Tr. 825, *per* Finch, C.J., at p. 1235.

There was a lack of any clear distinction between the Statutes of Parliament and the Ordinances of the King in Council long after the establishment of the Model Parliament at the end of the thirteenth century. The Lex Regia or Statute of Proclamations, 1539, gave the King wide but not exclusive powers of legislating without reference to Parliament by proclamation which had replaced the ordinance as a form of legislation. This statute did not give to the King and Council power to do anything that they pleased by royal ordinance, but was a genuine attempt by the King and Parliament to deal finally with the obscure position of the authority possessed by proclamations. It safeguarded the common law, existing Acts of Parliament and rights of property, and prohibited the infliction of the death penalty for a breach of a proclamation.[1] Despite the repeal of this statute in 1547, both Mary and Elizabeth continued to resort to proclamations as a means of governing. The judicial powers of the Council, and in particular of the Court of Star Chamber, were available to enforce proclamations. The scope of the royal prerogative was largely undefined. It is a most difficult task for the constitutional historian to say at any given period prior to 1689 exactly what must be enacted by Parliament alone and what could be achieved by prerogative ordinance. Nor is this surprising when it is remembered that legislative power originally lay with the King in Council, and that the influence of the Council varied with the ability of the monarch to choose his counsellors. James I. made full use of this power, with the result that in 1611 Coke was consulted by the Council, along with three of his brother judges who were added at his request, for an expression of opinion on the legality of proclamations. The result of their considerations is to be found in the *Case of Proclamations* (1611), 12 Co. Rep. 74; K. & L. 78, and may be regarded as final.

(1) Ordinances and Proclamations.

"1. The King by his proclamation cannot create any offence which was not one before; for then he might alter the law of the land in a high point; for if he may create an offence where none is, upon that ensues fine and imprisonment.

"2. The King hath no prerogative but what the law of the land allows him.

"3. But the King for the prevention of offences may by proclamation admonish his subjects that they keep the laws and do not offend them upon punishment to be inflicted by law; the neglect of such proclamation aggravates the offence.

"4. If an offence be not punishable in the Star Chamber, the prohibition of it by proclamation cannot make it so."

A definite limit is thus put upon the exercise of the prerogative, the full force of which was only effective when the Court of Star Chamber and other conciliar tribunals were abolished in 1640. But the existing

[1] *H.E.L.*, Vol. IV., pp. 102–3.

prerogative powers were left undefined except that in Coke's opinion proclamations could no longer increase them. The gist of the *Case of Proclamations* is that the King is the Executive and his business the enforcement of the existing law; his prerogative is under the law, and Parliament can alone alter the law which the King is to administer.[1]

(2) Taxation.   The imposition of taxes is a matter for legislation. Inevitably taxation was a major issue between the Stuart Kings and Parliament. If the Crown could not levy taxes without the consent of Parliament, the will of Parliament must in the long run prevail. It had been conceded by the time of Edward I. that the consent of Parliament was necessary for direct taxation. The history of indirect taxation is more complicated, but it was established by the time of the Wars of the Roses that parliamentary consent was required for taxes on specific commodities. The regulation of foreign trade was, however, a part of the royal prerogative in relation to foreign affairs. There was no clear distinction between the imposition of taxes by way of customs duties and the prerogative powers in relation to foreign trade. There was a conflict of authorities. Parliament was feeling its strength and each side appealed to the law to decide what was really a political issue that had lain dormant so long as Tudor Kings worked in harmony with Parliament. "If it was no part of the Tudor theory of government that emergency powers should be used for the raising of revenue, neither was it a bonâ fide use of the power of the purse to attempt to remove foreign policy or the defence of the realm from the hands of the Crown." [2]

Case of Impositions.   In the *Case of Impositions* (*Bates' Case*) (1606), 2 St. Tr. 371; K. & L. 48, John Bates refused to pay a duty on imported currants imposed by the Crown on the ground that its imposition was contrary to the statute 45 Edw. 3, c. 4, which prohibited indirect taxation without the consent of Parliament. The Court of Exchequer unanimously gave a decision in favour of the Crown. The King could impose what duties he pleased for the purpose of regulating trade, and the court could not go behind the King's statement that the duty was in fact imposed for the regulation of trade.

Case of Ship Money.   In the *Case of Ship Money* (*The King* v. *Hampden*) (1637), 3 St. Tr. 825; K. & L. 50, John Hampden, Knight of the Shire of Buckinghamshire, refused to pay ship money, a tax levied for the purpose of furnishing ships in time of national danger. Counsel for Hampden conceded that sometimes the existence of danger will justify taking the subject's goods without his consent, but only in actual as opposed to threatened emergency. The Crown conceded that the subject could not be taxed in normal circumstances without the consent of

---

[1] Anson, *Law and Custom of the Constitution* (5th ed., Gwyer), Vol. I., p. 343.
[2] K. & L., p. 65.

Parliament, but contended that the King was the sole judge whether
an emergency justified the exercise of his prerogative power to raise
funds to meet a national danger. A majority of the Court of Exchequer Chamber gave judgment for the King.[1] The decision was
reversed by the Long Parliament, and this aspect of the struggle for
supremacy was concluded by the Bill of Rights:

> That the levying money for or to the use of the Crown by pretence
> of prerogative without grant of Parliament for longer time or in other
> manner than the same is or shall be granted is illegal.

The power of the Crown to dispense with the operation of statutes
within certain limits seems to have been a necessary one having
regard to the form of many ancient statutes and the irregular meetings of Parliament. So long, however, as the limits upon the dispensing power were not clearly defined, there was here a threat to the
legislative supremacy of Parliament. It could be contended that the
dispensing power was one of inseparable prerogatives which could
not be curtailed, but violations of the common law or statutory
enactments of the common law were probably not within the scope
of the royal dispensation. In the leading case of *Thomas* v. *Sorrell*
(1674), Vaughan 330, a distinction was drawn between dispensing
with laws which are not for the particular benefit or safety of third
persons and laws which are for such benefit or for the benefit of the
public as a whole. In *Godden* v. *Hales* (1686), 11 St. Tr. 1165;
K. & L. 66, the court upheld a dispensation from James II. to Sir
Edward Hales excusing him from taking the oaths and fulfilling the
other obligations imposed by the Test Act. It can be argued that the
decision could have been given without impairing the distinction
indicated in *Thomas* v. *Sorrell* and by drawing a distinction between
malum prohibitum (by statute) and *malum in se* from which there can
be no dispensation. The judgment was, however, based on wider
grounds and it was held that it was an inseparable prerogative of the
Kings of England to dispense with penal laws in particular cases and
upon necessary reasons of which the King is sole judge.

Fortified by the favourable decision in the latter case, James II.
proceeded to set aside statutes as he pleased. Hard though it may
be to define the dispensing power, there is no doubt that James over-
stepped all limits of legality in granting a suspension of the penal
laws relating to religion in the Declaration of Indulgence. The
validity of his act only came before the courts in an indirect way at
the trial of the Seven Bishops for seditious libel arising out of their
petitions to James against reading the declaration. The Bill of Rights
abolished the Crown's alleged power of suspending laws.

(3) Dispens-
ing and
Suspending
Powers.

[1] For analysis of the arguments of Counsel and the judgment, see "The Case
of Ship Money," by Sir D. L. Keir, 52 *L.Q.R.* 546.

Comparison should be made with the provision relating to the dispensing power:

(1) That the pretended power of dispensing with laws, or the execution of laws by regal authority, as it hath been assumed and exercised of late, is illegal.

(2) That from and after this present session of Parliament, no dispensation by *non obstante* of or to any statute, or any part thereof, shall be allowed, but that the same shall be held void and of no effect, except a dispensation be allowed of in such a statute, and except in such cases as shall be specially provided for by one or more Bill or Bills to be passed during this present session of Parliament.[1]

It is apparent from these provisions that, while James II.'s dispensations were regarded as illegal, earlier dispensations were not called in question. Further it was recognised that the power might be required by the Executive in future. For this provision was to be made by Parliament. Actually no such provision was made. In the *Case of Eton College* (1815),[2] there was upheld a dispensation granted by Queen Elizabeth to enable Fellows of the College to hold benefices up to a certain value in conjunction with their fellowships, notwithstanding College statutes which forbade this type of plurality.

(4) The Independence of the Judiciary.

So long as the tenure of judicial office depended upon the royal pleasure there was a risk of the subservience of the Bench. Judicial independence is, therefore, closely connected with parliamentary supremacy. No doubt some of the decisions, such as the *Case of Impositions* and *Thomas* v. *Sorrell*, should be accepted without accusing the Judiciary of bias. But it is more difficult to absolve the judges who favoured the Crown in *Hampden's Case* or in *Godden* v. *Hales*.

Act of Settlement, 1701.

It was left to the Act of Settlement, enacting a provision which was originally intended to have taken its place in the Bill of Rights, to ensure the independence of the Bench "that . . . judges' commissions be made *quamdiu se bene gesserint*, and their salaries ascertained and established; but upon the address of both Houses of Parliament it may be lawful to remove them." [3]

Earlier the executive power had been checked by the abolition in 1640 of all jurisdiction of the Council in common law matters, and of the Court of Star Chamber which had been used for the enforcement of prerogative powers.

Position at end of Seventeenth Century.

The result of the seventeenth-century conflict between the Executive and Parliament was that the Bill of Rights and the Act of Settlement gave to Parliament the supremacy on all points, while preserving the prerogative rights of the Crown in matters which had not

---

[1] No attempt was made to curtail the prerogative of pardon or the Attorney-General's power to enter a *nolle prosequi* (p. 245, *post*).

[2] Peere Wms. Report 53; for an account of this case, see Broom, *Constitutional Law*, 2nd. ed., pp. 503–5.

[3] Repealed by Statute Law Revision Act, 1881. See for similar provisions Supreme Court of Judicature Act, 1925, ss. 12, 13; Appellate Jurisdiction Act 1876, s. 6.

been called in question. But as yet there was absent the recognition of the principle that the King's Ministers could best be controlled by their presence in Parliament as members, and so responsible to Parliament. It was not until early in the eighteenth century that this began to be recognised and it was indeed essential if the will of Parliament was to prevail. The process of impeachment was too cumbrous and drastic to be used as the everyday method of ensuring that a Minister should not disregard the will of Parliament, but the ultimate solution of the collective responsibility of the Cabinet was not at first perceived. The Bill of Rights was the first great victory of Parliament. The Act of Settlement by attempting to exclude Ministers from the House of Commons showed how far from realisation was the solution of the problem of co-ordination between the Executive and Parliament. Thus in the eighteenth century the nature of the struggle changes. The absolute discretion of the Crown, which the events of the closing years of the seventeenth century had still left in many respects unimpaired, could not be left with the Crown and its Ministers in such a way as to enable them to govern without responsibility in those matters which still fell within the royal prerogative. The significance of the period from 1688 until after the Reform Act, 1832, lies in the development of ministerial responsibility to Parliament.

The first step was to ensure the individual responsibility of Ministers of the Crown to Parliament for their actions, and, secondly, collective responsibility for general policy and for the actions of other Ministers.[1] This responsibility is political, and not legal, though for his individual acts contrary to law each Minister was, and is, responsible to the courts. *Danby's Case* (1679), 11 St. Tr. 599, went a long way towards establishing the principle that a Minister cannot shelter himself from legal responsibility by a plea of obedience to the command of the Sovereign: cf. *Somers' Case* (1701), 14 St. Tr. 234.

Growth of Ministerial Responsibility.

But the collective responsibility of the Cabinet could not be developed until that body had emerged as the effective executive organ. Even in the reign of George III. membership of the Cabinet did not by itself entitle a Privy Councillor to take part in decisions on policy. There was a distinction between the efficient or confidential Cabinet, all the members of which received papers, and the outer circle of the Cabinet Council, the titular or external Cabinet. Anne, like her predecessors, retained a personal initiative in the Councils of the Crown, frequently presiding at meetings of the Cabinet, a body which had as yet no regular composition.[2]

[1] For fuller treatment of Ministerial Responsibility, see Chap. 4, *post*.
[2] Anson gives three such bodies under titles of: (1) The Cabinet, or Lords of the Cabinet Council. (2) The Committee of Council. (3) The Privy Council or Great Council. Anson, *op. cit.* 4th ed., Vol. II., Part I., p. 104.

Exclusion
of Office
holders.

It has been seen that the Act of Settlement at the end of the previous reign excluded the Ministers of the Crown, as holders of offices of profit, from membership of the House of Commons. At the same time it attempted to impose personal responsibility for executive acts on Privy Councillors. It is true that neither of these provisions came into operation, as they were repealed before the death of Anne, but they serve to illustrate the lack of appreciation of the modern solution.

Transition
to Cabinet
Government.

The real point of transition to Cabinet Government came with the accession of the House of Hanover. The absence of George I. from meetings of the Cabinet made it essential that a Minister should be selected to preside at these meetings. Here is to be found the beginning of the office of Prime Minister. Henceforth the leaders of the two great parties of State, Whigs and Tories, control the direction of policy by maintaining a majority of supporters in the House of Commons. The methods to which both the Whigs and the Tories freely resorted included the acquisition of pocket boroughs, the grant of pensions and the gifts of sinecure offices and government contracts. The long Whig supremacy illustrates the effectiveness of these weapons. When George III. tried through the King's friends to re-establish personal government, he did so on parliamentary lines. Since the Bill of Rights it was impossible for the Executive to govern without the support of Parliament. As long, however, as Parliament was unreformed, that support could be secured by the use of bribery and patronage, except in times of great popular feeling, as on the occasion of the loss of the American Colonies and the

Reform Act,
1832.

fall of Lord North's Ministry. With the coming of parliamentary reform in 1832 it was no longer possible to govern by these means, and indeed steps had been taken earlier on the initiative of Burke to purge the Commons of corrupt supporters of the Ministry by means of Bills abolishing old offices and disqualifying contractors and other placemen from membership. The necessity of parliamentary support which had existed since 1689, meant that the Executive must hold the same political views as the majority in Parliament. Gradually there was evolved an Executive responsive to the will of the majority of the electorate. It is true that at first "the electorate" meant principally owners of land. To-day it means every adult male and female.

Conclusion.

Thus executive power has become impossible without the support of Parliament, which support is only obtainable by winning the confidence of a vast electorate. Parliament has the final voice in legislation, as in taxation and expenditure, and a Ministry can be forced to resign by defeat or by the defection of some of its supporters in the House of Commons. In the past Parliament could not dismiss a King without a revolution. The Commons can now dismiss the Ministry which advises the Sovereign and ensure its replacement by another pledged to give effect to a policy approved by a majority of the electorate.

B.

Meaning of Legislative Supremacy.

From this brief historical summary we turn to an examination of the practical results of parliamentary supremacy. Dicey, after examining several illustrations from history and showing that there existed no competing authority, concluded that within the limits of physical possibility Parliament could make or unmake any law whatever. The courts can only interpret and may not question the validity of Acts of Parliament. No Parliament can bind its successor; otherwise the supremacy of succeeding Parliaments would be limited. So far as constitutional law consists of statutes, there is no Act which Parliament could not repeal. The Bill of Rights could be cast overboard by the same process as the Prevention of Damage by Pests Act, namely by a repealing measure passed in ordinary form. Parliament can override the decisions of the courts, if need be with retrospective effect. It could restore to the Executive unfettered power to legislate as freely as if the *Case of Proclamations* had never been accepted as representing the law. The most firmly established convention could be declared illegal by statute.

Legal Power Unlimited.

That Parliament can pass any law whatsoever and that no one Parliament can be bound by an Act of its predecessors nor bind its successors may be illustrated both by His Majesty's Declaration of Abdication Act, 1936 (this changed the succession to the Throne which had been secured by the Act of Settlement), and by the statutes which have from time to time fixed or prolonged the duration of Parliament's own life. The duration of Parliament has been fixed by successive Acts which each repealed its predecessor, the Meeting of Parliament Act, 1694,[1] the Septennial Act, 1715, and the Parliament Act, 1911, which is still in force. The Parliament elected in December 1910 was dissolved in 1918, having five times renewed its own existence, which was limited to five years by its own enactment, the Parliament Act, 1911. The Parliament elected in 1935 five times renewed its own existence by Prolongation of Parliament Acts.

Supremacy Illustrated.

Parliament alone possesses the power to legalise past illegality. This power denies supremacy to the courts and has been used by an Executive which has a secure majority in Parliament to reverse inconvenient decisions of an impartial Judiciary.[2] The conclusion of the First World War, in the course of which a number of illegal acts were inevitably committed by an over-zealous Executive in the interest of the prosecution of the war, was marked by the passage of two Indemnity Acts, the Indemnity Act, 1920, and the War Charges Validity Act, 1925. There are many other instances of retrospective

Indemnity Acts and Retrospective Legislation.

---

[1] Formerly the Triennial Act.
[2] See Provisional Collection of Taxes Act, 1913, p. 115, *post.*

legislation, *e.g.* the Enemy Property Act, 1953, ss. 1–3, relating to the making or withholding of payments and other dealings with property since the outbreak of war in 1939, Acts validating void marriages, the Building Societies Act, 1939, s. 3, validating advances made by building societies in excess of their powers. Retrospective laws are, however, "*prima facie* of questionable policy and contrary to the general principle that legislation by which the conduct of mankind is to be regulated ought, when introduced for the first time, to deal with future acts and ought not to change the character of past transactions carried on upon the faith of the then existing law. Accordingly the court will not ascribe retrospective force to new laws affecting rights unless by express words or necessary implication it appears that such was the intention of the legislature." [1] Retrospective laws may not only confirm irregular acts but also make void and punish what was lawful when done. In this category fell Acts of Attainder and in modern times taxation is occasionally imposed with retrospective operation to penalise widespread evasion which, though lawful when practised has violated the general intention of the legislature. Such Acts may be described as *ex post facto* laws rather than as retrospective laws.

Parliamentary Supremacy and the Dominions. Legislative supremacy means that the validity of an Act of Parliament cannot be questioned by the courts which are bound to accept as law the validity of all parliamentary enactments. [2] If Parliament made it a criminal offence for a Frenchman to smoke in the streets of Paris, the Act would not be enforced by the French courts, but an English court could enforce it against a Frenchman who came to this country and was prosecuted under it. The legislative supremacy of the Parliament of the United Kingdom (the Imperial Parliament) formerly extended throughout the King's dominions (the Dominions and the Colonies) and was applied by British courts in protectorates and those foreign countries in which the Crown exercises jurisdiction. [3] There was, however, a convention that Parliament should not legislate for a self-governing Dominion except at the request and with the consent of that Dominion. This convention was enacted as law by section 4 of the Statute of Westminster, 1931. [4] Does this enactment limit the legislative supremacy of Parliament? The question may be framed differently: Would the courts recognise the validity of a statute passed in contravention of section 4 of the Statute of Westminster? Or can Parliament repeal the section? In strict legal theory an affirmative answer can be given to both these

---

[1] Willes, J., in *Phillips* v. *Eyre* (1870), L.R. 6 Q.B. 1; K. & L. 492, at p. 499
[2] "If an Act of Parliament has been obtained improperly, it is for the legislature to correct it by repealing it; but, so long as it exists as law, the courts are bound to enforce it."—*Lee* v. *Bude and Torrington Rly. Co.* (1871), L.R. 6 C.P. 577, at p. 582.
[3] P. 442, *post*.   [4] Part X., Chap. 3, C.

questions so far as the courts of the United Kingdom are concerned. "It is doubtless true that the power of the Imperial Parliament to pass on its own initiative any legislation that it thought fit extending to Canada remains unimpaired; indeed the Imperial Parliament could, as a matter of strict law, repeal section 4 of the Statute. But that is theory and has no relation to realities." [1] The Statute of Westminster did not purport to abrogate the supremacy of the Imperial Parliament. Indeed it expressly preserved the right of the Imperial Parliament to amend the British North America Acts (which contain the Canadian constitution) and to pass legislation affecting the States of Australia.[2] It is, however, open to doubt whether the courts of either Canada or Australia would recognise as part of Canadian or Australian law legislation passed in contravention of section 4. The courts of South Africa would not recognise such legislation as part of the law of the Union. Indeed South Africa no longer recognises the supremacy of the United Kingdom Parliament and has enacted that no Act of the United Kingdom Parliament passed after December 11, 1931, shall extend, or be deemed to extend, to the Union as part of the law of the Union unless extended thereto by an Act of the Parliament of the Union.[3] In *Ndlwana* v. *Hofmeyr N.O.*, [1937] A.D. 229, the Supreme Court of South Africa described the Union Parliament as the supreme and sovereign law-making body of the Union and characterised as absurd the suggestion that section 4 of the Statute of Westminster could be repealed. "Freedom once conferred cannot be revoked." [4]

The supremacy of Parliament is not limited so far as British courts are concerned by the rules of international law. The courts have nothing to do with the question whether the legislature has or has not done what foreign States consider a usurpation. Neither are they concerned whether an Act of Parliament is *ultra vires* on the ground that it contravenes generally accepted principles of international law.[5] No statute will, however, be held to apply to aliens with respect to transactions outside British jurisdiction unless the words are perfectly clear.[6] In practice Parliament only enacts legislation which can be enforced and, in accord with international law, attempts to exercise authority only within its own territories,[7] or over

Territorial Jurisdiction.

---

[1] *British Coal Corporation* v. *The King*, [1935] A.C. 500, at p. 520.
[2] P. 468, *post*.
[3] Status of the Union Act, 1934, s. 2. See p. 460, *post*.
[4] [1937] A.D. 229, at p. 237. This case was overruled by the same Court in *Harris* v. *Minister of the Interior*, [1952] (2) S.A. 428; K. & L. 506, but the latter case expressly upheld the sovereignty of the Parliament of the Union.
[5] *Mortensen* v. *Peters* (1906), 8 F. (Ct. of Sess.) 93.
[6] *Cail* v. *Papayanni* (1863), 1 Moo. P.C. (N.S.) 471, at p. 474. For an example of prohibiting an activity abroad by whomsoever committed (election broadcasts), see Representation of the People Act, 1949, s. 80.
[7] Including British ships wherever they may be.

C*

its own citizens when abroad.[1] Indeed our territorial conception of law is stronger than that of most other countries and the extent to which citizens of the United Kingdom and Colonies are affected by English law while in foreign countries is small. A few serious crimes committed in a foreign State by citizens of the United Kingdom and Colonies are justiciable in this country, such as treason, murder, manslaughter, bigamy, piracy.[2] Any British subject employed by the Government of the United Kingdom in the service of the Crown who commits in a foreign country, when acting in the course of his employment, any offence which, if committed in England, would be punishable on indictment, can be proceeded against in England for that offence: Criminal Justice Act, 1948, s. 31 (1). The National Service (Foreign Countries) Act, 1942, which was repealed after the end of hostilities, empowered the Crown to impose military service on British subjects in foreign countries.

Future Parliaments cannot be bound. No Parliament can bind its successors. Otherwise succeeding Parliaments would not be sovereign or supreme. This rule is illustrated by *Vauxhall Estates* v. *Liverpool Corporation*, [1932] 1 K.B. 733, where it was held that provisions contained in a later Act (Housing Act, 1925, s. 46, which related to compensation for land compulsorily acquired), repealed by implication the provisions of an earlier Act (Acquisition of Land (Assessment of Compensation) Act, 1919, s. 7 (i)) which attempted to invalidate subsequent legislation so far as it might be inconsistent.[3]

Sovereign and Non-Sovereign Legislatures. A distinction must be drawn between Parliament and a colonial legislature. Colonial legislatures are sovereign within the limits of their powers,[4] but they are bound by the Colonial Laws Validity Act, 1865,[5] and other Acts of the Imperial Parliament which apply to the colonies, such as the British Nationality Act, 1948, and merchant shipping legislation. The Colonial Laws Validity Act, 1865, requires any amendment of a colonial constitution to be made "in the manner and form" required by imperial or colonial legislation in force at the time. The Privy Council held invalid an Act of the New South Wales Parliament which purported to abolish the Upper House of New South Wales in contravention of a previous Act of the same Parliament. That Act had provided that the Upper House might only be abolished by a Bill which before being presented for

---

[1] And not over the citizens of other States of the British Commonwealth for offences committed outside the United Kingdom, unless such offences are punishable when committed by an alien: British Nationality Act, 1948, s. 3. A citizen of a Commonwealth State, however, like an alien, is subject to English or Scots law when resident in the United Kingdom.

[2] Sir Arnold McNair, *Legal Effects of War* (Cambridge University Press), 2nd ed., p. 367.

[3] See also *Ellen Street Estates Ltd.* v. *Minister of Health*, [1934] 1 K.B. 590.

[4] P. 439, *post.*

[5] Pp. 448–9, *post.*

the royal assent had been approved by the electors at a referendum, and the requirement of a referendum could only be abolished by the same process.[1] In the High Court of Australia[2] it was suggested that if a similar provision were enacted in England and a subsequent Bill received the royal assent without a referendum having been held, the courts might be called upon to consider whether the supreme legislative power had in fact been exercised in the manner required for its authentic expression and by the elements in which it had come to reside. It was further suggested that it would be an unlawful proceeding to present such a Bill for the royal assent before it had been approved by the electors and that, if before the Bill received the assent of the Crown it was found possible to raise for judicial decision the question whether it was lawful to present the Bill for assent, the courts would be bound to hold it unlawful to do so. It is, however, submitted that the courts in the United Kingdom would never question the validity of an Act of Parliament which had been duly promulgated. The courts will certainly not consider whether or not prescribed forms have been followed in passing a Bill,[3] nor will the courts enforce an agreement preventing the submission to Parliament of matters which may be relevant to the passage of a Bill.[4] But in *Harris* v. *Minister of the Interior*, [1952] (2) S. A. 428; K. & L. 506, it was sought to challenge the validity of a South African Act on the ground that the procedure prescribed by the constitution had not been followed; the Supreme Court of South Africa held that the Union Parliament was a sovereign legislature but that the courts had power to declare invalid an Act passed by both Houses of Parliament and duly promulgated and published by the proper authority on the ground that the Act had not been passed by the special machinery required by the Constitution Act of the Union. Thus the

---

[1] *Attorney-General for New South Wales* v. *Trethowan*, [1932] A.C. 526; see p. 449, *post*.

[2] 44 C.L.R. 394, *per* Dixon, J., at p. 426.

[3] " All that the Court of Justice can do is to look at the parliamentary roll; if from that it should appear that a Bill has passed both Houses and received the royal assent, no court of justice can inquire into the mode in which it was introduced into Parliament, nor into what was done previous to its introduction, or what passed in Parliament during its progress in various stages through both Houses" : *Edinburgh and Dalkeith Rly. Co.* v. *Wauchope* (1842), 8 Cl. and F. 710, *per* Lord Campbell, at p. 725.

[4] *Bilston Corporation* v. *Wolverhampton Corporation*, [1942] 1 Ch. 391; K. & L. 13, where the court refused to grant an injunction to prevent the defendants from opposing a local Act in breach of an agreement not to oppose which had itself been embodied in another local Act; see note by Sir William Holdsworth in 59 *L.Q.R.* 2. The Local Government Act, 1933, s. 139, provides that a borough council shall not promote a Bill for the purpose of constituting the borough a county borough unless the population of the borough is 75,000 or upwards. It is, however, submitted that the courts would not interfere to prevent such a Bill being promoted, whatever the population of the borough, but would leave the matter to the vigilance of Parliament.

Union Parliament is sovereign, but must comply with its constitutional procedure when asserting that sovereignty.[1]

No rival authority.

It has been shown in discussing the struggle for supremacy in the seventeenth century that legislative supremacy requires that there should be no rival legislative authority. Neither the Crown[2] nor any one House of Parliament[3] can change the law. Neither devolution nor delegation of legislative authority infringes the supremacy of Parliament. Legislative supremacy does not require that only Parliament should legislate, but it means that other bodies should only legislate with the authority of Parliament.[4] There has been little enthusiasm in this country for devolution, whether regional (*e.g.* separate legislatures for Scotland and Wales) or functional (*e.g.* an economic legislature elected by trade and professional organisations). That devolution can be reconciled with parliamentary control is shown by the procedure devised for the consideration and passage of measures of the National Assembly of the Church of England.[5] It is recognised that a substantial delegation of legislative powers is inevitable in the modern State. Apart from minor legislative powers exercised by local authorities and other bodies with statutory powers to enact by-laws, wide powers of legislation are delegated to government departments. Such delegation may in the absence of proper safeguards lessen control by Parliament of legislation, but it does not impair supremacy. Parliament may take away the powers that it has given. Moreover, unless Parliament excludes the jurisdiction of the courts, delegated legislation will be held invalid if the powers conferred by Parliament are exceeded.[6]

Foreign Legislation.

We have considered the territorial limitations upon parliamentary sovereignty and how far the laws passed by Parliament have extraterritorial effect. It is also necessary to consider how far foreign laws are enforced or recognised in the United Kingdom. The courts refuse to investigate the validity of the acts of a foreign State done within its own territory,[7] and will recognise a transfer of property situated in that territory by a decree of that State, should the question of its ownership be raised in litigation here. The meaning and effect

---

[1] The Court overruled on the latter point its earlier decision in *Ndlwana* v. *Hofmeyr N.O.*, [1937] A.D. 229.

[2] P. 33, *ante*. [3] Pp. 115 and 122, *post*.

[4] For prerogative legislation see p. 352, *post*.

[5] Part XI. [6] Part VII., Chap. 2.

[7] *A. M. Luther Co.* v. *James Sagor and Co.*, [1921] 3 K. B. 532; *Princess Paley Olga* v. *Weisz*, [1929] 1 K. B. 718. Sir Arnold McNair suggests (*op. cit.*, p. 377) that the courts may investigate the constitutionality as opposed to the validity of the act of a foreign State, but it is submitted that such an investigation will only be made in most exceptional circumstances, *e.g.* where there is involved the freedom of a person living in the United Kingdom: *In re Amand* (*No.* 2), [1942] 1 K.B. 445. Nor, it is suggested, would an English court investigate a question of constitutionality which by the foreign law is reserved for a special constitutional court.

of a foreign decree is a question of fact to be determined by evidence. The courts do not recognise the validity of a decree of a foreign State or a foreign law purporting to affect property situated outside the territory of that State.[1]

It is only with the authority of Parliament that foreign jurisdiction can be exercised in this country. Such jurisdiction was granted during the Second World War to allied Governments in London over their armed forces stationed in this country.[2] In the case of members of the United States forces Parliament surrendered its own jurisdiction over crimes committed in the United Kingdom; United States of America (Visiting Forces) Act, 1942, which remained in force until 1954.[3] Parliamentary supremacy was not infringed when the Crown permitted the exiled Netherlands Government to legislate in the United Kingdom for its own subjects: *In re Amand* (*No. 2*), [1942] 1 K.B. 445. International law recognises that a State may legislate in respect of its own subjects wherever they may be, and it mattered not whether such legislation was enacted in Holland or in the United Kingdom. It could, however, only be enforced in the United Kingdom through the authority of Parliament. Amand, a Netherlands subject, was called up for military service by a Netherlands decree made in the United Kingdom. He was arrested in pursuance of an Order in Council made under the Allied Forces Act, 1940, which gave to the Netherlands authorities jurisdiction over their armed forces in the United Kingdom and lent assistance in enforcing that jurisdiction. The Divisional Court recognised that a valid Netherlands decree could apply to Netherlands subjects in the United Kingdom; but it was an Act of the United Kingdom Parliament and an Order in Council made thereunder that made Amand liable to arrest and detention and thus gave enforceability to the Netherlands decree.[4]

The seventeenth-century struggle for supremacy left its mark upon the interpretation of statutes by the courts. Lawyers are traditionally suspicious of any encroachment by the Executive and this is reflected in the attitude of the courts to the interpretation of penal statutes, and statutes imposing taxation or conferring new powers on the Executive. In *Attorney-General* v. *Wilts United Dairies* (1921), 37 T.L.R. 884; K. & L. 163, a charge imposed by the Food Controller during the First World War as a condition of the grant of a licence to deal in milk was held invalid. The High Court referred to the

Marginal notes: Second World War. Interpretation of Statutes.

---

[1] *The Jupiter* (No. 3), [1927] P. 122, at p. 144. Possible exceptions are laws affecting the transfer of ownership of foreign ships (McNair, *op. cit.*, p. 378) and requisitioning the property of nationals in time of war (McNair, *op. cit.*, p. 368).

[2] P. 406, *post*.

[3] See now Visiting Forces Act, 1952, p. 406, *post*.

[4] McNair, *op. cit.*, p. 374.

"historic struggle of the legislature to secure for itself the sole power to levy money upon the subject," and held that express words were required for any delegation of the power to tax.[1] The courts will not question the supremacy of Parliament, but it was understood by the lawyers when they allied themselves with Parliament that the common law should be preserved, and this understanding has influenced the interpretation of statutes to the present day.[2] Judicial interpretation of discretionary powers will be discussed in Part VII., but some leading principles of interpretation may be mentioned here to illustrate how loath the Judiciary has hitherto been to construe a statute as changing the basic principles of the common law.[3] Express terms are required to take away the legal right of the subject to compensation in respect of property compulsorily acquired: *per* Lord Atkinson in *Central Control Board (Liquor Traffic)* v. *Cannon Brewery Co. Ltd.*, [1919] A.C. 744, at p. 752. There is a presumption that Parliament does not intend to deprive a subject of his right of access to the courts in respect of his common law rights: *Chester* v. *Bateson*, [1920] 1 K.B. 829; K. & L. 31, where during the First World War it was held that a regulation debarring any person from applying to the courts without the consent of the Minister of Munitions to recover possession of premises occupied by a munitions worker was not validly made under a power to issue regulations for preserving the public safety and the defence of the realm. Express and clear words are required to effect any major constitutional changes: *Nairn* v. *University of St. Andrews*, [1909] A.C. 147; K. & L. 11, where at a time when women were not enfranchised generally it was held that express words were required to confer the vote on women graduates of a Scottish university, and that they could not be enfranchised simply by the use of the words "every person" in connection with the right to be registered as an elector.

Political Limitations. We have hitherto considered territorial limitations on parliamentary supremacy and the legal meaning of the term. There are also practical political limitations. It is essential to the working of a parliamentary democracy that the laws made by the representatives of the people should be obeyed. It follows that laws must not be enacted that would prove unenforceable owing to their being repugnant to the moral sense of the people. In theory, but not in practice,

---

[1] For an instance of a wide delegation of taxing power, see p. 101, *post*. Though the Crown may not without parliamentary sanction levy a charge in return for the performance of a public duty, the courts will enforce payment for the performance of a service which cannot be demanded as of right, *e.g.* the provision of protection by armed forces for merchant vessels trading in peace time in foreign waters which were infested with pirates: *China Navigation Co.* v. *Attorney-General*, [1932] 2 K.B. 197; K. & L. 93.

[2] K. & L. 8–12; Dicey, *op. cit.*, Introduction, p. lxix and note 1.

[3] "That principle of construction is now, I apprehend, discredited," "Liberty and the Common Law," by Lord Wright, 9 *C.L.J.* 3.

Parliament could enact a law condemning all red-haired males to death or making attendance at public worship illegal.

So too the immense complexity of the business of government makes it necessary that, while preserving its supremacy, Parliament should exercise it only after the major interests affected have been consulted. The modern State regulates the whole life of the community. The initiation of legislation is the function of the Executive, but prior consultation of major interests affected is an essential part of the legislative process. Indeed it is not uncommon in the case of delegated legislation for Parliament expressly to provide for consultation between a Minister and the organisations representing interests to be affected by the making of regulations. Legislation affecting industrial life is not passed without consultation with the major industrial organisations of employers and employed—employers' associations and trade unions. Such consultation ensures that legislation is passed with adequate knowledge of the problems involved and that Parliament is aware in advance how far it will secure the co-operation essential for its enforcement. It is of the highest importance that the persons or bodies consulted should be truly representative of the interests concerned, but not all interests—especially consumers—are organised. Similar consultation takes place before the passage of legislation directly affecting the professions, *e.g.* the medical profession had to be consulted before the initiation of the National Health Service; the Bar Council and the Law Society before the introduction of measures changing legal procedure. Numerous measures necessitate the co-operation of local authorities which is secured in advance by consultation between the Ministry of Housing and Local Government and the Associations of Municipal Corporations and of County Councils. There is a tendency for the Executive to face Parliament with "agreed measures." But consultation does not mean that the bodies whose advice is sought can dictate policy. It is for the Minister to weigh up that advice and to present the policy of the Government to Parliament. Consultation must not be allowed to hamper Parliament in reaching final decisions. No dictation to Parliament must be tolerated. Parliamentary democracy would not work if a minority attempted to influence national action, *e.g.* in the sphere of foreign policy, by organised obstruction or strikes. The practice of consultation is one of the factors which have stood in the way of the establishment of any rival to Parliament by means of functional devolution. An economic Parliament elected by sectional interests might easily become a rival claimant for supremacy.

Consultation of Interests affected.

Finally there must be mentioned the responsibility of Parliament to the electorate, the political sovereign. Some constitutions provide that constitutional changes shall only take effect with the consent of the electorate obtained by a referendum (a poll of the electorate).

Parliament and the Electorate.

The referendum need not be confined to constitutional issues. Other constitutions provide for the initiative—a device to enable the electorate to instruct Parliament to proceed with a measure. Our constitution does not find a place for any machinery of direct democracy, but the view that the party which has come into power after a general election has a mandate from the electorate to implement by legislation the whole of its election promises has been increasingly urged of late. Equally any departure from the mandate is apt to be criticised by the Opposition. There is danger in the doctrine of the mandate, especially when election programmes are settled largely by reference to the views endorsed by large gatherings at party political conferences; it is the duty of a Government to govern and it can hardly be the case that decisions on foreign relations or on the elementary duty of maintaining order can only be taken with reference to action authorised beforehand by an electoral mandate. Power gained and held by consent may well be stultified by too rigid reliance on the mandate. Legislative supremacy is not shared with the electorate. None the less, though the power exists, no Parliament, save in an emergency, would prolong its own life, and at regular intervals the electorate exercises its political supremacy by the choice of representatives. Parliament accordingly exercises its legislative supremacy with its responsibility to the electorate in mind. History has shown that Parliament is always sensitive to public opinion. Even in the eighteenth century when Parliament was not a truly representative assembly, public opinion made itself felt in times of national crisis, *e.g.* the dismissal of the Fox-North coalition and the call to power of the younger Pitt. Experience of direct democracy shows that the voter when confronted by an isolated issue on a referendum is slow to favour any change in the *status quo*. Parliamentary government makes for more flexible government and probably for truer and more effective concern for the public interest of the community as a whole.

CHAPTER 3.

THE RULE OF LAW.

THE supremacy or rule of law has been since the Middle Ages a principle of the constitution. It means that the exercise of powers of government shall be conditioned by law and that the subject shall not be exposed to the arbitrary will of his ruler.[1] There is much truth in the contention that "principles of the constitution" are only "political principles." The rule of law had a different interpretation under weak Lancastrian monarchs than under the Tudors. It has been said that "unconstitutional" may mean merely "contrary to tradition," but "the principles of 1689 have become part of the accepted theory of democracy" and "in the political sphere there is much in the Whig philosophy with which any democrat will agree, and which is, therefore, an accepted and, one might almost say, permanent part of the constitution." [2] But the rule of law is a concept of greater antiquity, although admittedly it had to be reconciled with the doctrine of parliamentary supremacy in the course of the seventeenth-century contest with the Crown.

In the Middle Ages the theory was held that there was a universal law which ruled the world. Bracton, writing in the first half of the thirteenth century, deduced from this theory the proposition that rulers were subject to law. We have seen[3] how the alliance between common lawyers and Parliament had a decisive effect upon the contest between Crown and Parliament. That alliance had its roots in the later Middle Ages. Mediaeval lawyers never denied the wide scope of the royal prerogative, but the King could do certain things only in certain ways. It was not until the seventeenth century that Parliament established its supremacy, but Fortescue, C.J., writing in the reign of Henry VI., had applied what later became the two major principles of the constitution—the rule of law and the supremacy of the Parliament—and relied upon the rule of law to justify the contention that taxation could not be imposed without the consent of Parliament. With the rise in the sixteenth century of the modern territorial State the mediaeval conception of a universal law which ruled the world gave place to the conception of the supremacy of the common law. The abolition in 1640 of the Court of Star

History of the Rule of Law.

[1] For historical summary, see *M.P.R.*, pp. 71–3.
[2] Jennings, *The Law and the Constitution*, 4th ed., p. 298.
[3] Pp. 32–6, *ante*.

Chamber ensured that the principles of the common law should apply to public as well as private law. The rule of law meant the supremacy of all parts of the law of England, both enacted and unenacted. The supremacy of the law together with the supremacy of Parliament were finally established by the Bill of Rights in 1689.

Dicey's exposition of the Rule of Law.

Of all writers on the constitution since Blackstone the most influential has been the late A. V. Dicey, whose lectures delivered as Vinerian Professor of English Law at Oxford and first published in 1885 under the title *Introduction to the Study of the Law of the Constitution*[1] have been studied by successive generations of statesmen, lawyers and a large section of those interested in public life. The constitutional law of 1955 differs in many respects from that of 1885, but the influence of Dicey remains a real force and there is no better way of distinguishing between the permanent and impermanent features of our constitution than by examining the principles of the constitution as expounded by Dicey and determining how far they hold good to-day. Of those principles which Dicey expounded that which has had most influence and at the same time has received most modern criticism is his exposition of the rule of law.[2]

Committee on Ministers' Powers.

One of the terms of reference of the Committee on Ministers' Powers appointed by the Lord Chancellor in 1929[3] was to report what safeguards were desirable or necessary in respect of the legislative and judicial powers of Ministers in order to secure the constitutional principles of the sovereignty of Parliament and the supremacy of the law. It was understood that what was meant by the supremacy of the law was the principle expounded by Dicey.

First of Dicey's three meanings of the Rule of Law:

Absence of Arbitrary Power.

Dicey gave to the rule of law three meanings: "it means in the first place, the absolute supremacy or predominance of regular law as opposed to the influence of arbitrary power, and excludes the existence of arbitrariness, of prerogative, or even of wide discretionary authority on the part of the government . . . a man may be punished for a breach of law, but he can be punished for nothing else." [4] This interpretation conveyed that no man is punishable or can be lawfully made to suffer in body or goods, except for a distinct breach of law established in ordinary legal manner before the ordinary courts of the land. In this sense the rule of law is contrasted with systems of government based on the exercise by persons in authority of wide arbitrary or discretionary powers of constraint.

---

[1] 9th ed., with Introduction by E. C. S. Wade (Macmillan), 1939.
[2] The reader should study Dicey, *op. cit.*, Chaps. IV., XII. and XIII., and Introduction, pp. lxvii to xciv; Jennings, *The Law and the Constitution*, 4th ed., Chap. II. and App. 2; and "Constitutional Government and the Rule of Law," by G. Godfrey Phillips, *J.C.L.*, 3rd series, Vol. XX., pp. 262 *et seq.*
[3] Part VII., Chap. 1.
[4] Dicey, *op. cit.*, p. 202.

The rule of law "means, again, equality before the law or the equal subjection of all classes to the ordinary law of the land administered by the ordinary law courts." [1] In this sense the rule of law conveys that no man is above the law; that officials like private citizens are under a duty to obey the same law; and (though this does not necessarily follow) that there are no administrative courts to which are referred claims by the citizen against the State or its officials.

Dicey contrasted the rule of law with the *droit administratif* of France. He was at pains to contrast the disadvantages involved by a system of administrative law and administrative courts to judge disputes between officials and citizens with the advantages enjoyed by Englishmen through the absence of such a system. He did not properly appreciate the working of the French system of *contentieux administratif* by the *Council d'État*.[2] This was indeed the only part of *droit administratif* with which he dealt. Nor did he pay much attention to the wide powers of the Executive which existed in England even in his day.[3] The law which regulates the powers and duties of public authorities and officials in this country is as much administrative law as the *droit administratif* of France even though its enforcement or supervision may be controlled by the same courts as the rest of English law.[4] But, although Dicey misinterpreted the meaning of *droit administratif*, his emphasis upon equality before the law served to stress that fundamental liberties can be protected by the common law—that police law is not law, and that freedom requires a legal system which protects essential liberties.

Finally the rule of law as expounded by Dicey means "that with us the law of the constitution, the rules which in foreign countries naturally form part of a constitutional code, are not the source but the consequence of the rights of individuals, as defined and enforced by the courts, that, in short, the principles of private law have with us been by the action of the courts and Parliament so extended as to determine the position of the Crown and of its servants; thus the constitution is the result of the ordinary law of the land." [5] By this is meant that the legal rights of the subject, *e.g.* his freedom of action and speech, are secured not by guaranteed rights proclaimed in a formal code but by the operation of the ordinary remedies of private law available against those who unlawfully interfere with his liberty of action, whether they be private citizens or officials. A person libelled may sue his defamer. Free access to courts of justice is an efficient guarantee against wrongdoers.

Margin notes:
Second meaning of the Rule of Law:

Subjection of Officials to the Ordinary Courts.

Droit Administratif.

Third meaning of the Rule of Law:

Constitution the result of the ordinary Law of the Land.

[1] Dicey, *op. cit.*, pp. 202–3.
[2] Dicey, *op. cit.*, 9th ed., Appendix, Section I. (4). For the *Conseil d'État*, see C. J. Hamson, *Executive Discretion and Judicial Control* (Stevens), 1954.
[3] But see Introduction to 8th edition and his article "Administrative Law in England," 31 *L.Q.R.* 148.
[4] Part VII., Chap. 1.   [5] Dicey, *op. cit.*, p. 203.

Each of these three meanings of the rule of law will be examined. How far Dicey's exposition was true of Dicey's time is primarily a question for the legal historian. We shall consider how far Dicey's exposition is true to-day in order to ascertain how far, if at all, the conception of the rule of law has a permanent value as a principle of the constitution.

Arbitrary Power and Discretionary Authority distinguished:

Absence of Arbitrary Power.

In considering Dicey's first meaning of the rule of law a distinction must be drawn between arbitrary power and discretionary authority. It is still an essential principle of constitutional government in the United Kingdom that there should be no arbitrary power to arrest or punish. It may be argued that, provided the law authorises the punishment of those who in the opinion of the Judiciary, or even the Executive, have acted in a manner contrary to the interests of the State, there is nothing contrary to the rule of law in inflicting such punishment. This, however, is to deny any real meaning or value to the conception of the rule of law. What is authorised by law cannot be illegal, but it may be contrary to the rule of law as a principle of constitutional government.[1] The essential feature of Dicey's first meaning of the rule of law remains a feature of the constitution to-day, viz. that, so far as punishment for offences is concerned, the citizen can foresee the consequences of his conduct and will not be punished save for a breach of the ordinary law. He will, moreover, be tried in the ordinary courts. The law of England knows nothing of exceptional offences punished by extra-ordinary tribunals. There are no special courts for the trial of crimes against the State. Judges have power to adjust sentences to the gravity of offences and the circumstances and past records of offenders. Maximum sentences for specific crimes are, however, laid down by law for nearly every criminal offence. The common law crime of public mischief provides dangerous scope for judicial discretion,[2] but in general so far as major crimes are concerned the definition of an offence—whether by common law or statute law—is fixed and can be ascertained.

"The Ordinary Law."

When Dicey referred to "ordinary law," he had in mind the common law or law enacted in Acts of Parliament. To-day criminal law includes innumerable offences which are created by statutory regulations. It is important that the individual should have the assurance that the law can be ascertained with reasonable certainty. A person who takes the trouble to consult his lawyer ought to be able to ascertain the legal consequences of his actions. The bulk and detail of the regulations enacted by government departments

---

[1] See review by Sir William Holdsworth of E. C. S. Wade's Introduction to Dicey in 55 *L.Q.R.* 585.

[2] *The King* v. *Manley*, [1933] 1 K.B. 529; see "Public Mischief," by W. T. S. Stallybrass, 49 *L.Q.R.* 183; *The Queen* v. *Newland*, [1953] 3 W.L.R. 827.

undoubtedly creates uncertainty.[1] The power to create offences must be delegated because the needs of the modern State require that innumerable regulations be made and enforced. In order, however, to secure as far as practicable conformity with the rule of law provision must be made for simplicity, publication and accessibility. As the result of parliamentary pressure the importance of these factors was drawn to the attention of all government departments in April 1943.[2] Legislation followed in 1946; this was designed to ensure adequate publicity for statutory instruments in and out of Parliament: Statutory Instruments Act, 1946.[3] It is, however, highly desirable that there should be more parliamentary counsel,[4] so that the drafting of regulations may receive the same care as that of statutes and the work entrusted to a single authority rather than to the legal staffs of separate departments. Only so can there be any safeguard that there will be no violation of the accepted principles of criminal liability under pressure of administrative expediency. In another way the growth of delegated legislation touches upon the principle of the rule of law. There is a close connection between the rule of law and parliamentary supremacy. So long as criminal law was based on either common law or statute law a man was only punishable for a breach of law which was either based on the ancient custom of the country or was enacted by the representatives of the people. If offences are to be created by regulations made by government departments or subordinate bodies, it is essential that there should be scrutiny by Parliament to ensure conformity with the will of the people as expressed by its representatives. The need of such scrutiny was recognised in 1944 when there was appointed a select committee of the House of Commons to scrutinise those classes of delegated legislation which are required to be laid before Parliament.

While as a citizen a man is subject only to the ordinary law, he Group Law. may also be subject to the special law affecting his particular calling which may be enforced by special tribunals. But no man can be judged by his fellow citizens except so far as Parliament has authorised it or, as in the case of domestic tribunals, the parties agree upon it: *Lee* v. *Showmen's Guild*, [1952] 2 Q.B. 329, 341. The armed forces are subject to a statutory code of military law or naval law in addition to the ordinary law of the land, and offences against that law are triable by courts-martial.[5] The clergy are subject to ecclesiastical law enforced by the ecclesiastical courts or other special tribunals established by statute.[6] Solicitors are subject to the disciplinary powers of a statutory body composed of members of the

[1] Dicey, *op. cit.*, 9th ed., Introduction, p. lxxiv.
[2] *H.C. Deb.*, 5th Series, Vol. 389, cols. 1646–1669.
[3] Part VII., Chap. 6.   [4] P. 109, *post*.
[5] Part IX., Chap. 2.   [6] Part XI.

profession, with a right of appeal to the High Court. The General Medical Council, which is also a body set up by statute, has power to try by a Disciplinary Committee, which sits with a legal assessor, members of the medical profession for unprofessional conduct and, as the one penalty which it may impose, has power to erase a doctor's name from the Medical Register. An appeal by the person whose conduct is investigated lies to the Judicial Committee of the Privy Council. The Dental Board has similar powers; there is a right of appeal to the High Court. Provided that there is no imposition of arbitrary punishments and that ordinary judicial methods are observed, "group law" is not inconsistent with the rule of law. Courts-martial follow legal forms and observe strict rules of procedure. A recent extension of "group law" is, however, open to criticism. Provision has been made by statute[1] to enable a substantial majority of persons engaged in a particular branch of agriculture to frame a scheme for the organisation of their industry which has the force of law and is binding on all producers in the industry concerned whether they voted for or against the proposal. Schemes provide for the establishment of marketing boards elected by the industry concerned which are given powers of control over the production and marketing of a particular commodity. These powers include the power for the board itself to punish for a breach of the provisions of a scheme. Marketing boards have been criticised on the ground that they are in the position of prosecutor, judge and jury in their own case; that their chairmen are usually without legal qualifications; and that they do not follow normal rules of procedure and evidence. In 1939 a departmental committee recommended[2] that allegations of offences should be heard by small disciplinary committees presided over by an independent chairman with legal qualifications, and that provision should be made for an appeal from a disciplinary committee to the High Court on a point of law; the first of these recommendations has been accepted.[3]

Discretionary Authority.
We must now consider discretionary authority as opposed to arbitrary power. If it is contrary to the rule of law that discretionary authority should be given to government departments or public officers, then the rule of law is inapplicable to any modern constitution. When Dicey wrote the first edition of his *Law of the Constitution*, the primary functions of the State were the preservation of law and order, defence and foreign relations. The exercise of discretionary authority in these spheres did not touch directly upon the citizen's daily life, nor did it frequently give rise to cases in the

---

[1] Agricultural Marketing Acts, 1931–33; *cf.* Herring Industry Acts, 1935–44.
[2] Report of the Departmental Committee on the Imposition of Penalties by Marketing Boards and Other Similar Bodies, 1939, Cmd. 5980.
[3] Agriculture Marketing Act, 1949, s. 5.

courts. To-day the State regulates the national life in multifarious ways. Discretionary authority in every sphere is inevitable. A citizen can still so regulate his conduct that he can in general foresee whether he is likely to appear as a defendant in a criminal court. A citizen cannot foresee how far the State will interfere with his freedom to enjoy his property. A piece of land may be compulsorily acquired for some vital national purpose not known at the time when the land was purchased. A time comes when the upkeep of a private road will be assumed by ratepayers as a public charge. Discretion to determine when that time has come must be given to someone—in this case the local authority. Again, a borough may have too many public houses and some must be closed as redundant. No one can with certainty foresee which houses the licensing justices will classify as redundant; it is a matter for their discretion exercised bonâ fide and in the public interest, but none the less it is a discretion which may result in injury to the existing rights of a licence-holder. It is this absence of foreseeability which has caused a critic to suggest that planning is inconsistent with the rule of law.[1] His view is that the rule of law means that "government in all its actions is bound by rule, fixed and announced beforehand—rules which make it possible to foresee with fair certainty how the authority will use its concise powers in given circumstances, and to plan one's individual affairs on the basis of this knowledge." Such certainty is not attainable in modern conditions. The rule of law, however, demands that, so far as is practicable, where an individual plans his affairs reasonably with due regard for public welfare, he shall receive compensation, if he suffers damage as the result of a change in the law or the exercise of a discretionary authority granted in the public interest. To enable the citizen to foresee as far as possible the consequences of his actions and as a safeguard against arbitrary official conduct the grant of discretionary authority should prescribe as a minimum the general lines on which it should be exercised and fix precisely its limits. In this way the exercise of power can be challenged for excess or abuse in the courts. Discretionary power should not mean arbitrary power, *i.e.* power exercised by an agent responsible to none and subject to no control.

Dicey's second meaning of the rule of law also requires careful examination. "Equality before the law" does not mean that the powers of the private citizen are the same as the powers of the public official. Here it will suffice by way of illustration to mention that the powers of arrest possessed by police constables are, and always have been, somewhat wider than those of private citizens.[2] It is not

Powers of Public Officers.

---

[1] *The Road to Serfdom*, by F. A. Hayek (Routledge), Chap. VI., "Planning and the Rule of Law."

[2] See *Christie* v. *Leachinsky*, [1947] A.C. 573; K. & L. 182, and Part VIII., Chap. I., at p. 365.

contrary to the rule of law that special powers should be given to public officers to enable them to perform their public duties.[1] What the rule of law requires is that powers should be defined by law and that any abuse of power or other wrongful act by public officers should be subject to control by the courts in the same way as any wrongful act committed by a private citizen. The orders of the Crown or of a superior officer are no defence to a prosecution for a crime or a civil action in respect of a tortious injury.[2] This is what Dicey meant by "equality before the law." [3]

It is not inconsistent with the principle of "equality before the law" that, as we have seen, certain groups of the community, *e.g.* soldiers[4] and clergy[5] are subject to laws which do not affect the rest of the community, because those laws apply to all members of a particular calling. They are subject like others to the general law, though they incur additional liabilities as well as privileges by reason of their calling.

Qualifications to Dicey's Second Meaning.

But the second meaning attributed by Dicey to the rule of law requires some qualification under current conditions. In the first place there remain, even after the operation of the Crown Proceedings Act, 1947, a few privileges and immunities (as distinct from powers of government) which are open to public authorities and their officers. So far as judicial authorities enjoy protection from being sued,[6] their immunities are conferred solely to ensure the impartial administration of the law and these cannot be regarded as qualifications of the rule of law. So far as these privileges relate to the position of the Crown as litigant they are mainly concerned with the conditions of service in the armed forces and the exigencies of the postal service. But the Crown also enjoys a wide privilege of refusing to disclose relevant documents or to answer relevant questions which arise in the course of litigation: Crown Proceedings Act, 1947, s. 28; *Ellis* v. *Home Office*, [1953] 2 Q.B. 135.

Secondly, in common with all civilised States, the United Kingdom affords immunities to the persons and the property of other States, their rulers and diplomatic agents, in the form of exemption from process in the courts, but not from legal liability as such: *Dickinson* v. *Del Solar*, [1930] 1 K.B. 376. The significance of those immunities, which on the authority of the International Organisations (Immunities and Privileges) Act, 1950, have been made capable of a wide

---

[1] Powers are sometimes conferred directly upon officials, but more frequently the powers exercised by officials are conferred either upon the Crown or upon Ministers or other public authorities. They are inevitably exercised through officials of the department or authority concerned.

[2] For the position of soldiers acting under orders, see Part IX., Chap. 2, B., *post.*

[3] Dicey, *op. cit.*, p. 194.

[4] Part IX., Chap. 2.

[5] Part XI.

[6] Part V., Chap. 2.

extension in favour of recognised international agencies and their officers, lies not so much in the licence to commit offences with impunity on the part of respectable diplomats who can be certain of other sanctions in that event, as in their possible extension to the trading activities of modern States. In this connection it may be noted that, although the immunity from process extends to State property destined for the public use since it rests upon the dignity of national States,[1] the House of Lords has left open the question of its application to State-owned trading ships; *Compania Naviera Vascongado* v. *SS. Cristina*, [1938] A.C. 485.[2]

In the third place there are one or two instances where internal political expediency has required the conferment of special immunities. In particular the Trade Disputes Act, 1906, s. 4 (1), prohibits the bringing of any action against a trade union in respect of a tort. This rule applies whether the trade union is sued in its own name or through its officers. It has always been impossible to bring an action against an unincorporated body as such, *e.g.* social clubs and many charitable institutions, though individual members or officers are, of course, liable for wrongful acts in which they take part: *Hardie and Lane Ltd.* v. *Chiltern*, [1928] 1 K.B. 663; but it was held (prior to the Trade Disputes Act, 1906) that an action could be brought against trade unions, which were given special statutory privileges not enjoyed by other unincorporated associations but were also subject to important disabilities:[3] *Taff Vale Railway* v. *Amalgamated Societies of Railway Servants*, [1901] A.C. 426. A trade union can, to a limited extent,[4] sue and be sued on its contracts, and an action for tort can be brought against individual members, unless acts normally wrongful are protected by some other statutory provisions, *e.g.* section 3 of the Trade Disputes Act, 1906, which removes liability for inducing a breach of contract, provided the act done is in contemplation or furtherance of a trade dispute. The immunity of trade unions is an immunity from all actions for tort and is not confined to acts done in contemplation or furtherance of a trade dispute: *Vacher* v. *London Society of Compositors*, [1913] A.C. 107. The trustees of a union may be sued in relation to union property vested in them provided that the action does not relate to a tortious act committed by or on behalf of a union in contemplation or furtherance of a trade dispute.

---

[1] *The Parlement Belge* (1880), 5 P.D. 197.

[2] P. 211, *post.*

[3] See Trade Union Act, 1871, which provided that the purposes of a trade union should not be deemed unlawful merely because they might be in restraint of trade and gave to trade unions a limited legal capacity.

[4] Thus a member who has been expelled in breach of the rules of his union cannot recover damages from the union: *Bonsor* v. *Musicians' Union*, [1954] Ch. 479.

It is as true to-day as when Dicey wrote that officials are not exempted from the jurisdiction of the ordinary courts and that, as we
have seen, the law of England knows nothing of exceptional offences
punished by extra-ordinary tribunals. There are no special courts
for the trial of crimes against the State or of civil claims against
officials. There are, however, as has been mentioned in discussing
the separation of powers, many special courts for the decision of
issues which may affect vitally the proprietary rights of citizens or
their entitlement to benefits. Special tribunals appointed by Ministers,
or even Ministers themselves acting through civil servants may determine questions of insurability; what compensation shall be paid for
the compulsory acquisition of land; whether a dairy farmer may sell
milk. How far is the existence of such special courts contrary to the
rule of law? It is submitted that the rule of law is satisfied, provided
that the tribunals are impartial and independent; that every man is
heard before a decision is given affecting his rights; that reasons are
given for decisions and reasonable regard is paid to precedent. It is inconsistent with the rule of law that a judicial issue (as distinct from a
purely administrative decision) should be decided by a Minister
interested in carrying out a policy affected by the issue.[1] Judicial decisions not referred to the ordinary courts should generally be entrusted to a tribunal with a chairman with legal qualifications, and
on points of law there should be provision for an appeal to the courts,
e.g. whether or not an individual comes within the definition of an
insured person. The essential requirements are, however, that decisions should be impartial and that those who give them should not
be liable to pressure from the Executive.

That these requirements are invariably satisfied at the present time
cannot be asserted with any confidence, but that they are accepted as
standards of what should be the normal procedure is important. It
will be seen later that the number of tribunals is considerable and
that their creation has been piecemeal. To expect absolute uniformity
of procedure in such circumstances would be unreasonable, but there
remains the need for vigilance particularly on the part of Parliament,
lest the grant of statutory powers of adjudication be accompanied
by a laxity of procedure so as to defeat the ends of justice under
cover of administrative convenience.

Dicey's
Third
Meaning of
the Rule
of Law
explained.

Finally there must be examined the third meaning of the rule of
law, viz. that private rights depend not upon a constitutional code,
but on the ordinary law. Dicey is here referring not to the mass of
rights derived from statutes, *e.g.* pensions, insurance, or free education, but to the fundamental political freedoms—"the common law

---

[1] The whole question of special tribunals, their merits and demerits, is discussed in Part VII., Chap. 5; and see Chap. 3 of W. A. Robson, *Justice and Administrative Law*, 3rd ed. (Stevens & Sons).

of the constitution "—freedom of the person, freedom of speech, freedom of association. The citizen whose fundamental rights are infringed may seek his remedy in the courts and will rely, not upon a constitutional guarantee, but on the ordinary law of the land. The right to personal freedom is protected by the writ of habeas corpus, the right of self-defence and the right to bring an action or a prosecution for wrongful arrest, assault or false imprisonment.[1] Freedom of speech means that a man may write or say what he pleases provided that his words are not treasonable, seditious, obscene or contrary to the law of defamation (libel and slander).[2] The writ of habeas corpus existed at common law, but was made effective by the Habeas Corpus Acts of 1679 and 1816. The right to arrest is governed partly by common law, partly by statutes, *e.g.* the Criminal Justice Act, 1925, s. 44. The law of libel is primarily common law, but various statutes give special privileges to the Press, *e.g.* the Defamation Act, 1952, which extends the defence of qualified privilege to reports of proceedings of a large number of public bodies. The Public Order Act, 1936, is an important part of the law of public meeting, but the basis of that law is the common law relating to trespass and nuisance.[3] The ordinary law may prove a more effective protection than constitutional guarantees contained in a written constitution which may be suspended in times of emergency.[4] "The unwritten constitution of England consists of a set of legal principles gradually evolved out of the decisions of our Courts of Justice in individual cases."[5] For this reason there must be watched jealously any encroachment upon the jurisdiction of the courts and any restriction on the subject's right of access to them. "By any such encroachment the principal safeguard provided by the constitution for the main tenance of the subject's rights is impaired."[5]

The rule of law remains a principle of our constitution. It means Conclusion. the absence of arbitrary power; effective control of and proper publicity for delegated legislation, particularly when it imposes penalties; that when discretionary power is granted the manner in which it is to be exercised should as far as is practicable be defined; that every man should be responsible to the ordinary law whether he be private citizen or public officer; that private rights should be determined by impartial and independent tribunals; and that fundamental private rights are safeguarded by the ordinary law of the land. If this be accepted, it is only necessary to contrast the state of affairs in the totalitarian States, with their apparatus of secret police and people's

---

[1] Part VIII., Chap. 1.
[2] Part VIII., Chap. 3.
[3] Part VIII., Chap. 3.
[4] Note the very limited effect of the so-called Habeas Corpus Suspension Acts; Dicey, *op. cit.*, pp. 229–32.
[5] *M.P.R.*, p. 73.

courts administering not law, but the orders of those who can dictate what is the people's will, in order to answer affirmatively the question —does the rule of law to-day remain a principle of the constitution? This does not mean that it is a fixed principle of law from which there can be no departure. Since Parliament is supreme, there is no legal sanction to prevent the enactment of a statute which violates the principle of the rule of law. The ultimate safeguard then is to be found in the acceptance of the principle as a guide to conduct by any political party which is in a position to influence the course of legislation.

CHAPTER 4.

CONVENTIONS OF THE CONSTITUTION.

"Constitutional law creates obligations in the same way as private law, but its reactions as to persons possessed of political power are extra-legal: revolutions, active and passive resistance, the pressure of public opinion. The sanction is derived from the threat of these consequences."—Vinogradoff, *Outlines of Historical Jurisprudence*, Vol. I., p. 120 (Clarendon Press).

IN discussing conventions as a source of constitutional law it is desirable first to examine the nature of the obligation and then to consider what compels obedience in the absence of the ordinary means of enforcing a legal rule through the orders of a court. The term "convention" has been accepted, largely through the influence of Dicey,[1] to describe this kind of obligation, whether it derives from custom, agreement or expediency. There is, however, no necessary connection with the notion of express agreement in the sense in which the term, convention, is used by international lawyers. Dicey discussed the rules for the exercise of the royal prerogative by Ministers of the Crown and those governing the relations between the two Houses of Parliament, rules based on custom or expediency rather than resulting from any formal agreement. Nowadays conventional rules have a wider ambit and govern (*inter alia*) the relations between the various members States of the British Commonwealth. Since the Statute of Westminster, 1931, the rules governing the full competence of their Parliaments to legislate are statutory, though the Statute gave effect to much that had hitherto rested on agreement. But otherwise the relations between the various States including the United Kingdom are conventional, *i.e.* based on agreements reached at Imperial Conferences which have been subsequently adopted by the various Governments.[2] More recently agreement has been reached at less formal conferences, usually at meetings attended by Prime Ministers or Ministers for Finance or External Affairs.

What is a Convention of the Constitution?

As well in the sphere of high policy as in the work of routine administration modern government demands a high degree of flexibility. In the case of an enacted constitution changes can be achieved by constitutional amendment, but amendment is normally difficult to procure, and in practice many changes are brought about without formal modification. In this process interpretation by the

Inadequacy of Legal Rules.

---

[1] *Law of the Constitution*, 9th ed., Chap. XIV; and see Introduction, pp. xcv et seq.
[2] *Report of Conference on Operation of Dominion Legislation*, 1930, pp. 19, 20, Cmd. 3479.

courts of the written law plays its part, though not always in the direction of adapting the law to present needs, but evolution by conventional rules is equally important. In the United Kingdom the legal framework of executive government has been adapted to other ends than those which it formerly served without any change in the law, not by judicial interpretation, for which opportunity seldom occurs where there is no enacted constitution, but by the growth of conventional rules. In this way has the Executive, the servant in law of the Crown, become subject to Parliament and through the House of Commons to the electorate, its political overlord. The whole conception of constitutional monarchy was thus developed without destroying the legal powers of the Crown, other than those doubtfully claimed by the Stuarts. Again parliamentary government means not merely that there is a legislature with capacity to enact all laws, but that co-operation between Ministers and Parliament is secured by rules which are largely conventional and are enforced by political rather than legal sanctions. Fear of loss of office or of reputation is the ultimate sanction which causes Ministers to observe this part of constitutional law, rather than fine or imprisonment. Equally, expectation of office and regard for their political reputations ensure observance on the part of the Opposition.

Scope of Conventions.
"Conventions are rules for determining the mode in which the discretionary powers of the Crown (or of Ministers as servants of the Crown) ought to be exercised." [1] So wrote Dicey seventy years ago. He was concerned to establish that conventions were "intended to secure the ultimate supremacy of the electorate as the true political sovereign of the state." He was therefore mainly concerned with rules governing the use of the prerogative. The complexity of modern government has caused innumerable statutory duties to be entrusted to the Executive. The older powers are still exercised in the name of the Queen, though convention entrusts them to Ministers. Modern statutes recognise the convention and confer the powers expressly on individual Ministers in many, but not in all cases. When Parliament gives a Minister discretionary power, that power is exercised by him as a matter of law, but it will none the less be a discretionary power exercised on behalf of the Crown. The conventions which impose individual and collective responsibility upon Ministers operate to secure that in the exercise of legal powers conferred upon him by statute a Minister shall be as responsible to Parliament as if he were exercising a prerogative power which is in law the sole responsibility of the Crown. But it is not only in the sphere of the discretionary powers of the Executive that conventions are an important source of constitutional law, and a fuller examination of their contents and application is required.

[1] Dicey, *op. cit.*, pp. 422–3. See Introduction, 9th ed., pp. xcv–xcvii.

The Queen acts upon the advice of her Ministers everywhere in the The Sovereign; Choice of Prime Minister. British Commonwealth. At home she receives advice from United Kingdom Ministers; elsewhere her Governors-General, to whom are entrusted most (and in the case of the Union of South Africa all) of her powers, act on the advice of the Ministers who form the Cabinet of each State. But there are some matters which fall to be determined by the exercise of her independent judgment, and in particular the appointment of a Prime Minister,[1] and in some circumstances the dissolution of Parliament. There are conventional rules which limit her range of choice of a new Prime Minister. The support of the party or coalition which may be expected to command a majority in the House of Commons is a condition precedent to acceptance of the office. It is perhaps safe to say that membership of the House of Commons is another. At all events no peer has held the office since Lord Salisbury resigned in 1902, and the choice of Mr. Baldwin (as he then was) in preference to Lord Curzon in 1923 may be regarded as establishing that no peer could again accept the office, so long as the House of Lords is constituted as at present.[2] The practice of the Sovereign first consulting the leader of the Opposition when a Government tenders its resignation on defeat in the Commons is well established and ensures the impartial position in politics which a constitutional monarchy should occupy. Yet the ultimate decision is the personal responsibility of the Sovereign, and in the task of selection precedent is not conclusive, and therefore the conventions lack the binding force which they possess in other fields. This does not mean that they can normally be disregarded, but that unforeseen circumstances may deprive them of their force on a particular occasion.

Closely connected with the choice of a Prime Minister is the power Dissolution of Parliament. to dissolve Parliament. Here the Sovereign is by convention bound to accept the advice of the Prime Minister, since the alternative is to dismiss him and with him all his ministerial colleagues, a step which would inevitably involve the Sovereign in political controversy. There could be no justification for the dismissal against its will of a Ministry which commanded a majority in the House of Commons, save on the ground that the majority no longer reflected the will of the electorate. A dissolution is the orthodox means of testing this. When a minority Government holds office, the position is more complicated,

---

[1] Sir Ivor Jennings, *Cabinet Government*, Chap. II, where all the precedents are discussed. The Sovereign may, of course, seek advice, but it is not ministerial advice in the constitutional sense. The choice is the personal responsibility of the Sovereign.

[2] Sir Harold Nicolson, *George V*, pp. 377 ff.; Sir Winston Churchill, *The Second World War*, Vol. I., at pp. 523–4, for an account of Lord Halifax's views on this point in 1940, which emphasise the practical difficulties confronting a Prime Minister who is a peer.

but here again it is for the Prime Minister to choose the occasion for appealing to the electorate. Should he persist in retaining office despite his rejection by the electorate, the Sovereign might be forced into the position of having to dismiss him, but it is safe to say that this would only be done on the advice of the leader of an opposition party prepared to take office in his place. A similar situation could arise if a Prime Minister who had failed to obtain the support of the new House of Commons after a dissolution demanded a second dissolution in the hope of solving the deadlock. Convention, in the sense of a rule based on expediency, thus prescribes the proper course for the Sovereign to take.

The Cabinet.

A number of the conventional understandings which Dicey, quoting from Freeman's *Growth of the English Constitution*, cited as belonging to "the code by which public life in England is (or is supposed) to be governed" are closely connected with the prerogative of dissolution which has just been mentioned.[1] For example, "a Cabinet when outvoted on any vital question may appeal once to the country by means of a dissolution," or "If an appeal to the electors goes against a Ministry, they are bound to retire from office and have no right to dissolve Parliament a second time." There is, however, one convention upon which rests the whole doctrine of ministerial responsibility—"The Cabinet are responsible to Parliament as a body for the general conduct of affairs," as Freeman put it. It is impossible to exaggerate the importance of understanding the consequences of this rule, which is the foundation of parliamentary government as it is known throughout the British Commonwealth. For this reason it is selected as the single illustration of the operation of conventions in relation to Cabinet government.

Meaning of Ministerial Responsibility.

Ministerial responsibility has for the constitutional lawyer two distinct meanings, the one strictly legal, the other, which is under consideration here, purely conventional in the sense that it is no part of the law as applied by the courts. It is as well first to explain the former meaning, which is an integral part of the law. Holders of office under the Crown (and Ministers all have this status) are personally liable in law for their acts. Moreover, as the Crown can do no wrong, every act of the Crown must be done through a Minister who can be made responsible and, if necessary, sued. Acts requiring the Sovereign's participation must be authenticated by a seal for the custody of which a particular Minister is responsible or be recorded in documents bearing the counter-signature of a Minister. The use of the various seals on forms for recording the royal assent is regulated partly by statute and partly by custom.[2] When it is said that Ministers are personally liable in law for their acts, this means that

---

[1] Dicey, *op. cit.*, 9th ed., p. 416.
[2] Anson, *op. cit.*, 4th ed., Vol. II., Part I, pp. 62–72.

they are responsible for acts which they commit or sanction in their individual capacity. In early times liability was confined to officers of low status. Impeachment was used against the holders of the great State offices, though for a while under the Tudors it fell into disuse, as responsibility was regarded as being solely to the King and not to the law. By the end of the seventeenth century it was firmly established that no official, high or low, could plead the orders of the Sovereign when charged with a breach of the law. The rule of responsibility to the law has not been successfully challenged since the Act of Settlement provided that a royal pardon could not be pleaded in bar of an impeachment *i.e.* to prevent a person being brought to trial by this procedure. The Sovereign can do no wrong, but those who commit wrongs in the course of executing the Sovereign's business are personally liable and since 1948 can make the Crown, which is represented for this purpose by a Minister, responsible in law for illegal acts or omissions.

To return to the conventional meaning of ministerial responsi- Develop-
bility, it is not the fear of legal liability, but the desire to operate the ment of
Collective
machinery of government on constitutional lines which influences Responsi-
Ministers in their conduct of affairs and their relationship with Par- bility.
liament. Accordingly there has been evolved since 1688 the rule of collective responsibility which rests upon convention alone. During the greater part of the eighteenth century the Cabinet was still a body of holders of high office whose relationship with one another was ill defined, and thus the body as a whole was not responsible to Parliament. The Government was the King's Government in fact as well as in name, and the King acted on the advice of individual Ministers. The advice tendered by a Minister might, or might not, agree with that acceptable to his nominal colleagues, some of whom were seldom, if ever, consulted by their Sovereign. Apart from the relatively homogeneous Ministries under Walpole's pre-eminent leadership Cabinets were formed of different groups with many different aims; this made collective responsibility impracticable. Moreover, the King sometimes consulted those who were out of office without the prior approval of his Ministers. Eventually the Representation of the People Act, 1832 (the great Reform Bill), brought realisation that for the future the Executive must hold the same political views as the majority in Parliament. The support of Parliament could no longer be secured by the expedients of sinecure offices, pensions, the gift of seats in rotten boroughs, and such-like devices which had not shocked eighteenth-century political morality. The Cabinet, all its members united by party ties, became the definite link between the King and Parliament and so acquired the whole control over the direction of public affairs. Thus collective responsibility developed later than the political responsibility of individual Ministers. Just as

D

it became recognised that a single Minister could not retain office against the will of Parliament, so later it became clear that all Ministers must stand or fall together in Parliament, if the Government was to be carried on as a unity rather than by a number of advisers of the Sovereign acting separately.

What Collective Responsibility involves.

By the middle of the nineteenth century collective responsibility, as it is understood to-day, was firmly established. Lord Salisbury said in 1878: [1] "For all that passes in Cabinet every member of it who does not resign is absolutely and irretrievably responsible and has no right afterwards to say that he agreed in one case to a compromise, while in another he was persuaded by his colleagues. . . . It is only on the principle that absolute responsibility is undertaken by every member of the Cabinet, who, after a decision is arrived at, remains a member of it, that the joint responsibility of Ministers to Parliament can be upheld and one of the most essential principles of parliamentary responsibility established."

This statement explains why it is essential to draw the veil of secrecy over all that passes in Cabinet even in times when the requirements of security do not necessarily impose the ban of silence. It is impossible to preserve a united front, if disclosures are permitted of differences which have emerged in arriving at a decision. The fate of the minority of Ministers on the occasion of the single departure from the rule of unanimity reinforces its validity. In 1932 a coalition Cabinet issued an announcement to the effect that they had agreed to differ over the tariff issue, while remaining united on all other vital matters of national policy. The dissenting Ministers were given leave to oppose the majority view by speech and by vote. The convention of Cabinet unanimity was, however, reinforced when those Ministers decided a few months later to resign on the cognate issue of imperial preference.[2]

Collective responsibility does not require that every Cabinet Minister must take an active part in the formulation of policy, nor that his presence in the Cabinet room is essential whenever a decision is taken. His obligations may be passive rather than active when the decision does not relate to matters falling within his own sphere of administrative responsibility. He must, however, be informed beforehand of what the proposal is and have an opportunity of voicing his doubts and objections. The size of modern Cabinets (in peace time) would alone seem to preclude active participation by each Minister in forming conclusions. A body of some twenty or more is too large for effective committee work, but in the nature of things Ministers in Cabinet are, or should be, concerned more with de-

---

[1] *Life of Robert, Marquis of Salisbury*, Vol. II., pp. 219–20.
[2] Jennings, *Cabinet Government*, pp. 260–2; Dicey, *op. cit.*, Introduction, pp. cxliii–cxliv.

cisions of principle rather than detail.[1] Collective responsibility does, however, mean that a Cabinet Minister, and his Parliamentary Secretary, must vote with the Government in Parliament and, if necessary, be prepared to defend its policy. Neither in Parliament nor outside can a Minister be heard to say that he is in disagreement with a Cabinet decision, or for that matter with a decision of a colleague taken without reference to the Cabinet.

The individual responsibility of a Minister to Parliament is more positive in character. Each in his own sphere bears the burden of speaking and acting for the Government. When a Minister announces that His Majesty's Government have decided that they are prepared to take a certain course of action, it does not follow that the decision has been referred to the Cabinet. No doubt it would have been on an important issue of policy; but if the decision relates exclusively to the sphere for which the Minister is responsible, it must be at his discretion whom he chooses to consult beforehand; it is in the exercise of that discretion that he may decide to act without previous reference to his Cabinet colleagues. Nowadays so complex are results of governmental action that it is safe to assume that the practice of prior inter-departmental consultation is firmly established at all levels, and the experience of war should serve to ensure that there is no relapse into departmental isolationism. Be this as it may, a Minister knows that he will ultimately have to rely upon the support of his Cabinet colleagues if political criticism becomes vocal, and he must temper his decisions by reference to that consideration. *Individual Responsibility.*

While collective responsibility ensures that the Queen's Government presents a united front to Parliament, individual responsibility in its political meaning ensures that for every act or neglect of his department a Minister must answer. Hence the rule of anonymity in the Civil Service is important. For what an unnamed official does, or does not do, his Minister alone must answer in Parliament and the official, who can not be heard in his own defence, is therefore protected from attack. This positive liability of a Minister is essential to the performance by Parliament, and more particularly by the House of Commons, of its rôle of critic of the Executive. No Minister can shield himself by blaming his official. "It would be new and dangerous constitutional doctrine if Ministers of the Crown could excuse the failure of their policies by turning upon the experts whose advice they have taken or upon the agents whom they have employed." [2] *Ministers and the Civil Service.*

Ministerial responsibility to Parliament was debated in the House of Commons in 1954. A public enquiry conducted by a Queen's

---

[1] The number is now eighteen; this reduction has been secured partly by excluding the three Service Ministers; the number includes the Defence Minister.

[2] *The Times*, Leading Article, November 21, 1949.

Counsel had been ordered by the Minister of Agriculture and Fisheries to enquire into the circumstances of the disposal of land which was no longer needed for the purpose for which it had been acquired by the State.[1] The enquiry had resulted in the exposure of a number of civil servants to severe public criticism. Speaking in the debate the Home Secretary reaffirmed that a civil servant is wholly and directly responsible to his Minister and can be dismissed at any time by the Minister—a "power none the less real because it is seldom used." He went on to give a number of categories where differing considerations apply:

(1) A Minister must protect a civil servant who has carried out his explicit order.

(2) Equally a Minister must defend a civil servant who acts properly in accordance with the policy laid down by the Minister.

(3) "Where an official makes a mistake or causes some delay, but not on an important issue of policy and not where a claim to individual rights is seriously involved, the Minister acknowledges the mistake and he accepts the responsibility although he is not personally involved. He states that he will take corrective action in the Department."

(4) "Where action has been taken by a civil servant of which the Minister disapproves and has no previous knowledge, and the conduct of the official is reprehensible, there is no obligation on a Minister to endorse what he believes to be wrong or to defend what are clearly shown to be errors of his officers." He remains, however, "constitutionally responsible to Parliament for the fact that something has gone wrong," but this does not affect his power to control and discipline his staff.[2]

Nor can a Minister throw responsibility on a ministerial colleague, once it is established that the matter under consideration is the responsibility of his own department. This responsibility under modern conditions may not be easy to determine, and there are many arguments in favour of rationalising the machinery of government, so that the lines of demarcation of functions, and therefore of responsibility, may be more clearly marked. Those who see virtue in associating standing committees of Parliament with the work of government departments are faced with the argument that the existence of such committees, even though in theory their functions would be advisory and not executive, would detract from ministerial responsibility and hinder the exercise of criticism in Parliament itself.

[1] Crichel Down Enquiry, Cmd. 9176, 1954.
[2] 520 H.C. Deb. cols. 1289 ff.

Thus far the doctrine of ministerial responsibility has been dis- Ministerial Responsibility in War.
cussed without reference to what has happened twice in the present
century to meet the exigencies of the two World Wars. The institution late in 1916 and again at the outbreak of war in 1939 of a War
Cabinet has raised some interesting questions. What has been said
about collective responsibility has assumed the existence of a body
of Ministers all sharing equally, whether their number be twelve or
twenty-four, responsibility for the direction of public affairs and acting together under the stimulus of an effective Opposition in Parliament. What happens then to the doctrine when the Cabinet consists
of some five to nine senior Ministers, while other Ministers (including in the First World War all the Ministers with departmental
responsibilities, except the Chancellor of the Exchequer) have no seat
in the Cabinet, though they are invited to attend when matters affecting their departments are considered? On both occasions the normal
number of departmental Ministers was considerably increased by
the necessity for setting up new departments arising out of the
demands of war.

On one view it can be maintained that only the members of a War
Cabinet are collectively responsible, together with such other
Ministers as may have been called into consultation for a particular
decision. Against this it may be said that the Ministers who are not
members of the War Cabinet have delegated for the time being the
power to take decisions to their colleagues in the War Cabinet and
thereby pledged themselves to stand or fall by what the Cabinet decides, although they may have had no right or opportunity of voicing
their point of view beforehand.

The question is perhaps of academic interest only. In war a
Government must take rapid decisions. A team of as many as forty
Ministers, some of them stationed abroad, others chosen not on
account of political experience, but by reason of business capacity
for a war job entrusted to a highly specialised department, could not
conceivably function as a supreme executive sitting together on every
occasion. Unity is secured by the urgency of the danger; political
differences may be suppressed for the time being. The absence of
regular opposition in Parliament reduces to a minimum the chances
of effective challenge. In these circumstances it is unlikely that a
clear definition of the position of Ministers outside the War Cabinet
can emerge. The question would only become one of practical importance if and when a similar type of Cabinet held office in times
when the parties were divided on traditional lines.

Despite the return to larger Cabinets in 1945 there remains the Ministers not in the Cabinet.
category of senior Ministers, most of them with full departmental
responsibilities, who are not in the Cabinet; in 1955 they numbered
sixteen against the eighteen in the Cabinet and under modern

conditions no substantial reduction seems probable. The parties are again sharply, and at the present time, equally divided. Since Ministers who are not in the Cabinet have been so classified on appointment, it cannot be said that they have agreed to delegating their authority to Cabinet colleagues. It is clear that they are bound by Cabinet decisions and must refrain from criticising or opposing them in public. But on matters outside their departmental responsibilities they are not consulted in advance. It may be said that such Ministers share the consequences of collective responsibility, but that their actual responsibility is not the same. Their rôle is negative, that of the Cabinet is positive.

The Civil Service.   It is the law that all servants of the Crown can be dismissed at the pleasure of the Crown. This rule is only enforced against civil servants in cases of misconduct or gross inefficiency, for convention requires that civil servants shall remain in office, despite a change of Government. There is thus ensured continuity in the operation of the administrative machine, and without it something like chaos might follow with each change of Ministry. Ministers, who so far as their legal status is concerned are, like civil servants, servants of the Crown, may in the last resort be dismissed on political grounds, though they normally go out of office on the Prime Minister tendering his resignation or resign on account of a difference of opinion with their colleagues. Political considerations do not justify the dismissal of a civil servant, but such a step, though unconstitutional, would undoubtedly be legal. Here then is an example of the way in which a convention can restrict the operation of a rule of law. It is a corollary of this convention that any civil servant who, however remotely, may be regarded as the agent of (or in contact with) a Minister must abstain from active participation in politics, lest his loyalty to his party should bring him into conflict with his loyalty to his Minister.[1]

The rules which govern the conduct of a civil servant do not often come before the courts, since in a matter which is at the discretion of the Crown the aggrieved civil servant has no legal remedy. They are to be found in Treasury Minutes, or in important matters like disqualification from parliamentary candidature, in Orders in Council. The contents of these rules closely resemble rules of law proper and are enforced as such by the heads of departments, but their character is largely determined by the need for securing continuity of administration and the exclusion of individual participation in political activity. The enforcement of such rules is not a

---

[1] Part IV., Chap. 6, for a discussion of the extent to which political activity may be allowed. Since 1947 a limited number of civil servants have been removed or transferred on account of membership of the Communist party, to ensure that they do not have access to confidential State papers.

matter for the courts, as it is the prerogative of the Crown to regulate the conditions upon which its servants are employed.

The law and custom of Parliament may be said in some respects to occupy a position midway between law, in the narrower sense of rules applied by the courts, and convention. Some part of the law of Parliament is contained in statutes; for example, the composition of the House of Commons is determined by the Representation of the People Acts; the powers of the House of Lords to reject Bills passed by the Commons are limited by the Parliament Acts, 1911 and 1949. Another part is contained in decisions of the courts, though it does not follow that Parliament will accept these as conclusive; under this head comes a parliamentary privilege when it is in conflict with the legal rights of the subject.[1] Much else, including all matters relating exclusively to internal procedure and discipline of members, is determined by each House for itself. Under this heading comes the rule which excludes peers who have no judicial qualifications from sitting in the House of Lords to determine appeals from the courts. This is purely conventional. The Standing Orders of the House of Commons are determined by the House itself. In form they are not readily distinguishable from a code of law, but no judge is concerned with their enforcement. Standing Orders provide for the course of legislation, for rules of debate, for safeguarding the rights of the House, especially with regard to supplies (money) and taxation. They are not comprehensive; other matters of ordering proceedings can only be ascertained by reference to precedents recorded in the Journals of the House. Standing Orders embody much that is important to the constitutional lawyer, such as the principle that the expenditure of public funds can only be proposed by a Minister of the Crown, a provision which, as has happened elsewhere in the Commonwealth, would be included in a written constitution.

If the narrow view of the distinction between law and convention be accepted, namely that law is limited to those rules which are applied by the courts, much of the law and custom of Parliament is properly included under conventions. But in so far as Parliament itself enforces this law and custom by requiring compliance with its procedural code and maintaining its privileges, the distinction is a thin one. Perhaps the answer is to be found in comparing the privileges of Parliament with the royal prerogative. There are many matters of prerogative, such as the conduct of foreign affairs, the dissolution of Parliament (otherwise than by efflux of time), the disposition of the Armed Forces, which cannot be challenged in the courts. So too with privilege, and generally with the unwritten law of Parliament, the evidence of what is part of the ancient law of Parliament is only to be found in declarations made by that body,

---

[1] Part III., Chap. 4.

and not in decisions of the courts. As will be seen later,[1] the subject of parliamentary privileges lies in a field where the relations between the House of Commons and the courts are not yet clearly determined.

**Common-
wealth
Relations.**

Lastly there is a fertile field for conventions in the rules and practices which influence and govern relations between the members of the British Commonwealth of Nations. There is still a prevalent but erroneous belief that the Statute of Westminster removed dominion status from the realm of convention to that of law. The Statute, however, conferred legal autonomy only in the exercise of the legislative function. It marked the end of a long period of evolution of inter-imperial relations by means of conventions which still apply in the executive sphere of government. Two well-established conventions are recited in the preamble to the Statute and section four, which prohibits the Parliament of the United Kingdom from legislating for another State within the Commonwealth without its express request and consent, merely gives legal sanction to an existing convention. This again serves to emphasise how slender may be the distinction between convention and law.[2]

It is in this field that conventions derive from express agreements which in the past have been reached at periodic meetings of Imperial Conferences. But it must be emphasised that such agreements have no sanction behind them, and indeed there have been occasions when no convention has resulted simply because one or other of the Governments represented at a conference has gone out of office before any step had been taken to implement the decisions reached which have not proved acceptable to its successor. In place of such conferences, the recent practice has been to hold meetings of Prime Ministers or of other Ministers concerned with common problems, such as finance and external affairs. Their deliberations help to fix policy, but are less likely to result in new conventions.

Why Conventions are observed.

Dicey concluded that the reason why conventions are observed was that a breach would almost immediately bring the offender into conflict with the courts and the law of the land.[3] Other writers find the answer less easy and criticise Dicey's reasoning, even in its application to the limited field of conventions governing the use of the royal prerogative. Sir Ivor Jennings in particular makes the point,[4] that the emphasis upon the courts is misplaced, because much modern law is created by statute and enforced by administrative authority.

---

[1] Part III., Chap. 4; and see especially May, *Parliamentary Practice*, 15th ed., Chap. IX.

[2] For an example of conventions being enacted as law and yet excluded from enforcement by action in the courts, see s. 4 (2) of Ceylon Constitution, 1947, cited in 65 *L.Q.R.* 469 in Sir Ivor Jennings' article, "The Making of a Dominion Constitution." The conventions are those relating to the exercise of the powers of the Crown on ministerial advice.

[3] Dicey, *op. cit.*, pp. 445–6, Introduction, pp. cxxxvi *et seq.*

[4] See *The Law and the Constitution*, 4th ed., Chap. III., sect. 2.

The same writer points out that the absence of a written constitution is responsible for the difficulty of dividing law and convention by a clear line which would separate rules within and without the constitution. With us all institutions of government have been established by custom or convention or by the authority of an institution so established, and that this is the case with Parliament itself. He argues that, since this is so, the explanation that a breach of convention may result in a breach of the law is unacceptable.

It was Dicey's argument that a breach of the law would usually follow from disregard of the usages by which ministerial responsibility to the House of Commons is maintained, but he was also mindful of political sanctions, as evidenced by his discussion of the so-called external limitations upon the sovereignty of Parliament. Breach of a convention in any case is far more likely to lead to political action than to proceedings in court being brought against the offender. The refusal of a defeated Ministry to resign, though ultimately it could lead to administrative action which Parliament would refuse to sanction or condone and thus lead to illegal acts for which the courts would give redress, would have much more rapid repercussions in the political field. It may safely be said that the effective sanction against defaulting Ministers is to be found in political censure rather than the force of the law as an immediate consequence. *Effective Sanction.*

It is of more importance to consider the motive which induces obedience in each field where conventions operate. The Sovereign is guided in the exercise of personal prerogatives by a recognition of the tradition of impartiality which has grown up round the throne and is the real safeguard to ensure a continuance of the monarchy. Ministers fear lest they may be compelled to resign by force of public opinion manifested by an adverse vote at the polls, or, even apart from an election, by estranging some or all of their supporters in the House of Commons. They may also be credited with the desire to govern in accordance with the traditions of representative government. In the sphere of Commonwealth relations, the knowledge that there are in the background the vital political issues of unity in the Commonwealth and defence secures moderation in the use to which independence, now fully conceded by the United Kingdom, is put by each member State. There is in fact a standard of political authority which commands obedience. Those who govern submit to the judgment of public opinion, which they may seek to influence, but cannot ultimately control. *Conclusion.*

D*

PART III.

PARLIAMENT.

Parliament, by Sir Ivor Jennings (Cambridge University Press).

An Introduction to Procedure of the House of Commons, 2nd ed., by Lord Campion (Philip Allan).

Parliamentary Practice, by Sir T. Erskine May, 15th ed. (Sweet & Maxwell). The standard work of reference.

Parliament; a Survey (George Allen and Unwin, 1952).

The Finance of Government, by J. W. Hills and E. A. Fellowes, 2nd ed. (Philip Allan).

CHAPTER 1.

THE COMPOSITION OF PARLIAMENT.

A.

The House of Lords.

The Two Houses.

PARLIAMENT consists of the Queen, the House of Lords and the House of Commons. The two Houses sit separately and are constituted on entirely different principles. They must, therefore, be considered separately. The process of legislation is, however, a matter for both Houses and it is important to appreciate at the outset that the two-chamber system is an integral part of the constitution. The Parliament Act, 1911, reduced the powers of the House of Lords and the Parliament Act, 1949, curtailed still further the powers of that House to exercise a temporary veto on legislation, nor does the House play any part in making or unmaking Governments; for the control of the Executive is the function of the House of Commons. Nevertheless its power of holding up the passage of legislation may be an effective check on hasty legislation and its rôle as a revising chamber is important, especially for securing amendments to Bills which have been subjected to closure in the House of Commons.

The House of Lords.

The House of Lords consists of (i) over eight hundred and twenty temporal, and (ii) twenty-six spiritual Lords of Parliament. The temporal peers are:

(*a*) Hereditary peers of the United Kingdom,[1] who include holders of titles created in the peerage of England before the Union

---

[1] Princes of the Blood Royal only sit in the House by virtue of hereditary peerages conferred upon them by the Sovereign, with the exception of the heir apparent, who, unless a minor, sits as Duke of Cornwall.

with Scotland in 1707 and in the peerage of Great Britain from 1707 to 1801 when the Union of Great Britain and Ireland, which lasted until 1922 took effect, and account for the bulk of membership.

(*b*) Sixteen representative peers of Scotland elected from their own number for each Parliament by the hereditary peers of Scotland in accordance with the provisions of the Act of Union of 1707.

(*c*) Representative peers of Ireland elected for life. Until the creation of the Irish Free State in 1922 the peers of Ireland had under the Act of Union with Ireland, 1800, the right to elect twenty-eight representative members of the House of Lords, but there have been no elections since the foundation of the Free State, and with the abolition of the office of Lord Chancellor for Ireland the machinery for their election ceased to operate.[1]

(*d*) Not more than nine Lords of Appeal in Ordinary appointed by the Crown on the authority of the Appellate Jurisdiction Acts, 1876–1947 to perform the judicial duties of the House of Lords and holding their seats in the House for life.

The English House of Lords before the Act of Union with Scotland consisted of all the hereditary peers of England and the Lords Spiritual. After the Act of Union there was created a peerage of Great Britain, and similarly after the Act of Union with Ireland, a peerage of the United Kingdom. A peer of the United Kingdom, as had a peer of England before 1707 and a peer of Great Britain between 1707 and 1801, has the right to sit in the House of Lords. *{The Hereditary Peers of England and the United Kingdom.}*

Temporal peerages are created by the Queen on the advice of her Ministers. They are, except the judicial peerages, hereditary peerages of the United Kingdom and, carry with them the right to a seat in the House of Lords. A hereditary peerage can be created either by the issue of a writ of summons to the House of Lords, followed by the taking of his seat by the recipient of the writ, or by letters patent, the latter method being invariably adopted since very early times.[2] A peerage created by letters patent descends according to the limitation expressed in the letters patent, which is almost always to the heirs male of the body of the grantee, *i.e.* to and through the male line in direct lineal descent from the grantee. A peerage created by writ of summons descends to the heirs general of the grantee, *i.e.* to his heirs male or female, lineal or collateral. Thus in the absence of a special limitation in the letters patent, it is only a peerage created by writ of summons which ever devolves upon a female. Where there is only one female heir, she becomes a peeress in her own right. Where, however, there are two or more female descendants of equal degree, the elder is not preferred to the younger, and both or all inherit as co-parceners. In such cases a peerage falls *{Creation of Peers.}*

---

[1] In 1954 the number was five.
[2] See specimen Letters Patent in Appendix C.

into abeyance. Such an abeyance may on the advice of the Committee of Privileges of the House of Lords, which on reference from the Crown decides claims to existing peerages, be terminated by the Crown in favour of one co-heir, or in process of time may become vested in one descendant of the last holder of the peerage. The House of Lords has during the present century resolved to restrict drastically the practice of advising the termination of abeyances. A dispute as to the right of a newly-created peer to sit is determined by the House itself, acting through the Committee of Privileges.

Special Remainders.
Where a grantee has no direct male heir of the body, the letters patent, in order to preserve a peerage from extinction, may limit the peerage to the daughter of the grantee and the heirs male of her body, in default of heir males of the body of the grantee.

Restrictions.
A peerage cannot be alienated or surrendered,[1] nor has a peerage any connection with the tenure of land. This last point was finally decided by the *Berkeley Peerage Case* (1861), 8 H.L.C. 21. A peerage cannot be created with a limitation of descent which is unknown to the law relating to real property : *Wiltes Peerage Case* (1869), 4 H.L. 126. It was decided in the *Wensleydale Peerage Case* (1856), 5 H.L.C. 958, that the Crown, although able to create a life peerage, cannot create such a peerage carrying with it any office of honour—a term which includes the right to a seat in the House of Lords. This case illustrates the importance of the distinction between a peerage and a lordship of Parliament. It was unfortunate that the decision shut the door on an attempt to strengthen the House of Lords without the need for legislation and without increasing the number of the hereditary peerage. The decision was given in spite of weighty arguments to the contrary. The view which prevailed was that, as the issue of a writ of summons followed by the taking of his seat by the recipient created a hereditary peerage, it was therefore impossible to allow one whose peerage was by letters patent limited to his life to take his seat.

Disqualifications.
An alien cannot receive a writ of summons to the House of Lords nor may a writ of summons be issued to a bankrupt peer. Neither an infant nor a woman may sit in the House of Lords. It was decided in the case of *Viscountess Rhondda's Claim*, [1922] 2 A.C. 339, that the Sex Disqualification (Removal) Act, 1919, gave no right to a peeress in her own right to receive a writ of summons to Parliament. A conviction for felony, if followed by a sentence of imprisonment for twelve months or upwards, disqualifies from sitting or voting until after pardon or completion of the term of punishment. A peer who is a civil servant is debarred by Treasury Minute from

---

[1] The Titles Deprivation Act, 1917, provided for peers and princes being deprived of their dignities and titles on account of their adherence to the enemy during the First World War.

speaking or voting, though he may, of course, take his seat in the House.

The right of the Crown to create new peers was an important weapon to enable the Crown on the advice of the Prime Minister of the day to compel the House of Lords to give way to the House of Commons in case of conflict. The Peerage Bill of 1719 attempted to limit the power of the Crown to create new peers, but the proposal was rejected. The passing of the Reform Bill in 1832 and the Parliament Bill in 1911 were procured by a statement that the King had consented to create peers in sufficient numbers to secure a majority for the Government in the House of Lords.[1] It seems improbable that this prerogative will again be invoked; the passing of the Parliament Act, 1911, was thought at the time to reduce the likelihood of this.[2]

Creation of Peers.

No new Scottish peerages can be created since the Act of Union of 1707. When a new Parliament is summoned, the Scottish peers elect sixteen of their number to represent them in the House of Lords. Scottish peerages in respect of which no vote has been given since 1800 have been struck off the electoral roll. It was at one time thought that the Crown could not confer upon a peer of Scotland a peerage of the United Kingdom entitling him to a hereditary seat in the House of Lords, but this view was rejected by the judges in 1782 in advising the House upon the claim of the Duke of Hamilton and Brandon.

The Peers of Scotland.

The Act of Union with Ireland, 1800, provided that the Irish peerage might be maintained to the number of a hundred. There has been no new creation since 1898. During the Union there were twenty-eight representative life peers of Ireland, and elections took place as and when vacancies occurred.

The Peers of Ireland.

The nine judicial peers appointed by virtue of the provisions of the Appellate Jurisdiction Acts, 1876–1947, to perform the judicial functions of the House of Lords are styled Lords of Appeal in Ordinary. They have the right to sit and vote for life, notwithstanding resignation from their judicial appointment. They are entitled to a salary of £9,000 per annum, so long as they perform their judicial work and must have held for two years high judicial office,[3] or have practised at the Bar for fifteen years.

The Lords of Appeal Ordinary.

The Lords Spiritual are twenty-six bishops of the Church of England; they hold their seats in the House of Lords until they resign from their episcopal office. The Archbishops of Canterbury and York and the Bishops of London, Durham and Winchester have the right to a seat in the House of Lords. The remaining twenty-one spiritual lords are the twenty-one other diocesan bishops having

The Lords Spiritual.

[1] Sir Harold Nicolson, *George V*, pp. 184 ff.
[2] P. 103, *post.* [3] Part V., Chap. I.

seniority of date of appointment.[1] When such a bishop dies or resigns, his place in the House of Lords is taken not by his successor, but by the next senior diocesan bishop.

The Summoning of Peers.

A summons to Parliament cannot be withheld from a peer who is entitled to it, and individual writs of summons are drawn up for both the temporal and spiritual lords of Parliament. Although peerages are now invariably created by letters patent, a writ of summons must be received for each Parliament before a peer is entitled to take his seat. The writ addressed to a bishop contains the praemunientes clause which instructs the bishop to warn the clergy of his diocese to be present and consent to whatever Parliament ordains. This clause is a reminder of the time when the clergy attended Parliament as a separate estate. The clergy always attended reluctantly and preferred to grant taxes in Convocation. Since the fourteenth century they have not, except for the spiritual peers, attended Parliament, and since the seventeenth century they have ceased to tax themselves. Writs of attendance are also issued to the High Court Judges and the Attorney-General and the Solicitor-General. It is in fulfilment of this summons that the Judges have, in the past, performed the duty of advising the House of Lords on points of law in particularly difficult cases.

B.

The House of Commons.[2]

The Constituencies.

The Representation of the People Act, 1948, distributed the parliamentary seats in the House of Commons into 625 single-member territorial constituencies. The House of Commons elected in 1945 contained 640 members; the new composition applied to the Parliament elected in February, 1950, in which the representation by 12 members of the universities has ceased. By the House of

---

[1] The Bishop of Sodor and Man is excepted and cannot take a seat.

[2] The law relating to elections is contained in three consolidating statutes, of which the Representation of the People Act, 1949, dealing with (*inter alia*) the franchise and the conduct of elections is the most important. This Act repeals and re-enacts in a single statute previous legislation relating to the franchise, the conduct of elections and corrupt and illegal electoral practices. The other Acts are the House of Commons (Redistribution of Seats) Act, 1949, and the Election Commissioners Act, 1949. In the text reference is made to the original statutes which introduced important changes into the law, such as the Ballot Act, 1872, the Representation of the People Acts, 1918 and 1948, and the Corrupt and Illegal Practices Prevention Act, 1883.

To cite only the consolidating Acts of 1949 would prevent an intelligible presentation of the development of the law relating to elections, but students who are concerned with the administration of this branch of law should consult the text of the Acts of 1949, for both parliamentary and local government franchise and elections. On the other hand the constituencies are contained in the Act of 1948 and have not been included in a consolidating Act.

Commons (Redistribution of Seats) Act, 1944, there were established four permanent boundary commissions, for England, Scotland, Wales and Northern Ireland. The Speaker is the chairman of each of the four commissions. The Act provided for (1) an initial general review by each of the commissions of the representation of the whole of that part of the United Kingdom with which they are concerned; and (2) a periodical review of constituencies by the commissions at intervals of not less than three nor more than seven years with a view to recommending redistribution in accordance with changes in the number of electors. Effect was given by the Representation of the People Act, 1948, to the initial general redistribution of seats, but hereafter redistribution will be effected by Orders in Council which will require an affirmative resolution of each House of Parliament for their approval. The review in 1954 resulted in the abolition of six constituencies and the creation of eleven new ones, all in England. This brought the membership of the House of Commons up to 630 from the next general election.[1]

The periodic review is intended to ensure that so far as is practicable the electorate of a constituency will not exceed or fall short of the electorial quota by more than approximately a quarter of the quota. The electoral quota means the number obtained by dividing the total electorate by the number of constituencies. The quota in practice is varied in each part of the United Kingdom by the requirement that the total number of seats in Great Britain must not be "substantially greater or less than 613" and that there shall be not less than 71 seats in Scotland and not less than 35 in Wales; the number of seats for Northern Ireland is fixed at 12.

Since 1929 every adult person has, apart from certain disqualifications, possessed the franchise, or the right to vote. Before 1832 the franchise in county constituencies was exercised only by those males possessing freehold property worth 40s. a year. By the Representation of the People Act, 1832, the county franchise was extended to long leaseholders and copyholders of property of the annual value of £10, and to all male leaseholders for terms of not less than twenty years and to occupiers of property of £50 annual value. The county representation was increased from 82 to 139 seats. Various further changes were made in the county franchise by the Representation of the People Act, 1867, and the Representation of the People Act, 1884, enfranchised all male householders and lodgers occupying rooms of

History of the Franchise (England and Wales)—the County Franchise.

---

[1] An attempt to challenge the validity of one of the Orders in Council, after it had been approved by both Houses, was rejected by the Court of Appeal on the merits; *Harper* v. *Secretary of State for Home Department*, [1955] 2 W.L.R. 316. Although it was denied in the House of Commons, there seems no valid reason why delegated legislation proposed by the Boundary Commission should not be reviewed by the courts. The Act itself forbids such review, once the Order in Council has been made.

the annual value of £10 unfurnished. The latter Act enfranchised many agricultural labourers.

The Borough Franchise.   The borough franchise before 1832 varied from borough to borough.[1] The most common qualifications were: tenure of land, membership of a corporate body, tenure of particular tenements, and in certain cases merely residence. The Act of 1832, in addition to disfranchising many boroughs and transferring the seats to counties and large towns, established for the boroughs a uniform occupation franchise for any male who occupied as owner or tenant any house, shop or other building of the annual value of £10. The Act of 1867, which enfranchised the artisan class, extended the franchise to any male householder occupying a separate dwelling-house, and to lodgers occupying lodgings of the annual value, unfurnished, of £10. The borough franchise was substantially unaffected by the Act of 1884. This Act was followed by a further redistribution of seats, based on the general principle of equal electoral districts, each returning a single member.

Representation of the People Act, 1918.   The Representation of the People Act, 1918, established a uniform franchise for county and borough constituencies. This Act also redistributed seats, increasing the total membership of the House, which was 658 in 1832 and 670 in 1885, to 707. The creation of the Irish Free State in 1922 reduced the membership to 615. The franchise was given to all adult males possessing the qualifications either of residence or of the occupation of business premises. The franchise was also given to women of thirty years of age who, or whose husbands, occupied, in accordance with the requirements as to occupation for local government franchise, land or premises of the annual value of not less than £5 or a dwelling-house. In the university constituencies[2] all male graduates were entitled to vote, and all women of the age of thirty who were either graduates, or would have been graduates, if their university had admitted women to degrees. Disqualification by reason of receipt of outdoor poor relief was abolished by the Act of 1918 for both the parliamentary and local government franchise.

The Modern Franchise.   A uniform qualification for men and women was introduced by the Representation of the People Act, 1928. The effect of this Act, which amended the Representation of the People Act, 1918, was that the franchise could be exercised by all adults possessing one or more of the following qualifications:

(*a*) Residence for a qualifying period of three months ending on June 1.

---

[1] See Ilbert and Carr, *Parliament*, Chap. II. (Home University Library).
[2] The Universities of Oxford and Cambridge returned burgesses to Parliament since the time of James I. All the universities in the United Kingdom were represented in the House of Commons elected in 1945.

(b) Occupation of land or premises for business purposes of the annual value of £10 for the same period.

(c) Being the husband or wife of an occupier of such land or premises.

(d) Graduate membership of a university in the United Kingdom.

In December 1944, there came into operation a system of registration which involved a departure from the normal qualification based on a period of residence. The wholly abnormal movement of population into the forces and other forms of national service necessitated the introduction of a qualification based either on the address of the elector recorded on his identity card (a war-time device) or on his membership of the armed forces raised in the United Kingdom.[1]

Further changes were made by the Representation of the People Act, 1945, following on the recommendations of the Speaker's Conference which reported in the summer of 1944. The qualification of the spouse to be registered as a business premises voter was abolished. The qualification for the parliamentary franchise automatically carried qualification for the local government franchise, which had hitherto been restricted to occupiers of land and premises. This Act also contained novel provisions to enable the greater part of the armed forces stationed in theatres of war and elsewhere abroad to vote by post at a general election. Only those in the most distant or isolated stations were restricted to voting by proxy.

Thus the exercise of the parliamentary franchise at the General Election in July, 1945, depended upon registration as an elector based upon one or more of the following qualifications:

(i) Registration in the National Register as a civilian resident at the address contained on the elector's identity card on the relevant date for compiling the register of electors.

or

Registration as a service elector, including members of the forces and of the merchant navy and civilian war-workers abroad.

(ii) Occupation of land or premises for business purposes on the relevant date for compiling the register.

(iii) Graduate membership of a university.

An elector could not at a general election vote in more than two constituencies, one of them had to be in virtue of the residential qualification. Nor could an elector vote in the same constituency in respect of two qualifications.

By the Representation of the People Act, 1948, the qualifications based on business premises and a university degree were abolished

---

[1] Or membership of the merchant navy or civilian war-workers abroad.

and so the last elements of plural voting disappeared; an elector can have only one vote nationally in parliamentary elections, and one vote only for each local government unit, *i.e.* county, borough, district or parish. The sole qualification is residence in a particular place on the qualifying date, October 10[1]; the old requirement of a qualifying period of residence is no longer operative and in place of reliance on the National Register a canvass is carried out by electoral registration officers. The separate registration of service electors remains in force.

The Register of Electors.
It is a condition precedent to exercising the vote that the elector should be placed upon the register of electors. The register is prepared once a year by the registration officer of each parliamentary borough and county. The registration officers in England and Wales are in the case of the county constituencies the clerks of the county councils, in the case of borough constituencies the town clerks. A new register comes into force on February 16 each year.[2] The register is prepared after a house to house canvass of residents and is published first in a provisional form to allow of claims and objections. A separate register which is compiled on information obtained from service declarations contains the names of members of the forces whether serving at home or abroad and of other Crown servants who are abroad on service, together with those of their wives resident abroad with them. The principle of registration is that a service voter shall be registered as if he was living at the address at which but for his service he would be normally resident.

Any person may claim to be placed upon the register, and anyone may object to such claims. An appeal lies from the decision of a registration officer to the County Court, and on a point of law from the County Court to the Court of Appeal. Once placed upon the register, any person not suffering from any legal incapacity imposed by common law or statute, such as infancy or insanity, is entitled to vote, even though not qualified for inclusion on the register by reason of residence or service under the Crown. The register is conclusive on the questions whether or not a person registered therein was on the qualifying date resident at the address shown; and whether or not a person registered is registered as a service voter.

Disqualifications for the Franchise.
The following are the various disqualifications for the franchise. The franchise may not be exercised by:

(*a*) Aliens, but citizens of the Republic of Ireland are not disqualified.

---

[1] In N. Ireland, September 15.
[2] Electoral Registers Act, 1953; the Act of 1948 provided also for an autumn register, but this was abolished by the Electoral Registers Act, 1949, as a measure of economy.

(*b*) Infants, *i.e.* a person who has not attained the age of 21 by the relevant qualifying date for compilation of the register.[1]

(*c*) Lunatics and idiots.

(*d*) Peers.[2]

(*e*) Persons convicted of treason or felony who have not completed their punishment or been pardoned provided that they were sentenced to imprisonment for more than twelve months.

(*f*) Persons convicted of corrupt and illegal practices at elections, suffer a temporary disqualification which is universal in its incidence in the case of a corrupt practice; local in the case of an illegal practice.[3]

The following are the main categories of persons who are disqualified from sitting and voting as members of the House of Commons:

(*a*) Aliens, but citizens of the Republic of Ireland are not disqualified.

Disqualifications for Membership.

(*b*) Infants.

(*c*) Lunatics and Idiots. By the provisions of the Lunacy (Vacating of Seats) Act, 1886, the committal or reception of a member must be reported to the Speaker. The Speaker obtains a report from the Lunacy Commissioners, followed by another report after an interval of six months, and, if the member is still of unsound mind, his seat is vacated.

(*d*) Peers.[4]

(*e*) Clergy ordained in the Church of England and Church of Ireland,[5] Ministers of the Presbyterian Church of Scotland, and Priests of the Roman Catholic Church.

(*f*) Persons holding pensions at the pleasure of the Crown, other than holders of civil, military and diplomatic service pensions.

(*g*) Bankrupts.[6]

(*h*) Persons guilty of corrupt or illegal practices, as provided by Parts II and III of the Representation of the People Act, 1949, which reproduces with amendments the law enacted by the Corrupt and Illegal Practices Prevention Act, 1883.[3] The disqualification

---

[1] See Electoral Registers Act, 1949, s. 2, for the voting rights of certain persons coming of age during the currency of the electoral register.

[2] An Irish peer, other than one who before 1922 had been elected as a representative peer (see pp. 75 and 77, *ante*), can exercise the franchise if he is a member of the House of Commons.

[3] P. 390, *post*.

[4] Peers of Ireland who had not been elected before the creation of the Irish Free State as representative peers in the House of Lords are eligible for membership except for Northern Ireland constituencies.

[5] *Re MacManaway*, [1951] A.C. 161; Report of Select Committee on Clergy Disqualification, H.C. 200 (1953).

[6] The disqualification lasts until five years after discharge, unless the discharge is accompanied by a certificate that the bankruptcy was not caused by the bankrupt's misconduct.

which is universal for a corrupt practice, but limited to a particular constituency in the case of an illegal practice, is for five years.

(*i*) Persons convicted of treason or felony who have not completed their term of punishment or been pardoned, provided that they were sentenced to imprisonment for more than twelve months. A sitting member so convicted does not vacate his seat until he is expelled by order of the House. A member convicted of a misdemeanour may be expelled by the House of Commons, but such expulsion does not amount to a disqualification.[1]

(*j*) Persons holding or undertaking certain contracts or commissions for, or on account of, the public service. Any person so disqualified is subject to a penalty of £500 for every day on which he sits or votes. The penalty is payable to a common informer, not to the Crown. In the case of *Sir Stuart Samuel*, [1913] A.C. 514, it was held by the Judicial Committee of the Privy Council, to which the question was referred, that this disqualification applied to a member of a firm employed by the Secretary of State for India in Council to purchase silver for the purpose of the Indian currency. An Act of Indemnity may be passed to relieve a member from the penal consequences of sitting and voting during the existence of such a disqualification. By the House of Commons Disqualification (Declaration of Law) Act, 1931, it was declared that this disqualification, which was imposed by the House of Commons (Disqualification) Acts, 1782 and 1801, extends only to contracts for the furnishing or providing money to be remitted abroad or wares and merchandise to be used or employed in the service of the public.

(*k*) By statute a large number of public bodies (not being offices under the Crown) exclude from their membership Members of Parliament; these bodies include the boards of all the principal nationalised undertakings. No sitting Member can, therefore, be appointed to such a body without vacating his seat.

Office-holders.

(*l*) The holding of certain offices under the Crown.

This disqualification requires more detailed discussion in view of the "archaic, confused and unsatisfactory condition of the law." [2] During the first half of the seventeenth century the House of Commons asserted and secured the recognition of its right to control its own composition. The principle underlying the decisions made by the House was that a position, the duties of which entail prolonged absence abroad, or even at home, is incompatible with the duties of a member. Many of the decisions of this period were confirmed by subsequent statutes.

---

[1] P. 124, *post*.
[2] *Report from the Select Committee on Offices or Places of Profit under the Crown*, H.C. 120 of 1941, and *The Times*, December 13, 1949, *Candidates and Members*, by G. Bing, M.P.

After the Restoration the House was concerned more with its relations with the Crown than with the desire to ensure that its members performed their duties. Moreover, whereas the earlier decisions of the House purported to declare existing law, it was now seeking to make new law and recognised the necessity of legislation. Fear of undue influence through the presence in the House of Commons of office-holders led to a series of Place Bills and in 1701, by a provision in the Act of Settlement, there was enacted the complete exclusion of the holders of offices of profit to take effect after the accession of the House of Hanover. This provision, which would have prevented the development of the Cabinet system, as we understand it, by excluding Ministers from sitting in the House of Commons, was repealed before it took effect.

The Succession to the Crown Act, 1707, which is the basis of the present law on the disqualification of office-holders, was intended to enable Ministers to keep their seats in the House of Commons and yet to exclude the bulk of office-holders. The Act disqualified from election persons accepting a "new" office created since 1705. The acceptance of an "old" office, *i.e.* pre-1705 office, though annulling the election of the person accepting it, left him eligible for re-election, unless disqualification was expressly attached by statute to the particular office. *Succession to The Crown Act, 1707.*

Nevertheless a considerable volume of legislation was required in order to convert the distinction between "old" and "new" offices into a distinction between ministerial offices, the holders of which should be eligible for membership, and non-political offices of profit, the holders of which should be excluded. A series of statutes disqualified or suppressed a great many old offices.[1] Another series provided for the eligibility of the ministerial heads of newly-created departments subject to the necessity of re-election. The necessity for re-election was abolished first in the case of particular offices and then in the case of all offices of which the holders were eligible for membership.[2] Finally the Ministers of the Crown Act, 1937, in effect repealed the Act of Anne so far as it still governed the ministerial offices then in existence. But the Act imposed certain numerical limits on the number of Ministers of different classes who could sit simultaneously in the Commons. In the result there has been secured a politically neutral permanent civil service and the presence in the House of Commons of sufficient Ministers to ensure co-operation between Parliament and the Executive, while placemen, *i.e.* those who were indebted to the Government for a means of livelihood, have disappeared. *Political and Non-Political Offices.*

It is not proposed to summarise all the statutes which disqualify *Particular Disqualifications.*

[1] See Anson, *Law and Custom of the Constitution*, 5th ed., Vol. I., p. 101.
[2] Re-election of Ministers Acts, 1919 and 1926.

the holders of particular offices. Judges of the High Court of Justice and of the Court of Appeal are excluded by the provisions of the Supreme Court of Judicature (Consolidation) Act, 1925, a disqualification which was already of long standing. Most civil servants are disqualified either by the House of Commons Disqualification Act, 1741, or by the Act of 1707. Moreover by Order in Council (Servants of the Crown (Parliamentary Candidature) Order, 1950), any civil servant seeking election to the House of Commons must resign office on announcing his candidature.

Section 27 of the Act of 1707 drew a distinction between service in the armed forces and other offices. A member who was a serving officer was not required to seek re-election on receiving a new commission. The position of officers in a force or corps created since 1705 was doubtful and accordingly section 4 of the Air Force (Constitution) Act, 1917, conferred a comprehensive exemption from disqualification on officers of the Royal Air Force. The current service regulations are contained in the Order in Council of 1950 and apply to other ranks as well as to officers. Their effect is to prevent officers and men of the regular forces from being elected, so long as they remain on the active list.[1] A Select Committee which reported in 1941 recommended that the disqualification of those on the active list in the forces and of civil servants should be made statutory.[2] A returning officer [3] is excluded from candidature for the constituency in which he is the returning officer, unless he has delegated all his duties to an acting returning officer. A temporary measure, the House of Commons Disqualification (Temporary Provisions) Act, 1941, which was renewed annually until 1944, exempted from disqualification any member of the House of Commons whose appointment to an office under the Crown was certified by the First Lord of the Treasury to be required in the public interest for purposes connected with the prosecution of any war in which His Majesty might be engaged.[4]

Limitation on number of Ministers in House of Commons. The law in regard to the number of Ministers who may sit in the House of Commons is now mainly based on the Ministers of the Crown Act, 1937, and later Acts creating new Ministries. The principles underlying this legislation are that ministerial office as such shall be no bar to membership of the House of Commons, but that there shall be a maximum number of Ministers and Parliamentary

---

[1] The House of Commons (Service in His Majesty's Forces) Act, 1939, enabled members to serve during the Second World War and enacted that no one should be incapable of sitting or voting in the House of Commons by reason only of membership of any of His Majesty's Forces. This temporary Act lapsed after the General Election, 1950.

[2] P. 84, note 2, *ante.*

[3] P. 92, *post.*

[4] The number exempted might not exceed twenty-five unless, as the result of an address from the House of Commons, an Order in Council so provided: Ministers of the Crown and House of Commons Disqualification Act, 1942.

Secretaries in that House, thus ensuring that there shall be a nucleus of Ministers in the Lords; for convention requires the presence of political office-holders in one or other House. In detail the legislation secures that no person is disqualified from sitting in the House of Commons by holding the office of Chancellor of the Exchequer, the seven Secretaries of State, First Lord of the Admiralty, President of the Board of Trade, Minister of Agriculture and Fisheries, Minister of Education,[1] Minister of Health, Minister of Labour and National Service, Minister of Transport or Minister of Supply.[2]

Similarly no disqualification attaches to the Lord President of the Council, the Lord Privy Seal, the Postmaster-General or the First Commissioner of Works [3]; but only three of the holders of these posts may sit and vote in the House of Commons at any one time. In 1937 it followed that if all the offices enumerated in the Schedule of the Act were filled, there must be at least three holders of them in the House of Lords, but subsequent legislation has removed any statutory minimum. The First Lord of the Treasury,[4] the Minister of Housing and Local Government, the Minister of Pensions and National Insurance, the Minister of Fuel and Power, the Minister of Civil Aviation, the Minister of Food and the Minister of Defence are all eligible to sit in the House of Commons as is the Chancellor of the Duchy of Lancaster who holds an "old" office. A Minister who is appointed to perform particular duties without being put in charge of a department may sit in the House of Commons, but not more than three such Ministers may sit and vote at the same time.[5] In this category in 1955 were one of the Ministers of State who assisted the Foreign Secretary, the Minister of State for Colonial Affairs and the Minister of State at the Board of Trade, together with two more such Ministers in the House of Lords, one for the Foreign Office and the other for Scotland. The number of persons entitled to sit and vote in the House of Commons while they are Parliamentary Under-Secretaries is fixed by statute.[6]

Where any of the permitted numbers is exceeded, an election is Penalties. not invalid, but only a Minister who held his office and was a member of the House of Commons before the excess occurred may sit or vote until the number is reduced by death, resignation or otherwise to the number entitled to sit and vote. A Minister who sits or votes

[1] Education Act, 1944,
[2] Ministry of Supply Act, 1939.
[3] Ministry of Works Act, 1942. The office is held *ex officio* by the Minister.
[4] The salaried post held by the Prime Minister: Ministers of the Crown Act, 1937, s. 4.
[5] Re-election of Ministers Act, 1919, s. 2, and House of Commons Disqualification (Declaration of Law) Act, 1935.
[6] The number of Parliamentary Under-Secretaries to Ministries specified in the Ministers of the Crown Act, 1937, must not exceed twenty-two: Ministers of the Crown (Parliamentary Under-Secretaries) Act, 1951, s. 1 (2).

when he is not so entitled is liable to a penalty not exceeding £500 for each day on which he so sits or votes.

The Ministers of the Crown (Emergency Appointments) Act, 1939,[1] rendered eligible for membership of the House of Commons any person appointed as a Minister of the Crown for the purpose of exercising functions in connection with the prosecution of any war in which His Majesty might be engaged. The Act also rendered eligible their Parliamentary Under-Secretaries with limitation as to numbers.[2]

Recommendation of Select Committee. The number of ministerial office-holders in 1955 was seventy, excluding the Government Whips, five of whom held paid offices as Lords of the Treasury, and the political officers of the Royal Household (in all another thirteen).[3] It is desirable that most, in fact all, the principal departments should be represented in the House of Commons. The Select Committee appointed in 1941[4] recommended that not more than sixty holders of ministerial officers should sit and vote in the House of Commons at the same time. They further recommended that not more than one Parliamentary Private Secretary should be appointed for any one government department and this was acted upon by Mr. Attlee's Governments. The practice was that each Minister and Parliamentary Secretary appointed his own Parliamentary Private Secretary (unpaid) from among members of his party in the House. They hold no ministerial office, but are naturally close supporters of the Minister whom they serve. Sir Carleton Allen[5] commented of the House of Commons in 1944 when it contained most of the Ministers and Parliamentary Secretaries of the largest Administration in our history that "at least one-third of the present House of Commons consists of Ministers and sub-Ministers or persons bound in one way or another to the policies and measures of different departments of Government, and thereby —most significant still—to the policies and measures of all the departments of the Government in which they serve."

Resignation. From early times a member of the House of Commons has by strict law been unable to resign his seat, and the acceptance of an office of profit under the Crown is still the only legal method of release from membership. The offices commonly used for this purpose are the Stewardship of the Chiltern Hundreds and the Stewardship of the Manor of Northstead, and these are since 1926 the only "old offices"

---

[1] Passed in permanent form, but rendered temporary by the Ministers of the Crown and House of Commons Disqualification Act, 1942.

[2] Subsequently varied by S.R. & O., 1942, No. 1131.

[3] For the duties of the Whips, see Ilbert, *Parliament*, p. 151. Certain posts in the Royal Household are political appointments and their holders act as additional Whips if in the House of Commons, or assist in government business in the House of Lords.

[4] P. 84, note 2, *ante*.   [5] *Law and Orders* (Stevens), p. 282.

under the Succession to the Crown Act, 1707, which still involve resignation.

Disputes as to qualification for membership are determined by the House itself.[1] Formerly it was necessary that the member chosen should himself be one of the body of electors represented. The law, however, was constantly disregarded and in 1774 was repealed. Property qualification for membership was abolished in 1858.

Disputed Qualifications.

Voting Methods.

In single-member constituencies each elector can vote for only one candidate. When there are more than two political parties seeking the votes of the electorate, this system of election makes little provision for the representation of minorities, and can lead to strangely anomalous results. It is mathematically possible for one party to obtain the largest aggregate of votes in the country and yet not win a single seat in the House of Commons. In 1922 the Conservative Party polled 38 per cent. of the votes cast in the election and obtained 347 seats in Parliament. In 1929 the Conservative Party again polled 38 per cent. of the votes cast, but obtained only 253 seats.

Various systems of voting have been suggested with a view to securing a better representation of minorities and a distribution of seats corresponding more nearly to opinion in the country. The most notable of these are the alternative vote and proportional representation. If the alternative vote were adopted, single-member constituencies would be retained, but the elector would be allowed to express his choice of candidates in order of preference. If no candidate obtained a clear majority, the lowest on the list would be eliminated, his votes being distributed according to the second preferences shown on the voting papers. While making it more probable that in each particular constituency the final choice would be the real choice of the electors, the alternative vote would not provide adequately for the representation of minorities in the country. Under proportional representation, a form of which, known as the single transferable vote, was formerly used in the university constituencies returning more than one member, the country would be divided into large constituencies, each returning several members. The elector would vote for the candidates in order of preference, and any candidate obtaining a certain quota of first preferences would be immediately elected. His surplus votes would be distributed to other candidates according to the second preferences expressed, and again any candidate then obtaining the quota would be returned and a similar distribution of

Alternative Vote.

Proportional Representation.

[1] After consideration by a Select Committee; p. 124, *post.*

his surplus would take place. This system would undoubtedly provide adequate representation of minorities, but the drawback to any such system is that the more variety of opinion is represented, the more difficult it becomes to secure a Government of any one party with a reasonable working majority in the House of Commons. The Speaker's Conference on Electoral Reform and Redistribution of Seats rejected by large majorities proposals for proportional representation and for the alternative vote.[1]

[1] 1944, Cmd. 6534.

CHAPTER 2.

THE MEETING OF PARLIAMENT.

PARLIAMENT is summoned by the Queen by royal proclamation,[1] and it is by the Queen that it is prorogued and dissolved. The modern practice is that the same proclamation both dissolves Parliament and summons a new one. The old Parliament is first prorogued and the dissolution immediately follows. The new Parliament can be summoned to meet not less than twenty clear days after the date of the proclamation.[2] Parliament cannot meet without a summons from the Crown. There is no express rule of law requiring an annual meeting of Parliament, though the Meeting of Parliament Act, 1694, requires Parliament to meet every three years. But in practice legislation relating to the essential business of governing the country, including taxation and the expenditure of public funds, is only passed for one year and must be renewed annually, thereby ensuring that there is a session of Parliament at least once a year. For some years past it has been the practice for the parliamentary session to be prorogued in the autumn after a short resumption of sittings following the summer recess. The new session is then after a short period of prorogation opened in November.[3] *The Crown and Parliament.*

After the summoning of Parliament by royal proclamation, individual writs are issued to the members of the House of Lords, and writs are issued to returning officers commanding them to cause an election of members of the House of Commons to be held. The returning officer gives notice of the place and times at which nomination papers are to be delivered and the date of the poll in the event of a contest. Nomination papers must be delivered by the eighth day after the date of the proclamation and the poll held on the ninth day thereafter. A candidate must be proposed and seconded by an elector, and eight other electors must sign his nomination paper. If there are more candidates than vacancies, a poll is ordered. Voting is by secret ballot, and each elector indicates his choice by placing a mark against the name of the candidate whom he favours. There are provisions enabling a person registered as a service voter to vote by post or by proxy. *Elections to House of Commons.*

[1] See Form of Proclamation in Appendix C., pp. 501–2.
[2] Representation of the People Act, 1918, s. 21 (3), which has survived the repeal of the remainder of that Act by the Representation of the People Act, 1948.
[3] In 1949 the session which opened in November, 1948, was not prorogued until mid-December.

Conduct of Parliamentary Elections.

Responsibility for the conduct of an election rests upon the returning officer, who in the case of a county constituency is the sheriff, in a borough constituency the mayor. Most of the duties of the returning officer are, however, discharged as statutory duties by the registration officer[1] or by a deputy appointed by him. From these duties are excepted any duty of the returning officer relating to the delivery of the writ and matters connected therewith, and such duties, as for example, the declaration of the poll, as the returning officer may reserve to himself. The cost of an election, as distinct from the election expenses of the candidates, which are limited by statute and subject to scrutiny after the election, is paid out of public funds in accordance with a scale prescribed by the Treasury.

By-elections.

When a vacancy occurs in the House of Commons during the course of a Parliament, the Speaker issues a warrant for the issue of a writ for the holding of a by-election. A motion for the issue of the writ is normally moved by the Chief Whip of the party which held the seat before the vacancy occurred.

Dissolution.

Parliament endures for five years, unless it is sooner dissolved by the Sovereign.[2] The Sovereign cannot exercise the prerogative of dissolution without the advice of the Prime Minister; Ministers may be dismissed, though dismissal would only be justified under modern conditions by wholly abnormal circumstances.[3] It has for some time been a convention of the constitution that the Sovereign will dissolve Parliament at the request of the Prime Minister. The right to request a dissolution is a powerful weapon in the hands of a Prime Minister, who may use it to threaten recalcitrant supporters with the expenses of an election, and to compel the House of Lords to give way to the House of Commons, unless they are prepared to face the unfavourable result of an appeal to the country. A Prime Minister, whose Government is defeated in the House of Commons on a major issue, is expected either to resign, or to request a dissolution. Whether the convention as to the right to a dissolution would survive the presence of three parties, each with a fair proportion of seats, it is difficult to determine. It may be that the Sovereign would refuse, should the occasion arise, to grant a dissolution at the request of a Prime Minister who had never had a clear majority in the House of Commons. But what happened in 1924 is a precedent to the contrary; King George V. granted a dissolution to the Labour Prime Minister who had taken office without a majority, but with the support of the Liberals who subsequently withdrew that support. Another situation, more probable under existing conditions, might raise the question of the right

---

[1] P. 82, *ante.*

[2] See *Cabinet Government*, by Sir Ivor Jennings (Cambridge University Press), pp. 382 ff. For prolongation of the life of Parliament by legislation, see p. 39, *ante.*

[3] Part II., Chap. 4.

of a Prime Minister to request a dissolution. If, after a general election, particularly one which followed a dissolution granted at his own request, a Prime Minister found himself with a very small majority in the new House of Commons, as actually happened in 1950, it may be that the Sovereign ought to satisfy himself that no alternative Ministry could be formed before granting a second dissolution. In practice no doubt the Prime Minister would himself so advise. If he did not, there is some authority including that of Lord Asquith and Oxford, for the view that the Sovereign would be entitled to seek advice from other Privy Councillors who might be willing to form a second Government. The dilemma is, if a new Prime Minister took office, he might himself have to seek an early dissolution. If this was granted to him after it had been refused to his predecessor, the political impartiality of the Sovereign would be endangered.

Until 1867 the death of the Sovereign affected the duration of Parliament. Since the Representation of the People Act, 1867, the duration of a Parliament has been independent of the life of the Sovereign. Similarly should Parliament be prorogued or adjourned at the time of the death of the Sovereign, it meets at once without summons. Should the Sovereign die after a dissolution, but before the day fixed for the meeting of the new Parliament, the old Parliament would assemble and sit for six months or until sooner dissolved: Meeting of Parliament Act, 1797, s. 3. **Demise of the Crown.**

Prorogation brings to an end, not the existence, but a session of Parliament. Prorogation is effected either by the Sovereign in person or by a Royal Commission, the latter being the normal method, and operates until a fixed date. Parliament may be recalled by proclamation at one day's notice during a prorogation, if an emergency occurs.[1] Prorogation terminates all business, and any public Bills which have not passed through all the stages in both Houses lapse. In the case of private Bills a resolution may be passed before the end of a preceding session directing that a particular Bill be held over till the next session, but public Bills have not hitherto been carried over in this way. **Prorogation.**

An adjournment of Parliament is effected by either House of Parliament for such time as it pleases, but does not put an end to any uncompleted business. The Sovereign may call upon Parliament to meet before the conclusion of an adjournment intended to last for more than fourteen days. In practice arrangements are made for terminating the adjournment of either House at short notice, should the Lord Chancellor or the Speaker be satisfied that the public interest requires it. **Adjournment.**

---

[1] Parliament (Elections and Meetings) Act, 1943, s. 34.

Opening of Parliament.

Parliament, after a dissolution or a prorogation, is opened either by the Sovereign in person or by Royal Commissioners. As soon as the Houses have assembled, the Commons are summoned to the House of Lords to hear the Speech from the Throne, and, at the opening of a new Parliament, are first bidden to choose a Speaker. After choosing the Speaker the House adjourns until the following day, when the election of the Speaker is announced to the Lord Chancellor in the House of Lords. When a new Parliament meets, the Lords take the oath of allegiance as soon as Parliament has been opened, and the Commons as soon as the Speaker has been approved by the Sovereign and has himself taken the oath.

The Speech from the Throne.

The first business of a new session of Parliament is the debate on the Speech from the Throne. The Speech, for which the Cabinet is responsible, announces in outline the Government's plans for the principal business of the session. It is delivered in the House of Lords either by the Sovereign or, when Parliament is opened by Commission, by the Lord Chancellor. In each House an address is moved in answer to the Speech, and the debate on this address provides an opportunity for a general discussion of the political situation. It is in this rôle that Parliament acts as the grand inquest of the nation and the private member has the chance of contributing to the debate without undue fear of the party whip. Before the address is moved, the ancient right of Parliament to deal with matters not brought before it by the Crown (the rule of redress of grievances before supply) is asserted by the formal first reading of an obsolete Bill; in the Lords usually a Bill for the better regulation of "Select Vestries"; in the Commons a Bill for the better preventing of "Clandestine Outlawries."

Lord Chancellor.

The Lord Chancellor presides over the House of Lords. This office may be, but in practice is not, held by a commoner, and the Woolsack on which the Lord Chancellor sits as Speaker of the House is technically outside the precincts of the House. In contrast with the impartial position occupied by the Speaker of the House of Commons, the Lord Chancellor is free to take part in the deliberations of the House of Lords. Indeed he may often be the principal spokesman for the Government, and then he vacates the Woolsack temporarily by stepping aside while speaking; he returns to stand in front of the Woolsack to put the question to the House. Only in his absence does a Deputy-Speaker preside.

The Speaker.

The chief officer of the House of Commons is the Speaker. Except when the House is in committee he is its Chairman and is responsible for the orderly conduct of debates. It is through the Speaker that the House communicates with the Sovereign. He issues writs for the filling of vacancies. He has the statutory duty of determining whether a Bill is a money Bill within the meaning of the Parliament

Act, 1911.[1] The Speaker is appointed at the beginning of each Parliament. The party with a majority in the House selects a candidate for the Speakership. Such selection is usually made after consultation with the other parties, in order that the selection may be the unanimous choice of the House. It is customary for the previous holder of the office to be re-elected, if he is again willing to serve. The Speaker's seat was until recently[2] not contested at an election. The result of this convention coupled with the nature of the duties of the office is to deprive the Speaker's constituency of active representation in the House. If a Speaker dies in office, all business comes to an end until a successor is appointed.

When the House of Commons is in committee, the chair is taken by the Chairman or Deputy-Chairman of Ways and Means, or by one of a Chairmen's panel of not less than ten members nominated by the Speaker for the purpose of providing Chairmen of Standing Committees.[3] These officers preside when a Bill is taken in committee by the whole House,[3] or when the House sits as a Committee of Supply or of Ways and Means.[4] The Chairman or Deputy-Chairman of Ways and Means presides over the House in the absence of the Speaker. Unlike membership of the Chairmen's panel, the Chairmanship and Deputy-Chairmanship of Ways and Means are party appointments. New appointments are made with every change of Government. By custom the holders of these two offices do not take an active part in debates in the House itself. *Chairman of Ways and Means.*

The chief permanent officer of the House of Lords is the Clerk of the Parliaments appointed by the Crown and removable only by the Crown on address from the House of Lords. The Gentleman Usher of the Black Rod enforces the orders of the House, and the Sergeant-at-Arms attends on the Lord Chancellor. Under the Clerk of the Parliaments are a Clerk Assistant and Reading Clerk appointed by the Lord Chancellor and removable only by an address from the House. *Permanent Officers of the House of Lords.*

The Clerk of the House of Commons or Under-Clerk of the Parliaments is appointed by the Crown; two Clerk Assistants are appointed by the Crown on the nomination of the Speaker. These officers are removable only by an address from the House. The Sergeant-at-Arms appointed by the Crown is responsible for attending upon the Speaker and enforcing the orders of the House, including warrants issued by the Speaker for commitment for contempt or breach of privilege. *Permanent Officers of the House of Commons.*

---

[1] P. 103, *post.*
[2] It is doubtful whether this convention can still be regarded as in force.
[3] P. 107, *post.*   [4] Pp. 110 and 114, *post.*

CHAPTER 3.

THE FUNCTIONS OF PARLIAMENT.

A.

Control of the Executive

IT has been shown in discussing the transition to Cabinet Government [1] that it is Parliament that makes and unmakes the Executive. In order to retain office and to secure the passage of legislation and the grant of supplies a Government must command support in the House of Commons, and the choice of a Prime Minister depends upon the ability to secure such support. Normally the Prime Minister is the leader of the party which has the largest number of supporters returned to the House of Commons, though sometimes two or more groups will combine to keep in office a Government either based on a coalition or on a party which could not alone command a majority. It is through their representatives in Parliament that the electorate controls the Executive. The growth of the party system and the increase in the size of constituencies and the number of the electorate has resulted in votes being cast more for a party and its leaders than for local representatives on their own merits. An elector votes as much to choose a Prime Minister as to choose his local member.

Control by the Electorate.

It is chiefly since the Reform Act of 1832 that there has been any control of the Executive by the people, and the degree of that control as well as the method of its exercise are still matters of dispute and subject to changing conventions. [2] It has become the custom for a Ministry defeated in the House of Commons to appeal to the electorate rather than to resign at once, and it has also become an established convention that, should a Ministry decide to offer its resignation rather than to ask for a dissolution, its successors should take the earliest opportunity to appeal to the electorate. A defeat at a general election involves in normal circumstances immediate resignation. These conventions might, however, quickly become obsolete, should the two-party system give place to a combination of groups or even to three or four parties. With more than two main parties there is a real risk of frequent defeat in Parliament, and parties tend

[1] Part II., Chap. 2, A.
[2] *Thoughts on the Constitution*, by L. S. Amery, pp. 13 ff, 2nd ed. (Oxford University Press), *The People and the Constitution*, by C. K. Emden (Clarendon Press).

to come together and break away again. It would be impossible for government to be carried on, should every change of Ministry due to a re-shuffling of parties be followed by a general election. It has been pointed out that, though a group system gives more accurate representation of opinion, it lessens the ultimate control of the electorate.[1] Not only do Parliaments tend to last their full time, but it is impossible with more than two parties for the electorate to express its opinion upon a definite issue. The degree to which the electorate can determine policy depends upon the honesty and skill with which the parties frame the issues at a general election. Some elections seem merely to involve a choice between two possible Prime Ministers. Others involve a clear verdict for or against a proposed legislative change. There is a tendency to regard as a convention the rule that no radical change of policy should be undertaken unless the issue has been before the electors at a general election. Whether the difficulty of framing particular issues at a general election will lead to the adoption of the referendum is a problem of the future, but hitherto the advocates of this device have received little support in this country. In this connection it should be remembered that it is not only at an election that opinion can be tested. It is more and more becoming the custom for a Government to sense the feeling of the House and of the public by publishing in advance of a Bill its proposals in the form of a statement of policy as a White Paper.

Under adult suffrage a Member represents about 60,000 electors. Political organisation on a scale which only a nation-wide machine can operate is essential to secure election. One reason for the disappearance of independent Members was because none of them could command such an organisation without which no candidate could hope to-day to succeed. Candidates are thus necessarily selected because of their acceptability as members of a party. Members of Parliament represent the whole community, responsible in the last resort, as Burke pointed out, to their own consciences. They are not mere delegates of their constituents. Neither legally nor morally has a constituency a right to recall its member. But a member who changes his party may be expected to offer his resignation. *Members and their Constituents.*

A further consequence of the party system is the voluntary submission of Parliament to the Cabinet. A Cabinet with a clear majority in the House of Commons can usually secure the passage of its legislation in substantially the form that it proposes, subject to the now restricted powers of the House of Lords to delay the passage of a measure. It can also take the whole of the available time for government business, to the exclusion of the private member. In former times Governments were frequently defeated in the House of Commons, and still more frequently were forced to withdraw *Power of the Cabinet.*

[1] C. K. Emden, *op. cit.*

measures by threats of revolt among their followers. To-day members are returned to Parliament with the assistance of their party; without this assistance they cannot hold their seats. The threat of a dissolution involving the expense of an election, and still more the threat of the withdrawal of the support of the party organisation, will, except in rare cases, ensure the maintenance of the Government in office, until it seeks a dissolution at a time chosen by itself.

Parliamentary control.   Although the real power to promote legislation rests with the Cabinet and, as will be shown, it is difficult for Parliament to keep any real control over expenditure, it must not be assumed that Parliament has no control over Ministers. The defeat of the Government in the Commons in practice seldom occurs, even in the case of one which commands only a small majority. Moreover, it is only defeat on a major issue which constitutionally compels resignation. Parliament, however, is a deliberative as well as a legislative assembly. Debates of real value may take place during discussions on expenditure which, though failing to alter immediate programmes, may influence subsequent policy. Motions can be moved asking for papers, or for the appointment of commissions or committees of enquiry. The daily question hour, during which questions are addressed to Ministers, provides an opportunity for concentrating public attention on topics of current concern. Parliamentary questions are also of value in securing the redress of individual grievances. The use of question hour for this purpose is a real constitutional safeguard. Civil servants are aware that departmental action for which they are responsible to their Minister may result in a parliamentary question which may embarrass him in the House. Important debates arise on the Address in reply to the Speech from the Throne at the opening of a session; on the Budget speech of the Chancellor of the Exchequer; on a formal motion of censure and on other occasions apart from the ordinary legislative business. Debates unconnected with the passage of legislation are particularly useful in the House of Lords for the discussion of imperial and foreign affairs. Forty members may at the end of question time move the adjournment of the House of Commons in order to discuss a definite matter accepted by the Speaker as of urgent importance. If so accepted, the motion is taken later the same day. The debates on the estimates, taken on Supply days, serve the purpose of providing occasions for general debates on administration and policy, although the scope of debate is limited by the rule that proposals for legislation may not be discussed. There is usually an interval of half an hour every day between the close of public business and the time fixed for the adjournment of the House. An adjournment motion is moved and the ensuing half-hour may be used for raising matters which cannot easily be dealt with by question and answer, though no division can be taken. Ministers inevitably pay attention to general feeling in Parliament as giving valuable indication of general feeling in the country. Parliament does not however exercise detailed supervision of the administrative services of Government. It has been suggested that the departments should have attached to them committees of Parliament chosen for their special knowledge of the work of a department or group of departments.[1] They would examine in detail departmental estimates, and to them would be committed all Bills brought forward by their respective departments. Without some such change of procedure, or some measure of devolution and the establishment of subordinate legislatures for, *e.g.* Scotland, Wales, the North of England, it is impossible to establish real parliamentary control. There is little likelihood of detailed control of departmental administration by committees of members, nor is the legislative organ necessarily appropriate for the exercise of this function. Public administration is a highly technical matter and the ordinary member of Parliament, even if he possesses the qualifications for the task, has not at his disposal all the information available to the departments or the means of collecting such information. Moreover, proposals for the establishment of greater parliamentary control by means of committees are resisted on the ground that they would interfere with ministerial responsibility and the right and duty of the Government to govern. As the parliamentary system works to-day, the composition of the House of Commons determines the choice of a Government. To that Government is entrusted the determination of matters of policy and general responsibility for administration through the various departments.

That the party system has strengthened the system of modern government is undeniable. But it has also increased the importance of the Opposition in the House of Commons. To the Opposition nowadays falls the greater part of the work of criticising the exercise of executive power, which is the traditional function of the House. Back-bench supporters of a Government may exert much influence in meetings of the parliamentary party but they will normally support the Government in the division lobbies. The Opposition, the main and perhaps the only minority party, can exert pressure through its leaders, some of whom will already have had experience in office, and most of whom are likely in due course to form a future government. Thus is ensured the criticism of leaders who are responsible for alternative policies. They are backed by supporters who are disciplined more or less satisfactorily by the party machine. Thus the Executive of the Opposition party has come to be regarded as a

Her Majesty's Opposition.

---

[1] Ramsay Muir, *How Britain is Governed* (Constable), pp. 231 *et sep.* ; Sir Ivor Jennings, *Parliamentary Reform* (Gollancz), Chap. IX.

shadow Cabinet. The constitutional importance of an official Opposition has been recognised by the grant of a salary from public funds to its leader: Ministers of the Crown Act, 1937, s. 5; by the grant to-day under the rules of procedure of a certain precedence for its business in the House of Commons, but more particularly by its adoption in the Parliaments of the member States of the Commonwealth. To quote a former Clerk of the House, Lord Campion,

> "The 'Official Opposition' is a standing proof of the British genius for inventing political machinery. It has been adopted in all the Dominion Parliaments; the lack of it is the chief weakness of most of the Continental systems. It derives, of course, from the two-Party system; but in its developed form it represents a happy fusion of the parliamentary spirit of toleration with the democratic tendency to exalt party organization. The system involves the discouragement of individual initiative almost as much on the Opposition back benches as on those of the Government Party, for party organization seems more adapted to frontal attack in mass formation than to individual sniping. While admitting the loss to parliamentary life resulting from the sacrifice of the independent private Member, it cannot be denied that under modern conditions the concerted action of the Opposition is the best means of controlling a Government—by criticizing defects in administration loudly enough for the public to take notice." [1]

B.

Legislation. [2]

Private Members' Bills.

When we speak of parliamentary supremacy [3] we mean that Parliament has the right to legislate on every topic and that no other body may legislate except with the authority of Parliament. We have seen [4] that there are many practical limitations to the legislative power of Parliament. The real power to legislate rests with the Cabinet, which is under the constant pressure of organised opinion of all kinds seeking redress or relief through legislation. A public Bill, *i.e.* a Bill of general application, as opposed to one affecting particular local or private interests, may be introduced by a private member, but has little chance of becoming law unless the Government will allot sufficient time to it later in the session, or adopt the measure as its own after the second reading. The Government can use its majority to secure priority for government business. Private members, if they are successful in a ballot, may move motions and introduce Bills on certain Fridays in the earlier part of a session,[5]

---

[1] *Parliament; a Survey*, Chapter I., at p. 30.
[2] Appendix A contains specimens of legislative forms.
[3] Part II., Chap. 2, B.
[4] *Ibid.*
[5] For questions of procedure, see *An Introduction to the Procedure of the House of Commons*, by Lord Campion (Philip Allan).

unless, owing to pressure of business, private members' time is annexed by the Government. Certain other Fridays are allotted for private members' motions. There is no difference in procedure in regard to introduction between a government Bill and a private member's Bill. Any public Bill[1] may be introduced without leave, in which case no discussion takes place until the second reading. The second and third reading of private members' Bills are taken on Fridays in the first part of a session, and members ballot for the opportunity to move the second reading of their Bills. A Bill may also be introduced under the "Ten Minutes Rule." This method is usually employed when the object of introducing a private member's Bill is to secure publicity for the subject-matter rather than to secure the passage of the Bill. A motion for leave to bring in the Bill is set down for consideration immediately after question time. Short speeches are made by the mover and one opposer and then the question is put. Private Members' time was suspended by sessional orders from 1939 to 1949.

The increasing complication of the business of governing the country has led to ever-growing readiness to delegate legislative powers, though it must always be remembered that these powers are conferred by Parliament and can be annulled or restricted by Parliament. The power to legislate, when delegated, is normally confined to matters of detail bordering upon administration, though in a sudden emergency power may be delegated to legislate on major matters. The latter is well illustrated by legislation of 1931 when there were enacted by Parliament during the administration of a National Government a number of statutes which delegated power to legislate on matters of principle, subject to a time limit as to the exercise of the delegated powers. The Gold Standard (Amendment) Act empowered the Treasury to legislate for the control of the exchange. The National Economy Act empowered the King in Council to effect reductions, including salary cuts, in certain public services. The Foodstuffs (Prevention of Exploitation) Act authorised the Board of Trade, subject to an annulling resolution by either House of Parliament, to control the supply and price of certain foodstuffs, while two other measures which were designed to check abnormal importations of manufactured articles and horticultural products delegated to governmental departments the power to impose duties, subject to affirmative resolutions by the Commons.[3]

The Import Duties Act, 1932, was a striking example of delegation in relation to taxation. This Act delegated to the Treasury the power to legislate on matters of taxation without fixing any time limit for

Delegated[2] Legislation.

---

[1] P. 107, *post*.   [2] Part VII., Chap. 6.
[3] The Abnormal Importations (Customs) Duties Act, 1931; Horticultural Products (Emergency Customs Duties) Act, 1931.

the exercise of the power. The Act established a general *ad valorem* duty on all goods imported into the United Kingdom apart from certain specified exempted articles. The Treasury, after receiving a recommendation from the Import Duties Advisory Committee, who were removable from office by the Treasury, but otherwise independent of parliamentary or executive control, might by order direct that goods should be added to or removed from[1] the list of exempted articles. Similarly the Treasury might, on the recommendation of the Committee, impose or remove by order additional duties on luxury articles or articles of a kind which are produced or likely to be produced in substantial quantities in the United Kingdom.[2] On the recommendation of the Board of Trade the Treasury might by order give preference to goods from particular countries. The Act arranged for preferential tariffs for goods imported from the Dominions and Colonies.[3] The Board of Trade might with the concurrence of the Treasury impose additional duties on goods from those foreign countries which discriminated against United Kingdom goods. All orders made under the Act had to be laid before the House of Commons. Orders imposing customs duties expired after twenty-eight days, unless approved by resolution of the House of Commons. Other orders ceased to have effect, if within twenty-eight days the House by resolution determined that they should be annulled.

The Royal Assent.

Parliament cannot legislate without the concurrence of all its parts, and therefore the assent of the Sovereign is required. The Sovereign not only summons Parliament and can dissolve Parliament, but must give his consent before any legislation can take effect. After a Bill has passed through all its stages in Parliament, it is sent to the Sovereign for the Royal Assent, which is given either by the Sovereign in person or by commission. In giving the royal assent ancient forms are used. A public Bill, unless dealing with finance, as also a private Bill other than one of a personal nature, is accepted by the words "La Reine le veult." The formula for the veto was "La Reine s'avisera." A Bill of a personal nature, *e.g.* a divorce Bill in former times, is assented to by the words "soit fait comme il est desiré." A financial Bill is assented to with the words "La Reine remercie ses bons sujets, accepte leur benevolence et ainsi le veult." The right of veto has not been exercised since the reign of Queen Anne. It may be said to have fallen into disuse as a consequence of ministerial responsibility. The veto could only be exercised on ministerial advice, and no Government would wish to veto Bills for which it was responsible or one for the passage of which it had afforded facilities

---

[1] Finance Act, 1932, s. 7.

[2] Since 1939 the requirement of previous recommendation by the Committee has been suspended by the Import Duties (Emergency Provisions) Act, 1939, s. 1.

[3] See also Ottawa Agreements Act, 1932, giving effect to agreements reached at the Imperial Conference, 1932.

through Parliament. The consent of the Sovereign is requested before legislation which affects any matter relating to the royal prerogative, *e.g.* to limit the power to create hereditary peerages is debated. Such consent ensures that the ensuing legislation will not be subject to veto.

Except as provided by the Parliament Act, 1911, all legislation needs the assent of both Houses of Parliament. A Bill, other than a Bill relating to the imposition or application of taxes, may be introduced in either House and must pass through all its stages in both Houses. Important Bills which do not raise acute political controversy are frequently introduced in the House of Lords, but the majority of Bills originate in the House of Commons. It had for long been part of the customary law of Parliament that the House of Lords might reject, but not amend a Bill which related to public finance (other than charges of local authorities). To amend such a Bill would be to trespass upon the exclusive right of the Commons to grant or refuse supplies to the Crown. Though constitutional convention demanded that, when the will of the people was clearly behind the Commons, the Lords must give way in the event of a deadlock between the two Houses, the right of the Lords to reject legislation proposed by the Commons was until 1911 undisputed. The rejection by the House of Lords of the annual Finance Bill in 1909 led to the passing of the Parliament Act, 1911, which was amended in 1949. By the provisions of that Act legislation may in exceptional circumstances be effected by the Queen and Commons alone. A Bill may be presented for the royal assent without the concurrence of the Lords:

> The House of Lords; Parliament Act, 1911.

(1) If the Lords fail within one month to pass a Bill which, having passed the Commons, is sent up endorsed by the Speaker as a money Bill before the end of the session; or

(2) If the Lords refuse in two (formerly three) successive sessions to pass a public Bill, other than a Bill certified as a money Bill, and if one year (formerly two years) has elapsed between the date when it was read a second time in the House of Commons in the first and the date when it was read a third time in that House in the second (formerly third) of those sessions.[1]

A Bill to extend the duration of Parliament is exempted from the provisions of the Parliament Acts, and in view of the increased power given to the House of Commons a provision was embodied in the Act of 1911 limiting the duration of Parliament to five, instead of seven, years.[2]

A money Bill is a public Bill which in the opinion of the Speaker contains only provisions dealing with either the imposition, repeal,

[1] The changes were made by the Parliament Act, 1949, p. 104, *post.*
[2] For Acts prolonging Parliament, see p. 39, *ante.*

remission, alteration or regulation of taxation; the imposition of charges on the Consolidated Fund, or on money provided by Parliament for the payment of debt or other financial purposes or the variation or repeal of such charges; supply; the appropriation, receipt, custody, issue or audit of public accounts, or the raising or guarantee or repayment of loans. Bills dealing with taxation, money or loans raised by local authorities or bodies for local purposes are not certifiable as money Bills. It is curious that the annual Finance Bill has not always been endorsed with the Speaker's certificate, nor are many Bills which are on their face within the definition.[1] The only Bills which have passed into law under the operation of the Parliament Act, 1911, are the Welsh Church Act, 1914, the Government of Ireland Act, 1914 and the Parliament Act, 1949. The first was repealed before coming into force; the second became law only with some modifications.

Parliament Act, 1949.
In October, 1947, the Parliament Bill was introduced.[2] It proposed to amend the Parliament Act, 1911, by limiting the suspensory veto of public Bills (other than money Bills) to two sessions and one year's interval between the second reading in the Commons on the first occasion and the third reading in the same House on the second occasion. The Bill, after passing the lower House, was rejected by the Lords towards the end of the 1947–48 session, after a delay during which the second reading in the Lords was adjourned for the purpose of holding a conference of party leaders drawn from both Houses. The purpose of the Conference was to find out whether agreement could be reached on the reform both of the composition and of the powers of the second chamber. Agreement was reached for the further consideration by the parties of proposals for the composition of such a chamber. These involved a constitution which would secure that there should be no permanent majority for any one political party, that heredity alone should not constitute a qualification for admission, that women should be admitted, and that life members whether drawn from hereditary peers or from commoners created life peers should be drawn from persons appointed on grounds of personal distinction or public service and styled lords of Parliament. No agreement was reached on the powers of the proposed second chamber to delay the passage of legislation. The Government offered to recommend that the interval of one year from

---

[1] See Hills and Fellowes, *The Finance of Government* (Philip Allan), 2nd ed., Appendix I.

[2] The Bill also contained a provision to give retrospective operation to the shortened period of the suspensory veto, the object being to ensure the passage of legislation for the nationalisation of the iron and steel industries, which was introduced in the 1948–49 session, before the end of the then current Parliament in 1950. The provision, which was enacted in 1949, proved to be unnecessary, as the Iron and Steel Act, as enacted in 1949, contained a provision suspending its operation until after the next general election.

the second reading should be extended, if the period should prove in a particular case to be longer, to nine months from the third reading of a Bill on the first occasion of its passage through the Commons. The Opposition favoured eighteen months from the initial second reading but might have accepted twelve months from the third reading. They refused to accept the nine months' proposal because it might not have left the Lords adequate time to consider a Bill, in view of the length of time which is taken in the Commons to pass a controversial measure.[1] After the rejection of the Bill by the Lords on second reading, a step which followed the breakdown of the Conference, the Government wound up the session in July, 1948. Parliament reassembled in September for a short session solely for the purpose of again passing the amending Bill through the Commons and presenting it in the Lords where it was rejected for a second time under the Parliament Act procedure. The third session started late in October. It was not until this session had run for twelve months that the Parliament Bill was again passed through the Commons. It was in due course rejected by the Lords and received the Royal Assent on December 16, 1949, being thus the third measure to become law in this way since the enactment of the original Parliament Act in 1911.

The effect of the Parliament Act is to leave the House of Lords with a suspensory veto over non-financial Bills, but with no power to prevent legislation proposed by the House of Commons. There have been innumerable proposals both for the reform of the House of Lords and for the amendment of the Parliament Act. In particular it has been urged that the duty of certifying a Bill to be a money Bill should be transferred from the Speaker to an impartial committee, and that there should be excepted from the provisions of the Parliament Act a Bill to abolish or alter the constitution of the House of Lords. Those who believe in the necessity of a second chamber with power to revise and insist on its revisions, and with power to compel the democratically chosen first chamber to appeal to the electors before introducing any drastic changes in the law, would welcome the repeal of the Parliament Act, but any such proposal would involve reform of the composition of the House of Lords. *Proposals for Amendment.*

It is agreed that it is not desirable as a matter of political expediency to give new powers or to restore old powers to the House of Lords as at present constituted on the hereditary principle. Many proposals have been made for a reformed House of Lords, *e.g.* the nomination of life peers by the Crown on the advice of the Government of the day, elections by large constituencies, or combinations of these and other methods. It has been found impossible to secure agreement *House of Lords Reform.*

[1] See Cmd. 7380 for *Agreed Statement on Conclusion of the Conference of Party Leaders, 1948.*

upon any proposal. But the Conference held in 1948 nearly reached agreement on proposals which retained the power to delay legislation and suggested no corresponding increase of power in other directions. The House of Lords as at present constituted performs competently the task of revising legislation which is not regarded as sacrosanct by the Government and of debating matters of public importance. A reformed House of Lords, if based upon the elective principle, would inevitably come into conflict with the House of Commons, while, if based on any other principle, its composition would in all probability incline to be predominantly conservative. It is noticeable that in those countries where a second chamber proves of most value the constitution is federal. The Lower House is elected on a population basis, while the Upper House normally represents the component parts of the federation and thus secures that the point of view of the component States is put forward.

Conflicts between Lords and Commons. Since the Parliament Act, 1911, the knowledge that the House of Commons can usually enforce its will upon the House of Lords has rendered less important the older methods for the solution of conflicts between the two Houses, though the opportunities for a conflict between Lords and Commons between 1912 and 1945 were few. Since then the Lords, except on the issue of the Parliament Bill itself, have avoided a direct clash, but on two important occasions the Government did not resist vital amendments made by the Lords. If the Lords accept without amendment a Bill sent up to them by the House of Commons, they announce to the Commons that they have agreed to the Bill. If they amend a Bill, they return it with a message that they agree to the Bill with amendments to which they desire the consent of the Commons. Apart altogether from the provisions of the Parliament Act, for the Lords to amend a financial provision is a breach of the privileges of the Commons. This rule is sometimes waived owing to the fact that so many Bills containing financial provisions raise issues of general political, as much as financial, importance. If the Lords amend a financial provision (not being a money Bill certified under the Parliament Act), the question of privilege is raised when the Bill is returned to the House of Commons, but the House may waive privilege and consider the amendments made by the Lords on their merits. In the past if the Commons disagreed with the amendments made by the Lords, there were two methods for attempting to effect an agreement. A formal conference could be held.[1] Alternatively a Committee of the House which was disagreeing with amendments could send to the other House a statement of their reasons, together with the amended Bill. A settlement would probably be reached by informal conferences between the party leaders.

---

[1] As to conferences, see Anson, *op. cit.*, Vol. I., p. 298.

The process of legislation is complicated. A distinction must be drawn between public and private Bills. The object of a public Bill is to alter the general law. A private Bill is a Bill relating to some matter of individual, corporate or local interest.[1] A private Bill must not be confused with a public Bill introduced by a private member. It will be convenient to state in outline the process by which a public Bill becomes an Act of Parliament.[2] It is presented and receives a formal first reading. It is then printed. Then follows a second reading. The debate on the second reading is a debate on the general merits of the Bill.[3] After receiving a second reading it is referred either to one of the Standing Committees nominated by the Committee of Selection, or in the case of measures affecting constitutional rights to a Committee of the whole House. Since this matter is decided by motion, the Government can successfully resist the Opposition's demand that the importance of a Bill justifies its being committed to a Committee of the whole House. In committee members may move relevant amendments, and may speak any number of times in support of or in opposition to such amendments. When a Bill is committed to a Committee of the whole House, the Speaker leaves the Chair, and his place is taken by the Chairman of Committees— the Chairman of Ways and Means—or his Deputy. Standing Committees, formerly limited to five, are now constituted as business requires. At the beginning of each session there is appointed a Committee of Selection of eleven members drawn from all the main parties. The Committee of Selection nominates the members of the Standing Committees. Parties are represented as nearly as possible in proportion to their representation in the House itself, a rule which prevented use being made of Standing Committees in the Parliament elected in 1950 when the Government had a majority of only six, and has restricted the use of such Committees in the subsequent Parliament for a similar reason. For each of these Standing Committees there is a nucleus of at least twenty members and from ten to thirty others may be added by the Selection Committee for the consideration of a particular Bill; the quorum is fifteen. The Committee for Scottish Bills, to which are committed all Bills dealing exclusively with Scotland, consists of all the members for Scottish constituencies with not less than ten nor more than fifteen other members. After the committee stage the Bill as amended is reported to the House and is again discussed. Further amendments and alterations may be made in the report stage, and, if necessary, the Bill may be recommitted to

---

[1] Private Bills are of two kinds, Local, *e.g.* those affecting a particular locality, and Private (in the strict sense), *e.g.* those affecting a particular body or individual.

[2] The procedure described is that of the House of Commons.

[3] The second reading debate on Scottish Bills takes place in the Standing Committee of Scottish members unless this course is opposed by ten or more members.

the Committee. Finally the Bill is submitted to a third reading. During the third reading debate only verbal alterations may be made.

Crown's recom- mendation and Financial Resolutions.   The recommendation of the Crown, which is a guarantee that the Government accepts responsibility for the charge, is required by Standing Orders dating from the early eighteenth century before the House of Commons will proceed upon any motion for a charge upon the public revenue. The rule is in the United Kingdom merely embodied in a Standing Order, but it is of fundamental importance and is expressly enacted in the constitutions of several Commonwealth States. Similarly the present Constitution of India requires the recommendation of the President. National expenditure is the responsibility of the Government, which must provide means to meet all approved expenditure. Moreover private members are by the existence of this rule saved from temptation to suggest expenditure for the benefit of their constituents or particular interests. A Bill of which the main object is the creation of a public charge can only be introduced in the House of Commons. Wherever a Bill (and most modern Bills include some incidental expenditure) authorises any expenditure, a financial resolution in Committee of the whole House is necessary. This rule is a survival from the days when the Speaker was a royal nominee and the House desired to discuss expenditure under the chairmanship of a member chosen by themselves. There was formerly an important distinction of procedure between Bills primarily concerned with expenditure and those only incidentally involving expenditure. In the former case, but not in the latter, it was necessary that a financial resolution in Committee of the whole House should precede the introduction of the Bill. The distinction is now of little practical importance, as Bills primarily concerned with expenditure follow the same procedure as Bills incidentally involving expenditure, provided that they are presented, or brought in upon an Order of the House, by a Minister of the Crown.[1] In that event, or when expenditure is only subsidiary to the main object of a Bill, the financial resolutions in Committee of the whole House may follow the second reading of the Bill. The financial clauses are printed in italics, and after the second reading the necessary financial resolutions must be agreed to in Committee of the whole House before any clause authorising a charge can form part of the Bill. Written instructions were given in 1938 to all departments and to the parliamentary counsel to draft financial resolutions in wide terms in order that discussion might not be unduly limited by being confined by the terms of the financial resolutions introduced by the Government. The House then goes into Committee on the Bill or sends it to a Standing Committee. When a Bill is introduced

---

[1] Other than a Bill imposing taxation, which must be preceded by a financial resolution in Committee of Ways and Means; see p. 115, *post*.

in the House of Lords, the financial clauses are printed, but are only moved in the Commons at a later stage. They are left out of the Bill to avoid questions of privilege, but are inserted in brackets to make the rest of the Bill intelligible.

The complicated stages through which a Bill must go and the amount of time involved have led, with the increase of the amount of business to which Parliament must attend and of the number of members who wish to speak, to the adoption of various methods of curtailing debates. The simplest method is that known as the "closure," first introduced to check obstruction by the Opposition. Any member may, either in the House or in Committee, move "that the question be now put." The chairman may refuse to put the motion on the ground that it is an infringement of the rights of the minority, but, if the motion is put and carried, it brings to an end the debate which is in progress. The motion "that the question be now put" is voted upon without debate. It can only be carried in the House itself if the number voting is not less than 100. Another method is known as the "kangaroo" closure. The Speaker has the power, when a Bill is being discussed on the report stage, to select from among the various amendments proposed those which shall be discussed. The chairman of a Committee of the whole House may exercise similar power, as since 1934 may the Chairmen of Standing Committees. More drastic still is the "guillotine." By resolution of the House, various periods of time are allotted to each stage of a Bill. At the end of each period the portion of the Bill in question is voted upon without further discussion. The guillotine can also be employed in Standing Committees by a Time Order passed by the House; this empowers a Business Sub-Committee of the relevant Standing Committee to allocate a time-table for the Bill within the period allowed and fixes the date on which the Bill has to be reported back to the House.[1] An allocation of time by agreement was substituted for the guillotine to deal with the Government of India Bill in 1935, and may be followed in other cases.

Almost all important Bills are brought forward by the Government of the day and are the result either of decisions of policy taken in the Cabinet or of the recommendations of departments. They are drafted by Parliamentary Counsel to the Treasury on instructions framed by the departments In spite of the skill of these highly trained experts modern legislation becomes increasingly obscure. The problems which the draftsman is called upon to solve by legislative formulae increase in complexity as Parliament tries more and

Closure.

Drafting of Bills.

[1] This procedure, first authorised in 1945, was applied to the Transport and Town and Country Planning Bills in 1947 and resulted in a large part of each Bill not being considered at all in committee. The result was that the Government, as well as the Opposition, tabled a very large number of amendments in the Lords.

more to regulate social and economic conditions. Moreover pressure on parliamentary time, and even more the desire not to renew debate in Parliament on a former controversial issue, result in legislation by reference to existing statutes. Then too amendments may be hastily introduced at the last moment in order to facilitate the passage of a Bill. On the other hand, the production of numerous consolidation Acts is materially assisting to elucidate the Statute Book, *e.g.* Local Government Act, 1933, Public Health Act, 1936, the Companies Act, 1948, and the Representation of the People and the Marriage Acts, 1949. Since 1949 a number of Consolidation Bills have been passed into law each year and a wide range of topics has been covered. An outstanding example is the Magistrates' Courts Act, 1952, which enabled the repeal in part or in whole of sixty-four earlier Acts.

C.

Financial Procedure.[1]

Parliament, and more particularly the House of Commons, has two main functions in relation to public finance, the grant of supply and the raising of revenue. No payment out of the Exchequer may be made without the authority of an Act of Parliament, and then only for the express purpose for which it has been appropriated by the statute. No taxation, charges or loans can be authorised except by or under the authority of an Act.

Supply.

In advance of the opening of the financial year on April 1 the requirements of the departments in the form of estimates of the expenditure required for the public services for the coming year are presented to Parliament and published about the end of February. Previous to presentation the estimates are revised by and agreed with the Treasury, whose function is to adjust the competing claims of the various services, so far as the expenditure is capable of adjustment. A great part, however, of the requirements of the civil departments is fixed by statutes which determine the scale of expenditure, except the expenses of actual administration. Thus the Treasury cannot by revision of the estimates scale down the rate of insurance benefits, or of pensions, or the grants-in-aid of local authorities' services where the expenditure incurred, though voted annually, is determined by the scale enacted in the Act which created the charge. In the event of disagreement between the Treasury and a department the final arbiter is the Cabinet.

Resolutions approving the various votes into which the estimates are divided are passed by the House of Commons in Committee of

[1] The reader should refer to J. W. Hills and E. A. Fellowes, *The Finance of Government*.

Supply.[1] This Committee, like the Committee of Ways and Means, is a Committee of the whole House, sitting under the Chairman of Ways and Means, or his Deputy, in place of the Speaker. Each vote can be discussed separately and is separately passed. The number of days allotted for consideration of the annual estimates, including votes on account and supplementary estimates, is regulated by standing orders. The number has been fixed at twenty-six, all of which must be taken before August 5. The estimates for the separate departments for Scotland are referred to the Scottish Standing Committee, with a limit of six days for debate. The Opposition choose which of the departmental estimates they desire to discuss.[2] Discussions on supply afford an opportunity for discussing the general policy of the Government. In modern form the ancient rule holds good that redress of grievances must come before supply. No subject may be discussed that would require legislation. On the last day but one of the days allotted for supply all outstanding votes are taken, and on the last day there is taken the report stage of all outstanding resolutions. The resolutions when agreed to are embodied in the annual Appropriation Act which authorises the issue from the Consolidated Fund of the grants appropriating the amounts required for the Supply services of the year.[3] The Act also limits the expenditure of each department to the sums set out against each item in a schedule to the Act, thus ensuring not only that expenditure does not exceed the sum voted but that it is only incurred for authorised purposes.[4] Before the Appropriation Act can be passed there must be also voted in Committee of Ways and Means[5] and agreed to on report resolutions authorising the withdrawal of moneys from the Consolidated Fund.

It has been said that no expenditure can be incurred without parliamentary authorisation, but the Appropriation Act is not passed until July or August. Each financial year is a water-tight compartment. It follows that money must be provided for the Government between April 1 and the passing of the annual Appropriation Act.

Votes on Account and Consolidated Fund Acts.

---

[1] The whole House sitting in Committee and adopting the less formal procedure of committee.

[2] When the House first goes into Committee of Supply each March on the Army, Navy, Air Force and Civil estimates respectively, a general discussion on the proposed estimate may take place on the question "that the Speaker do now leave the Chair." There is no limitation on the number of occasions when debate may arise on this motion, but each occasion is included in the 26 allotted days. They afford opportunity for discussing amendments dealing with particular aspects of the administration of the services concerned which are moved by private members selected by ballot.

[3] Part IV., Chap. 7, and specimen Vote of Supply scheduled to the Act in Appendix A, p. 496, *post.*

[4] For the functions of the Comptroller and Auditor-General and his reports to the Public Accounts Committee of the House of Commons, see Part IV., Chap. 7.

[5] The resolutions are treated as formal.

There are submitted to the Committee of Supply early in March votes on account of the civil and revenue departments. Similarly two or three of the votes from the estimates of each of the service departments are passed. Unlike the civil departments, these departments may temporarily use for one purpose money voted for another. The Committee of Ways and Means votes out of the Consolidated Fund a sum equal to the vote on account and the votes passed for the defence services, and there is enacted a Consolidated Fund Bill [1] authorising the withdrawal from the Consolidated Fund of the necessary sum. The sum formally authorised by the Appropriation Act is the total of the expenditure voted for the year less the sum already authorised to be withdrawn by Consolidated Fund Acts.

Supplementary Estimates. Where a department later considers that it will need to exceed its estimated expenditure, a supplementary estimate must be introduced in Committee of Supply. The resolutions of the Committee of Ways and Means authorising the withdrawal from the Consolidated Fund of the sums so voted are usually embodied in the Consolidated Fund Act which authorises the issue of the next year's vote on account and the sum is appropriated to specific objects in the next year's Appropriation Act. Except when a supplementary estimate relates to a change of policy or a new service, the policy of the service concerned can only be debated in so far as it is brought into question by the excess. These debates have been criticised as time wasting; but the fact that a supplementary estimate must be justified in debate does operate as a check on the departments in framing their original estimates.

Votes of Credit. In times of grave emergency there may be voted a lump sum not allocated to any particular object. Such votes are known as votes of credit. By this means the extra-ordinary expenditure in time of war is in the main voted. The method involves relaxation of the usual methods of Treasury control, and in consequence the estimates of the departments concerned with war expenditure are presented with a token figure inserted instead of the actual expenditure proposed.

Appropriations in Aid. There must also be mentioned appropriations in aid, the estimates for which appear side by side with the estimates of expenditure, though only the net amount of the latter is voted. Appropriations in aid are sums received by departments and retained to meet departmental expenditure. For example, the net vote on account of the Public Trustee is £10, a token figure for the purpose of preserving parliamentary control, the whole of his expenditure being met by appropriations in aid in the form of fees.

[1] It is sometimes necessary for more than one Consolidated Fund Act to be passed in anticipation of the annual Appropriation Act.

The financial procedure of the House of Commons in relation to sanctioning expenditure is adequate for the purpose for which it came into being, namely to ensure that money should only be spent with the authority of Parliament and for the purposes authorised by Parliament, but it provides no opportunity for real control of expenditure. Discussions in Committee of Supply afford an opportunity for a general discussion on the work of a department, but not for a detailed examination of departmental expenditure. A member may move to reduce, though not to increase a vote, but such motions are invariably treated by the Government as votes of confidence and are invariably withdrawn or rejected. The accounts are not presented in a form which is easily understood by members, nor are they well adapted for the ascertainment of comparative costs.[1] The passing of outstanding votes on the last two days of Supply may involve the approval without discussion of large items of public expenditure.

Procedure in Committee of Supply.

There was until the outbreak of the Second World War a Select Committee on Estimates drawn from all parties which could examine estimates already presented and suggest economies, but could not discuss policy. It did not have an opportunity to discuss estimates till after they had been presented and only dealt with a limited number of estimates each year. A Select Committee on Procedure which reported in 1932 recommended that the work of the Estimates Committee should be more closely linked with that of the Public Accounts Committee [2] which receives the Comptroller and Auditor-General's report on any unauthorised expenditure, and that four of the Supply Days should be allotted to the reports to Parliament of these two Committees. If committees were attached, as has been suggested, to departments, they could examine the estimates of their respective departments. But the adoption of this suggestion would involve touching upon policy and it is claimed by some that as a result the responsibility of the Executive would be diminished. During the First and Second World Wars there were appointed Select Committees of the House of Commons on National Expenditure. The committee appointed during the Second World War was confined to investigating expenditure directly connected with the war. Nevertheless, it covered a wide range of departmental expenditure and interpreted its terms of reference as enabling it to criticise freely the policy of the departments. Its frequent reports to Parliament received wide publicity in the press, and the resulting action of departments was also reported on by the committee. It also addressed a number of representations to the Prime Minister where on grounds of security it was precluded from issuing a public report. This committee repeated the previous recommendation for closer

Select Committee on Estimates.

[1] See Part IV., Chap. 7, and Hills and Fellowes, *op. cit.*, p. 36.
[2] P. 181, *post.*

co-ordination between committees examining estimates and the Public Accounts Committee. They also criticised the form of the national accounts which are kept on a cash basis described by the committee as "the penny note book system." [1] The Select Committee on Procedure reported in 1946 in favour of amalgamating the Public Accounts and Estimates Committees into a Public Expenditure Committee entrusted with the whole task of examining with the assistance of sub-committees the field of public expenditure. [2] But the Government declined to ask the House to adopt this recommendation.

Although the terms of reference of the Estimates Committee remain as in use from 1921 to 1939 the manner of working has altered. Drawing on the experience of the wartime National Expenditure Committee the Estimates Committee, which now consists of thirty-six members, appoints investigating sub-committees. The result has been that as many as fourteen separate reports have been presented by the full Committee to the House in a single session. Evidence is taken from officials, and not only from one or two high officials as formerly, but from those actually responsible for the details of expenditure as well as from non-official witnesses such as trade associations on the occasion of examination of the estimates of the Ministry of Food. Since 1945 there have been several debates on reports from the Committee on Supply Days. The Committee is concerned to see that the sums voted are well spent within the permitted maxima approved by the Committee of Supply. It can suggest economies which may be reflected in the estimates of succeeding years. It may be claimed that, subject to the limitation that it is ineffective to secure a reduction of a current estimate, the Committee now functions more effectively than in the inter-war period, despite the mounting size of public expenditure which cannot be curtailed except by legislation since it is largely due to statutory items which reflect accepted policy.

Ways and Means.

It has been shown that before any money voted on Supply can be withdrawn from the Consolidated Fund there is needed a resolution of the Committee of Ways and Means, but the more important function of that Committee is the raising of revenue. Revenue, like expenditure, is raised partly under statutes that continue until repealed, partly under the authority of annual statutes. The bulk of revenue is raised by the former method, though income tax and sur-tax, since the rates are fixed annually, are in theory exceptions. In contrast the bulk of expenditure is sanctioned annually. Shortly after the opening of the financial year in April, the Chancellor of the Exchequer "opens his Budget" in Committee of Ways and Means.

[1] H. C. 122 of 1944.
[2] H. C. 189 of 1946, paras. 42 and 43.

The traditional Budget statement falls into two parts. The first is a retrospect of the past year, comparing yield of revenue with estimated yield, and actual with estimated expenditure. The second part deals with (1) the estimated expenditure of the new year, which is already known to members and the public through the publication by March of the new year's estimates, and (2) the Chancellor's proposals for meeting it out of taxation on the existing basis, together with his intentions as to the imposition of new or the remission of existing taxation. These matters are closely guarded secrets until the Budget is opened, in order that steps may not be taken to forestall them, *e.g.* by dumping of goods or speculation on the Stock Exchange. In recent years as a result of the increased interest in and importance to the Government of economic affairs there has been published contemporaneously with the opening of the Budget by the Chancellor of the Exchequer a White Paper containing an analysis of the national income of the past year. From this practice, which may well be extended to include other information, such as a statement of capital expenditure, there has resulted a change in the character of the Chancellor's statement in the direction of making it as much a statement of financial policy as a mere review of the actual finance of the period.

Immediately after the annual Budget statement resolutions agreeing to the Chancellor's proposals are passed by the Committee of Ways and Means. These cover the rates of income-tax and sur-tax and new customs and excise duties. Other taxes, such as death duties, which endure until varied or abolished by a Finance Act, do not require the Budget resolutions. The taxing resolutions of the Committee of Ways and Means are finally embodied in the annual Finance Act, just as the resolutions of the Committee of Supply are embodied in the annual Appropriation Act. The effect of any changes made by the Finance Act may be made retrospective to the date of the Budget or any selected date. It was for long the practice to begin at once to collect taxes under the authority of resolutions of the Committee of Ways and Means. This practice was challenged in *Bowles* v. *The Bank of England*, [1913] 1 Ch. 57; K. & L., at p. 162, in which Mr. Gibson Bowles sued the Bank of England for a declaration that it was not entitled to deduct any sum by way of income-tax from dividends, until such tax was imposed by Act of Parliament. The decision given in favour of the plaintiff illustrates the fundamental principle maintained in *Stockdale* v. *Hansard*[1] that no resolution of the House of Commons can alter the law of the land. In 1913, however, there was passed the Provisional Collection of Taxes Act, which gives statutory force for a limited period to a resolution of the Committee of Ways and Means varying an existing tax or

Budget Resolutions.

[1] P. 122, *post.*

renewing a tax imposed during the preceding year. An Act confirming such resolutions must become law within four months from the date of the resolution. The Act only applies to resolutions for the variation or renewal of customs and excise duties, income-tax and sur-tax. Though the collection of other new duties may not be started until the Finance Act is passed, the Treasury may make regulations to ensure that they shall be paid in the event of their being given retrospective operation.[1] It should be noted that the control of the House of Commons over taxation is far more real than is its control over expenditure. The raising of moneys by loan charged on the public revenue (Consolidated Fund) also requires the authority of an Act of Parliament; examples may be found in the War Loan Acts, 1914–19, the Austrian Loan Guarantee Act, 1933, and the National Loans Acts, 1939–45.

D.

Private Bills.

A private Bill is a Bill to alter the law relating to some particular locality or to confer rights on or relieve from liability some particular person or body of persons (including particularly local authorities and statutory undertakers, *e.g.* water companies).[2] After preliminary advertisement of the objects of the Bill, deposit of plans and other documents in Parliament, with local authorities and in other specified places, a petition for the Bill together with a printed copy of the Bill must be deposited with Parliament by November 27 each year. There is thus only one opportunity a year for the promotion of a private Bill. Provided that the other elaborate formalities required by the Standing Orders of the House in which the Bill is introduced have been complied with, the Bill receives a first reading. The second reading of the Bill does not determine, as in the case of a public Bill, its desirability, but merely that, given that the facts stated in its preamble are true, it is unobjectionable from the point of view of national policy. If read a second time, the Bill is committed to a Committee of four members in the Commons or of five members in the Lords. The functions of the Committee are to examine the Bill from the point of view of national policy and to hold the balance as between competing local and private interests. The Committee stage is a quasi-judicial proceeding at which after certain formalities the opponents of the Bill may appear. The promoters and opponents of the Bill are heard, usually by counsel, and may call evidence. It is

---

[1] Finance Act, 1926, s. 6, *e.g.* regulations authorising customs officers to record the names of importers.

[2] For history of private Bill procedure, see O. C. Williams, *History of Private Bill Procedure*, Vol. I. 1949, H.M. Stationery Office.

first decided whether or not the facts stated in the preamble, which sets out the special reasons for the Bill, have been proved. If the preamble is accepted, the clauses are then taken in order. If the preamble is rejected, the Bill is dead. After the committee stage the Bill is reported to the House, and its subsequent stages are similar to those of a public Bill. A private Bill may be opposed in committee in both Houses. Private Bill procedure when a Bill is opposed is both expensive and necessarily takes time. This method of seeking statutory powers is of great importance to progressive local authorities who may seek for powers wider than those conferred by the Acts from which they derive the powers common to local authorities in general. There are, however, other means of obtaining statutory authority for the exercise of special powers, and in particular both a provisional order, confirmed by Confirmation Bill, and special ministerial orders made under statute may be mentioned as of importance to-day both to local authorities and statutory undertakings as sources of their powers.[1]

E.

Miscellaneous Functions.

The judicial functions of Parliament—the appellate jurisdiction of the House of Lords and the process of impeachment—are discussed elsewhere.[2]

Judicial Functions.

Another function of Parliament is the receiving of petitions. Any subject may petition the House of Commons, even if he seeks to impose a new charge upon the public funds, and the House decides whether or not to receive such petitions. Petitions must be presented by a member. They are referred to a select committee, which may direct their circulation among members. They may be, but very seldom are, debated.[3]

Petitions.

Either House may set up a committee to enquire into any matter of public importance, and a resolution to set up such an enquiry may be an expression of no confidence in the Government of the day. Such committees may be composed solely of members of Parliament or may have a wider composition. Under the Tribunals of Enquiry (Evidence) Act, 1921, both Houses of Parliament may resolve that it is expedient that a tribunal be appointed to enquire into a matter of urgent public importance. In pursuance of such a resolution a tribunal may be appointed by Her Majesty or by a Secretary of State. The instrument of appointment may confer all the powersof

Committees of Enquiry.

---

[1] Part VI., Chap. 3, at pp. 277–80, *post*, for the procedure hereon.
[2] Part V., Chap. 1.
[3] Petitions are also occasionally presented to the House of Lords.

the High Court with regard to the examination of witnesses and production of documents. A tribunal was appointed under this Act in 1936 to enquire into allegations of a leakage of Budget secrets. In 1948 such a tribunal investigated allegations of improper approaches to certain members of the Government.

Addresses of Removal. Certain officers, such as Judges of the Supreme Court, are removable upon the presentation of an address to the Crown by both Houses of Parliament. The proceedings in relation to such an address are of a judicial character.[1]

[1] P. 250, *post.*

CHAPTER 4.

PRIVILEGES OF PARLIAMENT.

Nature of Privilege.

PRIVILEGES are an important part of the law and custom of Parliament. They concern the relations of both Houses with the Queen, the courts, the public, and with one another. Except so far as it has been made statutory, a privilege is part of the common law and, therefore, neither House can create any new privilege, but must justify its claim on the authority of precedent. The courts, while reluctant to enquire into the exercise of privilege, so far as it concerns the internal proceedings of either House or their relations with one another, will not admit of its extension at the expense of the rights of the subject. For to do so would involve recognising that one House could change the law by its own resolution.

A.

House of Commons.

In order that neither the House collectively nor members individually may be obstructed in the performance of their duties, there have from earliest times been attached both to the House itself and to members thereof certain privileges and immunities.

Demand of Privileges.

At the opening of each session of Parliament the Speaker formally claims from the Crown for the Commons "their ancient and undoubted rights and privileges." Those particularly mentioned are "that their persons may be free from arrests and molestations; that they may enjoy liberty of speech in all their debates and may have access to Her Majesty's royal person whenever occasion shall require; and that all their proceedings shall receive from Her Majesty the most favourable construction." The right of access is a collective privilege of the House exercised through the Speaker. The grant of these privileges is formally conveyed through the Lord Chancellor.

Freedom from Arrest.

The privilege of freedom from arrest protects a member of Parliament from civil arrest in proceedings for a period of from forty days before to forty days after a meeting of Parliament. It does not protect from arrest on a criminal charge for an indictable offence nor from preventive detention by order of the executive authority under statutory powers, e.g. regulations made under Defence Acts in time of war.[1] Parliament has, however, always maintained the right of

---

[1] Report from the Committee of Privileges, H. C. 164, 1940. Detention as the result of words spoken in Parliament would be a violation of the privilege of freedom of speech; see p. 120, post.

receiving immediate information of the imprisonment or detention of any member, together with the reasons for his detention. In cases of imprisonment the House passes without debate a motion for expulsion of the convicted member. In the various Habeas Corpus Suspension Acts of the eighteenth and early nineteenth centuries[1] provision was always made that before a member was committed to prison or detained there must be obtained the consent of the House of which he was a member. The general history of the privilege shows that the tendency has been to narrow its scope; it does not protect from proceedings under the Bankruptcy Acts nor probably from arrest on a criminal charge for a non-indictable offence nor from proceedings for contempt of court. There is no protection in cases of refusal to give surety to keep the peace or security for good behaviour. In the case of John Wilkes the Court of Common Pleas held[2] that the privilege protected from arrest for seditious libel, but both Houses of Parliament ruled to the contrary. Since the abolition of imprisonment for civil debt (except where it is shown that a debtor has means to satisfy a judgment, but has neglected to do so)[3] the privilege has become of small importance. The privilege applied to members' servants until the passing of the Parliamentary Privilege Act, 1770.

Freedom of Speech.

Haxey's Case.

Strode's Case.

The privilege of freedom of speech, though so well established as to be unquestioned, is manifestly of the first importance. It is to-day the only substantial privilege. In 1397 one Haxey questioned the expenses of the King's household. Haxey was condemned in Parliament as a traitor, but this judgment was reversed after the accession of Henry IV. Though this case has long been cited as an authority on privilege, it is now agreed among historians that Haxey was not a member of the Commons.[4] In Henry VIII.'s reign one Strode was imprisoned by the Stannary Court of Devon for invading the province of that court by introducing a Bill in Parliament to regulate the tin mines of that county which were within that court's jurisdiction. He was fined and imprisoned, but an Act[5] was passed declaring that any legal proceedings "for any bill, speaking, reasoning, or declaring of any matter or matters concerning the Parliament should be utterly void and of none effect." *Strode's Case* was a conflict between Parliament and the Stannary Court, not a conflict between the Crown and Parliament. Until the seventeenth century privilege meant little more than the assertion of freedom to choose subjects of discussion

---

[1] P. 382, *post.*
[2] *The King* v. *Wilkes* (1763), 2 Wilson 151.
[3] P. 364, note 1, *post.*
[4] See J. F. Tanner, *Tudor Constitutional Documents* (Cambridge University Press), p. 555; T. F. Tout, *Chapters in Mediaeval Administrative History* (Manchester University Press), Vol. IV., pp. 18–19.
[5] 4 Hen. 8, c. 8; Statutes of the Realm, iii. 53.

(*e.g.* Elizabeth's marriage) in face of objection by the Crown. In the new century the right to criticise the King's Government came to a head when in 1629 Eliot, Holles and Valentine were convicted for seditious words spoken in the House of Commons and for tumult in the same place. The judgment was subsequently reversed in the House of Lords on the ground that words spoken in Parliament could only be judged in Parliament. Finally it was enacted by the Bill of Rights, 1689, "that the freedom of speech or debates or proceedings in Parliament ought not to be impeached or questioned in any court or place out of Parliament." No action will lie against a member of Parliament for words spoken by him in the course of parliamentary proceedings, and similarly no action will lie for any publication among members of Parliament by order of the House or in the ordinary course of parliamentary business. It was held in *Lake* v. *King* (1667), 1 Saunders 131, that an action would not lie for defamatory matter contained in a petition printed and delivered to members. *Sir John Eliot's Case.* *Bill of Rights.*

Disclosures made in Parliament either by speeches or questions may not be made the subject-matter of a prosecution under the Official Secrets Acts, 1911–39.[1] Unless there are express words in a statute overriding parliamentary privilege, no member may be proceeded against as the result of words spoken in the performance of his duty as a member of Parliament. The privilege of freedom of speech extends to words spoken outside the House of Commons if spoken in the essential performance of duty as a member, *e.g.* a conversation on parliamentary business in a Minister's private house. Conversely it does not extend to a casual conversation in the House of Commons on private affairs. A member may not without the consent of the House give evidence in a court of law concerning what passes in Parliament.[2] *Official Secrets Acts.*

In connection with the privilege of freedom of speech it is convenient to consider also the right of the House to secure privacy of debate, and to publish its debates and proceedings outside Parliament. By resolution of March 3, 1762, any publication of speeches made by members is a breach of privilege. The resolution has never been renewed, but breach of privilege is occasionally raised in cases of misreporting of speeches in the press; this aggravates the breach, of which usually no notice is taken in order that publicity may be given to proceedings of the House. The House has always enjoyed the right to exclude strangers. Until the eighteenth century the House resented and prevented any publication of accounts of its proceedings, but since the famous conflict between the House of Commons and John Wilkes, this privilege has not been insisted upon. The *Privacy of Debate.*

---

[1] *Report of Select Committee on Official Secrets Acts,* H. C. 101, 1939.
[2] *Ibid.*

House, however, may at any time resolve that publication is a breach of privilege. In time of war each House occasionally asserts its right to exclude strangers in order to go into secret session for security reasons.

Publication of Debates and Speeches. The right of the House to publish its proceedings otherwise than among its own members was at common law restricted by the ordinary law of defamation (libel and slander). In the case of *Stockdale* v. *Hansard* (1839), 9 A. & E. 1; K. & L. 127, Stockdale sued the publisher of certain reports containing defamatory matter, which were published by order of the House of Commons and were available for sale to the public. This was the second of a series of actions between the parties arising out of the repeated publication of the reports. The defendant was ordered by the House to plead that he had acted under an order of the House of Commons, a court superior to any court of law, whose orders could not be questioned; and further that the House of Commons had declared that the case was a case of privilege; that each House of Parliament was the sole judge of its own privileges; and that a resolution of the House declaratory of its privileges could not be questioned in any court of law. The Court of Queen's Bench rejected the defence, holding that only the Queen and both Houses of Parliament could make or unmake laws; that no resolution of any one House of Parliament could place anyone beyond the control of the law; and that, when it was necessary in order to decide the rights of private individuals in matters arising outside Parliament, courts of law should determine the nature and existence of privileges of the House of Commons. They held further that there was no privilege of the House of Commons which permitted the publication outside the House of defamatory matter. Similarly, although a member of Parliament may speak freely within Parliament, he may be liable to proceedings for defamation if he publishes his speech outside Parliament: *The King* v. *Creevey* (1813), 1 M. & S. 278. The decision of the Queen's Bench showed that there can be no finality on the issue of legality of a privilege so long as the House of Commons asserts exclusive jurisdiction and the courts deny it. The sequel to the case was the attempt of the sheriffs to recover for the plaintiff by lawful process of execution on the property of Hansard the £600 damages which the court had awarded to Stockdale in the third action of the series. The House had previously decided that Hansard should not plead and that the plaintiff should suffer for his contempt of the resolutions and authority of the House. The money recovered from Hansard was in the hands of the sheriffs when the parliamentary session of 1840 opened; they were aware of the resolutions of the Commons. The House first committed Stockdale and then, on the sheriffs refusing to refund the money to Hansard, also committed the two sheriffs for contempt, without expressing the real cause for the committal: *The Case of the Sheriff of Middlesex* (1840), 11 A. & E. 293; K. & L. 140. Thus it would seem that the power to commit for contempt of court which the High Court can exercise for whatever conduct it adjudges to amount to contempt cannot be denied to the House of Commons, itself a part of the High Court of Parliament.[1]

As will be seen later,[2] the right of the House of Commons to commit for contempt is not limited to the enforcement of accepted privileges. The House is thus in a position to adjudicate independently of the courts. What it cannot do is to legislate by resolution to create a new parliamentary privilege of which the courts must take notice. That can only be done by Act of the whole Parliament.

The case of *Stockdale* v. *Hansard* was followed by the Parliamentary Papers Act, 1840, which enacted that any proceedings in respect of defamatory matter contained in a publication made by authority of the House of Lords or the House of Commons would be stayed on the production of a certificate from an officer of the House. Thus Parliament as a whole made the law to conform with what the House of Commons had attempted, unsuccessfully so far as the courts were concerned, to declare lawful by its own resolution. This Act also protected in the absence of malice the publication of fair and accurate extracts from papers published under the authority of Parliament. Although not strictly connected with parliamentary privilege, it may be added that, unless a plaintiff can prove malice, a fair and accurate unofficial report of proceedings in Parliament is privileged, as is an article founded on proceedings in Parliament, provided that it is an honest and fair comment on the facts: *Wason* v. *Walter* (1868), L.R. 4 Q.B. 73; K. & L. 152. The interest of the public in the publication of parliamentary proceedings is of more importance than occasional inconveniences to individuals. This decision does not protect reports of detached parts of proceedings published with intent to injure individuals, nor does it protect the publication of a single speech which contains libellous matter: *The King* v. *Creevey* (*ante*). It was suggested in *Davison* v. *Duncan* (1857), 7 E. & B. 229, that a similar privilege attaches to the bonâ-fide publication of a speech by a member for the information of his constituents, but it is difficult to ascertain whether a speech is circulated only to constituents. *(margin: Parliamentary Papers.)*

The House of Commons has the right to control its own proceedings and to provide for its own proper constitution. Except in cases of crimes committed within the precincts of Parliament, the courts will not interfere with what takes place inside Parliament. The House *(margin: Right to Control Internal Proceedings.)*

---

[1] P. 127, *post.* It is otherwise if the committal warrant discloses a separate cause of action available to the person committed by the House.

[2] P. 125, *post.*

lays down its own rules for the regulation of its proceedings and has the power to enforce those rules. This question will be discussed more fully in considering the relations between the House of Commons and the courts.

Disputed Elections.

It was for long doubtful as to whether or not the House had the right to determine questions of disputed elections. A dispute arose upon this question between James I. and the House of Commons in 1604, when one Goodwin, an outlaw, was elected for Buckinghamshire. A compromise was effected, but the Commons exercised the right to determine such questions from 1604 to 1868. They were first determined by committees, but from 1672 were determined by the whole House. The growth of party government resulted in disputed election returns being settled purely by party votes. In 1770 the Parliamentary Privilege Act, commonly known as Grenville's Act, transferred the decision of these questions to a committee chosen by lot. In 1868 Parliament entrusted the duty of deciding disputed elections to the courts. The procedure is regulated by the Parliamentary Elections Act, 1868.[1] A petition against an election is presented to the High Court of Justice, and the trial of such petition is conducted by two judges of the High Court sitting in the borough or county in which the election took place. The determination of the court is notified to the Speaker, and is entered upon the journals of the House of Commons. Of recent years there has been an almost total disappearance of election petitions, a feature which reflects the improved standard of public morality and the political intelligence of the electorate, though no doubt the large number on the electoral roll of a modern constituency has also contributed to the disappearance of attempts to bribe the electors.

Goodwin's Case.

Grenville's Act.

Expulsion.

The House of Commons still retains the right to pronounce upon legal qualifications for membership, and to declare a seat vacant on such ground. The House may, however, as in the case of Mitchel,[2] refer such a question to the courts. The House of Commons cannot, of course, create disqualifications unrecognised by law, but it may expel any member who conducts himself in a manner unfit for membership. A constituency may re-elect a member so expelled, and there might, as in the case of John Wilkes, take place a series of expulsions and re-elections. Expulsion is the only method open to the House of dealing with a member convicted of a misdemeanour. In 1947 a member was expelled by the House after the Committee of Privileges had reported that he had been guilty of gross contempt in accusing his fellow members of disclosing for reward the proceedings of confidential party meetings held in the precincts of the House,

---

[1] Now replaced by the Representation of the People Act, 1949, Part III., without change in the law.
[2] (1875), I.R. 9 C.L. 217.

but not forming part of the formal business of Parliament. It was disclosed to the Committee that the member himself had been guilty of the misconduct in question and, except for a single case, could not substantiate any of the charges against his fellow-members which he had published in a periodical circulating among journalists.[1]

The House of Commons has the right to enforce its privileges and to regulate its proceedings by punishing those who offend against the House. A member guilty of disorderly conduct, who refuses to withdraw, may on being named by the Speaker be suspended from the service of the House either for a specified time or for the remainder of the session. Punishment may also take the form of an admonition by the Speaker, or in more serious cases of a reprimand by the Speaker, or of commitment to prison by order of the House. The House of Commons may, in virtue of its inherent and essential right to control its own proceedings and maintain its dignity, commit any person for contempt, but such commitment cannot be for a fixed term, as a prisoner is automatically entitled to release when the House is prorogued. In parliamentary language the term, breach of privilege, is sometimes used as synonymous with contempt, in the same sense as in contempt of court.[2] But it is clear that a member of the House or other person may be adjudged by the House of Commons to be guilty of contempt without the actual infringement of any parliamentary privilege. Thus in *Allighan's Case*[1] the Committee of Privileges reported that the unfounded imputation in regard to the proceedings of party meetings held in private within the precincts of the Palace of Westminster involved an affront to the House as such. But information about such meetings was not in itself a breach of privilege. This contusion of language is particularly unsatisfactory to a lawyer, because the issue cannot readily be tested in a court of law. If it arises in relation to the internal proceedings of the House, as is most likely, the High Court will decline to intervene. Similarly there is no power in the Court to enquire into the validity of a committal for contempt, as such, by the House. Only if the actual cause of the committal is disclosed and is proved to be unlawful can the court give redress.[3]

The right of the House of Commons to the exclusive control of financial measures,[4] and the right of impeachment [5] are more appropriately discussed when considering the financial and judicial functions of Parliament. It is convenient to refer here to the question of the payment of members of Parliament. Since 1911 every member not in receipt of an official salary has received a salary, which was raised from £400 to £600 a year by the Appropriation Act, 1937, and

Committal for Contempt.

Payment of Members.

---

[1] H.C. 138, 1947.
[2] P. 395, *post.*
[3] P. 127, *post.*
[4] Chap. 3, *ante.*
[5] P. 241, *post.*

in 1946 to £1,000.[1] This has been supplemented since 1954 by the right to claim a fixed rate of subsistence allowance while the House is in session. Members, too, are sometimes paid by private bodies, *e.g.* trade unions. Lord Shaw expressed the view that a contract to pay a man in return for his support in Parliament of the views of a particular person or party would be unenforceable as contrary to public policy: *Osborne* v. *Amalgamated Society of Railway Servants*, [1910] A.C. 87, at p. 110 ff. It is improper for a member to enter into any contractual agreement with an outside body limiting his complete freedom of action in Parliament. So the House decided in 1947 on a motion to approve a majority report from the Committee of Privileges.[2]

The Courts and Parliamentary Privilege.

Questions of privilege have been a source of conflict between the House of Commons and the courts. Parliament has always held the view that whatever matter arises concerning either House of Parliament ought to be discussed and adjudged in that House to which it relates and not elsewhere; and that the existence of a privilege depends upon its being declared by the High Court of Parliament to be part of the ancient law and custom of Parliament.[3] It has been seen that the courts, in the case of *Stockdale* v. *Hansard*,[4] maintained the right to determine the nature and limit of parliamentary privileges, should it be necessary to determine such questions in adjudicating upon disputes between individuals. In *Eliot's Case* the question whether or not the court could deal with an assault on the Speaker committed in the House of Commons was expressly left open when the judgment was declared illegal by resolutions of both Houses, but there is no authority showing that crimes committed in the precincts of Parliament cannot be punished by the ordinary courts.[5] In civil cases the test is whether the act alleged took place in the course of parliamentary business and as part thereof.[6] An act which is criminal can hardly form part of such business. The present relationship between the High Court and Parliament is made clearer by the cases centring round Mr. Bradlaugh. In *Bradlaugh* v. *Gossett* (1884), 12 Q.B.D. 271; K. & L. 144, the Court of Queen's Bench refused to declare void an order of the House of Commons preventing Charles Bradlaugh, who had been duly elected member for Northampton, from taking the oath. It was held that the House of Commons had the exclusive right to regulate its own proceedings, and that no court

---

[1] See pp. 148–9, *post*, as to members of the Commons who are in receipt of ministerial salaries.
[2] H. C. 118, 1947.   [3] May, *op. cit.*, Chap. IX.   [4] P. 122, *ante*.
[5] An attempt to convict members of the Kitchen Committee of the House of Commons of breaches of the licensing law failed, primarily on the ground of the right of the House to regulate its internal affairs: *The King* v. *Graham-Campbell, ex parte Herbert*, [1935] 1 K.B. 594; see p. 123, *ante*.
[6] See H. C. 101, 1939, p. 119, *ante*, note 1.

could interfere with the exercise of such right. The Parliamentary Oaths Act, 1866, permitted certain persons to make a declaration of affirmation instead of taking an oath. It was disputed whether or not Bradlaugh was a person entitled to make such a declaration. Any person making the declaration otherwise than as authorised by the Act could be sued for certain penalties. The House of Commons permitted Bradlaugh to make the declaration. It is pointed out in the judgment of Stephen, J., in *Bradlaugh* v. *Gossett* that, should the House of Commons have attempted by resolution to state that Bradlaugh was entitled to make the statutory declaration, such a resolution would not have protected him against an action for penalties:

> "We should have said that for the purpose of determining on a right to be exercised within the House itself, the House, and the House only, could interpret the statute; but that as regarded rights to be exercised out of, and independently of, the House, such as the right of suing for a penalty for having sat and voted, the statute must be interpreted by this court independently of the House." [1]

In an action against Bradlaugh for penalties which was successful —*Clarke* v. *Bradlaugh* (1881), 7 Q.B.D. 38; *Bradlaugh* v. *Clarke* (1883), 8 A.C. 354—it was held that the Parliamentary Oaths Act, 1866, and the Promissory Oaths Act, 1868, did not authorise Bradlaugh to make the declaration.

In *Paty's Case* (1704), 2 Lord Raymond 1105, Chief Justice Holt, in a minority judgment, held that a writ of habeas corpus would go to release anyone committed for contempt by the House of Commons where the cause of committal stated in the return to the writ was insufficient in law. This view of the law is accepted to-day. If, however, no cause for committal other than contempt of the House is shown in the return, the High Court is powerless. As it was said by Lord Ellenborough in *Burdett* v. *Abbot* (1811), 14 East 1: "If a commitment appeared to be for contempt of the House of Commons generally, I would neither in the case of that court nor of any other of the superior courts enquire further." This opinion prevailed in *The Sheriff of Middlesex's Case* (1840), 11 A. & E. 273; K. & L. 140. Thus the House possesses an arbitrary power of committal for contempt which cannot be enquired into by the courts, provided that the cause of the contempt is not stated. Such a power is not available to the Executive, both by reason of the Statute 16 Car. 1, c. 10, s. 8, which guarantees the writ of habeas corpus against committal by the King and his Council, and because the common law holds arbitrary imprisonment unlawful and does not recognise the plea of act of State as justifying imprisonment of a British subject by a Minister.

---

[1] The Oaths Act, 1888, now permits an affirmation in lieu of an oath in all places and for all purposes where an oath is required by law.

It appears, therefore, that there may be two views laid down as to the privileges of the House of Commons. The House may act upon one view when regulating its own proceedings and committing for contempt, while the court may act upon another view when privileges arise in civil disputes. It has, however, been pointed out many times by judges that the court will naturally pay the greatest attention to the views and customs of the House of Commons in deciding what are the privileges of that House. There is none the less a possibility of conflict which may affect the liberty of the subject.

B.

House of Lords.

Privileges of the House of Lords.

The privileges of the House of Lords are:

(*a*) Freedom from civil arrest for peers for a period of forty days before and after a meeting of Parliament, as in the case of members of the House of Commons.

(*b*) Freedom of speech.

(*c*) Freedom of access to the Sovereign for each peer individually.

(*d*) The right to commit for contempt. The House of Lords can commit a person for contempt for a definite term, and the imprisonment is not terminated by prorogation of Parliament.

(*e*) The right to exclude disqualified persons from taking part in the proceedings of the House. The House itself decides, through the Committee of Privileges, the right of newly elected peers to sit and vote.[1] Claims to old peerages are referred by the Crown to the House of Lords, and are also decided by the Committee of Privileges. That body is not bound by its own previous decisions.

[1] P. 76, *ante*.

PART IV.

THE EXECUTIVE.

Cabinet Government, 2nd ed., by Sir Ivor Jennings (Cambridge University Press).
George V.; His Life and Reign, by Sir Harold Nicolson (Constable).
Government and Parliament, by Herbert Morrison (Oxford University Press)
The New Whitehall Series (George Allen and Unwin).

CHAPTER 1.

THE CROWN.

Introductory.

To study the organs of State which exercise the executive and administrative functions is the most difficult task that a student of constitutional law has to perform. He is, of necessity, without that acquaintance with what takes place in Cabinet meetings or within government departments which could alone give him an intimate knowledge of the machine in operation. When dealing with the Legislature and the Judiciary he is studying organs which work in the public eye. Proceedings both in Parliament and in the High Court can be followed by readers of *The Times*. What happens in the departments and how they work is unknown to the general public. True that from time to time questions in Parliament or strictures from the Bench remind the public that Whitehall is encroaching on their liberty. Public relations officers do their best to explain the more glaring examples of individual hardship which result from a too rigid administrative machine. Occasionally a retired civil servant gives the world a glimpse behind the scenes, but convention normally forbids any active member of that service from writing of his work. For the average lawyer acquaintance with Whitehall is limited to interviews with subordinate officials, while others perhaps get no further than interviews with a local inspector of taxes or a national insurance officer.

There is too another difficulty. Terms are used which have no precise legal significance. Differences of form do not always represent differences of substance. The term, the Crown, represents the sum total of governmental powers and is synonymous with the Executive. Terminology.

F

In the exercise of some of the powers of the Crown the Sovereign may be called upon to exercise a personal discretion;[1] others are exercised by the Sovereign on the sole responsibility of Ministers; in the exercise of others the Sovereign plays no part, for the majority of statutory powers are conferred upon Ministers as such and are exercised by them in their official capacity, though they are none the less exercised on behalf of the Crown. There is only a formal difference between a power conferred upon the Queen in Council which is exercised on the advice of the responsible Minister concerned and a power conferred directly upon that responsible Minister. The Queen, the Queen in Council [2] and the several Ministers of State are legal titles. It is only comparatively recently that the terms, Government and Prime Minister, have appeared in statutes,[3] and then only in a context which assumes their meaning to be known. The terms, Executive,[4] Cabinet, Ministry and Administration are extra-legal. The Cabinet [5] is the body of principal Ministers with whom rests the real direction of policy. We speak of the Ministry or the Administration of a particular Prime Minister with reference to the full body of political office holders who from time to time hold the reins of government, *i.e.* the Ministers of the Crown and their Parliamentary Secretaries.

A.

The Sovereign.

Title to
the Crown.

Title to the Crown is derived from the Act of Settlement, 1701: "The Crown . . . shall remain and continue to the said most excellent Princess Sophia" (the Electress of Hanover, granddaughter of James I.) "and the heirs of her body being Protestant." The title to the Crown follows the hereditary principle, but the Queen in Parliament may alter the succession. The limitation to the heirs of the body means that the Crown descends, with certain exceptions, as did real property under the law of inheritance in force before 1926. This branch of property law recognised (*inter alia*) the right of primogeniture and preference for males over females. There are disqualified from the succession to the Throne Roman Catholics and those who marry Roman Catholics, and the Sovereign must join in communion with the Church of England. On the death of King George V. he was succeeded by his eldest son, the Prince of Wales and heir

[1] P. 63, *ante.*
[2] P. 136, *post.*
[3] *E.g.* Statute of Westminster, 1931 (Government); Ministers of the Crown Act, 1937 (Prime Minister).
[4] P. 15, *ante.*
[5] Chap. 3, *post.*

apparent [1] who became Edward VIII. On the abdication of Edward VIII. it was provided by His Majesty's Declaration of Abdication Act, 1936, that the member of the Royal Family then next in succession to the Throne (King George VI), then Duke of York and heir presumptive [2] should succeed and that Edward VIII., his issue, if any, and the descendants of that issue should not thereafter have any right, title or interest in or to the succession.

The style and titles of the Crown in the reigns of George V. and VI. were determined by Royal Proclamation under the Great Seal which was issued on the authority of the Royal and Parliamentary Titles Act, 1927. The Preamble to the Statute of Westminster, 1931, declared that it would be in accord with the established constitutional position that any alteration in the law touching the succession to the Throne or the Royal Style and Titles shall also require the consent of the Parliaments of all the Dominions.[3] By Royal Proclamation the King in 1948 omitted the title, Emperor of India, the assent of Parliament of the United Kingdom having been given thereto by the Indian Independence Act, 1947, s. 7 (2); the Dominions passed their own enactments. Before Queen Elizabeth II. succeeded her Father, the form of royal style and titles was "George VI. by Grace of God of Great Britain, Ireland and the British Dominions beyond the Seas, King, Defender of the Faith." The Accession Council (see *post*) acknowledged Queen Elizabeth "Queen of this Realm and of all Her other Realms and Territories, Head of the Commonwealth, Defender of the Faith." A new Royal Titles Act was necessary to give legal effect to this change, as the Royal Style and Titles Act of 1927, which had authorised the changes made by royal proclamation of that year had expired. Several constitutional developments had made a change in the legal title desirable; in particular the royal title had hitherto rested on the doctrine of the indivisibility of the Crown throughout the Commonwealth. That indivisibility had by 1952 ceased to be the fact, and in the case certainly of the Republic of India the law. Accordingly the Royal Titles Act, 1953, gave the assent of the Parliament of the United Kingdom to the adoption by the Queen by royal proclamation of her title for use only in relation to the United Kingdom and all other territories for whose foreign relations the Government of the United Kingdom is responsible, *i.e.* Colonies,

Style and Titles.

---

[1] The eldest son of a reigning monarch, who is Duke of Cornwall by inheritance and is invariably created Prince of Wales. There is no precedent for the latter title being conferred upon an eldest or only daughter who is the heiress presumptive.

[2] The person at any time next in succession. *E.g.* an only daughter is heiress presumptive, unless and till a son is born to the Sovereign. So, too, before his accession the late King was heir presumptive to his brother, Edward VIII., but would have ceased to be so on the birth of a child (male or female) to his brother.

[3] P. 465, *post*.

Protectorates and certain trust territories. It was left to the other States within the Commonwealth to enact their own form of title, as they had proclaimed it at the time of the accession. In the result the only description common to all States is "Head of the Commonwealth," though in each case there is reference to the Queen's Headship of her other realms and territories. India, in accordance with her republican form of constitution, issued no decree of proclamation, although she continued to recognise the Queen's Headship of the Commonwealth as her link with the rest of the Commonwealth. Pakistan, who had not proclaimed the Queen as sovereign of that country, has since decided to adopt a constitution in the form of an Islamic Republic.

Royal Marriages.

The Royal Marriages Act, 1772, by placing certain restrictions upon the right of a descendant of George II. to contract a valid marriage without the consent of the Sovereign, guards against undesirable marriages which might affect the succession to the Throne. Until the age of twenty-five the Sovereign's assent is necessary (except in respect of the issue of princesses who have married into foreign families). After that age a marriage may take place without consent after a year's notice to the Privy Council, unless Parliament expressly disapproves.

Accession and Coronation.

Accession to the Crown is a coming of a person into the position of the Sovereign, whereupon all subjects owe personal allegiance. There are two ceremonies which mark the accession of the new Sovereign. Immediately on the death of his precedessor the Sovereign is proclaimed, not by the Privy Council[1] as such, but by the Lords Spiritual and Temporal and other leading citizens, a body which is a survival of an old assemblage, which met to choose and proclaim the King. The Proclamation is afterwards approved at the first meeting of the new King's Privy Council. After an interval of time follows the Coronation, the ancient ceremony which gave religious sanction to title by election and brought to a close the interregnum, when no King reigned, between the death of one King and the election of his successor. Anson noted that, as the recognition of hereditary rights strengthened, the importance of the election and coronation dwindled, while the great practical inconvenience of the interregnum, the abeyance of the King's Peace, was curtailed.

The modern coronation ceremony is full of historical interest. There are three stages:

(1) The acceptance of their Sovereign by the people and the taking of the oath of royal duties by the Sovereign.

(2) The purely religious ceremony which includes the anointing and crowning.

(3) The rendering of homage in person by the Lords Spiritual and Temporal.

[1] P. 136, *post*.

It should be noted that the oath illustrates the contractual nature of the sovereign power and has survived both the extravagant prerogative claims of the Stuarts and the Revolution of 1688. The form of the Coronation oath was prescribed by the Coronation Oath Act, 1688, as amended by the Acts of Union. In place of the formal declaration against transubstantiation, the Accession Declaration Act, 1910, substituted a modified declaration of adherence to the Protestant faith. The oath taken by the Sovereign in 1937 and in 1953 was varied without statutory authority in order to recognise the equal status of Kingship of the various States of the Commonwealth.

The Regency Acts, 1937–1953, have made, for the first time, standing provision for the infancy, incapacity and temporary absence of the Sovereign from the realm. The Sovereign comes of age at eighteen; until he reaches that age, the royal functions are to be exercised by a Regent who will also act in the event of total incapacity of an adult Sovereign. The Regent will be the next person in the line of succession, who is not excluded from the succession by the Act of Settlement and is a British subject domiciled in the United Kingdom. The Regent, if the heir-apparent or heir-presumptive, must have attained the age of eighteen; if another person, the age of twenty-one. If a Regency should become necessary on the succession of a child of Queen Elizabeth II. and her husband, while under the age of eighteen, the Duke of Edinburgh, if living, will be the Regent. He will also become Regent in the event of a Regency during the present reign, until a child or grandchild of the Queen and the Duke can become Regent on attaining the age of eighteen. Regency is automatic on the succession of a minor; but in the case of total incapacity a declaration has to be made to the Privy Council by the wife or husband of the Sovereign, the Lord Chancellor, the Speaker, the Lord Chief Justice and the Master of the Rolls, or any three of them, that they are satisfied by evidence (including that of physicians) that the Sovereign is by reason of infirmity of mind or body incapable of performing the royal functions, or that for some definite cause he is not available for the performance of those functions. Such a declaration must be made to the Privy Council and communicated to the other Governments of the Commonwealth. A Regency may be ended by a similar declaration. A Regent may exercise all the royal functions, except that he may not assent to a Bill for changing the order of succession to the Crown or for repealing or altering the Act of Anne made in Scotland and entitled an Act for securing the Protestant Religion and Presbyterian Church Government.

The Regency Act, 1937, did not apply to those Dominions which at that date had accepted the main provisions of the Statute of Westminster, namely Canada and the Union of South Africa, nor to Eire.

Infancy and Incapacity.

While the declaration leading to the appointment of a Regent has to be communicated to the other Governments of the Commonwealth, separate legislation by each Parliament is necessary to make the Act applicable. Presumably the necessity, which arises from section 4 of the Statute, does not extend to Australia or New Zealand by reason of the later dates at which they adopted this part of the Statute, nor to the newer Dominions, but all are competent to enact their own legislation.

Illness and Temporary Absence.   In the event of illness which does not amount to total incapacity or of absence or intended absence from the United Kingdom, the Sovereign may appoint Counsellors of State to exercise such of the royal functions as may be conferred upon them by letters patent. There may not be delegated the power to dissolve Parliament otherwise than on the express instructions of the Sovereign (which may be conveyed by telegraph), or to grant any rank, title or dignity of the peerage. The Counsellors of State must be the wife or husband of the Sovereign, the four persons next in line of succession to the Crown (excluding any persons (a) disqualified from being Regent, or (b) being absent or intending to be absent from the United Kingdom during the period of delegation) and Queen Elizabeth, the Queen Mother. The heir apparent or heir presumptive may be a Counsellor of State, if not under eighteen years of age.

The functions of Counsellors of State during absence of the Sovereign from the United Kingdom do not extend to those functions which in relation to a Dominion are normally exercised by the King. Thus when the King visited South Africa in 1947 the Canadian Government announced that His Majesty had notified the Governor-General that he would continue to exercise personally in South Africa such functions in relation to Canada and the announcement made it clear that the Council of State was a body set up on the authority of an Act of the United Kingdom Parliament and therefore exercised no authority in Canada.

Demise of the Sovereign.   Formerly the death of the Sovereign involved the dissolution of Parliament and the termination of the tenure of all offices under the Crown, since Parliament meets on the personal summons of the Sovereign, and all offices are in theory held at his will and pleasure. The duration of Parliament is now independent of the demise of the Sovereign.[1] The Demise of the Crown Act, 1901, provided that the holding of any office should not be affected by the demise of the Crown and that no fresh appointment should be necessary.

Abdication.   Akin to a demise of the Sovereign is his abdication. In 1936 King Edward VIII. signed a declaration of abdication to which effect was given by His Majesty's Declaration of Abdication Act, 1936. This

[1] P. 93, *ante.*

Act enacted that there should be a demise of the Crown upon the Act receiving the royal assent and provided for the exclusion of Edward VIII. and his issue from the succession to the Throne. Prior to the signature of the declaration of abdication the King's intention had been communicated informally to the Dominion Governments by the Prime Minister of the United Kingdom. Upon signature the declaration was formally communicated to the Dominion Governments.[1]

No attempt can be made to list the duties which fall to the Sovereign to perform in person. Many formal acts of government require her participation. Many State papers require her signature and of the contents of others she is required to be informed. The Prime Minister keeps her informed of all conclusions of the Cabinet. As a constitutional monarch she is bound to act on the advice of her Ministers. She may, however, temper their counsel and offer guidance from her own fund of experience in affairs. But she cannot reject the final advice they offer without bringing about their resignation and replacement by other Ministers. Much light has been thrown upon the exact tasks which were performed by the Sovereign in the early part of the twentieth century by Sir Harold Nicolson's biography of King George V.[2] In particular it appears that the Sovereign, even before the days when Cabinet conclusions were first recorded and reported by the Secretariat, could insist upon the advice of the Cabinet being given in written form, if he felt that it was dangerous or opposed to the wishes of the people. This was so that the King could record in writing the misgivings and reluctance with which he followed the advice of his Cabinet.[3] The rôle of the Sovereign is to advise, encourage and warn Ministers in respect of the recommendations which they make. This is a rôle which increases in importance as experience is acquired in dealing with successive Ministers. The Private Secretary to the Sovereign must necessarily play an intimate rôle in conducting communications between the Sovereign and his Ministers. This office is filled on the personal selection of the Sovereign. Constitutional propriety forbids consultation by the Sovereign with Privy Councillors or others who are outside the ranks of Ministers in office unless it be with their consent. Equally it is not for the Queen to initiate action of her own accord. She holds formal meetings of her Privy Council, gives audiences, *e.g.* to her Ministers, receives the credentials of foreign diplomatic representatives, holds investitures and confers honours and decorations. Her patronage, exercisable on ministerial advice, is wide. Her consent is needed for all major appointments which are

Duties of the Sovereign.

---

[1] Pp. 465–6, *post.* For a brief account of the separate action taken by the Dominions.

[2] *George V.* (Constable, 1952).   [3] *Op. cit.,* p. 116.

made by the Crown on the advice of the Prime Minister, Lord Chancellor and other Ministers. The Queen and her Consort, and all the members of the Royal Family, play a leading part in the ceremonies of public life and the social life of the nation. Visits and short tours of residence in Commonwealth countries are becoming a normal part of the life of the Royal Family.[1] Finally and perhaps most important of all, the Queen is the constitutional and personal link that binds together the British Commonwealth of Nations; to her is owed allegiance by their peoples except in the case of the Republic of India.[2]

Private Property.

The Sovereign may hold private property in a personal capacity, *e.g.* the Sandringham estate in Norfolk. Such property, unlike Crown property,[3] is liable to taxes and rates, but in a personal capacity the Sovereign cannot be sued[4] or prosecuted.

B.

The Queen in Council.[5]

The King was formerly the sole repository, in theory of law, of executive power, which he executed by and with the advice of his Privy Council. Despite the many powers conferred by modern statutes on individual Ministers, the Order in Council remains a principal method of giving the force of law to acts of the Government. It has been seen that to-day the Queen executes a large number of documents, under her own hand or a facsimile thereof. But the Order in Council is the document in general use for giving effect to the more important executive orders. A Royal Proclamation is issued when it is desired to give wide publicity to the action of the Queen in Council, as for the purpose of dissolving a Parliament and summoning its successor. Nowadays Orders in Council are approved by the Sovereign at a meeting of the Council to which only

[1] Appendix C includes specimens of some documents which require the royal signature. For a fuller account of the functions of the Sovereign, see Nicolson, *George V.* (passim) ; Bagehot, *The English Constitution* (Clarendon Press), Chaps. II., III. ; Jennings, *Cabinet Government*, Chaps. II. and XI. ; Sir Sidney Low, *The Governance of England* (Fisher Unwin), Chap. XIV.

[2] Part X., Chap. 3, D. Pakistan has resolved to adopt a republican form of government.

[3] P. 185, *post.*

[4] Crown Proceedings Act, 1947, s. 40 (1). Some writers suggest that a petition of right (p. 332, *post*) could still lie against the Queen in her personal capacity, *e.g.* O. Hood Phillips, *Constitutional Law*, p. 402 (Sweet and Maxwell).

[5] See Baldwin, *The King's Council in the Middle Ages* (Clarendon Press), and Dicey, *The Privy Council* (Arnold Prize Essay) (Macmillan), for historical accounts of the Privy Council.

four or five members are summoned and are authenticated by the
signature of the Clerk of the Council. Constitutional history shows
both the decline in the advisory and judicial functions of the Council
and its supersession in the former capacity by the Cabinet. To-day
the acts of the Privy Council are purely formal and give effect to
orders, the contents of which are the responsibility of government
departments. These are orders made either under the prerogative,[1]
e.g. constitutional legislation for a colony, or under an Act of Parliament, *e.g.* orders giving effect to university and college statutes under
the Universities of Oxford and Cambridge Act, 1923.

Council Committees.

The Council, having ceased to be an advisory Council of the
Crown, is summoned for the purpose of making orders, issuing proclamations or performing formal State acts. A few traces remain of
its former advisory functions; the Committee for Channel Islands
business is a survivor of the old Standing Committees appointed by
the King at the beginning or in the course of his reign. Other committees are the Judicial Committee of the Privy Council[2] and a
committee to consider grants of charters to municipal and other
corporations. There are also Committees of the Privy Council for
Scientific and Industrial, Medical and Agricultural Research, each
with advisory councils of leading scientists. The Department of
Scientific and Industrial Research is linked to the first of these Committees. The Lord President of the Council, a Cabinet Minister,
is responsible for the work of this department, as also for the
activities of the Medical and Agricultural Research Councils and
of the Atomic Energy Authority, for all duties imposed by statute
on the Privy Council and for the formal business transacted by
the Privy Council Office under the Clerk of the Council.

Office of Privy Councillor.

Membership of the Privy Council is a titular honour. Appointments are made by the Sovereign on ministerial advice. By convention all Cabinet Ministers, in whom are vested the right and duty of
advising the Sovereign on all matters of government, become Privy
Councillors. Members of the Royal Family and holders of certain
high offices of a non-political character, such as Archbishops and
Lords Justices of Appeal, are sworn members of the Council. In
addition the office is a recognised reward for public and political
service, and appointments of this nature usually figure in the New
Year and Birthday Honours Lists. The Council numbers about
300 members at the present day. Members are entitled to the prefix,
"Right Honourable." They take an oath on appointment which
binds them not to disclose anything said or done "in Council,"
without the consent of the Sovereign. As all members of the Cabinet
are members of the Privy Council, it is this oath which, in addition
to their obligations under the Official Secrets Acts, 1920–1939, binds

---

[1] P. 138, *post.*   [2] Part X., Chap. 4.

to secrecy all present and past Cabinet Ministers, who may only disclose Cabinet proceedings and other confidential discussions if so authorised by the Sovereign.[1] Alienage is a disqualification, but on naturalisation an alien becomes qualified for membership: *The King* v. *Speyer; The King* v. *Cassel*, [1916] 1 K.B. 595; [1916] 2 K.B. 858.

Relation of Cabinet to Council.

The functions of the Privy Council are distinct from those of the Cabinet. The former is a body which gives formal approval to certain acts of the Government; the latter is deliberative. Although all members of the Cabinet are Privy Councillors, it is not as a Committee of the Council that they meet, but as "Her Majesty's Servants." The Cabinet is summoned by the Prime Minister. The Council is convened by the Clerk of the Council, whose office dates back to the sixteenth century. The only connecting link between the modern Cabinet and the Council is the oath and obligation of secrecy which binds Cabinet Ministers as members of the Council; but it should be remembered that the first use of the term, Cabinet, was to describe inner bodies of the Privy Council.

House of Lords as Council of the Crown.

The House of Lords is still in theory a Council of the Crown. It has not been summoned, as such, since 1688, but traces of its former function are preserved in the writ of summons. Moreover, it is the privilege of a peer to seek individual access to the Sovereign, though the privilege may not be used by peers as such for the purpose of tendering advice on their own initiative on matters of government.

C.

The Royal Prerogative.[2]

At most periods in our history the term, prerogative, has been used to connote rights and capacities of the Crown which have little in common with one another except that in the words of Blackstone they are based on that "special pre-eminence which the King hath, over and above all other persons, and out of the ordinary course of the common law, in right of his regal dignity." [3] This chapter is primarily concerned with those powers which may be exercised by the Crown without the authority of Parliament. It is none the less necessary to explain other uses of the word, prerogative, and to touch briefly on the history of the prerogative, some appreciation of which is essential for understanding the present law.

---

[1] *The Times*, 8 August, 1952.
[2] The student should study both the cases and introductory chapters in Keir and Lawson, *Cases in Constitutional Law*, pp. 43–75. We express our obligation to the authors, on whose historical summary we have freely drawn.
[3] I. Blackstone, *Commentaries*, 232.

The mediaeval King was both feudal lord and head of the State. As chief feudal lord and in theory the owner of all land the King had all the rights of a feudal lord and in addition certain exceptional rights over and above those of all other lords. Like other lords the King could not be sued in his own courts; as there was no lord superior to the King, there was no court in which the King could be sued. In addition the King as head of the State had powers accounted for by the need for the preservation of the State against external foes and an "undefined residue of power which he might use for the public good." [1] We have already seen [2] that mediaeval lawyers did not regard the King as being above the law. Moreover certain of the royal functions could only be exercised in certain ways. The common law courts were the King's courts and only through them could the King decide questions of title to land and punish felonies. Yet as the fountain of justice the King possessed a residuary power of doing justice through his Council where the courts of common law were inadequate. Normally mediaeval writers used the term, prerogative, only of those rights which appertained to the King as feudal lord, but sometimes it was used to include all those rights, powers and capacities which were derived from the King's pre-eminence.

The history of the royal prerogative is inseparably connected with the history of parliamentary sovereignty and the alliance between common lawyers and Parliament. In outline that story has already been told. [3] The common lawyers asserted that there was a fundamental distinction between what came to be called the ordinary as opposed to the absolute prerogative. The ordinary prerogative meant those royal functions which could only be exercised in defined ways and involved no element of royal discretion. Thus the King could not himself act as a judge; he must dispense justice through his judges: *Prohibitions del Roy* (1607), 12 Rep. 63; K. & L. 76. The King too could only exercise legislative authority through Parliament: *The Case of Proclamations* (1611), 12 Rep. 74; K. & L. 78. [4] The absolute or extraordinary prerogative meant those powers which the King could exercise in his discretion. It was round the absolute prerogative that the seventeenth-century struggle between King and Parliament centred. The King has undoubted powers to exercise discretion in the interest of the State, especially in times of emergency, but the claims of the Stuart Kings in this regard could not be reconciled with the growing claims of Parliament. [5] The absolute prerogative covered a wider field than the King's rights to take extraordinary action to meet emergencies. It was primarily around the King's emergency

[1] K. & L. 44.   [2] P. 49, *ante.*   [3] Part II., Chap. 2, A.
[4] P. 33, *ante.*   [5] P. 32, *ante.*

powers that the seventeenth-century struggle turned, but the rights to pardon a criminal or grant a peerage were also part of the absolute as opposed to the ordinary prerogative. They could be exercised at the King's discretion. The contest could not be settled as a matter of law and indeed involved the execution of one King and the expulsion of another. None the less the rival theories and very real difficulties involved are best understood by a study of the leading cases, most of which were decided in favour of the Crown. The great taxation cases, *Bates' Case* and *The Case of Ship Money* have already been discussed,[1] so too have the cases relating to the dispensing power, *Thomas* v. *Sorrell* and *Godden* v. *Hales*.[2] Another case of the first importance was *Darnel's* or *The Five Knights' Case* (1627), 3 St. Tr. 1; K. & L. 49; where it was held that it was a sufficient answer to a writ of habeas corpus to state that a prisoner was detained without cause shown *per speciale mandatum regis* (by the special order of the King). No better example can be given of the problem of the absolute prerogative. It was the law that the King had a right to exercise a power of preventive arrest which could not be questioned by the courts. In *Darnel's Case* this power was used to enforce taxation levied without the consent of Parliament. The right of Parliament to control taxation came into conflict with a prerogative power recognised by law. The arbitrary power of committal was declared illegal by the Petition of Right, 1628, and the Statute of 1640 (16 Car. 1, c. 10, s. 8) guaranteed to the subject the writ of habeas corpus against the King and his Council.

The Solution of the Problem.   The problem of the prerogative was solved in two stages. The first is that of the seventeenth-century struggle culminating in the Revolution Settlement of 1689. The Bill of Rights declared illegal certain specific abuses of the prerogative. Moreover the Settlement marked the final triumph of the view that there was no extraordinary prerogative above the law. It is in this sense that a prerogative power may be described as a common law power. Derived from this ancient pre-eminence of the Crown it is a power which the common law recognises as exercisable by the King. The powers so recognised are many and important, *e.g.* the right to summon and dissolve Parliament, the right to declare war and make peace. There was, however, even after 1689 scope for conflict between King and Parliament. The second stage is the growth of responsible government and the establishment of a constitutional monarchy, as it is understood to-day.[3] The meaning of responsible government has already been explained.[4] It became established that the prerogative powers could only be exercised through and on the advice of Ministers responsible to Parliament.

[1] P. 34, *ante*.
[2] P. 35, *ante*.
[3] P. 13, *ante*.
[4] P. 65, *ante*.

The Sovereign is still the personification of the State, and has The Prerogative to-day. always enjoyed by prescription, custom and law the chief place in Parliament and the sole executive power. The Act of Settlement affirmed the laws of England to be the birthright of the people and that "all the Kings and Queens who shall ascend the throne of this realm ought to administer the government . . . according to the said laws; and their officers and Ministers ought to serve them respectively according to the same." Parliament is summoned and dissolved by the Queen; the powers of Ministers are exercised for and on behalf of Her Majesty; the courts are the Queen's courts. The term, prerogative, is sometimes used to include both the common law and the statutory powers of the Crown. It is, however, preferable to confine it to common law powers. It is also sometimes used in the sense, that is now perhaps archaic, of certain of those attributes of the Sovereign which result from the headship of the State. Thus the term, prerogative of perfection, is used of the rule that the Crown can do no wrong; prerogative of perpetuity, of the rule that the succession of one Sovereign is simultaneous with the death of his predecessor. The living meaning of the prerogative to-day is, however, that group of powers of the Crown not conferred by statute but recognised by the common law as belonging to the Crown.

The prerogative powers of the Crown are with very rare [1] excep- The Exercise of the Prerogative. tions to-day exercised by the Government of the day. For their exercise, just as for the exercise of statutory powers, Ministers are responsible to Parliament and may be asked questions relating to those public duties for which the Sovereign is responsible, provided that the duties fall within the province of the particular Minister. To this there are some exceptions and in particular a question with regard to the exercise of the prerogative of mercy in capital sentences is not in order. For the exercise of a prerogative power the prior authority of Parliament is not required. Thus, to take but one example, the Crown may grant a new constitution to a colony which has no representative legislature without first consulting or even informing Parliament. Parliament may criticise Ministers for the consequences which result from the exercise of prerogative; Parliament too may abolish or curtail the prerogative by statute; [2] but in regard to the exercise of the prerogative Parliament has no right to be consulted in advance. Certain prerogative powers could of course only be exercised if the Government were assured of parliamentary support. The Crown may declare war, but no Government could take the risk of declaring war without being assured of popular support, and Parliament alone can vote supplies to enable war to be waged. Although the contents of the prerogative depend largely upon historical causes,

---

[1] *E.g.* the choice of a Prime Minister; see p. 63, *ante.*
[2] P. 145, *post.*

it will be found that they can be justified on grounds of convenience and political wisdom. Prerogative powers are mainly those the exercise of which cannot wisely be discussed in a deliberative assembly, *e.g.* the disposition of the armed forces; appointments to the Civil Service; the grant of honours to individuals. Even more is this true of the prerogative powers of the Crown in relation to foreign affairs which in this book are discussed as acts of State.[1]

The Prerogative and the Courts.

It has been said that prerogative powers are those powers which the law recognises as belonging to the Crown other than powers conferred by statute. If an individual disputes the validity of an act purporting to be done under the prerogative, the courts will investigate whether or not the alleged prerogative power exists. An important illustration of this is discussed at the end of this chapter. Once, however, the existence and extent of the power are established, the manner of its exercise can only be questioned in Parliament. The mere plea of State necessity will not, however, serve to protect any one accused of an unlawful act towards a subject. This is a cardinal principle of English law. "With respect to the plea of State necessity, or a distinction that has been aimed at between State offences and others, the common law does not understand that kind of reasoning, nor do our books take notice of any such distinctions": *per* Lord Camden, C.J., in *Entick* v. *Carrington* (1765), 19 St. Tr. 1030; K. & L. 174. There is a clear distinction between the mere plea of State necessity and reliance upon a prerogative power recognised by law.

The Prerogative and Acts of State.

By virtue of his pre-eminence as head of the State the King exercises numerous powers in the realm of foreign affairs. Acts done in the exercise of such powers are generally known as acts of State. Whether these powers may rightly be described as prerogative powers is a matter of argument. In this book they will be treated separately and the term prerogative powers will be confined to the power and authority of the King in relation to his own subjects, and not rights vested in him in relation to persons owing no allegiance to him.[2]

Powers relating to the Legislature.

We may now consider separately some prerogative powers. By virtue of the prerogative the Sovereign summons, prorogues and dissolves Parliament.[3] The royal prerogative to create peers may be used on the advice of the Government to ensure the passage of a Bill through the House of Lords.[4] The Sovereign has a right as an integral part of the Legislature to assent or refuse to assent to Bills.[5]

[1] Part IV., Chap. 10, A.
[2] See *per* Warrington, L.J., in *In re Ferdinand, Ex-Tsar of Bulgaria*, [1921] 1 Ch. 107, at p. 139.
[3] Part III., Chap. 2.
[4] P. 77, *ante.*
[5] P. 102, *ante.*

The Crown may by Order in Council or letters patent legislate under the prerogative for certain colonies.[1]

Lapse of time does not bar the right of the Crown to prosecute, but there are many statutes which impose a time limit. All criminal prosecutions are brought in the name of the Crown. The Crown may stop a prosecution by the entry of a *nolle prosequi*, a prerogative power exercised by the Attorney-General.[2] The Crown too may pardon convicted offenders or remit or reduce a sentence on the advice of the Home Secretary.[3] It is by virtue of the prerogative that the Crown grants special leave to appeal from British courts overseas to the Judicial Committee of the Privy Council.[4] But most States of the Commonwealth have abolished all appeals to the Privy Council. *(margin: Prerogatives relating to the Judiciary.)*

The Sovereign is commander-in-chief of all the armed forces of the Crown. The Navy, though its recruitment and discipline are regulated by statute (Naval Enlistment Acts, 1835 to 1884, and Naval Discipline Acts, 1866–8[5]), is a prerogative force maintained without any direct statutory authority. The Bill of Rights prohibits the keeping of a standing army within the realm in time of peace without the consent of Parliament, and this prohibition includes all forces serving on land. Thus the authority of Parliament is required to authorise the maintenance of the Army, the Royal Air Force and, for their employment ashore, the Royal Marines.[6] Their control, organisation and disposition are within the prerogative. All officers of the Army and Air Force hold their commissions from the Queen. Naval officers' commissions are Admiralty commissions, signed by two naval members of the Board of Admiralty; a facsimile of the Queen's signature is appended at the top. *(margin: Prerogatives relating to the Armed Forces.)*

The Sovereign appoints Ministers and Judges of the Supreme Court and makes appointments to all the principal offices in State and Church and to membership of Royal Commissions to enquire into matters of controversy. Appointments to all posts in the Civil Service are appointments to the service of the Crown, though made by and in the name of ministerial heads of departments. The Sovereign too is the sole fountain of honour and alone can create peers and confer honours and decorations. *(margin: Appointments and Honours.)*

Taxation, including local rates, is not payable in respect of income received by the Sovereign as such. Nor is it payable on Crown properties or in respect of income received on behalf of the Crown by a servant of the Crown in the course of official duties; *Bank voor Handel en Scheepvaart N.V.* v. *Administrator of Hungarian Property*, [1954] A.C. 584. *(margin: Immunities from Taxation.)*

---

[1] Part X., Chap. 2, A.   [2] P. 245, *post.*
[3] P. 245, *post.*   [4] Part X., Chap. 4.
[5] As subsequently amended.   [6] See Part IX., Chap. 1.

Monopolies.   Grants and monopolies by the Crown were bad at common law except in the case of patents for new inventions: *The Case of Monopolies* (1602), 11 Co. Rep. 84, where there was held void a grant of the sole right to make and import playing cards. The Statute of Monopolies, 1624, a declaratory Act, controlled the Crown's power to grant to first inventors the monopoly of working new inventions. This statute formed the basis of modern patent law, now regulated by the Patents and Designs Acts, 1907 to 1949. The Statute of Monopolies recognised the rights of corporations, companies and societies of merchants and in 1683 the court held that a grant of the sole right of trading to the East Indies was valid: *East India Co.* v. *Sandys* (The Great Case of Monopolies) (1685), 10 St. Tr. 371; but in 1694 the House of Commons resolved that, unless prohibited by Parliament, all subjects have an equal right of trading with the King's dominions. Since that date the grant of exclusive rights of trading has been by statute, *e.g.* to the East India Company set up in 1698.[1]

Miscellaneous Prerogatives.   Other prerogative powers, many of which are nowadays regulated by statute, relate to the creation of corporations by royal charter; the erection and supervision of harbours; the guardianship of infants and persons of unsound mind; the administration of charities; the right to mine precious metals; coinage; the grant of franchises, *e.g.* markets, ferries and fisheries; the right to treasure trove [2]; the sole right of printing or licensing others to print the Bible, the Book of Common Prayer and State papers.

The Prerogative in time of National Emergency.   The declaration of war and making of peace will be considered in connection with acts of State.[3] The extent of the prerogative powers in time of grave emergency cannot be precisely stated, and in modern times the Executive takes statutory powers to meet emergencies.[4] That the prerogative powers are wide was admitted by Hampden's counsel in the *Case of Ship Money* [5]; nor save in regard to taxation were they abridged by the Bill of Rights. In time of sudden invasion or formidable insurrection the King may demand personal service within the realm.[6] Either the Crown or a subject may invade the land of another to erect fortifications for the defence of the realm: *The Case of the King's Prerogative in Saltpetre* (1607), 12 Rep. 12; K. & L. 76, but this right, like the right to take all necessary measures to repel the King's enemies in time of war or to restore order in time of insurrection, should probably not be regarded as a prerogative power.[7] It is a duty rather than a right and is shared by the Crown with all its subjects.

[1] East India Company Act, 1698.
[2] P. 267, n. l, *post.*   [3] Part IV, Chap. 10.
[4] Part VIII., Chap. 2.   [5] P. 34, *ante.*
[6] Chitty, *Prerogatives of the Crown*, p. 49.
[7] Part IX., Chap. 2.

The Crown may under the prerogative requisition British ships in territorial waters in time of urgent national necessity, not restricted to invasion or imminent danger: *The Broadmayne*, [1916] P. 64, at p. 67; *Crown of Leon* v. *Admiralty Commissioners*, [1921] 1 K.B. 595.[1] By the right of angary according to international law and also British municipal law, the Crown may, in time of war, requisition any chattels (not only ships) belonging to a national of a neutral State found within the realm, but compensation must be paid [2]: *Commercial and Estates Co. of Egypt* v. *Board of Trade*, [1925] 1 K.B. 271. **Requisition.**

By the common law writ of *ne exeat regno* the Crown may restrain a person from leaving the realm to evade justice, *e.g.* an absconding debtor. The Crown may probably by virtue of the prerogative restrain a British subject from leaving the realm in time of war, or recall him from abroad, but in modern times entry and exit in time of war are controlled by statutory powers. *Ne exeat regno.*

Many prerogative rights have been regulated by statute. Thus the care of lunatics is now regulated by the Lunacy and Mental Treatment Acts, 1890 to 1930, and statutory regulations made thereunder. It was not, however, until 1920 that it was clearly established that, where statutory powers are conferred covering the sphere of a prerogative power, the Crown must proceed under the statutory powers and cannot rely upon the prerogative. Acts of Parliament may by express words abrogate a prerogative power; but the fact that a statute covers the sphere of a prerogative power merely suspends its exercise, but does not abrogate it. The relationship between prerogative and statutory powers was clearly laid down by the House of Lords in *Attorney-General* v. *De Keyser's Royal Hotel*, [1920] A.C. 508; K. & L. 86. **Prerogative Powers and Statute Law.**

> An hotel was required for the purpose of housing the administrative staff of the Royal Flying Corps during the First World War. The Army Council offered to hire the hotel at a rent, but, negotiations having broken down, possession was taken of the premises under the Defence of the Realm Acts and Regulations made thereunder. A petition of right was brought against the Crown claiming compensation as a matter of right for the use of the hotel by the army authorities. (At the time that the Army Council took possession the Royal Flying Corps had not been superseded by the Royal Air Force and was under the control of the War Office.)
>
> It was argued for the Crown that there was a prerogative to take the lands of the subject in case of emergency in time of war, and that no compensation was payable as of right for land so taken. This

---

[1] The right of requisition probably extends to British ships, wherever they may be: "The Power of the Crown to Requisition British Ships in a National Emergency," by Sir William Holdsworth, 35 *L.Q.R.* 12. Compensation is probably payable.

[2] "The Right of Angary," by Sir Ivor Jennings, 3 *C.L.J.* 1.

argument overlooked the provisions of the Defence Act, 1842, which had been incorporated into the Defence of the Realm Acts. These provisions imposed conditions upon the compulsory acquisition of land and provided for payment of compensation *as a matter of right* to persons whose land had been taken.

The argument on behalf of the owners of the hotel was that in fact the Crown had taken possession under the statutes and regulations and so could not fall back on the prerogative right, under which no compensation could be claimed, except as a matter of grace.

Both the Court of Appeal and the House of Lords rejected the argument of the Crown, and held that the prerogative had been superseded for the time being by the statute, and therefore the Crown was not in any event entitled to act under the prerogative. There can be no excuse for reverting to prerogative powers when the Legislature has given to the Crown statutory powers which cover all that can be necessary for the defence of the nation, and which are moreover accompanied by safeguards to the individual which are in agreement with the demands of justice. It may be noted in passing that the courts were prepared to hold, had it been necessary, that the alleged prerogative to requisition land in time of war without paying compensation had not been proved.

The Emergency Powers (Defence) Act, 1939, passed immediately before the outbreak of the Second World War expressly provided that the powers which it conferred should be additional to any powers exercisable under the prerogative (s. 9).[1]

[1] P. 354, *post.*

CHAPTER 2.

MINISTERS OF THE CROWN.

Introductory.

THERE have already been studied the Cabinet system in brief out-line; [1] the relationship between the Executive and the Legislature: [2] and the meaning of ministerial responsibility.[3] The story of the gradual development of the Cabinet system has been told.[4] It is now necessary to consider the composition and machinery of the Cabinet and the other organs of central government. The determination of policy and the general supervision and co-ordination of all aspects of government is, as we have seen, the responsibility of the Cabinet. The execution and often the initiation of policy is the task of the various government departments. Departments are presided over by Ministers who may or may not be members of the Cabinet. They are staffed by permanent civil servants. In addition to the government departments presided over by Ministers there are also, as has already been mentioned,[5] certain independent authorities exercising functions of central government, but not directly responsible to Parliament through a Minister of the Crown.

Ministers.

Ministers of the Crown are those members of the political party, or coalition of parties, in power who hold political office. They are appointed by the Crown on the nomination of the Prime Minister. The term, Minister, is usually confined to the holders of the chief political offices of State and the heads of government departments, but the Ministry includes also junior Ministers who hold subordinate office in the Government. Each ministerial head of a department has one or more Parliamentary Secretaries [6] and there are other junior ministerial posts, e.g. Junior Lords of the Treasury who act as Government Whips.[7] There is no legal limit to the number of Ministers, but salaries are provided by statute for only a fixed number of ministerial posts. To provide a salary for an additional Minister without special legislation necessitates special provision in the annual Appropriation Act, and such a method of increasing the number of political office-holders is not viewed with favour by the Public Accounts Committee.[8] It was, however, used during the Second World War, for example in the appointment of Ministers

---

[1] Part I., Chap. 2.
[2] Part II., Chap. 1, and Part III., Chap. 3.
[3] Part II., Chap. 4.   [4] Part II., Chap. 2, A.
[5] P. 17, *ante.* See Chap. 11, *post.*
[6] When the Minister is a Secretary of State, the Parliamentary Secretary is titled Parliamentary Under-Secretary of State.
[7] P. 88, *ante.*
[8] P. 181, *post* ; see Sir Ivor Jennings in 2 *Modern Law Review*, 145.

resident in the Middle East, Washington and North Africa, and of
the Minister of Reconstruction.

Ministerial Salaries.

Apart from the Lord Chancellor [1] and the Law Officers of the
Crown [2] the salaries of Ministers are regulated by the Ministers of
the Crown Act, 1937,[3] as amended by the Ministerial Salaries Act,
1946, or in the case of offices created since 1937 by separate Acts.
The Prime Minister, if, as he now invariably does, he also holds the
office of First Lord of the Treasury, receives an annual salary of
£10,000 and an annual pension of £2,000.[4] A salary of £2,000 a year
is payable to the leader of the Opposition—the leader of the party in
opposition to Her Majesty's Government having greatest numerical
strength in the House. The Chancellor of the Exchequer, the seven
Secretaries of State,[5] the First Lord of the Admiralty, the President of
the Board of Trade, the Ministers of Agriculture and Fisheries, Education, Health, Labour and National Service, Transport and Civil
Aviation, Supply, Housing and Local Government, Pensions and
National Insurance, Fuel and Power, Works and Defence receive
salaries of £5,000 a year. All these Ministers are not necessarily
members of the Cabinet, but their salary does not depend upon
Cabinet membership. The Lord President of the Council and the
Lord Privy Seal receive salaries of £3,000 a year raised to £5,000 a
year, if they are members of the Cabinet. The salary of the Chancellor of the Duchy of Lancaster, who receives £3,000 a year chargeable
to Duchy funds, may similarly be raised to £5,000 a year by Cabinet
membership. The salary of the Postmaster-General is £5,000. All
ministerial salaries are maximum salaries and there is expressly
preserved the right of the House of Commons to move the reduction
of a Minister's salary in order to call attention to a grievance or
censure the conduct of a departmental activity.[6]

Parliamentary Under-Secretaries.

The Ministers of the Crown Act, 1937, provided for the payment
of salaries to a maximum number of Parliamentary Secretaries and
five Junior Lords of the Treasury.[7] The Act as amended by (*inter
alia*) the Ministers of the Crown (Parliamentary Under-Secretaries)
Act, 1951, provides for the salaries of three Parliamentary Under-
Secretaries to the Treasury and the Scottish Office; two in the

[1] The Lord Chancellor receives £12,000, of which £4,000 is charged on the
House of Lords Vote and £8,000 on the Consolidated Fund: see Supreme Court
of Judicature Act, 1925, s. 12 as amended by the Judges' Remuneration Act, 1954.
[2] The Law Officers receive salaries of £10,000 (Attorney-General) and £7,000
(Solicitor-General), and no longer take fees for litigation.
[3] Except Ministers without portfolio, the Chancellor of the Duchy of Lancaster (except as to extra salary when in the Cabinet) and the Paymaster-General.
[4] Provided that he is not in receipt of any salary from public funds.
[5] P. 165, *post*.
[6] All salaries of £5,000 and upwards were voluntarily reduced at the request
of the Prime Minister in 1951 for reasons of economy; after three years they were
restored.
[7] P. 180, *post*.

Admiralty, the Board of Trade, the Foreign Office, the Home Office, the War Office, the Ministries of Agriculture and Fisheries, Transport and Civil Aviation, Pensions and National Insurance, and one each for other departments, including the Post Office. The salaries range from £3,000 (to the Parliamentary Secretary to the Treasury who ranks as an Under-Secretary but is traditionally the Chief Government Whip) to £1,500. Salaries of all Ministers in the Commons whose official salaries are less than £5,000 a year qualify to receive in addition £500 a year and attendance expenses as members of the House of Commons.[1]

The Ministers of the Crown (Transfer of Functions) Act, 1946, conferred the power to transfer by Order in Council the functions of one Minister to another and also to dissolve an existing government department.

It is a convention that ministerial office-holders should be members of one or other House of Parliament. Indeed such membership is essential to the working of parliamentary government. It ensures contact between the Executive and the Legislature and enables Ministers to expound policy. Moreover, it is essential to the working of the parliamentary system that members should be exposed to parliamentary questions not only from the Opposition, but also from members of their own party. It is not, however, a rule of law that a Minister must be in Parliament, and a Minister who is defeated at an election usually continues in office while seeking election in another constituency. As has been seen,[2] the provisions of the Ministers of the Crown Act, 1937, limit the number of Ministers in receipt of salaries who may sit at any one time in the House of Commons and thus ensure indirectly that there should be ministerial representation in the House of Lords. It has often been suggested that Ministers should be able to speak and defend their policy in either House of Parliament, thus enabling the best man, whether peer or commoner, to be appointed to any post. *Ministers in Parliament.*

However technical may be the work of a government department, its head is a Minister usually appointed because of his general capacity and political experience as a member of his party and not because of expert knowledge. Nowhere is the practice at first sight so open to criticism as in the case of the three Service Departments, the War Office, the Admiralty and the Air Ministry and the Ministry of Supply where scientific developments make their closest impact upon government. The positions of a solicitor-politician or a trade union leader in control of army affairs and a co-operative expert in charge of the Admiralty present more apparent anomalies than those of a university don at the Board of Education, or a financial expert as Chancellor of the Exchequer—to illustrate from office-holders of *Ministers and the Civil Service.*

---

[1] Ministerial Salaries Act, 1946, s. 3.   [2] P. 86, *ante.*

the present century. There is little doubt that the technical work of government can only be carried on by a permanent civil service (assisted by other expert Crown servants in the case of the Service Departments), enjoying security of tenure, so far as political fluctuations are concerned. The traditions of such service incline to routine methods and a cautious approach is dictated by the obligation to protect the Minister from criticism in Parliament. Again the higher officials have not the business man's expectation of pecuniary gain, nor perhaps the professional man's hope of fame and fortune. For the ministerial head of a department there is the political stimulus, the hope of public advancement, and the publicity afforded by criticism in Parliament, which he must answer, and from the press and public, who may, sooner or later, drive him and his colleagues from office.

In the case of the Service departments in particular, both the Cabinet and Parliament are more likely to acquiesce in the financial demands of a department, if they are presented by a civilian or non-expert who has no particular temptation towards excessive expenditure. Secretaries of State for War do not become famous on account of the amount of public money they cause to be expended, but a professional soldier, if put in a similar position at the head of the War Office in peace time, might be prejudiced from the outset by a desire to maintain his personnel and equipment at the highest margin of security. It is better that the technical advisers of these departments should not come direct to Parliament as the heads of the Service in which they have spent their professional lives, but should voice their demands through the political head of the department. What may be lost in departmental efficiency may be gained by the introduction of outside opinion and incentive.

CHAPTER 3.

THE CABINET.

THOUGH the existence of the Cabinet has been recognised by the provision in the Ministers of the Crown Act, 1937, of salaries for those Ministers who are members of the Cabinet, the Cabinet is an organ of government the existence of which rests upon convention. No statute or rule of common law regulates its composition or lays down its powers. The Cabinet consists of those Ministers whom the Prime Minister invites to join him in tendering advice to the Sovereign on the government of the country. Cabinet Ministers are chosen by the Prime Minister from the leading members of his party or in the case of a coalition from the two or more parties forming the coalition.

No Minister can claim by virtue of his office to be included in the Cabinet, though in peace time there may be said to be a convention that certain offices carry with them a seat in the Cabinet, *e.g.* the Lord Chancellor, the Chancellor of the Exchequer, the Secretaries of State,[1] the Minister of Defence, the Ministers in charge of departments responsible for the principal services, *e.g.* Education, Labour and National Service, Agriculture. In addition there are usually included in the Cabinet two or three members with few, if any, departmental responsibilities, *e.g.* the Lord President of the Council and the Lord Privy Seal. These Ministers, whose executive duties are very few, are free to assist the Prime Minister on special problems or to co-ordinate different aspects of a single problem.

Like the Cabinet the office of Prime Minister is conventional, though its existence has been recognised by statutes.[2] We have seen how the Prime Minister is chosen by the Sovereign.[3] It is customary for the Prime Minister to hold the office of First Lord of the Treasury though this practice has not been invariable. The Prime Minister may also hold other offices, *e.g.* Lord Salisbury was for a long time Prime Minister and Secretary of State for Foreign Affairs while the leader of the House of Commons was First Lord of the Treasury. Lord Salisbury who resigned in 1902 was the last Prime Minister to sit in the House of Lords. Since the passing of the Ministers of the Crown Act, 1937, it is probable that the Prime Minister will always hold the post of First Lord of the Treasury, and

---

[1] Since the appointment of a Minister of Defence, the Service Ministers who include the Secretaries of State for War and for Air have not sat in the Cabinet.

[2] Chequers Estate Act, 1917; Ministers of the Crown Act, 1937: see p. 148, *ante.*

[3] P. 63, *ante.*

the statutory association of these two offices recognises the <u>convention that the Prime Minister should be in the House of Commons in view of the fact that that House exercises financial control</u>. As First Lord of the Treasury the Prime Minister is head of the establishments board of the Treasury and <u>his approval is required for appointments to the principal civil service posts</u>, *i.e.* those of permanent heads or deputy heads of departments and principal financial and establishment officers. <u>The function of the Prime Minister has been described as primarily one of giving advice, particularly in discussion of policy questions before they come to the Cabinet.</u>[1] He is in specially close relations with the Foreign Secretary in whose department matters of political importance are of continuous occurrence and are of such a nature that they may have to be settled between the two Ministers before being brought to the Cabinet. <u>All the more important Crown appointments are filled on the Prime Minister's nomination</u>, *e.g.* the <u>highest judicial appointments and bishoprics.</u>[2] He also <u>advises the Crown in regard to the creation of peerages, appointments to the Privy Council and grant of honours for political and other general services,</u>[3] and <u>appointments to those university professorships which are in the gift of the Crown. He issues invitations to serve on Royal Commissions.</u> The ascendancy of a Prime Minister over his colleagues must vary with the personality of the particular Prime Minister, but it is <u>understood that Ministers who are not prepared to accept the Prime Minister's decision must tender their resignation.</u> It is understood to be quite exceptional for a Cabinet decision to be <u>taken by a majority vote</u>, though there have been occasions when this has happened in default of an agreed conclusion.[4] On the other hand a Prime Minister cannot govern without the aid of colleagues who command the confidence of Parliament and too many resignations may cause the fall of a Government. The Prime Minister may be described as *primus inter pares* rather than as an autocrat.

<u>Cabinets vary in size.</u> They must not be too large for efficient deliberation, and yet they must not exclude those Ministers who are responsible for major spheres of government. <u>Between 1919 and 1939 the usual size of the Cabinet was twenty to twenty-two. A Minister who is interested in a particular topic can always express his views to the Cabinet and, though not a member, will normally be invited to attend particular meetings at which matters relating to</u>

Size of
Cabinets.

---

[1] Sir Ivor Jennings, *Cabinet Government*, pp. 197 ff.

[2] Pp. 239, 456, *post*.

[3] Honours are also granted on the advice of other Ministers, *e.g.* the Secretaries of State for Foreign Affairs and the Colonies, and the heads of the Service departments. Similarly certain appointments are made on the recommendation of other Ministers, *e.g.* High Court judgeships on the recommendation of the Lord Chancellor.

[4] *Cf.* Jennings, *op. cit.*, p. 242.

his departmental responsibilities are discussed; it is not, however, always easy to say that an issue of policy may not affect departments other than those directly concerned. A major decision on policy may indirectly affect most aspects of government and in peace time it was usual, up to 1939, to include in the Cabinet all the heads of the major government departments. That this practice resulted in unwieldy Cabinets is now generally agreed. From the start of the Second World War the need for day-to-day decisions demanded a smaller Cabinet. The size of the post-war Cabinet has fluctuated between sixteen and twenty. The number of important departments with Ministers in charge is about thirty. There has thus resulted a division in classification of Ministers into Cabinet Ministers and Ministers not in the Cabinet; but the line of division is flexible.[1]

A major problem of government is to secure co-ordination. Cabinet Committees and committees of senior officials of the departments are designed to secure this. Most problems concern more than one department and should be presented to the Cabinet after agreement has been reached or at least after differences have been defined by the departments concerned. It is necessary to distinguish between the Cabinet and its ministerial committees which settle issues of policy, and committees of officials which co-ordinate and advise. In theory an official committee advises; the Cabinet or a ministerial committee decides; the department takes the necessary action. This does not mean that it is necessary that every question on which a committee is asked to advise should go subsequently to Ministers. Agreed recommendations may be implemented automatically by the departments concerned on the responsibility and authority of their respective Ministers—or, if the issue involved is not a major one, without specific ministerial authority. Ministerial committees perform a dual function: they dispose of business which is not important enough to come before the full Cabinet; and they focus the issues for decision if reference to the Cabinet is required. A short account of the organisation of Cabinet committees is given in the next Chapter. *Cabinet Committees.*

The Cabinet Secretariat was created during the First World War in 1917. "For the first time in the history of the Cabinet a Secretary was present to record the proceedings and keep the minutes of the Cabinet and of its numerous committees, and orderly methods based on those developed by the Committee of Imperial Defence were introduced, including agenda papers, the distribution (in advance of the meetings) of relevant memoranda and other material, the rapid communication of decisions to those who had to act on them; and the knitting up to the Cabinet, not only of government departments, but also of numerous committees combining a vast range of *The Cabinet Secretariat.*

[1] Pp. 65–70, *ante*, for discussion of collective responsibility.

inter-departmental business." [1] The conclusions prepared by the Secretary to the Cabinet and circulated to the Queen and all Cabinet Ministers are the only authentic record of Cabinet meetings. All Cabinet committees are served by members of the Cabinet Secretariat. Although the Secretariat has no executive functions like those of a department, it is a highly efficient instrument for securing inter-departmental co-ordination by ensuring that documents are circulated before meetings in a form which presents the issue to be decided, for reporting, distributing and following up decisions taken. There is also a Central Statistical Office, which provides a common and impartial statistical service for all departments.[2]

With the development of the committee system and the creation of the Cabinet Secretariat there has been combined with ministerial responsibility the strong points of the local government system—advisory committees and a recording department serving all the various committees (the office of the clerk to the council).[3] The efficiency of any large organisation depends very largely on proper co-ordination of departmental activities. There must be proper co-operation in both the framing of policy and its execution. Under the Cabinet system such co-operation is secured without impairing the responsibility of the individual Minister for the work of his department.[4] An influential committee not only frames policy but by calling for progress reports is able to ensure to a large extent that its policy is carried out. The experience of war led to the retention of a number of standing committees of the Cabinet.

Organisation for War. During both the First and Second World Wars it was found necessary to supersede the normal Cabinet by a small War Cabinet to take responsibility for the conduct of the war. In 1916 the War Cabinet consisted of five, later six, senior Ministers without departmental responsibilities, except the Chancellor of the Exchequer. The War Cabinets of 1939–46 were larger, varying between seven and ten, and included a number of senior departmental Ministers. Thus in 1944 the War Cabinet consisted of the Prime Minister (also Minister of Defence), the Lord President of the Council (Deputy Prime Minister), the Foreign Secretary (and leader of the House of Commons), the Chancellor of the Exchequer, the Minister of Labour and National Service, the Minister of Production, the Home Secretary and the Minister of Reconstruction. Other Ministers were invited to attend meetings for the discussion of matters with which their departments were concerned. As in the First World War, when over 250 persons in all were summoned on occasions, other persons

---

[1] *Haldane Memorial Lecture*, 1942, by Lord Hankey.
[2] Chap. 4, *post*.
[3] Though the clerk to a council is also an executive officer who himself has responsibility for co-ordination.
[4] Part II., Chap. 4.

than Ministers might be in attendance. Thus the Chiefs of Staff were frequently in attendance. Visiting Prime Ministers or their deputies from the Dominions and representatives of the Government of India attended from time to time. The Secretariat of the Committee of Imperial Defence was merged in the War Cabinet Secretariat of which the military members constituted the staff of the Prime Minister as Minister of Defence.[1]

There was no Ministry of Defence and the constitutional responsibilities of the three service Ministers remained in those spheres for which the Minister of Defence did not accept responsibility. In his task of supervision of the work of the Chiefs of Staffs Sub-Committee the Prime Minister was assisted by a Defence Committee. On the home front the Lord President's Committee was the most important element in the elaborate structure of Cabinet Committees and their attendant official committees. To plan for peace there was appointed later in 1943 a Minister of Reconstruction to co-ordinate the activities of the various departments concerned with civil planning. Like the Minister of Defence the Minister of Reconstruction was a Minister without a department.

---

[1] *The Organisation for Joint Planning*, 1942, Cmd. 6351.

CHAPTER 4.

CABINET ORGANISATION.

BRIEF reference has been made in the preceding chapter to Cabinet committees and to the Cabinet Secretariat. But for those readers whose interests lie in the field of government rather than the practice of the law, it is proposed here to discuss more fully the organisation of the Executive at the highest level. It has been said that "the personal responsibility of Ministers and the collective responsibility of the Cabinet supply strong inducements for clearing up all those inefficiencies that inevitably from time to time find lodgment in the complicated government structure." [1] With the experience of two world wars to draw upon much has been done to improve the higher organisation which now works at a very different standard of efficiency as compared with the Cabinets of fifty years ago.

Problem of Co-ordination. There are few problems of government that can be resolved within a single department. It is necessary then to devise machinery to enable agreement to be reached, or at least for differences to be defined clearly before a matter comes before the Cabinet. Only so can a coherent policy be evolved. Moreover, without such machinery decisions at the top level are unlikely properly to be implemented by departments; for they will not be fully understood unless departments have been brought into consultation at an early stage and given opportunity of representing their points of view from the administrative angle through high officials as well as from the policy angle through Ministers who are adequately informed of the administrative implications.

Cabinet Committees. It is the general practice of Governments not to disclose the functions or composition of Cabinet Committees, since decisions are those of the Government as a whole. But more information is available to the public about central organisation for defence than for other purposes of government.[2] Yet it is surprising that the public should know more about defence organisation than the organisation which determines other issues; for the former must be adapted to change over from peace to active hostilities when it at once becomes shrouded from public knowledge for the time being from considerations of security. But such is the strength of the tradition

---

[1] *British War Economy*, by Sir Keith Hancock and M. M. Gowing (H.M.S.O.), 1949, p. 88.

[2] *Central Organisation for Defence*, Cmd. 6923 (1946); *British War Economy* (*ante*), Chaps. III. and VIII., and Vol. II. (*Their Finest Hour*) of Sir Winston Churchill's *War Memoirs*, Chap. I., which describe the organisation of the War Cabinets of 1916–19 and 1939–45.

of anonymity that, apart from the organisation for defence, Governments are seldom willing to disclose the composition, or even the existence of ministerial committees appointed by the Cabinet, whether as standing committees or as *ad hoc* committees to consider a specific issue, lest the collective responsibility of the Cabinet as a whole be weakened as well as that of the Minister who is principally concerned. We can only infer then what approximately is the structure of the present peace-time Cabinet organisation by analogy from the defence organisation and the war-time structure as disclosed by the war histories. From time to time the veil is lifted to inform the House of Commons that a particular named or unnamed Cabinet committee is considering a specific issue; the composition of the committee is never disclosed. It is known that, in addition to the Committee of Imperial Defence (to be discussed later), there existed before the Second World War the Home Affairs Committee which considered the draft of all Bills promoted by the departments. This committee co-ordinated the views of other departments affected before the Bills went to the Cabinet for approval in the form recommended by the Committee. The Law Officers, who are not members of the Cabinet, attended the meetings, as did senior officials concerned with particular Bills. This machinery proved useful for giving effect to the principle of ministerial responsibility as well as lightening the agenda of Cabinets. The Legislation Committee, as the Committee was renamed for the greater part of the war, is in existence to-day, as we learn from occasional references in ministerial speeches.

Another valuable source of information is to be found in the addresses of ex-Ministers delivered to academic audiences. These cannot give an up-to-date picture of the current Administration, but they are generally speaking valuable because they reflect the considered judgment of elder statesmen and are the fruit of long and intimate contact with the working of the machinery of government. Among these may be mentioned the Romanes Lecture for 1946 delivered by Lord Waverley, then Sir John Anderson, a few months after he gave up the office of Chancellor of the Exchequer [1] and the chapter on "Machinery of Government" in Mr. L. S. Amery's *Thoughts on the Constitution*.[2] The young administrator, confused by the organisation into which he is plunged on entry, may usefully compare what is with what was and what should be, as described by former Ministers. Another document to be considered is the Report of the Machinery of Government Committee over which Lord Haldane presided in 1918.[3] This was a departmental committee

---

[1] *The Machinery of Government*, Clarendon Press, 1946.
[2] Chap. III., Oxford University Press, 2nd ed. (1953).
[3] Cmd. 9230, 1918.

appointed by the war-time Minister of Reconstruction. Its principal recommendation was the distribution of the business of the departments into ten main divisions by reference to their functions. The war had drawn attention to the piece-meal growth of departments which had accentuated, at a time when co-ordination of effort was imperative, the illogical and overlapping allocation of duties. The Report divided the business of government into ten heads. Without advocating that each division should be under a single Minister, the Report favoured a small Cabinet not exceeding twelve and the retention of the war-time Cabinet Secretariat.[1] A number of the existing departments reflect the influence of the Report, *e.g.* Transport and Civil Aviation, Labour and National Service, and Supply. But no radical reallocation of duties was attempted and the size of the Cabinet (as distinct from the War Cabinet) has only once, and that for a few weeks in 1931, been reduced to twelve or below. One reason for not implementing the Haldane Report lay in the absence of any firm proposals as to ministerial relations within the ten divisions and indeed the main reason was the difficulty of reconciling the recommendations with the doctrine of collective responsibility.

Reconstruction of the central organisation prompted by the experience gained during hostilities was considered from 1943 onwards by a Cabinet Committee of the Coalition Government on the Machinery of Government which, it has been stated, is still in being. But, as with all such committees, its conclusions have been for the information of Ministers and no reports have been published.

Committee of Imperial Defence.

We turn then mainly to central organisation for defence to trace developments which are believed to have their counterpart to-day in other spheres of central government. The Committee of Imperial Defence was created in 1904 as an outcome of defects in organisation disclosed by the Boer War; the Committee remained in being until the outbreak of war in 1939, though it was replaced during the First World War on the establishment of the War Cabinet in 1916. It was an advisory body without executive authority, but, because the Prime Minister was its Chairman, its recommendations carried due weight to such an extent that its agreed proposals were in the majority of cases automatically implemented by the departments concerned, without reference to the Cabinet, on the responsibility and authority of the respective Ministers.[2] The function of the Committee was to frame the fundamental principles which should govern imperial defence and to prepare detailed plans to ensure that all authorities both at home and overseas should in the event of war

---

[1] Pp. 153–4, *ante.*
[2] See *Royal United Services Institute Journal*, May 1939, lecture by General (now Lord) Ismay, who was for many years Secretary of the Committee of Imperial Defence.

work to a detailed and coordinated plan. The value of the work of
the Committee was proved in 1914 and again in 1939 by the existence
of detailed plans for the transition from peace to war. Although the
Committee was always elastic in its composition, successive Prime
Ministers nominated a nucleus of Ministers and senior officials who
came to form a panel of regular members. Under the Committee
itself was a network of sub-committees with which rested responsibility for working out details of policy. From 1924 onwards the
need for inter-Service planning which had become insistent with the
advent of the Royal Air Force resulted in the creation of the Chiefs
of Staff Committee as a sub-committee of the Committee of Imperial
Defence. This laid the foundation of the joint staff organisation for
planning and intelligence which was developed in the years before
1939 and on the outbreak of war was incorporated into the War
Cabinet organisation.

A body, no matter how well constructed, which has no executive
authority is incapable of taking decisions on major questions affecting policy which are properly matters for the Cabinet. Accordingly
in 1939 the Committee of Imperial Defence was replaced by the War
Cabinet itself, but its network of committees was taken over.
Blended with the civil committees, some of which had already been
created as part of the structure of the Committee of Imperial
Defence, there was thus ready for adaptation to wartime tasks a
complicated yet flexible instrument for coordination.

When Mr. Churchill, as he then was, became Prime Minister in
1940, he assumed the title of Minister of Defence without a separate
Ministry and without defining his duties as such Minister; for in
war responsibility for the mobilisation and direction of the whole
resources of the nation rests primarily on the Prime Minister.
Although no Ministry of Defence was created, the Prime Minister
was served by a small military Secretariat which had formerly served
the Committee of Imperial Defence. The executive organ was the
Defence Committee of the War Cabinet, presided over by the Prime
Minister in which, in addition to senior Ministers including the three
Service Ministers, sat the Chiefs of Staff. The last named also retained
their own separate committee structure for inter-Service planning and
intelligence. There is no need for present purposes to follow up the
effect of this organisation on the dual responsibilities of the Chiefs
of Staff, collectively to the Prime Minister as Chairman of the Defence Committee on whose behalf they issued unified operational
instructions and directives, and individually to the Service Ministers
who remained responsible for the day-to-day administration of the
Services. As an experiment in coordination of effort the machine
enabled the Prime Minister to provide the drive without which
successful operations cannot be conducted.

Defence Committee, 1940.

Minister
of Defence.

Unification of defence policy, or for that matter of any policy, can be achieved by the assumption of executive control by the Prime Minister. In peace-time another Minister can relieve the Prime Minister to a large extent without re-casting the main structure of the wartime organisation. Accordingly in <u>1947 a separate small Ministry of Defence</u> was created; the duties of the Minister are set out, *post*, at p. 171. Broadly he is under the Prime Minister responsible for the apportionment of the resources between the Services in accordance with the strategic policy laid down by the Defence Committee which has permanently replaced the Committee of Imperial Defence. Like all Cabinet Committees it must refer major decisions of policy to the Cabinet for approval. That it can under effective leadership relieve the full Cabinet of a great part of defence business more effectively than could the Committee of Imperial Defence, which was in theory at least an advisory body rather than a Cabinet Committee, cannot be doubted. At all events complicated though the structure is by the peculiar authority enjoyed collectively by the Chiefs of Staff, the organisation does show how a strong ministerial committee can exercise control in a wide, perhaps the widest field, of State policy.

Sir John
Anderson's
proposals.

It is then not surprising that the method of co-ordinating committees both in war and in peace has proved itself in the fields of economic and social policy and indeed whenever a problem which overlaps the bounds of responsibility of a single department is in issue. Equally important is it to determine the relationship with his ministerial colleagues of the Minister chosen to preside over such a committee. Any rigid grouping of functions is unlikely to be acceptable; for Prime Ministers may hold different views on how best to mould together the ministerial team. Nor is it solely a matter of personalities. Problems differ in importance from year to year. Lord Waverley made some tentative suggestions in his Romanes lectures.[1] In addition to Defence he proposed an Economic Relations Committee to cover external economic affairs including import and export policy and commercial and economic relationships with foreign countries and with other members of the British Commonwealth. By the addition of the relevant Ministers such a Committee could be enlarged to cover internal economic problems or alternatively a separate National Development Committee might be established. Other committees should include an External Affairs Committee to consider relationships with foreign countries and within the British Commonwealth which are not primarily of an economic or financial character. There would also be an appropriate committee representing the departments concerned with social services to cover the whole field of social welfare. The suggested plan included the retention of

[1] Anderson, *op. cit.*, pp. 13 ff.

the Legislation Committee with terms of reference enlarged to cover the review of all proposals for legislation whether by Bill, Regulation, or Order at the stage of formal drafting. Such a system was no doubt suggested by the experience of the Lord President's Committee of the War Cabinet which was the principal coordinating committee for home front affairs, during the greater part of the Second World War.[1] Flexibility of function can be secured not only by changing ministerial representation on Cabinet Committees but also by the use of the small *ad hoc* committee to report on specific problems. It is often important that similar committees should exist at the official level not to decide but to report to Ministers.

With regard to the Minister chosen to preside over a Cabinet Committee the choice would seem to lie between a non-departmental Minister, such as the Lord President of the Council or the Lord Privy Seal, or a departmental Minister who has a predominant interest in the matters allocated to a particular group. Personality and endowments may ensure that such a Minister occupies a commanding position, but in constitutional theory he ought to be on a parity with his Cabinet colleagues If a group of Ministers within the Cabinet were to exercise by reason of their chairmanship of committees supervisory powers over the departmental Ministers who sit with them on a committee, the responsibility of the latter to parliament for the conduct of their departments might be weakened.[2] Within the departments it would be impractical to serve two masters in the person of the supervising Minister and the departmental Minister, nor could a Minister in practice supervise without a duplication of staff with those of the departments.[3] Such an expensive expedient could only slow down the machinery of government and from time to time would inevitably cause friction and indecision. Another solution of the difficulty might be to select as chairman for the day the Minister whose department was most closely concerned with the principal item on the agenda. It is clear that if the principle of supervising Ministers were accepted as a regular feature, there would be a much smaller Cabinet and the status of the departmental Ministers as such would be permanently weakened; indeed they might become effectively no more than parliamentary secretaries to the supervising Minister. There is much to be said for a smaller Cabinet, as Lord Haldane proposed as far back as 1919.

Supervising Ministers.

---

[1] Hancock and Gowing, *op. cit.*, pp. 215–23, for a discussion of the War Cabinet system including the Lord President's Committee.

[2] Sir Winston Churchill's Administration which was formed in 1951 contained two co-ordinating Ministers during the first two years of its existence. Both had seats in the House of Lords and there was some confusion as to their effect upon departmental responsibility in the Commons so far as concerned the Ministers whose departments had been placed under a Minister for Co-ordination.

[3] Anderson, *op. cit.*, pp. 12–13.

G

But the experience of the years from 1940 to 1945 shows that this can be obtained without introducing supervising Ministers. For the existence of the War Cabinet did not, in the opinion of one of its members, involve any derogation from their responsibility to Parliament and to the public for matters within their departmental sphere of those Ministers who were not members of the Cabinet.[1]

Decentralisation. On the other hand the increasing complexity of modern government has resulted in too much centralisation with the attendant evils of indecision, delay and even frustration; these evils are felt most on the periphery. It is generally recognised that Parliament cannot be burdened with further tasks and that the load on the parliamentary machine is already excessive. The solution lies in limiting the control to be exercised from the centre, at all events in matters of internal government. The experience of the new public corporations entrusted with the administration of the socialised services and industries suggests this. The greater the measure of dispersal, the easier should be the problem of coordination of policy at the highest level; for the Cabinet could be relieved of many problems of administration which at present come before it and confine its attention to major questions of policy. Less emphasis would have to be placed on the doctrine of ministerial responsibility as applied to departmental Ministers. In turn there should be more reliance on the courts including independent administrative tribunals for the redress of individual grievances resulting from administrative intransigence. There are as yet few signs of any such solution.

Cabinet Secretariat. The Cabinet Secretariat serves all Cabinet Committees whether standing or *ad hoc.* Under the Secretary to the Cabinet are two deputy secretaries, one civil, the other military who together act as joint secretaries of the Defence Committee. A small body of assistant secretaries are seconded from the departments for a fixed period to provide the services for the Cabinet Committees. This interchange ensures a steady flow of officials who are trained both in departmental administration and in the work of coordination at the top level. Upon technical matters especially in the sphere of economics and pure science a government needs more guidance than the presence of experts in a single department is likely to provide. The employment of advisers from outside the government service supplies part of the deficiency. For the rest the need for authoritative guidance in technical matters is met by the following organisations: the Central Statistical Office which is part of the Cabinet Secretariat, the Economic Planning Board and the Economic Section of the Treasury under the direction of the Chancellor of the Exchequer in his capacity of Minister for Economic Affairs, the Advisory Council on Scientific Policy, the Defence Research Policy Committee under

[1] Anderson, *op. cit.*, p. 11.

the Chairmanship of a scientist of high standing which is placed under the Minister of Defence, and the four principal scientific bodies, the Department of Scientific and Industrial Research, the Medical Research Council, the Agricultural Research Council and the Atomic Energy Authority, which are responsible to the Lord President of the Council.

CHAPTER 5.

THE CENTRAL GOVERNMENT DEPARTMENTS.

ADMINISTRATIVE government at the centre is carried out mainly by departments. A list of the departments follows, together with a brief statement of their principal functions.[1] No attempt has been made to cover in detail the vast field of activity of the Central Government.

Organisation of Departments.

A department is presided over by a Minister who in the case of all the more important departments was up to 1939, in peace time, a member of the Cabinet. He is assisted by a Parliamentary Secretary [2] who, though included among members of the Government, is not a Minister in the strict sense but an official who is exempted by statute from disqualification from membership of the House of Commons; he (or she) is invariably a member of one House or the other.

The Permanent Secretary [3] is the senior civil servant in the department. Under him are one or more Deputy Secretaries and a hierarchy of administrative officers graded as Under-Secretaries, Assistant Secretaries, Principals and Assistant Principals. It is the administrative staff who are responsible for executing policy and on them, particularly the higher grades, the Minister must be able to rely for disinterested and impartial advice.

Government Departments.

(a) *The Treasury.*[4]—The Treasury is the Central Department. Its functions fall into two distinct divisions: (a) Finance, (b) Supply and Establishments. It is under the second head that the Treasury exercises a predominating influence over the expenditure, and therefore over the policy, of the departments and over the whole Civil Service.

(b) *Departments presided over by Secretaries of State.*—Something must be said about the office of Secretary of State. There are now seven Secretaries of State, who preside over some of the more important departments. For all but peers and privy councillors the Secretary of State is the only avenue of approach for the subject to the Sovereign, save by petition. Whereas departments may be approached by direct communication, this is not so in the case of

---

[1] For the Lord President, see p. 137, *ante*. For a fuller account of the functions of the various departments, see Jennings, *Cabinet Government*, Appendix III.

[2] Where the Minister is a Secretary of State, the Parliamentary Secretary is designated Parliamentary Under-Secretary of State. There may be more than one Parliamentary Secretary; see p. 148, *ante*.

[3] Where the Minister is a Secretary of State, the Permanent Secretary is designated Permanent Under-Secretary of State and the Under-Secretaries Assistant Under-Secretaries of State.

[4] Chaps. 6 and 7, *post*. For composition of Treasury Board, see p. 180, *post*.

approach to the Sovereign. Similarly, authentic communications by the Sovereign to his people are normally countersigned by a Secretary of State. It is interesting to note that the duties of Secretaries of State are legally interchangeable and independent of any distinction on account of the departments over which they preside. In practice each Secretary of State limits his functions to those traditionally related to his own department and many powers are conferred by statute on a particular Secretary of State, *e.g.* on the Secretary of State for War by the Defence Act, 1842.[1] Documents signed by a Secretary of State do not indicate that they are signed by any particular Secretary, the signature being followed by the words "One of Her Majesty's Principal Secretaries of State."

The office of Secretary of State springs from a humble origin, and it is not easy to say at what precise moment in history the King's Secretary became a definite office. In the Tudor period the Secretary became a channel of communication for home and foreign affairs, and the office seems to have grown in importance, largely perhaps on account of the personal rule of the Tudors. From about 1540 two Secretaries of State were appointed, but not at first as an invariable practice. It was when the Privy Council sought to combine deliberative and executive functions that the office assumed its present importance. The Secretaries of State ceased in fact, though not in law, to be servants of the King and his Council and became one of the motive forces in the Cabinet. On two occasions before 1782 a third Secretaryship was added for the time being. It was in that year that the Home Office and the Foreign Office came into existence as separate departments. For some 150 years there had been a Secretary of State for the Northern Department, in charge of business relating to the Northern Powers of Europe, and another for the Southern Department, which embraced France and the Southern countries. Ireland fell to the senior Secretary, while the Colonies and Home Affairs came under either.[2] On March 27, 1782, the Foreign Office came into existence as a result of a circular letter addressed by Fox to the representatives of Foreign Powers in London, to the effect that he had been entrusted with the sole direction of foreign affairs, while his colleague, the Earl of Shelburne, had been appointed Principal Secretary of State for Domestic Affairs and the Colonies. The Home Secretary from that date took precedence over all other Secretaries. At that time he had very few of the statutory powers and duties which subsequent legislation has conferred upon him. The other Secretaryships of State may be said to have been

History of Secretaryships of State.

---

[1] The Act speaks of the "principal officers of the Ordnance," whose powers and duties have been vested in the Secretary of State for War by subsequent enactments.

[2] But compare the account in Anson, *op. cit.* (4th ed.), Vol. II., Part I., pp. 178 ff.

created out of this Secretaryship. In 1794 a Secretary of State for War was appointed, who in 1801 took over the Colonies. In 1854 a separate Secretary of State for the Colonies was appointed on account of the Crimean War. In 1858, as the result of the Indian Mutiny, Indian affairs were entrusted to a Secretary of State for India. It was not until 1918 that another Secretaryship was created, namely, that for Air. In 1925 the Secretary of State for the Colonies was appointed to a separate Secretaryship for Dominion Affairs, the Colonial Office and the Dominions (now the Commonwealth Relations) Office being henceforth organised in separate departments, though the offices were, until 1930, held by the same holder. In 1926 the Secretary for Scotland, who, as head of the Scottish Office, controlled much of the internal government of Scotland, assisted by subordinate departments, was given the status of Secretary of State. Consequent on the Government of Burma Act, 1935, a ninth Secretaryship was added which was held by the Secretary of State for India until 1947 when that office lapsed consequent on the creation of the new Dominions of India and Pakistan and on the secession early the next year of Burma the Burma Secretaryship also ceased to exist and its holder was transferred to the Colonial Office as a second Minister with the title of Minister of State for Colonial Affairs, without a seat in the Cabinet.

The Home Office.—The Home Office is responsible for internal order and for all functions of internal government not assigned to some other department. Its functions include the control of aliens,[1] naturalisation,[2] police regulations for the county and borough police forces,[3] the administration of the Children and Young Persons Acts, and the Shops Acts, the control of the sale of poisons, intoxicating liquors, explosives and firearms, the enforcement of safety regulations for places of public entertainment, and the functions of the United Kingdom Government in relation to Northern Ireland, the Channel Islands and the Isle of Man. The Home Office is the central administrative authority for supervising the registration of electors and the conduct of both parliamentary and local elections. It has certain statutory duties in relation to fire brigades and the war-time National Fire Service which has since been transferred to county and county borough administration was under its direct control. The Home Secretary is the official channel of communication between the Crown and the Church of England, though in regard to Crown appointments to the chief ecclesiastical posts the King is advised by the Prime Minister.[4] Since 1951 he has also held the office of Minister for Welsh Affairs; in this capacity he is assisted by a second Parliamentary Under-Secretary of State.

---

[1] Pp. 199–201 *post.*   [2] Pp. 196–7, *post.*   [3] Pp. 189–90, *post.*
[4] Crown livings are mainly in the gift of the Lord Chancellor.

In regard to the administration of justice the Home Secretary shares with the Lord Chancellor[1] and the Law Officers of the Crown[2] a part of those duties which in continental countries would be performed by a Minister of Justice. These duties are discussed in Part V., Chap. 2. The Home Office as the department responsible for the maintenance of order has a general responsibility for the administration of the criminal law and has special functions in relation to advising courts of summary jurisdiction. The Home Secretary is by statute placed in control of the Prison Commission and the Metropolitan Police.

The Foreign Office.—The Secretary of State for Foreign Affairs is responsible for foreign affairs and relations with Foreign States. He is assisted by two Ministers of State as well as by two Parliamentary Under-Secretaries. The powers of the Crown in this sphere are prerogative powers and, while the Foreign Secretary is primarily responsible for their exercise, they are, like all prerogative powers, exercised subject to the collective responsibility of the Cabinet as whole to which all major decisions are referred. The Foreign Office controls Her Majesty's Foreign Service created in 1943 by the amalgamation by Order in Council into one service of the staffs of the Foreign Office and Diplomatic Service, the Commercial Diplomatic Service and the Consular Service. The Foreign Office is responsible for the exercise by the Crown of foreign jurisdiction[3] in territories falling outside the spheres of the Colonial or Commonwealth Relations Offices.

The Commonwealth Relations Office.—This department was organised as a separate office for Dominion Affairs in 1925 and was renamed by Order in Council in 1947. Until 1930 it remained under the same Secretary of State as the Colonial Office. It is concerned with the relations between the United Kingdom and the other Members of the Commonwealth, the Central African Federation, Basutoland and the Protectorates of Bechuanaland and Swaziland. The last three territories are administered by a High Commissioner who also holds the independent office of High Commissioner of the United Kingdom Government in the Union of South Africa.[4]

The Colonial Office.—This department deals with all the Colonies, the protectorates, other than the territories administered by the High Commissioner in South Africa (*ante*), and the trust territories. It is responsible for so much of colonial legislation as is enacted by Orders in Council, and exercises a wide patronage over appointments in the Overseas Service.[5] The Secretary of State is assisted by a Minister of State.

---

[1] Pp. 172 and 247, *post.*
[2] Pp. 173–4, *post.*
[3] P. 443, *post.*
[4] P. 474, *post.*
[5] Part X., Chap. 2.

The War Office.[1]

The Scottish Office.—The Secretary of State for Scotland is responsible (with some exceptions) so far as Scotland is concerned for all the functions which in England and Wales are discharged by the Home Secretary, the Minister of Agriculture and Fisheries, the Minister of Health, the Minister of Education and (in part) the Minister of Transport. He has in addition duties corresponding to some of those of the Lord Chancellor. He is also the mouthpiece of Scottish opinion in the Cabinet and elsewhere. His office, in which he has the assistance of a Minister of State, is discharged through four main departments of equal status each under a permanent Secretary—the Department of Agriculture for Scotland, the Scottish Education Department, the Department of Health for Scotland and the Scottish Home Department. The day-to-day administration of these departments is conducted from Edinburgh and the London office of the Scottish Office is mainly a parliamentary and liaison office. It may be said that the Scottish Office is responsible for most of the functions of government relating to Scotland which can be handled on a geographical basis. Economic functions, *e.g.* those of the Treasury and the Board of Trade, the Ministry of Supply, and defence are administered by Ministers for the United Kingdom as a whole.

The Air Ministry.[1]

(c) *Departments presided over by Senior Ministers.*

The Admiralty.[1]

The Board of Trade.—The Board, still in form a Committee of the Privy Council for Trade and the Plantations constituted by an Order in Council in 1786, consists of a body of permanent commissioners. The President is the ministerial head and the Board never meets in its corporate capacity, but acts through the President or some officer designated by him. The work of the department is divided between foreign and domestic matters. The former are handled by the Commercial Relations and Treaty Department and include the negotiation of trade agreements with other countries. The promotion of overseas trade is the responsibility of a Minister of State. As regards internal trade a group of divisions regulates industry and manufacturers and deals with production policy in all cases not specifically allocated to another department, *e.g.*, Ministry of Fuel and Power. Other functions are the administration of bankruptcy, company law and patents and designs.

The Ministry of Health.[2]—The Ministry is responsible for the administration of the services under the National Health Service

---

[1] For the three Service Departments, see p. 172, *post*
[2] See also Part VI.

Act, 1946, and generally for all questions concerning the physical and mental health of the nation, including vital statistics. The department supervises those few health services which since 1948 have remained the responsibility of local authorities.

The Ministry of Education.—The promotion of education and the development of educational institutions are the principal duties of this department. The Minister is charged with securing the effective execution by local authorities under his direction and control of the national policy of providing a varied and comprehensive education service in every area. This duty does not extend to university education.

The Ministry of Agriculture and Fisheries.—Except that the Minister is also responsible for the Ordnance Survey and, jointly with the Secretary of State for Scotland, for Forestry, the name sufficiently explains the functions of the department. The Commissioners of Crown Lands are a body corporate charged with the management of land held by right of the Crown; the Minister of Agriculture and Fisheries is First Commissioner. He is also (1954-55) Minister of Food pending the winding-up of that department which from 1939 was responsible for food rationing and bulk purchase of food-stuffs.

The Ministry of Labour and National Service.—This department is responsible for all questions relating to conditions of labour and employment. During the Second World War it administered all regulations relating to compulsory national service and is now responsible for the administration of the National Service Acts, 1948–54.[1] The rôle played by the Minister in recent years has emphasised the importance of keeping industrial disputes out of party politics. Starting with Mr. Ernest Bevin in 1940 successive Ministers seem to have established a convention that whoever presides over this Department will keep as aloof as possible from the more heated party political controversies. Moreover Her Majesty's Opposition have contributed to this understanding, more particularly in recent years during the tenure of office of Sir Walter Monckton who has markedly abstained from party controversies outside and inside the House; he has been supported in his policy by his immediate predecessor now on the Opposition benches.

The Post Office.—To this department is entrusted a State monopoly of the postal and telecommunication services of the country. Since there are post offices throughout the country, the Post Office is utilised for many services provided by the Government which involve local dealings with the public. Among these may be mentioned the issue of certain licences, the collection of certain taxes, the payment

---

[1] Pp. 405, 409–11, *post.*

G*

of pensions and of family and service allowances, the sale of insurance stamps, the issue of savings certificates and the conduct of a savings bank business. The British Broadcasting Corporation operates under Royal Charter, which gives it a semi-independent status, with a body of Governors who are appointed by the Crown. The Postmaster-General, under whose licence the stations and services are operated, replies to questions in Parliament relating to its services, but he does not control day-to-day administration. By the Television Act, 1954, the Independent Television Authority is placed in similar relationship with the Postmaster-General.

The Ministry of Transport and Civil Aviation.—It is the task of this department to regulate and improve the means of locomotion and transport. On its creation in 1919 there were transferred from the Board of Trade the regulative powers relating to railways, canals, roads and harbours. Its exercise of powers under the Road Traffic Acts, 1930–34, is among its more important functions. During the Second World War there were transferred to this department the functions of the Board of Trade in relation to the mercantile marine which had in 1939 been transferred to the newly created Ministry of Shipping.[1] The Minister appoints and has powers of general direction over the Transport Commission, the State corporation which has monopoly powers over much of public inland transport (except by air). In 1944 a Minister of Civil Aviation was appointed to take charge of the functions of the Air Ministry relating to civil aviation and the two State airways corporations. The separate department was merged in the Ministry of Transport in 1952.

Ministry of Pensions and National Insurance.—This department was established by the Ministry of National Insurance Act, 1944, to administer all State insurance services. It also administers the scheme of disablement and dependents' pensions for the Armed Forces, mainly those arising out of casualties of the First and Second World Wars.

Ministry of Housing and Local Government.—A Ministry of Town and Country Planning was created by statute in 1943. In 1951 the title of the department was changed, first to Local Government and Planning, and later to Housing and Local Government, on the transfer from the Ministry of Health, itself in part successor to the Local Government Board since 1917, of responsibility for the housing programme and the general supervision of local government; this includes responsibility for financing local authorities from the Exchequer.

Ministry of Supply.—This department was created in July 1939 by the Ministry of Supply Act, 1939. The primary function of the de-

---

[1] During the Second World War entitled Ministry of War Transport.

partment is to provide supplies for the Army and Air Force either by purchase or manufacture. It also administers the controls on certain raw materials of strategic importance. The Admiralty is its own supply department.

The Ministry of Works.—This department provides buildings throughout the country to house government departments and is responsible for repair and maintenance. It is entrusted with the care of royal palaces and royal parks. Since 1940 it has also exercised important powers in relation to building and the building industry, including the power to sanction by licence the erection and repair of buildings.

The Ministry of Fuel and Power.—This department was constituted as a war-time Ministry in 1942 by the transfer of the functions of the Board of Trade and Ministry of Transport in relation to mines, oil, gas and electricity undertakings. It controls the distribution of solid fuels and operates coal rationing. The department was made permanent in 1945.

(*d*) *The Ministry of Defence and the Service Departments.*

The Ministry of Defence.—Responsibility for a unified defence policy for the three armed services rests upon the Minister of Defence, who is, under the Prime Minister, deputy Chairman of the Defence Committee of the Cabinet. The functions of the Minister and his department, which was created in 1947 in succession to the war-time defence secretariat of the War Cabinet organisation, are

(*a*) the apportionment of available resources of man-power and material between the three services in accordance with the strategic policy laid down by the Defence Committee. This includes the framing of general policy to govern research and development and the correlation of production programmes;

(*b*) the settlement of questions of general administration on which a common policy for the three services is desirable;

(*c*) the administration of inter-service organisations, such as Combined Operations Headquarters and the Joint Intelligence Bureau.[1]

The three Service Ministers are like other departments presided over by Ministers of Cabinet rank who are responsible to Parliament; the First Lord of the Admiralty, the Secretary of State for War and the Secretary of State for Air. Each Service is, however, directed by a board or council composed, partly of experts, partly of civilians over which the responsible Minister presides. There are thus combined ministerial responsibility and expert direction. The responsible Minister may override his colleagues.

---

[1] Cmd. 6923, 1946, para. 26.

The Admiralty.—The Board of Admiralty are Commissioners for executing the office of Lord High Admiral. The Board consists of the First Lord of the Admiralty, several naval experts (including the Five Sea Lords and Vice-Chief of Naval Staff), the Parliamentary Secretary to the Admiralty, the Financial Secretary to the Admiralty, the Civil Lord and the Permanent Secretary to the Admiralty. The Parliamentary and Financial Secretary and Civil Lord are members of Parliament. The Permanent Secretary is the chief civil servant in the Admiralty.

The War Office.—The Secretary of State for War presides over the Army Council which controls the Army as the Board of Admiralty controls the Navy. The Army Council is composed of military members, including the Chief, Vice-Chief and Deputy Chief of the Imperial General Staff, the Adjutant-General to the Forces, and the Quarter-Master General to the Forces, and three civilian members: the Secretary of State, the Parliamentary Under-Secretary of State and Financial Secretary and the Permanent Under-Secretary of State (a civil servant).

The Air Ministry.—The Secretary of State for Air presides over the Air Council similarly constituted to the Army Council. It consists of service members, including the Chief of the Air Staff, and three civilian members, the Secretary of State and the Parliamentary and Permanent Under-Secretaries of State for Air.

The administration and organisation of the Territorial Army [1] and Auxiliary Air Force is assigned to county associations presided over by the Lord-Lieutenant of each county.

The Meteorological Service comes under the Air Ministry. The Coastguard Service is under the Board of Trade, but may be taken over by the Admiralty in an emergency when officers and men become subject to the Naval Discipline Acts.

The Lord Chancellor.—The Lord Chancellor is a member of the Cabinet in peace time. The Lord Chancellor is Speaker of the House of Lords,[2] and has the custody of the Great Seal. He presides as a judge over the two highest courts in the realm, the House of Lords and the Judicial Committee of the Privy Council. His duties in connection with judicial appointments and the general administration of justice will be discussed in Part V., Chap. 2. The Lord Chancellor is responsible for the Land Registry and Public Trustee Office. Despite its judicial nature the office has remained political in that it is held by an eminent member of the Bench or Bar adhering to the party in office. A previous political career is not an indispensable qualification and three Chancellors have in the present century been appointed

---

[1] P. 408, *post.*   [2] P. 94, *ante.*

from the Bench without having been members of the House of Commons.[1]

Lord President of the Council.[2]

Lord Privy Seal.—The duties of this office have been abolished by statute. The holder usually sits in the Cabinet without specific departmental duties.

Chancellor of the Duchy of Lancaster.—Apart from patronage this office is virtually a sinecure office and is used for the appointment of a Minister, sometimes with a seat in the Cabinet, who can be free of departmental duties. The revenues of the Duchy belong to the Sovereign as Duke of Lancaster.

The Law Officers' Department.—All government departments either have departmental solicitors or use the services of the Treasury Solicitor. The Home, Foreign, Colonial and Commonwealth Relations Offices have legal advisers. The Law Officers of the Crown, the Attorney-General and Solicitor-General, represent the Crown in courts of justice, and act as legal advisers to the Government on more important matters. They are assisted by Junior Counsel to the Treasury who are practising barristers and hold no political office. As representing the Crown, the Attorney-General and Solicitor-General take part in many judicial or quasi-judicial proceedings relating to the public interest, such as proceedings relating to the administration of charities and income tax. The appointments are political and are conferred on successful barristers who are supporters of the party in power. The Attorney-General has sometimes been a member of the Cabinet, but in view of his duties in connection with prosecutions [3] it is generally regarded as preferable that he should remain outside the Cabinet as the Government's chief legal adviser. In addition to the salaries of their offices the Law Officers formerly drew substantial sums in fees for Crown litigation, though private practice was prohibited. But the salaries are now fixed at £10,000 for the Attorney-General and £7,000 for the Solicitor-General with no fees. Advancement to judicial or political office is more or less assured to the holders of either appointment, but the supposed claim of the Attorney-General to appointment as Lord Chief Justice would seem to have little foundation. Only twice since 1875 has the Attorney-General been appointed directly to the latter office. The Attorney-General is the head of the English Bar. The Dean of the Faculty of Advocates is head of the Scots Bar. The Lord Advocate and the Solicitor-General for Scotland are the Law Officers for Scotland.

---

[1] A succinct account of this office is given by Lord Schuster in 11 *C.L.J.* 175, (1949).

[2] P. 137, *ante.*   [3] Part V, Chap. 2.

Certain duties, *e.g.* consent to certain types of prosecutions, such as offences under the Official Secrets Acts, 1911–1939, are by statute imposed upon the Attorney-General or the Lord Advocate. In the event of absence or illness or with special authority these duties may be carried out by the Solicitor-General or Solicitor-General for Scotland respectively.[1]

The Treasury Solicitor.—The Department of the Treasury Solicitor is responsible for the legal work of those departments which have neither legal advisers nor solicitors to the department on their staff. In other cases it undertakes litigation only, leaving the other legal work to the department's own legal adviser. Generally speaking when a department becomes responsible for administering a statutory code, such as the National Insurance Acts, 1946, it sets up its own legal department. The Department of the Treasury Solicitor is not a centralised legal advisers' office, but one which is responsible for a large residue of the legal work of government. The Treasury Solicitor holds office as Procurator-General and Treasury Solicitor. As Queen's Proctor he may intervene in divorce proceedings to prevent abuse of the processes of the court.

Minor Departments.—There are in addition a number of minor departments, *e.g.* the Public Trustee, the Land Registry, the Paymaster-General's Office,[2] the Stationery Office,[3] the Charity Commissioners and the Public Record Office. Offices of State connected with the Royal Household, such as the Lord Chamberlain, the Keeper of the Privy Purse and the Master of the Horse, are personal appointments by the Sovereign. Other Household posts are filled by Government patronage.

War-time Ministries.

Several Ministries were created during the Second World War under the Ministers of the Crown (Emergency) Appointments Act, 1939, which made provision for the appointment of Ministers for the purpose of the prosecution of the war and for the transfer of functions to such Ministers from other departments. The Minister of Labour became also Minister of National Service. The Home Secretary became also Minister of Home Security with a separate Parliamentary Secretary and staff constituting the Ministry of Home Security. The Minister of Transport became Minister of War Transport with control of all land and sea transport. There were created also the Ministry of Aircraft Production to carry out the supply functions of the Air Ministry, the Ministry of Economic Warfare, the Ministries of Information, of Food and of Fuel and Power.

---

[1] Law Officers Act, 1944.
[2] The Paymaster-General is a Minister.
[3] The Chancellor of the Exchequer is the Minister responsible for this office. See also for other subordinate departments connected with the Treasury, p. 181, *post.*

The last-named has become a permanent department. The Ministry of Production was created to co-ordinate the requirements of the various supply departments and the Minister of Production was a member of the War Cabinet. In 1942 there was appointed a Minister of Reconstruction,[1] without a separate Ministry, to co-ordinate plans for post-war construction. The Secretary of State for Foreign Affairs was assisted by a Minister of State. Ministers Resident [1] were appointed to various posts abroad, *e.g.* the Middle East, the Mediterranean, West Africa, and (for supply purposes) in Washington.

[1] These appointments were not made under the Ministers of the Crown (Emergency Appointments) Act, 1939, but under the Prerogative; their salaries were provided through a vote scheduled to the annual Appropriation Act.

CHAPTER 6.

THE CIVIL SERVICE.

What is a
Civil
Servant?

THE departments are staffed by administrative, professional, technical, executive and clerical officers who constitute the Civil Service. Civil servants are all servants of the Crown. There is no comprehensive definition of a Crown servant. A person appointed by another Crown servant under the authority of a statute may be a Crown servant as much as one appointed directly by the Crown. The facts of each appointment must be considered.[1] The lawyer is particularly concerned with the definition of an officer of the Crown contained in s. 2 (6) of the Crown Proceedings Act, 1947, which limits proceedings against the Crown in tort to the act, neglect or default of an "officer who has been directly or indirectly appointed by the Crown and was at the material time paid in respect of his duties as an officer of the Crown wholly out of" the revenues of the Central Government as there defined.

Civil
Service
Grades.

There are various grades in the Civil Service. Within each grade are established, *i.e.* pensionable, non-established and temporary appointments. The main groupings are 1. Non-industrial (other than manipulative). 2. Minor and manipulative grades. 3. Industrial. From the constitutional point of view interest is confined to the 4,300 members of the administrative grade of group 1 who are assisted by some 80,000 professional, scientific and technical officers, 61,000 members of the executive grade together with 300,000 clerks and typists. The remainder, totalling some 650,000 in 1954, are accounted for mainly by workers in the Post Office, the Service Departments and the Ministry of Supply. The Administrative Class forms the highest grade of permanent officials and by them are taken all important decisions, except on matters of policy which are decided by a Minister or the Cabinet as a whole.

Organisation
within
Departments.

The administrative work of a department is usually carried out under divisions or branches, each in charge of a senior administrative officer, assisted by administrative, executive and clerical officers. The nature of a department's functions will determine the range of professional and technical officers employed. For example, the Ministry of Health naturally employs a large staff of medical practitioners; the Ministry of Education contains an inspectorate of

[1] N. E. Mustoe, *Law and Organization of the British Civil Service* (Pitman), Chap. I.

schools. Scientific advisers are found in many departments. It is to be observed that the professional and technical staffs are not directly concerned with the formulation of policy. Accordingly they occupy in the civil service hierarchy a status inferior to their equivalent in rank in the administrative grade, which is reflected not only in their salaries, but in the extent to which their services are made use of in matters closely related to their specialised knowledge. It is a subject of criticism that, especially in scientific matters, the civil departments have no body equivalent to the Army Council or Board of Admiralty, where professional opinion is represented at the highest level. In defence of the present system it may be argued that the specialist may take too narrow a view and that the administrator is more capable of interpreting specialised knowledge in its application to national policy. It is, however, doubtful how far under modern conditions the administrator is capable of sustaining the burden which is placed upon him by the complexity of the issues, where specialised knowledge is required in the formation of a judgment.

The Civil Service in its present form, though its numbers have increased out of all proportion with the advent of social and other State services, dates from 1855. From 1870 patronage as a mode of recruitment for the administrative and executive classes was replaced by entry through competitive examinations of a general character. Professional and technical officers are recruited by special examination or by selection by boards after an interview. Appointments are normally terminable at the pleasure of the Crown and the conditions of employment are regulated by Orders in Council. The Civil Service Commission conducts the entrance examinations under regulations made by itself and approved by the Treasury. As we have seen, a servant of the Crown may be dismissed at pleasure and has no remedy, but his tenure is in fact secure. A person who holds a pensionable post is only dismissed for misconduct and then there are safeguards for his protection. Salaries, if not expressly provided by statute, as in the case of a few of the higher appointments, are regulated by the Treasury or fixed by Order in Council. Only the total sums required for payment of salaries appear in the annual estimates of the departments laid before Parliament. Pensions and superannuation payments are authorised by statute, but no recourse can be had to the courts to enforce payment of pensions, or to afford a remedy for wrongful dismissal either against the Crown, the Treasury, or the head of the department concerned. Civil servants are not in the employment of their departments, all being equally, from the highest to the lowest, in the service of the Crown.

Tenure of Appointment.

The law of the Civil Service is contained in the Orders in Council and regulations made thereunder and in Treasury circulars or minutes addressed to the permanent heads of departments. There is

Law of the Civil Service.

an appeal against dismissal to the head of the department. Negotiations as to conditions of service are in the lower grades conducted through Whitley Councils and arbitration in Industrial Courts; but the Treasury retains final control and embodies the agreements or awards in Treasury circulars.

Political
Activities
of Civil
Servants.

Reference has already been made to the prohibition on parliamentary candidature which is imposed upon servants of the Crown by the Order in Council of 1950.[1] In 1949 a departmental committee reviewed the whole question of the existing limitations on the political activities of civil servants.[2] Its proposals were varied after later discussions with the staff side of the Civil Service National Whitley Council and brought fully into force in 1954. It is recognised that the political neutrality of the Civil Service is a fundamental feature of British democratic (*i.e.* constitutional) government. Accordingly participation in national politics is barred not only for the administrative and professional grades, but for many of the executive and clerical staffs who work with them under changing political Ministers. This restricted category, comprising some 11 per cent. of the whole Civil Service, are in general allowed with permission to take part in local government. A second category, totalling some 26 per cent., may take part in all political activities, except parliamentary candidature, subject to accepting a code of discretion since they are working as public servants under the Government of the day; but all in this category are eligible for permission to undertake national as well as local political activities. The rest of the minor and manipulative grades and the industrial grade are free to engage in political activities, national and local, except when on duty, or on official premises or while wearing uniform, subject, however, to the provisions of the Official Secrets Acts relating particularly to unauthorised disclosure of information acquired from official sources. The restriction on political liberty, especially in the first category, is no doubt severe, but public confidence in the integrity of the Civil Service is so important that it is probably better to draw no distinction between those who are in daily touch with Ministers of the Crown and those who work in close contact with them in the Departments.

Treasury as
Central
Department.

Each major department is separate, but for the general control of the Civil Service the Treasury acts as a central department and controls the general organisation and conditions of the Civil Service through its Establishments Division under the authority of the First Lord of the Treasury. The Permanent Secretary to the Treasury is head of the Civil Service and advises the Prime Minister on those

---

[1] P. 86, *ante*.
[2] Report of the Committee on the Political Activities of Civil Servants (the Masterman Committee), Cmd. 7718, 1949 and Cmd. 8783, 1953, recommending with variations the implementation thereof. Establishment Circular 26/53; see XXXII. *Public Administration*, 324 ff.

higher appointments which require his consent.[1] The Establishments Division of the Treasury secures uniformity and advises departmental establishment officers. The number and salaries of each category of departmental officers require Treasury approval. Treasury circulars or minutes are also sometimes issued on matters of discipline and other matters where uniformity of practice between departments is essential.[2]

The Civil Service Commission was created in 1855 following the Northcote-Trevelyan Report on the Civil Service; this recommended *(inter alia)* that all posts should be filled by open competitive examination. It was not until 1870 that open competition was introduced as the normal method of recruitment. By this means the original objective of the Commission, namely the avoidance of patronage, has ever since been achieved. The present authority of the Commission is derived from an Order in Council of 22nd July, 1920, which provides that "the qualifications of all persons proposed to be appointed, whether permanently or temporarily, to any situation or employment in any of Her Majesty's establishments shall . . . be approved by the Commissioners. . . ." The main functions of the Commissioners derive from the royal prerogative and in practice they are independent of control and subject to no influence or pressure, political or otherwise, in testing and selecting candidates. The Commissioners also conduct the examinations for entry into the Armed Forces with a view to regular commissions, and the First Commissioner is also Chairman of the Overseas Service Appointments Board.

Civil Service Commission.

[1] P. 152, *ante.*
[2] Royal Commission on the Civil Service (1929), *Minutes of Evidence,* Appendix I., p. 27, cited by Sir Ivor Jennings, *Cabinet Government,* p. 135.
The position of the Treasury as a central department is emphasised by its control over Parliamentary Counsel to the Treasury, who draft Bills for all departments, and over the Treasury Solicitor, who conducts Crown litigation on behalf of many other departments.

CHAPTER 7.

PUBLIC FINANCE.[1]

IN this Chapter there will be considered the manner of raising and spending the national revenue with particular reference to the administration of the Treasury. Parliamentary control of expenditure and taxation has already been described in Part III., Chap. 3, and in Chap. 6 of this Part there have been mentioned the functions of the Treasury as the central department of the Civil Service.

Treasury Board. The office of Treasurer was first put into commission in 1616. Since 1714 it has always been in commission. The Treasury Board, as are the Commissioners for executing the office of the Lord High Admiral, *i.e.* the Admiralty, is a body of Commissioners. The Board is created by letters patent under the Great Seal and is composed of a number of individuals appointed by name. In practice they are the First Lord of the Treasury (an office normally taken by the Prime Minister), the Chancellor of the Exchequer (Under Treasurer) and the Assistant Government Whips (Junior Lords of the Treasury).[2] The Board never meets, individual members being responsible for the business transacted. Treasury warrants are generally signed by two of the Junior Lords. The Chancellor of the Exchequer is the Finance Minister, not by virtue of his membership of the Board, but by separate patents of office. He is invariably a member of the House of Commons where he is assisted by the Financial Secretary to the Treasury. He answers in Parliament not only for financial and general civil service matters, but also for the various service departments which come under his control. Since 1947 the Chancellor of the Exchequer has been given a wide responsibility for the general direction of economic policy, both external and internal. He has the assistance in this sphere of a ministerial Economic Secretary and of the Economic Planning Board, an official committee, and an Economic Section. In the execution of policy the President of the Board of Trade is in particular closely concerned.

The Chancellor of the Exchequer.

Before discussing the part played by the Treasury in revenue matters, it is necessary to give a brief account of the public offices which work in connection with the Treasury.

---

[1] See generally Hills and Fellowes, *The Finance of Government*, 2nd ed., and *The Treasury* (The Whitehall Series), and for the history of the Exchequer and the office of Treasurer, see Anson, *Law and Custom of the Constitution* (4th ed.), Vol. II., Part II., pp. 172 ff.

P. 88, *ante*.

(1) The department charged with responsibility for the collection of customs and excise duties is the Board of Customs and Excise, while direct taxation, such as income tax, sur-tax, estate duty and stamp duties, are the responsibility of the Board of Inland Revenue. These subordinate departments are placed by statute under Treasury direction. The Post Office is also a department concerned with the collection of revenue on a large scale.

The Board of Customs and Excise and the Board of Inland Revenue.

(2) In addition to the important function of auditing public accounts, the Comptroller and Auditor-General can alone authorise the Bank of England to give credit to the Treasury for payments out of the Consolidated Fund, which is the account at the Bank of England through which all the public revenue passes. He will only give this authority when satisfied that the requirements of the Treasury have been sanctioned by Parliament. As auditor of the public accounts, this officer examines the accounts of departments annually to ensure that public money is spent for the purpose for which it was voted and reports to a standing committee of fifteen members of the House of Commons, called the Public Accounts Committee, which, in turn, makes its report to the House. The report, though not usually debated by the Commons, assists control by the Treasury. The Comptroller draws attention to any excess of authorised expenditure, as well as to unnecessarily extravagant or irregular items in the accounts of a department. The importance of this office is such that the salary attached to it is not subject to the annual vote of Parliament, but is charged on the Consolidated Fund by an Act which does not require annual renewal. In this respect the Comptroller and Auditor-General is in the same position as the Supreme Court judges, and, like the judges, he holds his office during good behaviour, but can be dismissed by the Queen upon an address presented by both Houses of Parliament. He is ineligible to sit in the House of Commons.[1]

Comptroller and Auditor-General.

(3) The office of Paymaster-General is usually held by a junior Minister. Payments on account of the public services are made to the Paymaster-General by the Bank of England, and he pays out the money to the departments and other persons authorised by the Treasury.

Paymaster-General.

There may also be mentioned the Royal Mint, responsible for coinage, and the Public Works Loan Board, which advances money to local authorities for the purpose of authorised capital expenditure.

The main functions of the Treasury in relation to public finance are:

Functions of Treasury.

(1) The imposition and regulation of taxation, including the preparation of the annual Finance Bill, and the collection of revenue.

[1] Exchequer and Audit Departments Acts, 1866, 1921 and 1950.

(2) The control of public expenditure, including supervision of the departmental estimates.

(3) The provision of funds to meet the public services, including the exercise of borrowing powers.

(4) The management of the public debt.

The whole of the national revenue is Crown revenue, but the raising and spending of revenue is subject to the control of the House of Commons. This, in the first place, means that, with unimportant exceptions, the Crown cannot raise any money except by the authority of an Act of Parliament. Secondly, public money cannot be expended without the consent of Parliament, and it is the rule of the House of Commons to appropriate revenue to specific purposes of departmental expenditure (Supply). The procedure in relation to Supply Bills has already been dealt with in Part III, where some comment will be found on the ineffectiveness of parliamentary control so far as securing economy of expenditure is concerned.[1]

It has long been provided by Standing Orders of the House of Commons that no charge can be placed upon the public revenue except on the recommendation of the Crown signified by a Minister. The same rule prevails with regard to taxation. A private member may move to reduce a tax, but not to increase it. Thus the Government of the day is responsible for all taxation and expenditure, and no private member can propose that the public funds be utilised for any public purpose that is not approved by the Government.

Consolidated Fund.

All the revenue collected for the National Exchequer is paid into the Consolidated Fund, and all payments for national purposes come out of this fund. In calculating its supply requirements for the forthcoming year a department has to show in its estimates the amount expected as departmental receipts (appropriations-in-aid).[2] These will reduce the amount of the department's total of supply money to be voted by Parliament out of the Consolidated Fund. But like votes of supply, appropriations-in-aid must receive parliamentary sanction in the annual Appropriation Act, and if the estimate of receipts under this head is exceeded, the surplus is surrendered to the Exchequer. A private member may not move in Committee of Supply to reduce an appropriation-in-aid.

Expenditure: Consolidated Fund Services.

The expenditure of the country is grouped under two heads, namely, Consolidated Fund Services and Supply Services. The Consolidated Fund Services are payments under statutes which make a recurrent grant, either for a fixed number of years or without limitation of time. Payments on account of the Supply Services have to be voted each year by the House of Commons. The principal item of expenditure under the heading, Consolidated Fund Services,

[1] Part III., Chap. 3.   [2] P. 112, *ante.*

is the interest upon, and management of, the National Debt. It is obvious that credit which depended for its security on annual review by Parliament would not prove attractive to lenders. Accordingly government loans are charged under statutes which give permanent authority for meeting the obligations incurred to lenders. The National Debt is in normal times reduced by application of (*a*) any surplus of national income over expenditure on March 31, the end of the financial year (the Old Sinking Fund), and (*b*) any saving in the permanent annual charge for interest (the New Sinking Fund).

The Queen's Civil List [1] was granted to the Queen by the Civil List Act, 1952, for her reign and six months after, and accordingly is a Consolidated Fund Service. The Civil List is the annual income granted to the Sovereign to provide the privy purse and household expenses. It is granted at the beginning of each reign in lieu of the ancient hereditary revenues, including the income from Crown lands, which are on each occasion first surrendered to Parliament by the Crown. The present amount of the Civil List is £475,000. Although a system of appropriations, under which parliamentary grants of supplies were assigned for specific purposes, was adopted for general use from 1689 onwards, many items of public expenditure continued to be met out of the hereditary revenues of the Crown and thus escaped parliamentary control. By 1830 the Civil List had been cut down to the personal requirements of the Sovereign, and other public expenditure came under the control of Parliament. The Act of 1952 also made provision for the Duke of Edinburgh, Her Majesty's younger children and certain other members of the Royal Family. Others, including the Queen Mother, were provided for in the Civil List Act, 1937, on the accession of King George VI. The Duke of Cornwall enjoys separate provision out of the revenues of the Duchy of Cornwall; the Act of 1952 appropriates the bulk of these to the Queen during his minority, as part of the Civil List Grant of £475,000.

The sum of £2,500 per annum is charged upon the Consolidated Fund by the Act for Civil List pensions awarded each year to distinguished persons or their dependants who are in poor financial circumstances, but despite the name these pensions have nothing to do with the Civil List.

The salaries of those officials whom it is desired to make more independent of parliamentary control than the ordinary departmental officials are also made by statute Consolidated Fund payments. Whereas the total amount needed for salaries by each government department comes under annual review by Parliament, the salaries of the Lord Chancellor (as a judge),[2] the Speaker of the House of

Civil List.

Salaries charged on Consolidated Fund.

---

[1] For history of Civil List, see Anson, *op. cit.* (4th ed.), Vol. 2, Part II., pp. 195 ff.

[2] Part of the salary is charged to the House of Lords Offices Vote.

Commons, the Comptroller and Auditor-General, the Lords of Appeal in Ordinary, the judges of the Court of Appeal, the High Court of Justice and the County Courts and the Metropolitan Magistrates are charged on the Consolidated Fund. There is thus no special opportunity of criticising in Parliament each year the work of these officers, as in the case of those who are paid from the Supply Services, and this practice tends purposely to preserve their independent position.[1]

Supply Services. The Supply Services, as we have seen,[2] fall under three main heads, the Armed Forces of the Crown, the Civil Services and the Revenue Services. The financial year runs from April 1 to March 31, except for the purposes of income tax and sur-tax, where the period is April 6 to April 5. Each year in the autumn the government departments submit to the Treasury an estimate of their expenditure for the ensuing year. Each estimate is closely scrutinised by the Treasury and cannot be submitted to the House of Commons until it has received Treasury approval. In this way the Treasury is able to a limited extent to check a tendency to extravagance on the part of the spending departments. No doubt a strong Chancellor of the Exchequer can make administration as economical as possible. But it must be remembered that the Treasury must assist in carrying out the policy of the Cabinet. Successive Cabinets by introducing legislation which involves expanding expenditure are really responsible for increasing items. Policy is apt to be synonymous with expenditure, and therefore the opportunities for the Treasury to curtail expenditure are largely confined to curtailing the expenses of administration. If, for example, the Cabinet decides to increase old age pensions by statutory amendment, the estimates of the Ministry of Pensions and National Insurance, when submitted to the Treasury, must show the increase resulting from the extended benefit. The Treasury may insist that the administrative expenses be restricted—and Treasury control is in this sphere effective—but it has no control whatever over the statutory rate of benefit, once it is approved by Parliament. A strong Chancellor of the Exchequer may, however, as a member of the Cabinet, use his influence with his colleagues by indicating that he is unable to find the money to carry their proposed policy into effect. In the past this has been effective to curtail expenditure on the fighting services, none of which is incurred on the authority of permanent Acts. Nowadays all capital expenditure on the public services is allocated under a system of priorities.

Treasury Sanction. No proposal involving the expenditure of public funds is nowadays presented to the Cabinet until it has been examined both by the

---

[1] The salaries of members of the National Assistance Board are charged on the Consolidated Fund. See p. 220, *post*.
[2] Part III., Chap. 3, C.

Treasury and any other department which may be concerned with the proposal. Indeed all proposals involving an increase in departmental expenditure on any new service require Treasury sanction.[1] Thus the financial implication of any policy which it is proposed to put into effect is ensured full examination.

The annual examination of the estimates by the Treasury also enables the Chancellor of the Exchequer to prepare the annual Budget statement in time for presentation to the House of Commons early in the new financial year.[2] An examination of the estimates can alone enable the Chancellor of the Exchequer and his advisers to determine whether or not additional taxation will have to be imposed, or again, whether the requirements of the ensuing year will enable him to remit some portion of the existing taxation.

Estimates.

The decline in Treasury control which is due to the causes described has important results. The Treasury (or indeed the department concerned) is debarred from financial control over a new State service, once the measure initiating it has been placed upon the statute book. No alteration of policy is possible, except by the inelastic method of repealing or amending Acts, and a Government will seldom risk the unpopularity of a reversal of policy which would deprive the electors of an established service. The control exercised over the estimates by the House of Commons has long ceased to be more than formal. It is idle to maintain that there is any safeguard in the rule that there shall be no expenditure of public funds without the sanction of the House of Commons, so long as that House itself sets the pace by passing legislation which involves automatic increases in expenditure. Treasury control is thus ineffective in relation to those departments which are committed to fixed statutory charges.[3]

Decline in Treasury Control.

The revenue of the Crown is divided into ordinary and extra-ordinary, the latter being derived mainly from taxation. The principal item of "ordinary" revenue is the income derived from Crown lands, which in the main have long since been surrendered to the public. The net rents and profits so derived are paid into the Consolidated Fund. The Crown is also, as part of its "ordinary" revenue, entitled to property found without any apparent owner. The most important illustration of this is the property of an intestate who dies without a spouse or blood-relations entitled to take under the Administration of Estates Act, 1925, ss. 46 and 47, as amended by the Intestates' Estates Act, 1952.

Revenue: Ordinary Revenue.

[1] For Treasury control, see Sir Ivor Jennings, *Cabinet Government*, Chap. VII.
[2] Part III., Chap. 3, C.
[3] The functions of the Treasury in relation to war-time expenditure are substantially modified and control has to be relaxed, especially with regard to war service expenditure.

Extra-
ordinary
Revenue.

The "extraordinary" revenue derived from taxation falls under several heads. The greater part of the sum raised annually by taxation is imposed by provisions in Finance Acts which do not require renewal, but stand until repealed or amended. The rate of income tax is, however, fixed each year.

Indirect
Taxation.

The following are the most important items of indirect taxation, *i.e.* taxation which is, generally speaking, capable of being passed on to the consumer by the taxpayer.

Customs
Duties.

(1) Customs duties are levied upon commodities imported into this country from other countries. Preferential rates are granted to products of the Commonwealth and the Colonies. With the abandonment of free trade in 1931, there was employed a novel and striking form of delegated legislation for controlling this mode of taxation; see Import Duties Act, 1932.[1]

The Customs and Excise Act, 1952, contains a code of regulations and imposes penalties upon those who attempt to evade the duties. Dutiable goods may only be imported free of duty if they are deposited in a warehouse, the owner of which has entered into a bond with the Crown that the proper duties will be paid if, and when, the goods are released for sale at home. The provision of bonded warehouses is particularly useful for enabling goods intended for re-exportation to other countries to escape duty.

Excise
Duties.

(2) Excise duties are imposed upon commodities produced for consumption in this country. The revenue officials have important powers of entry and search to check evasion of the tax. The term, excise duty, is not used strictly in the sense of a tax on commodities, but also covers a number of taxes in the form of licences to manufacture certain articles, *e.g.* beer and spirits; licences to carry on certain occupations, *e.g.* pawnbroker, money-lender, and retailer of beer, spirits, wine and tobacco; and licences to use certain articles, *e.g.* for keeping a dog, or driving a motor-car. Other duties under this heading are purchase tax levied on retail sales and the duty on entertainments.

Drawback.

As an equivalent to the bonded warehouse in the case of imported goods, excise duties in the strict sense are generally subject to drawback, *i.e.* repayment of the duty if the goods are exported to a foreign country. The exporter of beer is allowed a drawback on the excise duties paid on the manufacture. The object is to enable British manufacturers to compete in foreign markets with foreigners who may not have had to pay duties on the same commodities. In the case of a customs duty on an article in the raw state, which is imported into this country for manufacture and then re-exported in the finished form, the manufacturer can claim repayment of the

[1] Pp. 101–2, *ante.*

customs duties paid on importation. Tobacco to be manufactured
into cigarettes for exportation is an example of this.

A direct tax may be broadly described as one which falls on the
actual person who pays the tax. Direct
Taxation.

(3) Estate duty becomes payable to the Crown on the death of
an individual leaving property the value of which exceeds £3,000.
The duty is paid both upon property which the deceased enjoyed,
and upon the interests to which others succeed on account of his
death. It is payable by the personal representatives on all the property of the deceased, whether land, money or goods. Death
Duties.

(4) Stamp duties are levied upon certain legal instruments, such
as instruments of transfer of land or stock and shares. Stamp
Duties.

(5) The income tax is the direct tax which not only yields the
largest sum of public revenue but affects directly the pay packet of
the majority of workers in the country and all who derive their
income from securities. By the Income Tax Act, 1952, income is
treated as falling under separate heads, called schedules, for the purpose of assessment to tax. In general income tax is levied on all
income arising in the United Kingdom and on the income of residents
in the United Kingdom wherever it arises. Income Tax
and Sur-tax.

There is a standard flat rate of income tax, but there are important
allowances and deductions which have the effect of making income
tax a graduated tax. The tax applies to the income of trading companies and all corporate bodies (charities excepted) as well as to that
of individuals.

Sur-tax, an additional tax, is a graduated tax on the income of
individuals above a certain figure. At present the tax is levied on the
excess of income over £2,000, the rate rising with the amount of
such excess. There are additional taxes on the profits of trading
corporations.

From a constitutional point of view something must be said about
the administration of these taxes. The Commissioners of Inland
Revenue are charged with the general management of the taxes
and represent the interests of the Crown, *i.e.* the general body of
taxpayers. The duties of the Commissioners in each district (the
civil parish is the normal unit) are carried out by Inspectors, whose
areas cover a number of adjoining districts. Inspectors are civil
servants with an expert knowledge of tax law who are responsible
for details concerning assessments and for dealing with claims and
allowances. Also under the Commissioners of Inland Revenue are
collectors of taxes. In each district there is a body, known as the
General Commissioners (Commissioners of the General Purposes
of the Income Tax); this body, which contains no official element,
holds office independently of the Inland Revenue Commissioners,
and is a tribunal interposed between the Crown and the individual Administra-
tion of
Income Tax.

taxpayer, from whose ranks its members are drawn. It is the duty of the General Commissioners, subject to certain important exceptions, which include assessments to sur-tax,[1] to confirm assessments of taxation, and to hear appeals by the taxpayer and the Revenue authorities on questions of law and fact. If a taxpayer so wishes, he may (and usually does) appeal to the Special Commissioners rather than to the General Commissioners. From the General or Speical Commissioners appeals lie on points of law only to the Chancery Division of the High Court, thence to the Court of Appeal and the House of Lords.

[1] Made by the Special Commissioners of Income Tax (see p. 345, *post*).

CHAPTER 8.

THE POLICE.

ALTHOUGH the constable is an officer with powers long known to the common law and part of the special powers of the modern police officer are exercised by him as a constable, the professional police forces only date from the first half of the nineteenth century.[1] *Local Police Authorities*

The Metropolitan Police, whose jurisdiction extends over a fifteen-mile radius from Charing Cross is the only police force in the United Kingdom which is under the direct control of the Home Secretary, who is the police authority. The executive head is the Commissioner of Police for the Metropolis, who is appointed by the Crown and is the disciplinary authority. The Commissioner makes appointments and has powers of suspension and dismissal. The City of London Police are an independent force, but the appointment of the Commissioner (Chief Officer) must be approved by the Home Secretary. The Court of Common Council is the police authority.

Elsewhere in England and Wales the Police are organised as county or county borough forces. The local police authority for a county is the Standing Joint Committee, so called because its members are drawn half from the County Council and half from the Justices of Peace in Quarter Sessions, who had sole responsibility from 1839 when the county police force was first authorised until 1889 when the County Councils came into existence.[2] In a county borough the authority is the Borough Council acting through the Watch Committee. The local authority determines the size of its force and has the powers of appointment and of dismissal; these powers are in counties exercised by the Chief Constable as disciplinary authority; in boroughs they are exercised by the Watch Committee. The authority pays the salaries and wages of members of its force, though the scale of payments is fixed on a national basis.

The central administrative control of the Home Secretary is important. The appointment of the chief officer of police (Chief Constable) by the police authority is subject to the approval of the Home Secretary. The Police Act, 1919, s. 4, provides that "it shall be lawful for the Secretary of State to make regulations as to the *Home Secretary and Local Police Forces.*

[1] For a short account of the history of the police and parish constables, see Hart, *Introduction to the Law of Local Government and Administration* (Butterworth), 5th edition, Chap. 24. The control exercised by the Home Secretary is described in *The Home Office* volume of *The New Whitehall Series* (George Allen and Unwin).

[2] See County Police Act, 1839; Local Government Act, 1888, s. 9.

government, mutual aid, pay, allowances, pensions, clothing expenses and conditions of service of all members of all police forces within England and Wales, and every police authority shall comply with the regulations so made." These regulations can only be made after consultation with the Police Council, a body constituted by the Act, on which representatives of police authorities and of all ranks of the police force sit. In 1954 a new form of Police Council was set up; it is composed of representatives of the official and the staff sides (on Whitley Council lines [1]) under an independent chairman; in the event of disagreement over scales of pay there is provision for reference to three arbitrators. There is a uniform system of police pensions throughout the country: Police Pensions Act, 1921. Any member of the police force who feels aggrieved by the decision of the local police authority to dismiss him or require him to resign may appeal to the Home Secretary against such dismissal: Police (Appeals) Act, 1927. The Police (Appeals) Act, 1943, extended the right to appeal to questions of reduction in rank or rate of pay. In addition to regulation under the Police Act, 1919, which constitutes a system of legislation on all points of police administration, the Secretary of State exercises considerable control through the purse. Since 1856 a grant has been made out of the funds of the Exchequer towards the police expenses of local authorities, but the payment of this grant is, by statute, made conditional on the Home Secretary's certificate that the force is efficient in numbers and discipline. Inspectors of Constabulary have proved powerful instruments in maintaining efficiency. As the amount of the grant is one-half of the whole expenses, it is clear that no local authority can afford to forgo its certificate of efficiency. Both the Metropolitan and City of London Police are in receipt of similar grants, the balance of expenditure in the case of the former being contributed by the Councils whose area is included in the Metropolitan Police District.

Amalgamation of Forces. The existence of a number of independent police forces has often been criticised. With modern means of locomotion criminals need have no local associations, and on the grounds of efficient administration there is much to be said in favour of amalgamations on a large scale. Many voluntary amalgamations took place before 1939. The Defence (Amalgamation of Police) Regulations, 1942, made provision for the compulsory amalgamation of certain police forces as a war-time measure. Before 1947 the number of separate police forces was even greater than at present since 47 non-county boroughs had their own forces. The Police Act, 1946, which merged these borough forces into the appropriate county force,[2] provided for further amalga-

---

[1] P. 178, *ante.*
[2] Except in the case of Cambridge and Peterborough which on population grounds were treated as county boroughs for police purposes only.

mations, both voluntary and compulsory at the instance of the Home Secretary, in the latter case with the safeguard that no compulsion can be enforced upon a public authority having a population of over 100,000 to amalgamate with a larger authority without its consent. The idea of a national police force is repugnant to the English tradition of local government, and on constitutional grounds there are obvious objections to equipping the Executive with the equivalent of the continental gendarmerie. Not even in detective matters is there a national force, although for the purpose of unravelling complicated crimes the Criminal Investigation Department of the Metropolitan Police has a great advantage over local forces. The assistance of this department is available to the local forces, but it rests with the local force to decide whether or not assistance shall be invoked in any particular case which may arise in its area.

It is not easy to define the precise status of a police officer. Though appointed by a local authority and liable to dismissal by them, he is not in the legal sense their servant. On appointment a constable is sworn in before a justice of the peace. His oath requires him to scrve the Sovereign as a constable; he is bound to obey the orders of the justices. Though subject in some respect to local supervision and required to obey certain local police regulations, a police officer is as such a servant of the State or ministerial officer of the central power.[1] "The powers of a constable as a peace officer, whether conferred by statute or by common law, are exercised by him by virtue of his office and cannot be exercised on the responsibility of any person but himself . . . a constable, therefore, when acting as a peace officer, is not exercising a delegated authority, and the general law of agency has no application." [2] A police authority, therefore, cannot be made liable in respect of tortious acts of a member of a police force which have been occasioned by the exercise of such powers.[3] It may be otherwise if the officer has committed a tort when employed on duties of a different character on behalf of his own authority. Nor is the Crown liable; for, even if an officer is a servant of the Crown, the police are not paid wholly out of moneys provided by Parliament and are not, therefore, within the definition of servants of the Crown for the purpose of imposing vicarious liability in tort: Crown Proceedings Act, 1947, s. 2 (6). A police officer has been held to be "a person holding office under His Majesty" for the purpose of the Official Secrets Acts.[4] On the other hand a local authority has been held entitled to recover damages for injuries done

Legal Status of a Police Officer.

[1] *Fisher* v. *Oldham Corporation,* [1930] 2 K.B. 364.
[2] *Enever* v. *The King (Australia)* (1906), 3 C.L.R. 969, at p. 977.
[3] *Fisher* v. *Oldham Corporation, ante.*
[4] *Lewis* v. *Cattle,* [1938] 2 K.B. 454; for criticism of this decision, see Sir Ivor Jennings in 2 *Modern Law Review,* 73.

to a police officer whereby the authority lost his services and the officer became entitled to a special disability pension payable by the authority.[1]

Special Constables.

The authorities charged with the preservation of the peace have for long had power to appoint special constables to supplement the regular police force in an emergency. Nowadays this power is exercised by two or more justices of the peace. Able-bodied male residents between the ages of twenty-five and fifty-five may be enrolled, notice of appointment being given to the Home Secretary and the Lord-Lieutenant of the county. Special constables may be appointed apart from an actual or apprehended emergency, and the Special Constables Acts, 1914 and 1923, made provision for the maintenance of a special constabulary reserve on a permanent footing.

[1] *Bradford Corporation* v. *Webster*, [1920] 2 K.B. 135; but see now *Attorney-General for New South Wales* v. *Perpetual Trustee Co. Ltd.*, [1955] A.C. 457, where it was held that a police constable is a holder of a public office and not a servant for whose loss of services a police authority can sue.

CHAPTER 9.

ALLEGIANCE AND NATIONALITY; ALIENS; EXTRADITION; FOREIGN ENLISTMENT.

A.

Allegiance and Nationality.

ALLEGIANCE may be natural or local. British subjects owe allegiance to the Queen at all times wherever they may be. The subjects of the Queen owe her allegiance and the allegiance follows the person of the subject. He is the Queen's liege wherever he may be, and he may violate his allegiance in a foreign country just as he may violate it within the realm: *The King* v. *Casement*, [1917] 1 K.B. 98. The holders of certain public offices are required by statute to take the oath of allegiance, viz. Ministers of the Crown, certain high officers of State, members of both Houses of Parliament, judges and justices of the peace, the bishops and clergy of the Established Church of England and members of the armed forces who are serving on regular engagements.[1] Local allegiance is owed by all aliens within the realm and the Queen's protection. It was held in the celebrated treason case of the Second World War: *Joyce* v. *Director of Public Prosecutions*, [1946] A.C. 347, that allegiance was owed by the holder of a British passport, which had been obtained on false statements, notwithstanding that he, being an American citizen, had gone to Germany and there committed treasonable acts in time of war. He had at no time, it would appear, contemplated putting himself while abroad under the protection of the Crown.[2] Allegiance is probably owed by enemy civilians within the realm in time of war and possibly by prisoners of war interned within the realm.[3] It is not owed before their capture by alien enemies coming to invade the realm.[4]

A resident alien's duty of allegiance does not cease when the Queen's protection is temporarily withdrawn, owing to the occupation of the British territory where he is residing by enemy forces in time of war. In *De Jager* v. *Attorney-General of Natal*, [1907]

---

[1] National Servicemen do not take the oath; they sign a declaration regarding their obligations under the Official Secrets Acts, 1911–39.

[2] See 9 C.L.J. 330 and 10 C.L.J. 54 for articles sustaining and attacking this decision by Professor H. Lauterpacht and Professor Glanville Williams respectively.

[3] McNair, *Legal Effects of War*, 3rd ed., p. 16.

[4] *Ibid.*, pp. 17, 54–5. The offence of treason is based on a breach of allegiance, but the war-time Treachery Act, 1940, applied to any person within the realm.

H

A.C. 326, a resident alien was held guilty of treason, who, in such circumstances, joined an invading force, although that force was composed of nationals of his own country.

Protection. The extent of the Queen's duty to provide protection cannot be precisely defined. It is a duty which cannot be enforced by the courts so far as the provision of protection for British subjects in foreign parts is concerned. If special protection is given by the armed forces of the Crown, the subject can be required to pay for it by process of law enforcing an agreement to make payment: *China Navigation Co.* v. *Attorney-General*, [1932] 2 K.B. 197; K. & L. 93. Indeed, the only recognition of the nature of the duty within the realm is to be found in the recognition by the courts that there is no obligation upon an individual to pay for ordinary police protection: *Glasbrook Bros.* v. *Glamorgan County Council*, [1925] A.C. 270, where an obligation to pay for special police protection to private property was enforced, though no such action would lie for ordinary services rendered by the police for the maintenance of public order.

British Nationality; Law before 1949. Prior to the operation of the British Nationality Act, 1948, which came into force on January 1, 1949, in the United Kingdom and throughout the Colonies, the status of a natural born British subject, who was born on or after 1915 was governed by the British Nationality and Status of Aliens Act, 1914–43.[1] The Act recognised two principal criteria, place of birth and the nationality of the father as qualifications for nationality, *i.e.* membership as a citizen of the State. The status of British subjects born before 1915 was governed mainly by the common law which was based upon the place of birth (*jus soli*), and by the Naturalisation Act, 1870.

The Act of 1914–43 was also enacted in statutes, which with some exceptions, especially as regards conditions of naturalisation, were identical, by the Parliaments of Canada, Australia, New Zealand and South Africa, the only Dominions with legislative competence in 1914 to enact separate nationality laws. Thus all British subjects had a common status, which rested on the basis of common allegiance to the Crown, and this was recognised by the legislation of different parts of the Commonwealth, as it later came to be called. The principle of a common code system was observed and alterations by any one of the five States could only in practice be made after consultation and agreement with the other four.

Even before the addition to the Commonwealth of India, Pakistan and Ceylon (to whose territories as well as to those of Southern Rhodesia and until 1948 of Burma the United Kingdom Act applied) the common code system was becoming unworkable in practice. Canada in 1946 passed a Citizenship Act which laid down conditions

---

[1] It is convenient to refer to the Act of 1914 and the several amending Acts as a single statute.

for the acquisition and loss of Canadian, as distinct from British, citizenship; it also enacted that all Canadian citizens were British subjects and that all persons who were British subjects by the law of any other part of the Commonwealth should be recognised as British subjects in Canada.

These principles of separate citizenship for each State of the Commonwealth and mutual recognition of that qualification for the status of British subject or Commonwealth citizen—the terms have the same meaning in law—are accepted by the British Nationality Act, 1948.[1] We are not here concerned with the current law of other Commonwealth States or with the special position of a national of the Republic of Ireland who enjoys the status of a British subject within the United Kingdom and the Colonies.[2] The Act accordingly provided that after 1948 citizenship of the United Kingdom and Colonies should describe the qualification for British nationality of those nationals whose status was determined by the legislature of the United Kingdom Parliament, *i.e.* nationals of the United Kingdom, the Channel Islands, the Isle of Man and of all the Colonies, as distinct from the other States of the Commonwealth and of Southern Rhodesia which enjoys legislative independence for this as for other purposes. *Act of 1948.*

The Act repeals all the nationality provisions of the Act of 1914–43 and, unlike that Act, determines the status of all persons alive at the date of its coming into operation. But, except for some important changes with regard to married women, the qualifications for citizenship of the United Kingdom and Colonies closely resemble those laid down for the common status of British subjects by the previous Act.

These qualifications are— *Qualifications for U.K. Citizenship.*

1. Birth in the United Kingdom or the Colonies, with exceptions in the case of children born (*a*) to non-citizen fathers who are in enjoyment of diplomatic immunity from suit and legal process; (*b*) to enemy alien fathers where the birth occurred in a place under occupation by the enemy (s. 4).

2. Descent. This qualification safeguards the citizenship of a person born abroad whose father is a citizen of the United Kingdom and Colonies at the time of the birth.

There are certain provisions which apply where the father himself acquired citizenship by descent; these limit citizenship to the child in those cases where

(*a*) the child is born or his father was born in a protectorate, protected state, mandated territory or trust territory or any

[1] Cmd. 7326 (1948) gives a summary of the main changes which were subsequently enacted.
[2] British Nationality Act, 1948, s. 3 (2); Ireland Act, 1949, s. 2 (1).

place in a foreign country where by treaty, capitulation, grant, usage, sufferance, or other lawful means, Her Majesty then has or had jurisdiction over British subjects; or

(b) the child's birth having occurred in a place in a foreign country other than a place such as is mentioned in the last foregoing paragraph, the birth is registered at a United Kingdom consulate within one year of its occurrence, or, with the permission of the Secretary of State, later; or

(c) the child's father is, at the time of the birth, in Crown service under Her Majesty's Government in the United Kingdom; or

(d) the child is born in any country mentioned in sub-section (3) of section 1 of the Act in which a citizenship law has then taken effect and does not become a citizen thereof on birth (*i.e.* another State of the Commonwealth (s. 5).

3. Registration.—A citizen of another State in the Commonwealth is entitled to be registered (without fee) as citizen of the United Kingdom and Colonies if he satisfies the Home Secretary that—

(i) he has been ordinarily resident in the United Kingdom for twelve months immediately preceding, or

(ii) he is in the service of the Crown under the Government of the United Kingdom.

There is a discretion to refuse registration in the case of an applicant who has renounced or been deprived of citizenship and seeks re-admission. The Home Secretary may cause minors who are children of United Kingdom citizens to be registered upon the application of their parents or guardians; other minors may be registered at the discretion of the Home Secretary in special circumstances which are not defined (ss. 6–9).

4. Naturalisation. Aliens and persons living under the protection of the Crown in protectorates or trust territories (British protected persons) may apply for a grant of citizenship by naturalisation if they have satisfied certain qualifications, which are in the case of an alien:—

(a) that he has either resided in the United Kingdom or been in Crown service under Her Majesty's Government in the United Kingdom, or partly the one and partly the other, throughout the period of twelve months immediately preceding the date of the application; and

(b) that during the seven years immediately preceding the said period of twelve months he has either resided in the United Kingdom or any colony, protectorate, United Kingdom mandated territory or United Kingdom trust territory or been in Crown service, or partly the one and partly the other, for periods amounting in the aggregate to not less than four years; and

(c) that he is of good character; and

(d) that he has sufficient knowledge of the English language, and

(e) that he intends in the event of a certificate being granted to him—

(i) to reside in the United Kingdom or in any colony, protectorate or United Kingdom trust territory; or

(ii) to enter into or continue in Crown service under Her Majesty's Government in the United Kingdom, or service under an international organisation of which Her Majesty's Government in the United Kingdom is a member, or service in the employment of a society, company or body of persons established in the United Kingdom or established in any colony, protectorate or United Kingdom trust territory (s. 10 and 2nd schedule).

A British protected person must satisfy the requirements as to character, linguistic ability and intention to reside or to serve in the Crown Service, but he need only have resided for twelve months prior to the application or be in the service of the Crown at the time of such application.

Citizenship may also be acquired by incorporation of territory in which event the Crown is empowered to specify by Order in Council the persons who shall be citizens of the United Kingdom and Colonies by reason of their connection with that territory (s. 11).

The position of a married woman is the same as that of a single woman. Thus a woman who is a citizen of the United Kingdom and Colonies will not, as was the case before 1949, lose her citizenship by marrying an alien. Such a woman who was married before 1949 re-acquires her citizenship automatically (s. 14). A woman who is before marriage an alien, or a British protected person, is entitled after marriage to a citizen of the United Kingdom and Colonies to be registered as a citizen; she is required to take the oath of allegiance (s. 6 (1)). She can only be deprived subsequently of citizenship if the Home Secretary is satisfied that the registration was obtained by fraud, false representation or concealment of a material fact, a provision which applies to all who acquire citizenship by registration or naturalisation. A woman who before marriage is a citizen of another State in the Commonwealth is entitled to registration as a citizen of the United Kingdom and Colonies (see under Registration, *ante*).

A married woman is under no disability in the matter of acquiring or losing citizenship. An alien woman married to an alien husband can apply for naturalisation in her own right (s. 10). If a married

Women.

woman who is a citizen of the United Kingdom and Colonies also possesses another citizenship, she will be free to renounce her citizenship of the United Kingdom by registering a declaration, as can any other citizen of the United Kingdom (s. 19).

Common-
wealth
Citizenship.

The Home Secretary both in the case of applications for naturalisation and those for registration where he is given a statutory discretion has the right to refuse an application without giving any reasons. Nor can his refusal be called in question in any court of law, though he can, of course, be questioned in Parliament.

The nationality laws of the other States of the British Commonwealth are determined exclusively by their own Parliaments. The scheme of legislation which has been adopted by agreement is that each State shall define its own citizens and shall declare those citizens to be British subjects or Commonwealth citizens, at its option. Thus the legislation of most, but not all States, which have passed nationality statutes up to the present contain a common clause, the substantial effect of which is to ensure that all persons recognised as British subjects or Commonwealth citizens shall be so recognised throughout the Commonwealth; see *e.g.*, s. 1 of the British Nationality Act, 1948.

Deprivation
of
Citizenship.

It is only persons who have acquired the status of citizenship by registration or by naturalisation who can be deprived of citizenship of the United Kingdom and Colonies. Apart from the case of revocation of registration or of a certificate of naturalisation on the ground that it has been obtained by fraud (s. 20 (2)), a provision to which reference has been made in relation to alien women marrying citizens of the United Kingdom, the Home Secretary may revoke letters of naturalisation granted to aliens or British protected persons, but not the registration of citizens of other States in the Commonwealth, if he is satisfied that such a person—

(*a*) has shown himself by act or speech to be disloyal or disaffected towards Her Majesty; or

(*b*) has, during any war in which Her Majesty was engaged, unlawfully traded or communicated with an enemy or been engaged in or associated with any business that was to his knowledge carried on in such a manner as to assist an enemy in that war; or

(*c*) has within five years after becoming naturalised been sentenced in any country to imprisonment for a term of not less than twelve months (s. 20 (3)).

Other provisions relate to naturalised citizens who reside continuously for seven years and upwards in foreign countries (s. 20 (4)).

The Home Secretary may only exercise his powers of deprivation if he is satisfied that it is not conducive to the public good that a naturalised citizen should continue to have that status. Provision is made for a judicial enquiry before the citizenship is revoked under s. 20 (2) or (3) and such enquiry may be granted in other cases.

Nationality acquired by birth, as well as that acquired by natura- **Divesting of** lisation, may be divested. This was not so at common law. Acquisi- **Citizenship.** tion of nationality of a foreign State does not, as it did under the Act of 1914, automatically cause loss of United Kingdom citizenship. Section 19 provides for renunciation by declaration in the prescribed manner. The Home Secretary may withhold registration of the declaration if it is made during war by a person who is also a national of a foreign State. It was decided in *The King* v. *Lynch*, [1903] 1. K.B. 444, that a British subject who had taken the oath of allegiance to the enemy in the Boer War had not thereby lost his British nationality and that his attempt to become naturalised as an enemy subject was ineffective. He was accordingly convicted of treason.

There is no authority upon the effect of an attempt by a British subject to become naturalised to a non-enemy State in time of war.[1] But under s. 19 of the Act of 1948 the attempt, if made by a United Kingdom citizen in order to renounce his citizenship, can only succeed if the Home Secretary is willing to register the declaration.

B.

Aliens.

An alien has full proprietary capacity, except that he may not **Status of** own a British ship. He may not exercise the franchise, parliamentary **Aliens.** or local, nor may he hold a public office. An alien has no right to be admitted into the Queen's realms and territories.[2] It is probable that the Crown may even in time of peace expel an alien under the prerogative.[3] The expulsion of aliens is now, however, regulated by statutory powers.

The admission and deportation of aliens is governed by the pro- **Admission,** visions of the Aliens Order, 1953, made under the powers conferred **Supervision** by the Aliens Restriction Acts, 1914 and 1919.[4] Articles 1 and 4 of the **Deportation.** Order prevent leave being given to an alien to land in the United

[1] McNair, *Legal Effects of War* (3rd ed.), p. 23.
[2] *Musgrove* v. *Chung Teeong Toy*, [1891] A.C. 272.
[3] McNair, *op. cit.*, p. 34; but see Dicey, *op. cit.*, p. 225.
[4] The Act of 1914 applied only in time of war, imminent national danger, or grave emergency. It was extended for one year in time of peace by the Act of 1919, which is itself renewed each year by an Expiring Laws Continuance Act.

Kingdom, unless he complies with certain conditions, *e.g.* that he is in a position to support himself and his dependents, or that it is not undesirable on medical grounds that he should be permitted to land. A British protected person [1] is not an alien for the purposes of the Aliens Order; nor is a citizen of the Republic of Ireland, nor a member who is serving in the United Kingdom in the armed forces of any of the North Atlantic Treaty Powers.

The regulations fall under three heads:

1. *Admission.*

The immigration officers have a general discretionary authority to grant or to refuse leave to land to any alien coming from outside the United Kingdom, but they must not grant leave to land to any alien who fails to fulfil the conditions laid down in the Aliens Order, 1953. In the case of any alien seeking admission with a view to taking employment, leave to land cannot be granted, unless the alien is able to produce a permit issued to his prospective employer by the Ministry of Labour and National Service.

2. *Supervision.*

The registration and supervision of registered aliens is carried out by the police under Home Office instructions and is compulsory after three months' residence. The Acts permit of drastic supervision and restrictions in the event of war or a major emergency.

3. *Deportation.*

The Home Secretary has power to order the deportation of any undesirable alien, if he considers it is conducive to the public good. He may consult an advisory committee in the case of proposed deportations which are based on any grounds other than landing in the United Kingdom without permission or failure to observe the conditions imposed on landing. The functions of the committee are exclusively advisory, and the Home Secretary is not bound to consult the committee in every case where he proposes to make an order for deportation under the general discretionary power conferred by Article 20 (1) and (2) of the Aliens Order 1953. In the case of an alien convicted of a criminal offence, the power of deportation is usually exercised on a recommendation for the expulsion of any convicted alien which the court can make under the regulations. The High Court will restrain an excess of this power. Thus if the Home Secretary ordered the deportation of a British subject in the belief that he was an alien, the subject could have the issue of alienage or non-alienage determined in habeas corpus proceedings: *Eshugbayi Eleko* v. *Government of Nigeria*, [1931]

[1] P. 196, *ante.*

A.C. 662, at p. 670. There is no power to expel from the United Kingdom a British subject, no matter of which State in the Commonwealth he may be a citizen.[1] Similarly it seems the court could go behind an order for an alien's arrest, which though valid on its face, was a mere sham not made bonâ fide: *The King* v. *Superintendent of Chiswick Police Station, ex parte Sacksteder,* [1918] 1 K.B. 578. A deportation order, being an administrative act and not a judicial one, cannot, however, be quashed by certiorari [2] on the ground that the Home Secretary held no enquiry: *Ex parte Venicoff,* [1920] 3 K.B. 72; K. & L. 351.

Alien enemies are inevitably in time of war subject to drastic restrictions imposed either under the prerogative, the Aliens Restriction Acts or Defence Regulations. Under the prerogative the Crown has the right to intern, expel or otherwise control an enemy alien at its discretion. But an enemy alien who has been permitted to remain in this country is within the Queen's protection and may sue in the Queen's courts. A person residing voluntarily on enemy territory, including territory occupied by the enemy,[3] or carrying on business in such territory is, on the other hand, debarred from suing in the United Kingdom, whether he be an enemy, a neutral or a British subject.[4] Such persons are enemies in the sense that they are on the other side of the line of war, and it is trade with enemies in this sense that is forbidden in time of war by the Trading with the Enemy Acts and also by common law.[5] Such persons can, however, be sued and, if judgment goes against them, they can appeal. The outbreak of war does not automatically bring about confiscation of enemy private property, but the Crown may before the conclusion of peace confiscate the property of an alien enemy (in the national sense) by the ancient procedure of inquisition of office.[6] It is customary to vest enemy private property in a custodian of enemy property and to provide for its disposition by peace treaty.[7] A cause of action which has accrued to any one who becomes an enemy on the outbreak of war is suspended, so long as a state of war exists.

Alien Enemies.

---

[1] The Commonwealth States in most cases and many colonies impose restrictions on entry against non-resident British subjects.

[2] P. 320, *post.*

[3] *Sovfracht (V.O.)* v. *N. V. Gebr. Van Udens Scheepvaarten Argentuur Maatschappij,* [1943] A.C. 203.

[4] *Porter* v. *Freudenberg,* [1915] 1 K.B. 857.

[5] Magna Carta. Cl. 41 provided that on the breaking out of war merchants of the hostile State who may be in England shall be attached without damage to their bodies or goods until it be known how our merchants are treated in such hostile State; and if ours be safe, the others shall be safe also.

[6] McNair, *op. cit.,* p. 125.

[7] See Distribution of German Enemy Property Act. 1949, which provides for collection and distribution without a peace treaty.

C.

Extradition.

Extradition relates to the surrender by one State to another of persons who are fugitives from justice. The delivery of the accused or convicted person is made on the request of the State seeking to secure the fugitive's person. It is possible for a person accused, or convicted in his absence, of a crime under the law of State A to be surrendered by State B, where he resides, as a fugitive criminal from State A without ever having been present in State A, and this is true even of a national of State B, if the relevant treaty provides for the extradition of nationals: *The King* v. *Godfrey*, [1923] 1 K.B. 24, where the court ordered the surrender of a British subject to the Swiss authorities on a charge under Swiss law of false pretences alleged to have been made in Switzerland by the partners of the accused to which he, a resident in England, was an accessory. There is no formulated rule of public international law on the subject of extradition, but the need for it is recognised by practically all civilised States as a matter both of morality and expediency; of morality since mankind deprecates escape from the consequences of, at all events, serious crime; of expediency in that no State desires to become a haven of refuge for the underworld.

Extradition is controlled by two factors, namely (1) statute law defining the grounds of, and the procedure for, surrender of criminals and (2) treaties with foreign States. In order to secure the surrender, both the municipal law and the provisions of the particular treaty must be satisfied. Thus in *The Queen* v. *Wilson* (1877), 3 Q.B.D. 42, it was held that section 6 of the Extradition Act, 1870, which provided that every fugitive criminal shall be liable to surrender must be interpreted in light of the treaty with Switzerland, which excluded at that time the surrender by Great Britain and Switzerland of their own nationals.

No proceedings can be taken unless an extradition treaty has been concluded with the foreign State which seeks the surrender of the fugitive, or into whose territory the fugitive has escaped or is sheltering from British justice. The Extradition Acts of 1870 to 1935,[1] which define extraditable offences and the procedure for surrender, require that the terms of a treaty be brought into force by means of an Order in Council. About fifty treaties have been concluded by the United Kingdom. In some cases there is no provision for the extradition of nationals of the contracting parties (though it is not essential that there should be reciprocity in this respect and British policy is to surrender a national without requiring reciprocity), *e.g.* an Italian who is wanted on a criminal charge in this country will not

[1] See Counterfeit Currency (Convention) Act, 1935, s. 4.

be extradited from Italy, if he has succeeded in escaping thither. This restriction does not, of course, affect any remedy which his own State may have against a national in respect of his crimes committed in the United Kingdom. There is one exception to the category of crimes in respect of which extradition proceedings may be brought under the treaties. No person accused of a purely political offence can be extradited. It is not, however, easy to define a purely political offence—*The Queen* v. *Castioni*, [1891] 1 Q.B. 149; *The Queen* v. *Meunier*, [1894] 2 Q.B. 415—for such an offence may, or may not, involve violence; and if it is a crime of violence, it may be political on the ground of being incidental to a political disturbance, in which case extradition will not be ordered by the English courts, or committed merely to satisfy private vengeance, as with an isolated act of bomb-throwing by an anarchist. In the latter case the offender is not permitted to shield himself behind the exception. If the requisition for surrender has in fact been made with a view to a prosecution of a political character, although based on a non-political criminal charge, such as larceny or aggravated assault, the court must refuse the requisition: *The Queen* v. *Governor of Brixton Prison, ex parte Kolczynski*, [1955] 2. W.L.R. 116.

The process for securing the extradition of an offender who has Procedure. escaped to this country is as follows: the diplomatic representative of the country desiring extradition of a fugitive offender makes a request to the Foreign Office for his arrest, sending at the same time evidence on which the charge is based, or, if the person has already been convicted in the country where he committed the crime, evidence of his conviction and sentence. The Foreign Office forwards the request to the Home Office, whereupon the Home Secretary, unless he considers the offence to be a political one, issues an order to the Chief Metropolitan Magistrate at Bow Street, who, in turn, issues his warrant for the criminal's arrest to the Metropolitan Police. This process may be curtailed, as the Extradition Acts provide for a warrant being issued on sworn information prior to the order for proceedings by the Home Secretary; but the order must be made later, if proceedings are continued. All cases have to be investigated before the Chief Magistrate or another of the Metropolitan Magistrates sitting at Bow Street. In the event of the magistrate deciding that the offender should be committed to prison to await his surrender, fifteen days must elapse, during which the offender may apply to the High Court for his release by means of a writ of habeas corpus. The surrender will not be ordered unless the offence alleged is one which substantially coincides with an indictable offence under English criminal law. It may also be refused on the following grounds:

(1) Insufficient evidence of identity.
(2) That the offence is not within the treaty.

(3) That the offence alleged is not against the law of the country requesting the surrender.

(4) That no *prima facie* case has been made out.

(5) That the offence is purely political, or that the surrender is sought for a political object.

Section 19 of the Extradition Act, 1870, restricts the offences for which a surrendered person may be tried here to such crimes as may be proved by the facts on which the surrender is grounded: see *The King* v. *Corrigan* (1930), 47 T.L.R. 27. For example, a person surrendered by France on facts which supported a charge of arson could not after surrender be tried for forgery without being given an opportunity of first returning to France.

The surrender of fugitive criminals to, or by, Commonwealth States and Colonies is dealt with by the Fugitive Offenders Act, 1881. The procedure authorised is similar to that for extradition, but is simpler. Political offences are not excluded, and there is no diplomatic application, but in practice all applications go through the Home Office and, as the case may be, the Commonwealth Relations or Colonial Office. Both the Extradition Act, 1870, and this Act operate in overseas territories of the Crown and thus apply to a Commonwealth State until altered by the Parliament of that State.

D.

Foreign Enlistment.

To enable the Government of a neutral State to fulfil its obligations towards a belligerent State it is necessary for the former to control and sometimes to prohibit certain activities of its nationals. The Foreign Enlistment Act, 1870, which applies to the Colonies and, until repealed or re-enacted locally, to the other States of the Commonwealth, prohibits (*a*) enlistment by a British subject in the military or naval service of any foreign State at war with a friendly State; (*b*) quitting by such person from Her Majesty's dominions for that purpose; (*c*) building, equipping or despatching a ship with intent or knowledge that it will be used in such military or naval service; (*d*) preparing or fitting out any naval or military expedition to proceed against the dominions of a friendly State. The last two prohibitions (*c*) and (*d*) apply to any person, subject or alien, within Her Majesty's dominions.

Breach of a blockade imposed by a foreign State and the carriage of contraband are normally [1] permitted by English law when the United Kingdom is neutral, though the Crown will not protect its nationals against the seizure by a belligerent of the property involved.

[1] See, however, Merchant Shipping (Carriage of Munitions to Spain) Act, 1936.

CHAPTER 10.

FOREIGN AFFAIRS.

A.

Acts of State.

THOSE acts of the Crown which are done under the prerogative in the sphere of foreign affairs are known as acts of State.[1] Instances of acts of State are the declaration of war,[2] the making of peace, and the recognition of foreign Governments. The term, "act of State," means "an act of the Executive as a matter of policy performed in the course of its relations with another State, including its relations with the subjects of that State, unless they are temporarily within the allegiance of the Crown." [3] Such an act is not justiciable by the courts: *Republic of Italy* v. *Hambros Bank Ltd. and another*, [1950] Ch. 315, where the court refused to adjudicate on, or to take cognisance of a financial agreement between Italy and the United Kingdom. It gives rise neither to contractual rights nor claims in tort. The term "act of State" has also been defined as follows: "an exercise of sovereign power" which "cannot be challenged, controlled or interfered with by municipal courts. Its sanction is not that of law, but that of sovereign power, and, whatever it be, municipal courts must accept it, as it is, without question"; *per* Fletcher Moulton, L.J., in *Salaman* v. *Secretary of State for India*, [1906] 1 K.B. 613, at p. 639. Such matters as fall properly to be determined by the Crown as acts of State in this sense are not subject to the jurisdiction of the municipal courts, and rights alleged to be acquired thereunder, *semble* even by British subjects, cannot be enforced by such courts.[4] Acts resulting from a treaty of cession or by reason for annexation of territory fall into this class; such acts may confer a title to property on the Crown which must be accepted by municipal law: *West Rand Central Gold Mining* v. *Co. The King*, [1905] 2 K.B.

---

[1] P. 142, *ante*.

[2] But should the Crown come to any person not being a native of England, the nation is not obliged to engage in war for the defence of territories not belonging to the Crown of England without the consent of Parliament: Act of Settlement, 1701.

[3] " Act of State in English Law," by E. C. S. Wade, *British Year Book of International Law*, 1934, p. 98.

[4] See *Rustomjee* v. *The Queen* (1876), 2 Q.B.D. 69, at p. 73; K. & L. 106, and *Civilian War Claimants' Association* v. *The King*, [1932] A.C. 14 (no right of subjects to sums payable to the State as reparations under the Treaty of Versailles, 1919).

391, at p. 409. In this case a British corporation failed to establish by petition of right the right to enforce against the Crown a claim for a wrong inflicted upon it by the Government of a State (the former South African Republic) which had been extinguished by acts upon the part of the Crown which were acts of State, namely, conquest and annexation. No interference with the rights of British subjects enforceable in British courts was thereby involved, and it lay within the discretion of the Crown to determine which, if any, of the liabilities of the extinguished State it was prepared to assume. In *Nabob of the Carnatic* v. *East India Company* (1792), 2 Ves. Jun. 56, there was dismissed a bill in equity founded upon treaties between the Nabob and the Company; the treaties were political and made between a foreign Power and subjects of the Crown acting as an independent State under charter and statutory powers; they were therefore not subject to the jurisdiction of the courts.[1]

Effect of Acts of State on British Subjects. The Crown cannot justify in a British Court an interference wherever taking place with the existing rights of British subjects by the plea of act of State, but an alleged right may be unenforceable because it is placed outside the jurisdiction of the municipal courts by the operation of such an act: *West Rand Central Gold Mining Co.* v. *The King (ante)*. Thus the treaty-making power of the Crown does not dispense with the necessity for legislation where the creation of a treaty requires a modification of the existing rights of subjects.[2] On the other hand, acts which are within the undoubted power of the Crown may indirectly have an effect upon private rights. Thus the declaration of war will render it illegal to carry out existing contracts with alien enemies; the recognition of a foreign Government may affect the result of a lawsuit depending upon the validity or otherwise of a foreign decree confiscating property abroad [3]; the recognition of the diplomatic status of a foreigner will render him immune from suit by a subject in a British court.

Act of State as Defence to Action in Tort. The plea, act of State, can be raised as a defence to an act, otherwise tortious or criminal, committed abroad by a servant of the Crown against a subject of a foreign State or his property, provided that the act was authorised or subsequently ratified by the Crown. The use of the term in such a case is in the nature of a special defence qualifying the rule of municipal law which normally prevents a wrongdoer setting up that his tortious act was done by command of the Crown.

This defence is illustrated by *Buron* v. *Denman* (1848), 2 Ex. 167; K. & L. 102.

> A naval commander stationed on the coast of Africa was ordered by the Governor of a British colony to secure the release of British

---

[1] For acts of State in protectorates, see p. 443, *post*.
[2] Pp. 213–4, *post*.   [3] P. 216, *post*.

subjects detained as slaves on foreign territory. He exceeded his instructions, since, in addition to releasing the slaves, he set fire to a barracoon belonging to a Spaniard who was trading in slaves at the place. The Spaniard brought an action in the English courts against the officer, but, the proceedings having been reported to the Home Government, the Crown adopted the act of the officer. The court held that the subsequent ratification by the Crown was equivalent to prior authorisation and that no action lay in respect of an act of State.

But such a defence is not available against a British subject. Thus in *Walker* v. *Baird*, [1892] A.C. 491; K. & L. 115:

> An action for trespass was brought against a naval captain who had seized the respondent's lobster factory under Admiralty orders with the object of enforcing the terms of a treaty with France. The lobster factory was situated on British territory. Held that the defence that the matters complained of were acts of State and so could not be enquired into by the courts was untenable and that legislation would have been required to legalise such action.

In this case the Crown tried unsuccessfully to establish the right, as an incident of its treaty-making power, to compel its subjects to recognise the provisions of a treaty having for its object the preservation of peace. The Privy Council, however, held that the allegations contained in the statement of defence did not bring the case within the limits of this proposition and refused to decide the point.

Nor can an act of State be pleaded as a defence to a wrongful act against an alien, the subject of a friendly State, resident on British territory.

Johnstone v. *Pedlar*, [1921] 2 A.C. 262; K. & L. 117.

> An American subject was arrested by the Dublin police (before the establishment of the Irish Free State) and subsequently sentenced to a term of imprisonment for illegal drilling. At the time of his arrest a considerable sum of money was found on his person. Having served his sentence, the prisoner sued the police for the return of his money. The police put in at the trial a certificate by the Chief Secretary for Ireland confirming the seizure of the money to the effect that the seizure was ratified on behalf of the Crown as an act of State. Held that the alien had a legal remedy for the recovery of the money, his status being as regards civil rights assimilated, with minor exceptions, to that of a subject.

It is arguable that, in the case last cited, the defence of act of State might have prevailed, had the Crown formally withdrawn its protection owing to the alien's treasonable acts. On the other hand, it can also be contended that the defence of act of State is never available against aliens (other than enemy aliens unless they are within the realm with consent of the Sovereign) in respect of acts done within British territory. This view was expressed *obiter* by Scrutton, L.J., in *Commercial and Estates Co. of Egypt* v. *Board of Trade*, [1925] 1 K.B. 271, at p. 290. The point was left undecided in *Johnstone*

v. *Pedlar* (*ante*). An alien resident abroad may, of course, persuade his Government to seek redress by diplomatic means.

An act of State authorised by a foreign ruler may empower a British subject to seize British-owned goods on a British ship in foreign territorial waters: *Carr* v. *Fracis Times and Co.*, [1902] A.C. 176. It will not, however, be regarded by a British court as a justification of a wrongful act committed under the British flag outside the jurisdiction of the foreign ruler: *The Queen* v. *Lesley* (1860), Bell C.C. 220.

B.

State Immunity.

The immunity of Heads of State and State property may be classified under three heads :

(*a*) Immunity of Heads of States.

(*b*) Diplomatic and consular immunity.

(*c*) Immunity in respect of public property of a foreign State.

The immunity is one from legal process, and its nature may be illustrated by the following case:

Mighell v. *Sultan of Johore*, [1894] 1 Q.B. 149.

> The Sultan, while visiting this country, became engaged to a young woman to whom he disclosed his identity as being that of Mr. Albert Baker. The Sultan having failed to fulfil his promise of marriage, the lady attempted to serve a writ on him for breach of promise of marriage.
>
> Held that as a ruler of an independent foreign State, Johore being so regarded for this purpose, the Sultan was immune from process, unless he submitted to the jurisdiction.

The Parlement Belge (1880), 5 P.D. 197, laid down the important principle, that as a consequence of the independence of every sovereign authority a State will decline to exercise any of the territorial jurisdiction of its courts over the person of any sovereign or ambassador, or over the public property of any State destined for the public use, or over the property of any ambassador, even though the sovereign, ambassador or property be within its territory. This statement was occasioned by the seizure, under process of the Admiralty Division (to secure redress for collision damage), of a packet steamer which had collided with a ship of a British subject. The vessel was the property of the King of the Belgians and carried mails for his Government, as well as private passengers and merchandise.

The immunity may be waived by an unequivocal act of submission: *Duff Development Co.* v. *Government of Kelantan*, [1924] A.C. 797; K. & L. 104. It is an immunity, not from liability, but from local jurisdiction. Accordingly when a foreign diplomatic agent on being sued for damages for negligent driving waives his immunity, upon instructions from his superior, and judgment is entered against him, his policy of motor-car insurance is enforceable by means of third party procedure against the insurance company, even though he could not have been sued except upon his own voluntary submission : *Dickinson* v. *Del Solar*, [1930] 1 K.B. 376. Even in face of a contractual agreement to submit to the jurisdiction, a State can claim immunity in an English court, but not if the undertaking to submit has been given to the court at the time when the other party has asked the court to exercise jurisdiction over the State in question: *Kahan* v. *Pakistan Federation*, [1951] 2 K.B. 1003, which left open the question whether Pakistan was a foreign sovereign State for this purpose.

Heads of States consist of Monarchs and Presidents. A Monarch of a foreign State visiting this country with the knowledge of the Government is afforded certain honours and enjoys certain protection and immunities. In particular, he cannot be subjected to the criminal jurisdiction of the courts, nor compelled against his will to plead in a civil court. He may, of course, himself be a plaintiff. Under the so-called doctrine of extra-territoriality he is immune from all taxation and his residence is inviolable. The position of a President is less certain, but it may be assumed that, having regard to the increasing number of important States having this type of ruler, the practice does not differ substantially from that adopted in the case of visiting Monarchs. (*a*) Immunity of Head of State.

The immunity of diplomatic representatives is part and parcel of that enjoyed by the heads of the States which they represent, though some writers attribute it to the necessity of such persons being free from the local jurisdiction, in order the better to perform the duties they owe to the accrediting country. In English law the Diplomatic Privileges Act, 1708, provided that:— (*b*) Immunity of Diplomatic Representatives.

> "all writs and processes that shall at any time hereafter be sued forth or prosecuted whereby the person of any ambassador or other publick minister of any foreign prince or state authorised and received as such by Her Majesty her heirs or successors, or the domestick or domestick servant of any such ambassador or other publick minister may be arrested or imprisoned or his or their goods or chattels may be distrained or seized or attached shall be deemed and adjudged to be utterly null and void to all intents constructions and purposes whatever."

This Act is declaratory of the common law and international practice, and behind it lies the principle accepted by the courts in *The Parlement Belge* (*ante*). The person of a diplomatic envoy is inviolable and is protected by the criminal law, which makes interference with State envoys a misdemeanour. The protection is extended to their families, staffs, official residences, papers and mails.

With regard to domestic servants there is some uncertainty. The extent of the immunity from criminal process could probably be examined by a court; its absolute character in civil proceedings is well established. The immunity can be waived by the head of a diplomatic mission. But a diplomatic envoy is expected to conform to the law of the land, unless it is likely to interfere with the free conduct of his duties. He is liable to be recalled on representation made to his home Government by the Foreign Secretary.

Scope of Immunity.

The principal consequences of the extra-territoriality granted to diplomatic envoys by municipal law are: [1]

(*a*) Immunity of domicile, so far as is necessary for the independence and inviolability of envoys.

(*b*) Exemption from civil and criminal jurisdiction; even the issue of a writ of summons is void: *Musurus Bey* v. *Gadban*, [1894] 2 Q.B. 352.

(*c*) Exemption from being a witness on subpoena.

(*d*) Exemption from police orders and regulations.

(*e*) Exemption from taxation, including income tax on their emoluments and on private income derived from abroad, customs duties and local rates.

The Diplomatic Privileges (Extension) Act, 1941, extended diplomatic immunity to the representatives of allied Governments established in this country during the Second World War. The Diplomatic Privileges (Extension) Act, 1944, enabled the Crown to concede further extensions to international organisations and their officers. This Act was amended in 1946 to give effect to a general convention on privileges and immunities of the United Nations, including its councils and other organs, and also to make provision for the immunities, privileges and facilities to be enjoyed by the International Court of Justice. A further amendment was made in 1950 consequent on the agreement embodied in the Statute of the Council of Europe to confer immunities upon members of Parliaments appointed to sit in the Consultative Assembly at Strasbourg. The Acts of 1944, 1946 and 1950 were replaced by the International Organisation (Immunities and Privileges) Act, 1950, a consolidating statute. The Diplomatic Immunities (Commonwealth Countries and Republic of Ireland) Act, 1952, conferred upon the High Commissioners of those countries and on their official staffs the same immunities as are enjoyed by the envoys of foreign States and their official staffs. In the case of citizens of the United Kingdom who are members of such staffs immunity can only be claimed for their official acts.

[1] Oppenheim, *International Law* (Longmans), Vol. I., 8th ed. (Lauterpacht), pp. 788–805.

Consular immunities are not of great importance, and their extent is inconsiderable.

It was in connection with immunity of State property that *The Parlement Belge* (*ante*) was decided. The law relating to ships (other than men-of-war) which enjoy immunities in international law may be summarised as follows: [1]

(c) Immunity in respect of Public Property of a Foreign State.

(i) A British court of law will not exercise jurisdiction over a ship which is the property of a foreign State; nor can any maritime lien attach, even in suspense, to such a ship, so as to be enforceable against it, if and when it is transferred into private ownership.

(ii) Ships which are not the property of a foreign State, but are chartered or requisitioned by it or otherwise in its possession and control,[2] may not be arrested by process of the Admiralty Court while subject to such possession and control, nor will any action lie against the foreign State; . . . but when the governmental possession and control cease to operate and the ship is redelivered to her owner, an action *in personam* will lie against him in respect of salvage services rendered to her while in governmental possession and control when he has derived a benefit from those services.

From the case of *The Porto Alexandre*, [1920] P. 30—a case of salvage—it appears that this immunity extends to the freight earned by such ships, and presumably to the cargo itself, if publicly owned. It is, however, not certain whether immunity attaches to all ships owned, chartered or requisitioned by States when engaged in trading, or only to ships so owned, chartered or requisitioned when "dedicated to public uses": *Campania Naviera Vascongado* v. *S.S. Cristina*, [1938] A.C. 485, where three members of the House of Lords indicated that if and when the main point involved in *The Parlement Belge* (*ante*) and *The Porto Alexandre* (*ante*) (both decisions of the Court of Appeal) came to the House of Lords it would be open to the House to take a different view.

A sovereign State's user, direction or control of chattels cannot be the subject of proceedings in the courts here. In *United States of America* v. *Dollfus Mieg et Cie, S.A.*, [1952] A.C. 582, an action for conversion of gold bars was stayed by the House of Lords because it violated the immediate right to possession of Governments who were bailors of the gold bars defined under a contract of bailment with the Bank of England. But it is not enough for a foreign Government merely to assert a claim to property; the court must be satisfied that conflicting rights have to be decided in relation to that claim before staying the action: *Juan Ysmail & Co. Inc.* v. *Indonesian Government*, [1954] 3 W.L.R. 531, where the claim

---

[1] See Oppenheim, *op. cit.*, Vol. I., 8th ed., pp. 856–7.
[2] See *Government of the Republic of Spain* v. *S.S. Arantzazu Mendi*, [1939] A.C. 256.

to immunity was rejected on the ground that the title of the Government was manifestly defective.

Importance
of Immunity
in respect of
Property.

The subject of immunity, while part of international law, is of constitutional importance, because, as has been remarked earlier, the immunities enjoyed constitute a class of persons outside the ordinary law of the land. So long as the immunities were confined to the persons of sovereigns or other rulers and their representatives, they were comparatively unimportant. The same cannot be said of their extension to property. As Scrutton, L.J., said in *The Porto Alexandre (ante)*:

> " No one can shut his eyes . . . to the fact that many States are trading, or are about to trade, with ships belonging to themselves; and if these national ships wander about without liabilities, many trading affairs will become difficult; but it seems to me the remedy is not in these Courts. *The Parlement Belge* excludes remedies in these courts. But there are practical commercial remedies. If ships of the State find themselves on the mud because no one will salve them when the State refuses any legal remedy for salvage, their owners will be apt to change their views. If the owners of cargoes on national ships find that the ship runs away and leaves them to bear all the expenses of salvage, as has been done in this case, there may be found a difficulty in getting cargoes for national ships. These are matters to be dealt with by negotiations between Governments. . . ."

The Brussels Convention of 1926 entered into by the United Kingdom and other maritime States embodied the general principle that ships and cargoes operated and owned by States for commercial purposes shall be subject in time of peace to ordinary maritime law. The convention has not yet been ratified by the United Kingdom or by the United States, both of whom still allow jurisdictional immunities to State-owned ships engaged in trade. Its ratification would involve legislation.

C.

Treaties.

Terminology.

No one but the Queen can conclude a treaty. The term, treaty, is used somewhat loosely of all international engagements in written form, but it must be remembered that such engagements are as capable of classification as documents in municipal law. Thus, just as it would be incorrect to describe the effects of a simple contract in writing and a conveyance as identical, so a commercial agreement with another State differs from a treaty of cession or from a law-making treaty. A more exact terminology of international agreements confines the term, treaty, to the more solemn agreements, such as treaties of peace, alliance, neutrality and arbitration. The term, convention, is used of multilateral law-making treaties, *e.g.* the

Hague Conventions or the treaties concluded under the auspices of the League of Nations, such as the Slavery Convention, 1926. Agreements declaratory of international law are sometimes styled declarations, *e.g.* the Declaration of London, 1909. A protocol denotes a treaty amending or supplemental to another treaty. The term, pact, has been made familiar by the Peace (Kellogg-Briand) Pact of Paris, 1928.[1]

At first sight the treaty-making power appears to conflict with the constitutional principle that the Queen by prerogative cannot alter the law of the land, but the provisions of a treaty duly ratified do not by virtue of the treaty alone have the force of law. The assent of Parliament must be obtained and the necessary legislation passed before a court of law can enforce the treaty, should it conflict with the existing law. Many treaties, however, such as treaties of guarantee have nothing to do with the municipal law. In practice it must be remembered that treaties are concluded on the advice of Ministers, who will normally be in a position to command a majority in Parliament. Once a treaty has been made, Parliament can neither change nor reject it without in effect passing a vote of censure on the Government that made it. There is then no difficulty in obtaining from Parliament any consequential amendment of the law which the treaty may involve. Treaties involving the cession of territory were at one time thought to be exempt from this necessity of obtaining implementation by Parliament, just as are declarations of war. But nowadays treaties of cession are either made conditional on confirmation by Parliament (Anglo-Italian (East African Territories) Act, 1925), or are subsequently submitted to Parliament for express approval (Anglo-Venezuelan Treaty (Island of Patos) Act, 1942). It is easy to see that such treaties may sometimes involve an alteration in the substantive rights of subjects, particularly those who live in the ceded territory, in respect of their nationality. Moreover the assumption of part of the national debt appropriate to the ceded territory will normally involve a charge on the public funds of the State to which the territory is ceded, and this, in the case of the United Kingdom, requires parliamentary sanction. Treaties affecting belligerent rights are excepted from this requirement, as waging war comes under the prerogative. Thus the Hague Conventions which modify the rights of the Crown when engaged in maritime warfare and also the law administered in British Prize Courts, are recognised by the courts without legislation.

The question—When do British treaties involve legislation?—may be answered by the following summary: [2]

Constitutional Requirements.

---

[1] See Sir Arnold McNair, *The Law of Treaties*, Clarendon Press, Part I., Chap. 1.

[2] McNair, *op. cit.*, Part I., Chap. II.

(1) Treaties which, for their execution and application in the United Kingdom, require some addition to, or alteration of, the existing law.[1] Thus a treaty which purported to confer immunity upon privately owned foreign merchant ships may deprive a British subject of his remedy and so constitute an alteration of his legal rights which can only be made enforceable by statute. The Queen will not be advised to ratify such treaties unless and until such legislation has been passed, or Parliament has given the necessary assurance that it will be passed. A treaty imposing upon the United Kingdom a liability to pay money, either directly or contingently, usually falls within this category, because, as a rule, money cannot be raised or expended without legislation.

(2) Treaties requiring for their application in the United Kingdom that new powers which it does not already possess shall be given to the Crown. Extradition treaties are in this category. Without statutory authority arrest by the Crown of a person accused of the commission of a crime in a foreign State with a view to his surrender can be challenged successfully by writ of habeas corpus.

(3) It is the practice, and probably by now may be regarded as a binding constitutional convention, that treaties involving the cession of territory require the approval of Parliament given by a statute.

Formalities of Treaty-making. The first step in negotiation of a treaty is the issue of a document known as a Full Power to one or more representatives, *e.g.* the Foreign Secretary, another Minister of the Crown or an Ambassador or other diplomat. The negotiating States submit their respective Full Powers for verification. On the conclusion of the treaty the representatives, styled plenipotentiaries, sign and seal the formal document. The final stage is ratification, which means the sealing of the instrument of ratification by the Sovereign and the exchange or deposit of the treaty at an agreed place. Ratification is a requirement which normally depends upon express provision being made in the treaty; it is an act of the Executive in exercise of the royal prerogative and is not a parliamentary process. There is no general rule of international law that a treaty needs formal ratification, but it is not the practice of the United Kingdom Government to enter into a treaty unless they mean to ratify it in due course. Treaties requiring ratification by the Crown are usually laid before Parliament for twenty-one days before the instrument of ratification is submitted to the Sovereign,[2] but there is no legal requirement that the consent of Parliament is required before a treaty is either made or ratified by

---

[1] This principle was declared in *The Parlement Belge* (1879), 4 P.D. 129, though on appeal the case was decided on a different ground. The point was raised but not determined, in *Walker* v. *Baird*, [1892] A.C. 491; K. & L. 115; p. 207, *ante*.

[2] The so-called Ponsonby Rule which dates the practice from 1924.

the Sovereign. A treaty prima facie operates from the date when it enters into force and this date, in the absence of contrary provision, is the date when the formalities of ratification have been completed. In the case of inter-governmental agreements, as distinct from treaties made between heads of States, ratification is not in practice required. Such agreements operate from the completion of exchange of deposit of signed copies. It should be noted that ratification is the act of the Crown, not of Parliament.[1]

D.

Declarations by the Executive relating to Foreign Affairs.

There are certain matters, chiefly relating to foreign affairs, where the declaration of the Government is treated as a conclusive statement binding upon the courts. Such declarations may be described as acts of State. They relate to matters which it falls to the Crown to determine:

(*a*) Recognition of States or Governments: *Aksionairenoye Obschestvo, A. M. Luther* v. *J. Sagor & Co., Ltd.*, [1921] 3 K.B. 532.

(*b*) Status of foreign States or Governments: *The Dora*, [1919] P. 105; *Duff Development Co.* v. *Government of Kelantan*, [1924] A.C. 797; K. & L. 104.

(*c*) The question whether a person is entitled to diplomatic status: *Engelke* v. *Musmann*, [1928] A.C. 433.

(*d*) The existence of a state of war: *Janson* v. *Driefontein Consolidated Mines*, [1902] A.C. 484; *The King* v. *Bottrill, ex parte Kuechenmeister*, [1947] K.B. 41.

(*e*) The extent of British territory: *The Fagernes*, [1927] P. 311.

The question of the recognition or status of a foreign State is one for public international law, but the fact of recognition may have an important bearing on the result of litigation in English courts.[2] Once the court has decided that the law of a foreign State is to be applied in accordance with the English rules of private international law, recognition of that State determines what foreign law (the current law of the State so recognised) is to be applied.

In *Duff Development Co.* v. *Government of Kelantan* (*ante*), the House of Lords reaffirmed that it had

> for some time been the practice of the courts to take judicial notice of the sovereignty of a State and for that purpose (in any case of uncertainty) to seek information from a Secretary of State; and when such information is so obtained, the court does not permit it to be questioned by the parties.

Recognition.

[1] McNair, *op. cit.*, Part I., Chaps. VII and XIII.
[2] Oppenheim, *International Law, op. cit.*, vol. I. pp. 124–52 for the subject of Recognition of States as International Persons.

For most purposes it is immaterial whether recognition is *de facto*, *i.e.* provisional and therefore liable to be withdrawn, or *de jure*. Legislative and other internal acts of a State which is recognised *de facto* are treated by the courts of the United Kingdom on the same footing as those of a State which has been recognised *de jure*.[1]

In *Krajina* v. *Tass Agency*, [1949] 2 All E. R. 274, it was held by the Court of Appeal that the certificate of the Soviet ambassador stating that the press agency was a Department of the Soviet Government entitled the agency to assert the immunity normally attaching under international law to a department of a foreign State, *semble* even if the agency has a separate legal entity. Accordingly a writ for libel was set aside. The sequel of this decision was the appointment of a departmental committee to inquire into the state of immunities under English law and to make recommendations having regard to the wide functions of a modern State. Since this country expects and usually receives reciprocity in the matter of State immunity, the questions of policy raised by the enquiry may have wide repercussions.[2]

In *Aksionairenoye Obschestvo, A. M. Luther* v. *J. Sagor & Co., Ltd. (ante)*, the recognition of the Soviet Government as a *de facto* government caused the Court of Appeal to find for the defendants, although it was expressly stated that the decision of the lower court in favour of the plaintiff was correct because at the time that it was given the Soviet Government had not been recognised by the British Government. The title of the defendants depended upon a confiscatory act by the Soviet Government in Russia operating on property then within Russian jurisdiction. Once the Soviet Government had been recognised, the validity of its decrees could not be impugned unless they were held to violate public policy, as understood in English law. Effect would be given to its legislative and executive acts retroactively as well as for the future; it would not be given unconditionally *e.g.* if its meaning were called in question in evidence.[3]

Diplomatic
Status.
In *Engelke* v. *Musmann (ante)* a statement made at the invitation of the court by the Attorney-General on the instruction of the Foreign Secretary as to the status of a person claiming immunity from process in the civil courts by reason of diplomatic privilege was accepted as conclusive. Such immunity is enjoyed by virtue of local municipal law which adopts the rules of international law, and it is for the court to determine whether such immunity shall be enjoyed by the person claiming it. But the fact of a person holding a position which would entitle him to diplomatic immunity is peculiarly within

---

[1] But cf. *Haile Selassie* v. *Cable and Wireless Ltd.* (No. 2), [1939] Ch. 182— no entitlement by State succession in case of *de facto* rule by occupation of territory by another State.
[2] The Report (Cmd 8460, 1951) was, however, limited to diplomatic immunity.
[3] See *Bank of Ethiopia* v. *National Bank of Egypt and Liguori*, [1937] Ch. 513, and p. 44, *ante*, note 7.

the knowledge of the Foreign Office, and the statement of that fact by or on behalf of the department is regarded by the courts as conclusive. There was no attempt in this case by the Foreign Office to interfere in the litigation; it merely furnished a record of what had been done by virtue of prerogative powers in recognising the diplomatic status of one of the parties, apart altogether from the litigation in question.

In *Janson* v. *Driefontein Consolidated Mines (ante)*, the plaintiff's right to recover depended upon whether war had broken out before his loss occurred. The declaration of the Executive upon this point was accepted as conclusive. "By the law and custom of this country the Sovereign alone has the power of declaring war and peace" : *The Hoop* (1799), 1 C. Rob. 196, *per* Lord Stowell, at p. 199. It follows that it is for the Crown to determine whether war exists. *Existence of War.*

In *The Fagernes*, [1927] P. 311, the Court of Appeal accepted the Attorney-General's statement, made on the instructions of the Home Secretary, that a place where a collision at sea had occurred was not claimed to be within the limits to which His Majesty's jurisdiction extended. The collision occurred in the Bristol Channel several miles from the nearest land. The effect was to non-suit the plaintiff. *Extent of British Territory.*

More complicated is the acceptance by the courts of declarations by the Executive in regard to reprisals in time of war. By international law every belligerent must establish a prize court to determine claims in regard to captured ships and aircraft. Prize courts may be established by authority from the Queen or the Admiralty. In the United Kingdom the jurisdiction is by statute vested in the Admiralty Division of the High Court in London; in practice they are set up in colonial territory on the authority of the Prize Courts Act, 1894, and elsewhere on that of the Prize Act, 1939. Within the United Kingdom, as elsewhere, a prize court administers international law. A British prize court is bound by an Act of Parliament, but not by an Order in Council purporting to enlarge the rights of the Crown, though it will apply an Order in Council modifying those rights: [1] *The Zamora*, [1916] 2 A.C. 77. The Crown may by Order in Council recite facts showing that a case exists for reprisals (additional restrictions over and above those normally sanctioned by international law). A prize court will accept as conclusive the facts recited and will give due weight to an Order in Council as showing what in the opinion of the Executive is the only means of meeting an emergency, but this will not preclude the right of any party to contend, or the right of the court to hold that the reprisals taken are unlawful as entailing on neutrals an unreasonable degree of inconvenience: *The Zamora, ante.* *Reprisals.*

[1] *Cf.* the right of the Crown to grant a licence to trade with the enemy: *The Hoop (ante)*.

CHAPTER 11.

PUBLIC BOARDS AND OTHER GOVERNMENTAL AGENCIES.

No account of the present-day machinery of government would be complete without some general consideration of:—

A. (i) the many statutory authorities with executive and regulatory functions of government which for various reasons are not directly under the control of a Minister answerable to Parliament for their administration;

   (ii) the public corporations which have been created since 1945 for the main public utility services (except water) and for the coal industry.[1]

B. The large number of bodies with advisory functions which are associated with the work of government departments.

A.

Boards and Commissions.[2]

History.   Independent organs of government have a long history. In the eighteenth century, when central control had been weakened through the curtailment of the powers of the Privy Council in the preceding century, there were innumerable bodies of commissioners created by statute, as often as not by private Acts, which enjoyed limited but autonomous powers for such purposes as police, education, paving, lighting and improvements of various kinds. They indulged freely in experiments and developments which were sometimes extra-legal in the sense that they lacked authorisation by Parliament. They were free from any effective administrative control by the Central Government; and the cumbersome control which could have been exercised through the courts by the prerogative writs was seldom invoked. These bodies were essentially local in character. It was not until after the Reform Act, 1832, that there emerged a few notable experiments in autonomous administration covering the whole country. With the passing of the Reform Act ministerial responsibility, as it is understood to-day, began to take shape. Yet

---

[1] The iron and steel industry was nationalised in 1949 and denationalised by the Iron and Steel Act, 1953.

[2] For this subject see *Public Enterprise* and *Problems of Nationalised Industries* (both edited by W. A. Robson) (George Allen and Unwin).

two years later, as a result of the Report of the Poor Law Commission, there was set up one of the most striking experiments in the administrative field without such responsibility. The Poor Law Commissioners, the Three Kings of Somerset House, enforced upon the local administration of poor law relief strict central control by means of orders and an inspectorate. No Minister answered for them in Parliament. This is not the place to discuss the history of this short-lived experiment, nor that of other examples taken from the nineteenth century, such as the General Board of Health or the Railway Commissioners. Non-departmental Boards formerly found favour in Scotland, and in greater variety in Ireland before 1920. In the early years of the present century the Insurance Commissions and the Road Board afford examples of this type of organisation in the United Kingdom. It is noticeable that the fate of most such bodies has in the past been that their functions eventually have been transferred to a government department.

The years between the wars saw great activity in this field of governmental machinery, and since 1945 the public corporation has emerged as the chosen instrument for the public control of certain basic industries and public utilities. The constitutional consequences of entrusting functions to bodies which are not directly responsible to Parliament require examination, but in a field which is still experimental it is important to avoid dogmatic conclusions, as the changing pattern of these corporations shows. So far as it is possible to generalise, recent developments may be said to be due to several motives: (1) The decision to follow a policy of nationalising a basic industry; (2) the desire to keep a public service, and particularly one which is concerned with the administration of State benefits, as far removed from political influence as possible; (3) the recognition that civil service methods are not suitable for the conduct of an enterprise on a commercial basis. The independent authority is a compromise designed to avoid political fluctuations on the one hand and the rigours of bureaucratic control on the other. There are, however, some further reasons why experiments have been made in this field. Thus concentration, particularly at high level, on a particular activity is easier to achieve in the case of an independent board concerned with the administration of a single functional activity than it can be in a government department dealing with several functions. Decisions at the top can be more quickly taken and are less liable to be changed by subsequent political fluctuations. Again, the device is a convenient means of securing uniform administration in a field which within the departmental machine is the responsibility of different Ministers in each part of the kingdom, as is the case with agriculture. A board too may be the means of preventing the overloading of the departmental organisation or, in the alternative, the increase

Reasons for recent Developments.

in the already formidable number of departments and with it the number of ministerial posts to be filled by Members of Parliament. Fuller use may be made of expert knowledge in a particular field if the responsibility is concentrated in a small body of persons experienced in that field who are not under ministerial direction, at all events as regards day-to-day administration.

The Problem of Ministerial Control.

But, whatever the motives for their creation or the advantages which may accrue in administrative convenience and efficiency, it is necessary for the constitutional lawyer to watch the growth of these experiments in relation to their cumulative effect on ministerial responsibility for national policy. There is little doubt that these agencies have their part to play in modern government, provided that each operates in a clearly defined field. But should they encroach upon matters of national policy which ought to be determined by Ministers directly responsible to Parliament? If the answer is No—and our tradition suggests that answer—then it is important to retain some form of direct control by Ministers over the policy-making activities of these agencies. This does not mean that for every act of day-to-day administration the Minister should be responsible, but that a general power of direction should be retained and that the board should not be irresponsible in the realms of policy and finance.

National Assistance Board.

To illustrate the problem the centralised administration of public assistance by the National Assistance Board since its creation in 1934 may be considered. The Board is an independent body of not more than six members. It is the duty of the Board to assist persons who are without resources or whose resources, including benefits receivable under the National Insurance Act, 1946, must be supplemented in order to meet their requirements. Originally created to supplement the unemployment insurance scheme of benefits, it has taken over what remained of the old poor law from the local authorities since 1948. It acts through its own local officers and local advisory committees. The Board has discretionary powers as to the scale of allowances, which can, however, only be altered with the approval of Parliament, which is given by affirmative resolutions of each House; Parliament can reject but cannot amend the regulations laying down the scale. The Minister of National Insurance is not in law entitled to interfere with the day-to-day administration of the Board, which is conducted by its officers, nor can he direct its decisions. He receives an annual report from the Board which it is his duty to present to Parliament, and to defend if debate ensues. The Minister is not, however, responsible for decisions of the Board's officers in individual cases of relief. For these there is provided a local appeal tribunal whose decision is conclusive for all purposes. The regulations of the Board are laid in draft before Parliament by the Minister, together with his reasons for differing from the proposals, should such a situation arise. Thus, in a field where highly controversial political issues arise, the Minister occupies an ambiguous position in relation both to the Board and to Parliament.

It must be emphasised that this illustration is not typical. Indeed it would be misleading to regard it as anything more than an empirical essay into an uncharted field. Nevertheless after a stormy start the Board has worked well in conditions which hitherto have been favourable to its operations. Whether it could survive a long period of substantial unemployment is doubtful. It is perhaps more profitable to suggest some of the considerations which have to be taken into account in order to reconcile independent authority with ministerial responsibility, since it is undesirable to lay down rigid rules for the operation of institutions where flexibility and variety are essential if the practical aim for their establishment is to be achieved. *Considerations of Responsibility.*

1. In general the public interest should be represented by a Minister who is responsible to Parliament for broad policy.

2. There should be as little interference as possible by the Minister with day-to-day administration.

3. The Minister should be required to approve general schemes and regulations and should have power to issue general directions on policy.

4. Where a board is financed from public funds, financial control is required in the form of approving capital expenditure and annual estimates. Even where a board is not dependent on public funds, such control is desirable, if its operations are conducted without responsibility to the general public at whose cost as consumers charges are borne.

5. To compensate for the measure of independence from day-to-day ministerial control, appointments to boards and commissions which are normally made by the Minister, should include persons of high standing who can exercise a detached and impartial judgment. They should not normally be confined to persons expert in the special work of the independent authority.

6. Mutual confidence between the Minister ultimately responsible and the members of the authority is required. This can be attained by staggering vacancies at fixed intervals, thus ensuring continuity of association between the authority and the Minister and his department.

7. There should be a means of resolving deadlocks between the Minister and the authority. Perhaps this can only be attained through a power of dismissal, though its exercise by the Minister save in the last resort would destroy the independence of the authority.

This is not the place to attempt any classification of independent agencies. It may, however, help to an appreciation of the *Types of Independent Authorities.*

constitutional problem if some examples are given of the kind of function which has been entrusted to such bodies. It is only by surveying the field that any conclusion can be drawn whether or not their existence tends to the establishment of a fourth arm of government, whose functions cannot aptly be fitted into the traditional pattern of executive, legislative and judicial.

In the first place there are a number of authorities which administer purely governmental services and make discretionary payments out of public funds. Such are the National Assistance Board and the War Damage Commission, which, while subject to Treasury direction in general matters, exercised a wide discretion whether the owners of buildings destroyed or damaged by enemy action should receive a value payment or a sum based on the cost of the work of restoration or repair.

In a comparable category are the authorities, such as the British Council and the Arts Council of Great Britain which receive grants from public funds to expend at their discretion on cultural activities. Arguments which are valid for condemning the use of agencies not responsible to Parliament in a field so susceptible of political controversy as unemployment relief cannot be readily sustained against their use where questions of taste are paramount. So far as the British Broadcasting Corporation is an organ for entertainment and culture it belongs to this category.

It is, however, with the third category of independent boards that the constitutional lawyer is most concerned. The production of coal, the railways and other related transport services, the production and distribution of electricity and gas, the overseas air-transport services and for a short period the production and distribution of iron and steel, have all since the end of the Second World War, been entrusted by Parliament to public corporations. Nor is this list exhaustive. Private ownership has disappeared and each corporation operates as a monopoly without the stimulus of competition (except in the case of air routes served by foreign air lines). The board of directors responsible to the shareholder who looks for financial results has been replaced by responsibility to Parliament, as representing the Exchequer, which contributes the capital and may have to bear the losses on working, and to the consumer public. There is no rigid pattern for the constitution of these corporations, but in all the Acts which have created these authorities there are to be found provisions which recognise that it is in the long run only through a Minister of the Crown that responsibility to Parliament can be adequately enforced. This is not the place to examine the constitution of each corporation. The pattern which has emerged so far is that as Minister has the power to appoint and in certain conditions to dismiss members of the corporation itself; after consulting the corporation he can give general directions when the national interest so requires; his approval and that of the Treasury is required for financing capital expenditure; reorganisation schemes require his consent. But with day-to-day administration, including the appointment and dismissal of the higher executive officials, he is not concerned. Most of the corporations function through regional organisations and the very size of their undertakings demands some measure of decentralisation. The National Coal Board, the first of the nationalised corporations, retained both by law and by administrative practice, a greater measure of central control than has been found expedient in the case of the corporations set up later. Centralised control makes ministerial direction easier; it may, on the other hand, clog the machine and increase the inevitably high costs of administration. Hence the tendency has been to increase the powers of the regional units at the expense of the central body. For example the Area Gas Boards are left relatively free from control by the Central Gas Council, whose members are, apart from the chairman and vice-chairman, all the chairmen of the Area Boards, but in this case appointments to the Area Boards are made by the Minister.

So far it would appear that Ministers have not exercised their powers of giving general directions to any great extent. In Parliament they have more or less successfully avoided responsibility for day-to-day administration. But the relationship to Parliament of the corporations is still in process of evolution. The constitutional problem remains. How can a public authority financed by the taxpayer be controlled by Parliament, except through a responsible Minister of the Crown? It must also be noted that the new authority does not fit naturally into the age-long triple classification of governmental functions—executive, legislative and judicial; this classification is unsuited to any industrial or commercial undertaking. But so far as relations with Parliament are concerned it can be fitted, as the case of the General Post Office shows, into the traditional executive machine, should necessity require.[1] *Relationship to Parliament.*

Criticism has been rife; excessive centralisation, absence of effective constitutional or financial control, the increase in Government patronage are some of the grounds for this. One question, in particular, needs an answer—if decentralisation into independent units is desirable, how can the already weak parliamentary control be strengthened? Following the recommendations of a Select Committee of the House of Commons a sessional Select Committee was set up by the House in the 1954–55 Session[2]; its terms of reference include the duty to inform Parliament about the current

[1] See generally 10 M.L.R. (1947), at pp. 233 and 377, *The New Public Corporations and the Law,* by Professor W. Friedmann.
[2] H.C. 332, 1952 and H.C. 235, 1953.

policy and practice of certain nationalised industries. The Committee
will not be concerned with matters which have been decided by a
Minister or which clearly involve his responsibility to Parliament,
nor with matters of day-to-day administration or terms of employment. Within its limited powers it is hoped by the Government that
the Committee will seek "to set up a tradition of conduct which will
result in its being regarded (by the nationalised industries) not as
an enemy or critic, but as a confidant and a protection against
public pressure, as well as a guardian of the public interest." Doubt
is permissible as to whether a body composed of party politicians
can hope to achieve this high aim.

Legal
Status.

To the lawyer other features are of interest. The principal powers
and duties of the corporations are expressed by their constituent Acts
in terms so general that it is doubtful whether they could be enforced
by any legal process. So to a measure of political and financial irresponsibility must be added irresponsibility in law for non-feasance,
though there remains the possibility of the courts restraining an *ultra
vires* exercise of power. In *Tamlin* v. *Hannaford*, [1950] 1 K.B. 18; K.
& L. 15; the Court of Appeal rejected the view that the British Transport Commission was the servant or agent of the Crown, notwithstanding that the Minister of Transport had statutory powers
of control over the Commission which were greater than those
possessed by any shareholder over a company incorporated under
the Companies Act, 1948. It would seem that this decision governs
the status of the other public corporations, unless, as is the case with
the Central Land Board, they are expressly made to act by and on
behalf of the Crown or are directly placed under the Ministers of the
Crown, as in the case of the Prison Commission which is directly
under the Home Secretary. The courts have also had to consider, in
the context of bequests to medical institutions, what is the meaning
in law of the term, nationalisation, postulated as an event divesting
gifts made to hospitals as private institutions. But these considerations are not very helpful in determining what special status in law
a nationalised corporation has. In *Tamlin* v. *Hannaford* the Court
of Appeal was attracted by the analogy of a limited liability company.
Although the Court found that the Minister had been given by
Parliament powers over the corporation at least as great as those
possessed by the principal shareholder in a one-man private company, it held that the Transport Commission was not the agent of
the Minister and in the eyes of the law it was its own master and
answerable as fully as any other corporation. Thus it would seem
that, since public corporations are mainly constituted on lines similar
to the Transport Commission and have the same relationship with
a Minister, they cannot be treated as enjoying any of the privileges
and immunities of the Crown; that their servants are not civil

servants; and that their property is not Crown property. Their liabilities at common law and by statute are the same as those of corporations which are not identified with organs of government.[1]

The fourth and last group is the most diversified. It is concerned with a variety of economic controls of enterprises, the ownership of which remains in private hands. Of these the agricultural marketing boards have attracted most attention. These are organisations, of the guild type, set up for the internal regulation of production with a view to saving an industry from financial decline. They have been criticised on account of their price-fixing powers, since the consumer is unrepresented, and by reason of their disciplinary jurisdiction over the producers, whose membership is compulsory. The future of these bodies is uncertain; during the war only the Milk Marketing Board remained in active operation after the establishment of the Ministry of Food. Some other boards are again in operation. Other bodies are concerned more with planning and reorganisation, though they usually possess additional functions of an executive character. Finally under this heading come a number of licensing, registration and rate-fixing bodies, exercising powers of a quasi-judicial character, such as the Area Traffic Commissioners who license operators of public service vehicles and approve the routes for such vehicles. The Transport Tribunal, which in the railway sphere has replaced the Railway Rates Tribunal, is an expert body presided over by a lawyer, which is concerned with fixing charges, a task which is neither wholly administrative nor judicial.

No doubt there will be many experiments in this field in the immediate future and other questions will have to be answered besides that of the degree of ministerial control. One perhaps should be mentioned here—whether the public interest can be served if in addition to the Civil Service and the local government service there exists a third form of public service, what may be called the public corporation service. This at present, while too diversified to be called a separate service, enjoys greater freedom with regard to recruitment and conditions of service than the two older services.

There are many boards which, while separately constituted from the departments to which they are attached, are directly under a Minister of the Crown. The Prison Commission, the Forestry Commission and the executive bodies of the National Health Service, the Regional Hospital Boards and the Regional Executives for general medical, dental and ophthalmic services are cases in point. All these are specialised agencies of government which for convenience of administration have been severed from the general departmental

Boards under Ministers.

---

[1] Both the Transport Commission and the British Electricity Authority have been successfully prosecuted; in both cases the proceedings were brought against divisional organs (Railway Executive and Yorkshire Electricity Board).

I

organisation. Their existence raises no special problem in relation to ministerial responsibility. It is, however, to be noted that the Regional Hospital Boards, and not the Minister, are by the National Health Services Act, 1946, s. 13, expressly made liable for any liabilities, including tortious liability, in the exercise of their statutory functions on behalf of the Minister.

B.

Advisory Bodies.[1]

Why consultation is needed.

To secure observance a law must command consent of the governed. To secure that consent a freely elected House of Commons passes the law. Neither Parliament nor the government department which is charged with the duty of preparing a Bill or regulations are necessarily, or even usually, in a position to decide of their special knowledge what detailed provisions, or in some cases what general policy will command acceptance. It is for a Minister, having consulted the Cabinet when important questions of policy arise, to determine what shall be the contents of a Bill. It is for him to explain and justify the contents, clause by clause, accepting modifications, maybe, in the course of its passage through Parliament. It is, however, but rarely that Parliament rejects a Bill because it cannot accept the general principles which are contained in the legislation. Indeed, no Government could long survive if this happened. It is important therefore, to consider briefly some of the means whereby information is obtained by a Government to enable it to perform its duty of preparing legislation.

Royal Commissions and Departmental Committees.

When it is apparent that a change in the law is desirable and the issue is one which the Government considers requires preliminary enquiry, it is usual to appoint a departmental committee, or, if the matter is of high import and time is not of the essence, a Royal Commission, to enquire into the matter and to report to the Government on all aspects of the problem. The former method is usually followed, but the latter naturally enjoys greater prestige. For example, the vital issue of the causes for a declining birth-rate was referred to a Royal Commission on Population with the object of advising on long-term policy. The conditions under which there are cared for children who lack parental care was investigated by a departmental committee. While a Royal Commission is appointed by royal warrant and a departmental committee by a Minister, in either case the personnel to conduct the enquiry is selected by the departments

[1] *Advisory Bodies*, edited by R. V. Vernon and N. Mansergh (Allen and Unwin) contains a comprehensive account of the various consultative bodies.

most closely concerned with the proposed legislation. Members are chosen, partly from their record of public service, partly by reason of their knowledge of the problem under investigation. They are drawn mainly from outside the ranks of government servants.

When the investigating body has delivered its report, it is for the Minister, or the Government as a whole, to decide how far the recommendations are acceptable, and if so, in what form they should be presented to Parliament. The function of an extra-governmental body is purely advisory, and this is equally true of the consultative committees to which reference may now be made.

The practice of consultation with extra-governmental organisation has grown rapidly in the present century. It is inevitable that the increase in the functions of government should have made the need for expert advice felt by the administrator. Nor is the need confined to projected legislation, though consultative committees have proved particularly valuable in the task of framing regulations. The function of such committees is to enable the Minister to ascertain informed opinion before he comes to a decision, whether that decision involves an executive or a legislative act. In some cases there is a statutory obligation on a Minister to consult a standing committee or named association, though it is seldom that the advisory body can take the initiative without the matter being referred to it by the Minister. The majority of these bodies are, however, appointed at the discretion of a Minister, because he feels the need for advice. Under this heading come most of the committees associated with the Ministry of Health, which between 1919 and 1938 numbered one hundred and twenty-five. By 1949 the total of all advisory bodies had swollen to about seven hundred.

Consultative Committees.

An illustration of the type of body which a Minister must consult is the Police Council. Regulations relating to conditions of service in the police forces can only be made, under section 4 of the Police Act, 1919,[1] after the Home Secretary has consulted the Council, a body constituted under the Act, on which sit representatives of local police authorities and of all ranks of the police.[1] The Education Act, 1944, required the Minister of Education to establish central advisory councils for education, one for England and one for Wales, to advise not only on any questions referred to them by the Minister, but also upon any matters of educational theory and practice as the councils think fit. The Education Councils replace the Consultative Committee of the former Board of Education, a body which, though lacking the power to take the initiative, made reports at the request of the President of the Board, upon which were based, first the reorganisation of primary education, and later the expansion of secondary education which is intended to raise the status of modern and

Examples of Consultation.

[1] P. 190, *ante.*

technical schools to an equality with county secondary and grammar schools. The Minister of Health is advised in the central administration of the national health service by a Central Council upon such general matters relating to that service or any services provided by the local health authorities as the Council thinks fit and upon any questions which he may refer to them.

The National Insurance Advisory Committee advises upon questions referred to it by the Minister in relation to his functions under the National Insurance Act, 1946, and also has certain duties given to it by that Act; in particular the Minister must submit to the Committee the draft of any regulations which he proposes to make under the Act before their submission to Parliament. The Committee after due advertisement must consider any objection made to the draft and report on the draft to the Minister who is required when laying the regulations before Parliament in whatever form he then decides to make them, also to submit the report of the Advisory Committee and the reason (if that be the case) why he has not given effect to the report of the Committee. Thus are secured the independent views of a representative committee whose advice the Minister will not lightly reject and, if he does not accept it, the Minister must inform Parliament of the reason.

Consultative bodies influence fundamental reforms, as well as serve as a source of expert knowledge on technical matters. Research and the collection of information are important functions for which departments need the assistance of outside organisations. As yet it is only tentatively that the device has been applied to the field of private law, but the Law Revision Committee,[1] first appointed by the Lord Chancellor in 1934 and re-constituted in 1952, after a thirteen-year interval, as the Law Reform Committee, the committee on the law of defamation (1939) and the several post-war committees on procedure and specific topics of substantive law mark a beginning of what may become a systematic advisory service to secure a continuous watch on anomalies in the field of the civil law and its administration. There is, however, urgent need for reconsideration of some branches of the criminal law, *e.g.* the complex law of larceny. This is an appropriate field for the Home Secretary rather than the Lord Chancellor.

[1] P. 248, *post.*

PART V.

THE JUDICIARY.

The Machinery of Justice 2nd. ed., by R. M. Jackson (Cambridge University Press).
History of English Law, especially Vol. I., by Sir W. S. Holdsworth (Methuen), for reference.

CHAPTER 1

THE COURTS.

MAGISTRATES, or justices of the peace, are appointed in each county, and for such of the larger boroughs as have their separate commissions of the peace,[1] by the Crown on the recommendation of the Lord Chancellor, who is advised as to counties by the Lord-Lieutenant, with the assistance of an advisory committee, and as to boroughs by separate advisory committees. Men and women are eligible. They are not paid for their services but may receive certain allowances for travel and lodging. Their duties are mainly judicial, but certain administrative functions remain to them as a residue of the many such functions which county justices and to a less extent borough justices formerly performed. Any court of summary jurisdiction consisting of two or more justices sitting in a petty sessional courthouse forms a court of petty sessions. Juvenile courts for the trial of young offenders are constituted from special panels of suitably qualified justices appointed by justices of each county petty sessional division or borough magistrates' court out of their own number. A juvenile court consists of not more than three justices drawn from the panel and must hold its sittings at a different time from those of the ordinary summary court and preferably in a different room. Domestic proceedings [2] are also tried by not more than three justices, of whom one should be a man and one a woman. The hearing of domestic proceedings is separated from other business and, as in juvenile courts, the general public is excluded. In the metropolitan police district of London paid metropolitan magistrates sit alone and have a somewhat wider jurisdiction. They are appointed by the Crown on the recommendation of the Lord Chancellor. Many of the larger towns in the provinces have stipendiary magistrates. The retiring age for justices of the peace is seventy-five, at which age

Justices of the Peace.

---

[1] P. 271, *post.*
[2] Separation and maintenance proceedings and proceedings under the Guardianship of Infants Acts, 1886 and 1925.

they are transferred to a supplemental list and only permitted to exercise functions such as authenticating documents and giving certificates; they may take no part in judicial business. It is the practice by the terms of their appointment to require metropolitan magistrates to retire at seventy, subject to a possible extension for two years. When a justice of the peace is incapacitated by age earlier than seventy-five or infirmity or some other reason, the Lord Chancellor may place his name on the supplemental list.[1]

Justices' Clerks.

Since the middle of the nineteenth century every bench of magistrates has had the assistance of a salaried clerk in the transaction of its judicial and administrative functions. The clerk advises the magistrates, since the vast majority of them are unacquainted with the law or legal procedure on appointment, on matters of court practice and points of law. He may not, however, himself adjudicate and therefore the magistrates must make up their own minds as to the guilt or innocence of an accused person rather than seek the advice of the clerk on that issue. The clerk, who is nowadays normally a solicitor in whole time employment as such is appointed by the Magistrates Courts Committee for the county or borough which has a separate commission of the peace. This Committee since 1953 has been given the responsibility for the administrative details of magistrates' courts as well as arranging for instruction to be given to newly appointed justices.

Summary Jurisdiction.

Innumerable minor offences are tried by magistrates exercising summary jurisdiction in county and borough Petty Sessional Courts. A large number of indictable offences (such as thefts and other offences under the Larceny Act, 1916), can also be tried summarily on the application of the prosecution, should be accused desire it and the magistrates consider it expedient. Conversely, where an offence triable summarily is punishable with more than three months' imprisonment, the accused may elect to be tried by a jury at Quarter Sessions. A person convicted summarily of an indictable offence may be committed in custody to Quarter Sessions if the magistrates are of opinion that greater punishment than they have power to inflict should be inflicted. All offences other than homicide, committed by young persons under seventeen may be tried summarily in the juvenile court. Petty Sessional Courts also conduct preliminary enquiries into indictable offences to determine whether or not an accused person should be committed for trial.[2] A coroner's court, which conducts enquiries (inquests) into the cause of violent or unnatural death or where the cause of death is unknown, may commit for trial on a charge of homicide.[3]

[1] Justices of the Peace Act, 1949, s. 4.
[2] A single justice may commit for trial.
[3] P. 267, *post.*

From the justices sitting in Petty Sessions an appeal against a con- Appeals
viction lies to the justices of the whole county sitting in Quarter from Magistrates.
Sessions, or where a borough has its own Court of Quarter Sessions
from Borough Petty Sessions to Borough Quarter Sessions sitting
with the Recorder as sole judge. Such an appeal is a rehearing of the
case. The prohibitive cost to the appellant of such appeals led to the
passing of the Summary Jurisdiction (Appeals) Act, 1933. This Act
provided that in fixing the amount of recognisances to be entered
into by appellants account shall be taken of their means and that
such recognisances shall merely be conditioned to prosecute the
appeal and not to pay costs, and further provided for the granting of
legal aid to appellants. Means are also to be taken into account
when a party is ordered to pay costs. Appeals to County Quarter
Sessions are heard by an appeals committee of justices having
special qualifications. From Quarter Sessions a further appeal lies
on a point of law by means of a case stated at the request of the
defendant or the prosecution for the opinion of the Queen's Bench
Division of the High Court, or a case may be stated by the justices
in Petty Sessions without any preliminary appeal to Quarter Sessions. Such appeals are heard by a Divisional Court of three judges
of the Queen's Bench Division.

The value of associating laymen with the administration of justice Suggested Reforms.
and the resulting economy to the State is obvious. The system,
which was upheld by a large majority of the members of the Royal
Commission which reported in 1948, is not without its critics.[1]
Many benches of magistrates are efficient and fair, but there may be
too great a readiness to accept police evidence, and to rely upon
guidance from the professionally qualified clerk. It is true that the
majority of persons elect to be tried summarily rather than to await
trial at Quarter Sessions by a jury, but this can be attributed to
the natural desire to avoid delay. Lay magistrates are perhaps too
aware of local prejudices and personalities. A recent reform has
been the appointment of whole-time clerks serving areas formed by
grouping county divisions and the smaller boroughs into areas that
can conveniently be served by a whole-time clerk.[2] The substitution
of paid stipendiary magistrates for unpaid justices was rejected by
the Royal Commission. It would involve great expense, in addition
to losing the value of the association of laymen with the administration of criminal law.[3]

Charges of treason, felony and misdemeanour are triable on Criminal Courts Quarter Sessions.

[1] Cmd. 7463, 1948.
[2] *Report of the Departmental Committee on Justices' Clerks*, 1944, Cmd.
6507 recommended this practice.
[3] For criticism of Magistrates' Courts and suggested reforms, see Jackson,
op cit., pp 139–53 and the Report of the Royal Commission. The Justices of the
Peace Act, 1949, removed some of the grounds of criticism.

indictment (formal written accusation). Indictable crimes are tried with a jury at Quarter Sessions or Assizes or at the Central Criminal Court. Quarter Sessions has criminal jurisdiction over indictable offences committed within the county or borough, but certain offences are excluded, *i.e.* treason, murder, offences, other than burglary, which can be punished with life imprisonment and certain other offences which are of considerable gravity or likely to involve difficult questions of law, *e.g.* bigamy. Conversely, as has been seen, some of the less serious indictable crimes may be tried summarily.[1] Quarter Sessions may transmit to Assizes any case which it considers should more properly be tried at Assizes owing to the gravity of the charge or the difficulty of the point of law involved. A County Quarter Sessions may apply to the Lord Chancellor for the appointment of a chairman and deputy-chairman with legal qualifications (a barrister or solicitor of ten years' standing), to whom a salary may be paid. Quarter Sessions presided over by a chairman or deputy-chairman so appointed, or one who has held judicial office as defined in the Administration of Justice (Miscellaneous Provisions) Act, 1938, may try certain crimes which must normally be tried at Assizes. Nearly all Courts of County Quarter Sessions have taken advantage of these provisions to acquire extended jurisdiction. The Quarter Sessions of those boroughs which have their own Courts of Quarter Sessions are presided over by a Recorder, a practising barrister, as sole judge.[2] The Recorder is appointed by the Crown and is paid out of borough funds a salary prescribed by the Crown. He sits with a jury.

Assizes.

Criminal cases committed to Assizes are tried by petty juries before judges of the Queen's Bench Division travelling the seven circuits into which England and Wales are divided. These Courts of Assize are branches of the High Court of Justice. The Judges trying criminal cases on circuit derive their authority from commissions of oyer and terminer and general gaol delivery. The former gives power to try all prisoners against whom an indictment may be preferred; the latter gives power to try all prisoners in gaol or who have been released on bail. These commissions are sometimes issued to Queen's Counsel and other Special Commissioners who are not judges of the High Court. Assizes are normally held three times a year in each county and in a few large towns which have their own Assizes. In Manchester, Leeds and Liverpool the Assizes are held four times a year. At the Winter and Summer Assizes civil business is taken as well as criminal, but except in a few large towns the Autumn Assize is confined to criminal business. Judges taking civil business at Assizes derive their authority from commissions of assize and have the unlimited jurisdiction of the High Court, but

[2] P. 230, *ante.*   [2] P. 271, *post.*

the jurisdiction of the Chancery Division is scarcely ever exercised by the Assize Judges. Divorce, but not as a rule Probate or Admiralty jurisdiction is exercised at Assizes and judges of the Probate, Divorce and Admiralty Division may go on circuit for that purpose.

The Central Criminal Court at the Old Bailey acts as the Court of Assize for criminal business for London, Middlesex and part of the Home Counties. The judges are the judges of the Queen's Bench Division, one of whom in rotation attends each of the monthly sessions of the Court, the Recorder of London, the Common Sergeant, and one of the other judges of the City of London Court. *Central Criminal Court.*

The Queen's Bench Division of the High Court of Justice also possesses criminal jurisdiction. The jurisdiction is mainly supervisory and derived from the ancient Curia Regis. Certain offences of a special nature, *e.g.* crimes committed abroad by public officials are tried in the Queen's Bench Division, unless the High Court (acting through the Queen's Bench Division) directs trial at the Central Criminal Court. Where owing to local prejudice it is impossible to secure a fair trial, the Queen's Bench Division may direct that a case be tried either at the Central Criminal Court or some other court of Assize or Quarter Sessions than the court which would otherwise have jurisdiction. The Queen's Bench Division may by order of certiorari [1] quash for an error of law the proceedings of Quarter Sessions or any inferior tribunal. Cases of grave importance are sometimes removed into the Queen's Bench Division in order to secure a trial at bar before three judges, as when Sir Roger Casement was tried for treason in 1916.[2] A trial may be ordered before three judges of the Queen's Bench Division sitting at the Central Criminal Court instead of a trial at bar. The original, as opposed to the supervisory, jurisdiction of the Queen's Bench Division, is rarely exercised. *Criminal Jurisdiction of Queen's Bench Division.*

With the exception of offences tried summarily at Petty Sessions criminal cases are tried by a jury unless the accused pleads guilty to the charge.[3] Such juries are known as petty juries and consist of twelve householders. Criminal proceedings in respect of indictable crimes (other than the considerable number of less serious indictable offences which can be tried on the application of the prosecution and by consent of the accused at Petty Sessions) begin with a preliminary enquiry by magistrates, before whom an information is laid either by the police or a private prosecutor. It is the duty of the magistrates holding the preliminary enquiry to decide whether or not there is a case to go to trial. It is also for the magistrates to decide whether to commit the accused to Assizes or Quarter Sessions where both have *Preliminary Enquiries; Grand and Petty Juries.*

---

[1] Part VII., Cha . 3.
[2] *The King* v. *Casement*, [1917] 1 K.B. 98.
[3] See Jackson, *op. cit.*, pp. 236–50 for a critical account of the jury system.

I*

jurisdiction. Magistrates may not commit to Assizes a case triable at Quarter Sessions, unless they are of opinion that the case is unusually grave or difficult or that serious delay or inconvenience would result from committal to Quarter Sessions. There is also power to avoid delay by committal to the Assizes or Quarter Sessions of an adjoining county. Until 1933 committal for trial by a magistrate was followed by the presentation of a bill of indictment to a grand jury of not more than twenty-three nor less than twelve "good and loyal men" of the county—in practice justices of the peace and others of standing—selected by the Sheriff. The grand jury dated from the presentment of accused persons initiated by the Assizes of Clarendon (1166) and Northampton (1176). If the grand jury considered that there was a prima facie case to answer, they found a true bill and an indictment was presented to the petty (or trial) jury. Though regarded by some as a valuable constitutional safeguard, it was considered as an unnecessary waste of time and money that the careful investigation before magistrates should be followed by a further and necessarily less thorough enquiry by a grand jury. Grand juries were abolished in 1933. An indictment may now be presented to a petty jury either (*a*) where the prisoner has been committed for trial by a magistrate, or in the case of a murder or manslaughter by a coroner's court,[1] or (*b*) where a direction or consent of a judge of the High Court has been obtained, or (*c*) by order of the judge of any court in which the prisoner is suspected to have committed perjury.

Court of Criminal Appeal.

From both Assizes and Quarter Sessions an appeal lies against conviction or sentence (but not against acquittal) to the Court of Criminal Appeal. This court, which consists of the Lord Chief Justice and the judges of the Queen's Bench Division, is usually constituted by three judges, the minimum number required by statute. A single judgment of the court is delivered. Appeal lies to it as of right on a question of law, and by leave of the court itself or of the trial judge on a mixed question of law and fact or against sentence. There is no power to order a new trial. From the Court of Criminal Appeal an appeal lies, either by the Crown or by the accused, to the House of Lords on a point of law certified by the Attorney-General to be of exceptional public importance.

County Courts.

County Courts, the chief lower courts for the trial of civil disputes, are presided over by judges appointed by the Queen on the advice of the Lord Chancellor. England and Wales are divided into fifty-four circuits; the number of judges is eighty, as a maximum. The judge usually sits alone, but when fraud is alleged, the defendant may apply for trial by a jury of eight which may also be had for the trial of certain classes of action remitted from the High Court, *e.g.*

[1] P. 267, *post.*

defamation. The qualification for appointment is at least seven years' standing as a barrister. An appeal lies to the Court of Appeal. County Court judges retire at seventy-two, with an extension to seventy-five at the discretion of the Lord Chancellor. County Court jurisdiction[1] is local and limited. In general, only those cases can be tried in the County Court in which the amount involved does not exceed £400, but there are some exceptions to this rule. Where cases are brought in the High Court which could have been brought in the County Court, there are provisions penalising the plaintiff in costs.

The Court of Aldermen [2] appoints the Recorder of London who acts as a judge of both the Central Criminal Court and the Mayor's and City of London Court. The appointment of the Recorder must be approved by the Crown before he can exercise his judicial functions. The Mayor's and City of London Court is the County Court for the City. It is an amalgamation of two courts, the Mayor's Court with a jurisdiction unlimited as to amount and the City of London Court, a court for small cases. There sit as judges, in addition to the Recorder, the Common Sergeant and two judges of the City of London Court, one of whom is also a judge of the Central Criminal Court. Appeals lie to the Court of Appeal. *(margin: City of London Courts.)*

Certain boroughs have ancient courts which exercise civil jurisdiction. Their jurisdiction is sometimes larger in regard to amount than that of the County Court. The most important are the Liverpool Court of Passage, the Salford Hundred Court and Bristol Tolzey Court. Appeals from the Court of Passage and Salford Hundred Court lie direct to the Court of Appeal; from other borough courts appeals lie to the Queen's Bench Division. *(margin: Borough Courts.)*

Civil cases outside the jurisdiction of the County Courts are tried in the High Court of Justice, including the Assize Courts. There were, before 1875, several superior courts, each with its own special province, though between the three Common Law Courts there was much overlapping. The Common Law Courts were the Court of King's Bench, originally concerned with offences against the King's peace, the Court of Common Pleas for the trial of cases between subjects and the Court of Exchequer for the trial of matters touching the revenues of the Crown. Both the Court of King's Bench and the Court of Exchequer had invaded the original province of the Court of Common Pleas. There were also the Court of Chancery, exercising the equitable jurisdiction of the Chancellor, the Admiralty Court, the Court of Probate and the Court of Divorce and Matrimonial Causes, and the Chancery Courts of the Counties Palatine of Lancaster and Durham. The Court of Appeal from the three *(margin: Superior Civil Courts before 1875.)*

---

[1] For account of County Court jurisdiction, see Jackson, *op. cit.*, pp. 23–29.
[2] Part VI., Chap. 2, D.

Common Law Courts was the Court of Exchequer Chamber.[1] Chancery appeals immediately prior to the Judicature Act went to two Lords Justices in Chancery, sitting with or without the Lord Chancellor.

Judicature Act, 1873. By the Judicature Act, 1873 (now the Supreme Court of Judicature (Consolidation) Act, 1925), all these Courts (except the two Palatine Courts) and the Courts of Assize were amalgamated into the Supreme Court of Judicature, consisting of the Court of Appeal and the High Court of Justice. The Act was chiefly directed to the reorganisation of court machinery. So far as the substantive law was concerned it marked the fusion of law and equity. The High Court of Justice was divided into five Divisions: Queen's Bench; Common Pleas; Exchequer; Chancery; Probate, Divorce and Admiralty. These Divisions have now been reduced to three: Queen's Bench; Chancery; Probate, Divorce and Admiralty. The jurisdiction of the High Court is unlimited as to amount. Judges of the High Court are appointed by the Crown, on the recommendation of the Lord Chancellor. They must be barristers of at least ten years' standing. There is no retiring age.

High Court Judges. The number of puisne judges (judges of the High Court other than the Lord Chancellor, Lord Chief Justice and Master of the Rolls) must not be less than twenty-five nor more than thirty-nine. A puisne judge must be a barrister of at least ten years' standing. Unless the number falls below twenty-five, the Queen may not be advised to fill a vacancy unless the Lord Chancellor with the concurrence of the Treasury[2] advises that the state of business requires that the vacancy should be filled. A judge of the High Court is attached to such Division as the Lord Chancellor may direct, but not less than seventeen judges must be attached to the King's Bench Division, not less than five to the Chancery Division, and not less than three to the Probate, Divorce and Admiralty Division. The Lord Chancellor may with the consent of the judge concerned transfer a judge from one Division to another, but no judge may be transferred from the Queen's Bench Division without the consent of the Lord Chief Justice, who presides over that Division, or from the Probate, Divorce and Admiralty Division without the consent of the President of that Division.

Queen's Bench Division. The Queen's Bench Division is concerned with every class of common law action, in addition to its criminal and appellate jurisdiction and its power to supervise inferior courts and judicial bodies

---

[1] The judges of the two Common Law Courts other than the court from which the appeal came, *e.g.* Queen's Bench appeals came before the judges of the Common Pleas and Exchequer.

[2] The necessity of Treasury concurrence has been criticised as an infringement of the independence of the Judiciary.

by means of the prerogative orders which will be discussed later.[1] It exercises the jurisdiction of the three former Common Law Courts. It acts as the Assizes for London and Middlesex, so far as civil business is concerned, and countless cases are tried in London in the Queen's Bench Division which might equally be tried on circuit at Assizes. It is for a Master, an officer of the court who deals with the preliminary stages of an action, or a District Registrar of the High Court who carries out the duties of Masters in certain provincial towns to decide whether an action shall be tried in London or at Assizes. Cases in which many local witnesses are concerned are best tried in the county in which the dispute arose. Trials take place both before a judge and jury, and before a judge alone. There is a right to a jury in cases involving charges of fraud, unless there is involved a prolonged investigation of accounts or documents or a scientific or local investigation which cannot conveniently be made with a jury, or in cases of libel, slander, malicious prosecution, false imprisonment, seduction or breach of promise of marriage. In all other cases it is for the court in its discretion to decide whether trial shall be by a jury or by a judge alone.[2] A jury trial in civil cases is not nowadays often requested. The history of the jury links it with cases now tried in the Queen's Bench Division. Elsewhere it is sometimes used in contested probate and divorce cases. Even in actions for negligence where juries were formerly favoured, the majority of trials to-day are by a judge alone. In cases tried with a jury matters of law are for a judge, matters of fact are for the jury.[3] Until 1949 juries were either common or special. A special juror had a higher property qualification and either party could apply for a special jury in any civil case where trial by jury was appropriate. The theory was that a more intelligent verdict could be obtained from a jury with higher qualifications; the objection which has prevailed was that political bias in one direction was more likely to influence such juries. Special juries were abolished by the Juries Act, 1949; the term, common jury has thus become obsolete, but a City of London special jury for the trial of commercial cases in the Queen's Bench Division can still be obtained.[4]

The old Court of Chancery exercised the equitable jurisdiction of the King's Chancellor, delegated to him by the King in Council. This jurisdiction supplemented the common law by granting new remedies such as injunctions and specific performance and dealing also with matters, *e.g.* trusts, of which the common law courts took no cognisance. Equity, originally an elastic system for meeting

Chancery Division.

---

[1] Part VII., Chap. 3, and Part VIII., Chap. 1.
[2] Administration of Justice (Miscellaneous Provisions) Act, 1933, s. 6.
[3] For merits and defects of trial by jury, see Jackson, *op. cit.*, pp. 65-9.
[4] Juries Act, 1949, ss. 18, 19, 20.

hard cases, had developed an important body of law almost as fixed as the common law. As a result of the Judicature Act any judge of the High Court may sit in any Division, and any Division may give any remedies available, whether they are based on the common law or on equity. Each Division, however, has in practice its own particular business, and to the Chancery Division there are specifically assigned those matters formerly dealt with by the courts of equity. They include partnerships, mortgages, trusts, the specific performance of contracts and the administration of the estates of deceased persons. Company business also is administered by the Chancery Division. There is also assigned to this Division the revenue and bankruptcy jurisdiction of the High Court. The Lord Chancellor, who is President of the Supreme Court of Judicature, though still nominally president of this Division, has long ceased to sit. The Chancery Courts of Lancaster and Durham have a jurisdiction over Chancery suits which is limited as to area but unlimited as to amount. An appeal lies from them direct to the Court of Appeal.

Probate, Divorce and Admiralty Division. The business of the Probate, Divorce and Admiralty Division presided over by the President of that Division is apparent from its name. On the Admiralty side it exercises the jurisdiction of the old Court of Admiralty, and is concerned with maritime matters [1] and particularly collisions at sea. [2] On the probate side it takes the place of the Court of Probate, which in 1857 took over from the ecclesiastical courts the granting of probate of wills and letters of administration. On the divorce side it grants the matrimonial remedies formerly granted by the Court for Divorce and Matrimonial Causes. Divorce jurisdiction in undefended cases has also been given to Commissioners, who exercise the powers of High Court judges, both in London and in the Provinces where the local County Court judge is generally appointed to act in addition to his usual duties. Until 1857 the ecclesiastical courts could grant decrees of judicial separation, but could not dissolve marriages. The matrimonial business of those courts was transferred in that year to the newly constituted Court for Divorce and Matrimonial Causes, which was also given the new power of decreeing a dissolution of marriage. There is little in common between the three sides of this Division save that both probate and divorce business were originally exercised by the ecclesiastical courts, and that the law administered by all three sides of the Division is more influenced by Roman law than by either common law or equity. The combination of probate and divorce with admiralty is due, not to logic, but expediency. When the new

[1] Actions relating to the carriage of goods by sea are usually tried in the Queen's Bench Division in what is known as the Commercial Court, *i.e.* before a judge appointed to try commercial cases. The procedure is simple and speedier than that ordinarily employed in the Queen's Bench Division.
[2] For jurisdiction in prize in time of war, see p. 217, *ante*.

High Court was formed, this Division was the residuary legatee of the old courts. A Divisional Court of two judges of this Division hears appeals from the justices in matrimonial matters under the Summary Jurisdiction (Separation and Maintenance) Acts, 1895 to 1949.

Except where it is limited by statute there is a right of appeal from any Division of the High Court to the Court of Appeal. The judges of the Court of Appeal are the Lord Chancellor, the Lord Chief Justice, the Master of the Rolls, the President of the Probate, Divorce and Admiralty Division, the Lords of Appeal in Ordinary, if qualified to be Lords Justices,[1] ex-Lords Chancellors (all the above are ex-officio members of the Court), and eight Lords Justices of Appeal. All these judges are appointed by the Crown on the recommendation of the Prime Minister. There usually sit the Master of the Rolls and the Lords Justices. The Court sits in divisions up to four in number, each usually consisting of three judges. Additional judges may be drawn, when necessary, from the High Court. The Master of the Rolls presides over one division of the Court, a senior Lord Justice over the others, but the Lord Chancellor may appoint a Vice-President of the Court to preside in one division in the absence of an ex-officio member. The qualification of a member of the Court of Appeal is fifteen years' standing as a barrister or a judgeship of the High Court. There is no retiring age for members of the Court. Ordinary judges of the Court of Appeal may sit as judges of the High Court, and, if appointed after 1938, may be required so to sit. *Court of Appeal.*

From the Court of Appeal an appeal by leave of the Court or of the House of Lords lies to the House of Lords, the supreme tribunal of England and Wales, Scotland and Northern Ireland, in which is vested the ancient jurisdiction of the High Court of Parliament. Besides its normal appellate jurisdiction the House of Lords formerly had an active jurisdiction in criminal cases, as a court of first instance. It tried those impeached by the House of Commons and peers accused of treason or felony or misprision of either; the privilege of peers, which could not be waived by the accused, to be tried by their fellow peers was abolished in 1948. The sittings of the House of Lords for judicial business are ordinary sittings of the House, but in practice since *O'Connell's Case* [2] it has been a conventional rule that no lay peer shall take part in the exercise of appellate jurisdiction. In 1948 the House by motion authorised the hearing of appeals by the Appellate Committee. This expedient, to which resort was first made in order to permit a judicial business being conducted away from the Chamber in consequence of building operations rendering the sittings inaudible, has also changed the *House of Lords.*

1 This excludes Scottish Lords of Appeal.
2 *O'Connell* v. *The Queen* (1844), 11 Cl. & Fin. 155.

ancient practice which prevented the conduct of judicial business while the House was sitting as a deliberative assembly. The Committee reports back to the House and thus enables judgment to be delivered by members of the Appellate Committee in the full Chamber. In that the practice might prevent the Lord Chancellor from presiding over the Committee when his presence was required on the Woolsack, this breach with tradition was regarded by some as an undesirable innovation. The Law Lords are the Lord Chancellor, the nine Lords of Appeal in Ordinary who are appointed by the Crown on the recommendation of the Prime Minister[1], ex-Lord Chancellors and other peers who hold or have held high judicial office in a Superior Court in the United Kingdom or in the Judicial Committee of the Privy Council.[2] The Lords of Appeal receive salaries and are bound to sit; the other Lords serve voluntarily. A Lord of Appeal must have held high judicial office for two years or have been a practising barrister (or advocate in Scotland) of fifteen years' standing. There is no age for retiring. There is a convention, but no more than a convention, that ex-Lord Chancellors in receipt of pensions should serve when requested to do so by the Lord Chancellor. On the hearing of appeals there must be present three Law Lords. The House usually sits in divisions of five or three. Appeals may be heard when Parliament is prorogued. Before 1876 there were frequently only one or two peers with judicial experience, and the Lords frequently summoned the judges of the High Court [3] to advise them on questions of law, but since the creation in that year of the Lords of Appeal in Ordinary this practice has tended to fall into disuse. The judges were last summoned in a civil case in 1898 and in 1935 on the last occasion of the trial of a peer for felony.

Comparison with Judicial Committee of the Privy Council.

It is interesting to compare the procedure of the House of Lords with that of the Judicial Committee of the Privy Council, the final court of appeal from the overseas territories.[4] In the House of Lords dissenting opinions are expressed. In the Judicial Committee one speech only is delivered, expressing the opinion of the majority of the judges, should there be any difference of opinion. The House of Lords is moved that an appeal be allowed or dismissed and the order made is entered in the Journals of the House. The Judicial Committee humbly advises Her Majesty and the decision is formally embodied in a subsequent Order in Council.[5] The House of Lords is bound by its own decisions. The Judicial Committee is in theory and, to a modified degree, in practice free from

---

[1] Appellate Jurisdiction Acts, 1876–1947. Unless the number drops to six, vacancies can only be filled if the state of business so requires.

[2] *E.g.* who have been Lords of Appeal, Judges of the Supreme Court or of the Court of Session in Scotland.

[3] P. 75, *ante.*   [4] Part X., Chap. 4.

[5] For specimen, see Appendix C, p. 503, *post.*

precedent. In 1929 the Judicial Committee examined the validity of one of their own decisions given two years previously: *Wigg and Cochrane* v. *Attorney-General of the Irish Free State*, [1927] A.C. 674; *Re Transferred Civil Servants' (Ireland) Compensation*, [1929] A.C. 242.

When the House of Lords sat as a court of first instance lay peers could take part in the business. A barrister who is a peer may practise before the House of Lords in appeals, when the House is a court in which there only sit peers with judicial qualifications. He was unable to practise before the House when it was trying peers on criminal charges: *In re Lord Kinross*, [1905] A.C. 468. _Lay Peers and Barristers._

The Commons may impeach any person before the Lords for any crime or political misdemeanour. Before the full development of ministerial responsibility impeachment was a useful weapon enabling the Commons to call to account Ministers appointed by and responsible to the Crown. There has, however, been no impeachment since 1805. The Commons now have direct control over Ministers and so do not need to employ the cumbrous weapon of impeachment. By the Act of Settlement, 1701, a pardon from the Crown cannot be pleaded in bar of an impeachment, but it is nevertheless open to the Crown to pardon one who has been successfully impeached. _Impeachment._

It was at one time doubtful whether the House of Lords could try civil cases as a court of first instance. The exercise of such jurisdiction in the case of *Skinner* v. *East India Company* (1666), 6 St. Tr. 710, in the reign of Charles II., led to a prolonged dispute between Lords and Commons. Since that time no attempt has been made to exercise it. About the same time the case of *Shirley* v. *Fagg* (1675), 6 St. Tr. 1122, established the right of the Lords to hear appeals from the Chancery Court. _No Civil Jurisdiction in First Instance._

The Sheriff Court, roughly corresponding to the County Court in England, but with a wider jurisdiction which is not subject to any pecuniary limit, is the most important lower civil court in Scotland. The Sheriff, who is a lawyer usually in practice in the Court of Session, acts mainly as an appeal judge, the ordinary work being performed by several Sheriffs-Substitute. There is a further appeal to the Inner House of the Court of Session if the value of the cause exceeds £50. There is also a Justice of the Peace Civil Court for debts up to £5. Justices, are appointed on the recommendation of the Secretary of State for Scotland. _The Courts of Scotland:[1] Civil Courts._

The Court of Session has jurisdiction over the whole country. Originally emanating from the King's Council it assumed its present form in 1532 on the establishment of the College of Justice of which its judges, advocates and writers to the Signet are members. The _Court of Session._

[1] See W. I. R. Fraser, *Outline of Constitutional Law* (Hodge), 2nd ed., Chaps. XIII. and XIV,

judges are Senators of the College and number fifteen. Five (Lords Ordinary) sit as judges of First Instance (the Outer House). The remainder (Inner House) sit in two divisions presided over by the Lord President and the Lord Justice-Clerk respectively. From the Inner House an appeal lies to the House of Lords.

Criminal Courts.   In cases of breach of the peace and other petty offences the justices in Justice of the Peace Courts in the counties and in Police Courts in the burghs have jurisdiction of a limited kind. There is an appeal to Quarter Sessions from the former courts and from both on questions of law to the High Court of Justiciary.

The bulk of the criminal work is done by the Sheriff Court. This Court has jurisdiction to try any common law crime not expressly excepted, and all statutory offences assigned to it, provided that the maximum penalties are adequate (summary—three months' imprisonment or £25 fine; under solemn procedure with a jury—two years' imprisonment). Appeal lies to the High Court of Justiciary, which is also the highest criminal court of first instance. The court consists of the fifteen Senators, who are also Lords Commissioners of Justiciary. They go individually on circuit as well as sitting in Edinburgh. Appeals against conviction by the Court are heard by three or more of its judges, but there is no further appeal to the House of Lords.

Prosecutions in Scotland.   Private prosecutions are very rare for common law offences, *e.g.* homicide, theft. Nor can a private person prosecute for such an offence or a statutory offence punishable with imprisonment without the option of a fine except by leave of a public prosecutor, unless there is express statutory provision. Every criminal court has a public prosecutor who is in the High Court and by solemn procedure in the Sheriff Court the Lord Advocate, in the latter court for summary offences a Procurator-Fiscal. As in England there are special provisions for summary trial of offences committed by juveniles.

CHAPTER 2.

THE JUDICIAL FUNCTION.

THE courts are the Queen's courts; "all jurisdictions of courts are either indirectly or immediately derived from the Crown. Their proceedings are generally in the King's name; they pass under his seal, and are executed by his office," but it is "impossible as well as improper that the King personally should carry into execution this great and extensive trust," [1] and further, as has been seen,[2] the British understanding of the separation of powers demands that the Judiciary should be independent of the Executive. It is enacted that the royal command shall not disturb or delay common justice, and that, although such commands are given, the judges are not therefore to cease to do right in any point.[3] Jurors must be duly empanelled and returned; excessive bail must not be imposed nor cruel and unusual punishments inflicted.[4] The early Kings delivered justice in their own courts. The delegation of this duty to judges was an early and inevitable result of the growth of the business of government and the development of a system of law requiring specialised knowledge. In 1607 James I. claimed the right to determine judicially a dispute between the common law courts and the ecclesiastical courts. That the right of the King to administer justice himself no longer existed was decided by all the judges headed by Coke: *Prohibitions del Roy* (1607), 12 Co. Rep 63; K. & L. 76:

> "The King in his own person cannot adjudge any case, either criminal, or treason, felony, etc., or betwixt party and party, concerning his inheritance, chattels or goods, etc., but this ought to be determined and adjudged in some court of justice according to the law and custom of England. God had endowed His Majesty with excellent science and great endowments of nature, but His Majesty was not learned in the laws of his realm of England, and causes which concern the life, or inheritance, or goods or fortunes of his subjects, are not to be decided by natural reason, but by artificial reason and judgment of law, which law is an art which requires long study and experience, before that a man can attain to the cognizance of it. The law is the golden met-wand and measure to try the causes of the subjects; and which protected His Majesty in safety and peace."

Of this case Dicey wrote: [5] "Nothing can be more pedantic, nothing more artificial, nothing more unhistorical, than the reasoning by

---

[1] 1 Blackstone, *Commentaries*, Book I., Chap. VII.
[2] Part II., Chap. 1.
[3] Statute of Northampton, 1328. [4] Bill of Rights, 1689.
[5] *Law of the Constitution*, 9th ed., p. 18.

which Coke induced or compelled James to forgo the attempt to withdraw cases from the courts for His Majesty's personal determination. But no achievement of sound argument or stroke of enlightened statesmanship ever established a rule more essential to the very existence of the constitution than the principle enforced by the obstinacy and the fallacies of the great Chief Justice."

The creation of New Courts. A similar limitation of the prerogative is found in the rule that the Crown can no longer by the prerogative create courts to administer any system of law other than the common law. The common lawyers were the allies of Parliament in the struggle with the Stuarts, and the victory of Parliament meant the disappearance of the prerogative courts of the Star Chamber and the High Commission. Even the Court of Chancery barely escaped the destructive ardour of the Commonwealth. In the case of *In re Lord Bishop of Natal* (1864), 3 Moo. P.C. (N.S.) 115; K. & L. 81, the Judicial Committee held that the Crown had no power to create by letters patent a metropolitan see of Cape Town endowed with coercive authority and jurisdiction over a suffragan bishop.

" It is a settled constitutional principle or rule of law, that, although the Crown may by its prerogative establish courts to proceed according to the common law, yet it cannot create any new court to administer any other law."

Thus the creation of a court of equity in a settled colony [1] would require an Act either of the Imperial Parliament or the Colonial Legislature. Similarly no extraordinary tribunals can be established in this country without parliamentary sanction.

The Executive and Criminal Proceedings. The vast majority of criminal prosecutions are instituted either by the police, a government department or a local authority, *e.g.* the revenue authorities for customs offences, but any person may initiate a prosecution whether or not he has been injured by the alleged crime. Certain prosecutions may, however, only be instituted with the consent of the Attorney-General, *e.g.* certain offences against the State, under the Official Secrets Acts or Public Order Act, 1936, or offences where great harm might be occasioned by a vexatious charge, *e.g.* offences under the Punishment of Incest Act, 1908.

Director of Public Prosecutions. The Director of Public Prosecutions—a barrister or solicitor—is appointed by the Home Secretary and works under the general supervision of the Attorney-General who makes regulations for the conduct of his office, with the approval of the Home Secretary and the Lord Chancellor. The Director prosecutes in certain types of cases, where he is required by regulations to prosecute, *e.g.* all

---

[1] Part X., Chap. 2. Section 4 of the British Settlement Act, 1887, provides for the conferment of jurisdiction by Order in Council on any court in any British possession in respect of matters arising in any British settlement as therein defined.

murder cases and in certain other grave crimes, when so directed by the Attorney-General, and also where it appears to the Director himself that he ought to take over a particular case because of its difficulty. He is required to prosecute for election offences under the Representation of the People Act, 1949, Part III, of which consolidates the Acts of 1883–95 relating to the prevention of corrupt and illegal election practices.

The desirability or otherwise of a prosecution is never in ordinary circumstances brought before the Cabinet, but a political offence, such as sedition, may raise political issues, so as to cause the question of a prosecution to be considered by the Cabinet.[1] If the Attorney-General considers that the strict exercise of his duty to prosecute at his individual discretion would be against the public interest, it is his duty to consult the Cabinet.[2] But the responsibility for the decision to prosecute rests with the Attorney-General, free from any pressure by his colleagues. Formerly the Home Secretary could direct a prosecution; it is nowadays recognised that the Home Office is not a prosecuting authority. *Political Crimes.*

The Attorney-General may at any time stop a criminal prosecution by the entry of a *nolle prosequi*. This power is used to stop vexatious private prosecutions, but normally when it is decided not to press a prosecution, no evidence is offered and acquittal follows as a matter of course. Its exercise is open to criticism by the Legislature, and any abuse is prevented by the ordinary principle of ministerial responsibility: *The Queen* v. *Allen* (1862), 1 B. & S. 850. A private prosecutor can only withdraw a charge by leave of the court. *Nolle Prosequi.*

Criminal proceedings may similarly be prevented by the exercise of the royal prerogative of pardon. This power is ordinarily exercised by the Sovereign after sentence on the advice of the Home Secretary, when there is some special reason why a sentence should not be carried out. The Home Secretary acts on his individual responsibility in tendering his advice. Until 1908 English law provided no adequate means of reviewing judicially the judgment of a criminal court,[3] and accordingly the method of rectifying any injustice was by the grant of a pardon. Thus the Minister was forced into the position of a final court of appeal in criminal cases, without possessing any of the ordinary powers of a court of law, such as taking evidence on oath. The Criminal Appeal Act, 1907, established the Court of Criminal Appeal—a similar court was established for Scotland in 1928—and *The Prerogative of Pardon.*

[1] Jennings, *Cabinet Government*, pp. 217–9; 177 H.C. Deb. 581–704; 483 H.C. Deb. 683–90.

[2] Sir Patrick Hastings, Attorney-General, 177 H.C. Deb. 599.

[3] By the Crown Cases Act, 1848, the practice of the judges of holding informal meetings from time to time to discuss difficult questions arising at criminal trials was regularised by the institution of the Court for Crown Cases Reserved. This court had power to determine points of law reserved by the trial judge solely at his own discretion.

thus the Home Secretary and the Secretary of State for Scotland are relieved of responsibilities which it was inconvenient that they should discharge. The prerogative of pardon is essentially an executive act and should not involve judicial issues. But the prerogative still remains and is in particular exercised by the Home Secretary in relation to death sentences, all of which by long-standing custom are reviewed. By section 19 of the Criminal Appeal Act, 1907, the Secretary of State, on the consideration of any petition for the exercise of the prerogative, may (*a*) refer the whole case to the Court of Criminal Appeal, and the case shall then be heard and determined by the court, as in the case of an appeal by the person convicted, or (*b*) if he desires the assistance of the court on any point arising in the case refer that point for their opinion thereon.

Types of Pardon. Pardons under the prerogative are of three sorts:

(1) A free pardon rescinds both the sentence and the conviction.[1]

(2) A commutation, or conditional pardon, substitutes one form of punishment for another. A capital sentence is usually commuted to penal servitude for life, if the Home Secretary advises an exercise of the prerogative.

(3) Remission reduces the amount of a sentence without changing its character, *e.g.* reduces a sentence of imprisonment from six months to two months, or remits part of a fine.

In addition to the above three modes of pardoning, there is a power to reprieve or respite sentence. This postpones the carrying out of a sentence, and is largely resorted to in capital cases pending the formal grant of a commutation, or conditional pardon; the Secretary of State can signify the King's pleasure in this way by an order under his own hand, whereas the more formal modes, which formerly to have full legal effect had to be passed under the Great Seal, still require a warrant under the royal sign manual, countersigned by the Secretary of State.

Limitations on Prerogative of Pardon. The prerogative of pardon closely resembles the dispensing power. It can only be exercised subject to the following limitations:

(1) The offence must be of a public character, and the Crown has no power to remit judgment in suits between subject and subject.

(2) The pardon cannot be used as a licence to commit crimes. It can, however, be pleaded in bar of an indictment, or, after verdict, in arrest of judgment, except that under the Act of Settlement, 1701, a pardon may not be pleaded in bar of an impeachment by the Commons in Parliament. Nor can the Queen pardon the unlawful committal of any man to prison out of the realm: Habeas Corpus Act, 1679. By common law the commission of a public nuisance cannot be pardoned until the nuisance has been abated.

[1] For specimen, see Appendix C, p. 509, *post.*

(3) A pardon only relieves from the penalty resulting from criminal proceedings, but not from the conviction, unless a free pardon is granted.

No motion will be accepted by the Speaker criticising in the House of Commons the Home Secretary by reason of his refusing to recommend a reprieve or pardon while the sentence is pending.

There are two main distinctions between the English judicial system and that of continental countries. In continental countries judgeship is a career. The young judge starts his career in one of the lowest courts and hopes to advance through judicial office and other posts under the Ministry of Justice to the highest courts. In England judges— both of inferior and superior courts—are appointed from practising members of the Bar. On the other hand the vast majority of justices of the peace who sit in the magistrates' courts are laymen. The judges have a tradition of independence and their affinities are with the Bar rather than the Executive and its servants. They are, too, less concerned with promotion. Few county court judges reach the High Court Bench. Promotion from the High Court to the Court of Appeal involves no increase in salary. *Bench and Bar.*

The other main distinction is the absence of a Ministry of Justice. Appointments to the High Court Bench, to county court judgeships and to recorderships of borough quarter sessions[1] are made on the recommendation of the Lord Chancellor who has himself always had experience as a practising barrister. The administrative business of the Supreme Court and the appointment of court officials is partly in the hands of the Lord Chancellor and partly of the judges.[2] Rules of the Supreme Court are made by the Rules Committee consisting of the Lord Chancellor and other judges with two practising barristers and two practising solicitors. The secretariat is the Lord Chancellor's department. The Lord Chancellor appoints the County Court Rules Committee and may alter or disallow the rules made by it. He may appoint a similar committee for magistrates' courts. The Lord Chancellor too, as we have seen, appoints and removes lay magistrates. In the Lord Chancellor's Office there are departments for the County Courts and for Justices of the Peace. He may grant separate Courts of Quarter Sessions to boroughs with a population of over 65,000 and upon his recommendation are appointed metropolitan and stipendiary magistrates. In the exercise of judicial patronage the Lord Chancellor acts on his personal responsibility and the doctrine of collective ministerial responsibility does not arise. Proposals for law reform relating to the field of private law (contract, *Lord Chancellor.*

[1] The Recorder of the City of London is appointed by the Court of Aldermen, and a few boroughs where Quarter Sessions have no criminal jurisdiction have the right to appoint their own recorder.
[2] Primarily the Presidents of the various Divisions of the Supreme Court.

tort or property) are the responsibility of the Lord Chancellor. In 1934 there was established a Law Revision Committee to advise on changes in private law, where references are made to them by the Lord Chancellor. This committee produced a number of reports up to 1939 and most of its recommendations have become law. Under the name of the Law Reform Committee it was revived in 1952, but since 1945 it has also been the practice to appoint committees *ad hoc* to consider changes in special topics of law and procedure.

Judicial duties of the Home Secretary. Other duties performed by a Minister of Justice elsewhere fall to the Home Secretary. The administrative arrangements for metropolitan courts are under the control of the Home Office and the Home Secretary confirms appointments of clerks to justices which are made by magistrates' courts' committees. Magistrates' courts are independent judicial authorities and in the exercise of their judicial functions can be controlled only by the Queen's Bench Division through the prerogative orders.[1] The Home Office, however, exercises the function of securing uniformity by means of advisory circulars in regard to such topics as sentences and the collection of fines, and sometimes containing advice in regard to the interpretation of statutes and regulations. The general administration of magistrates' courts is the responsibility of the Home Secretary. The Home Secretary is responsible for the probation system and the care of juvenile delinquents, and through the Prison Commission for the administration of prisons and Borstal institutions for the treatment of young offenders. He is also responsible for deciding whether a prisoner who has been certified as insane shall be discharged from the Broadmoor Institution, a mental hospital for criminals which is administered by the Board of Control (Ministry of Health). Approved schools to which persons under seventeen may be sent on conviction and remand homes are inspected by the Home Office.

Advocates of a Ministry of Justice argue that the present division of responsibility between the Lord Chancellor and Home Secretary is illogical and results in no one Minister being responsible for reform. On the other hand, to entrust all judicial appointments to a Minister of Justice might lead to obvious evils such as political appointments to the Bench and promotion by seniority rather than appointments based on merit.

The Judges and the Constitution. The primary function of the Judiciary is to determine disputes either between subjects or between subjects and the State. Judges must apply the law and are bound to follow the decisions of the Legislature as expressed in statutes. In interpreting statutes and applying decided cases they do, however, to a large extent make,

[1] Part VII., Chap. 3.

as well as apply, law. In countries where there is a written constitution (*e.g.* United States) which cannot be overridden by the ordinary process of legislation, the Judiciary is in a special sense the guardian of the constitution and may declare a statute to be unconstitutional and invalid. In England the chief constitutional function of the Judiciary is to ensure that the administration conforms with the law. The supremacy of the will of the people as expressed by their representatives in Parliament rests upon the rule of law enforced by the courts.

It is clearly desirable that judges should not only be independent of the Government, but also free from liability to vexatious actions for acts done in the exercise of their duty. It is better that private persons should suffer injuries than that judges should be influenced, to however slight a degree, in the dispensing of justice by fear of the consequences. These considerations apply to the judges of any country, but they apply with still greater force to the judges of a country in which individual rights and constitutional liberties depend upon the decisions of the ordinary courts and are not guaranteed by any formal constitution. *Judicial Independence.*

In the exercise of such powers as that of issuing the prerogative writ of habeas corpus[1] or in the trial of actions for false imprisonment and malicious prosecution the judges are in a position to control officers of the Government in the interest of the liberty of the subject. It is essential that they should be free from any fear of dismissal by the persons whom they may be asked by a litigant to control. Judges of the High Court and of the Court of Appeal, with the exception of the Lord Chancellor, are appointed by the Crown to hold their offices during good behaviour, subject to a power of removal by Her Majesty on an address presented to Her Majesty by both Houses of Parliament: Supreme Court of Judicature Act, 1925, s. 12.[2] A similar provision applies to Lords of Appeal: Appellate Jurisdiction Act, 1876, s. 6.[3] Judges' salaries are fixed and are charged and paid out of the Consolidated Fund[4]: Supreme Court of Judicature Act, 1925, ss. 13 and 15; Judges' Remuneration Act, 1954. The salary of the Lord Chancellor is such yearly sum as with the amount payable to him as Speaker of the House of Lords (£4,000) makes up the sum of £12,000 a year; the salary of the Lord Chief Justice is £10,000 a year; of Lords of Appeal and the Master of the Rolls £9,000 a year; of Lords Justices of Appeal and Judges of the High Court £8,000 a year. The salaries of County Court judges are *Appointment and Dismissal of Judges.*

---

[1] Part VIII., Chap. 1.
[2] For similar repealed provision of the Act of Settlement, see p. 7, *ante*. Prior to the Act of Settlement judges were from 1625 to 1640 and after 1688 appointed during good behaviour and thus tenure of office was not at the King's pleasure.
[3] P. 240, *ante*.   [4] P. 182, *ante*.

£2,800 a year and of Metropolitan Magistrates £2,500 [1]; these salaries are also charged on the Consolidated Fund.

Procedure for Removal. Offices held during good behaviour could formerly in the event of misconduct be determined without an address to the Crown by *scire facias*, criminal information or impeachment.[2] An address to the Crown for the removal of a judge must originate in the House of Commons. The procedure is judicial and the judge is entitled to be heard. There is only one instance of the removal of a judge by this method since it was introduced by the Act of Settlement. County Court judges are appointed by the Lord Chancellor from barristers of at least seven years' standing and may be removed by him for inability or misbehaviour. Magistrates may be removed from the commission of the peace by the Lord Chancellor, though in practice a magistrate is not removed unless his conduct becomes scandalous.[3]

Judicial Salaries. The Act of Settlement provided that the salaries of the judges shall be ascertained and established, though this principle was not fully implemented until the Judicature Acts in the nineteenth century. It is perhaps unsatisfactory that, though an address by both Houses of Parliament is required to secure the removal of a judge, under the provisions of the Parliament Act, 1911, the House of Commons alone might reduce a judge's salary by any amount.[4] Under the constitutions of the Commonwealth of Australia and of the Republic of Ireland judges' salaries may not be diminished during tenure of office.

Scotland. Judges of the Court of Session are appointed by the Crown for life and cannot be removed except on grounds of misconduct (*ad vitam aut culpam*): Claim of Right, 1689. There is no statutory provision for the removal of judges of the Court of Session, but sheriffs, sheriffs-substitute and stipendiary magistrates may be removed by the Secretary of State for Scotland on a report by the Lord President and the Lord Justice-Clerk.

Judicial Immunity from Civil Actions. It is a general proposition of the common law that no action will lie against a judge for any acts done or words spoken in his judicial capacity in a court of justice. "It is essential in all courts that the judges who are appointed to administer the law should be permitted to administer it under the protection of the law independently and

---

[1] Judicial Officers (Salaries) Act, 1952. All judicial salaries are pensionable, subject to various qualifying periods of service before a pension can be claimed as of right.

[2] The processes of *scire facias* and criminal information were abolished in 1947: Crown Proceedings Act, 1947, 1st Schedule. For impeachment, see pp. 241, *ante*.

[3] For supplemental list, see p. 230, *ante*.

[4] Judges' salaries were included in salary reductions effected by Order in Council made under the National Economy Act, 1931; see Sir William Holdsworth in 48 *L.Q.R.* 25; E. C. S. Wade in *Law Times*, April 2 and 9, 1932. and reply by Sir William Holdsworth, *Law Times*, May 7, 1932.

freely, without favour and without fear. This provision of the law
is not for the protection or benefit of a malicious or corrupt judge,
but for the benefit of the public, whose interest it is that the judges
shall be at liberty to exercise their functions with independence
and without fear of consequences": *Scott* v. *Stansfield* (1868), L.R.
3 Ex. 220, *per* Kelly, C.B., at p. 223. It can be argued from the
authorities that the judge of a court of record is not liable for anything done or said in the exercise of his judicial functions, even if he
exceeds his jurisdiction.

In the case of acts done within the jurisdiction the immunity
exists, however malicious, corrupt or oppressive be the acts or words
complained of: *Anderson* v. *Gorrie*, [1895] 1 Q.B. 668; K. & L. 236.
Immunity does not attach to a ministerial, as opposed to a judicial,
act. Thus an action lies for a wrongful refusal to hear a case, but
not for a wrongful decision: *Ferguson* v. *Earl of Kinnoull* (1842),
9 Cl. & F. 251; K. & L. 280. Moreover a judge is not liable where
he exceeds his jurisdiction owing to a mistake of fact, unless he ought
to have known the facts ousting his jurisdiction: *Calder* v. *Halkett*
(1839), 3 Moo. P.C. 28. A similar immunity to that of judges
attaches to the verdicts of juries: *Bushell's Case* (1670), 6 St. Tr. 999;
and to words spoken by parties, counsel and witnesses in the course
of judicial proceedings. *[Scope of Immunity.]*

The same immunity exists in the case of inferior courts, *e.g.* county
courts and magistrates' courts: *Law* v. *Llewellyn*, [1906] 1 K.B. 487,
where it was held that no action lies against a justice of the peace
in respect of defamatory words spoken by him when exercising
judicial functions. Even when a justice is sued in respect of his
performance of administrative duties, it is necessary to prove that
he acted maliciously and without reasonable or probable cause.[1]
When a magistrate acts outside his jurisdiction it is unnecessary to
prove malice, but no action may be brought in respect of anything
done under a conviction until the conviction has been quashed.[2]
The absolute protection given to members of courts acting within
their jurisdiction attaches also to members of tribunals which have
the attributes of a court, *e.g.* a court-martial.[3] Where a tribunal does
not have the attributes of a court, its decisions and words spoken in
the course of its proceedings are privileged only in the absence of
malice, even though it is under a duty to act judicially, *e.g.* London
County Council when sitting to grant music licences: *Royal Aquarium
and Summer and Winter Garden Society Ltd.* v. *Parkinson*, [1892]
1 Q.B. 431: K. & L. 202. *[Inferior Courts.]*

[1] Justices Protection Act, 1848, s. 1; *Everett* v. *Griffiths*, [1921] 1 A.C. 631, at
p. 666. Crown Proceedings Act, 1947, s. 2 (5), absolves the Crown from liability
for the acts of any person discharging judicial duties or executing judicial process.
[2] Justices Protection Act, 1848, s. 2. See L. A. Sheridan, *Protection of Justices*,
14 M.L.R. 267.   [3] And to counsel, witnesses and parties.

Scotland.   In Scotland a magistrate or justice of the peace will be liable in damages for acting without or in excess of jurisdiction provided that the conviction has been quashed and malice and want of reasonable and probable cause established: Summary Jurisdiction (Scotland) Act, 1908, s. 59. The action must be brought within two months of the proceedings complained of.

Criminal Liability of Judges.   The criminal law punishes corruption, neglect of duty or misconduct in the execution of judicial duties. The overriding importance of the protection of the liberty of the subject is shown by the fact that a High Court judge who unlawfully refuses to issue a writ of habeas corpus during vacation is liable to a fine of £500 to be paid to the person detained.

> *Note.*—No attempt has been made to give more than an outline of the judicial organisation. For a full account together with criticisms and suggestions for reform the student should read *The Machinery of Justice*, by R. M. Jackson (2nd edn.) (Cambridge University Press) and, as regards magistrates' courts the Report of the Royal Commission on Justices of the Peace, 1946–48 (Cmd. 7463, 1948).

PART VI.

LOCAL GOVERNMENT.

Principles of Local Government Law, 3rd ed., by Sir Ivor Jennings (University of London Press).
An Introduction to the Law of Local Government and Administration, 5th ed., by W. O. Hart (Butterworth).
Local Government, by Sir John Maud (Home University Library).
The Development of Local Government (3rd ed.) by W. A. Robson (George Allen and Unwin).

CHAPTER 1.

GENERAL FEATURES.

A.

Development of Local Government.

IT is doubtful whether even the oldest of our central organs of government can be traced back to an earlier time than the reign of William the Conqueror, but our present counties and parishes find their origin in the shires and hundreds, vills or townships of pre-Norman days. The central government of England was largely superimposed upon existing local organisation. Modern legislative reforms have recognised local government as an established fact and our present local government areas, outside the industrial towns, largely reflect ancient conditions.[1]

Antiquity of Local Government.

In the early Middle Ages each county or shire had its court or governmental assembly, presided over by the sheriff as the royal representative and composed of the freemen of the county. The county court performed general governmental as well as judicial functions. Within the county were hundred courts similarly composed and under the supervision of the sheriff. The manorial courts of the feudal system were the courts of the smaller units, the vill and the township. Boroughs which obtained charters from the Crown possessed varying degrees of autonomy. The justices in eyre, royal judges with wide powers both administrative and judicial, controlled the local courts by means of periodic visitations. From the time of Henry II. onwards royal justice began to cover the whole

Early Middle Ages.

[1] For the history of Local Government, see Hart, *op. cit.*, Part I., Chap. I.

country through the circuits of justices of assize and general gaol-delivery. The local and manorial courts were superseded and with them the office of sheriff lost much of its former importance.

Justices of the Peace.

From the fourteenth century the newly created justices of the peace acquired administrative as well as police powers. The parish, an ecclesiastical unit, also became the unit of local administration, just as in earlier times the feudal manor had given an organisation to the vills or townships. It was the parish which was liable for the repair of roads and later for the administration of the Elizabethan poor law. Justices exercised control over the parish and its officers. The justices themselves were controlled by the Council and the Court of Star Chamber, but this influence disappeared with the curtailment by the Long Parliament in 1640 of the powers of the former body and the abolition of the latter.

Eighteenth Century.

No attempt was made after the Revolution Settlement in 1689 to re-impose central administrative control. Apart from the boroughs, which were largely autonomous acting under their charter powers, general local administration was in the hands of the county justices sitting in Quarter Sessions. Judicial control existed by means of the prerogative writs of mandamus, certiorari and prohibition issued by the Court of King's Bench.[1] It was during this century that there was developed the device of the *ad hoc* authority—a separate body for a particular service as opposed to the general administrative authorities, the justices. At first by means of local Acts and later by public measures applying to the whole country Parliament sanctioned the creation especially in urban areas of *ad hoc* authorities for different purposes, *e.g.* commissioners of sewers and improvement commissioners.

Era of Reform.

With the Report of the Poor Law Commissioners in 1834 there opened an era of local government reform. By the Poor Law Act, 1834, there were established *ad hoc* authorities (boards of guardians) to administer the reformed poor law and at the same time there was re-imposed central control through the Poor Law Commissioners —a body of three officials of the Central Government with no Minister responsible to Parliament for their activities.[2] Other reforms followed. The boroughs underwent a drastic reorganisation under the Municipal Corporations Act, 1835, and became reformed units of administration governed by councils elected on a uniform franchise, though the enlargement of their powers came later, especially from the Public Health Act, 1875.

Elected all purposes Authorities.

By the end of the nineteenth century the all purposes authority elected on a wide franchise was in the process of superseding the

[1] Part VII., Chap. 3.
[2] Their functions were in 1847 transferred to a Poor Law Board responsible to Parliament through its President, a Minister of the Crown.

ad hoc authority as the administrative agency of the main services of local government. The Municipal Corporations Act, 1882, like the Act of 1835, was primarily concerned with internal organisation and corporate property. The Act of 1835 had secured that all borough councils should be elected on a wide franchise. The 1882 Act was a consolidating measure and conferred few powers of local government. While it strengthened the organisation of the more efficient authorities and thus indirectly contributed to the super-session of the *ad hoc* authority, it did not result in any considerable transfer of powers. The Local Government Act, 1888, transferred to elected county councils the administrative powers of Quarter Sessions. The Local Government Act, 1894, converted into elected urban district councils the urban sanitary authorities which had been set up under various Public Health Acts and established elected rural district councils, to which were transferred the public health functions of the boards of guardians. Thus highways and public health became services of the all purposes authorities. Early in the twentieth century education, and in 1929 the poor law, thenceforth known as public assistance, were transferred to such authorities.

Ad hoc authorities were, however, established for various purposes through the nineteenth century, *e.g.* the school boards by the Education Act, 1870, which endured until the larger all purposes authorities became local education authorities in 1902. The principal remaining *ad hoc* authorities, the boards of guardians, were abolished by the Local Government Act, 1929, which transferred their functions to county and county borough councils, but *ad hoc* authorities remained for a few special purposes, *e.g.* land drainage. Moreover for certain purposes *ad hoc* districts not corresponding to the normal county districts have been created, *e.g.* the catchment areas for land drainage administered by river boards. Under the Education Act, 1944, the local education authorities are the county and county borough councils. In order to preserve and extend local initiative in the county areas county councils were required to draw up schemes of divisional administration for the delegation of certain of their functions to divisional executives. Boroughs and urban districts with a population of not less than 60,000, or a school population of not less than 7,000, could claim to be excepted and be given the functions elsewhere performed by a divisional executive. In special circumstances the Minister may confer a similar right on other boroughs or urban districts.

For many matters too co-operation between areas is essential for administrative efficiency and economy and the principle of the *ad hoc* authority has tended to reappear in the shape of joint committees or joint boards. A joint committee, *e.g.* a maternity and child welfare committee of two public health authorities, is a committee to

Joint Committees and Boards.

which different authorities appoint representatives who are responsible to the appointing authorities. The use of joint committees enables services to be administered in areas most fitted to produce efficiency without any sacrifice of the convenience and symmetry secured by the maintenance of a uniform system of all purposes local authorities. A joint board, *e.g.* a board set up by the Minister of Housing and Local Government to govern two or more districts unified for any public health purposes, is, when once appointed, a separate entity with powers of its own.[1]

Central Control.

The Poor Law Act of 1834 imposed central control upon local authorities and the poor law under its modern name of public assistance remained, until its abolition by the National Assistance Act, 1948, a service where direct control was imposed, but in modern times the control was that of a Minister responsible to Parliament and not that of an independent board.[2] The Municipal Corporations Acts of 1835 and of 1882 and the Local Government Acts of 1888 and 1894 imposed but little central control, but in respect of particular services, *e.g.* public health, housing, education and town and country planning there has been a steady advance towards central control partly by indirect, though effective, means.[3] In 1872 there was established the Local Government Board and as a result poor law and public health came under one central control though only in the case of the poor law was the control direct.

B.

Characteristics of Local Authorities.

What is Local Government?

There is no hard-and-fast dividing line between the services administered by central and local government. In the main matters of local rather than national importance are entrusted to local authorities, but many services are administered by the local representatives of central authorities which, had they been established earlier, might have been entrusted to local authorities. Some modern services, *e.g.* national insurance, widows', orphans' and old age pensions and national assistance are so administered. Nevertheless, new functions are also constantly placed up on county and county borough authorities by Parliament, usually accompanied by provision out of the Exchequer to meet part of the cost. Older services, *e.g.* public health, police and highways, are mainly administered by locally elected bodies. Education, which in a strictly logical system should be a national service, is administered by the local education authorities, but by inspection, regulation and supervision

---

[1] Hart, *op. cit.*, pp. 135–8.   [2] P. 254, *ante*, note 2.
[3] Pp. 260–63, *post*.

the Minister of Education since 1944 controls and directs the execution by local education authorities of a national policy.

The prerogative plays no part in local government, and local authorities, though representative bodies chosen by popular election, have not the autonomy of Parliament. Even on matters admittedly of local rather than national interest they cannot determine their own powers. These powers are derived from statutes and exercised subject to the *ultra vires* rule. Within the limits of its powers a local authority may act as it pleases provided that it performs the specific administrative duties imposed upon it and subject always to the pressure that the central government can bring to bear through supervision, withholding of grants, and, in the last resort, by the exercise of default powers.

Powers of Local Authorities.

Up to the Second World War the cleavage due to party issues was less marked in local than in national affairs, though there were party divisions, at all events in London and most boroughs. Politics play an increasing part in local elections, but the policy of a council is less susceptible to changes due to political influence. There is more continuity of personnel. Members are elected for fixed periods and usually are re-elected from time to time if they offer themselves for re-election. County and borough councils elect aldermen, who hold office for a longer period than elected councillors and consequently may have considerable sway in the direction of policy and preservation of continuity. The chairmen of all local authorities and of their principal committees tend to be men with long experience of the work.

Party Politics.

Local elected authorities mainly perform administrative functions. Within their powers they determine policy and they have power to enact by-laws, subject to the sanction of the appropriate government department. They are, however, chiefly concerned with the maintenance of public services which they are by law required to administer. The work of the larger councils is conducted through committees. Most matters are initiated in committee. Even the general policy of a council arises on a committee report rather than at the outset by resolution of the council. Most communications addressed to a council are sent to the appropriate committee and are never seen by the council as a whole. It would be impossible to carry on the work of the larger local authorities if the committee system had not been adopted.

Committees.

No payment is made generally to members of elected local authorities in return for their services. But the Local Government Act, 1948, permits reasonable travelling and subsistence allowances to be paid in certain cases which except in the case of county and rural district councils exclude allowances for attendance at ordinary meetings of the council or its committees. In addition financial loss allowances

Local Government Officers.

K

may be paid to members to cover loss of earnings and additional expense (other than travel and subsistence) incurred on approved council business; this includes attendance at meetings. Elected councillors render only part-time service. It is difficult for busy men and especially for those who are employees to give much time to local government work, and the days of a leisured class with ample time for gratuitous public service have passed away. Inevitably there results an increase in the influence of the paid official. The direction of policy is the task of the elected representative; its execution that of the permanent official. A local government officer is more closely controlled by the committee to which he is responsible than are civil servants by Ministers. Committees do not confine themselves to policy, but supervise the administrative work for which they are responsible. Where there is a capable chairman of a committee, there is little danger that the permanent official will direct policy overmuch. Indeed there is more danger that committee members will be too active in matters of routine which are better left to permanent officials.[1]

Appointment of Officers. The officers of local authorities are not members of a single public service, as are civil servants, but a local authority recruits its staff independently, and at present the system of recruitment falls short of the carefully contrived system of the Civil Service. Officers are responsible to the elected bodies by which they are appointed, though in some cases the appointing authority is anomalously not liable for the acts of its servants where the latter are guilty of negligence in the performance of duties placed by statute upon them as agents of the central government.[2] There is an obligation to appoint certain officials. Thus both a county and a borough council must appoint a clerk, a treasurer, a medical officer of health and a surveyor. A borough must also appoint a sanitary inspector. A county council and a county borough council must also appoint a chief education officer and a children's officer.

The Redistribution of Functions. We have seen how by 1930 the *ad hoc* authority had for the time being, with a few exceptions, been superseded by the all purposes authority. There is, however, no finality in the distribution of functions between the various authorities. The Central Government encroaches upon local authorities, and larger authorities absorb the powers of smaller authorities. Certain matters once reasonably entrusted to local authorities become of importance to the nation as a whole or require the application of a uniform national policy. Certain services are used by the nation as a whole and cannot rightly remain a charge upon local areas. Thus relief of the able-bodied unemployed became a national service with the setting-up

[1] *Cf.* Jennings, *op. cit.*, Chap V. (1).
[2] *Stanbury* v. *Exeter Corporation*, [1905] 2 K.B. 838; Part VII., Chap. 2.

of the Assistance Board in 1934, and certain trunk roads were transferred in 1936 to the Minister of Transport. The importance of fire services to the Civil Defence during the Second World War led to their amalgamation into a National Fire Service under the Home Office, but in 1948 the Service was again transferred to local authorities (county and county borough councils). As reconstruction plans began to take shape there was seen a marked tendency to deprive local authorities, and particularly the smaller ones, of their powers in the interests of efficiency and uniform administration. Even where there is no pressure for the transfer of powers to the Central Government, there is pressure for the transfer of vital services to the larger authorities and the creation of larger areas. Since 1945 the larger authorities (county and county borough councils) have lost to the Central Government their hospital and public assistance services and in borough areas all the electricity and gas undertakings of the local authorities were transferred to nationalised boards in 1948. County councils have acquired responsibility for (*inter alia*) town and country planning and fire services, the former at the expense of the district councils. All borough councils have acquired new powers in relation to the provision of entertainments, publicity services and civic restaurants. The National Health Service has added a range of *ad hoc* authorities under the direction and control of the Minister of Health and has deprived local authorities of certain public health powers as well as of the hospital services.

It is difficult to equate the comparative inefficency and penury of a poor agricultural county or a small borough in a rural area with the efficiency and wealth of a prosperous and autonomous urban area of the size, say, of Birmingham. On the other hand as areas become larger, local patriotism becomes less and there is no longer direct contact between the citizen and his local councillor. If the smaller bodies are shorn of all their effective powers, it will no longer be worth the while of good men to stand for election. The nation has gained much from the use of local government as a training ground for national politics, and national life would be impoverished if the smaller authorities disappeared or became ineffective. There is, however, a widespread belief that the smaller authorities do not attain an adequate standard of efficiency and that they are in too close contact with their constituents to apply their powers fearlessly where individual rights are affected. In 1945 a pronouncement by the Government on local government organisation advocated the retention of the present system of areas with the continued establishment of joint boards or joint committees where co-ordination of services between two or more areas is necessary. Such a policy does not, however, rule out ultimate integration of the joint bodies in any area into a single co-operating unit, if experience should show this to

Problem of Areas.

be desirable.[1] The report of the Local Government Boundary Commission for 1947 [2] contained a description of the causes of weakness in local government and put forward some far-reaching recommendations for reform. The dissolution of the Commission in 1949 was accompanied by a statement of the Minister of Health that the review of the structure and functions of local government was a constant preoccupation of the Government but no indication was given that the review would result in action at an early date.[3]

C.

Central Control.[4]

Ministry of Housing and Local Government.   The general supervision of the work of local government authorities in England and Wales when it is not, as with education, for example, administered by another Ministry has been undertaken since 1951 by the Ministry of Housing and Local Government; this department also has a general responsibility for financial grants by the central government to these authorities. Its other main tasks are the housing programme, which is executed by district councils, the new towns, through the agency of development corporations and the control of land use in accordance with the town and country planning legislation. All these functions were given to the department by Orders in Council made under the Ministers of the Crown (Transfer of Functions) Act, 1946, which enables the adjustment of departmental organisation by delegated legislation. The functions of the Ministry of Housing and Local Government as the chief central department concerned with local government administration were formerly exercised by the Ministry of Health, itself the successor in 1919 of the Local Government Board which was created in 1872.

Ministry of Health.   The Ministry of Health was established by the Ministry of Health Act, 1919, in order to centralise under one department the control of matters affecting public health. The department took over the work of the old Local Government Board and of the National Insurance Commissioners and some functions of other departments, *e.g.* the Board of Control supervising the care of mental patients, which was formerly under the Home Office. The Local Government Board had as its chief functions (1) the control of poor relief; (2) powers in relation to public vaccination; (3) general control over the registration of births and deaths, and (4) supervision, with some

---

[1] *Local Government in England and Wales during the Period of Reconstruction.* 1945 Cmd. 6579.
[2] H.C. 86, 1948, pp. 264–5, *post.*
[3] H.C. Deb., Vol. 460, cols. 760–63.
[4] See Jennings, *op. cit.,* Chap. VIII., and Hart, *op. cit.,* Part II.

control, of the administration of public health and local government in general, chiefly by supervising the work of local authorities, by inspection by medical officers and by grants-in-aid. The Ministry of Health is now responsible for the general health of the community and for the administration of the national health service. Its place as successor to the Local Government Board in relation to the local authorities generally has been taken by the Ministry of Housing and Local Government.

The task of the Ministry of Education, which in 1944 replaced the Board of Education, is to promote the education of the people and the progressive development of institutions devoted to that purpose. It is the duty of the Minister to secure the effective execution by local authorities under his control and direction of the national policy for providing a varied and comprehensive educational service in every area of England and Wales. Thus there is exercisable direct control by a central department over a service which essentially depends upon a national rather than local policy, but which continues to be administered by a local representative authority.

Ministry of Education.

The Ministry of Transport controls the exercise of the highway functions of local authorities, largely through grants given for the construction and upkeep of the roads for which they are responsible.

Ministry of Transport.

It has been seen [1] how there was a growing tendency during the nineteenth century towards greater central control of local authorities. Despite the creation in 1872 of the Local Government Board with a Minister at its head the degree of control exercised to-day was not achieved until the Local Government Act, 1929, which reduced the local taxation income of local authorities and led to a reconsideration of the relations between the Exchequer and local authorities. The methods of control are many and various. By-laws [2] require the confirmation of the Ministry of Housing and Local Government or sometimes of another Minister, *e.g.* those relating to law and order which need the approval of the Home Secretary. The sanction of a government department is required before a local authority may exercise its borrowing powers.[3] The accounts of local authorities are audited by district auditors who are appointed by the Minister of Housing and Local Government.[4] Inspection by officers of the Central Government (*e.g.* of schools by Her Majesty's inspectors on behalf of the Ministry of Education; of police forces by the Home Office [5]) is a condition precedent to grants for specific services. The Minister of Housing and Local Government is empowered, subject to the approval of the House of Commons, to

Methods of Control.

---

[1] P. 256, *ante.*
[2] P. 280, *post.*
[3] P. 284, *post.*
[4] Pp. 284-5, *post.*
[5] Part IV., Chap. 8.

reduce any exchequer equalisation grant if he is satisfied that a council has failed to maintain a reasonable standard of efficiency and progress or that its expenditure has been excessive or irrecoverable.[1] This power operates as a potential threat rather than as a weapon to be used in practice, since its use would throw into chaos the local administrative machine and lead either to the abandonment of services, at all events in part, or to an intolerable increase in local taxation. Statutes affecting local government usually give powers to a department to make the necessary regulations and orders to bring the statute into effect. Frequently local authorities are required to prepare schemes and submit them for approval. Frequently statutes provide that an appeal from the decision of a local authority shall lie to the appropriate central department. Sometimes the Minister may, where a local authority fails in its duties, either act himself or transfer the function concerned to some other authority. Central control has hardened since the end of the Second World War and has been accompanied by the loss of important local services. The block grant from the Exchequer has been replaced by equalisation grants calculated by a procedure to be outlined later which keeps the financial relationship under continuous review. Rating valuation and assessment have passed to officers of the Commissioners of Inland Revenue. In the important and costly service of education supervision by the Board of Education has been replaced by control and direction by a Minister of Education. Contributions from the Exchequer exceed revenue derived from rates. New towns are being planned by *ad hoc* development corporations and not by the local authority of the area. The remnant of the old poor law has become national assistance administered by a national board. Hospital services have been transferred to *ad hoc* regional bodies acting under the control of the Minister of Health. Municipal electricity and gas services have been nationalised. To facilitate control by Whitehall some of the remaining local services have been transferred from district councils to county councils and county boroughs. Town and country planning, police and fire services, education (so far as some large district councils were formerly authorities for elementary schools) are instances in point.

Conclusion.   It will be seen that the methods of central control are both numerous and effective. None the less local administration and to a limited extent the framing of policy remain functions of local authorities. The Ministry of Housing and Local Government secures the co-operation of local authorities and the relationship is one of friendly partnership. But for such a relationship local authorities could obstruct the objects of central policy by the adoption

---

[1] Local Government Act, 1948, s. 6.

of a *non possumus* attitude. Local authorities are not branches of departments in Whitehall, though they operate some of the central services on an agency basis, as in the case of domestic fuel rationing. Their members are elected by the districts which they serve. Their services are administered by their own officers and the quality of administration varies from area to area.

CHAPTER 2.

ORGANISATION AND GENERAL DUTIES OF LOCAL AUTHORITIES.

Local Authorities.

THE Local Authorities in England and Wales [1] are:

1. Councils of the administrative counties (County Councils).

2. Councils of boroughs which are county boroughs (County Borough Councils).

3. Councils of county districts (Borough Councils, Urban and Rural District Councils).

4. Parish Councils and Parish Meetings.

The county borough is a self-contained area. The county is divided into districts and may be described as a two-tiered authority, if the parish authority be ignored.[2] Thus a rural parish will be in the rural district of X in the administrative county of Y and the county and district councils will both exercise authority in the parish for different purposes.

Review of Areas.

Under the Local Government Act, 1933, ss. 139–146, as amended by the Local Government Boundary Commission (Dissolution) Act, 1949, a county council has a discretion or can be required by the Minister of Housing and Local Government to review at any time after 1951 the status and boundaries of county districts and parishes. Proposals submitted by counties require confirmation by the Minister. Where a borough objects to any proposal affecting the borough, an order by the Minister is subject to special parliamentary procedure under the Statutory Orders (Special Procedure) Act, 1945.[3] A new county borough can only be constituted by private Act of Parliament and must have an estimated population of 75,000. Extensions of such boroughs are made by ministerial order which is subject to the special procedure of the Act of 1945. By the Local Government (Boundary Commission) Act, 1945, a Local Government Boundary Commission was constituted to conduct county reviews and also to handle the creation and extension of county boroughs, the union of contiguous county boroughs and that of county boroughs and counties. The Minister of Health had power to give general

[1] The Standing Joint Committee of the County Council and Quarter Sessions is the local police authority, except in boroughs possessing a separate police force which is administered by the Watch Committee of the Council. For Police, see Part IV., Chap. 8.

[2] The functions of parish councils and parish meetings (p. 272, *post*) are strictly limited.

[3] P. 280, *post*.

directions to the Commission, which required parliamentary approval by an affirmative resolution. The orders of the Commission were to be final except those relating to the status or boundaries of counties or county boroughs, which were subject to the special parliamentary procedure. The Act was repealed in 1949 because the Government decided against giving the Commission any power to alter the structure of local government or to vary the functions of the different classes of authorities. Without the removal of these limitations it was difficult to implement the alteration of areas. The Report of the Commission for 1947 [1] contained proposals which would have involved the creation of a new type of authority, a one-tier administrative county, for the areas of twenty of the most populous county boroughs, and a change in the allocation of functions to other or additional county boroughs, which would become part of the administrative county and look to the county for certain services, *e.g.* police and fire, though otherwise largely autonomous as at present. [2]

A.

Organisation of Counties.

It is one of the most confusing features of local government that different institutions are called by the same name. The county affords an example. For parliamentary purposes, for local administration and taxation and for military organisation, the term " county " is used to describe areas which are not necessarily co-terminous. The term is also used of the local civil court, the county court, though here the divisions make no pretension of corresponding with the county as depicted on the map of England. Again, the term is used to distinguish those boroughs which, by virtue of possessing a population of a certain size, are separated for administrative and parliamentary purposes from the area of the county in which they are situated. The county borough of Salford is in the county palatine of Lancaster, the county borough of Croydon in the county of Surrey; yet for local government administration these places are, practically speaking, units separate from their respective counties.

Terminology.

Apart from the administrative services of the elected authorities, the organisation of the county comprises other offices:

Formerly a military representative of the King and, as such, commander of the local militia, yeomanry and volunteer forces, the Lord-Lieutenant is appointed by commission. He is usually the President of the county Territorial Army and Auxiliary Air Force

The Lord-Lieutenant.

---

[1] H.C. 86, (1949).　　　　[2] For current proposals, see Preface.

K *

Association. Otherwise little remains of his official military duties, except the power to recommend appointments to first commissions in the Territorial Army.[1] He may appoint not more than twenty Deputy-Lieutenants, subject to the Crown's power to decline approval. The Lord-Lieutenant is the head of the county commission of the peace, and *custos rotulorum* (keeper of the records). He recommends to the Lord Chancellor with the assistance of an advisory committee, suitable persons in the county for appointment as justices of the peace, except in such county boroughs and boroughs as have a separate commission of the peace.

The Sheriff.   The Sheriff is also a royal representative, who in former times played a far more important part in county affairs than to-day. As conservator of the Queen's Peace he had the duty to suppress riots, to repel invasion and pursue felony and could call on the *posse comitatus* [2] to assist him. He is still, however, the Crown's agent for the execution of processes of law. He summons juries, executes the judgments of the superior civil courts and is responsible for the carrying out of death sentences.[3] As a revenue official he collects the Crown debts, such as fines imposed by higher courts and forfeited recognisances and bonds. He is the returning officer in the county parliamentary elections to whom writs for the election of members of Parliament are addressed. His duties, as such, may be, and generally are performed by the clerk of the county council as acting returning officer. He is in attendance on the judges of Assize. Some traces remain of the Sheriff's greater importance in former times. The office is compulsory. Selection is by the Crown from among three persons for each county nominated by a special court which meets annually on November 12. One of these names is subsequently "pricked" by the Queen at a special meeting of the Privy Council. This court is a kind of reproduction under a modern statute of the old Exchequer. Those entitled to sit are the Lord Chancellor, the Chancellor of the Exchequer, the Lord President of the Council, and other Privy Councillors, the Lord Chief Justice and the High Court judges. The qualification for the office is the holding of sufficient land within the county to answer for any damages that may be awarded against the Sheriff for neglect of duty. Various persons are exempted from the office, such as members of Parliament and officers on the active list of the regular forces. The expenses of a

[1] For position of Territorial Army during and since Second World War, see p. 409, *post*.

[2] The county levy, now obsolete.

[3] Other sentences of criminal courts are carried out by prison officials or the police, but the Sheriff remains responsible for carrying out any order unless the duty is imposed on someone else: *The King* v. *Lydford*, [1914] 2 K.B. 378. Committals for contempt of court are carried out by the tipstaff, an officer of the court. The Sheriff executes judgments of civil courts through the bailiff, a Sheriff's officer.

Sheriff are such that in these days many qualified persons seek to be excused. No remuneration is payable, though the Sheriff is entitled to certain fines and a percentage of the Crown debts collected.

The Sheriff must appoint an Under-Sheriff and a Deputy-Sheriff. In practice he performs none but the ceremonial duties of his office in person. His legal representative for local business is the Under-Sheriff, usually a solicitor, whose firm practises in the county town. The Deputy-Sheriff is the Sheriff's London agent, who must have an office within one mile of the Inner Temple Hall. The purely ministerial work, such as levying executions, is carried out by bailiffs. The Under-Sheriff. The Deputy-Sheriff.

The Coroner is appointed by the county council. It is his duty to hold enquiries into cases of sudden death and discovery of treasure trove.[1] His salary is paid out of county funds. Larger counties appoint more than one coroner, the county being divided for this purpose into districts. Coroners must be barristers, solicitors or legally qualified medical practitioners of five years' standing: Coroners (Amendment) Act, 1926. Some cities and boroughs have the right to appoint their own coroners. The Coroners' Rules, 1953, require inquests to be held in public and in general aim at restricting inquests to relevant matters without restraining the discretion of the coroner as to the conduct of proceedings. The Coroner.

Justices of the peace for the county, as we have already seen, are appointed by the Crown, advised by the Lord Chancellor on the recommendation of the Lord-Lieutenant, who is assisted by an advisory committee. All the justices of the county are qualified to adjudicate at Quarter Sessions.[2] Justices of the Peace.

The county is divided into separate divisions for petty sessional purposes.[3] We are not concerned here with the judicial duties of the quarter and petty sessions.[4] Since the Local Government Acts of 1888 and 1894, only a few administrative powers remain vested in justices of the peace. They have, however, certain powers in connection with mental hospitals, visiting prisons and the administration of the licensing law.

Until the Local Government (Clerks) Act, 1931, the clerk of the peace, to which office appointment was made by the standing joint committee of the county council and the county quarter sessions, was also the clerk of the council of the administrative county, holding the latter more important office by virtue of tenure of the former. By that Act appointments to the two offices are made by separate Clerk of the Peace.

---

[1] Treasure trove, which consists of objects of gold or silver which have been hidden and of which the original owner cannot be traced, is the property of the Crown. The finder receives back the objects or their market value, provided he reports his discovery promptly to the Coroner of the district.

[2] P. 232, *ante*, for provisions as to chairmen and jurisdiction.

[3] P. 229, *ante*.   [4] Part V., Chap. 1.

bodies, the county council appointing its own clerk, quarter sessions its clerk of the peace. The two offices may still be, and usually are, held by the same person. The clerk of the peace is an officer of the judicial county and acts as clerk of quarter sessions. The clerk of the county council is also the electoral registration officer of the parliamentary county, but not of the separate parliamentary boroughs within the county. Boroughs with separate courts of quarter sessions appoint their own clerks of the peace.

The County Council. The administrative county came into existence in 1888. The Local Government Act of that year had for its principal object the transfer of county administrative business from the justices of the peace sitting in quarter sessions to elected bodies. The same Act created the county borough which, for most administrative purposes, is a separate county, while remaining for other purposes, *e.g.* judicial, within the geographical county in which it is situated. Including London, which is a separate unit, there are sixty-two administrative counties in England and Wales, and eighty-three county boroughs. It is not proposed to give separate treatment to the county borough.[1] As we have seen, the trend of development is to centralise local services under the administrative county and county borough to the exclusion of the lesser local authorities, some of which (boards of guardians) have been superseded, and others (district councils) deprived of some of their important powers, for example, planning and highways, but public health, as distinct from the local health services, and housing are still administered by the county districts.[2]

Composition of County Council. In each administrative county there is an elected county council, and in each county borough there is an elected borough council. The county council consists of a chairman, aldermen and councillors, in the proportion of one alderman for every three councillors. A county council must hold four meetings in a year, including the statutory annual meeting. The chief executive officers [3] are the clerk of the council, the county accountant, the medical officer of health, the surveyor, the chief education officer, the children's officer, the chief fire officer, and other officials, technical experts and inspectors with qualifications suitable to their specialised spheres. The chief constable of the county is appointed, subject to the approval of the Home Secretary, by the standing joint committee of the county council and quarter sessions. It may be remarked that the clerk of

---

[1] See Local Government Act, 1933, s. 139 as amended by the Local Government Boundary Commission (Dissolution) Act, 1949, for the conditions for the creation of new county boroughs, and see p. 264. *ante.*

[2] There has been a tendency in modern legislation to give to county councils some power of co-ordination and oversight over certain functions of district councils, *e.g.* housing, sewage and water supply, coupled with powers of financial assistance.

[3] See Local Government Act, 1933, Part IV., for officers of local authorities.

the council is the officer upon whom largely depends the efficiency of county administration. He is usually a solicitor with special training in local government work.

Local authorities may appoint committees for general or special **Committees.** purposes, and may delegate to a committee any of their functions, except the power to levy rates or borrow money. A committee may, with the exception of the finance committee, include, up to one-third of its number, persons who are not members of the local authority. Committees must be appointed by county councils for the following purposes: finance, education, public health, agriculture, child welfare, health, mental deficiency and fire brigades.

A county council has power to delegate to the Council of a county **Delegation.** district as agent those of its functions for which it is not required by law to appoint a committee, but may not delegate the power to levy a rate or borrow money. Local authorities may establish joint committees and joint boards; the latter are separate authorities for the management of permanent services, *e.g.* a port health authority.

The principal powers and duties of county councils relate to high- **Powers and** ways, including county bridges, main [1] and classified roads and all **Duties.** roads in rural districts; education; town and country planning; fire protection; police; certain local health and agricultural services; child welfare; and certain national assistance services. They also control the activities of the district councils in public health. In addition there are a large number of minor administrative services provided and regulative duties performed by a county council. County borough councils are organised in the same way as non-county borough councils. They have the powers of county councils and in addition the powers which non-county boroughs exercise as county districts, *e.g.* they are urban sanitary authorities. Thus they are all-purpose authorities.

B.

Organisation of Boroughs.

Municipal boroughs, of which there are some 420 in England and **Boroughs.** Wales, are corporations consisting of a mayor, alderman and local government electors. They are governed by a council, to which the electors elect every year councillors to represent them for triennial periods; the councillors elect the aldermen for periods of six years, one half of the number retiring every third year; the number of aldermen is one-third of the councillors. The mayor is elected

---

[1] Trunk roads are maintained by the Minister of Transport, who may delegate his functions to local highway authorities.

annually by the councillors and aldermen together. The borough council thus consists of the mayor, aldermen and councillors.

Charters. Boroughs are, and always have been, created by royal charter, but they are subject, like the statutory authorities, to the provisions of the Local Government Act, 1933, regulating their constitution and general powers. A charter of incorporation is sought by an urban district council by petition to the Queen. The petition is considered by a committee of the Privy Council; notice of the petition must first be given to the county council concerned and to the Ministry of Housing and Local Government. The effect of the charter when granted is, apart from transitional arrangements, *e.g.* for initial elections, to extend the relevant provisions of the Local Government Act, 1933, to the new borough.

Committees. Borough councils like county councils work through committees but, unlike county councils, they are not obliged by statute to appoint certain committees for particular purposes [1] except that in county boroughs, which have a separate police force, they must appoint a watch committee to supervise the borough police.[2]

Executive Officers. The senior official of the borough council is the town clerk, who, like the clerk of the county council, is the head of the council staff. He is its legal adviser, and countersigns all orders for payments made out of the general rate fund of the borough. His office is essential for the due performance by the council of its duties. The other officials are the borough treasurer, the medical officer of health, the surveyor, the sanitary inspector, the chief constable (in county boroughs which possess a separate police force) and other officers such as technical experts and inspectors.

Work of the Borough Council. The functions of the borough council which is not a county borough are those of a county district. Thus the council is the local authority under the Public Health Acts. It is also the housing authority and maintains the non-county roads. The corporate lands and buildings are vested in it with powers of management. County boroughs possess a separate police force managed by the watch committee of the council. Many of the most important powers of the larger boroughs are derived from general Acts giving adoptive powers or from private Acts. Powers acquired in this way relate to public utility undertakings, such as water services, the running of omnibuses and tramways, the provision of docks, harbours and markets, civic restaurants, entertainments, and other amenities of a public character.

Cities. Every city is also a municipal borough. Certain towns have at various times been called " cities " by royal charter or letters patent. Such towns are usually the cathedral towns of ecclesiastical dioceses or very large towns such as Leeds and Bradford. There are also a

---

[1] P. 269, *ante.*   [2] P. 189, *ante.*

few counties of cities, or counties of towns, formerly regarded as counties by themselves. At the present day these have separate sheriffs, and in some cases separate commissions of assize.

Most of the larger boroughs have a separate commission of the peace, justices being appointed by the Crown advised by the Lord Chancellor on the recommendation of the borough advisory committee. The majority of such boroughs have their own court of quarter sessions over which a recorder presides.[1] The mayor, who is elected annually by the council, is a justice *ex officio* for the borough or, if it has no separate commission of the peace, for the county. The grant of a separate commission of the peace enables the borough justices to act as a separate petty sessional division, and in practice the county justices do not sit as a rule at the borough petty sessions.[2] Borough justices have their own clerk and borough quarter sessions a clerk of the peace. A borough having a separate commission of the peace may apply to the Crown for the appointment of a stipendiary magistrate whose appointment is recommended by the Lord Chancellor.[3]

Commissions of the Peace.

C.

Organisation of Urban and Rural Districts.

The administrative county, which does not include the county boroughs, is divided into urban and rural county districts. The former comprise both municipal boroughs and urban areas not forming part of a borough (urban districts). Each of these county districts has its elected council. As regards administrative powers the two types of urban authorities do not greatly differ, but there are some differences between the powers of urban and rural district councils. Both are pre-eminently public health authorities, but the latter have somewhat smaller powers. Both rural and urban district councils were established by the Local Government Act, 1894. They replaced a confusing variety of public bodies which sprang up during the nineteenth century, such as local boards of health and rural sanitary authorities. They were, in a reorganised form, the sanitary authorities which were established in 1872. Their powers are exclusively statutory and are derived mainly from the Public Health Acts, 1875 to 1936, the Housing Act, 1936, the Highways Act, 1835,

Urban and Rural District Councils.

---

[1] P. 232, *ante.*

[2] County justices probably have no jurisdiction where a borough possesses a separate court of quarter sessions, and cannot sit at borough petty sessions where the borough was exempt before the Municipal Corporations Act, 1835.

[3] A stipendiary may also be appointed on application by the county council for the whole or any part of a county, or a joint county and borough area may be constituted for this purpose.

and subsequent Acts. They are accordingly the local public health, highway (in urban districts) and housing authorities, subject in the case of highways to important powers vested in the county council. Urban councils have powers to regulate buildings and streets, to provide water, public parks, libraries and allotments. Many powers can be obtained by the adoption of Acts empowering the provision of public amenities or conferring increased regulative powers on the council. Both urban and rural district councils have been since 1925 the rating authorities, but the rating valuation and assessment have now passed to the central government. County councils have to address their demands for rates (precepts) to the district councils. The chief officer of both urban and rural district councils is the clerk, usually, like the town clerk and the clerk to the county council, a solicitor.

Parish Councils. In rural areas only there is a further unit—the parish council— elected by the local government voters of the civil (as distinct from the ecclesiastical) parish. The parish council is entrusted with the management of parish property and certain public health powers. More extensive powers may be obtained under certain adoptive Acts, *e.g.* the provision of street lighting, recreation grounds, public baths and wash-houses, and libraries (the latter in default only of provision of library facilities by the county council).

Parish Meeting. All rural parishes have parish meetings, but in smaller parishes there is no parish council and the parish meeting exercises some of the powers of a parish council. The parish meeting is the only example of direct, as opposed to representative, government to be found in England.

D.

Local Government of London.

Administrative County of London. The administrative county of London was created, like other administrative counties and county boroughs, by the Local Government Act, 1888, and the metropolitan boroughs, which cover the same area, by the London Government Act, 1899. The London Government Act, 1939, for most purposes takes the place for London of the Local Government Act, 1933.

City of London. The City of London stands apart. It is unaffected by the Municipal Corporations Acts and is still governed partly under its old charters. Its status is that of a metropolitan borough with special privileges; the London County Council is the local education authority. The lord mayor, aldermen and common councillors form the Court of Common Council. The aldermen and common councillors are elected at the wardmotes, the former for life, the latter annually, by the local government electors] of the ward;

formerly membership of a ward was confined to the liverymen of the city companies or guilds. For some purposes the Court of Aldermen forms a separate council. The lord mayor and aldermen are *ex officio* justices of the peace; each sitting alone has the powers of two justices sitting elsewhere in petty sessions.

The metropolitan borough councils, though acting as the public health authorities for their areas, do not stand in the same relation to the London County Council as do the councils of non-county boroughs to their county councils. The London County Council is the education authority for the whole area. It is also the housing authority, though the borough councils have certain powers under the Housing Act, 1936. The subject of local government in the Metropolis is too specialised for further treatment in this book. It may, however, be noted that certain local services for London are provided by separate authorities, *e.g.* the Metropolitan Police controlled by the Home Secretary, the water supply by the Metropolitan Water Board, passenger traffic by the London Transport Executive, while the river Thames, up to a point beyond the metropolitan area, its docks and wharves, comes under the Port of London Authority. The size of the greatest urban centre in the world is sufficient to justify the existence of a distinctive organisation for local government purposes. *London County Council and Metropolitan Borough Councils.*

E.

Scotland.

The Secretary of State, as the head of the Scottish Department of Health, takes the place of the Minister of Housing and Local Government as regards the local government of Scotland, which has a separate history. The reforms of 1929 were applied by the Local Government (Scotland) Act, 1929, in modified form and the Local Government (Scotland) Act, 1947, is the counterpart of the Local Government Act, 1933, which only applies to England and Wales. *Department of Health.*

Elected town councils date only from 1833, though many of them then took the place of corporations with ancient charters. County councils were introduced, as in England, in 1889, replacing the justices of the peace and the commissioners of supply. The Local Government (Scotland) Act, 1929, abolished a number of *ad hoc* authorities in favour of the elected councils. The district council corresponds to the English parish council. The local government franchise embraces all parliamentary electors, as in England,[1] and ratepayers, being the owners and occupiers of heritable property of £10 annual value, lodgers with a similar qualification and all inhabitant occupiers *Local Councils.*

[1] P 275, *post.*

of dwelling-houses, if not registered as parliamentary electors. Registration as an elector or residence are in general the qualifications for election to a council. Any person who has a pecuniary interest in a contract with the council is disqualified from discussing or voting on any question relating thereto. The services, and methods of administration and of control in the main resemble those in force in England. There are important differences in regard to licensing jurisdiction. There are no aldermen. As in England and Wales one-third of the town councillors retire each year and county councillors are elected every three years at a single election.

No attempt has been made to discuss in detail in this brief outline of local government organisation the powers and duties of the various authorities in relation to the services rendered by them. Hart, *Introduction to the Law of Local Government and Administration*, contains a full account of the whole subject-matter in England and Wales. The reader is also referred to Wright and Hobhouse, *Local Government and Local Finance* (9th edition, Oakes and Dacey), for a concise account of the various services administered by local authorities and to Chapters 18–19 which describe the negotiating machinery for conditions of service for officers and the central associations of local authorities. These associations play an important part in negotiations with government departments upon all aspects of local government.

CHAPTER 3.

LOCAL GOVERNMENT ELECTIONS, LEGISLATION AND FINANCE.

THE Local Government Act, 1933, contains a uniform code for the constitutions of local authorities and provides them with a framework of powers of a general character, thereby repealing a large number of statutory provisions governing separate authorities and amending the law as far as necessary to produce uniformity. It does not deal with specific statutory powers relating to particular services, such as public health or education.

A.

Local Government Elections.

Prior to 1945 the local government franchise rested on the occupation of land or premises. The right to vote at a local government election was thus broadly coincident with liability to assessment for rating purposes. The Representation of the People Act, 1945, giving statutory force to the recommendations of the Speaker's Conference of the previous year, extended to parliamentary electors as such the right to be registered and to vote as local government electors. The Act did not, however, assimilate the two franchises, since it preserved the previous local government franchise both in England and Wales and in Scotland for those owners and occupiers who do not qualify for the parliamentary franchise by reason of residence in the qualifying premises and for peers who are disqualified from voting at parliamentary elections. Thus the total number of local government electors outnumber the parliamentary electors. These qualifications were continued by the Representation of the People Act, 1949, and may be summarised as follows :

1. (i) Residence on the qualifying date in the area; or

(ii) if not so resident, occupation as owner or tenant of any rateable land or premises in the area of the yearly value of not less than £10.

Only British subjects or citizens of the Republic of Ireland of full age who are not under any legal incapacity are entitled to be registered.

Local Government Franchise.

2. Members of the forces wherever serving and other Crown servants employed outside the United Kingdom, and their wives residing with them may also be registered, as if they were resident at the address at which they would be residing but for their service. Electors in this class may vote by proxy.

The register is published once a year on February 16 as a register of parliamentary and local government electors, those who are only qualified to vote at local government elections being marked to indicate that fact. The qualifying date for inclusion in the register is the preceding October 10.

Qualifications for membership.

There are three qualifications for elected membership as councillors of local authorities, which is confined to British subjects and citizens of the Republic of Ireland of full age:

(i) Registration as a local government elector within the area of the local authority;

(ii) Ownership of freehold or leasehold property within the area;

(iii) Residence for the whole of the twelve months before the election within the area of the authority.

Aldermen, who, as has been stated, are elected by the councillors of county and borough councils, must either be elected councillors or qualified so to be; the office of councillor is vacated on election as an alderman.

Disqualifications.

The chief disqualifications are:

(i) The holding of paid office under the council concerned or any of its committees;

(ii) Bankruptcy, unless certified not to be attributable to the debtor's misconduct, or composition with creditors.

(iii) Imprisonment for an offence for not less than three months without option of a fine within five years before election, or since election;

(iv) Surcharge (consequent upon disallowance of expenditure) of more than £500 by a district auditor within the same periods; [1]

(v) Conviction under enactments relating to corrupt or illegal practices at elections.

Formerly it was a disqualification to have an interest in a contract placed by the authority: *Lapish* v. *Braithwaite*, [1926] A.C. 275. But such a pecuniary interest now only disables a member of a council from speaking or voting on any question with respect to the contract: Local Government Act, 1933, s. 76. Beneficial interest in stock or shares of a contracting company is deemed to be such an interest. [2] Interests and those of a spouse have to be disclosed to the clerk of the authority, who is under a duty to keep a record of

---

[1] P. 284, *post.*

[2] Ownership of even a small fraction of shares has to be disclosed, but does not disable a member from speaking or voting: Local Government Act, 1948, s. 131.

such disclosures. A member is not disabled from voting because of his interest in a question as a ratepayer or tenant of a council house or as an ordinary consumer of municipal water; nor does any liability attach because of an interest in any matter relating to the terms on which the right to participate in any service, including the supply of goods, is offered to the public.

Councillors are elected to county councils triennially in single member electoral divisions. Elections are held for each administrative county as a whole every third year between April 3 and April 15. County aldermen are elected by the councillors for six years, one-half retiring by rotation at every triennial election of the council.

County Council Elections

Councillors of borough councils, whether county or non-county boroughs, are elected every year in May, on a date between May 3 and May 15 which is fixed annually by the Home Secretary, for three years, one-third retiring by rotation each year. Aldermen are elected by the council (*i.e.* by the councillors and non-retiring aldermen) for six years, one-half retiring triennially.

Borough Council Elections.

The councillors of district councils likewise hold office for three years and retire by thirds each year, but the county council may, on the application of the district council, provide for simultaneous retirement every third year. The elections for these councils are held in the period May 3 to May 15, the actual date being fixed by the county council.

Urban and Rural District Council Elections.

B.

Legislation affecting Local Authorities.

A local government authority is a body corporate constituted by Act of Parliament and endowed with statutory powers. Municipal corporations form an exception in that they are created by royal charter which incorporates the inhabitants i.e. the mayor, aldermen and burgesses, the authority itself not being incorporated; the charter can only confer upon the corporation the status permitted by the Local Government Act, 1933, and cannot enlarge the statutory powers of the authority.[1] County councils, urban and rural district councils, parish councils and meetings have all been created by statute. The Acts which constituted these bodies differed in character. The Municipal Corporations Act, 1882, regulated all the activities of the corporation, as such, acting through the borough council, but did not affect the existing statutory functions of the council as the authority for public health, highways or other special services. On the other hand, the Local Government Act, 1888,

Constituent Acts.

[1] *Cf.* Attorney-General v. Leicester Corporation, [1943] Ch. 86; a borough council may have unrestricted power to expend its rate fund but, without statutory authority, it cannot in so doing interfere with existing private rights.

enacted general provisions to cover all the functions of the county councils which were set up by the Act. The Local Government Act, 1933, provided a general code for the constitution and common powers of all local authorities and accordingly effected substantial amendments to the earlier Acts. By common powers are meant such matters as making by-laws, holding property, making contracts, the audit of accounts and finance. Rating valuation and exchequer grants are governed by the Local Government Act, 1948.

Acts relating to particular Services.

Acts relating to the functions of local authorities confer the special powers necessary for their performance; they can be divided into general Acts and adoptive Acts.

General Acts.

By the first type of statute a local authority is given many compulsory powers and duties which it is both empowered and under a legal duty to perform, as for example its chief powers and duties under the Public Health Acts, 1875 and 1936, as public health authority, or under the Education Act, 1944, as local education authority. Even in a general Act some of the powers may be optional.

Adoptive Acts.

An adoptive Act confers powers which may be utilised by a local authority at its option; once adopted the powers must be exercised as rigidly in conformity with the terms of the statute as those conferred by a general Act strictly so-called. By way of example the Public Libraries Acts, 1892 and 1919, may be cited. The local authorities which are given the opportunity of adopting the Acts need not do so, unless they so elect, but having elected, the library facilities provided are limited by the terms of the Acts. Another example is contained in the Local Government Act, 1948, s. 132, which authorises the provision of entertainments of various kinds or a contribution towards the cost of such activities.

Private Acts.

The legislation discussed above is enacted by means of public general Acts. We must now examine private or local Acts. The private Act has been one of the means whereby Parliament has exercised control over local administration. The constituent and general Acts for this purpose are a comparatively modern method, dating from the period succeeding the Reform Act, 1832. Private Bill legislation is much older; the process was utilised by local authorities most actively during the nineteenth century and is still freely resorted to for the purpose of acquiring additional powers peculiar to a local authority's own area. It is to be observed that, despite the introduction throughout local government of representative councils elected on a wide suffrage, Parliament has never been prepared to concede to these bodies the right of determining the powers needed for the local requirements of their areas without reference to the legislature. Some critics consider that local administration should be unfettered in matters where neither national interests nor the interests of other authorities are involved. A private or local Act of Parliament, though it passes at one stage through an essentially different type of procedure in Parliament resembling litigation between its promoters and opponents,[1] is as much the law of the land as a public general Act. The difference lies in the local effect of the law it enacts. Herein lies its utility for enabling a local authority to obtain parliamentary sanction for powers not exercisable under a general or adoptive Act. The larger municipalities can thus enlarge their powers by this method. Private Bills promoted by municipalities are usually of the omnibus type and embrace a great diversity of provisions. To take an example at random, the Nottingham Corporation Act, 1929, is entitled:

> An Act to authorise the Lord Mayor, Aldermen and Citizens of the City of Nottingham, and County of the same City,[2] to construct sewerage and sewage disposal works, street works and waterworks, to purchase lands compulsorily for various purposes, to extend the limits of the Corporation for the supply of water, to empower the Corporation to run trolley vehicles on further routes, to confer further powers upon the Corporation with regard to streets and buildings and the health and good government of the City and for other purposes.

In addition to the promotion of private or local Bills there are other ways open to local authorities, as well as to undertakings seeking statutory powers for the conduct of services, whereby statutory powers of local application can be obtained. The oldest of the methods, which dates from the mid-Victorian legislation relating to public health, is known as provisional order procedure. A provisional order is an order made by a Minister under authority conferred by an enabling Act on the application of a local authority or statutory undertaker where Parliament has sanctioned this course for a particular purpose. The order is provisional in the sense that it requires express confirmation by Parliament before it operates to confer the powers sought. This is given by a Provisional Order Confirmation Bill, which is a public Bill introduced by, or on behalf of, the Minister concerned. Opponents of the order may be heard at two stages. In the first place, if any objections are put forward by interested parties as a result of the advertisement of the application which is a necessary preliminary to its promotion, the making of the order by the Minister is preceded by a public enquiry. This is conducted by an official appointed by the Minister who is usually an officer with specialised knowledge of the matter at issue. Again, while the Confirmation Bill is pending in either House of Parliament, a petitioner can appear before the select committee to which the Bill is referred. The procedure thereafter follows the lines of that for private Bills. It has been used extensively under Acts relating to public health, water supplies and the extension of boundaries of local

Provisional Orders.

---

[1] Part III, Chap. 3, D.   [2] P. 271, *ante.*

authorities. It is less expensive than the promotion of a private Bill and usually ensures that the promoter can learn the strength of the opposition he is likely to meet at an early stage. At the same time it preserves to Parliament the right, which is seldom exercised in practice, to reject or to amend the Confirmation Bill. The Acquisition of Land (Authorisation Procedure) Act, 1946, provides a uniform procedure for the compulsory purchase of land by local and other public authorities for various statutory purposes; it has replaced in many cases earlier procedure by provisional order.

Ministerial Orders.

The second method requires either no action by Parliament or only a simple resolution of each House before the order becomes law. While Parliament can reject the order either by passing a resolution for its annulment or by declining to approve an affirmative resolution, where this requirement is prescribed, it cannot amend any provision that is contained in an order. This type of order is made by a Minister to confirm a scheme put before him by the applicant after a public enquiry where the Act provides for objectors being heard in this way. It is sometimes called a special order or simply a ministerial order. An example is to be found in the confirmation by the Minister of Housing and Local Government of a clearance scheme made by a local authority under the Housing Act, 1936. From the point of view of the opponents of the scheme, the objection to this procedure is that there is no opportunity of putting their case before a select committee in Parliament, if the Minister overrules the objections which they have put forward at the public enquiry.

Special Parliamentary Procedure.

Neither of these methods is wholly appropriate where both a measure of central control by Parliament is desirable on grounds of national policy and at the same time speedier action is required than is available for the passage of an opposed Provisional Order Confirmation Bill. In 1945 provision was made, which, while preserving the right of interested parties to be heard before a parliamentary committee on objections to detail, affords an opportunity to any member of Parliament to raise on the floor of the House any question of general policy that may be involved: Statutory Orders (Special Procedure) Act, 1945, which applies to any future statutory powers for any authority to make or to confirm orders where the power is required to be subject to " special parliamentary procedure." [1]

By-Laws.

By-laws are an important means whereby a local authority exercises its regulative functions. A county council and a borough council possess statutory power to make by-laws for the good rule and government of their areas and to prevent and suppress nuisances not already punishable, but no local authority has an inherent power to initiate legislation to acquire new powers by this means. The

[1] For details including application to provisional order procedure contained in earlier Acts, see Hart, *op. cit.*, pp. 313–6.

Public Health Acts, 1875 and 1936, and other statutes confer upon public health authorities statutory power to make by-laws and regulations. There are various restrictions on the power to make by-laws, such as a limit on the penalty to be prescribed for breach. By-laws normally require confirmation by the Minister of Housing and Local Government or by the Home Office, as the case may be. In consequence of this requirement it is the practice to adopt, with or without modification, model sets of by-laws drawn up by the confirming authority. The courts may declare a by-law invalid, either as being *ultra vires* or as being an unreasonable exercise of power: *Kruse* v. *Johnson*, [1898] 2 Q.B. 91; K. & L. 38.[1] The Town Police Clauses Acts, 1847 and 1889, consolidate the usual provisions which were formerly to be found in local Acts for the police regulation of towns. The Acts enable a variety of by-laws to be made for traffic control, public vehicles, street regulation, lighting and kindred subjects.

C.
Local Government Finance.

There are four principal sources of revenue available to meet the needs of a local authority: (i) rates, (ii) contributions from the Central Government and other local authorities, (iii) loans, and (iv) fees, charges and income from trading undertakings and from estates.

Sources of Revenue.

Rates are a species of local taxation payable by the occupiers of land and buildings. The amount varies with the annual value of the property. There are certain total or partial exemptions. Agricultural land no longer pays rates, while property used for productive, industrial or freight-transport purposes is rated at a quarter of the normal figure.[2] The purpose of these exemptions is to relieve industry of some of its burdens.

Rates.

A rate is assessed upon the annual value of land or buildings. This value represents the rent at which the property might reasonably be expected to let from year to year, less the annual cost of repairs, insurance and other expenses. The law thus assumes the existence of a hypothetical tenant, and calculates what sum he would be prepared to pay for a lease on such terms. Special methods are provided for calculating the value of large undertakings, such as waterworks, harbours and mines. Railway and canal properties of the Transport Commission and properties of the British Electricity

Rateable Value.

[1] P. 309, *post*; see also *Parker* v. *Bournemouth Corporation* (1902), 86 L.T. 449.
[2] Rating and Valuation (Apportionment) Act, 1928, and the Local Government Act, 1929, ss. 67 and 68.

Authority and its area boards are not liable to be rated, but the authority concerned is liable for an annual payment in lieu of rates which is divisible among local authorities.

Mode of Assessment. The district councils are the rating authorities for all purposes of local government. Rating is thus a principal function of the councils of all boroughs (including county boroughs), urban districts and rural districts. County councils address their demands for rates to meet county expenses to the rating authorities in their areas. In rural areas these expenses constitute the major part of the total rate. A valuation list, containing particulars of all interests in land, including buildings, within the rating area and the names of the occupiers, is prepared, not by the rating authority as formerly, but by a valuation officer selected by the Commissioners of Inland Revenue. Objections may be made to the valuation officer who must revise the draft list after the period for objections has passed. There is an appeal to the local valuation court, a tribunal of three drawn from a local valuation panel, and thence to the Lands Tribunal [1] or the case may by agreement be referred to arbitration. The valuation list remains in force for five years. [2] The rating authority levies a rate to meet the expenses of a fixed period, usually six months, on the current list. The rate is a uniform amount in the £ on the assessment of each unit (hereditament) of land and buildings. This is the general rate for the district and includes the expenses both of the rating authority itself, of the county council and other precepting authorities. Special rates are leviable on the same basis on separate areas in rural districts, *e.g.* where a charge has been incurred under an adoptive Act, such as for street lighting, which only benefits a particular part of the district. In urban areas such expenses are included in the general rate, since the services are in theory available for all ratepayers. The water rate is levied separately on a different basis. Parish councils are restricted as to their normal expenditure to the proceeds of a fixed rate which must not exceed 8*d.* in the £ of rateable value, exclusive of expenditure on powers under adoptive Acts but including debt charges. Payment of rates is enforceable only by summary proceedings before justices of the peace for a distress warrant.

Contributions from the Central Government. Before 1930 certain national taxes and the proceeds of certain licences collected by county and county borough councils were granted to those bodies out of the local taxation account of the Exchequer. Various grants were also made for education, for modern health ser-

---

[1] P. 346, *post.*

[2] The first valuation list under this procedure is expected to come into force in 1956; formerly valuation was the duty of the rating authority, subject to confirmation by a representative local assessment committee. See Local Government Act, 1948, Part III., as amended by the New Valuation Lists (Postponement) Act, 1952.

vices and for the upkeep of the roads, the latter from the proceeds of motor registration, taxes and fines for motoring offences. By the Local Government Act, 1929, there was paid annually to the councils of counties, county boroughs and county districts, in lieu of most of these sources of revenue and to compensate for losses from the rating relief given to industry, contributions to local government expenses from funds provided by Parliament. These were called general exchequer grants. The total amount contributed from the Exchequer for this purpose was determined by a national fund or pool, called the general exchequer contribution, provided out of general taxation. It consisted of three items: (1) An amount equal to the total losses of all counties and county boroughs on account of such rating relief, (2) an amount equal to the total losses on account of discontinued grants for separate services, and (3) an amount fixed periodically by Parliament; Local Government Act, 1929, s. 86. The block grants under (3) were determined by an elaborate formula of weighted population so as to take into account varying local conditions and requirements, such as the numbers of children under school age and of unemployed persons. The system was designed to make a general contribution from the Exchequer towards the cost of local services adapted to the needs of each area. The police, housing and education grants and some of the road grants from the Central Government were not affected by the Local Government Act, 1929, and are still paid separately for each of these services.

A new system of block grants, the distribution of which is dependent more upon rateable value than under the formula of weighted population was introduced by the Local Government Act, 1948, Part I. The method is to lay down a standard of financial resources needed by each county and county borough and to provide for the attainment of that standard by equalisation grants from the Exchequer. The Central Government thus becomes in effect a ratepayer in the area of those local authorities where resources fall below the standard. Out of the grant county councils make annual payments on a capitation basis to each of their county district councils, including non-county boroughs. The standard of resources is calculated each year partly by a new formula of weighted population which takes into account school age population and, in the counties, road mileage in relation to actual population. By dividing the total weighted population into the total rateable value for England and Wales the national average of rateable value per head is ascertained and that is taken as the minimum standard of resources. In counties or county boroughs where the local rateable value per head of weighted population falls short of the national average, the equalisation grant makes up the difference each year.

Exchequer Equalisation Grants.

The system is thus flexible. For the first five years a system of transitional grants, on a diminishing scale, operated to secure some net gain to all local authorities. The object of this was to compensate for losses due to transfers of local government services to the central government which accordingly no longer attracted the grant in aid and to a revised method of calculating education grants.

Loans.

Just as a trading company increases its capital by borrowing on the security of its assets to finance further developments, so a local authority, subject to strict statutory regulations, may raise loans for the purpose of financing its permitted activities. The security offered is that of the fund formed by the revenue under the authority's control. The power to borrow may be conferred in three ways. A general power of borrowing for purposes which local authorities are empowered to carry out is given by the Local Government Act, 1933. Its exercise is subject to the sanction of the Minister of Housing and Local Government, or in the case of transport undertakings only, the Minister of Transport. In the second place, loans authorised by local Acts are raised by the larger urban authorities; in this way powers may be obtained over and above those conferred by the general law. Borrowing powers conferred by local Acts may be made exercisable without the sanction of the Minister, if the estimates are proved before the select committee of Parliament which considers the Bill, but returns of the expenditure of the money so borrowed must be made to him. Thirdly, a provisional order may confer borrowing powers, in which case the previous consent of a government department is required, as well as parliamentary sanction. Local authorities can borrow from the Public Works Loan Commissioners, a body which was created in 1817 for the purpose of advancing money to municipal bodies, or from independent sources of finance, including the raising of a loan on the open market.

Other Revenue.

Other sources of revenue may be briefly noted: profits from public utility undertakings (chiefly confined to urban authorities), *e.g.* water, omnibus and tramway undertakings, markets; income from other corporate property and miscellaneous fees.

Audit.

Departmental control over local authorities in finance is not exclusively exercised through the payment of the general exchequer grants. District auditors who are appointed by the Minister of Housing and Local Government conduct annual audits of the accounts of local authorities, with an important exception in the case of the general accounts of some of the boroughs. These auditors, though civil servants, are not mere agents of the Minister and in the performance of their duties exercise a quasi-judicial function. Expenditure incurred without statutory authority must be disallowed by the auditors, as well as excessive expenditure upon lawful objects. Illegal payments are surcharged personally upon those who have authorised them—the elected representatives. A surcharge of over £500 disqualifies the person surcharged from membership of the local authority concerned.[1] In the case of boroughs expenditure on public assistance, education and housing, if a housing subsidy is payable, is subject to district audit. Other municipal accounts are audited by two borough elective auditors and a mayor's auditor, unless the borough has adopted either the system of district audit or a system of professional audit as authorised by the Local Government Act, 1933, s. 239. In the metropolitan boroughs all accounts are subject to district audit.

[1] For appeals from district auditors, see p. 329, *post*.

PART VII.

ADMINISTRATIVE LAW

Report of the Committee on Ministers' Powers (H.M. Stationery Office, 1932. Cmd. 4060) (cited as *M.P.R.*).

Principles of Administrative Law, by J. A. G. Griffith and H. Street (Pitmans).

Cases in Constitutional Law, by Sir David Keir and F. H. Lawson, Section V. 4th ed. (Oxford University Press).

Concerning English Administrative Law, by Sir Cecil Carr (Oxford University Press).

Law of the Constitution, by A. V. Dicey, 9th ed., Appendix, Section I. (Macmillan).

Justice and Administrative Law, by W. A. Robson, 3rd ed. (Stevens).

Governmental Liability, by H. Street (Cambridge University Press).

CHAPTER 1.

THE NATURE AND CLASSIFICATION OF POWERS.

Introductory. ADMINISTRATIVE law is the law relating to the organisation and services performed by the various administrative agencies of government. It deals with the powers of all such bodies and determines their rights and duties. In every State it has been the experience of the present century that there has been a vast increase in the activities of government and therefore of the volume and importance of administrative law. It is in the field of discretionary powers over persons and property that disputes most frequently arise. Hence came the tendency of some lawyers to confine the term, administrative law, to jurisdiction of a judicial nature exercised by administrative authorities over the rights and property of private individuals. The question, how far can the courts control the exercise of discretionary power is one of the most difficult problems which engage the attention of the lawyer. But he is equally concerned with the important constitutional issues which are raised by the relationship between Parliament and the various administrative agencies. Ministerial responsibility lies at the root of representative government; it may be impaired if too wide a scope is given to an independent agency. The supremacy of Parliament is weakened by the unrestricted delegation to the Executive of power to legislate. The independence of the judges becomes merely academic in importance if control over adjudication should pass from their hands. The more rapidly the functions of government expand, the more important it is to safeguard principles which may easily be overlooked in the pressure to devise an expedient to overcome some urgent administrative problem. Not the least useful task of the lawyer is to watch the form of legislation, whether it be by Bill or by statutory instrument, at its inception, and to test its merit by reference to established constitutional usage. Nor need such a task necessarily imply blind opposition to every innovation. Both the Minister and the civil servant may be ready to look impatiently upon the lawyer as obstructing the realisation of policy. Especially is this so, if the lawyer takes his stand in the past and is blind to changing social conditions. It is important that the lawyer of to-day should fill the rôle of a constructive, and not merely a destructive, critic in the process of reconciling individual liberty with the public interest. The rule of law is still the basis of political liberty, as it is understood by the European Democratic States and in the United States and throughout the British Commonwealth of Nations. But just as our legal forefathers in the seventeenth century helped to secure that liberty by their contribution to the parliamentary cause, so lawyers to-day can secure the survival of the rule of law by their insistence upon the impartial administration of government agencies, especially in the field where the private rights of the individual appear to conflict with public interest.

It is not easy for the lawyer trained in the conception of rights and duties under the Common Law to reconcile the discretionary powers of the administrator, which only too often resemble arbitrary power, with the rule of law which demands the foreseeability of the consequences of an act. The civil servant, with an eye always open to the political consequences of his acts on his Minister, may be as averse as the lawyer from a departure from precedent, though he may be less aware of the impact of administrative action on the individual. An understanding, therefore, of the administrative process is as vital to the lawyer as an appreciation of the rule of law is for the public servant. Where disputes arise, it is the judicial approach to their solution which is the more likely to secure a feeling of justice done. But if the lawyer is to play his part in this work it is necessary to define the limits of discretionary power. We, therefore, start by examining the nature of powers conferred by Parliament upon public authorities and proceed to consider the extent of judicial review of their exercise. This leads on to an account of the powers of administrative courts and similar tribunals which have not so far taken their place in the hierarchy of courts of law. The subject of the Crown as a litigant is to-day less obscure than formerly, and it is convenient, if illogical, to postpone discussion of the subject until after judicial review of powers has been considered. A chapter on delegated legislation concludes this Part. Statutory instruments are one of the

Administration according to Law.

two main sources of administrative law, the other (Acts of Parliament) has been dealt with in Part III.

Legal Powers.

Legal rights in the strict sense are the benefits which are derived by the individual from legal duties imposed upon other persons. A legal power is the ability to affect the legal relations of other people. The exercise of the legal powers with which public authorities are mainly concerned may affect the rights of individual citizens, even though they are exercised for the good of the public in general. The legality of such exercise depends on whether or not the power, which has been conferred by statute has been exceeded. The capacity to challenge the exercise of a power belongs primarily to those who may be adversely affected by it as individuals because their rights may be injured. This means that the power can be challenged by any one to whom the authority owes a duty not to exceed the power. If a power is exceeded, the excess may expose the authority to common law liability in tort; for example a government inspector who enters private premises without authorisation to do so may be sued for damages for trespass. But more often the remedy sought is not to redress tortious injury, but simply to restrain the unlawful exercise of power rather than to redress actual loss to the plaintiff. A ratepayer has a right to challenge expenditure out of the rate fund of his local authority for a purpose not authorised by law because he has an interest and the authority is under a duty to him and to all the other ratepayers not to exceed its powers: *Prescott* v. *Birmingham Corporation*, [1955] Ch. 210, where a ratepayer successfully challenged the validity of free municipal transport for certain classes of elderly residents at the expense of the general body of ratepayers.

For the most part the conferment of a power on a public authority does not create any duty to the individual because powers are given to enable services to be provided for the good of the public as a whole and do not create any rights enforceable by action in favour of any individual. In particular an individual cannot usually force by an action in the courts a public authority to exercise a power which has not been exercised when or as it should have been, unless he can show that the default constitutes a breach of duty owed to him as an individual.[1] At the same time, unless by express words or by necessary inference a power authorises injury to be inflicted upon the property or the person of an individual, the existence of a power does not *ipso facto* authorise the commission of a tort or breach of contract.[2] Challenge in the courts to the exercise of a power may come in cases where it is alleged that there is no such power, or that the power has been exceeded or used for an unauthorised purpose. Since most powers are discretionary, *i.e.* exercisable at the discretion

[1] *East Suffolk Catchment Board* v. *Kent*, [1941] A.C. 74; K. & L. 332.
[2] *Geddis* v. *Proprietors of Bann Reservoir* (1878), 3 App. Cas. 430, 455.

of the authority, the court cannot be asked to substitute its own discretion for that of the authority. For this would defeat the intention of the statute which has entrusted the discretion to a particular agency. But there may be cases where the court can say either that the discretion has not been exercised at all or that a proposed exercise is not a lawful exercise of the discretion because the authority has taken a wrong view in law of the nature of the discretion, *e.g.* by acting on irrelevant considerations: *The Queen* v. *Boteler* (p. 296, *post*). or that it has been abused, *e.g.* from corrupt motives and, therefore, in effect has not been exercised; or, if the record of the proceedings so discloses, *e.g.* from the reasons given, that the exercise of the power has been carried out by an error in law. Nor, where the power authorises interference with private property, can the owner sue for the resulting loss in the absence of a breach of duty to use care (negligence) in exercising the power.[1] But if a discretionary power can be exercised without infringing private rights, the courts will as far as possible require the power to be exercised so as to protect those rights, *e.g.* without the exercise constituting a nuisance at common law.[2] These propositions will be illustrated in the description of powers which follows and in the succeeding chapters which examine the relationship between the courts and public authorities.

It is necessary for Parliament when conferring a power to determine upon whom it should be conferred and what safeguards should be imposed on its exercise. Such a decision will largely be based on consideration of each particular power and the belief that it will best be exercised by some particular body or person, *e.g.* a Minister, a court of law or an independent statutory body. It is obvious that in a complex modern society powers and duties must be entrusted to public authorities which are not possessed by private individuals. "A sanitary inspector can enter my house to inspect my drains; my employer can not. A sheriff can summon me to serve on a jury; my friends can not." [3] The powers of public servants are usually powers which they exercise on behalf of the Crown or of Ministers or of local authorities; powers are rarely conferred by statute on subordinate officers themselves. But private citizens and public authorities and their officers alike must justify the exercise of a power in the same way; the power must be shown to have originated either from a statute or the common law and to be exercised according to law.

If A.B. does an act which affects the rights of his neighbour, C.D., he must be able to justify his act, if need be, in a court of law. He must exercise his power in the manner prescribed by law, and

Powers of
Private
Citizens.

[1] *Hammersmith Railway Co.* v. *Brand* (1869), L.R. 4 H.L. 171.
[2] *Metropolitan Asylum District* v. *Hill* (1881), 6 App. Cas. 193; K. & L. 19.
[3] Jennings, *The Law and the Constitution*, 4th ed., p. 296.

L

for the purpose for which the law has sanctioned it. Suppose that A.B., inconvenienced by a branch of C.D.'s tree overhanging his garden, wishes to remove the branch, he must first consider his legal position. Having satisfied himself that he is permitted by law to remove the branch, he must then consider in what particular way the law permits him to do it. Can he, if he wishes, enter his neighbour's garden for the purpose? Can he lop it off without notice? Sometimes the exercise of a power is optional; sometimes there is a legal duty to exercise it. A citizen has duties as a member of the public. Every man is under a duty to assist in quelling a breach of the peace, if called upon to aid a constable; he would, for example, be under a duty to assist a police officer who called upon him to assist in arresting a violent offender.[1]

Authority for acts of Public Authorities. If A.B. instead of being a private citizen is the holder of a public office, *e.g.* a collector of taxes, or a justice of the peace, his official acts must be justified in the same way. For every act performed in the course of a public duty there must be legal authority; or, as it is frequently put, a public authority or public servant must act *intra vires*. Just as a power must be shown to originate either from statute or at common law, so either the statute or common law will determine how it must be exercised and whether the person upon whom a power is conferred is compelled to exercise it or is merely given a discretion to exercise it. The tax collector must be able to show, if his authority is challenged, that Parliament, or a body entrusted by Parliament with the levying of taxation, has conferred the power to collect taxes on holders of his office or on the Crown or the department which he serves; further, he must collect them only in accordance with certain statutory rules. By accepting office he comes under a duty to collect taxes, exercising his power in the manner allowed by law. The same is true of the justice of the peace. He is a member of the Judiciary and administers in particular much of the criminal law. He also performs certain other duties and exercises powers of an administrative character. He is empowered by the Magistrates' Courts Act, 1952, and various Criminal Justice Acts to deal judicially with certain offences within limits defined by Parliament. He is under a duty to exercise these powers if called upon to do so, and he can be controlled, if need be, by process in the courts compelling him to exercise his powers or not to exceed them.

Classification of Powers— Statutory and Common Law. The majority of governmental powers are to-day derived from statute. Innumerable statutory powers are entrusted to the Queen in Council, to individual Ministers or to government departments, to public authorities or to holders of public offices. The chief common law power of the Executive is the royal prerogative [2] whereby

[1] P. 366, *post*.   [2] Part IV., Chap. 1, C.

Ministers of the Crown are able to exercise on behalf of the Crown certain vital functions of government without express parliamentary authority, thought subject to subsequent political responsibility to Parliament. The exercise of prerogative powers is usually less fettered than is the exercise of statutory powers, since the manner in which statutory powers are to be exercised is in general specifically prescribed.

Governmental powers may be classified in accordance with the three functions of government[1] *i.e.* legislative, administrative and judicial, though it is often impracticable to distinguish clearly between legislative and administrative or between administrative and judicial, power.[2] The body upon which a power is conferred affords no reliable test of the nature of the power. The Queen in Council exercises legislative, administrative and judicial powers. Some of the functions of the Judiciary are administrative. It may be said that legislation is the making of general rules of conduct, but generality is a question of degree. If the Postmaster-General issues instructions for the guidance of all head-postmasters, is he exercising a legislative or an administrative function? [3] The legislative form may be used to deal with individual cases, *e.g.* an Act of Parliament indemnifying an individual from the consequences of an illegal act.[4]

Classification of Powers—Legislative, Administrative and Judicial.

The exercise of judicial functions involves investigations, deliberations and the making of findings and other pronouncements on the rights and liabilities of parties.[5] These rights and liabilities are determined by settled procedure and their content is governed by a fixed objective standard. The extent of the discretion which the court can exercise is thus usually strictly limited. But the administrator, even when he is engaged in settling a dispute, will not be so circumscribed, unless he is expressly empowered by statute to give decisions on a point of law. His discretion enables him to take what he thinks is the right course in all the circumstances, *i.e.* to decide according to policy, which may have more regard to public interest than private rights. The term quasi-judicial has been used by courts to describe a process which is partly judicial as well as administrative.[6] That part of the process which has a judicial element may be described as "quasi-judicial," or the whole power may be described as a "quasi-judicial" power. Thus the exercise of an administrative power, *e.g.* the

Judicial Powers.

---

[1] Part I., Chap. 2.
[2] Jennings, *op. cit.*, Appendix I.
[3] Jennings, *op. cit.*, 1st ed., p. 14.
[4] *E.g.* Arthur Jenkins Indemnity Act, 1941.
[5] See *Administrative Tribunals and the Courts*, by D. M. Gordon, 49 L.Q.R. 94.
[6] See 10 C.L.J. 216 (1949) for article by H. W. R. Wade, *Quasi-judicial and its Background*, which accepts the inevitability of this inelegant term to describe functions which lie on the borderline between judicial and administrative spheres.

confirmation by a Minister of an order made by a local authority, must frequently be preceded by a public enquiry by an official appointed by the Minister. The holding of the enquiry involves the hearing of evidence, and this resembles the judicial process. It must be conducted in accordance with certain rules known as rules of natural justice. The decision whether or not to confirm the order involves the exercise of a discretion; the Minister must take into account the findings at the enquiry, as well as other relevant factors, *e.g.* general policy in regard to similar orders. Thus the Minister, while to some degree he may be acting as a judge, arrives at his decision not by applying any fixed rule of law, but by exercising his own judgment as to what in all the circumstances is fair and just, having regard to the public interest as well as the private rights of any objectors. "Though the act of affirming a clearance order is an administrative act, the consideration which must precede the doing of the act is of the nature of a quasi-judicial consideration." [1] In general it may be said that a power involves a judicial element whenever it involves the decision of a dispute. When the decision primarily involves the application of law to facts, it is a judicial process. When the final decision primarily involves an exercise of discretion based on policy, it is a quasi-judicial process. Another view is that a tribunal which bases its decision on policy or expediency is legislating and suggests that the true distinction is between a judicial tribunal which looks to law to guide it and an administrative one which is a law unto itself. [2] To draw the line is not easy, and as a result it has been suggested that a judicial decision is merely a decision which is in fact exercised by the courts in accordance with strict legal procedure, whereas a quasi-judicial decision is given by an administrator or an administrative court entitled to follow its own procedure provided only that the rules of natural justice are observed. [3] Frequently it is determined only as a matter of expediency whether a decision shall be entrusted to a judge or to an administrator, [4] but it is submitted that when the law is being applied to facts (*e.g.* does a citizen fall within the definition of an injured person under a particular statute?) a strictly judicial function is exercised, whether it is in fact exercised by judge or administrator. It is important to use terms accurately. If classification is by function or substance, we use the terms "judicial" and "quasi-judicial" as showing the nature of the decision to be given. If classification is by procedure, we use the term "judicial" when a decision is given by a

---

[1] *Errington* v. *Minister of Health*, [1935] 1 K.B. 249, at p. 273.
[2] See 49 L.Q.R. 94 and 419 for article by D. M. Gordon, *Administrative Tribunals and the Courts.* ; see his definition of a judicial tribunal at p. 106.
[3] Jennings, *op. cit.*, 4th ed., pp. 277–88.
[4] Pp. 341–4.

judge following ordinary legal procedure, and the term "quasi-judicial" when a decision is given by an administrator after hearing the opposing parties. There are various purposes for which it is necessary to decide the meaning of the term, judicial. Thus the High Court can only issue orders of certiorari and prohibition when there is a duty to act judicially in determining matters which affect legal rights. Again the rules of natural justice only apply when judicial procedure is enjoined. The absolute protection afforded from liability in tort to judges and magistrates can be claimed in relation to the exercise of their judicial powers. The value of the expression, quasi-judicial, in these contexts is that it has brought within the ambit, certainly of the first two purposes, the proceedings of bodies which can only by a strained interpretation be regarded to as exercising judicial functions as defined at the beginning of this paragraph.

The following examples illustrate some types of governmental powers:

1. Special Constables Act, 1914, s. 1 (1).

Her Majesty may, by Order in Council, make regulations with respect to the appointment and position of special constables . . . and may, by those regulations, provide—

(*a*) that the power to authorise the nomination and appointment of special constables . . . may be exercised although a tumult riot or felony has not taken place or is not immediately apprehended; and

(*b*), (*c*), (*d*) (other purposes for which the regulations may be made); and (*o*) for such supplemental and ancillary matters as may be necessary or expedient for the purpose of giving full effect to the regulations.

Legislative Power conferred on the Sovereign in Council.

2. Police Act, 1919, s. 4 (1).

It shall be lawful for the Secretary of State to make regulations as to the government, mutual aid, pay, allowances, pensions, clothing, expenses and conditions of service of all police forces in England and Wales, and every police authority shall comply with the regulations so made.

Legislative Power conferred on a Minister.

The difference between legislation by Order in Council and legislation by a Minister is one of form, not of substance. In both cases the content of the legislation is framed by a department.

3. Diseases of Animals Act, 1950, s. 15.

The Ministry of Agriculture and Fisheries may if it thinks fit in any case cause to be slaughtered any animals affected by foot and mouth disease.

Administrative Power conferred on a Department.

The Minister is empowered at his discretion to implement the statutory policy of slaughter to eradicate the disease; provided that the infection is confirmed, an order to kill the cattle cannot be challenged.

Quasi-Judicial Power conferred on a Minister.

4. Housing Act, 1936, s. 26, and Third Schedule which deals with the submission of clearance orders in connection with housing schemes prepared by local authorities.

> Third Schedule, para. 5:
>
> If no objection is duly made . . ., the Minister may, if he thinks fit, confirm the order with or without modification; but in any other case he shall, before confirming the order, cause a public local enquiry to be held and shall consider any objection not withdrawn and the report of the person who held the enquiry and may then confirm the order either with or without modification.

The public enquiry for the hearing of objections resembles a judicial process so far as it includes the requirement to hear evidence and the Minister has the duty of exercising a kind of judicial function (quasi-judicial), since he must consider the objections and the report of the inspector whom he has appointed to conduct the enquiry before he makes up his mind. But he applies no substantive rule of law in his decision to confirm or to reject. If there are no objections, the Minister is exercising a power which is purely administrative; he can please himself whether or not to confirm and he cannot be challenged in a court to justify his decision.

Discretionary nature of administrative powers.

The exercise of powers involves in most cases the exercise of discretion by the administrator. Where a single imperative course of action is prescribed, *e.g.* to pay compensation for the slaughter of animals affected by foot-and-mouth disease, we speak of a ministerial duty because the law gives the Minister no option but to pay. Discretion involves a choice between two or more courses of action. The judge performing the judicial function of applying an existing rule of law to the facts as found by him (or by the jury) is in a different position from the administrator, unless the administrator is, as is sometimes the case, given a judicial function by statute. The administrator is entitled to arrive at his decision by reference to considerations of policy. There may be precedents which he does not care to ignore. But within the limits of the statutory power which gives him the discretion, he is free to do so if he chooses and his decision cannot be challenged in a court of law on the ground that he has disregarded precedent or the weight of evidence. The forum where his decision can be criticised is Parliament.

Again, it may be the duty of the administrator to exercise his discretion in initiating action. The judge must await a dispute before he can function at all. It is the duty of the administrator to conduct or to supervise the conduct of a particular branch of governmental activity. His is the discretion when to act and, usually, how to act.

Discretionary powers can be challenged on such grounds as excess or irregularity, but there are a few where the language of the statute seems to confer an absolute discretion on the administrator. Under the British Nationality Act, 1948, the Home Secretary may grant a certificate of naturalisation to an alien who satisfies certain conditions. Even if those conditions are satisfied, his discretion is absolute and against his refusal there can be no appeal to a court of law.[1] During the Second World War power was given to the Home Secretary by a defence regulation [2] to detain anyone whom he had reasonable cause to believe came within one of the specified categories which included persons of hostile origin or association. In *Liversidge* v. *Anderson*, [1942] A.C. 206 [3] the plaintiff who had been detained under the regulation brought an action against the Home Secretary for false imprisonment. It was held by the House of Lords, Lord Atkin dissenting, that the court could not enquire into the grounds for the belief which led to the making of the detention order; the matter was one for executive discretion. In regard to a political and not triable issue an objective test of reasonableness could not be applied, but only a subjective test. The statement of his belief by the Home Secretary was accepted as conclusive. Lord Wright, however, appeared to accept the view expressed in an earlier case by Tucker, J. (as he then was), that the applicant for a writ of habeas corpus was entitled to challenge the *bona fides* of the Home Secretary by affirmative evidence: *Stuart* v. *Anderson and Morrison*, [1941] 2 All E.R. 665. Perhaps this case may be regarded as an example of a discretion theoretically open to question but in practice absolute. The Home Secretary must have reasonable cause to believe, but the court cannot go behind his statement that he had such reasonable cause to believe. In every case the degree of discretion conferred by a statute or regulation must be determined by reference to the statute or regulation in question. In *Nakkuda Ali* v. *Jayaratne*, [1951] A.C. 66; K. & L. 378, the Judicial Committee held that there was no general principle that a court could not examine whether reasonable grounds in fact existed and not merely in the mind of the official concerned. It is simply a question of the width of the discretion; all can be challenged for excess.

The exercise of most discretionary powers may be questioned in the courts. This does not mean that the courts can review the exercise of discretion and substitute their own decision for that of the body or person to whom a discretion has been entrusted: *Associated Provincial Picture Houses Ltd*. v. *Wednesbury Corporation*, [1948] 1 K.B.

---

[1] British Nationality Act, 1948, s. 10 (i) and Second Schedule.
[2] Defence Regulation 18B; see Part VIII., Chap. 2.
[3] For full discussion of this and other Regulation 18B cases, see Part VIII., Chap. 2, *post*, and K. & L. 262.

223; K. & L. 292, where the court declined to interfere with a condition imposed by the corporation in a licence granted for opening a cinema on Sundays on an allegation that the condition was unreasonable. In the absence of provision for an appeal the merits of a decision cannot be challenged in the courts. The cases which come before the courts are mainly those where discretionary powers have been improperly exercised and it is with the type of exercise of power which involves judicial review that the lawyer is primarily concerned. It must, however, always be remembered that the main control of discretionary powers is by administrative agencies. Senior officials control their subordinates and all officials are responsible to the Minister who presides over the department. It is always open to a person aggrieved to apply to the Minister for a review of a departmental decision. Sometimes it is specifically provided by statute that the decision of an administrative tribunal requires ministerial confirmation or is subject to an appeal to the Minister concerned.[1] Nor is judicial review the sole or even the main external control. Persons aggrieved by administrative decisions will more frequently appeal to their member of Parliment than to the courts and by means of parliamentary questions and other opportunities for criticism [2] the House of Commons is able to exercise reasonably effective control. Individual grievances are frequently raised on the motion for the adjournment [2] and the possibility of a parliamentary question is an ever present cause of anxiety to civil servants. It must also be borne in mind that those powers, the exercise of which is subject to judicial review, are not normally exceeded or abused. It is the abnormal case which comes before the courts. Just, however, as the courts will prevent an administrator from exceeding his statutory power (acting *ultra vires*), so they will prevent the wrongful exercise of a discretion unless it is in terms absolute. Such a wrongful exercise of discretion may arise from consideration of irrelevant issues, from failure to consider relevant issues, from an erroneous application in law of the power, *e.g.* by wrongly interpreting the statute which granted it, or from improper motives.[3] In practice it is not easy to determine this in the case of a public authority which cannot be required to disclose its administrative procedure or to produce its files in court. In *The Queen* v. *Boteler* (1864), 4 B. & S. 959; K. & L. 291, justices refused to order a parish to contribute to the expenses of its poor law union because they disapproved of the Act of Parliament which had annexed the parish to the union. The High Court ordered the justices to issue a contribution order and Cockburn, C.J. said:

[1] Chap. 5, *post.*   [2] Part III., Chap. 3.
[3] For further consideration of grounds for judicial review, see Chap. 2 B, *post.*

"I do not intend in the slightest degree to encroach upon the doctrine that, where magistrates have a discretionary power to decide whether they will do an act or not, this court will not order them to do it when they have exercised their discretion upon the merits of the matter. But it is clear upon the facts of the present case that they have not exercised that discretion which in law they will have been justified in exercising. . . . They proceeded upon the ground that the annexation of this place to the union was unjust, in other words that the operation of the Act of Parliament under which that was effected was unjust. Their decision virtually amounts to this—'we know that upon all other grounds we ought to issue the warrant, but we will take upon ourselves to say that the law is unjust, and therefore we will not issue it.' That is not a tenable ground on which this court can allow magistrates to decline to exercise their discretion according to law."

The magistrates had exercised their discretionary power after taking into consideration a matter which was wholly extraneous to their exercise of juridiction to decide whether or not to make the order, namely their disapproval of the policy of the Act of Parliament.

CHAPTER 2.

JUDICIAL CONTROL OF POWERS.

Reasons for
stressing judi-
cial control.

THE remainder of this Part (Part VII.) will be concerned with judicial control of the exercise of powers by administrators or by administrative courts and with delegated legislation. These are the aspects of administrative law which are of primary interest to the lawyer. They involve the principles of separation of powers, parliamentary sovereignty, the rule of law and the right of access to the courts. They are the topics which raise the fundamental difficulty of reconciling liberty with government. The lawyer, bred in the traditional system of English law with its emphasis upon the supremacy of Parliament and the right of the individual to defend his rights in the courts, is concerned to watch critically the delegation of law-making powers to the Executive and the adjudication of disputes by tribunals not hitherto recognised as part of the established machinery of the State. But it must not be supposed that legislation and adjudication are the only or indeed the main functions of the Executive. Its task is to govern by providing and administering the public services. The removal of legislative power to a central authority subordinate to Parliament and the establishment of a system of administrative courts to settle those justiciable issues which are now decided by administrators or tribunals appointed by administrators would still leave the bulk of administrative work to be performed, as at present, by the government departments and other bodies which enjoy a greater or less degree of autonomy in these matters. The main functions of administrators are planning, co-ordinating, supervising and generally exercising a discretion as regards alternative courses of action which are not of a character susceptible of adjudication in court. The real control of these functions lies with the House of Commons and not with the courts.

Ministers'
Powers
Report.

"The most distinctive indication of the change of outlook of the government of this country in recent years has been its growing preoccupation, irrespective of party, with the management of the life of the people. A study of the Statute Book will show how profoundly the conception of the function of government has altered. Parliament finds itself increasingly engaged in legislation which has for its conscious aim the regulation of the day-to-day affairs of the community, and now intervenes in matters formerly thought to be entirely outside its scope. This new orientation has its dangers as well as its merits. Between liberty and government there is an age-long conflict. It is of vital importance that the new policy, while truly promoting liberty by securing better conditions of life for the people of this country, should not, in its zeal for interference, deprive them of their initiative and independence which are the nation's most valuable assets." [1]

These words, cited at the beginning of the *Report of the Committee on Ministers' Powers*, aptly summarise the policy of the State in modern England and draw attention to the risk inherent in such policy. That this feature of modern government is equally true of the United States of America is shown by the following pronouncement by Chief Justice Hughes of the Federal Supreme Court:

"The distinctive development of our era is that the activities of the people are largely controlled by government bureaux in State and Nation. It has well been said that this multiplication of administrative bodies with large powers has raised anew for our law, after three centuries, the problem of 'executive justice,' perhaps better styled 'administrative justice.' A host of controversies as to private rights are no longer decided in courts." [2]

The Committee on Ministers' Powers, to which reference has been made, was appointed in 1932 at a time when a storm of criticism was being directed against the departments by the Bench and Bar, by prominent academic lawyers at Oxford and a small group of lawyers and others in the House of Commons. The appointment of the Committee coincided with the publication of an essay by the Lord Chief Justice, Lord Hewart.[3] This essay contained criticism which was mainly destructive by a judge who considered that the courts were losing their historic control of administration through the King's Bench Division. The terms of reference to the Committee were to consider the powers exercised by, or under the direction of (or by persons or bodies appointed specially by), Ministers of the Crown by way of (*a*) delegated legislation, and (*b*) judicial or quasi-judicial decision, and to report what safeguards were desirable or necessary to secure the constitutional principles of the sovereignty of Parliament and the supremacy of the law. The Committee, which vindicated the Civil Service from the charge of bureaucratic tyranny, made many constructive recommendations on the topics of delegated legislation and administrative justice. Though no Government has formally adopted its recommendations, its influence has been seen in changes made in drafting Bills which confer powers on departments and, in particular, in the establishment by the House of Commons in 1944 of the Select Committee on Statutory Instruments (at that time called Statutory Rules and Orders).[4] In some cases the recommendations of the Committee on Ministers' Powers have not been

[1] *Report of the Committee on Finance and Industry*, Part I., Chap. I., para. 8, p. 415 (Cmd. 3897, 1931), cited *M.P.R.*, p. 5.
[2] See *Cases on Administrative Law*. Edited by Felix Frankfurter and J. F. Davison. Preface. (C.C.H. University Casebook Series, New York).
[3] *The New Despotism* (Benn).
[4] Pp. 358–9, *post*.

accepted, *e.g.* in 1946 the Statutory Instruments Act repealed the Rules Publication Act, 1893. The Committee had recommended an extension of the provisions of the latter Act relating to antecedent publicity for proposed delegated legislation.

A.

Liability in Tort and Contract.

The chief function of the courts in relation to the control of public authorities is to prevent an excess or abuse of statutory power. But it is also the function of the courts to enforce contracts and redress tortious injuries, and to punish crimes. In this section of this chapter there will be discussed the liabilities of public authorities and their servants.

Individual
Liability.

In the absence of statutory immunity every individual is liable for the commission of wrongful acts and for such omissions of duty as give rise to actions in tort at common law or for breach of statutory duty. Obedience to orders does not normally constitute a defence [1] whether the orders are those of the Crown,[2] a local authority,[3] a limited company or an individual employer. The constable who finds himself a defendant in an action for false imprisonment cannot plead that he was acting under the orders of his sergeant in effecting a wrongful arrest. It is, however, seldom that officials of public authorities are sued in tort in respect of acts done in the course of duty without the employing authority being joined as defendant. A plaintiff usually sues the authority because (*a*) the authority is a more substantial defendant, and (*b*) certain statutes [4] exempt the servants of a local authority from being sued in respect of acts done *bona fide* in the course of duty. Actions against servants of the Crown were more common owing to the exemption of the Crown itself from liability for tort prior to the operation of the Crown Proceedings Act, 1947.[5] The Constables Protection Act, 1751, protects constables who act in obedience to the warrant of a magistrate and do not exceed the authority of the warrant, even though the magistrate has acted without jurisdiction in issuing the warrant. Officers of the court are protected, unless the cause is clearly outside the jurisdiction of the court: *The Case of the Marshalsea* (1613), 10 Co. Rep. 76a; K. & L. 201. A sheriff also who executes a judgment is protected at common law, as is the judge who gave it, subject to the same condition. A constable who arrests a person, other than a person charged

---

[1] For the position of members of the armed forces under criminal law, see Part IX., Chap. 2, B.

[2] Chap. 4, *post.*   [3] *Mill* v. *Hawker* (1875), L.R. 10 Ex. 92.

[4] Public Health Act, 1875, s. 265; Public Health Act, 1936, s. 305; Food and Drugs Act, 1938, s 94; National Health Service Act, 1946, s. 72.

[5] Chap. 4, *post.*

with felony, when an invalid warrant has been issued, but without having the warrant in his possession, has no protection. The Criminal Justice Act, 1925, s. 44, allows arrest without the warrant being in the constable's possession at the time, but this section only applies where a lawful warrant has been issued and the Constables Protection Act does not justify what would apart from the invalid warrant, be an unlawful arrest: *Horsfield* v. *Brown*, [1932] 1 K.B. 355. The Custom and Excise Act, 1952, s. 280, affords revenue officers a considerable measure of protection where there is probable cause for the seizure and detention of property as liable to forfeiture.

A public authority (including, with some exceptions, departments of the Central Government), is, like any other employer, liable for the wrongful acts of its servants or agents committed in the course of their employment.[1] It was established by the leading case of *Mersey Docks and Harbour Board Trustees* v. *Gibbs* (1866), L.R. 1 H.L. 93; K. & L. 240, that the liability of a public body whose servants negligently execute their duties is identical with that of a private trading company. In spite of the argument that a corporation should not be liable for a wrongful act, since a wrongful act must be beyond its lawful powers and therefore not attributable to it, it is clear that a corporation is, like any other employer, liable for the torts of its employees acting in the course of their employment. A hospital authority (now a regional hospital board) will be liable for negligence in the performance of their professional duties of those physicians and surgeons who are employed by the authority under a contract of service; equally where the authority employs a specialist under a contract, not of service, but for services to be rendered by him as an independent contractor, it is liable to the patient for his negligent treatment: *Cassidy* v. *Minister of Health*, [1951] 2 K.B. 343, esp. at p. 364; *cf. Collins* v. *Hertfordshire County Council*, [1947] K.B. 598. Where, however, the employee's act is *ultra vires* the corporation, there must be express authority from the corporation.[2] Those who are apparently the employees of a public authority are not always acting in that capacity when committing acts which constitute torts. They may be acting altogether outside the course of their employment "on a frolic of their own." Officials, too, may be acting under the control of a central authority, even though appointed by a local authority, or may be performing an independent public duty cast upon them by the law after their appointment; in neither case is the employing authority vicariously liable: *Stanbury* v. *Exeter Corporation*, [1905] 2 K.B. 838, where a local authority was held not liable for the

Liability of Public Authorities.

---

[1] For fuller treatment of this topic, see Dicey, *op. cit.*, Appendix, Section I., pp. 539–41.
[2] See Winfield, *Text-book of the Law of Tort* (Sweet & Maxwell), 6th ed. pp. 126–8.

negligence of an inspector, who, though appointed by it, was acting at the time under an order of the Board of Agriculture: *Fisher* v. *Oldham Corporation*, [1930] 2 K.B. 364, where a local authority was held not liable for a mistake made by a constable in arresting the wrong person, though the constable was appointed by the watch committee which paid him and could dismiss him. Whether a police officer makes an arrest under the wide powers conferred upon him at common law or under the statutory enlargement of his powers, he does not act as the servant in law of the local police authority.[1]

Statutory Justification.
Where Parliament has expressly authorised something to be done, the doing of it cannot be wrongful. Compensation for resulting damage is usually provided by Parliament. Certain presumptions are, however, observed in the interpretation of statutes. In particular it is assumed that, when discretionary power is given to a public body to perform some administrative act, there is no intention to interfere with private rights, unless the power is expressed in such a way as to make interference inevitable. A case which illustrates this is *Metropolitan Asylum District* v. *Hill* (1881), 6 App. Cas. 193; K. & L. 19. Statutory powers which authorised the construction of a smallpox hospital in Hampstead were held not to have sanctioned the erection of the building in such a way as to constitute a nuisance at common law in the absence of express words or necessary implication in the statute. At pp. 212–13 Lord Watson said:

> "I do not think that the Legislature can be held to have sanctioned that which is a nuisance at common law, except in the case where it has authorised a certain use of a specific building in a specified position, which cannot be used without occasioning nuisance. . . . Where the terms of the statute are not imperative, but permissive, when it is left to the discretion of the persons empowered to determine whether the general powers committed to them shall be put into execution or not, I think the fair inference is that the Legislature intended that discretion to be exercised in strict conformity with private rights and did not intend to confer licence to commit nuisance in any place which might be selected for the purpose."

If, however, the exercise of a statutory power, and *a fortiori* of a statutory duty, inevitably involves injury to private rights, or if express powers are given to do something in a particular way which must involve injury, *e.g.* to construct a building upon a particular site for a particular purpose, there is no remedy unless the statute makes provision for compensation: *Hammersmith Railway Co.* v. *Brand* (1869), L.R. 4 H.L. 171. The negligent performance of a statutory duty or exercise of statutory powers may, however, be tortious; and where the exercise of a statutory power necessarily involves injury, care must none the less be taken to avoid aggravating the injury by negligent execution: *Geddis* v. *Proprietors of Bann Reservoir*

---

[1] P. 191, *ante.*

(1878), 3 App. Cas. 430, at pp. 455–6. Where a statutory power can be exercised in a manner either hurtful to an individual or in a manner innocuous to an individual "that man or body will be held to be guilty of negligence if he chooses, or they choose, the former mode of exercising his power or their power, and not the latter, both being available to him or them": *Lagan Navigation Co.* v. *Lambeg Bleaching Dyeing and Finishing Co.*, [1927] A.C. 226, *per* Lord Atkinson at p. 243. Thus in *Fisher* v. *Ruislip–Northwood Urban District Council,* [1945] K.B. 584, it was held that a statutory power to erect air-raid shelters on the highway could only be exercised subject to a duty to take reasonable care to safeguard the public user of the highway by such special lighting as was permissible, even though ordinary street lighting was at that time prohibited; a motorist had been injured through colliding with an unlit shelter.

Hitherto we have been considering negligent and other wrongful acts which render the doer liable at common law to an action for damages. The omission to perform a statutory duty sometimes gives rise to tortious liability. The mere omission to perform a duty imposed by statute may give no cause of action to an individual who claims that he has suffered loss thereby. For the duty may be owed only to a higher public authority and not to members of the public as such.[1] There must be distinguished too a statutory power which, though it does not create a duty to the individual which enables him to compel its exercise, may be challenged where negligence can be shown in its execution. Sometimes a statutory duty coincides with a common law duty and then the common law right to claim damages for its breach remains, unless it is taken away by the statute. Sometimes a statute creates a duty and imposes a penalty for failure to perform it. In such event it must be discovered from the interpretation of the statute whether the remedy for breach of duty is limited to the penalty provided by the statute or whether there is also an action in tort available to a person injured by the breach. *Prima facie* a person injured by a breach of a statutory duty can sue unless it can be established by considering the statute as a whole that no such right was intended to be given;[2] but the general object of the statute must be looked at to see if the plaintiff has suffered the kind of harm which it is the object of the Act to prevent. Usually there is no such right where the duty is that of a statutory authority which owes a duty only to the general public and not to individuals.[3] Where the

Statutory Remedies.

---

[1] *East Suffolk Catchment Board* v. *Kent,* [1941] A.C. 74; K. & L. 332.
[2] *Monk* v. *Warbey,* [1935] 1 K.B. 75, at p 81; *Cutler* v. *Wandsworth Stadium Ltd.,* [1949] A.C. 398.
[3] E.g. *Atkinson* v. *Newcastle Waterworks Co.* (1877), 2 Ex.D. 441, no liability where plaintiff's house was burned down because of failure to maintain pressure in water pipes; *Saunders* v. *Holborn District Board,* [1895] 1 Q.B. 64, no liability where damage caused by failure to clear street refuse.

duty is an absolute one, there is an absolute liability upon the person concerned, and this applies to public authorities, *e.g.* the obligation to fence dangerous machinery imposed by the Factories Act, 1937. If the workman is injured, the employer is punishable by fine and is also liable in civil proceedings for damages. The employer can thus only protect himself from liability to pay damages by insuring against the risk. For injuries, however, incurred in cases where the liability is determined under the Coal Mines Act, 1911, s. 102, there is no such absolute liability to penalties under the criminal law or to pay damages in civil proceedings if it is shown that it was not reasonably practicable for the defendant (nowadays the National Coal Board) to avoid or to prevent the breach of duty. In the case of the common law duty to repair a highway, which was transferred by statute from the inhabitants of a parish to the elected local highway authority, an action lies against a highway authority for misfeasance [1] (*e.g.* the imperfect filling of a trench) but not for non-feasance [2] (mere failure to repair); but there is liability for breach of a statutory duty, *e.g.* to repair a bridge which is not part of the highway;[3] and for failure to remove a defective tram-track from a highway.[4] A breach of duty is usually punishable on indictment as a misdemeanor but such cases are now rare.[5] An indictment lies in respect of a public nuisance where the breach constitutes a nuisance to the public generally. Such an indictment can be brought for failure to repair a highway.

Public Authorities Protection Act, 1893.

The Public Authorities Protection Act, 1893, as amended by the Limitation Act, 1939, s. 21 (1) formerly protected the acts of public servants from challenge in the courts after a short lapse of time. No action could be brought against any person (which term included public authorities and servants of the Crown) for any act done in pursuance or execution, or intended execution of any Act of Parliament, or of any public duty or authority, or in respect of any neglect or default in the execution of any such Act, duty or authority, unless it was commenced before the expiration of one year [6] from the date on which the cause of action accrued. Further, in the event of the defendant being successful there were penal provisions as to costs.

The policy of the Act, which replaced one hundred and eight separate statutory provisions containing varying periods of limitation for actions against various public bodies and officials, was judicially explained in the following terms: "By the limitation which it imposes it prevents belated and in many cases unfounded actions. In this way it . . . prevents one generation of ratepayers from being

---

[1] *Shoreditch (Mayor of)* v. *Bull* (1904), 90 L.T. 210.
[2] *Cowley* v. *Newmarket Local Board*, [1892] A.C. 345.
[3] *Guilfoyle* v. *Port of London Authority*, [1932] 1 K.B. 336.
[4] *Simon* v. *Islington Borough Council*, [1943] K.B. 188.
[5] *The King* v. *Pinney* (1832), 5 C. & P. 254; K. & L. 418.
[6] For criminal proceedings the period of limitation was six months.

saddled with the obligations of another, and secures steadiness in municipal accounting": *Bradford Corporation* v. *Myers*, [1916] 1 A.C. 242, per Lord Shaw, at p. 260. In practice the application of the twelve months limit for bringing an action resulted in public servants and their employers escaping liability for negligence in circumstances where servants not paid out of public funds would have been liable. After a departmental committee[1] had recommended the repeal of the Act, there was substituted by the Law Reform (Limitation of Actions) Act, 1954, a period of limitation of three years (in place of the usual six years) in all actions involving personal injury or brought under the Fatal Accidents Act, 1846, for liability in negligence, nuisance or neglect of duty (including a contractual and a statutory duty). This provision put all defendants, whether private citizens or public authorities on the same footing.

Since the repeal of the Public Authorities Protection Act, which required prosecutions for criminal proceedings against public authorities to be started within six months, there are no general immunities from criminal process available to such bodies. But so far as the departments of central government are concerned, the Crown cannot be prosecuted, though its servants as individuals cannot plead its orders as a defence to criminal liability.

B.

Excess and Abuse of Powers.

It has been shown that the main control of administrative powers is that exercised by higher administrative agencies and through ministerial responsibility to Parliament, but that the courts can exercise control when a power is exceeded or abused.[2] When a power is exceeded, any acts done in excess of the power will be invalid as being *ultra vires*. The *ultra vires* doctrine cannot be used to question the validity of an Act of Parliament; but it is effective to control those who exceed the administrative discretion which an Act has given. The simplest example of the application of the *ultra vires* rule is where an act is done in excess of a power, or where jurisdiction to adjudicate upon a dispute is exceeded.

Ultra Vires Rule.

The application of the rule may be illustrated by three examples:

(1) A public authority upon which a power is conferred, exceeds that power by doing an act which is not authorised by the statute: *Attorney-General* v. *Fulham Corporation*, [1921] 1 Ch. 440. The borough council of Fulham arranged to benefit the housewives of the borough by installing a municipal laundry with the latest contrivances

[1] Report of the Committee on the Limitation of Actions, Cmd. 7740, 1949.
[2] P. 296, *ante.*

worked by corporation officials. Under the Baths and Wash-houses Acts, 1846 and 1847, the council had power to establish a wash-house, where people could wash their own clothes. A ratepayer tested the question whether the new laundry was *intra vires* this power and sought by an injunction to restrain the corporation from conducting the laundry as a business. It was held that the statutory power was confined to the establishment of a wash-house and that it was *ultra vires* for the Fulham Corporation to wash the clothes itself, that is, by its servants. Thus were the women of Fulham deprived of the benefit of an up-to-date municipal laundry.

(2) An authority may be given by Parliament the power to legislate on conditions contained in the enabling Act. Such legislation, which will be by statutory instrument in the form *e.g.* of regulations made by the appropriate Minister or other authority, must not contain provisions which conflict with such conditions. Thus s. 3 of the National Service Act, 1948, which relates to transfers of national servicemen during part-time service after the completion of the period of service with the regular forces, provides:

> The Service Authorities shall by regulations make provision for enabling or requiring a person serving in any auxiliary force during his part-time service, or during service performed in lieu thereof, to be transferred to any other auxiliary force; so, however, that such regulations shall not provide for the transfer of any person to the royal naval reserve, the royal naval volunteer reserve, the royal marine forces volunteer reserve, the royal air force volunteer reserve or the royal auxiliary air force except at his own request.

Any attempt by, for example, the Secretary of State for Air to obtain involuntary reinforcements for the Auxiliary Air Force by means of a regulation made under this section would be held *ultra vires* if challenged in the courts, as was a prohibition on certain imports made by proclamation under s. 43 of the Customs Consolidation Act, 1876, in *Attorney-General* v. *Brown*, [1920] 1 K.B. 773.

(3) Under the Housing Act, 1925,[1] the Minister of Health was empowered to confirm improvement schemes submitted by local authorities in accordance with the provisions of the Act. A scheme was submitted for confirmation which was not within the Act in that it left the local authority free to sell or lease land compulsorily acquired without restricting the use to which the land should be put. It was held that the Minister's jurisdiction was confined to confirming schemes which were within the Act: *The King* v. *Minister of Health, ex parte Davis*, [1929] 1 K.B. 619. The scheme was *ultra vires* and, had he confirmed it, the Minister would have acted in excess of his jurisdiction.

A later illustration is afforded by *Jackson, Stansfield and Sons* v.

[1] Since repealed. The present law is contained in the Housing Act, 1936, ss. 25 and 26 and Schedules 1, 2 and 3.

Butterworth, [1948] 2 All E. R. 558, when an oral (instead of a written) licence to repair buildings was held not to comply with a Defence Regulation (56A) relating to the issue of such licences.

The courts will intervene not only to prevent powers being exceeded, but also to prevent their being abused. Control of the improper exercise of powers may also be regarded as an application of the *ultra vires* doctrine. The exercise of a discretion without taking into account all relevant considerations is equivalent to a failure to exercise it. The exercise of a power for an improper purpose is not an exercise of a power conferred for purposes defined in the statute which confers it. Acts which are *prima facie* lawful may be invalidated, if they are done for a wrong purpose or by a wrong procedure. The exercise of a quasi-judicial power in abuse of the rules of natural justice is tantamount to a failure to exercise it at all. It must, however, again be stressed that where a discretion is committed to an administrator, whether it is of a quasi-judicial character or not, no appeal based solely on the merits of the decision lies to the courts. Provided that the discretion is exercised legitimately, the courts cannot substitute their discretion for his.[1] The only appeal is to higher administrative authority or by raising the matter in Parliament.

Any exercise of a power for an improper purpose is invalid as not being done *bona fide*. A distinction must be drawn between purpose and motive. Where an exercise of a power fulfils the purposes for which the power was given, it matters not that those exercising it were influenced by an extraneous motive. The distinction is best illustrated by reference to decided cases. The Municipal Council of Sydney was empowered to acquire land compulsorily for the purpose of extending streets or improving the city. The council purporting to exercise this power acquired land, not for the purpose of an extension or improvement, but with the object of taking advantage of an anticipated increment of value. The acquisition of the land was an invalid exercise of the power: *Municipal Council of Sydney* v. *Campbell*, [1925] A.C. 338. In another case, the Westminster Corporation was empowered to construct public conveniences. Underground conveniences were designed so that the subway leading to them provided a means of crossing a busy street. It was sought to restrain the Corporation from proceeding with the work on the ground that the real object was the provision of a crossing and not of public conveniences. The court refused to intervene. "It is not enough to show that the Corporation contemplated that the public might use the subway as a means of crossing the street. In order to make out a case of bad faith, it must be shown that the Corporation constructed the subway as a means of crossing the street under colour and pretence of providing public conveniences not really wanted":

Abuse of Powers.

Improper Purposes.

[1] P. 295–6, *ante*

Westminster Corporation v. *London and North Western Railway Co.*, [1905] A.C. 426, *per* Lord Macnaghten, at p. 432. Similarly the court refused to intervene when the Brighton Corporation improved a road which it had power to improve for the public benefit, although the motive of the improvement was largely to induce an automobile club to hold races upon it: *The King* v. *Brighton Corporation, ex parte Shoesmith* (1907), 96 L.T. 762. From *Arthur Yates & Co. Pty. Ltd.* v. *Vegetable Seeds Committee* (1945), 72 C.L.R. 37; K. & L. 299, it would seem that the exercise of powers of an administrative organisation of a subordinate character such as a wartime State seed control body may be challenged simply on the ground that it has acted for an inadmissible or ulterior purpose; on the other hand such a challenge cannot succeed against a representative body whose function is legislative rather than administrative. The seeds committee had issued general orders prohibiting the sale of seeds of certain descriptions; it was held that the *bona fides* of the committee in making the orders could be challenged, whereas in similar circumstances the good faith of a legislature could not be called in question in a court of law.

Discretion may not be delegated or surrendered.   An authority to which the exercise of discretion has been entrusted by statute cannot delegate that exercise to another unless upon the construction of the relevant statute it is clear that responsibility remains with the delegating authority acting through a subordinate in exercising the discretion: *Allingham* v. *Minister of Agriculture and Fisheries*, [1948] 1 All E.R. 780; K. & L. 336, where it was held that an agricultural executive committee could not delegate to one of its officers its discretion regarding the issue of cropping orders given to farmers: *Ellis* v. *Dubowski*, [1921] 3 K.B. 621; K. & L. 357.

Nor may a discretion be surrendered, whether the surrender takes the form of contracting in advance to exercise it in a particular way or of pre-judging the way in which it shall be exercised. Thus the licensing committees of the justices have full discretion in licensing matters, but it is their duty to hear all applications and to apply their minds in each case presented to them, whatever general policy they may have decided upon. Each applicant must have the opportunity of urging that the general policy should not be applied in the particular circumstances of his case. Even so extensive a discretion must be exercised in a judicial manner: *Sharp* v. *Wakefield*, [1891] A.C. 173.

Nor can a discretion be taken away by orders from a superior: *Simms Motor Units Ltd.* v. *Minister of Labour*, [1946] 2 All E.R. 201, where a National Service Officer who had been given a wartime statutory power to reinstate dismissed employees at his discretion failed to exercise his discretion, but applied instead a general instruction given to him by his Minister to the effect that he should reinstate in all cases of a particular type, thus negativing the exercise of the discretion.

Excessive expenditure upon a lawful object may be illegal: *Roberts* v. *Hopwood*, [1925] A.C. 578, where the court held invalid a payment of wages by the Poplar Borough Council which fixed an arbitrary rate for wages without regard to existing labour conditions. But the courts will not interfere with the discretion of local authorities as to payment of wages, unless the authority has taken extraneous considerations into account in fixing the rate: *In re Decision of Walker*, [1944] K.B. 644, But the general rate fund cannot be used to subsidise free municipal transport for elderly citizens at the expense of the ratepayer generally, in the absence of statutory authorisation: *Prescott* v. *Birmingham Corporation*.[1] Just as irrelevant considerations must not be taken into account (*The Queen* v. *Boteler*[2]), so relevant considerations must not be overlooked (*Roberts* v. *Hopwood*, *ante*). Similarly a decision will be quashed where the adjudicators have in error not addressed themselves to the real point to be decided: *The King* v. *Board of Education*, [1910] 2 K.B. 165 (affirmed *sub nomine Board of Education* v. *Rice*, [1911] A.C. 179). So, too, the courts intervened where licensing justices of a borough, who were empowered to fix an earlier closing hour in particular localities, made a general rule for earlier closing hours throughout the borough without reference to the needs of the particular localities concerned.[3]

Unlike other delegated legislation by-laws made by subordinate bodies may be declared invalid not only because they are *ultra vires*, but also because they are unreasonable.[4] The courts will not, however, treat the by-laws of a public authority as unreasonable unless they are manifestly oppressive, whereas the by-laws of a trading concern, such as a water company, will be rigorously scrutinised. In *Kruse* v. *Johnson*, [1898] 2 Q.B. 91; K. & L. 38, a by-law of the Kent County Council prohibiting the playing of musical instruments or singing in the highway within fifty yards of a dwelling-house to the annoyance of the inmates was held to be good. The Court held that it should be slow to condemn as invalid on the ground of supposed unreasonableness any by-law made by a body legislating under the delegated authority of Parliament within the extent of the authority given to the body to deal with matters which concerned it. But a by-law will be held *ultra vires* if it is repugnant to the general law of the land: *Powell* v. *May*, [1946] K.B. 330, where a County Council had attempted to make unlawful something that was expressly exempted from the prohibitions imposed by statutes relating to betting.

Margin notes: Local Authority Discretion. By-Laws.

---

[1] P. 288, *ante*.　　　　[2] P. 296, *ante*.

[3] *Macbeth* v. *Ashley* (1874), L.R. 2 H.L.Sc. 352, cited by Lord Halsbury, L.C., in *Sharp* v. *Wakefield*, [1891] A.C. 173 at p. 180.

[4] The court will not interfere with the exercise of legislative power by the Central Government, except on grounds of *vires*: *Attorney-General for Canada* v. *Hallet and Carey Ltd.*, [1952] A.C. 427.

Control of
Quasi-
Judicial
Powers.

It has already been shown that an excess of jurisdiction may be restrained by the courts, and that a power to confirm a valid scheme may not be exercised by confirming an invalid one. Other examples of excess of jurisdiction in the exercise of quasi-judicial powers are:

(1) A borough council made an order for the compulsory acquisition of land under section 1 of the Housing Act, 1930, which authorised the acquisition of land for the purpose of clearance. Before the order had been confirmed the owner had demolished the houses on the land. The council none the less applied for confirmation. It was held that the order could only be confirmed for the purpose of clearance which was not the purpose for which its confirmation was sought: *Marriott* v. *Minister of Health*, [1937] 1 K.B. 128.

(2) The Minister of Transport was empowered to hear appeals from traffic commissioners in respect of the grant of licences for public service vehicles. While upholding a decision of the commissioners to grant a licence, the Minister decided that the licence should be revoked at such time as other provision was made for services on the road in question. It was held that the Minister in laying down conditions for the future was exercising an original jurisdiction which had not been conferred upon him, instead of an appellate jurisdiction, and that his order was, therefore, invalid: *The King* v. *Minister of Transport, ex parte Upminster Services*, [1934] 1 K.B. 277.

C.

Natural Justice.

Procedure of
Administra-
tive Courts.

The most frequent cause for judicial interference with the exercise of judicial and quasi-judicial powers is a disregard of what are known as the rules of natural justice. These rules do not require that the proceedings of an administrative court must be conducted as in a court of law or in accordance with the strict rules of evidence, but they seek to ensure that justice shall not only be done, but also be seen to be done. The leading case on this topic is *Local Government Board* v. *Arlidge*, [1915] A.C. 120; K. & L. 369.

> The Hampstead Borough Council had made a closing order in respect of a house which appeared unfit for human habitation. The owner appealed to the Local Government Board in the manner prescribed by the Public Health Act, 1875,[1] under which the Board might make such order in the matter as might seem equitable, and the order so made would be binding and conclusive on all parties. After a public local enquiry the Board dismissed the appeal. Arlidge applied to the courts to declare the decision to be invalid, mainly on

[1] For present procedure of appeal to the County Court, see Housing Act, 1936, s. 15.

the grounds that the order in which it was embodied did not disclose which of the officials of the Board actually decided the appeal; that he, the plaintiff, did not have an opportunity of being heard orally by that official; that he was not permitted to see the report of the inspector who conducted the public enquiry on behalf of the Board. It was held by the House of Lords, reversing the Court of Appeal, that Arlidge could not object to the order on these grounds, since Parliament having entrusted judicial duties to an executive body must be taken, in the absence of any declaration to the contrary, to have intended it to follow the procedure which was its own and was necessary if it was to be capable of doing its work efficiently. Furthermore, Parliament had empowered the Board to frame rules to regulate its own procedure. So long as the officials dealt with the question referred to them without bias, and gave the parties an opportunity of presenting the case in adequate form, the Board could follow its own particular methods of procedure which were necessary, if it were to do its work efficiently, even though that procedure did not follow meticulously that of a court of law.

Similarly in *Board of Education* v. *Rice*, [1911] A.C. 179, Lord Loreburn laid it down that in disposing of an appeal the Board of Education was bound to act in good faith and to listen fairly to both sides, since that was a duty which lay on everyone who decided anything. The Board was not, however, bound to follow the procedure of a trial. It could obtain information in any way it thought best, always giving a fair opportunity to those who were parties in the controversy to correct or contradict any relevant statement prejudicial to their view.

When the courts are competent to adjudicate upon a dispute between a citizen and a public authority, *i.e.* when the public authority in the exercise of its discretionary powers is under a duty to act judicially and cannot simply determine the issue by an administrative decision, the rules of natural justice must be observed. A man must not be judge in his own cause. Both sides must be heard (*audi alteram partem*). These rules do not admit of precise definition. They have been described by Lord Selborne in *Spackman* v. *Commissioners of Public Works* (1885), 10 App. Cas. 229.

Rules of Natural Justice.

> "No doubt in the absence of special provisions as to how the person who is to decide is to proceed the law will imply no more than that the substantial requirements of justice shall not be violated. He (the administrator) is not a judge in the proper sense of the word; but he must give the parties an opportunity of being heard and stating their case and their view. He must give notice that he will proceed with the matter and he must act honestly and impartially and not under the direction of some other person or persons to whom the authority is not given by law. There must be no malversation of any kind. There would be no decision within the meaning of the statute if there were anything of that sort done contrary to the essence of justice."

Again, Swift, J., explained the duty of a person holding a public enquiry,[1] and the statement applies to any "person or body charged with the duty of deciding"; he must take care that the views of both the contending parties and the contentions they submit and the evidence they proffer are given proper weight; that nothing is done against the instinct which every citizen possesses to offend against which is said to be contrary to natural justice. The courts will not intervene merely because an irregularity has occurred (*e.g.* the asking of an improper question in examining a witness), but only if there is a departure from natural justice which goes to the root of the matter and renders the enquiry a nullity.[2]

No man a judge in his own cause.

It is an elementary principle that bias must be eliminated from influencing judicial decision. Without the consent of all parties no judge can adjudicate an issue in which he has any personal or proprietary interest at stake. The judge who is a shareholder in a company which appears before him as litigant must decline to hear the case, save by consent: *Dimes* v. *Grand Junction Canal* (*Proprietors of*) (1852), 3 H.L.C. 759. An extreme instance is furnished by *The King* v. *Sussex Justices, ex parte McCarthy*, [1924] 1 K.B. 256, which shows that the possibility of a suspicion of bias, even where none actually influenced the decision, is a ground for allowing an appeal.

> The acting clerk to the justices was a member of a firm of solicitors who were to represent the plaintiff in civil proceedings pending as a result of a collision in connection with which the applicant was summoned for a motoring offence. The acting clerk did not in fact advise the justices in the decision at which they arrived to convict the applicant, but retired with the bench. It was held that, as the clerk's firm was connected with the case in the civil action, he ought not to advise the justices in the criminal matter and therefore could not, had he been required to do so, properly have discharged his duties as clerk.
>
> The conviction was accordingly quashed, despite the fact that the clerk had actually taken no part in the decision to convict, the bench not asking for his opinion or advice.

On the other hand, in *The Queen* v. *Rand* (1866), L.R. 1 Q.B. 230; K. & L. 358, the Court of Queen's Bench refused to set aside a certificate given by justices in favour of the Bradford Corporation merely on the ground that two of the justices were trustees of societies which had invested funds in bonds of the Corporation. The question how far the rule that a man should not be judge in his own cause should prevent the settlement of disputes being entrusted to Ministers

---

[1] *Marriott* v. *Minister of Health, ante.*

[2] In *General Medical Council* v. *Spackman*, [1943] A.C. 627, Lord Atkin suggested that the requirements of natural justice might be more strict, *e.g.* when the name of a professional man was being removed from the register, than, *e.g.* where a school was being closed. See also *Russell* v. *Duke of Norfolk*, [1949] 1 All E.R. 109, at p. 118, for the application of the rules of natural justice to a domestic tribunal (Stewards of the Jockey Club) and pp. 314–5, *post*, for exclusion of the rules on the ground that the act under review was done in a purely executive, *i.e.* administrative, capacity.

whose departments are responsible for the execution of a policy which may be opposed to the interests of an opposing party cannot easily be solved; for it is important that the interests of the general public should be safeguarded as well as those of the individual applicant or objector. It is essential that a court shall be without bias, through fear, favour or other interest; but a dispute arising as an incident in the administration of a public service cannot, by reason solely of prejudice to private rights, be isolated from the general responsibility of the department concerned. Where a Minister has to decide such a dispute, it is all important that he should explain the reasons by which he seeks to justify his decision, if it is adverse to the private citizen concerned. The explanation may not satisfy, but it will at least prevent an abuse of the power which might result from an absence of any obligation to justify it. Dictators do not explain; responsible administrators can and should justify their actions. But, as yet, there is no general rule of law to require this.

An equally elementary principle of justice is that no party ought *Audi alteram* to have his case decided without being afforded an opportunity of *partem.* hearing the case which he has to meet as well as stating his own case. "Even God himself did not pass sentence upon Adam before he was called upon to make his defence. 'Adam,' says God, 'where art thou? Hast thou not eaten of the tree that thou shouldst not eat?' "[1] In *Cooper* v. *Wandsworth Board of Works* (1863), 14 C.B. (N.S.) 180; K. & L. 366, the court held invalid a demolition order, justifiable in itself, which was made by the Board without giving notice to the owner of the property or affording him an opportunity of being heard. There is, however, no obligation, unless a statute so provides,[2] that a hearing should be oral: *Local Government Board* v. *Arlidge, ante.* Even in a court of law evidence may in proper circumstances be given by affidavit.

The *audi alteram partem* rule is not observed where evidence is Housing Acts given by one party without an opportunity being given to the other Cases. party to contradict it. The application of this principle has caused difficulty where the Minister of Health has under the Housing Acts both executive and quasi-judicial duties. In *Errington* v. *Minister of Health,*[3] [1935] 1 K.B. 249, the court quashed an order of the Minister because of a failure to act quasi-judicially. The Minister was empowered under the Housing Act, 1930,[4] to confirm, after

---

[1] *Dr. Bentley's Case* (1723), 1 Stra. 557.
[2] *E.g.* Electricity Supply Act, 1919, s. 22 (1), which provided a right of being heard.
[3] For comment on this decision, see *Frost* v. *Minister of Health,* [1935] 1 K.B. 286, and Note by E. C. S. Wade in 51 *L.Q.R.* 417; see also *Robins & Son, Ltd.* v. *Minister of Health,* [1939] 1 K.B. 537; *Stafford* v. *Minister of Health,* [1946] K. B. 621.
[4] See now Housing Act, 1936, 3rd Schedule.

holding a public enquiry, clearance orders made by local housing authorities. Confirmation orders could be challenged on the ground that they were not within the powers of the Act. The Minister was thus in the position of having to decide a contest between the owners of the property affected by the proposed order and the local authority. After an enquiry had been held, but before the order had been confirmed, there took place further communications on the subject-matter of the enquiry between the Ministry and the local authority without the knowledge of the owners who had objected to the order being confirmed. Furthermore, an official of the Ministry viewed the property in the company of officials of the local authority and formed an opinion upon it in the absence of the owners. It was held that an order made after an enquiry based on additional evidence obtained in the absence of the objectors was not within the powers of the Act. Before, however, an objection is lodged, the Minister may make such enquiries as he thinks fit, and the making of such enquiries will not invalidate a subsequent confirmation order, even though an objection is lodged at a later date: *Frost* v. *Minister of Health*, [1935] 1 K.B. 286. "In so far as the Minister deals with the matter of the confirmation of a clearance order in the absence of objection by the owners, it is clear that he would be acting in a ministerial or administrative capacity and entitled to make such enquiries as he thinks fit to enable him to make up his mind." Sometimes the Minister is faced with two duties and has to reconcile an executive duty under one section of an Act with a quasi-judicial duty under another. The fact that he had under consideration an objection to the confirmation of a clearance order did not debar the Minister from fulfilling his statutory duty to advise a local authority on handling overcrowding, despite the fact that the area involved by the clearance order was part of the area discussed in connection with overcrowding: *Offer* v. *Minister of Health*, [1936] 1 K.B. 40, a decision which was also based on the fact that no objection had yet been lodged, see *Frost's Case, ante*; *Horn* v. *Minister of Health*, [1937] 1 K.B. 146, a decision which was based on the fact that at the interview complained of the Minister did not discuss the particular site involved. It would appear that the Minister may perform his executive duties without being restricted by the need to have both parties before him, although they overlap his quasi-judicial duties, but that he (or his officers) must act judicially when the act done (*e.g.* an interview) is specifically related to the subject-matter of quasi-judicial proceedings.

Scope of Rule.

It is necessary that the Minister should be under a duty to act judicially at some stage, before the considerations which have just been discussed will apply. Thus in *Franklin* v. *Minister of Town and Country Planning*, [1948] A.C. 87; K. & L. 360, the duty of selecting sites for new towns which is placed upon the Minister by section 1 of the New Towns Act, 1946, was treated by the House of Lords as a purely executive decision, notwithstanding that the Act prescribed certain methods for the discharge of that duty. These included the obligation to consider the report of a public enquiry which the Minister was bound to convene if objections were made and not withdrawn. It is difficult, if not impossible, to reconcile this decision of the House of Lords with the Housing Act cases which have been discussed.[1] There is a superficial distinction to be found in that the housing procedure involves the participation of two administrative authorities, whereas it is for the Minister alone to take the initiative and to decide the issue in the case of selecting a new town. But the common law conception of natural justice which requires a man to be heard in objection to administrative invasion of his private property has never depended on the two-tier administration, *i.e.* one authority confirming or rejecting the proposals of another. It is fallacious in such cases to regard the Minister (the confirming authority) as a "judge" : he decides according to policy at the national level, just as the local authority decides at the local level. The doctrine of natural justice was worked out by the courts long before central control of local authorities came into being in the form made familiar by the Housing Acts and similar measures: see for example *Cooper* v. *Wandsworth Board of Works* (*ante*) and *Urban Housing Co.* v. *Oxford City Council*, [1940] Ch. 70[2]. In the last-mentioned case Lord Greene, M.R. (at p. 85) stated that a local authority's decision to demolish a wall under statutory power was a quasi-judicial decision and this statement was wholly in accordance with the earlier cases. There is another ground for criticism of *Franklin's Case*, namely that the Minister on the evidence had prejudged the issue. The Housing Act cases were not concerned with any charge of bias on the part of the Minister but whether the judicial part of the procedure, namely the public enquiry, was properly conducted in accordance with the rule, *audi alteram partem*. In all these cases the duty to hold a public enquiry was prescribed by statute. But the rule is a common law obligation, even although it is not possible closely to define when the obligation will be implied. The rule is not specifically laid down in any Act of Parliament; on the other hand no Act says that it shall not apply. The following are some of the considerations which may lead a court to infer that there is an obligation to hear all parties :

---

[1] See "Quasi-judicial and its Background," by H. W. R. Wade, 10 C.L.J. 216, 234 ff, where the view is taken that *Franklin's Case* implies a shift from the natural justice rules of the common law.

[2] H. W. R. Wade, in "The Twilight of Natural Justice ?", 67 L.Q.R. 103, at p. 110.

1. Where the relevant power uses language appropriate to a decision being given in a court after a sitting;
2. Where there is a power conclusively to decide questions of law and of fact and so to ascertain existing rights;
3. Where destruction or demolition of property is involved in the exercise of the power;
4. Where the power is given to an authority which ordinarily acts as a court; and
5. Where the exercise of the power may involve a final decision that a man has been guilty of discreditable conduct.

As in all matters of construction these considerations may be displaced by contrary intention. Nor does any implied duty relate to what is involved by a hearing.[1]

Publication of Reasons.
The Committee on Ministers' Powers suggested two further principles of natural justice: (*a*) that the reasons for a decision should be made known to the parties, (*b*) that when a public enquiry is held as a means of guiding a Minister to a decision, the report of the inspector who holds the enquiry should be made available to the parties heard. Neither of these suggested principles can be regarded as rules of law. But, in response to public pressure, some departments have adopted the practice of communicating the decision in a letter which sets out the reasons which have led the Minister to decide the dispute in the way he has. Appeals to the Minister of Housing and Local Government against the refusal of a local planning authority to allow an alteration to a building or to the use of land are dealt with in this way. It was held in the case of *Denby* (*William*) & *Son* v. *Minister of Health*, [1936] K.B. 337, that there is no legal obligation to publish an inspector's report. Since a Minister is not bound to follow the recommendation in the report and usually has to take extraneous matters into consideration, it is difficult to see what object would be achieved by making publication a legal requirement. On the other hand there is much to be said for requiring a Minister to explain his reasons and in particular to say why he has come to a decision which differs from the course of action recommended to him in the report. The alternative might be to transfer the duty of deciding to the inspector who presides at a public enquiry. His decision should not be binding on the Minister, who could overrule it, giving reasons for so doing. In that case the original decision of the inspector should be published. Sometimes a statute has required publication of reasons; *e.g.* the Restriction of Ribbon Development Act, 1935, s. 7 (4), which has since been repealed, in connection with appeals from highway authorities, required the Minister of Transport to publish a summary of facts as found by him and of his reasons for the decision.

[1] For an elaboration of this conclusion see note by R. B. Cooke in 1954 C.L.J. pp. 14–19.

CHAPTER 3.

METHODS OF JUDICIAL CONTROL.

HITHERTO we have considered the principles which regulate the review of administrative powers by the courts. There must now be examined the different procedures by which the jurisdiction of the courts can be invoked. A review may take place incidentally in the course of a prosecution for an offence under a statutory regulation. It is a defence to a prosecution for an offence created by a regulation that the regulation is *ultra vires* and so invalid. Again, a civil action may be based on a claim for damages for an act which, unless justified by statutory authority, would be a wrongful act. Apart from review in the course of ordinary litigation, there are several means of directly invoking the jurisdiction of the courts to check excess or abuse of powers.

Methods of Control.

At common law the principal machinery of review was provided by the prerogative writs—mandamus, certiorari and prohibition. These prerogative writs have now been replaced by judicial orders obtained by a more simple procedure of application to the Queen's Bench Division of the High Court.[1]

Orders of Mandamus, Certiorari and Prohibition.

Mandamus is a peremptory order, issuing out of the Queen's Bench Division of the High Court, commanding a body, or person, to do that which it is its, or his, duty to do. The issue of the order cannot be required as of right; it is entirely a matter for the discretion of the court, which "will render it as far as it can the supplementary means of substantial justice in every case where there is no other specific legal remedy for a legal right; and will provide as effectually as it can that others exercise their duty wherever the subject-matter is properly within its control"—*per* Lord Ellenborough, C.J., in *The King* v. *Archbishop of Canterbury* (1812), 15 East 117, 136. The order does not lie against the Crown. If a government department is acting as agent of the Crown and is responsible only to the Crown, having no duty to the subject in the matter, it is not amenable to the orders of the court in the exercise of its prerogative jurisdiction in granting or refusing mandamus: *The Queen* v. *Lords of the Treasury* (1872), L.R. 7 Q.B. 387.[2] But mandamus will lie to enforce the performance of a public duty which has been imposed by statute on a department

Mandamus.

---

[1] Administration of Justice (Miscellaneous Provisions) Acts, 1933, s. 5 and 1938, s. 7.
[2] *Cf.* for a failure to enforce by action a duty owed to the Crown: *Gidley* v. *Lord Palmerston* (1822), 3 Brod. & B. 275.

of government or its servants provided that the applicant can show that the duty is one which is owed to him and not merely to the Crown; in the former case his remedy lies in having his grievance ventilated in the House of Commons, but he has no remedy in the courts: *The Queen* v. *Special Commissioners for Income Tax* (1888), 21 Q.B.D. 313, at p. 317. The distinction turns upon the rule that no third party (the complainant) can compel an agent (the department) to perform a duty which is owed not to him, but solely to the principal (the Crown). Against other bodies or persons mandamus will only be granted where the duty is in the nature of a public duty and especially affects the rights of an individual, provided that there is no more appropriate remedy. Thus mandamus will not lie if there is an alternative remedy in a domestic tribunal: *The King* v. *Dunsheath, ex parte Meredith*, [1951] 1 K.B. 127. The applicant must have demanded performance of the duty and been refused. The duty must be an imperative, and not a discretionary one, but there may be an imperative duty to exercise a discretion one way or another, such as the duty of a magistrates' court to hear and determine a case which falls within its jurisdiction. The exercise of such discretion is enforceable by mandamus.

It was held in *The King* v. *Housing Tribunal*, [1920] 3 K.B. 334, that mandamus lay against the tribunal to compel it to hear and determine an appeal. Its previous decision had been given without hearing the applicants and was accordingly brought up and quashed by certiorari.[1] Again, where there had been an irregular election of aldermen to a newly created borough council, mandamus to hold a lawful election was the appropriate remedy: *In re Barnes Corporation, ex parte Hutter*, [1933] 1 K.B. 668. Mandamus has also been obtained by a ratepayer to compel the production of the accounts of a local authority for inspection by his agent: *The King* v. *Bedwelty Urban District Council, ex parte Price*, [1934] 1 K.B. 333, notwithstanding that the officers of the council concerned were liable to prosecution, which, even if successful, could only have resulted in a fine and could not have secured the production of the accounts. Where, however, a statute prescribes a specific remedy, *e.g.* complaint to a Minister, mandamus will not lie: *Pasmore* v. *Oswaldtwistle Urban District Council*, [1898] A.C. 387.

Extension of Remedy.   At one time the operation of mandamus was confined to a limited class of cases affecting the administration of public affairs, and in particular it was invoked to compel inferior courts to proceed in matters within their jurisdiction or public officers to perform their legal duties. But many Acts of Parliament, mainly private or local Acts, which confer powers and obligations upon public utility undertakings of all descriptions, normally require the execution of

[1] P. 320, *post*.

certain works for the benefit of private persons, *e.g.* landowners who may have been dispossessed of their property or some of its amenities by the undertaking. An Act may impose the duty of erecting a bridge over a new railway, or of constructing a road in place of one which has been stopped up. The execution of works of this description is enforceable by mandamus at the instance of persons aggrieved. By the Rules of the Supreme Court, Order LIII, an action for mandamus may be substituted for the judicial order of mandamus in cases where private rights have been affected by failure to perform the duty; this remedy does not lie where the judicial order is appropriate; it is merely ancillary to an action brought for the purpose of enforcing a private right in respect of which litigation has arisen, but the duty sought to be enforced must be one of a public character, as in the illustrations given above.

An order of prohibition issues out of a superior court (Queen's **Prohibition.** Bench Division) primarily to prevent an inferior court from exceeding its jurisdiction, or acting contrary to the rules of natural justice, *e.g.* to restrain a judge from hearing a case in which he is personally interested. It does not matter that the inferior court administers a different law from that of the High Court; thus it lies against ecclesiastical courts and lay against the old Admiralty courts prior to the Judicature Acts. For many years past it has also been granted against Ministers of the Crown and public authorities in general to control the exercise of judicial or quasi-judicial functions. It does not lie against private bodies, such as a social club, *e.g.* in relation to the expulsion of a member.

It is not clear what are the precise limitations of the writ; but it **Scope of** is certain that it will lie against a body exercising public functions, **Remedy.** but it cannot be used to restrain legislative powers or those powers which cannot be challenged in a court of law because they are purely executive in character. An attempt to invoke prohibition (together with certiorari) against the National Assembly of the Church of England and its legislative committee to restrain that body from proceeding with the Prayer Book Measure, 1928, was unsuccessful, on the ground that neither the Assembly nor the committee was empowered to act, or did in fact attempt to act, judicially in matters affecting the interests of the subject: *The King* v. *The Legislative Committee of the Church Assembly, ex parte Haynes-Smith*, [1928] 1 K.B. 411. Nevertheless, the tendency is to enlarge the scope of the effectiveness of the writ. The courts exercise the power of controlling any body of persons to whom has been entrusted a "judicial" power of imposing obligations upon others. The case of *The King* v. *Electricity Commissioners, ex parte London Electricity Joint Committee*, [1924] 1 K.B. 171; K. & L. 282, is of particular interest in this connection:

The Commissioners possessed statutory powers enabling them to draw up schemes for improving the existing organisation for the supply of electricity in districts. A scheme was not to become operative until a public enquiry had been held and other conditions fulfilled. A writ of prohibition was granted to prevent the holding of an enquiry on the ground that the scheme to be presented at the enquiry was *ultra vires.*

A public body, which could not be regarded as a court of law, was attempting to exercise powers which affected the rights of private companies responsible for the existing supply of electric current. It could not be regarded as exercising legislative, but judicial, functions in proposing to arrive at a decision on a scheme which would affect the rights of the electricity undertakings. Clearly in this sense judicial has a wide meaning not referable exclusively to what is done within the jurisdiction of a court of justice. The judgment of Atkin, L.J., as he then was, deserves careful study as affording many illustrations of the circumstances in which the courts have granted the writ in the past. It is also made clear that the common requirement of confirmation by a higher authority, even where the approval has to be that of the Houses of Parliament, does not put an order of a local authority outside the category of a judicial proceeding which can be restrained by means of prohibition. Atkin, L.J., said: "In the provision that the final decision of the commissioners is not to be operative until it has been approved by the two Houses of Parliament I find nothing inconsistent with the view that in arriving at that decision the commissioners themselves are to act judicially and within the limits prescribed by Act of Parliament, and that the courts have power to keep them within those limits." The case should also be studied in connection with certiorari.

Certiorari.

Certiorari issues to remove a suit from an inferior court which adminsters the same law into the Queen's Bench Division of the High Court. It does not lie to review the decisions of a court exercising separate jurisdiction in a limited sphere, such as an ecclesiastical court, though prohibition will lie to restrain such a court from exceeding its jurisdiction: *The King* v. *Chancellor of St. Edmundsbury and Ipswich Diocese*, [1948] 1 K.B. 195. The reason for this distinction is that the High Court does not exercise ecclesiastical jurisdiction (apart from any special statutory provisions) and, therefore, is not competent to review a decision on ecclesiastical law; it can, however restrain any court which goes beyond the sphere of its own jurisdiction. It may be used before a trial to prevent an excess or abuse of jurisdiction and formerly to remove the case for trial to a higher court.[1] It is invoked also after trial to quash an order which has

[1] Removal of trial to another assize or quarter sessions court is now governed by the Administration of Justice Act, 1938, s. 11 (3). No order of certiorari is now required.

been made without jurisdiction or in defiance of the rules of natural justice. While it is only applicable to review a judicial act, "judicial" is again used in the widest sense and is not confined to acts of bodies which would ordinarily be considered courts. "The power of obtaining an order of certiorari is not limited to judicial acts or orders in a strict sense, that is to say, acts or orders of a court of law sitting in a judicial capacity. It extends to the acts and orders of a competent authority which has power to impose a liability or to give a decision which determines the rights or property of the affected parties": *Local Government Board* v. *Arlidge*, [1915] A.C. 120, at p. 140. The applicant must show a special grievance over and above that suffered by the public at large. In *The King* v. *Hendon Rural District Council, ex parte Chorley*, [1933] 2 K.B. 696, certiorari was granted at the instance of an adjacent owner to quash a decision of a district council giving permission for development of land in an area where, under a town-planning scheme, such permission might have given rise to a claim for compensation payable by the ratepayers. It was shown that a member of the council interested in the use of the land had voted on the resolution. The rule lay against a county council which had given an applicant permission under its statutory powers as a licensing authority to do that which he was expressly forbidden to do by statute, *e.g.* to open a cinema on a Sunday: *The King* v. *The London County Council, ex parte The Entertainments Protection Association, Ltd.*, [1931] 2 K.B. 215. In *General Medical Council* v. *Spackman*, [1943] A.C. 627, the House of Lords quashed a decision of the General Medical Council removing a doctor's name from the medical register. The Council which was under a statutory obligation to hold a "due enquiry" had refused to hear fresh evidence to dispute a finding by the Divorce Division of the High Court that the doctor had committed adultery with a patient.[1]

It would seem that an order might be subject to certiorari even if approved by an affirmative resolution of both Houses of Parliament. A resolution of the two Houses is not an Act of Parliament.[2]

Certiorari is frequently sought along with prohibition, so that not merely may an *ultra vires* act be reviewed (certiorari), but its operation may also be restrained (prohibition). Prohibition restrains a tribunal from proceeding further in excess of jurisdiction. It lies wherever any act remains to be done in respect of which the prohibition can operate: *Estate and Trust Agencies (1927), Ltd.* v. *Singapore Improvement Trust*, [1937] A.C. 898, where prohibition lay to prevent demolition of a building under a decree made in the exercise of a

Prohibition, Certiorari and Mandamus Contrasted.

[1] The Medical Act, 1950, s. 18 (2), prevents the re-trial of the issue of adultery by the Disciplinary Committee of the Council which is bound to accept the decision of the High Court.
[2] See the judgments of Atkin and Younger, L.JJ., in *The King* v. *Electricity Commissioners*, p. 319, *ante*.

M

quasi-judicial function. Certiorari formerly required the record or order of the court to be sent up to the Queen's Bench Division to have its legality enquired into, and, if necessary, to be quashed. The operation of the orders may overlap; there may be a record to remove into the higher court and also an excess of jurisdiction left to prevent.

> "Wherever any body of persons, having legal authority to determine the rights of subjects and having the duty to act judicially, act in excess of their legal authority, they are subject to the controlling jurisdiction of the King's Bench Division exercised in these writs." *Per* Atkin, L.J., in *The King* v. *Electricity Commissioners*, [1924] 1 K.B. 171 at p. 205; K. & L. at p. 283.

What is the duty to act judicially?

There have been (*a*) some important decisions arising out of applications for certiorari on the meaning of the duty to act judicially, and (*b*) one decision which has restored certiorari as a means of challenging an error of law which is disclosed in the record of an inferior court acting within its jurisdiction. It would seem that these decisions apply equally to applications for prohibition. As a result of these cases, all of which are recent, it would seem that the higher courts which at times have been reluctant to intervene in a dispute between a citizen and a government department arising out of the operation of controls [1] have nevertheless now enlarged their jurisdiction to review decisions not merely for an excess of power, but because they have been reached in error as to the law which they are properly seeking to enforce. In *Nakkuda Ali* v. *Jayaratne*, [1951] A.C. 66; K. & L. 378, the Judicial Committee declined to accept that a government controller was under any duty to act judicially before deciding to revoke a licence in textiles. Without such a licence trade in textiles in Ceylon had been prohibited by a defence regulation. The controller had power under the regulation to cancel a licence where he had "reasonable grounds to believe that any dealer is unfit to be allowed to continue as a dealer." The Court, as we have seen, did not follow the decision in *Liversidge* v. *Anderson* [2] and therefore was not prevented from enquiring into the reasonableness of the belief of the controller. But it decided that the controller was not acting judicially in exercising his power of revocation. Unless he was required so to act, certiorari would not apply. The Court treated the decision to revoke as executive action and therefore there was no obligation of the controller even to hear the application. He could simply cancel the licence as he had done after informing the applicant that he was suspected of certain irregularities. Mr. Wade and others have rightly regarded this case as showing the inadequacy of certiorari as a means of redressing disputes between private citizens and government

[1] See two articles by H. W. R. Wade, "Quasi Judicial and its Background," 10 C.L.J. 216, and "The Twilight of Natural Justice?" 67 L.Q.R. 103.
[2] P. 295 *ante*.

departments which may arise out of State regulated activities. The courts, however, do not yet seem able to offer any certain test as to what is a judicial and what an administrative function, the former alone being subject to challenge. It is clear that, when there is a duty to grant a hearing, the function is judicial. In *The Queen* v. *Manchester Legal Aid Committee, ex parte R. A. Brand & Co. Ltd.*, [1952] 2 Q.B. 413; K. & L. 323, a Divisional Court granted an order of certiorari to quash a legal aid certificate which had originally been granted to a bankrupt and later renewed in favour of his trustee in bankruptcy, a professional man of substance. The court held that the local committee which had issued the certificate was under a duty to act judicially although there was no dispute before them to settle.

"The true view, as it seems to us, is that the duty to act judicially may arise in widely different circumstances which it would be impossible, and, indeed, inadvisable, to attempt to define exhaustively. Where the decision is that of a court, then, unless, as in the case, for instance, of justices granting excise licences, it is acting in a purely ministerial capacity, it is clearly under a duty to act judicially. When, on the other hand, the decision is that of an administrative body and is actuated in whole or in part by questions of policy, the duty to act judicially may arise in the course of arriving at that decision. Thus, if, in order to arrive at the decision, the body concerned had to consider proposals and objections and consider evidence, then there is the duty to act judicially in the course of that inquiry."

As the cases stand at present the remedy may be excluded on the construction of a particular statute on the ground that the power is administrative and that its exercise does not involve a duty to act judicially; this has the effect of excluding the operation of the rules of natural justice and in particular the requirement to hear both sides before deciding the issue. On the other hand, the legal aid case shows that the courts are unwilling to give up their controlling power over an administrative body whenever the power which is challenged is one that can be decided solely on the evidence and apart from extraneous questions of policy, such as the grant of legal aid. A legal aid committee is an administrative body unconcerned with questions of policy and it must act judicially in deciding the application solely on the facts of the particular case before them and apart from any extraneous considerations, such as the undesirability of the type of litigation contemplated.

Moreover, the scope of certiorari has been widened by the decision of the Court of Appeal in *The King* v. *Northumberland Compensation Appeal Tribunal, ex parte Shaw*, [1952] 1 K.B. 388; K. & L. 312, for report in lower court. In this case certiorari issued to quash the decision of an inferior tribunal acting within its jurisdiction; it had given reasons for its decision which were bad in law due to a wrong interpretation of the statute law which the tribunal was administering. Thus it seems that an error of law can be reviewed by certiorari, provided that the error is disclosed on the record of the decision. This is not to say that the High Court can substitute its own discretion for that of the body to which Parliament has entrusted the exercise of the power, nor can the decision be reviewed if no reasons have been given. A tribunal may very well misdirect itself as to the law without disclosing error in the record as when it gives a decison without stating any reasons. On the other hand, the record may disclose an error in law without expressly stating it, the error being revealed, as in the case cited, by inference from the decision reached; the tribunal had assessed compensation of a displaced officer on a scale which could only have been determined by a misreading of the Act authorising the compensation.

In accordance with the principles already stated these judicial orders do not provide a means of appealing against the proper exercise of a discretionary power by a body to which a discretion has been entrusted by statute. That the court has no power to substitute its own discretion for that of the administrative body is clear from the following passage:

> "It is a fundamental rule of this court that they will not, either by a process of certiorari or mandamus, presume to act as a court of appeal by means of either of these two proceedings. For a certiorari where jurisdiction is in question, the court must be satisfied that there is neither an absence of jurisdiction nor an excess of jurisdiction and to allow an order of mandamus to go there must be a refusal to exercise the jurisdiction. The line may be a very fine one between a wrong decision and a declining to exercise jurisdiction; that is to say, between finding that a litigant has not made out a case, and refusing to consider whether there is a case": *The King* v. *The Licensing Authority for Goods Vehicles for the Metropolitan Traffic Area, ex parte B. E. Barrett, Ltd.*, [1949] 2 K.B. 17, at pp. 21–22, *per* Lord Goddard, C.J.

Illustrations of operation of Certiorari and Prohibition. — Two earlier decisions of the Court of Appeal illustrate the working of certiorari and prohibition. They both arose out of housing schemes prepared in terms which were not authorised by the Housing Act, 1925.[1] In *The King* v. *Minister of Health, ex parte Davis*, [1929] 1 K.B. 619,[2] a property owner in the area affected by the proposed scheme successfully applied for a writ of prohibition to prevent the Minister proceeding to consider the scheme with a view to confirmation. The scheme contained provisions *ultra vires* the Housing

---

[1] For present procedure for challenging a clearance order or compulsory purchase order, see Housing Act, 1936, 2nd Schedule; and see *In re Bowman, South Shields (Thames Street) Clearance Order*, [1932] 2 K.B. 621, a case under the Housing Act, 1930.

[2] P. 306, *ante*.

Act, and, therefore, it was not within the jurisdiction of the Minister to confirm it. The Act only contemplated the submission to the Minister of *intra vires* schemes for confirmation.

In the second case, *The King* v. *Minister of Health, ex parte Yaffé,* [1930] 2 K.B. 98, the scheme had been confirmed by the Minister after modification by him. The writ of prohibition was, therefore, of no avail to prohibit confirmation. But the applicant applied for a writ of certiorari to review the Minister's decision. In this he was successful in the Court of Appeal. Although the Housing Act provided that the Minister's order, when made, should have statutory effect as if enacted in the Act, it was held that this did not prevent the validity of the order being enquired into by the court. The Act only contemplated orders having statutory effect, if the scheme presented had been drawn up in strict compliance with its terms. The decision was reversed by the House of Lords on the facts: *Minister of Health* v. *The King,* [1931] A.C. 494; K. & L. 36. The principle was, however, confirmed that, while the provision makes the Minister's order speak as if it were contained in the Act, the Act in which it is contained is the Act which empowers the making of the order. If, therefore, the order as made conflicts with the Act, it will have to give way to the Act.

An interesting illustration of the use of both orders in the same proceedings is to be found in *The King* v. *Paddington and St. Marylebone Rent Tribunal, ex parte Bell London and Provincial Properties Ltd.,* [1949] 1 K.B. 666. The case is also a useful example of the interpretation of the wide wording of a statute in relation to the history of the Act and the reasons which led to its enactment. A borough council purported to use on a wholesale scale its powers of referring to a tribunal set up under the Furnished Houses (Rent Control) Act, 1946, tenancies of all furnished flats wherever two or more successful applications by tenants in the same block had been decided in favour of the tenants.[1] A Divisional Court granted prohibition to restrain the use of the tribunal as a general rent-fixing agency, irrespective of complaints by tenants, and certiorari to quash eight cases which had been selected by the tribunal out of over three hundred cases relating to the same block of flats, on the ground that such selection could not convert an invalid reference into a valid one. In none of the cases had any enquiries been made by the council to establish a *prima facie* case. Certiorari also lay to quash the decisions in the eight cases because the reason given by the tribunal for reducing the rents was based on their inspection of the premises but was not even referred to at the

Both Orders in same Proceedings.

---

[1] The main jurisdiction of these tribunals (see also p. 305, *post,*) is to fix a fair rent between a landlord and his tenant; proceedings are normally instituted by the tenant for a reduction of the rent.

hearing, thus depriving the owners of any opportunity of dealing with it.

Importance of Writs.

Thus these orders, despite parliamentary formulae to prevent administrative acts being questioned in the courts, are still important. They provide means of questioning the legality, but not the discretion, of judicial or quasi-judicial decisions (in the broadest sense) of public bodies, including government departments, as well as of the ordinary courts (other than the High Court, Assize Courts and the Central Criminal Court) and of administrative courts.

Statutory Machinery for Challenge.

It was formerly a frequent practice to provide by statute for the challenge by certiorari of orders which owing to the absence of a judicial element could not be challenged by certiorari at common law. Thus the Local Government Act, 1888, and the Municipal Corporations Act, 1882, provided for the challenge by certiorari of orders for payment out of county and borough funds respectively. To-day it is more frequent and indeed usual to take away the right of proceeding by certiorari and substitute a simpler statutory procedure which can sometimes only be exercised for a limited time after the making of an order. Thus the Local Government Act, 1933, ss. 184 and 187, provides (in lieu of the procedure by certiorari just mentioned) that any person aggrieved by an order for payment out of county or borough funds may apply to the High Court, which may give such directions as it thinks fit, and the order of the court is final. The Housing Act, 1936, s. 15, provides for an appeal to the county court within twenty-one days of the making of a demolition or closing order in respect of particular premises. A further appeal lies to the Court of Appeal on a point of law. A different procedure applies in regard to clearance orders affecting whole areas and compulsory purchase orders: Housing Act, 1936, 2nd Schedule. A period of six weeks is allowed during which an order which has been confirmed by the Minister of Housing and Local Government may be challenged in the High Court. Challenge is restricted to two grounds only: (*a*) that the order is not within the powers of the Act, (*b*) that the requirements of the Act have not been complied with and that, as a result, the objector has been substantially prejudiced. These orders may not be questioned by certiorari, at all events unless there is an excess of jurisdiction,[1] and, except as provided in the Act, may not otherwise be questioned in any legal proceedings whatsoever. In a case which turned upon a similar provision contained in the Public Works Facilities Act, 1930, it was stated by Branson, J., that, even when an order was not within the powers of the Act, it was necessary for the applicant to show that he had been prejudiced: *In re City of Manchester* (*Ringway Airport*) *Compulsory Purchase Order* (1935), 153 L.T. 219. This case was, however, doubted by

---

[1] *E.g.* if the Minister had used his powers for a totally extraneous purpose.

the Court of Appeal in *Horn* v. *Minister of Health*.[1] The better opinion appears to be that it is so important that justice should not only be done, but should be seen to be done,[2] that, though the High Court undoubtedly has a discretion, an order will be quashed whenever it is outside the powers of the Act. Where a procedure for challenge is provided by statute, it is frequently laid down that cases should be heard by a single judge of the High Court appointed by the Lord Chancellor, from whom an appeal usually lies to the Court of Appeal. This provision applies to the appeals against clearance orders under the Housing Act, 1936.

The High Court may grant an injunction to restrain a person from acting in an office to which he is not entitled, and may also declare the office to be vacant. This procedure takes the place of the ancient procedure of an information in the nature of a writ of quo warranto, but the principles which governed the former procedure still apply: Administration of Justice (Miscellaneous Provisions) Act, 1938, s. 9. By this means those who have improperly assumed to exercise an office may be removed. In *The King* v. *Speyer*, *The King* v. *Cassel*, [1916] 1 K.B. 595; [1916] 2 K.B. 858, quo warranto proceedings were employed to question the legality of the appointment of naturalised British subjects to the Privy Council. The Act of Settlement had limited the prerogative power to create Privy Councillors by excluding those born abroad, but subsequent legislation had removed this disability so far as naturalised subjects were concerned. Quo warranto proceedings lay "for usurping any office, whether created by charter alone, or by the Crown with the consent of Parliament, provided the office be of a public nature and a substantive office, not merely the function or employment of a deputy or servant at the will and pleasure of others": *Darley* v. *The Queen* (1845), 12 Cl. & F. 520—office of City Treasurer of Dublin. Under the Local Government Act, 1933, s. 84, a local government elector may initiate proceedings either summarily or in the High Court to question the right of a person to act as a member of a local authority. The High Court may declare that the office is vacant and order the payment of penalties. A court of summary jurisdiction may impose a fine not exceeding £50 for each conviction of a person who acts while disqualified. *(Improper Assumption of Office.)*

An injunction may be claimed against a public authority by any individual who can show that he will suffer special damage as the result of contemplated illegal action, *e.g.* a public nuisance, or that he has suffered such special damage as the result of action which it *(Injunctions.[3])*

---

[1] P. 314, *ante.*

[2] *Errington* v. *Minister of Health*, [1935] 1 K.B. 249, *per* Maugham, L.J., at p. 280. This case was decided under a similar provision of the Housing Act, 1930.

[3] For a discussion of the scope of this remedy and of declaratory judgments, see article by Professor W. Friedmann, 22 *Australian Law Journal*, 446–53.

is not too late to restrain. An injunction may be obtained to restrain any *ultra vires* act, *e.g.* to restrain an improper expenditure of borough funds: *Attorney-General* v. *Aspinall* (1837), 2 My. & Cr. 406. An injunction can be obtained for these purposes by the Attorney-General, either at his own instance or at the instance of a relator (one who informs). A relator need have no personal interest in the subject-matter of the claim except his interest as a member of the public. The Attorney-General must be joined as a party where the individual complaining can show no special damage to himself. It is at the discretion of the Attorney-General whether or not to proceed. If the public body is doing an act which tends to injure the public, it is the right of the Attorney-General to intervene, and he will be successful, even though he cannot prove that injury will result from the act complained of. A relator action, as these proceedings are called, lies to restrain an illegal act, even though its validity could be tested by certiorari: *Attorney-General* v. *Tynemouth Corporation*, [1899] A.C. 293; or though the infringement of public rights could be visited with other penalties: *Attorney-General* v. *Sharp*, [1931] 1 Ch. 121. There are two cases where a person can sue without joining the Attorney-General: *Boyce* v. *Paddington Borough Council*, [1903] 1 Ch. 109: (1) if interference with the public right also constitutes an interference with the plaintiff's private right, *e.g.* where an obstruction upon a highway is also an interference with a private right of access to the highway: *Lyon* v. *Fishmongers Co.* (1876), 1 App. Cas. 662; (2) where no private right of the plaintiff is interfered with, but he, in respect of his public right, suffers special damage peculiar to himself from the interference with a public right, *e.g.* where as a result of a public nuisance a plaintiff's premises have been rendered unhealthy and incommodious: *Benjamin* v. *Storr* (1874), L.R. 9 C.P. 400.

Declaratory Judgments.　A declaratory judgment may serve to restrain both the Crown and public authorities generally from illegal conduct. Such a judgment cannot, like an injunction, or a judicial order, such as certiorari, be directly enforced, but a public body is not likely to disregard a decision of the High Court that its course of action is unlawful. In the case of the federal constitutions of the British Commonwealth and also in the United States it may be used to elucidate the constitutional validity of statutes. Order XXV., r. 5, of the Rules of the Supreme Court provides that:

> "No action or proceedings shall be open to objection on the ground that a merely declaratory judgment or order is sought thereby, and the court may make binding declarations of right whether any consequential relief is or could be claimed, or not."

It would appear that a declaration can be obtained that the judgment of an inferior tribunal is invalid as being in excess of jurisdiction, unless an alternative remedy is available. This "remedy" has enabled trade unions and their members to obtain relief, though they are prevented from directly enforcing certain contracts by the Trade Union Act, 1871, s. 4. It is also an obvious convenience in a dispute between a ratepayer and his local authority or between two local authorities to be able to have the law determined in its application to a particular case without seeking a coercive remedy. Somewhat similar is the practice of local authorities agreeing to state a case on points of law for the decision of the court. An action for a declaratory judgment or the statement of a special case must be based on a concrete case which has arisen. The courts will not give answers to questions propounded in the form of hypothetical cases. Nor can the judges be asked to give advisory opinions on points of law.[1] The remedy by declaration has the advantage that it may be valuable when other remedies are spent. Thus in *Barnard* v. *National Dock Labour Board*, [1953] 2 Q.B. 18,[2] where the Board had delegated its disciplinary powers to a port manager without statutory authority, certiorari did not lie to quash an order which suspended certain dock workers because an application for that remedy would have been out of time. But the court, without laying down the bounds of its jurisdiction, expressed itself competent and willing to declare any injustice as unlawful in the absence of any available remedy and further to restrain that injustice by an injunction. The court stated that this discretionary relief would only be used sparingly, without defining the bounds of its application; it is, however, available against domestic as well as administrative courts.[3]

An example of the check which may be imposed upon the exercise Surcharge. of discretionary power is to be found in the surcharge upon the individual members of a council which is responsible for excessive or illegal expenditure. The power of disallowance and surcharge is vested in district auditors who are appointed by the Ministry of Health, but enjoy independence from his control in the exercise of their powers.[4] A right of appeal from a surcharge ordered by a district auditor lies to the High Court, but an alternative right of appeal lies to the Minister of Health if the amount of the surcharge does not exceed £500. An unsuccessful appeal to the High Court cannot be followed by an appeal to the Minister.[5] Both the court and the Minister have a power to remit the surcharge and this power may be

---

[1] See *Consultation of the Judiciary by the Executive*, by E. C. S. Wade, 46 L.Q.R. 169; and p. 479, *post*, for references to the Judicial Committee of the Privy Council.
[2] *Cooper* v. *Wilson*, [1937] 2 K.B. 309 for an early example of this jurisdiction, and compare *Toowoomba Foundry Proprietary Ltd.* v. *The Commonwealth* (1945), 71 C.L.R. 545 at p. 584.
[3] *Lee* v. *Showmen's Guild*, [1952] 2 Q.B. 329.
[4] Part VI., Chap. 3, C.
[5] *The King* v. *Minister of Health, ex parte Dore*, [1927] 1 K.B. 765.

exercised on application by the persons surcharged, even if there is no appeal from the auditor's decision, on the ground that they acted reasonably or in the belief that their action was authorised by law. The court and the Minister have discretion as to costs and may order their payment out of the fund to which the accounts relate. In *Roberts* v. *Hopwood*, [1925] A.C. 578,[1] Lord Atkinson said at p. 595:

> "A body charged with the administration for definite purposes of funds contributed in whole or in part by persons other than the members of that body owes, in my view, a duty to these latter persons to conduct that administration in a fairly businesslike manner with reasonable care, skill, and caution, and with due regard to the interests of those contributors who are not members of the body."

Because local bodies have discretionary powers to fix wages for their employees, they must not, since they are handling public money, use it unreasonably, even for a lawful purpose.

Exclusion of the Jurisdiction of the Courts.

The jurisdiction of the courts to control excess or abuse of powers may be excluded by express words in a statute.[2] Thus it may be provided that confirmation of an order by a Minister shall be conclusive evidence of compliance with a statute,[3] and that the validity of a statutory order shall not be questioned in any legal proceedings whatsoever. Where, however, it is merely stated that an order shall have effect as if enacted in the Act which authorised it, the courts may none the less hold the order invalid if it is inconsistent with the provisions of the Act. If an order conflicts with the Act which sanctions it being made, it must give way to the Act: *Minister of Health* v. *The King*.[4] In this case the House of Lords distinguished the earlier judgment in *Institute of Patent Agents* v. *Lockwood*, [1894] A.C. 347; K. & L. 35, where the House had upheld the validity of general rules made by the Board of Trade. In both cases definite views were expressed as to the effect of the words "shall have effect as if enacted in this Act." In both cases these views were *obiter dicta*. It is, however, clear that in the later case the House of Lords was of the opinion that the words did not validate an order which was plainly inconsistent with the Act.[5] The Committee on Ministers' Powers expressed the view that, even where it is provided that the confirmation of an order shall be conclusive evidence of compliance

---

[1] P. 307–8, *ante.*

[2] Chap. 5, *post*, for arguments for and against such exclusion.

[3] *Ex parte Ringer* (1909), 25 T.L.R. 718.

[4] P. 325, *ante.*

[5] In the earlier, but not the later, case the rules required had to be laid before Parliament, which could annul them by negative resolution. The House of Lords did not, however, distinguish the two cases on this ground. For full discussion of these two cases, see *The Parliamentary Powers of English Government Departments*, by John Willis (Harvard University Press, 1933), and Note in 60 *L.Q.R.*, at p. 325, by Sir Carleton Allen, who regards the question as still open.

with the Act, an order could be questioned if the Minister making it was acting altogether outside his province.[1] It is, however, suggested that, if there are added the words "and shall not be questioned in any legal proceedings whatsoever,"[2] the jurisdiction of the courts is effectively excluded.

[1] *M.P.R.*, p. 40.

[2] These words have not yet been considered by the Court of Appeal or House of Lords; see, however, *Ex parte Ringer,* p. 330, *ante.*

CHAPTER 4.

PROCEEDINGS BY AND AGAINST THE CROWN.

Fundamental Rules. THERE were two main rules which governed until 1948 the complicated law relating to the liability of the Crown and its servants: (1) the rule of substantive law that the King could do no wrong; (2) the procedural rule that the King could not be sued in his own courts—a rule derived from the feudal days when a lord could not be sued in his own court.

What is the Crown? It is necessary to consider separately (*a*) contractual and (*b*) tortious liability, but first it must be emphasised that the term " Crown " included all the departments of the Central Government, and, unless a statute expressly provided otherwise,[1] a Minister of the Crown retained the immunity of the Crown when as agent of the Crown he performed duties or exercised powers conferred upon him by statute in his own name. The shield of the Crown only covered what may be described as the general government of the country.[2] Thus the immunity of the Crown was generally not enjoyed by independent statutory authorities which are not presided over by a Minister of the Crown,[3] *e.g.* the British Broadcasting Corporation and the agricultural marketing boards. In some cases, however, these bodies acted on behalf of the Crown and thus shared the immunity of a government department, *e.g.* the Assistance Board and the Livestock Commission. It was necessary to examine in each case the particular Act of Parliament which established the body concerned.

Contractual Liability: Petition of Right. It was, however, essential that the subject should be able to obtain his rights under a contract made with a government department. The remedy was a petition of right, which was originally a remedy available only for the recovery of property, but was made available to enforce any contractual obligation. The practice was governed by the Petitions of Right Act, 1860. A petition of right lay in respect of any claim arising out of contracts by which the Crown could be bound, but not in respect of claims arising out of tortious acts. It lay also for the recovery of real property, for damages for breach of contract:

---

[1] P. 335 n.2 *post.*

[2] " Liability for Acts of Public Servants," by Sir W. Harrison Moore, 23 *L.Q.R.*, p. 12. *Mersey Docks Trustees* v. *Cameron* (1861), 11 H.L.C. 443, at p. 508.

[3] Part IV., Chap. 11.

Thomas v. *The Queen* (1874), L.R. 10 Q.B. 31, and to recover compensation under a statute: *Attorney-General* v. *De Keyser's Royal Hotel*, [1920] A.C. 508; K. & L. 86. It probably lay for recovery of a chattel.[1] It was a condition precedent to the hearing of a petition by the court that it should be endorsed with the words *fiat justitia* by the Crown on the advice of the Home Secretary, who acted on the opinion of the Attorney-General. There was no appeal against the refusal of the *fiat*. A judgment in favour of a suppliant on a petition of right took the form of a declaration of the rights to which the suppliant was entitled and, being always observed by the Crown, was as effective as a judgment in an ordinary action, though execution could not be levied against Crown property.

The Crown Proceedings Act, 1947,[2] which came into force on January 1, 1948, enables the appropriate government department, or in the alternative where no department is named for the purpose of legal process the Attorney-General, to be sued both in the High Court and in a county court by ordinary process under rules of court in all those cases where a petition of right or a special statutory procedure (some of these were of great antiquity and extreme complexity) had hitherto been required. The ordinary rules of agency apply; thus an agent need only have ostensible authority to bind the Crown and there is no rule requiring the actual authority of the Crown.

The Law since 1948.

But it is not every contract entered into by the Crown which gives a right to redress for its breach. Thus, if the contract expressly provides that money payments thereunder are to be made out of monies provided by Parliament, such provision is a condition precedent to liability under the contract, but it is not necessary that specific appropriations shall be made in advance to meet the obligations of the Crown. Any damages awarded against the Crown will, however, only be recoverable if appropriation is made by Parliament in the usual way.[3] This applies whether the liability is in contract or in tort; nor, as will be seen, can execution to enforce a judgment be levied against Crown property. There is, moreover, a rule of law, the exact extent of which it is not easy to determine, that the Crown cannot bind itself so as to fetter its future executive action: *Rederiaktiebolaget Amphitrite* v. *The King*, [1921] 3 K.B. 500; K. & L. 221, where the court held unenforceable an undertaking by the Government promising freedom from detention to a Swedish ship trading with Great Britain during the First World War. But the defence of executive necessity probably only "avails the Crown where there is an

---

[1] Winfield, *op. cit.*, 5th ed. p. 84.
[2] For text, see K. & L. 209–19. Section 1 relates to contracts.
[3] See H. Street, *Governmental Liability*, pp.84–92. For Appropriation, see p. 111, *ante.*

implied term to that effect or that is the true meaning of the contract":
Robertson v. *Minister of Pensions*, [1949] 1 K.B. 227, at p. 231. At
all events the defence has no application to ordinary commercial
contracts made by the Crown.[1] Those who make contracts on behalf
of the Crown, as its agents, are in accordance with the general
rule of law not liable personally: *Macbeath* v. *Haldimand* (1786),
1 T.R. 172.

Service
under the
Crown.

No servant of the Crown can normally claim damages for wrongful dismissal; for it is part of the prerogative that the Crown only
employs its servants at its pleasure. The Crown relies on its freedom
to dismiss its servants at will in the public interest; thus the relationship between the Crown and its servants is unilateral and does not
give the servant a right of action for dismissal. In the absence of
statutory provision [2] civil servants may be dismissed at pleasure:
Dunn v. *The Queen*, [1896] 1 Q.B. 116; K. & L. 220, where Lord
Herschell said:

> "Such employment being for the good of the public, it is essential
> for the public good that it should be capable of being determined at
> the pleasure of the Crown, except in certain exceptional cases where
> it has been deemed to be more for the public good that some restric-
> tion should be imposed on the power to dismiss its servants."

Having failed in his petition of right, Dunn sued the servant of the
Crown who had engaged him, for damages for breach of warranty
of authority. It was held that no action lies against a Crown servant for breach of warranty of authority, but the decision can be
supported on the narrower ground that Dunn must be deemed to
have known that the officer who had engaged him had no power
in law to engage him for a fixed period: *Dunn* v. *Macdonald*,
[1897] 1 Q.B. 401.[3] Where an office is abolished in statute, a Crown
servant has no claim, even though the terms of his engagement
expressly state that he can only be dismissed for "cause": *Reilly* v.
The King, [1934] A.C. 176, where it was said (*obiter*), at p. 179, that a
term would not be implied that the Crown could dismiss at pleasure,
if the contract prescribed the period of employment and provided
expressly for dismissal for cause.

Security of
Tenure.

The security of the Civil Service depends upon convention rather
than law.[4] The agreements reached between the Treasury and representatives of the staffs of government departments in joint councils
(Whitley Councils) and afterwards confirmed by the Treasury do
not give rise to contractual rights: *Rodwell* v. *Thomas*, [1944] K.B.

---

[1] Street, *op. cit.*, pp. 98–9; J. D. B. Mitchell, *The Contracts of Public Authorities*,
pp. 27–32 (London School of Economics).

[2] *E.g.* the statutory provision that judges hold office during good behaviour,
Part V., p. 249, *ante*; see also *Gould* v. *Stuart*, [1896] A.C. 575, where the New
South Wales Civil Service Act, 1884, was held to override the general rule.

[3] Discussed in K. & L., p. 196.   [4] Part II., Chap. 4.

596. No remedy exists where an officer appointed under statutory authority loses his office through its premature termination by Act of Parliament without compensation, since the agreement has become impossible of performance: *Reilly* v. *The King, ante.* Members of the armed forces [1] cannot sue for arrears of pay, for no engagement between the Crown and members of the armed forces can be enforced by a court of law: *Leaman* v. *The King*, [1920] 3 K.B. 663; *Kynaston* v. *Attorney-General* (1933), 49 T.L.R. 300.

The rule that "the Crown can do no wrong" made it impossible before 1948 to sue the Crown either in respect of wrongs expressly authorised by the Crown or in respect of wrongs committed by servants of the Crown in the course of their employment: *Viscount Canterbury* v. *Attorney-General* (1842), 1 Ph. 306. The actual wrong-doer, who is usually a subordinate official, could, and still can, be sued, but the Crown as his employer was not liable vicariously, nor the superior officer who is directly responsible for the employment. A superior official is not responsible for wrongs committed by his subordinates unless he has expressly authorised them; for all the servants of the Crown are fellow-servants of the Crown and not of one another: *Raleigh* v. *Goschen*, [1898] 1 Ch. 73; *Bainbridge* v. *Postmaster-General*, [1906] 1 K.B. 178. The actual wrongdoer cannot, however, plead the orders of the Crown as a defence. In practice the Treasury Solicitor usually defended an action against a subordinate official and the Treasury, as a matter of grace, paid damages if he was found liable. In 1942 the Lord Chancellor appointed an independent person to certify (if the plaintiff so desired) whether a subordinate was acting in the course of his employment. This enabled the plaintiff before proceeding with his action against the actual tortfeasor to determine whether or not he could expect the Crown to stand behind the defendant and meet any damages which the court might subsequently award to him against the defendant personally. But the big flaw remained that nobody could sue the Crown, the largest employer of labour in the country, on the same basis as an ordinary employer could be sued for the torts of a servant committed in the course of employment. Until 1948 government departments enjoyed the immunity of the Crown unless a statute expressly provided otherwise. Various statutes attempted to simplify proceedings against particular departments, but the varying methods adopted caused great perplexity.[2]

Tortious Liability; the Law before 1948.

---

[1] For civil pay, see *Lucas* v. *Lucas and High Commissioner for India*, [1943] P. 68 which followed the same rule, but see "A Civil Servant and his Pay," by D. W. Logan, 61 *L.Q.R.* 240, and *Sutton* v. *Attorney-General* (1923), 39 T.L.R. 294, where the House of Lords treated civil pay as recoverable in contract so long as it was not sued for on the basis of recovering for wrongful dismissal.

[2] See 3rd ed. pp. 266–67 and *Minister of Supply* v. *British Thomson Houston Co.* [1943] K.B. 478.

With certain important exceptions the Crown Proceedings Act, 1947, s. 2, establishes against the Crown liability in tort as if it were a private person of full age and capacity; it can be made liable for the torts of its servants or agents. The action is brought against the appropriate government department, the Treasury being responsible for publishing a list of the departments and naming the solicitor for each department to accept process on its behalf; in cases not covered by the list the Attorney-General may be made defendant. As in the case of actions for breach of contract or recovery of the property of the subject from the Crown, the trial follows that of an ordinary High Court or County Court action, except that

(*a*) judgment against the department cannot be enforced by the ordinary methods of levying execution or attachment; but the department is required to pay the amount certified to be due as damages;

(*b*) in place of an injunction or a decree of specific performance, remedies which are sanctioned by imprisonment for default, and, therefore, inappropriate, the court makes an order declaratory of the rights of the parties;

(*c*) similarly there can be no order for restitution of property, but the court may declare the plaintiff entitled as against the Crown.

The principal exceptions from liability in tort relate to the Post Office and the Armed Forces. Neither the Crown, nor an officer of the Crown (save at the suit of the Crown) can be held liable for any act or omission in relation to a postal packet (unless it is registered), or to a telephonic communication (s. 9). Similar immunity is given both to the tortfeasor and to the Crown in respect of acts or omissions causing death or personal injury which are committed by a member of the armed forces while on duty, where the plaintiff is himself (*a*) a member of the forces who is either on duty at the time or, if not on duty as such, is on any land, premises, ship, aircraft or vehicle which is being used for the purposes of the armed forces, and (*b*) the injury is certified by the Minister of Pensions as attributable to service for purposes of pension entitlement (s. 10).

Apart from these specific exceptions which give immunity not only to the Crown, but to the servant, the liability of the Crown is restricted to the torts of its officers as defined in the Act (s. 2 (6)). The definition requires that the officer shall (*a*) be appointed directly or indirectly by the Crown and (*b*) be paid in respect of his duties as an officer of the Crown at the material time wholly out of the Consolidated Fund,[1] moneys provided by Parliament, the Road Fund or a fund certified by the Treasury. This excludes for example the police.[2] There is also immunity for acts done by officers acting in a judicial capacity or in execution of judicial process (s. 2 (5)).

[1] P. 182, *ante*.   [2] P. 191, *ante*.

The Crown is liable as an employer for tortious breach of common law duty by its officers or in respect of ownership and occupation of property, *e.g.* for negligence. It is also liable for breach of a statutory duty, provided in the latter case that the Act is one which binds the Crown, such as the Factories Act, 1937. There is no liability enforceable by action in the case of statutory duties which only bind the Crown or a Minister, and not other persons, such as the duty placed upon the Minister of Education by s. 1 of the Education Act, 1944, to promote the education of the people.[1]

An action for a declaration[2] may be brought against the Crown without claiming any consequential relief, *e.g.* where a wrong is merely threatened: *Dyson* v. *Attorney-General*, [1911] 1 K.B. 410, but not to determine purely hypothetical questions which may never arise; *e.g.* as to whether there is a contingent liability to a tax: *In re Barnato, Joel* v. *Sanger*, [1949] 1 Ch. 258. Formerly the scope of this remedy in Crown proceedings was doubtful and it could not be used to prejudge an issue which might have had to be adjudicated in a petition of right for breach of contract or detention of property by the Crown: *Bombay and Persia Steam Navigation Co.* v. *Maclay* [1920] 3 K.B. 402, at p. 408.

The rule that Acts of Parliament do not bind the Crown, *i.e.* that the Crown is not to be prejudiced as to its prerogatives, unless the particular statute so enacts either by express words or by necessary implication, has an important bearing on the liability of the Crown for breach of statutory duty[3]: *Food Controller* v. *Cork*, [1923] A.C. 647; *Bank Voor Handel en Scheepvaart NV* v. *Administrator of Hungarian Property*, [1954] A.C. 584. It is by the operation of this rule that Crown property is exempt from local rates and income tax. Here, again, the term "the Crown" includes all those departments which can be regarded as exercising functions which emanate from the Crown or form part of the general government of the country, but the mere fact that premises are used for public purposes does not result in exemption. Thus exemption from income tax was accorded in respect of a building used for Assizes and as a county police station: *Coomber* v. *Justices of Berks* (1883), 9 App. Cas. 61; but exemption from rates was not accorded to the outfall works of a county council acting as sewerage authority: *L.C.C.* v. *Erith (Churchwardens) and Dartford Union Assessment Committee*, [1893] A.C. 562. Where a statute does not apply to the Crown or its servants acting in the course of duty, there is no liability on the part of the individual

Application of Statutes.

---

[1] XXVI *Canadian Bar Review*, pp. 387 ff., at pp. 390–91.

[2] See pp. 328–9, *ante,* for the scope of relief by declaratory judgments.

[3] It has been held that when a statute is enacted "for the public good," the Crown is not bound by implication, unless to exclude the Crown would wholly frustrate the purpose of the Act; *Province of Bombay* v. *Municipal Corporation of Bombay*, [1947] A.C. 58.

servant for a breach of the statute, for he has committed no offence: *Cooper* v. *Hawkins*, [1904] 2 K.B. 164, where it was held that a statutory restriction fixing a speed limit did not apply to the driver of a War Office vehicle, as the statute neither expressly nor impliedly bound the Crown.[1]

Inter-
locutory
Process.

Discovery of documents, which is an important interlocutory proceeding to enable a party to inspect all documents in the possession or control of his opponent which relate to any of the matters in question in the action, could formerly not be used against the Crown. By s. 28 of the Act of 1947 the court may make an order for discovery against the Crown. Refusal to disclose particular documents or even the existence of such documents on the ground that to do so would be injurious to the public interest is open to the Crown. Objection, if the decision is taken by a Minister or in his absence by the permanent official at the head of his department, will not be overruled by the court; *Duncan* v. *Cammell, Laird & Co., Ltd.*, [1942] A.C. 624, esp. at p. 642; K. & L. 193. Refusal to disclose matters on the ground that to do so would be injurious to the public interest is also a valid objection on the part of the Crown in litigation to which the Crown is not a party. Objection may be taken not only to disclosing a particular document, but also on the ground that it is one of a class of documents which must be treated as confidential, *e.g.* in order to guarantee freedom and candour of communication on public matters in confidential reports;[2] but the desire to avoid public criticism is not by itself a good ground for objection. Similar rules apply to interrogatories, *i.e.* written questions to obtain information from the other party on material facts. In practice, therefore, the court cannot examine the documents if the decision to object is taken by the Minister and the value of discovery or interrogatories against the Crown is questionable.

History of
Reforms.

It is of interest to outline the steps which led to the important reforms which have been described. The whole question was as far back as 1921 referred to a Crown Proceedings Committee, which reported in 1927 in the form of a draft Bill.[3] Under this Bill it was recommended (*a*) that the Crown should be liable in tort; (*b*) that the Crown itself should enjoy the protection of the Public Authorities Protection Act, 1893,[4] in the same way that servants of the Crown were protected under the existing law; (*c*) that petitions of right should be abolished and that proceedings by and against the Crown should be

---

[1] See Road Traffic Act, 1930, s. 121 (2), for the present law enforcing liability against the Crown in respect of mechanically propelled vehicles.
[2] See *Ellis* v. *Home Office*, [1953] 2 Q.B. 135, for an illustration of the harsh operation of this rule.
[3] *Crown Proceedings Committee Report* (Cmd. 2842), 1927.
[4] Repealed by Law Reform (Limitation of Actions) Act, 1954, see p. 305, *ante*.

assimilated, as far as possible, to ordinary civil proceedings; (*d*) that costs should be awarded to and against the Crown; (*e*) that discovery should with proper safeguards be available against the Crown. The Report met with the support of lawyers and was endorsed by the Committee on Ministers' Powers who reported in 1932 that the whole position of the Crown in litigation gave rise to "a lacuna in the rule of law." Little progress was made with implementing the draft Bill. By the Administration of Justice (Miscellaneous Provisions) Act, 1933, it was provided (*a*) proceedings by the Crown (though not proceedings against the Crown) could be instituted in the County Court; (*b*) debts due to the Crown could, without prejudice to procedure by means of information, be recovered by proceedings instituted by an ordinary writ of summons; (*c*) costs could be awarded to or against the Crown in any civil proceedings to which the Crown was a party.[1] The Limitation Act, 1939, made the ordinary periods of limitation for bringing an action applicable to proceedings by and against the Crown with one exception.[2] The opposition to the adoption of the Report as a whole continued in official and ministerial circles until after the Second World War. The remaining recommendations were implemented by the Crown Proceedings Act, 1947. The principal argument advanced against this reform was that juries would award excessive damages to successful plaintiffs, being influenced by the knowledge that the capacity of the Crown to pay was limitless.

The immediate cause of the introduction of the Bill which was enacted as the Crown Proceedings Act, 1947, was the hardship caused to scores of litigants by the refusal of the House of Lords in *Adams* v. *Naylor*, [1946] A.C. 543 to accept the liability of the nominated defendant. The practice of nominating a defendant was one method whereby the Crown mitigated as an act of grace the rigour of its immunity at law where the actual wrongdoer could not be ascertained. In the case cited the court refused to give judgment against an army officer who had been nominated to accept service of the writ in respect of injuries to children in a derelict minefield on the coast, simply because he was the officer in charge of the area. No negligence could be proved against him personally and, therefore, he was not guilty of any breach of duty; accordingly the case was dismissed leaving the injured parties without any legal redress against the Crown, the real occupier. It followed that a superintendent of a government factory, as such, could not be made defendant in cases

---

[1] If the Crown seeks leave to appeal to the House of Lords, leave may be conditional on payment of the respondent's costs of the appeal in any event; see e.g. *Marriott* v. *Minister of Health*, [1937] 1 K.B. 128, at p. 143.

[2] Previously there was no period of limitation for actions by the Crown, except that for the recovery of land the period was 60 years. For this type of action it is now 30 years, instead of the ordinary period of 12 years.

of neglect by the Crown as the occupier under duty to take safety precautions: *Royster* v. *Cavey*, [1947] 1 K.B. 204.

Scotland.   The Act applies to Scotland with the substantial variations which are caused by the differences in Scots law and civil procedure. Thus the liability of the Crown in tort is reproduced in Scotland by liability in reparation; the Lord Advocate is the proper person to sue and be sued on behalf of the Crown or a department of government; the sheriff's court replaces the county court. The procedure by petition of right never had any application in Scotland, but the ordinary forms of actions for payment or declaration are, as hitherto, used against the Lord Advocate in cases of contractual liability.

CHAPTER 5.

ADMINISTRATIVE JUSTICE.

THE last three chapters have been devoted to the control of the courts over the administration. It is now necessary to say a little about the various administrative courts to which fall the task of determining the greater part in volume of disputes between the citizen and the State. It has already been shown by examples how these courts may be prevented from an excess or abuse of their powers by the High Court granting the judicial orders which have replaced the prerogative writs (other than habeas corpus) and particularly certiorari and prohibition. England has for many centuries had courts that can be called special. Mediaeval merchants had their courts of pie poudre; the tin miners of Devon and Cornwall had their courts of Stannaries. Most of the old special courts have been absorbed in the common law system, though ecclesiastical courts have survived. But the same growth of governmental activities and introduction of new services provided by the State that has led to an increase in the volume of delegated legislation has led to the creation of numerous special tribunals for the settlement of disputes or determination of rights. The introduction of each new social service has involved both delegated legislation and administrative justice. Thus the National Insurance Act, 1911, which may be regarded as introducing a new type of governmental function, provided for the adjudication of disputes by an administrative authority.[2] Innumerable issues of a judicial or quasi-judicial kind arise in the course of administration of the public services, particularly those which affect the individual welfare of large sections of the community. The administration of many services, *e.g.* housing, highways, town-planning, can only be carried on by the compulsory (if need be) acquisition of privately owned property. The owners are involved in disputes with governmental authorities, central and local, and means have to be devised for the settlement of such disputes. Again, legislation may confer the right to sickness or disablement benefits as under the National Insurance Acts, 1946. A tribunal must be able to determine whether a claimant is entitled to a service pension. Sometimes the determination of disputes is entrusted to a Minister or his

Adminis-
trative
Courts.[1]

---

[1] For an account of Administrative Courts, see W. A. Robson, *Justice and Administrative Law* (3rd ed.), Chap. 3, and R. M. Jackson, *The Machinery of Justice* (2nd ed.), Chap. VI. A long list is given in 1 *British Journal of Administrative Law* (1954), pp. 60 *ff.*, showing with which department each court is connected. It is exceptional to appoint a civil servant as a member of an administrative court.

[2] *M.P.R.*, p. 96.

agent, as at first instance in the case of entitlement to benefits under national insurance rather than to a special tribunal. Usually this is not so when the issue is strictly judicial (an issue involving the application of law to facts) rather than quasi-judicial (an issue usually involving the ascertainment of facts but where the final decision must be mainly related to administrative policy). Similarly an appellate administrative court is usually preferred to appeals being heard by the Minister or his agent, even if no question of law is involved. National insurance again provides an illustration in its local appeal tribunals, from which appeal lies on a point of law to a judicial Commissioner. Where a Minister is himself required to decide an issue on an appeal, it is frequently laid down that before giving a decision, *e.g.* confirming a compulsory purchase order under the Housing Act, 1936, which is opposed, he must hold a public enquiry through one of his officers.

Reasons for Administrative Justice.

The reference of disputes to administrative courts, the members of which are frequently appointed by Ministers, has caused anxiety to those who cherish the sanctity of the common law—and they are not exclusively confined to the legal profession—lest the position of the judiciary and the influence of the law should be impaired. Modern problems cannot, however, be solved by a rigid application of the doctrine of separation of powers; there must be considered what Lord Greene called [1] the functional capacity of the judicial machine. Constitutional machinery must be suited to its intended product and must be able to satisfy the demands made upon it.[2] The right of access to the courts has been and is a bulwark of our liberties and must be preserved, but we shall not assist its preservation by asking the Judiciary to undertake tasks which do not fall within its proper sphere. Many tasks performed by the Judiciary involve the exercise of discretion. In particular this applies to the passing of sentence upon a convicted criminal. A judge as well as another man may exercise discretion fairly and wisely, but in general "the Judiciary is not concerned with policy," nor is it for the Judiciary to decide what is in the public interest.[3] Modern planning involves the grant of powers which are not suitable for reference to the courts. "Questions which involve the conferring of rights or the taking away of rights on the basis of what a tribunal thinks is reasonable on the facts of the individual case are not, in general, suitable for decision by a court of law." [3] There is a widespread feeling too that litigious procedure does not produce the right atmosphere for the

---

[1] "Law and Progress," Haldane Memorial Lecture, published in 94 *Law Journal*, October 28, November 4, and November 11, 1944; and Lord Greene's judgments in *Johnson (B) & Co. (Builders), Ltd.* v. *Minister of Health*, [1947] 2 All E. R. 395 and in *Robinson* v. *Minister of Town and Country Planning*, [1947] K.B. 717.

[2] Lord Greene, *op. cit.*   [3] *Ibid.*

working of a social insurance scheme. The courts too are expensive and not speedy. The implementation of a new policy necessitates the speedy, cheap and decentralised determination of a very large number of individual cases. For such work the courts are not suited. Moreover some judges, influenced by the principle of interpretation that the common law can only be changed by express words or necessary intendment,[1] have approached the task of interpreting the social legislation of the present century on too narrow a basis, in that they may have failed to adapt the individualistic tradition of the common law to the conception of liberty as it is understood in the welfare State of to-day. The judges cannot, however, be fairly blamed so long as they are confined to fixed rules for interpreting the meaning of statutes and are not allowed to examine the purpose of the legislation, except so far as it is ascertainable from the words of the statute. None the less Parliament, aware of judicial methods of interpretation, tends to entrust the determination of disputes arising from social legislation to administrative courts rather than to the courts. The difficulty has been well put by Dr. Jackson:[2] "Social legislation can rarely be comprehended by seeing its effects as solely an issue between two individuals, but the isolated issue is the centre of traditional common-law technique." On the other hand, as Lord Greene pointed out, the Legislature must not adopt vague language in the hope that the judges will, somehow or other, interpret it in such a way as to make it work. "Policy is not the concern of the Judges save in so far as the manifest objects of the statute, as appearing on its face, may provide a context pointing to one interpretation rather than another."

The necessity for administrative justice must not, however, lead us to underrate the merits of our traditional legal system. Jurisdiction ought not lightly to be given to administrative courts rather than to the courts of justice and, so far as is practicable, the merits of the traditional system should be embodied in the new. It is unnecessary to stress the value of an independent judiciary administering the law in open court. To some extent independence can be secured by entrusting to the Lord Chancellor the appointment of chairmen of tribunals. Many appointments are, however, made by the Ministers responsible for the administration of the services in question and are appointments for a short period of years. There cannot be the same degree of independence when a paid member of a tribunal is eligible for re-appointment by a Minister. It is not, however, the practice to appoint civil servants and there is no evidence of pressure being brought to bear by Ministers on the members of administrative courts any more than it is ever used on magistrates' courts by the Home Office. But the legal system based on centuries of experience

Merits of the Ordinary Courts.

---

[1] See, however, p. 46, *ante*, note 3.   [2] Jackson, *op. cit.*, 2nd ed., p. 235.

ensures that irrelevant material is excluded and that decisions are given in accordance with accepted principles. Lawyers are trained to apply principles and weigh evidence. The courts follow precedent and publish the reasons for their decisions. Some of these features are lacking in many administrative courts. The right to be represented by a professional advocate is an important feature of the legal system, which is usually excluded before such tribunals as do not contain a lawyer or senior civil servant as chairman.[1]

Varied functions of Administrative Courts.

The functions of special tribunals are too various to permit of classification. They embrace, *inter alia*, the determination by local appeal tribunals of rights to benefits under the Insurance Acts; the fixing of rents by local furnished rents tribunals; the granting of licences by the Area Traffic Commissioners under the Road Traffic Act, 1930; the fixing of fares and freight rates by the Transport Tribunal; the imposition of penalties for the enforcement of a marketing scheme in a particular industry by a marketing board. Bodies like the Area Traffic Commissioners exercise administrative as well as quasi-judicial duties. Some in the past, such as the Railway and Canal Commission and the Railway Rates Tribunal, which have now been superseded by the Transport Tribunal, have been courts of record and followed closely the procedure of a court of law; the majority are more informal and flexible in their methods, although their procedure is usually (but not always) prescribed by rules.

General Considerations.

In regard to administrative courts irrespective of their functions the following questions are of importance to the constitutional lawyer: (*a*) Do they determine strictly judicial or only quasi-judicial issues? (*b*) Are their decisions final? We have seen that, unless a statute provides for an appeal, the jurisdiction of the High Court over administrative courts is confined to the control of excess of jurisdiction and the enforcement of the rules of natural justice, unless an error of law is disclosed on the record.[2] Sometimes an appeal lies from one court appointed by a Minister to another so appointed or even to the Minister in person; sometimes there is an appeal on fact and law; sometimes on law only; sometimes an appeal lies to the County Court; sometimes to a single judge of the High Court whose decision is final; sometimes to the High Court and thence to the Court of Appeal and House of Lords; sometimes there is no appeal. Each case must be determined by reference to the terms of a statute, for the common law made no provision for appeals. (*c*) How are they appointed? Sometimes a ministerial tribunal is appointed by the Minister concerned in the dispute; sometimes by the Lord Chancellor; sometimes by the Lord Chancellor and the Minister acting together. (*d*) Who are their personnel? Sometimes tribunals are composed of government officials; sometimes provision is made

---

[1] See e.g. S.I., 1948, No. 1144, Reg. 13.   [2] P. 323–4, *ante*.

for an independent chairman with legal qualifications who sits with representatives selected from panels drawn from employers and employed persons respectively. In at least one case, the furnished rents tribunal, no qualifications are prescribed and the Minister of Housing and Local Government has complete freedom of choice. There is in England no scientific system of administrative tribunals, for the simple reason that, like all our institutions, they have been evolved piecemeal to solve an urgent problem rather than in pursuance of a blue-print system. Suggestions for a system of administrative courts have twice been rejected by authoritative committees.[1] There are those who advocate the establishment of an Administrative Division of the High Court for the redress of grievances arising out of administration. If it is intended to limit jurisdiction to points of law, this proposal is merely an extension of what happens already in *e.g.* tax appeals, which lie to the Judges of the Chancery Division who take the revenue cases. If it means that the High Court is to review the decisions of administrators on merits, irrespective of a point of law, it has already been pointed out that there are limits to the functional capacity of the judicial machine, if its independence is to to be preserved. The merits and demerits of special tribunals can better be appreciated after some consideration of the various types of tribunal that have been established.

The Special Commissioners of Income Tax hear appeals on income-tax matters from the rulings of inland revenue officials. They are a body of whole-time officials appointed by the Treasury and hold office during pleasure. The Commissioners can be required to state a case for the opinion of the High Court on a point of law. Of this body the Committee on Ministerial Powers stated:[2] "By common consent this tribunal gives general satisfaction by its impartiality, in spite of the fact that its members are not only appointed by the Treasury, but may, when not performing judicial duties, actually act as administrative officials. All we can say about it is that it is a standing tribute to the fair-mindedness of the British Civil Service; but the precedent is not one which Parliament should copy in other branches of administration." *Special Commissioners of Income Tax: (Judicial)*

The Transport Tribunal has jurisdiction over the fares and rates charged by the Transport Commission and determines important questions of policy relating to the carriage of passengers and merchandise. The Tribunal consists of three members appointed on the oint recommendation of the Lord Chancellor, the President of the *Transport Tribunal: (Administrative)*

---

[1] The Committee on Ministers' Powers and the Departmental Committee on the Imposition of Penalties by Marketing Boards and other Similar Bodies (p. 54, *ante*).

[2] *M.P.R.*, pp. 86-7. The Committee on Ministers' Powers regarded the Commissioners as a specialised court, but they are more properly regarded as an administrative tribunal; see Jackson, *op. cit.*, p. 295.

Board of Trade, and the Minister of Transport. One member must be experienced in commercial affairs, one in transport matters and the president must be an experienced lawyer. The president holds office during good behaviour, but can be removed on the joint recommendation of the three appointing Ministers. The other members hold office for seven years and are then eligible for re-appointment.

Agricultural Land Tribunals (Administrative).

Under the Agriculture Act, 1947, as amended by the Agriculture (Miscellaneous Provisions) Act, 1954, regional Agricultural Land Tribunals are set up to which farmers can appeal (*inter alia*) against dispossession orders of the Minister, against directions as to the provision of equipment for land under supervision, against proposals to retain land in the possession of the Minister, or against proposals relating to the sub-division of agricultural land. The subject matter of these appeals relate to considerations of policy rather than of law. But there is a power to refer any questions of law to the High Court. The Chairman of each Tribunal must be a barrister or solicitor of standing who is appointed by the Lord Chancellor; he appoints two other members, one from each of two panels representative of the farming and agricultural land-owning communities respectively; the panels are drawn up by the Lord Chancellor.

Lands Tribunal.

The Lands Tribunal Act, 1949, set up two Lands Tribunals, one for Scotland and one for the rest of the United Kingdom. The Tribunals are given jurisdiction over a variety of matters relating to the valuation of property, including the assessment of compensation for compulsory acquisition of land and rating appeals from the local valuation courts. The jurisdiction can be enlarged by Order in Council. The President of the Lands Tribunal, who must have held judicial office or be a barrister of standing, is like the other members appointed by the Lord Chancellor.[1] These members must be barristers, solicitors or persons qualified by professional experience in the valuation of land. There is no fixed composition for the Tribunals; this is varied according to the particular case as the President may determine. Thus a single surveyor may sit or the President together with members who are lawyers and surveyors. On the application of any party a case may be stated on a point of law for determination of the Court of Appeal; otherwise the decision of the Lands Tribunal is final.

The establishment of the Lands Tribunal is of great interest because it represents an attempt to collect the decision of disputes relating to a variety of kindred matters into the hands of a single court for determination. This may well be a pointer to a solution of the problem of administrative justice on the lines of a

---

[1] The President and members of the Lands Tribunal for Scotland are appointed by the Lord President of the Court of Session.

series of higher administrative courts, each covering a range of specialised but related jurisdictions.

The Discipline Committee under the Solicitors Act, 1932, affords an example of a professional tribunal. It is a committee established for the purpose of hearing applications against solicitors, either to strike them off the roll or to compel them to answer allegations made against them by clients. Solicitors are officers of the court and, therefore, are properly subjected to a disciplinary code of conduct by State machinery. This committee is appointed by the Master of the Rolls. For hearing of applications there sits a board of at least three members who are practising solicitors. The committee has power to order a solicitor to be struck off the roll, to suspend him from practice or to order him to pay costs. It acts as a judicial body hearing formally applications by complainants, administering oaths and generally conducting its procedure as a court of law. Every order made by the committee must be prefaced by a statement of the findings in relation to the facts of the case. An appeal from an order of the committee lies to the High Court. *Professional Tribunals; Discipline Committee (Solicitors): (Judicial).*

Claims for benefit under the National Insurance Act, 1946, are submitted to an insurance officer appointed by the Minister of National Insurance. The insurance officer may either allow the claim or refer the matter for decision to a local tribunal which consists of two members, each drawn from a representative panel, one of persons representing employers and insured persons other than those who are in employment, the other of employed persons, together with a chairman who is appointed by the Minister and need not be a lawyer. Provision is made for appeals from the decisions of local tribunals to the National Insurance Commissioner, a senior barrister who is appointed by the Crown; the decision of the Commissioner is final. The same Act provides that certain questions, but not a direct claim to benefit, may be decided by the Minister who may, if he wishes, refer the matter to a single judge of the High Court. From a decision by the Minister there is a right of appeal to the High Court judge whose decision is final. *National Insurance Appeals (Judicial).*

The Road Traffic Act, 1930, as subsequently amended, entrusted the grant of licences for public service passenger vehicles to area traffic commissioners (now the Licensing Authorities for Public Service Vehicles) appointed by the Minister of Transport. The Road and Rail Traffic Act, 1933, gave to the same commissioners the power to grant licences for goods vehicles on roads. In the former case there is an appeal from the decision of the commissioners to the Minister; in the latter case to the Transport Tribunal [1] (formerly to a special appeal tribunal). *Appeals under Road Traffic Acts (Administrative).*

---

[1] P. 345, *ante*.

Service
Pensions
Appeals
(Judicial).

Under the Pensions Appeal Tribunal Acts, 1943 and 1949 (which relate to pensions for disability in the armed forces), there is an appeal from decisions of the Minister of Pensions to a tribunal appointed by the Lord Chancellor. A tribunal consists normally of a legal chairman, a medical practitioner and a representative of the claimant's service; but, when an appeal relating to degree of disablement is heard, an additional medical practitioner takes the place of the legal chairman. Either the claimant or the Minister may with the leave of the tribunal or of the High Court appeal on a point of law from the tribunal to a single judge of the High Court appointed by the Lord Chancellor. The appointment of particular judges to hear appeals under particular statutes ensures familiarity with the subject-matter and the policy involved.

Registration
of Dairy
Farms
(Adminis-
trative).

Under the Food and Drugs (Milk and Dairies) Act, 1944, dairy farmers must be registered and the Minister of Agriculture and Fisheries may refuse to register or may cancel the registration of a dairy farmer whose premises are not in a condition that will allow him to comply with the Minister's regulations. The decision is left to the Minister, but he is assisted by a fact-finding tribunal appointed by himself and must accept as conclusive the decision of a majority of the tribunal on the facts. The decision thus is ministerial and based on administrative policy. The procedure before the tribunal is quasi-judicial and to that the rules of natural justice will be applied by the High Court.

Summary.

The future of administrative justice is still uncertain. Speculation is out of place in a book which is concerned with present practice. But the following recommendations would perhaps win fairly general acceptance.

1. Judicial issues should not be entrusted to Ministers and when they are entrusted to ministerial tribunals, there should be legal chairmen, preferably appointed by the Lord Chancellor as in the case of the Lands Tribunal.

2. Administrative decisions which involve issues in dispute with individual citizens are frequently entrusted to Ministers. The rules of natural justice cannot normally be applied so as to prevent a Minister from adjudicating upon a dispute on the ground that he is interested in the policy involved. Final decisions on policy must be taken by Ministers responsible to Parliament. Before, however, a Minister can exercise a discretionary power, the facts must be established. The finding of facts cannot always easily be divorced from the advice that must be given to a Minister on policy and in such cases it is difficult to improve upon the expedient of a public enquiry. Wherever possible the finding of facts should be entrusted to an independent fact-finding tribunal. It has been suggested that tribunals of this character might be selected from panels of suitable

persons with legal chairmen; and with an official of the department concerned as an assessor.[1]

3. The supervisory jurisdiction of the High Court should be vigilantly maintained and there should always be a right of appeal to the High Court on points of law within a short stated time.[2]

4. The reasons for decisions should be made available to the parties and epitomes of leading cases should be published.[3] The Committee on Ministers' Powers also strongly recommended [4] that the reports of inspectors who hold statutory public enquiries should be published. Judicial opinion has, however, been very doubtful of the wisdom of this recommendation, mainly on the ground that the recommendations of the inspector are not the only factor in determining the issue.[5]

5. The right to be represented by counsel or solicitor is one of the surest defences of the subject and it ought not to be taken away save in cases of a very simple description, and even in these a party should be entitled to have someone to appear for him.[6]

Lord Greene, thus summed up the matter: "It is only certain classes of questions which are suitable for submission to a special tribunal to the exclusion of the courts. In deciding whether a case falls within these classes, it is relevant to consider the number of individuals likely to be affected and their probable pecuniary position; the necessity or otherwise of providing a speedy and inexpensive procedure and one affording opportunities for decentralisation; whether the questions likely to arise are predominantly questions of fact, and whether expert knowledge and experience are desirable for their decision; and the extent to which the jurisdiction is to be based on discretion rather than on fixed rules and precedents. In all cases there should be a right of appeal to the courts on questions of law. In no circumstances should the power of the courts to restrain a special tribunal from exceeding its jurisdiction be taken away. Each particular piece of legislation should be considered in relation to its special character in the light of the foregoing principles." Since this view was expressed there has emerged a policy of preferring local tribunals of three to the exclusion of the ordinary courts to determine most matters of dispute arising out of the administration of the social services which have since 1945 been considerably extended. Even as the final arbiter on points of law the specialised commissioner is preferred to the High Court or any other appellate tribunal. In one case no appeal of any kind is allowed and

---

[1] Lord Greene, M.R., *op. cit.*   [2] *M.P.R.*, p. 98.
[3] *M.P.R.*, p. 116.   [4] *M.P.R.*, p. 106.
[5] *M.P.R.*, pp. 103–107; *Denby (William) and Son* v. *Minister of Health*. [1936] 1 K.B. 337.
[6] *Cf.* Lord Greene, *op. cit.*

local tribunals set their own standards. This is the case of the furnished rents tribunals which are empowered to fix the rent of furnished houses and to determine certain other matters between landlord and tenant in a sphere where hitherto only law administered by the ordinary courts has prevailed; the Furnished Houses and the Landlord and Tenant (Rent Control) Acts, 1946 and 1949.

The conclusion of the whole matter is perhaps that no hard-and-fast rules can be laid down. The rule of law can exist without a single system of judicature, provided that the essential requirements of justice are observed. Nevertheless it is vital to the maintenance of law in any society that matters shall not be left to determination at the whim or fancy of local tribunals who are guided by no fixed standards of conduct. In this way only too easily can tribunals degenerate into people's courts responsible only to the orders of a dictatorial Minister.

CHAPTER 6.

DELEGATED LEGISLATION.[1]

THE function of legislation—the making of general rules—is a function of Parliament. When Parliament delegates that function we speak of delegated legislation. The term is used of (a) the exercise of a legislative power delegated by Parliament, or (b) the rules or regulations passed as the result of the exercise of a delegated legislative power.[2] The by-laws made by local authorities or the Transport Commission are delegated legislation. Professional bodies too may be given power to enact delegated legislation, e.g. the Council of The Law Society (the governing body of the solicitors' profession) is given power by the Solicitors Act, 1932, to make regulations for the compulsory attendance of articled clerks at schools of law. This chapter is, however, concerned primarily with the exercise of legislative functions by government departments and such independent authorities as the wages councils or the agricultural marketing boards.[3]

What is Delegated Legislation?

Delegated legislation is not a new development. *The Report of the Committee on Ministers' Powers* gives examples of delegation of legislative powers in the sixteenth, seventeenth and eighteenth centuries.[4] The bulk of delegated legislation has, however, been enormously increased to meet the needs of the modern State. So long as the State existed mainly for the purpose of preserving order by repelling external aggression, administering justice and preventing crimes, Parliament was able to provide the necessary legislation. Nowadays social welfare and economic problems of a national and international character form as important a part of the business of government as the older function of preserving the peace and security of the realm. The Government provides services to advance the social welfare of the population and directly or indirectly controls the economic resources of the State. The provision of social services involves the making of detailed regulations to provide for benefits for a great variety of classes of persons. The exercise of economic control involves the imposition of a variety of restrictions and positive duties. Parliament no longer has the time nor indeed the necessary data to

Growth of Delegated Legislation.

---

[1] Reference should be made to *M.P.R.*, Section II. For emergency legislation 1939–1949, see Part VIII, Chap. 2. See also R. C. FitzGerald, *Safeguards in Delegated Legislation*, 27 C.B.R. 550–74.

[2] *M.P.R.*, p. 15.   [3] P. 54, *ante*.

[4] *M.P.R.*, pp. 10–15.

enable it to produce the mass of detailed regulations which the present functions of the State require. It is impossible to foresee all possibilities and flexibility is essential. As a result Parliament tends to lay down general principles and to entrust to Ministers the task of forming the regulations necessary for their amplification. The annual volume of public general statutes for 1937 occupied just over a thousand pages; statutory rules and orders for the same period occupied about 2,400 pages, though not all the latter are printed and published. By 1947 the two volumes of statutes contained over 2,000 pages; no fewer than 2,916 statutory instruments were issued in the numbered series, filling three volumes. There has been some decline in these figures in recent years, but statutory instruments far exceed in volume the statute book.

Original Legislation distinguished. Delegated legislation should be distinguished from general legislation enacted by a process other than the normal method of passing an Act of Parliament. Prerogative legislation by Order in Council or Letters Patent is still utilised by the Colonial Office as a principal mode of legislating for newly acquired territory and for enacting colonial constitutions. The annexation of Kenya as a colony was effected by this means in 1920.[1] In form prerogative Orders in Council do not differ from those issued under the authority of an Act of Parliament, which are delegated legislation proper, and for their contents the Government, and not the Privy Council, is politically responsible. Nevertheless they are examples of legislation by the Queen in Council and do not require the prior authority of Parliament in the form of an enabling Act.

Forms of Delegated Legislation. Delegated legislation by Ministers of the Crown takes one of two forms: (*a*) the statutory Order in Council, (*b*) the departmental regulation. Both are called statutory instruments; they were formerly known as statutory rules and orders. For both the department concerned is responsible. In the former case "the formal legislative act is made more national by being united with the traditions of the King in Council." [2] Regulations appear under many names: regulations, rules, orders, warrants, schemes, by-laws. The term "rules" is appropriate to an instrument regulating procedure;[3] "by-laws" imply that provisions, though of a general nature, are to have effect only in a limited area; the term "order" is used to cover varying forms of legislation as well as executive orders, though the Committee on Ministers' Powers recommended that (except for Orders in Council) it should be confined to instruments exercising executive power or giving judicial and quasi-judicial decisions, and that the term "regulation" should be used to describe an instrument by

---

[1] See Appendix C, p. 502, *post.*
[2] *M.P.R.*, p. 26.
[3] *E.g.* Rules of court—delegated legislation enacted by the Judiciary.

which the power to make substantive law is exercised.[1] No scientific distinction of nomenclature has in fact been adopted, nor has there been uniformity in the terms used in different Acts of Parliament or by different departments. Some improvement has been effected since 1943 as a result of criticism in Parliament and elsewhere; but the Select Committee for scrutinising statutory instruments [2] has again recommended that for the convenience of Parliament and the public the different classes of delegated legislation should be classified under separate designations.[3]

Delegated legislation is an inevitable development in the modern welfare State for the following reasons:

Justification of Delegated Legislation.

(1) *Pressure upon parliamentary time.* If Parliament attempted to enact all legislation itself, the parliamentary machine would break down, unless there was a radical alteration of the rules of debate on consideration of Bills. The granting of power to legislate to a department which is administering a public service under statutory powers can obviate the need for amending Bills to a large extent.

(2) *Technicality of subject-matter.* Legislation on technical topics necessitates prior consultation with experts and interests concerned.[4] The giving of the power to make regulations to Ministers facilitates such consultation.[5] Bills are confidential documents and their actual text cannot be disclosed until they have been presented to Parliament and read a first time. Thereafter they can only be altered by formal amendment at the committee or report stages. No such secretive custom need obscure the preparation of delegated legislation unless security considerations arise.

(3) *The need for flexibility.* An important scheme providing for a state-regulated and state-aided educational service or a system of national insurance benefits demands that something less cumbrous and more expeditious than an Act of Parliament shall be available to amplify the main provisions, to meet unforeseen contingencies and to facilitate adjustments that may be called for after the scheme has been put into operation. Delegated legislation fills those needs. The National Health Insurance Act, 1911, would have been a dead letter, had it not been followed over a two-year period by delegated legislation amplifying its provisions. The present national insurance scheme was enacted by Parliament two years before it was brought into operation, a step which was preceded by a great volume of regulations made under the parent Acts.

(4) *State of Emergency.* It has always been recognised that in times of emergency the Government needs to take action quickly and

---

[1] *M.P.R.*, p. 64.   [2] P. 358, *post.*
[3] H.C., 113 of 1944.   [4] P. 361, *post.*
[5] *M.P.R.*, Vol. II., Evidence, p. 120.

in excess of its normal powers. In most continental States provision is made for the suspension in times of emergency of those constitutional guarantees which with us are dependent on the safeguards provided by the common law. In the United Kingdom Parliament both enlarges the discretionary powers of the Government by a general enabling Act and at the end of the emergency, if need be, protects its officers from vexatious actions in the courts by passing an Indemnity Bill legalising any illegalities committed *bona fide* during the period. The Government relies mainly on delegated legislation for the exercise of emergency powers, although the Crown still possesses an ill-defined residue of prerogative power capable of use in time of national danger. Thus during the First and Second World Wars wide legislative powers were conferred by the Defence of the Realm Acts, 1914–15, and the Emergency Powers (Defence) Acts, 1939–40. The powers under the latter Acts so far as economic controls are concerned have been continued by a series of Supplies and Services Acts from 1945 onwards. These Acts enable defence regulations to be used as legislative instruments to regulate the post-war economy and to provide for current defence requirements in any part of the world. The Emergency Powers Act, 1920, a permanent Act, enables the Executive to legislate subject to parliamentary safeguards in the event of an emergency which threatens to interfere with the supply of food and other essential services on an extensive scale, but the powers are inadequate to put the country on a basis of war-time government.[1]

Exceptional Types of Delegated Legislation.   Criticism centres upon particular types of delegated legislation.

(a) *Matters of principle.* There is a clear threat to parliamentary government if power is delegated to legislate on matters of general policy, or if so wide a discretion is conferred that it is impossible to be sure what limit the legislature intended to impose.[2] If power is delegated to legislate on matters of principle, it is essential to maintain parliamentary control over the exercise of the power. If the power of the courts to declare delegated legislation *ultra vires* is to be of any real value, the delegated power must obviously be defined with reasonable strictness. Critics of the departments are apt to forget that every effort is usually made to ensure that regulations are drawn in such a way as to provide for all possible contingencies and thus eliminate the elements of uncertainty and inability on the part of persons affected to foresee the consequences of the enactment. Acts of Parliament conferring powers are frequently wide in their

---

[1] Pp. 381–389, *post.*

[2] The Committee on Ministers' Powers cited the vague power given to the Minister of Health to "make such rules, orders and regulations as he may think fit for the management of the poor," Poor Law Act, 1930, s. 136 (now repealed); *M.P.R.*, p. 31; see also Sir Cecil Carr, *Concerning English Administrative Law*, p. 38.

terms; regulations made under them usually avoid vague propositions and when they sub-delegate powers, *e.g.* to local authorities, they do so in full and clear terms. Indeed, the citizen is more troubled by the bulk and complexity than by the generality of delegated legislation.[1]

(*b*) *Delegation of taxing power.* We have seen how vital to parliamentary supremacy is the function of imposing taxation.[2] None the less the working of a tariff system has been found impracticable without delegation.[3] The five measures of 1931 previously [4] referred to were subject to a time limit, but the Import Duties Act, 1932,[5] contained no time limit. Under that Act the House of Commons surrendered to the Treasury the power to impose *ad valorem* duties and to alter the free list. Control by the House of Commons is retained by enacting that Treasury orders should lapse after forty days, unless earlier confirmed by a resolution of the House.

(*c*) *Sub-delegation.* The technique of a delegate sub-delegating the power to legislate was encouraged by the terms of the Emergency Powers (Defence) Act, 1939, s. 1 (3) that "Defence Regulations may provide for empowering such authorities, persons or classes of persons as may be specified in the Regulations to make orders, rules and by-laws for any of the purposes" for which the Regulations could be made. This provision also applies to current regulations made under the post-war Supplies and Services Acts, 1945–51. On occasions this has resulted in legislative action at four removes from the parent Act, as when general licences were authorised under directions issued, which directions were given under the authority of orders made under a Defence Regulation which in turn was made under the Act of 1939. Action at four removes from the direct authority of Parliament has been condemned as tending "to postpone the formulation of an exact and definite law" and as encouraging "the taking of powers meanwhile in wider terms than may ultimately be required." [6] It also increases the number of civil servants who are authorised to make general laws under their own signatures.

It is doubtful whether (apart from express authority) the practice of interpreting an initial delegation of the power to legislate as authorising the making of other categories of instruments by the relevant Minister himself or by other bodies is as a matter of law valid. It certainly makes control by the ordinary constitutional

---

[1] See, however, *Blackpool Corporation* v. *Locker*, [1948] 1 K.B. 349, *esp. at* p. 362.
[2] Part II., Chap. 2.
[3] Carr, *op. cit.*, p. 40.
[4] P. 101, *ante.*
[5] Pp. 101–102, *ante.*
[6] Third Special Report of the Select Committee on Statutory Rules and Orders, H.C. 186 (1945–46) para. 16.

methods difficult. This mischief can best be cured by the use of precise limitations in the parent Act.

(*d*) *Retrospective operation.* In discussing the supremacy of Parliament mention has been made of legislation having retrospective operation.[1] To change the character of past transactions carried out on the faith of the then existing law is repugnant to the conception of the rule of law. If on occasions it is inevitable that Parliament should yield to the proposals of a Chancellor of the Exchequer to stop a leakage in the revenue with effect from a date a few months earlier, this should be done by Parliament itself and not be entrusted to delegated legislation, where there is no procedure apt for securing amendment of the new law. Such legislation can only be justified if Parliament has the opportunity of debating the matter as one of principle on second reading and of amending the proposal in committee, if need be.

(*e*) *Exclusion of the jurisdiction of the courts.* We have seen that the jurisdiction of the courts is confined to declaring delegated legislation *ultra vires*.[2] The real control over delegated legislation must be parliamentary and administrative. Parliament can define powers clearly and scrutinise through a small committee the regulations made in pursuance of delegated powers. Ministers can see that departments and subordinate bodies under their control act reasonably in the exercise of their powers. The courts can only ensure that powers are exercised *bona fide* and for the purposes defined in Acts of Parliament. They cannot ensure that they are exercised reasonably in the wide sense. None the less the control of the courts is important and should only exceptionally be excluded. The Committee on Ministers' Powers expressed the view that in exceptional cases challenge was undesirable, *e.g.* planning orders under which the title to property is affected or stock regulations under which money may change hands. They recommended, however, that, when a regulation or order cannot remain indefinitely open to challenge, *e.g.* a clearance order, there should be an initial period of challenge of at least three and preferably of six months.[3]

(*f*) *Authority to modify an Act of Parliament.* Sometimes power is delegated to modify a statute. The passing of a complicated and far-reaching statute may involve minor alterations in numerous local Acts. Particularly criticised has been the so-called " Henry VIII. Clause " enabling a Minister to modify the Act itself so far as necessary for bringing it into operation.[4] The use of this clause has in practice been innocuous and its abandonment would mean that

---

[1] Pp. 39–40, *ante*.   [2] Pp. 305–306, *ante*.

[3] *M.P.R.*, p. 62; Carr, *op. cit.*, p. 48; see Housing Act, 1936, 2nd Schedule. and p. 326, *ante*.

[4] *M.P.R.*, pp. 36–38; Carr, *op. cit.*, pp. 41–47.

once an Act had been passed, no defect in its provisions could be modified without amending legislation. None the less the Committee on Ministers' Powers recommended that the " Henry VIII. Clause " should never be used except for the purpose of bringing an Act into operation and that it should be subject to a time limit of one year from the passing of the Act. It is clearly dangerous in principle to permit the Executive to change an Act of Parliament. A recent illustration of the use of the clause is to be found in the Representation of the People Act, 1945, which has since been repealed. Section 12, which gave the Secretary of State power to make supplementary orders for the purpose of restarting local elections which had been suspended during the war, provided that the orders should have effect notwithstanding anything in any enactment, including the Act itself. The reason for the provision was the insoluble problem of securing a formula which would cover the retirement by rotation of the councillors who served during the war, some of whom had been elected before the war, while others had been co-opted to fill vacancies.

A real safeguard against abuse of power to legislate must be sought in parliamentary control. If this control is to be effective, there must be adequate machinery for its exercise. Sometimes it is provided that regulations shall be laid before Parliament without prescribing what action can be taken by Parliament; sometimes that they may be annulled by negative resolution of each House within a specified period, usually without prejudice to the validity of any action previously taken under the regulation; sometimes that they shall not operate until approved by an affirmative resolution, usually of both Houses, sometimes of the House of Commons only if the regulations relate to financial provisions; sometimes regulations are laid in draft; but usually they are immediately operative. Where a regulation is merely laid before Parliament, a member of the House of Commons who wishes to move its annulment must find time during the ordinary sittings of the House; this is as a rule impracticable. When regulations are expressly made liable to annulment within a stated period, a motion for annulment is exempted business and may be taken after the normal close of business, if a private member moves the prayer (*i.e.* a resolution requiring that an Address be presented to Her Majesty for the revocation of the instrument) and can obtain enough supporters to "keep a House." If the prayer is successful, the regulation is not thereby revoked, but provision is made for revocation, if the Government so decides, by Order in Council. The Statutory Instruments Act, 1946, s. 5 (1) provides that the validity of anything previously done under the instrument shall not be affected, but that no further proceedings, *e.g.* prosecutions for breach, shall be taken under it after the date of the resolution. When an

Safeguards: (1) Parliamentary Control.

affirmative resolution is required, the onus is on the Government to present orders for approval. The Committee on Ministers' Powers recommended [1] that, except when an affirmative resolution is required, there should be uniform procedure in regard to all regulations required to be laid before Parliament, viz. they should be open to annulment—not amendment—by resolution of either House without prejudice to the validity of any action already taken under the regulation.[2] The Select Committee (*post*) has recommended that the procedure of confirmation by affirmative resolution should apply to all regulations imposing taxation or modifying the terms of a statute. It is, however, a matter of controversy how far effective parliamentary control can be exercised without placing upon Parliament a task which it is unfitted to perform, namely the detailed supervision of administration. It is not only in relation to delegated legislation that this arises; we have already discussed it briefly in connection with the nationalised industries.[3]

(2) Scrutinising Committee. The Committee on Ministers' Powers had further recommended the appointment of a small Standing Committee of each House to consider and report on Bills conferring law-making powers and on regulations and rules made in pursuance of such powers and laid before Parliament. The former function would appear to be unnecessary so long as Bills are adequately considered in committee.[4] In 1944 there was appointed a Select Committee of the House of Commons to consider every statutory rule or order laid or laid in draft before the House upon which proceedings may be or might have been taken in either House of Parliament in pursuance of any Act of Parliament (*i.e.* requiring confirmation or subject to annulment). The function of the Committee is to consider whether the attention of the House should be drawn to any regulation on any of the following grounds:—

(1) that it imposes a charge on the public revenues or contains provisions requiring payments to be made to the Exchequer or any Government Department or to any local or public authority in consideration of any licence or consent, or of any services to be rendered, or prescribes the amount of any such charge or payments;

[1] *M.P.R.*, p. 67.
[2] In 1944 it was discovered that the National Fire Service Regulations originally made in 1941 had not been laid before Parliament. The Fire Services (Emergency Provisions) Act, 1941, required that they should be laid before Parliament "as soon as may be," and provided for annulment by a negative resolution. Lawyers disagreed as to whether the failure to lay invalidated the regulations. *Ex abundanti cautela* an Act was passed to validate the regulations and acts done under them and to indemnify those responsible: National Fire Service Regulations (Indemnity) Act, 1944. See now Statutory Instruments Act, 1946, s. 4, *post*, at pp. 359–361.
[3] Part IV., Chap. 11.   [4] Part III., Chap. 3., B.

(2) that it is made in pursuance of an enactment containing specific provisions excluding it from challenge in the courts, either at all times or after the expiration of a specified period;

(3) that it appears to make some unusual or unexpected use of the powers conferred by the Statute under which it is made;

(4) that it purports to have retrospective effect where the parent Statute confers no express authority so to provide;

(5) that there appears to have been unjustifiable delay in the publication or in the laying of it before Parliament;

(6) that there appears to have been unjustifiable delay in sending a notification to Mr. Speaker under the proviso to subsection (1) of section four of the Statutory Instruments Act, 1946, where an Instrument has come into operation before it has been laid before Parliament;[1]

(7) that for any special reason its form or purport calls for elucidation.

The Select Committee is assisted by the Speaker's Counsel. The Committee may require the department concerned to submit an explanatory memorandum or to send a representative to explain a regulation to the Committee. Before a report is made to the House drawing special attention to any regulation an opportunity must be given to the department concerned to furnish orally or in writing such explanations as it may think fit. The Committee, known as the Scrutinising Committee, is appointed each session. Its official title is now the Select Committee on Statutory Instruments. In addition to routine reports on its examination of batches of statutory instruments, the Committee has made several proposals relating to its sphere of action and from one of these there resulted the Act about to be discussed. It has only found it necessary to call the attention of the House to objectionable features, as defined by its terms of reference, in the case of a very small proportion of the thousands of instruments which it has examined in the six years of its existence. In the House of Lords a Special Orders Committee was set up as far back as 1925. This Committee examines all instruments which are subject to affirmative resolution procedure.

An obvious safeguard when a legislative power is delegated is (3) Publicity. adequate publicity. The Statutory Instruments Act, 1946, which came into force on January 1, 1948, repealed the Rules Publication Act, 1893. The latter Act was designed to secure antecedent publicity for the more important statutory instruments of some, but not all government departments. The provisions of the Act of 1946,

[1] P. 360, *post.*

which only applies to direct delegated legislation,[1] may be summarised as follows:—

(1) All documents by which power is conferred by Act of Parliament to make, confirm or approve orders, rules, regulations or other sub-legislation by Order in Council or by a Minister under a power expressed to be exercisable by statutory instrument are known as statutory instruments (s. 1).

Thus the confused nomenclature of delegated legislation remains, except that statutory instruments replace statutory rules and orders as a collective title.[2]

(2) There is a uniform procedure for numbering, printing, publishing and citing statutory instruments (s. 2).

(3) It is a defence in proceedings for contravention of a statutory instrument to prove that it had not been issued by the Stationery Office at the date of the alleged contravention, unless it is shown by the prosecutor that reasonable steps have been taken to bring the purport of the instrument to the notice of the public or of persons likely to be affected by it or of the person charged (s. 3 (2)).[3]

In *Johnson* v. *Sargent*, [1918] 1 K.B. 101, it was held that a statutory instrument (unlike an Act of Parliament) did not take effect until it became known. This decision had given rise to doubts which the above provision is designed to remove. The point is an important one because current administrative practice relies upon the immediate enforceability of certain types of control, *e.g.* price schedules which for obvious reasons cannot be given publicity in advance. In practice, however, the police or other local enforcement agency are as likely as the offender to be ignorant of the change in law for some while after it has been made.

(4) A statutory instrument which is required to be laid before Parliament must be laid in both Houses before it comes into operation. If this cannot be done for reasons which are essential, the Lord Chancellor and the Speaker must be notified forthwith and an explanation given to them why copies were not laid before the instrument came into operation (s. 4 (1)).

This stricter provision takes the place of a power to make provisional rules and thereby on grounds of urgency to avoid the requirements of the Rules Publication Act as to antecedent publicity. Every copy must show on the face of it the date of operation and information as to compliance with the requirement of laying before Parliament (s. 4 (2)).

---

[1] There is no obligation to publish sub-delegated legislation (p. 355, *ante*), and *Blackpool Corporation* v. *Locker* (*loc. cit.*).

[2] P. 352, *ante*.

[3] See *The Queen* v. *Sheer Metalcraft Ltd.*, [1954] 1 Q.B. 586.

(5) In the case of instruments which are subject to annulment in pursuance of a resolution of either House, a uniform period of forty days (exclusive of any time during which Parliament is dissolved, prorogued or adjourned for more than four days) is prescribed within which a prayer for annulment may be moved by a member.[1]

One way of avoiding a clash between a department exercising legislative powers and the interests most likely to be affected is to provide for some form of prior consultation.[2] Without formal obligation much direct consultation takes place between departments and associations representing local government, industry, trades or professions. Nor is consultation limited to delegated legislation. Proposed Bills, but not the actual text, may be the subject of lengthy discussions before they are introduced in Parliament. Antenatal publicity as required by the repealed Rules Publication Act has largely been rendered unnecessary by the development of this departmental practice. In some cases the practice is made obligatory and specified interests must be consulted. In others the legislation has to be prepared by the affected interest and the Minister confirms or approves the resulting instrument which may take the form of a scheme. Perhaps the most significant development is to be found in the requirement of the submission of draft regulations to a statutory advisory body, particularly where as in the case of national insurance the interests affected are nation-wide. The work of the National Insurance Advisory Committee has already been outlined.[3]

Consultation of Interests.

A development is the growth of what has been described as "administrative quasi-legislation." [4] Government departments have adopted the practice of issuing pronouncements stating the official point of view on doubtful points in statutes, or announcing concessions that will be made in the application of statutes to individual cases. In 1944 the Chancellor of the Exchequer presented to Parliament a twenty-page list of extra-statutory war-time concessions given in the administration of inland revenue duties.[5] The Finance Acts remain on the statute book, but certain provisions cease to represent the law as applied in practice. Sometimes arrangements made administratively affect the rights of one subject against another. Thus under section 29 of the now repealed Workmen's Compensation Act, 1925, it was a defence to a claim by a workman for damages at

Administrative Quasi-Legislation

---

[1] As recommended by the Select Committee on Statutory Instruments (H.C. 113 of 1944).
[2] See *Delegated Legislation—Some Recent Developments*, by J. A. G. Griffith, 12 M.L.R. 306–318.
[3] Part IV., Chap. 11. For details of the initial tasks of the Committee, see 12 *M.L.R.* 312–313.
[4] "Administrative Quasi-Legislation," by R. E. Megarry, 60 *L.Q.R.*, p. 125.
[5] Cmd. 6559, 1944.

common law that he had accepted compensation under the Act. In 1942, the Home Secretary announced in the House of Commons that employers' organisations and insurance interests generally had agreed not to raise this defence, provided that proceedings were started within three months of the accident. As a result the necessity for remedial legislation was avoided. Thus without any change being made in the law a substantial change was made in the advice which a solicitor should give his client. It is at least essential that there should be some systematic publication of administrative notifications.[1]

[1] As to publication of decisions of administrative tribunals, see Chap. 5, *ante*.

PART VIII.

THE CITIZEN AND THE STATE.

Law of the Constitution, by A. V. Dicey, 9th ed., Part II. (The Rule of Law), Chaps. V., VI. and VII., and Appendix, Section II. (MacMillan).
History of English Law, by Sir W. S. Holdsworth, Vol. X., pp. 644–713 (Methuen).
Freedom under the Law, by Sir Alfred Denning, Chaps. I. and II. (Stevens).
The Problem of Power, by Lord Radcliffe (Reith Lectures).

CHAPTER 1.

FREEDOM OF PERSON AND PROPERTY.

Introductory.

WE have already seen [1] that under the constitution there are no formal guarantees of liberty apart from the declarations of rights contained in the ancient charters and the restrictions on the arbitrary power of the Crown imposed by the Revolution Settlement of 1689. The citizen may go where he pleases and do or say what he pleases, provided that he does not commit an offence against the criminal law or infringe the rights of others. If his legal rights are infringed by others, *e.g.* by trespassing upon his property or defaming his reputation, he may protect himself by the remedies provided by the law. It is in the law of crimes and of tort and contract, part of the ordinary law of the land, and not in any fundamental constitutional law, that the citizen finds protection for his political liberty, whether it is infringed by officials or by fellow-citizens. In times of emergency the Executive is accorded special powers by Parliament, but there are no formal guarantees—such as are to be found in a constitutional code formally enacted—which have to be suspended. It follows that a text-book on constitutional law can only deal in bare outline with the law relating to the fundamental freedoms, such as freedom of the person, free speech, free elections. For detail the student must turn to text-books covering the branch of the law concerned. Freedom of speech means that a man may say whatever will not expose him to a prosecution or a civil action for defamation. To know what utterances will so expose him the citizen must familiarise

No constitutional Guarantees.

---

[1] Part I., p. 5, *ante*: Part II., pp. 58–59, *ante*.

himself with the intricacies of the law of defamation. The enjoyment of property is conditioned by the common law principle that one must use one's property in such a way as not to inflict injuries upon one's neighbour. The advent of the Welfare State has brought other features into the legal relationship between citizens and Government. The various social services have each created their legal and administrative problems; for example, disputed claims on the National Insurance funds, liability to patients of hospitals and of medical practitioners in the health service, restrictions designed to ensure the better use of land and a higher standard of production on the farms. The liabilities in contract and tort of public authorities and the means of adjusting private rights with the public interest by litigation have been referred to in earlier chapters. But it is necessary to emphasise that there is a wide field of economic relationship which has still found no place in constitutional law. This must explain, although it does not excuse, the omission of any discussion of the part played by the State in industrial relations as well as of any discussion of the striking movement away from contract to status which has resulted from the standardisation, although not necessarily directly imposed by the State, of so many aspects of current conditions of civilisation.

A.

Personal Freedom.

Justification for Imprisonment.

A BRITISH subject cannot claim his freedom to be guaranteed, but he can, nevertheless, protect himself by proceedings in the civil and criminal courts against those who interfere with his liberty. A privilege is of little use unless it is protected and enforced. Under English law interference with freedom, *i.e.* physical coercion and restraint, can only be justified on certain grounds. If none of these be present, the person detained has a cause of action for damages for false imprisonment against his goaler, or he can prosecute him for assault. The principal grounds are:

(1) Arrest and detention pending trial, when permitted by law, on a criminal charge.

(2) Sentence of imprisonment or detention imposed after due trial by a court, *e.g.* in a Borstal Institution after conviction on a criminal charge, or committal to an approved school.

(3) Imprisonment for civil debt[1] and for contempt of court, including imprisonment for contempt of either House of Parliament.

---

[1] Since the Debtors Act, 1869, imprisonment for debt is confined to the case of persons of proved capacity to pay who decline to obey the order of the court to satisfy a judgment debt or other order of a court for payment.

(4) Detention under the law relating to lunacy and mental deficiency, or detention of a child in need of care or protection under the Children and Young Persons Acts, 1933 and 1938.

(5) The exercise of parental authority over an infant. A husband has no such authority over his wife: *The Queen* v. *Jackson*, [1891] 1 Q.B. 671.

The extent of the power of arrest and the kindred power of search has been discussed in many leading cases of constitutional importance. An arrest may lawfully be effected by a police officer who acts on a written warrant for arrest granted by a justice of the peace or other judicial authority who is empowered to issue warrants after application (an information) supported by a statement on oath outlining the alleged offence. The warrant must indicated specifically the person whose arrest is to be effected. There is no power to issue a general warrant to search for and to arrest an unnamed person. *Arrest with Warrant.*

More complicated is the extent of the power and duty of police officers and private persons to arrest without warrant where they suspect that a crime has been committed or to prevent the commission of a crime. The Executive has no power to interfere, through the police or otherwise, with the personal freedom of the subject by means of arbitrary arrest; for the plea of an act of State is no defence to an action brought by a subject in defence of his private rights [1]: *Entick* v. *Carrington* (1765), 19 St. Tr. 1030; K. & L. 145. There are, however, numerous occasions where arrest without warrant is justified either by common law or statute.[2] The powers of a police officer are somewhat wider than those of a private citizen. Anyone, whether police officer or private citizen, is required by law to arrest any person who in his presence commits a treason or felony or dangerous wounding.[3] A police officer must, and a private person may, also prevent such crimes, and indeed any breach of the peace, by detaining temporarily any person plainly about to commit such an offence. There is also a power to arrest without warrant any person reasonably suspected of having committed treason or a felony or dangerous wounding. In such a case, however, a private citizen would have no defence to an action for false imprisonment if the crime in question had not in fact been committed by anyone: *Walters* v. *W. H. Smith & Son, Ltd.*, [1914] 1 K.B. 595. An illegal arrest without a warrant for a petty offence cannot be subsequently justified on the grounds that there was a reasonable suspicion that the *Arrest without Warrant.*

---

[1] P. 142, *ante.*
[2] Kenny, *Outlines of Criminal Law*, 16th ed. Pp. 473–476.
[3] It has for a long time not been the practice to prosecute a private person for failure to arrest a felon, unless he has been called upon by a police officer for assistance. The duty, however, exists.

person arrested had in fact committed a felony. A person on being arrested without a warrant is entitled to be told then and there on what grounds he has been detained unless he is caught in the actual commission of an offence, such as burglary.[1] Any passer-by may be called upon to assist a constable who has seen a breach of the peace committed by more than one person or who has been assaulted or obstructed in the arrest of a felon and has had reasonable necessity for calling upon others to assist him. To refuse assistance in such circumstances is a misdemeanour: *The Queen* v. *Brown* (1841), Car. & M. 314; K. & L. 428. It has been held that a police officer may enter private premises to prevent a breach of the peace, and *per* Hewart, C.J., to prevent the commission of any offence that he reasonably believes is imminent or is likely to be committed: *Thomas* v. *Sawkins*, [1935] 2 K.B. 249,[2] where police officers successfully maintained their right to be present, though not invited by the organisers, at a meeting held on private premises which the general public had been invited by advertisement to attend. Numerous statutory provisions authorise a police officer to arrest without warrant in particular cases.[3]

Questioning of suspected persons.
In 1912 the judges of the King's Bench Division drew up certain rules to govern the taking of statements from persons who may subsequently be put on trial after questioning conducted by the police. The rules, which are known as the Judges' Rules, have not the force of law, but statements obtained contrary to the rules may, and normally will, be rejected by the judge at the trial.[4] The constitutional importance of the rules lies in the protection which they afford against a confession being made under duress by an accused person or without being aware that any statement he may make after being taken into custody can be used in evidence against him, as well as in his favour, at his trial. These rules are not the least important of the safeguards contained in the rules of evidence relating to criminal cases which secure a fair trial and thus they are an important part of the protection afforded to the citizen against an abuse of power by the police.

General Warrant Cases.
The principle that a plea of the public interest does not justify a wrongful act was established by the eighteenth-century cases known as the *General Warrant Cases*. The practice of issuing general warrants to arrest unspecified persons and to search property is said to have originated with the Court of Star Chamber. It is obviously

---

[1] *Christie* v. *Leachinsky*, [1947] A.C. 573; K. & L. 182.

[2] For discussion of this case, see "*Thomas* v. *Sawkins*: A Constitutional Innovation," 6 *Cambridge Law Journal*, 22, and Dicey, *op. cit.*, pp. 573–575.

[3] Kenny, *op. cit.* pp. 474–476. The complicated state of the common law was clarified by the House of Lords in *Christie* v. *Leachinsky* (*ante*).

[4] For the text of the Judges' Rules, see Archbold, *Criminal Pleading, Evidence and Practice*, 33rd ed. p. 414–415.

a powerful weapon to assist an embarrassed Executive to obtain material upon which to formulate charges against persons suspected of hostility towards the Government. At a later stage the practice was authorised by the Licensing Act, 1662, for use by a Secretary of State to prevent publication of unlicensed material, and such warrants continued after the lapse of that Act in 1695. The *General Warrant Cases* arose out of the attempt of George III.'s Government to stifle the political activities of John Wilkes and the publication known as the *North Briton*. Even at a later date the severity of the law against seditious publications was maintained largely by executive action, but the cases decided once and for all the illegality of general warrants and thus deprived the Executive of a formidable instrument of oppression.

Of these three cases *Leach* v. *Money* (1765), 19 St. Tr. 1002, decided that a general warrant to arrest unnamed persons (the printers and publishers of the *North Briton*), against whom a charge had not yet been formulated, was illegal; *Wilkes* v. *Wood* (1763), 19 St. Tr. 1153, that the papers of an unnamed person could not be seized on a warrant of this description; *Entick* v. *Carrington* (1765), 19 St. Tr. 1030; K. & L. 174, that there was no inherent power in the Secretary of State as a Privy Councillor [1] to order an arrest except in cases of treason, and that a general warrant as to the papers of a named person was illegal. The sequel to these cases was a successful action against Lord Halifax as the Secretary of State who had issued the warrants. A modern decision has, however, seriously diminished the protection afforded by *Entick* v. *Carrington* in cases where the police have effected the lawful arrest of one man, but are in search of evidence of the commission by a different person of another offence. The police have a right by common law to search the person of anyone who is arrested on a warrant and in practice the search extends to anything in the possession and control of arrested persons which may be relevant to the charge brought against them. It is also customary to search all persons taken into custody on a serious charge, whether arrested on a warrant or not. In *Elias* v. *Pasmore*, [1934] 2 K.B. 164, it was held that upon the arrest by lawful process of an accused person the police can search the premises where the prisoner is arrested and seize material which is relevant to the prosecution for *any* crime committed by *any* person, not merely by the prisoner himself.[2] The decision does not, however, justify the wholesale seizure of the contents of the premises except in so far as any of the contents are evidence of the commission of an offence by someone.

There are a number of cases where search warrants may lawfully be issued under the authority of a statute. Such cases in effect form

Search Warrants.

---

[1] All Privy Councillors are now Justices of the Peace and can therefore commit for any indictable offence.
[2] See "Police Search," by E. C. S. Wade, 50 *L.Q.R.* 354.

exceptions to the rule that general warrants are illegal. The oldest and, indeed, one which was admitted in *Entick* v. *Carrington* (*ante*) to exist at common law, permits the search of premises which are suspected of being made a receptacle for stolen goods: *Jones* v. *German*, [1896] 2 Q.B. 418.[1] The more important from the constitutional point of view are those conferred by the Official Secrets Act, 1911, s. 9; and the Incitement to Disaffection Act, 1934, s. 2 (2); the former provision reads as follows:

> (1) If a justice of the peace is satisfied by information on oath that there is reasonable ground for suspecting that an offence under this Act has been, or is about to be committed, he may grant a search warrant authorising any constable named therein to enter at any time any premises or place named in the warrant, if necessary, by force, and to search the premises or place and every person found therein and to seize . . . anything which is evidence of an offence under this Act having been or being about to be committed. . . .
>
> (2) Where it appears to a superintendent of police that the case is one of great emergency and that in the interests of the State immediate action is necessary, he may by a written order . . . give to any constable the like authority. . . .

In the Incitement to Disaffection Act, 1934,[2] a High Court Judge is substituted for a justice of the peace, and elaborate restrictions are imposed upon the right to search (s. 2 (2)–(4)).

Under the authority of various statutes (some seventy in all) search warrants may be issued, *e.g.* for explosive substances intended to be used for felonious purposes; for unlicensed firearms; for forged documents and instruments of forgery; for counterfeit coins and coinage tools; for goods which infringe the provisions of the Merchandise Marks Act, 1887; for obscene books and pictures. Search for a woman or girl detained for immoral purposes, or for ill-treated or neglected children, may also be authorised by warrant. In certain special cases under the Larceny Act, 1916, s. 42 (2), any constable may be authorised in writing by a chief police officer without a justice's warrant to search premises for stolen property.

Remedies for Infringement of Freedom. For interference with freedom of the person on any grounds other than those permitted by law, the subject has four types of remedy, if the first may properly be called a remedy at all. These are: self-defence, a prosecution for assault, an action in respect of wrongful arrest, and the prerogative writ of habeas corpus. The remedies are available equally against an official or a private fellow-citizen.

Self-Defence. Self-defence is an extra-judicial remedy. If a charge which does not justify arrest without a warrant has been expressly made, the

---

[1] Extended to goods obtained by other fraudulent practices by the Larceny Act, 1916, s. 42 (1).

[2] P. 395, *post*.

person charged is entitled to resist arrest whether by a police officer or a private citizen, but the right to resist is limited by the duty to submit to arrest by a police officer, even though the reason for arrest is not at once given. Resistance to an arrest which is made on insufficient grounds is justifiable if the officer conceals some other ground for arrest which he later brings forward in justification of having made the arrest. But if a police officer arrests without a warrant a person for a felony without notifying the charge and the person arrested knows that he is a police officer, resistance which causes the death of the officer cannot be justified and the person resisting, even though innocent of the felony for which he has been arrested, may be guilty of murder.[1] It is inexpedient to resort to self-defence to resist arrest by a police officer, because, if the resistance cannot be justified on this ground, the consequential assault of the officer is aggravated by reason of his being a policeman. Although the law is by no means clear, self-defence does not appear to mean that the use of any amount of necessary force is lawful. The amount of force used must not merely be necessary for the protection of liberty, which includes freedom from interference both for one's person and property, but also proportionate to the harm it is intended to avert. For example, if a person, walking along the coast alone, is compelled to turn aside from his path by the aggression of three men who accost him, he is not at liberty to shoot them dead, merely because they threaten to assault him if he does not turn back. But if the came person is surrounded by the trio on the top of Beachy Head and they gradually force him to the cliff's edge, thereby imperilling his life, it is both necessary for the protection of his person and also proportionate to the harm which he desires to avert from himself, namely death, that he should shoot his aggressors. There is some authority for saying that a man who is set upon in his own house may shoot to kill anyone who seeks forcibly to evict him, because he cannot reasonably be expected to retreat further. In *The King* v. *Hussey* (1925), 41 T.L.R. 205, a conviction for unlawful wounding was quashed, the circumstances being that the tenant shot his landlord through the keyhole, while the latter and some friends were seeking forcibly to evict him.

A civil action for damages lies for assault or false imprisonment; further, an action for malicious prosecution may be maintained by any person who is prosecuted for an offence in the criminal courts maliciously and without reasonable and probable cause. These remedies may be used against anyone, including public officials, police officers and keepers of mental hospitals. In addition, criminal proceedings may be brought for assault, and it is in the criminal law

Prosecution for Assault and Action in respect of Wrongful Arrest.

---

[1] *Christie* v. *Leachinsky, ante, per* Lord du Parcq, at p. 601, citing *The King* v. *Woolmer* (1832), 1 Mood. 334.

that the greater safeguard of the subject is provided against his fellow-citizen's interference with personal liberty.[1]

Prerogative Writ of Habeas Corpus.

It is not sufficient that the subject should be able to defend himself or pursue his remedy under the ordinary law in the courts. For he may be detained by order of the State, or, for that matter, by an individual, and so not to be in a position to institute legal proceedings. Accordingly the law of England provides in the writ of habeas corpus a process by which a person who is confined without legal justification may secure release from his confinement.[2] The wrongdoer is not thereby punished, but the person imprisoned procures his release and is then at liberty to pursue his remedies against the wrongdoer in the ordinary way. The writ of habeas corpus is with one exception available to all persons within the King's protection, including any alien enemies who may be permitted to be at large in time of war. It is not, however, available to an enemy who is a prisoner of war nor to an interned enemy alien, nor can a notice of intended internment be challenged by application for the writ.[3] The following passage from Blackstone describes the nature of the process, namely, the prerogative writ of habeas corpus:

> The great and efficacious writ, in all manner of illegal confinement, is that of *habeas corpus ad subjiciendum*, directed to the person detaining another, and commanding him to produce the body of the prisoner, with the day and cause of his caption and detention, *ad faciendum, subjiciendum et recipiendum*, to do, submit to and receive whatsoever the judge or court awarding such writ shall consider in that behalf. This is a high prerogative writ, and therefore by the common law issuing out of the Court of King's Bench not only in term time, but also during the vacation by a *fiat* from the chief justice or any other of the judges and running into all parts of the King's dominions; for the King is at all times entitled to have an account, why the liberty of any of his subjects is restrained, wherever that restraint may be inflicted.[4]

Again, Broom says:[5]

> "This great constitutional remedy rests upon the common law declared by Magna Carta and the statutes which affirm it, rests, likewise, on specific enactments ensuring its efficiency, extending its applicability, and rendering more firm and durable the liberties of the people . . . and the right to claim it cannot be suspended, even for one hour, by any means short of an Act of Parliament."

[1] Certain prosecutions require the consent of the Attorney-General (*e.g.* prosecutions under the Official Secrets Acts), but in general any person may initiate a prosecution for any criminal offence.

[2] For the equivalent of the process in Scotland see p. 376, *post*, and the Criminal Procedure (Scotland) Act, 1887, s. 43, superseding the Act of 1701 "for preventing wrongous imprisonment and against order and delays in trials" which now only applies to persons in prison on a charge of treason.

[3] *The King* v. *Vine Street Police Superintendent, ex parte Liebmann*, [1916] 1 K.B. 268; Sir Arnold McNair (*Legal Effects of War*, 3rd ed., Cambridge University Press) suggests (p. 56, note 5) that the reason is to be found in the prerogative of the Crown to wage war and incidentally to capture enemy persons and hold them in captivity.   [4] 3 Bl., *Commentaries*, p. 131.

[5] See *Constitutional Law*, 2nd ed., p. 223, cited by Lord Shaw of Dunfermline in *The King* v. *Halliday, ex parte Zadig*, [1917] A.C. 260 at p. 296.

The writ of habeas corpus is obtainable by any person on behalf Procedure.
of the prisoner as well as by the prisoner himself. This is an important safeguard, though in practice every facility is granted to a
person in prison to make application for the writ, if he so wishes.
The procedure is as follows:[1]

Application is made *ex parte* supported by an affidavit to the
Divisional Court or in vacation or in a case concerning the custody
of an infant to the Judge in Chambers. If *prima facie* grounds are
shown, the Court or Judge ordinarily directs that notice of motion be
given or a summons issued. Argument on the merits of the application then takes place on the day named. If the Court decides that
the writ should issue, it orders the release of the prisoner or the handing over of the infant to the applicant, and this order is sufficient
warrant for the release. Under this practice there is no need to produce the prisoner in court at the hearing and no return to the writ
is actually made. The Court or Judge has power on the *ex parte*
application to order the issue of the writ forthwith; this power it
uses in exceptional cases, particularly where there is danger of the
person detained being taken outside the jurisdiction; where this is
ordered, argument as to the legality of the detention takes place on
the return to the writ.[2]

This procedure may be illustrated by the following documents
which were cited by Lord Finlay in *Secretary of State for Home
Affairs* v. *O'Brien*, [1923] A.C. 603; K. & L. 273.

IN THE COURT OF APPEAL [3]

ON APPEAL FROM THE HIGH COURT OF JUSTICE
KING'S BENCH DIVISION

Friday the 13*th day of April* 1923.

ENGLAND.—Upon reading the affidavit of Art O'Brien and the
several exhibits therein referred to it is ordered that Monday the 23rd
day of April instant be given to His Majesty's Secretary of State for
Home Affairs to show cause why a writ of habeas corpus should not
issue directed to him to have the body of Art O'Brien immediately
before this Court at the Royal Courts of Justice London to undergo
and receive all and singular such matters and things as this Court
shall then and there consider of concerning him in this behalf.

Upon notice of this order to be given to His Majesty's Secretary of
State for Home Affairs in the meantime.

---

[1] R.S.C. Order LIX., rules 14 to 22.
[2] This was the ordinary procedure at an earlier date.
[3] The Divisional Court refused the writ; hence the appeal, which was not
treated as being in a criminal cause or matter (see p. 373, *post*).

IN THE COURT OF APPEAL

ON APPEAL FROM THE HIGH COURT OF JUSTICE
KING'S BENCH DIVISION (ENGLAND)

Wednesday the 9th day of May 1923.

Upon reading the affidavit of the Right Honourable William Clive Bridgeman and upon hearing Mr. Attorney-General of Counsel for His Majesty's Secretary of State for Home Affairs and Mr. Hastings of Counsel for Art O'Brien it is ordered that a writ of habeas corpus do issue directed to His Majesty's Secretary of State for Home Affairs commanding him to have the body of Art O'Brien immediately before this Court at the Royal Courts of Justice London to undergo and receive all and singular such matters and things as this Court shall then and there consider of concerning him in this behalf. And it is ordered that the said Secretary of State for Home Affairs be allowed until the 16th day of May instant within which to make his return to the said writ.

With liberty to apply,
BY THE COURT.

Efficacy of Writ against the Executive.

The case from which the above documents are taken illustrates the efficacy of the writ to put an end to unlawful detention at the hands of the Executive and to free the prisoner to pursue his ordinary remedies in the courts against those responsible for his imprisonment. The order for O'Brien's detention was made by the Home Secretary, a member of the United Kingdom Government, and authorised arrest in England, deportation to the newly-established Irish Free State and handing over to the Government there, over which the United Kingdom Government had no control. Thus the order made in England was plainly illegal. Moreover the House of Lords recognised that the Home Secretary could not give effect to the order to produce O'Brien in the High Court in London without the assistance of the Government of the Free State.[1] Thus the writ affords a guarantee for questioning the legality of detention which is effective only so long as the prisoner is not sent out of the country; against this event the Habeas Corpus Act, 1679 (*post*), provides severe penalties.

Successive Applications for Writ.

It has been confirmed in a curious case which came before the Judicial Committee of the Privy Council from the West Coast of Africa, *Eshugbayi Eleko* v. *Government of Nigeria*, [1928] A.C. 459, that successive applications for the writ to be issued may be made by

---

[1] Cf. *Zabrovsky* v. *G.O.C. Palestine*, [1947] A.C. 246, where the applicant was detained outside the jurisdiction of the Government of Palestine which had ordered the arrest, but under orders which were lawful both in Palestine, so far as deportation and exclusion were concerned and as to detention in Eritrea, the place of imprisonment.

an applicant to every court or judge having jurisdiction to hear applications. In this case a tribal chieftain, whose deportation had been ordered, sought to apply for the writ to one judge after another of the High Court of Nigeria, and the Privy Council upheld his right so to apply. Moreover, on each application, the case has to be decided on its merits. This illustrates the important constitutional safeguard that the writ of habeas corpus affords. An applicant may thus, by way of renewed application, take his case before every judge of the High Court of Justice, until he has exhausted all the available judges, but not, except by way of appeal, to the Court of Appeal: *In re Carroll*, [1931] 1 K.B. 104.[1] He may appeal from a decision of the High Court, or of a judge thereof, refusing the issue of the writ, or discharge under the writ, to the Court of Appeal, and thence to the House of Lords: *ex parte Woodhall* (1888), 20 Q.B.D. 832; *cf. Re Clifford and O'Sullivan*, [1921] 2 A.C. 570; K. & L. 459.[2] But if the matter is one the direct outcome of which may be the trial of the applicant and his possible punishment for a criminal offence by a court claiming jurisdiction in that regard, the matter is a criminal cause and there is no appeal, since the Court of Appeal has only a civil jurisdiction: *Amand* v. *Home Secretary and Minister of Defence of Royal Netherlands Government*, [1943] A.C. 147, where a Netherlands subject who was liable to be charged with an offence against the military law of his country was held not to be entitled to appeal against a refusal of the writ.[3] Nor has the Court of Criminal Appeal any jurisdiction because there has been no conviction or resulting sentence against which to enter an appeal. It has been held that no appeal lies to the Court of Appeal in the case of a person for whose deportation application has been made under the Fugitive Offenders Act, 1881, and who applies unsuccessfully for the issue of the writ in the Queen's Bench Division: *The King* v. *Governor of Brixton Prison, ex parte Savarkar*, [1910] 2 K.B. 1056. This ruling is also applicable to a person whose extradition has been ordered.

If any court has ordered the release of the applicant from custody after hearing the merits of the case, there is no appeal from the order of that court available to the respondent, *i.e.* the person who is ordered to obey the writ by discharging the prisoner, and this is so whether the person detained in custody has actually been released under the order or is still detained: *Cox* v. *Hakes* (1890), 15 App.

Effect of Writ.

---

[1] But see "Habeas Corpus Procedure," by R. F. V. Heuston, 66 *L.Q.R.* 79, where it is argued that an application is only renewable before a different court, not another judge of the same court.

[2] Pp. 425–426, *post.*

[3] See "A Note on Habeas Corpus," by Lord Goddard, 65 *L.Q.R.* 30, pointing out that the old writ of error did not apply to decisions arising out of the prerogative writs before 1875 when appeals under statutory provisions superseded writs of error.

Cas. 506; *Secretary of State* v. *O'Brien (ante)*.[1] An appeal by the respondent will, however, lie in those cases where habeas corpus proceedings are employed as a means of determining which of two or more persons has the right to the custody of a child: *Barnardo* v. *McHugh*, [1891] A.C. 388. Disobedience to the writ is punishable by fine or imprisonment for contempt of court, and the offender may be exposed to heavy penalties recoverable by the person injured. Not only is the writ used against governors of prisons to prevent a prisoner being detained in custody without trial, but by this means a wife may question the legality of her husband's detention of herself, or parents may establish that a child is detained in an institution, such as an orphanage or rescue home, contrary to their wishes: *Barnardo* v. *Ford*, [1892] A.C. 326.

History of Writ of Habeas Corpus.[2]   In origin the writ of habeas corpus enabled a court to bring before itself persons whose presence was necessary for some legal proceeding pending before it. Such a writ can be used for many purposes; for example to assert jurisdiction against a rival court and to release persons imprisoned by order of such a court in excess of the jurisdiction. Thus it came to be a writ by which persons unlawfully imprisoned could get released. Constitutional statesmen of the seventeenth century saw in this writ and particularly in the variety known as habeas corpus *ad subjiciendum* an instrument to check arbitrary arrest and made it more efficient. The writ was to issue out of the King's Bench or Common Pleas. Further in 1628 the Petition of Right declared that the decision in *Darnel's Case*[3] was not the law and that the King could not imprison *per speciale mandatum* without showing cause. In 1640 the Star Chamber Abolition Act,[4] imposed the same requirement on commitments by the Council or any conciliar court.

The Act of 1679 made the writ of habeas corpus *ad subjiciendum* effective for protecting the liberty of the subject by providing for speedy enquiry into the legality of imprisonment on a criminal charge and for speedy trial of a person remanded in custody on such a charge.[5] The provisions of the Act may be summarised as follows:

The writ must issue from the Lord Chancellor or any of the judges of the superior courts in term or in vacation, unless the prisoner is committed on conviction for a crime or by some legal process (ss. 3 and 10).

---

[1] A release from detention on the ground that the prerequisites of lawful detention under Defence Regulations had not been complied with was no bar to a subsequent valid order for detention: *The King* v. *Home Secretary, ex parte Budd*, [1942] 2 K.B. 14.

[2] *H.E.L.*, I., 227–228; IX., 108–125.

[3] P. 140, *ante*.

[4] 16 Car. I., c. 10, s. 8.

[5] *H.E.L.*, IX., pp. 112–125.

The term is to be specified within which the return of the writ must be made and within which the court must adjudicate upon the writ (ss. 2 and 3).

There can be no re-committal for the same offence of a person who has secured his release by the writ (s. 6).

Provision is made in cases of treason or felony for speedy trial or release on bail (s. 7).

Evasion by transfer of a prisoner to another gaol or to a place outside the jurisdiction of the court, *i.e.* to Scotland, Ireland or abroad, is prohibited (ss. 9 and 12).

The Act, however, did nothing to check the evil of a judge or magistrate requiring excessive bail as a condition of release. The Bill of Rights ten years later merely declared that "excessive bail ought not to be required." [1] Nor had the court power to examine the truth of any return made by the gaoler.

The Act of 1679 only applied to detention on a criminal charge. Later the writ became commonly used, but without the benefit of the provisions of this Act, to secure relief from imprisonment by private persons or on other than criminal charges, such as imprisonment for military service. The Act of 1816 applied the provisions of the earlier Act to persons deprived of their liberty otherwise than on a charge of crime, or by imprisonment for debt or on process in a civil suit (it was not till later in the century that these latter forms of imprisonment were greatly modified). In civil cases to which the Act applied the judge was given power to enquire into the truth of the facts set out in a return to the writ. This provision was not applied to criminal cases by the Act, but the strict rule of incontrovertibility has been relaxed by the judges.[2] The Habeas Corpus Act, 1862, precluded the writ from issuing to any colony or other overseas territory in which there is a court with authority to grant and issue the writ and with power to ensure its execution. So to-day the writ cannot be issued by the High Court to any member State in the Commonwealth or to any of the principal colonial territories.

The writ of habeas corpus protects the citizen in two ways from an arbitrary Executive. If the cause of detention shown to the court is insufficient, the prisoner must be discharged forthwith; but even if the cause is sufficient, by means of the writ the prisoner can secure a speedy trial and so prevent the Executive from detaining him for as long as is considered expedient. In the case of treason or felony a prisoner must be released on bail, if he is not indicted at the next Assizes after his committal, unless the witnesses for the Crown cannot appear. If he is not indicted and tried at the next subsequent

Act of 1816.

Double Purpose of Writ.

---

[1] P. 376, *post.*
[2] Church, *Writ of Habeas Corpus*, pp. 212–213—an American work published in 1884.

Assizes, he must be discharged from custody. The Assizes Relief Act, 1889, ensured the speedy trial of all persons committed to Quarter Sessions, whether charged with felony or misdemeanour. Curiously there is no similar provision in respect of misdemeanants committed to Assizes.

Bail.

Bail may be granted either by justices or by the High Court; in the latter case the application is made to a Judge of the Queen's Bench Division sitting in chambers. Before a person is committed for trial, the justices conducting the preliminary investigations have discretion as to bail in case of both alleged felony and misdemeanour, and the High Court will be slow to interfere with this discretion. Justices who refuse bail must inform the accused upon committal for trial, other than for treason or murder, of his right to apply to the Queen's Bench Division.[1] The High Court has discretion to refuse bail in all cases.[2] The High Court may grant bail to a person who has given notice of appeal to Quarter Sessions from a conviction or sentence by a court of summary jurisdiction, as can the summary court. Bail may also be granted where application has been made for a case to be stated for the opinion of the High Court on a point of law or for review by an order of certiorari.[3] It cannot be granted to a person who has been convicted summarily of an indictable offence, but has been sent to Quarter Sessions for sentence by reason of his previous character.

Dicey: Views on Habeas Corpus.

The net result of the habeas corpus procedure is that " while the Habeas Corpus Act is in force, no person committed to prison on a charge of crime can be kept long in confinement, for he has the legal means of insisting upon either being let out upon bail, or else of bring brought to speedy trial." [4]

Safeguards in Scotland.

The writ of habeas corpus has no counterpart in Scots Law, but there is statutory provision to ensure the speedy trial of a person who is held in custody on a criminal charge. The Criminal Procedure Act, 1887, s. 17, gives to a person arrested on any criminal charge the right to have access to a lawyer and to obtain a delay of 48 hours in his examination before the magistrate (Sheriff-substitute) to allow of the attendance of the lawyer. The same Act by section 43 provides that a person who has been committed for trial must receive an indictment within 60 days of commitment; or, if he has been in prison for 80 days, he must be brought to trial and the trial concluded within 14 days in all from the date of commitment, unless the delay is due to the illness of the accused or some other sufficient cause for which the prosecution is not responsible.

[1] Magistrates' Courts Rules, S.I. 1952, No. 2190, rule 9.
[2] *The King* v. *Phillips* (1922), 38 T.L.R. 897.
[3] Criminal Justice Act, 1948, s. 37, which extends the powers of the High Court and of Quarter Sessions.
[4] Dicey, *op. cit.*, p. 218; for suspension of Act, see p. 382, *post.*

B.

Enjoyment of Property Rights.

The right freely to enjoy property is conditioned by the obligations which the law imposes upon the owner or occupier. The common law recognises obligations to neighbours and others and these have been supplemented by statutory duties relating to the use of land and other forms of property. Recently the conception of ownership of land and buildings, so far as concerns the relationship between the individual owner and the State has been radically changed, without, however, altering the obligations which occupation of land imposes in relation to neighbouring owners. That is to say the modification of proprietary rights has not changed the common law duties with regard to nuisance, negligence or trespass so far as they affect land and buildings. The Town and Country Planning Acts, 1947–54, restrict the value of all land to its existing use, which means to agricultural use, except where the land has already been developed by building. Moreover any change of user after 1947 can only be made with permission of the planning authority, which is the county council or county borough council, as the case may be. Parliament has, moreover, by both public and local Acts, sanctioned the compulsory acquisition of land for stated public purposes on terms of compensation. Thus an owner of land may be compelled to suffer its acquisition by another, whether it be by the State or by a local authority. A public corporation, such as the Transport Commission, if it proposes to extend a line of railway may acquire land compulsorily by promoting a private Bill in Parliament. The Town and Country Planning Act, 1947, considerably enlarged the powers of local planning authorities to acquire land for the purposes of that enactment, including the implementation of development plans approved for their areas. A discussion of freedom of enjoyment of property is therefore bound to take account of the processes whereby the owner may be compelled to exchange his right freely to enjoy his land for a sum of money representing the value of that right on a scale calculated by statutory standards. Originally fixed on a scale as if for damages for trespass, later the valuation was on the basis of a free market, but it has now been reduced by the existing use formula of the Town and Country Planning Acts.

Duties of Property Owners.

Property may be compulsorily acquired for public purposes where a statute so authorises. Without statutory authority the central government has no power to acquire land except by agreement with the owner, while a local authority requires statutory authority even for acquisition by agreement since it is only for the purpose of its statutory services that acquisition by a local authority is lawful.

Compulsory Purchase of Land.

The same is true of the public corporations like the Transport Commission. Powers of compulsory purchase may be given either by an Act of Parliament authorising the acquisition of specific property for a specific purpose or by orders made under an Act conferring general powers to be exercised for purposes and under conditions laid down in the Act. In the latter case land can be acquired by a public utility undertaking (statutory undertaker, such as a waterworks company) or a local authority on an order made by a Minister, or sometimes under a scheme confirmed by him. Thus the authority of a department of the central government is required in all such cases. Under older Acts the order is usually subject to express confirmation by Parliament, but under modern Acts the confirmation by the Minister may be final or subject only to annulment by Parliament on the grounds of the general public interest, a step which is rarely taken.

Compensation.

Where a statute authorises the compulsory acquisition of property, it is the invariable practice to provide for the payment of compensation. It is an established rule of construction that express words are required to authorise the taking of property without payment: *Newcastle Breweries* v. *The King*, [1920] 1 K.B. 854.[1] A code governing the procedure for compulsory acquisition and the payment of compensation is contained in the Lands Clauses Acts (Lands Clauses Consolidation Act, 1845, and subsequent amending Acts). These Acts [2] are, unless expressly excluded or varied, automatically included in all Acts which authorise the compulsory acquisition of land. But where land is acquired by a government department, local authority or non-profit-making public body, compensation is, unless a statute otherwise provides, assessed not under the Lands Clauses Acts, but on a less favourable basis to owners under the Acquisition of Land (Assessment of Compensation) Act, 1919. A statute may provide for a different basis of compensation, *e.g.* under the Housing Act, 1936, s. 40, the owner of property acquired for slum clearance purposes is in general only compensated to the extent of the site value of his property and not in respect of houses to be demolished thereon. The Acquisition of Land (Authorisation Procedure) Act, 1946, provides a general code for compulsory purchase applicable wherever the power to authorise purchase by a local authority is conferred on any department of central government. Under the Acquisition of Land (Assessment of Compensation) Act, 1919, compensation was assessed by an official arbitrator chosen from a panel appointed by a reference committee, but this

[1] The decision, though not the principle mentioned, was disapproved in *Hudson Bay Co.* v. *Maclay* (1920), 36 T.L.R. 469, at p. 478, and *Robinson* v. *The King*, [1921] 3 K.B. 183, at p. 197.

[2] Other codes regulate acquisition for particular purposes, *e.g.* Railways Clauses Consolidation Act, 1845; Waterworks Clauses Act, 1847; Towns Improvement Act, 1847, and various Military Land Acts.

method has been superseded by the Lands Tribunal Act, 1949, which replaces the arbitrator by a central tribunal appointed by the Lord Chancellor. This court, the members of which must be lawyers or surveyors, has other jurisdiction in matters relating to land valuation.[1]

Under the prerogative there is power to deprive the subject of possession of his property for the defence of the realm in time of national danger: *Attorney-General* v. *De Keyser's Royal Hotel Ltd.*, [1920] A.C. 508; K. & L. 86. The various precedents extending back to the seventeenth century point to a usage of payment, but Lord Dunedin, in the case cited, did not consider that such usage imposed an obligation upon the Crown to pay compensation. There are permanent Acts which govern the acquisition or requisition [2] of land for defence purposes (Defence Acts, 1842 to 1873), and under these Acts compensation is payable. During both the First and Second World Wars additional powers were taken. The Defence of the Realm Act, 1914, provided for the suspension by regulation of any restrictions on the acquisition of land contained in the Defence Acts, though the Crown was not thereby relieved of the obligation to pay compensation (*De Keyser's Hotel Case, ante*). The specific purposes for which regulations could be made under the Emergency Powers (Defence) Act, 1939,[3] included (*a*) the taking possession or control on behalf of His Majesty of any property, (*b*) the acquisition on behalf of His Majesty of any property other than land. The Emergency Powers (Defence) Act, 1940, authorised the making of regulations requiring persons to place their property at the disposal of His Majesty. No regulations were, however, made under this Act authorising the acquisition as distinct from the requisition of land. The acquisition by the Crown of land requisitioned for war purposes is governed by the Requisitioned Land and War Works Acts, 1945 and 1948. The assessment of compensation for the use of land and the acquisition of other property during the Second World War was regulated by the Compensation (Defence) Act, 1939.[4] During the First World War it was held (in *De Keyser's Hotel Case, ante*) that the Crown could not compel an owner of requisitioned property to accept a rent assessed on an *ex gratia* basis by a non-statutory tribunal, the Defence of the Realm Losses Commission. Under the Act of 1939 two specialised tribunals were established—a General

Defence.

---

[1] P. 346, *ante*.

[2] Requisition, as opposed to acquisition, implies temporary occupation.

[3] P. 384, *post*.

[4] This Act affords a good example of administrative quasi-legislation (p. 361, *ante*). The Act excludes fair wear and tear from the Crown's liability to make good damage done. The Treasury has ruled that fair wear and tear may be taken into account. It may be suggested that the proper course would have been to amend the Act by deleting the exclusion. As it is, the subject has no right enforceable by law to claim for fair wear and tear.

Claims Tribunal and a Shipping Claims Tribunal. Both tribunals may be compelled by the High Court to state a special case for the opinion of the court on a point of law.

General Restrictions on Use of Property and Freedom of Contract.

The law does not allow a private owner unlimited and unlicensed use of his property. The old writ of trespass and its extensions by means of actions on the case provided the common law with the means of resisting invasion of proprietary rights. Trespass to land and conversion of goods are civil wrongs and, if malicious injury be inflicted, are also statutory criminal offences. The owner or occupier may not use his land so as to constitute a nuisance either to the public at large or to his neighbour in particular. Adjoining owners are liable for the support of adjacent land, but not buildings thereon, in the absence of a right of support being acquired. There is a liability accruing from the escape of dangerous things. Both as to land and other forms of property there are numbers of statutory restrictions on use or disposition, which are imposed by such statutes as Public Health Acts, 1875–1936; Petroleum Act, 1934; Coal Industry Nationalisation Act, 1946, and the Town and Country Planning Act, 1947. No building can be erected without approval of the plans by the appropriate authority. The relationship of land-lord and tenant is for the most part controlled by statutes which restrict freedom of contract with the object of protecting the tenant. Freedom of contract in other spheres is often restricted; employers are required to contribute for the benefit of their employees as well as on account of themselves and their families to the national insurance scheme and also to contribute to the insurance of their employees against industrial injuries received in the course of employment. Under war conditions all production and manufacture were under the control of agencies of the Central Government and many of these controls were continued into the post-war economy, though the majority have now been abandoned or relaxed, without, however, the power to re-impose them being rescinded in many cases.

The catalogue of restrictions which are now a permanent part of the welfare State must not lead to the inference that similar restraints exist in the sphere of political, as compared with economic liberty. Freedom of the person from arrest, freedom of speech in all its aspects could be made subject to restrictions in the same way as restraint has been imposed upon freedom of contract in the economic sphere, namely by Parliament. But the climate of political opinion is the constitutional safeguard against an abuse of the legal power of Parliament to destroy what has been built up over centuries by Parliament itself and no less by the Judiciary in restraining the powers of the Executive. That the legal power exists is illustrated by the account of emergency powers which follows.

CHAPTER 2.

EMERGENCY POWERS IN PEACE AND WAR.

A.

Emergency Powers Act, 1920.

PARLIAMENT has sanctioned, by the Emergency Powers Act, 1920, a modified form of rule by regulation in the event of emergency. The power is surrounded by the safeguard of parliamentary control, which distinguishes it from the old claims to legislate independently of Parliament by virtue of necessity. The power is only exercisable when a state of emergency prevails. It is for the Executive to declare such a state, but the circumstances in which it can do so require careful consideration.[1]

Before it is lawful to declare a state of emergency, action must have been taken or threatened which is calculated to deprive the community, or any substantial portion of it, of the essentials of life by interfering with the supply and distribution of food, water, fuel or light, or with the means of locomotion. The state of emergency is declared by proclamation, which can only remain in force for one month, though in practice the period may be continued indefinitely by the issue of a new proclamation. The proclamation must be forthwith communicated to Parliament. If Parliament is not sitting, it must be summoned within five days. So long as the proclamation is in force, regulations may be made by Order in Council for securing the essentials of life to the community. Such powers may be conferred on government departments and on the police as may be deemed necessary for the purpose of preserving peace or for securing and regulating the supply and distribution of necessities and maintaining the means of transport. But the regulations must stop short of imposing compulsory military service or industrial conscription, and no regulation may make it an offence for anyone to take part in a strike or peacefully to persuade others to do so. Regulations may provide for the trial by courts of summary jurisdiction of persons guilty of offences against the regulations, subject to maximum penalties. The regulations must be laid before Parliament and expire after seven days, unless a resolution is passed by both Houses providing for their continuance. The Act does not suspend the writ of habeas corpus and expressly prohibits the alteration of any existing procedure in criminal cases or the conferring of any right to punish

State of Emergency.

[1] The text of the Act is given in K. & L., pp. 429-430.

by fine or imprisonment without trial. The Trade Disputes and Trade Unions Act, 1927, which was passed as a direct result of the General Strike of 1926, aimed at preventing a repetition of such an event by making illegal sympathetic strikes or lock-outs, if conducted on a scale calculated to coerce the Government, by persons in trades not affected by any existing dispute. The Act was, however, wholly repealed in 1946.

Up to 1949 there was only one adequate opportunity of considering the effectiveness of the Act of 1920,[1] but the occasion was so important, namely, the General Strike and the Coal Strike, 1926, that it may be regarded as having provided an effective means of suppressing internal disorder on a large scale. In 1948 a state of emergency was declared in consequence of a dockers' unofficial strike in London and elsewhere, but the strike ended at once and no regulations under the Act were made, but on July 11, 1949, for the same cause an emergency was again declared and regulations came into force; these enabled the Government to take over the working of those London docks which were affected by the strike.

B.

Emergency Powers in Time of War.

It has always been recognised that times of grave national emergency demand the grant of special powers to the Executive. There are times when it would be dangerous to maintain the normal limitations imposed by judicial control. At such times arbitrary arrest and imprisonment are legalised by Act of Parliament. Modern war demands the abandonment of personal liberty in that the duty of compulsory national service necessarily takes away for the time being the right of the individual to choose his occupation. It was not, however, until the present century that conscription, even in time of war, was introduced in Great Britain.

Habeas Corpus Suspension Acts.

In former times it was the practice in times of danger to the State to pass what were popularly known as Habeas Corpus Suspension Acts.[2] These Acts in effect prevented the use of the writ of habeas corpus for the purpose of insisting upon speedy trial or the right to bail in the case of persons charged with treason or other specified offences. They did not suspend generally the use of habeas corpus proceedings and, as soon as the period of suspension in relation to particular crimes was passed, anyone who for the time being had been denied the assistance of the writ could seek his remedy in the

---

[1] In time of war far wider powers are needed: see Section B, *post*.
[2] Dicey, *op. cit.*, pp. 229–237.

courts by an action for false imprisonment or malicious prosecution. Suspension did not legalise illegal arrest; it merely suspended a particular remedy in respect of particular offences.   Accordingly it was the practice at the close of the period of suspension to pass an Indemnity Act, in order to protect officials concerned from the *Indemnity* consequences of any incidental illegal acts which they might have *Acts.* committed under cover of the suspension of the prerogative writ. During a period of emergency many illegalities may be committed by the Executive in their efforts to deal with a critical situation. The object of suspension was to enable the Government to take steps which, though politically expedient, were, or might be, not strictly legal. An Indemnity Act legalises all such illegalities and so supplements a Suspension Act which may not have given to the Executive all the power that it required.

Neither during the First nor Second World Wars was there any *First World* direct suspension of habeas corpus. The Defence of the Realm Acts, *War.* 1914–15, empowered the Executive to make regulations by Order in Council for securing the public safety or for the defence of the realm. It was held that this general power was wide enough to support a regulation authorising imprisonment without trial: *The King* v. *Halliday, ex parte Zadig*, [1917] A.C. 260; K. & L. 26.

> The House of Lords held that a regulation was valid which authorised the Secretary of State to detain a British subject on the grounds of his hostile origin or association. It was contended on behalf of Zadig, who was a naturalised British subject, that some limitation must be put upon the general words of the statute delegating power to the Executive; that there was no provision for imprisonment without trial, and indeed the Defence of the Realm Act, 1915, had expressly provided for the trial of British subjects in a civil court by a jury; that general words in a statute could not take away the vested right of a subject or alter the fundamental law of the Constitution; that the statute being penal in nature must be strictly construed and that no construction should be adopted which was repugnant to the constitutional tradition of the country. The majority of the court swept aside these arguments and held that on the construction of the Act the Executive had unrestricted powers. Lord Craigmyle (Lord Shaw of Dunfermline as he then was) delivered a dissenting judgment which has been preferred by some; he declined to infer from the delegation of a power to make regulations for public safety and defence that Zadig could be detained without a trial and indeed without being accused of any offence, save that he was of hostile origin or association as defined by the regulation; Parliament had not expressly said in words any one of these things.

A person detained under a valid regulation giving unrestricted power to detain cannot subsequently bring an action for false imprisonment in order to test the merits of his detention. Thus, though habeas corpus proceedings are not suspended, there is a greater infringement of liberty in giving the Executive unrestricted power to detain than in suspending habeas corpus proceedings in respect of particular charges.

Wide, however, as were the powers of the Executive, it was still practicable to challenge a regulation in the courts. Two cases deserve mention. In *Attorney-General* v. *Wilts United Dairies, Ltd.* (1921), 37 T.L.R. 884; K. & L. 163,[1] an attempt by the Food Controller to impose a charge was held invalid on the ground that the regulation challenged conferred no express power to impose charges upon the subject. Doubt was also expressed whether a regulation conferring such a power would have been within the general power to make regulations for the public safety or the defence of the realm. In *Chester* v. *Bateson*, [1920] 1 K.B. 829; K. & L. 31, there was held invalid a regulation which deprived a citizen of the right of access to the courts. The regulation empowered the Minister of Munitions to declare an area in which munitions were manufactured, stored or transported to be a special area. The effect of such declaration was to prevent any person without the consent of the Minister from taking proceedings for the recovery of possession of, or for the ejectment of a tenant of, any dwelling-house in the area, if a munition worker was living in it and duly paying rent. It was held that Parliament had not deliberately deprived the citizen of resort to the courts and accordingly that a regulation framed to forbid the owner of property access to legal tribunals was invalid, unless it could be shown to be a necessary or even reasonable way of securing the public safety or the defence of the realm.

Despite the wide powers conferred by the Defence of the Realm Acts numerous illegalities were undoubtedly committed and after the War there was passed a wide Indemnity Act, the Indemnity Act, 1920, and a separate Act relating to illegal charges, the War Charges Validity Act, 1925.

Second World War.

The legislators of 1939 took pains to close the gaps left in 1914–15 and specific powers were taken to avoid the effects of all the decisions of the First World War (except *Chester* v. *Bateson, ante*), which had restricted the powers of the Executive. No attempt was made to prohibit access to the courts, but the powers given were so wide that such a precaution was unnecessary. The Emergency Powers (Defence) Act, 1939, empowered the making of regulations by Order in Council which appeared necessary or expedient for the public safety, the defence of the realm, the maintenance of public order, the efficient prosecution of any war in which His Majesty might be engaged and the maintenance of supplies and services essential for the life of the community. There followed a list of particular purposes for which regulations could be made without

[1] P. 45, *ante*.

prejudice to the generality of the five general purposes; [1] these included power to make provision for the trial of offenders against the regulations and for the detention of persons by the Secretary of State in the interests of the public safety or the defence of the realm (a tribute to the dissenting judgment of Lord Shaw in *The King* v. *Halliday, ante*), and for authority to enter and search any premises. The case of *Attorney-General* v. *Wilts United Dairies, Ltd.* (*ante*), was not overlooked and the Treasury was empowered to impose charges in connection with any scheme of control under Defence Regulations. Treasury regulations imposing charges required confirmation by an affirmative resolution of the House of Commons. Other regulations had to be laid before Parliament "as soon as may be" after they were made and could be annulled by negative resolution within twenty-eight days. Orders made on the authority of Defence Regulations were not subject to any special form of parliamentary control. In addition to the Emergency Powers (Defence) Act there were passed within a few weeks of the outbreak of war some sixty temporary Acts, most of which suspended or amended provisions of permanent Acts relating to various public services.

The Emergency Powers (Defence) Act, 1939, expressly forbade the imposition by regulations of any form of compulsory military service or industrial conscription. Compulsory service was imposed by separate National Service Acts.[3] The ban on the imposition by Defence Regulations of industrial conscription was removed by the Emergency Powers (Defence) Act, 1940. This Act enabled Defence Regulations to require persons to place themselves, their services and their property at the disposal of His Majesty as might appear to him to be necessary or expedient for any of the general purposes enumerated in the Act of 1939. Defence Regulation 55 made under the Act of 1939 had provided for the control of industry, but not of the labour employed in industry. Under the Act of 1940 the directions under Defence Regulation 58A provided for the transfer of labour from less essential civil work to work more closely connected with the war effort. Individuals were thereby directed to take up particular employment with a named undertaking. There followed Essential Works Orders restricting discharge or resignation from employment in essential occupations. Control of Engagement Orders provided that engagement of men and women within certain age groups could only be made through the State employment exchanges. The Control of Engagement Orders were reimposed in 1947 until March, 1950, and, by the device of changing the object for

Industrial Conscription.

---

[1] For regulations affecting property, see p. 379, *ante*.
[2] For trial by court-martial and war zone courts, see Part IX., Chap. 3.
[3] Part IX., Chap. 1.

which Regulations could be used, large numbers of Defence Regulations relating to production, transport and commodity rationing have been continued on the authority of a series of Supplies and Services Acts.[1]

The Courts during the Second World War.

Access to the courts was not barred. The courts could not, however, consider whether a particular regulation was necessary or expedient for the purposes of the Act which authorised it. It was left to His Majesty to make such regulations as appeared to him to be necessary or expedient for these purposes: *The King* v. *Comptroller-General of Patents, ex parte Bayer Products*, [1941] 2 K.B. 306,[2] which disapproved the earlier decision in *E. H. Jones (Machine Tools), Ltd.* v. *Farrell and Muirsmith*, [1940] 3 All E.R. 608. The courts could, however, hold an act to be illegal as being not authorised by the regulation relied upon to justify it. Thus in *John Fowler & Co. (Leeds), Ltd.* v. *Duncan* (1941), 57 T.L.R. 612, it was held that an order authorising a controller to control financial transactions in connection with an undertaking did not authorise him to direct the undertaking to increase its bank overdraft.

Regulation 18B.

Most relevant of all the Defence Regulations to personal liberty was Regulation 18B. We have seen [3] that Parliament expressly empowered the Executive to make regulations for detention without trial in the interests of public safety or the defence of the realm. Under Regulation 18B the Home Secretary was empowered to detain anyone whom he had reasonable cause to believe came within specified categories of suspects (including persons of hostile origin or association) and that by reason thereof it was necessary to exercise control over him. Facilities were given to persons detained to make objections to an advisory committee appointed by the Home Secretary. The Home Secretary was obliged to report to Parliament monthly the number of persons detained and the number of cases in which he had not followed the advice of the advisory committee. It was open to the subject to challenge detention by application for a writ of habeas corpus, but such applications had little chance of success in view of the decision of the House of Lords in *Liversidge* v. *Anderson*, [1942] A.C. 206.[4] In spite of a powerful dissenting judgment by Lord Atkin the House of Lords took the view that the power to detain could not be controlled by the courts, if only because considerations of security forbade proof of the evidence upon which detention was ordered. The words "had reasonable cause to believe" only meant that the Home Secretary must direct personal attention to the matter. It was sufficient for him to have a belief which in his mind was reasonable. The courts would not enquire into the grounds for his belief, although apparently they

---

[1] P. 387–9, *post.*   [2] See also *Progressive Supply Co.* v. *Dalton*, [1943] Ch. 54.
[3] P. 385, *ante.*   [4] P. 295, *ante.*

might examine positive evidence of *mala fides* or mistaken identity.[1] Stress was laid upon the high position of the Home Secretary and his responsibility to Parliament. Indeed, the House of Lords appeared to go very near to upholding the doctrine of State necessity so decisively rejected in the eighteenth century in *Entick* v. *Carrington*.[2] In another case decided at the same time the House of Lords held that a mistake on the part of the advisory committee in failing, as was required by the regulation, to give the appellant correct reasons for his detention did not invalidate the detention order: *Greene* v. *Secretary of State for Home Affairs*, [1942] A.C. 284. In only one case did a person who had been detained under the regulation secure his release by means of habeas corpus proceedings. An order was made for the detention of the applicant on the ground that he was connected with a fascist organisation. He was wrongly informed that the order had been made on the ground of his being of hostile association. The Divisional Court ordered his release. His triumph was, however, short-lived, as the Home Secretary made a new order for his detention.[3]

The Emergency Powers (Defence) Acts, 1939–40 expired in February, 1946, though the Emergency Powers (Transitional Provisions) Act, 1946, had previously extended to the end of 1947 a small residue of defence powers; some of these in turn were extended temporarily, others made permanent and others not continued in force by the Emergency Laws (Miscellaneous Provisions) Act, 1947, and later enactments. Although the majority of the regulations relating to defence and to the public safety had been revoked after the end of hostilities, it was apparent that the regulations by which for example industry was controlled and commodities rationed could not be quickly revoked. Accordingly the Supplies and Services (Transitional Provisions) Act, 1945, following the pattern of war emergency legislation, enabled legislation by defence regulation to continue for a further period of five years and thereafter annually, if both Houses of Parliament so determine by resolution, for the purpose of maintaining, controlling and regulating supplies and services so as—

Emergency Powers Since 1945.

(*a*) to secure a sufficiency of those essential to the well-being of

---

[1] *Per* Lord Wright, at p. 261, approving the judgment of Tucker, J., in *Stuart* v. *Anderson*, [1941] 2 All E. R. 665. In the United States the Supreme Court took the view that the test to be applied in any judicial review of action taken to meet the war emergency was whether the action was necessary for that purpose. Thus, however wide was the general protective measure against persons of enemy origin and association it did not justify detention of a person admitted by the Government to be a loyal citizen of the United States, albeit of Japanese ancestry; *Hirabayashi* v. *United States*, 320 U.S. 81 (1943); *Ex parte Endo*, 323 U.S. 283 (1944).

[2] P. 367, *ante*; see "Regulation 18B and Reasonable Cause," by Sir Carleton Allen, 58 *L.Q.R.* p. 232.

[3] *The King* v. *Home Secretary, ex parte Budd*, [1942] 2 K.B. 14. See also *The Times*, May 28, 1941.

the community or their equitable distribution or their availability at fair prices: or

(*b*) to facilitate the demobilisation and resettlement of persons and to secure the orderly disposal of surplus material; or

(*c*) to facilitate the readjustment of industry and commerce to the requirements of the community in time of peace: or

(*d*) to assist the relief of the suffering and the restoration and distribution of essential supplies and services in any part of Her Majesty's dominions or in foreign countries that are in grave distress as the result of war.

In 1947 in view of the rapidly deteriorating economic situation the following additional purposes were added by the Supplies and Services (Extended Purposes) Act, 1947:—

(*a*) for promoting the productivity of industry, commerce and agriculture;

(*b*) for fostering and directing exports and reducing imports, or imports of any classes, from all or any countries and for redressing the balance of trade; and

(*c*) generally for ensuring that the whole resources of the community are available for use, and are used, in a manner best calculated to serve the interests of the community.

In 1951 the Supplies and Services (Defence Purposes) Act further enlarged the purposes of the Act of 1945, which now also apply:—

(*a*) for providing or securing supplies and services required for the defence of any part of Her Majesty's territories or any territory under her protection or jurisdiction, or for the maintenance or restoration of peace and security in any part of the world, or for any measures arising out of a breach or apprehended breach of peace in any part of the world; and

(*b*) for preventing supplies or services being disposed of in a manner prejudicial to such matters.

Thus over a wide field of government legislation by regulations has in peace-time taken the place of legislation by Bill. In form this type of delegated legislation does not differ from the usual type of minsterial regulation-making power which is the inevitable feature of every major Act. But the general character of the powers are so wide, whereas delegated legislation is normally restricted within defined limits and for relatively narrow purposes, that the consequent relaxation of parliamentary control is significant. Parliament cannot amend nor in practice can it reject what the Minister decrees. The only concession to parliamentary control was contained in the Supplies and Services Act, 1945, which extended the annulment procedure to all orders and other instruments made under powers conferred by Defence Regulations.[1] Hitherto only the regulations themselves had been subject to this device for securing the attention of Parliament to ministerial legislation and incidentally bringing it within the terms of reference of the Select Committee on Statutory Instruments.[2] Many of the resulting regulations have been revoked, especially in the field of economic controls, but the power to rule by regulation, if need be, still remains; for example, if it again became necessary to ration domestic foodstuffs, no new legislation by Parliament would be required before the Government could act.

[1] S. 4 (1).   [2] P. 358, *ante*.

CHAPTER 3.

LIBERTY OF DISCUSSION.

IN this Chapter there will be discussed those aspects of freedom which are particularly associated with democracy. "Without free elections the people cannot make a choice of policies. Without freedom of speech the appeal to reason which is the basis of democracy cannot be made. Without freedom of association electors and elected representatives cannot band themselves into parties for the formulation of common policies and the attainment of common ends." [1]

Free Elections.

As early as the thirteenth century the Statute of Westminster I. of 1275 provided that there shall be no interference with free elections by force of arms, malice or menaces. In modern times the Ballot Act, 1872, provided for secrecy of elections. This Act is the keystone of our electoral law and the principles contained in it are sacrosanct. [2] This Act, along with all the main statutes relating to election law, has been repealed and re-enacted by the Representation of the People Act, 1949, which provides, as we have seen, a code of this branch of the law both for parliamentary and for local elections. A series of Corrupt and Illegal Practices Prevention Acts, which have been re-enacted in Parts II. and III. of the Act of 1949, imposed penalties on those who attempt to influence elections by bribery, treating, intimidation, excessive expenditure or other practices forbidden by law. [3] Of late years, partly owing to the size of the electorate, partly no doubt owing to the better political education of the public, these Acts have been rarely invoked. Where a candidate has secured election and he or his election agent has committed or acquiesced in corrupt or illegal practices, he may be unseated on a petition which is heard by two judges of the Queen's Bench Division.

Freedom of Association.

The crime and tort of conspiracy are the principal restrictions which English law places upon freedom of association for political purposes. A criminal conspiracy is an agreement to do an unlawful act or to do a lawful act by unlawful means. The definition of conspiracy as a civil tort has caused infinite judicial perplexity. [4] The law of

---

[1] Sir Ivor Jennings, *Cabinet Government* (Cambridge University Press), p. 13.

[2] Nevertheless a temporary modification was necessary in order to give members of the forces, seamen and war workers abroad the right to vote by post or by proxy at a general election held under war conditions: Representation of the People Act, 1945, Part IV.

[3] The law relating to elections may be studied in Parker, *Election Agent and Returning Officer*, 5th Ed. (Chas. Knight & Co., Ltd.).

[4] See *Crofter Hand Woven Harris Tweed Co.* v. *Veitch*, [1942] A.C. 435.

conspiracy must be studied in text-books of criminal law [1] and the law of torts.[2] There should be studied also the law relating to trade unions and to industrial disputes. One general restriction of constitutional interest may be mentioned here. The Public Order Act, 1936, s. 2 (1),[3] makes it an offence to take part in the control or management of any association of persons organised or trained and equipped (*a*) for the purpose of enabling them to be employed in usurping the functions of the police or of the armed forces of the Crown, or (*b*) for the purpose of enabling them to be employed for the use or display of physical force in promoting any political object, or in such manner as to cause reasonable apprehension that they are organised and either trained or equipped for that purpose. The same Act by section 1 (1), forbids the wearing without police permission in any public place or at a public meeting of uniform signifying association with a political association or the promotion of a political object.

The attitude of English law towards freedom of discussion is that a speaker or writer has no special protection to enable him to give free expression to his opinions, but that there is no restriction which can interfere with this freedom, unless he oversteps the bounds set by law, and, in particular, by the law of defamation. The law throws the risk on the speaker, writer and publisher. _{Freedom of Speech.}

Freedom of Speech.

The law of defamation is divided into slander, *i.e.* defamation in a transitory form, by word or gesture, and libel, *i.e.* defamation either in a permanent form, such as the printed word, or by sound or television broadcast. Without embarking on a technical discussion of this branch of law it may be said that there can be no defamation, so far as liability for damages in a civil action is concerned, unless the defamatory matter be published to a third person, but there may be criminal liability, even if the words are only published to the person defamed. The basis of liability in the latter case rests on the probability of a breach of the peace. Generally speaking, there is no remedy to restrain in advance the publication of alleged defamatory matter. The ordinary remedy is an action for damages, coupled, if necessary, with an injunction to restrain further publication.[4]

Law of Defamation.

Some occasions are privileged and then there is no liability for defamation. Privilege is of two kinds, (*a*) absolute, (*b*) qualified. Qualified privilege may be rebutted on proof of malice. Examples of communications which are absolutely privileged are statements made in the course of judicial [5] or parliamentary proceedings,[6] communications between a Minister of the Crown and the Crown

Privilege.

---

[1] *E.g.* Kenny, *op. cit.*, Chap. XXII.
[2] *E.g.* Winfield, *Text-book of the Law of Tort*, Chap. XVII.
[3] The text is given in Dicey, *op. cit.*, p. 635.
[4] For unintentional defamation, see Defamation Act, 1952, s.4; offer of amends may exclude damages.
[5] P. 251, *ante*.   [6] P. 121, *ante*.

or another Minister,[1] military reports, communications between solicitor and client, and documents published by authority of Parliament.[2] Qualified privilege attaches to, *e.g.*, communications made in pursuance of a legal, social or moral duty to a person who has an interest in receiving the communication.[3]

The Press.

The Press may be said to be in much the same position as the ordinary individual. Under the prerogative and later by the Licensing Act, 1662, printing was a monopoly and was only permitted under licence. But since 1695, when the Act was not renewed, the liberty of the Press has consisted in printing without licence, subject to the consequences of the ordinary law. It is not surprising that the Press figures largely in the cases relating to the law of defamation. There are, however, a number of enactments which give the Press some not unimportant advantages.[4]

Special Defence open to Press.

The defence of apology is only available in an action for libel contained in a public newspaper or other periodical publication; the defendant must prove (1) that the libel was published without actual malice and without gross negligence, and (2) that before the commencement of the action, or at the earliest opportunity afterwards, he inserted in such newspaper or publication a full apology for the libel. (3) Moreover, there must be a payment made into court by way of amends, which precludes any other defence denying liability being pleaded: Libel Act, 1843. In practice this defence is not used.

Press Reports.

Qualified privilege attaches to reports in newspapers [5] or broadcasts from within the United Kingdom of a wide range of matters of general public interest transacted at home, in the Commonwealth or by international organisations: Defamation Act, 1952, s. 7, and Schedule. Some such reports are privileged without explanation or contradiction; others are subject to the publication, if the plaintiff so desires, of a reasonable letter or statement by way of contradiction. Only matter which is of public concern and the publication of which is for the public benefit attracts this protection. Unofficial reports of parliamentary debates and judicial proceedings whether or not they are published in a newspaper also enjoy qualified privilege at common law. Reports of proceedings in courts of justice must be fair and accurate, not prohibited by order of the court, and not blasphemous, seditious or immoral. Such reports are also subject to the provisions of the Judicial Proceedings (Regulation of Reports) Act, 1926, which prohibits the publication of indecent matter, and in the case of reports in newspapers of matrimonial cases, restricts what may lawfully be published to a bare summary of the names of the parties,

---

[1] *Chatterton* v. *Secretary of State for India*, [1895] 2 Q.B. 189, at p. 191.
[2] P. 123, *ante*.   [3] Winfield, *op. cit.*, pp. 348–54.
[4] See *e.g.* Defamation Act, 1952, s. 4, which is not limited to newspaper defendants.
[5] Defined so as to include monthly as well as daily and weekly journals.

their legal advisers, the witnesses, a statement of the matter at issue, submissions, together with the decision thereon, on points of law, and the judgment. In connection with criminal libels the Press enjoys some protection, and in particular an order of a judge of the High Court is required before a newspaper can be prosecuted for criminal libel. Such a prosecution is very rarely sought.

But it cannot be said that these defences amount to a special law for the Press, especially when it is noted that any defendant in an action for defamation can plead as his defence honest and fair comment on the facts of a matter of public interest. Nowadays offences by the Press are tried in the ordinary civil and criminal courts. In general the State is content to leave the public expression of opinion to the working of the ordinary law, subject only to the regulation under the Act of 1926 of certain types of judicial reports. **No special Law of Press.**

Stage plays performed in Great Britain must be approved by the Lord Chamberlain, an officer of the Royal Household, who appoints an examiner of plays to perform this duty which, although made statutory by the Theatres Act, 1843, is an interesting relic of the royal prerogative being exercised in the interest of public morals. Theatres are licensed by the principal local authorities,[1] as are premises for the exhibition of films, but the latter control is based on safety requirements rather than on order and decency. Control may be exercised over actual films to be shown in licensed premises by making the licence conditional on the showing of films which carry the approval of the British Board of Film Censors, an official body maintained by the trade which is usually presided over by a distinguished retired public servant. **Licences for Entertainments.**

Although prosecutions for blasphemy are nowadays very rare, the State is vigilant to check the corruption of public morals by the publication of obscene material. There are two distinct proceedings in criminal law designed for this purpose. It is at common law a misdemeanor to publish an obscene libel, *i.e.* a publication which contains matter tending to deprave and corrupt those whose minds are open to such immoral influences and into whose hands a publication of this sort may fall.[2] **Obscenity and Blasphemy.**

There is also a procedure which is aimed at preventing the sale of obscene publications without punishing the seller, the author, or anybody else, for a criminal offence. The Obscene Publications Act, 1857, gives the police the power to seize on a justices' warrant obscene publications with a view to securing from a court of summary jurisdiction their condemnation and an order for destruction of all copies found on the premises. It is for the court, that is to say, two or more justices of the peace, to be satisfied, after reading the books or inspecting the illustrations, that the contents, including the

---

[1] In London (parts of) and other places with a royal residence, theatres are licensed by the Lord Chamberlain.
[2] *The Queen* v. *Hicklin* (1868), L.R. 3 Q.B. 360.

obscene material, are calculated to deprave and corrupt. This in the case of the common law offence has to be proved by the prosecution. Under the statutory procedure the court has to satisfy itself that the material is obscene and must then order the destruction of the publication. This form of censorship is open to question as different courts may reach different conclusions. Moreover it does not follow that a prosecution of the responsible publisher, author or seller will be undertaken as a consequence of the order for destruction.

Sedition.

The State retains in its armoury certain little-used weapons to deal with offences against itself. It is a misdemeanour to publish words or documents with seditious intent. On one view the definition of sedition [1] is wide enough to cover almost every act of disaffection or disloyalty whether to the State or the Established Church, but prosecutions for seditious offences, though they were frequent in the eighteenth century, are rare and juries are unwilling to convict for the expression of opinion relating to public affairs. In practice it is essential for a successful prosecution to prove a clear incitement to violence as well as the publication of defamatory words. [2]

Official Secrets Acts.

The Official Secrets Acts, 1911 to 1939, confer drastic powers which are capable of being used to prevent the Press and its contributors from commenting upon affairs of public interest. In addition to conferring wide powers of search upon suspicion [3] the Acts make it an offence to communicate to any person (other than a person to whom communication has been authorised) any information entrusted in confidence by any person holding office under the Crown. The information need not relate to any matter of national importance and its truth or public interest is immaterial. Thus it would be an offence to reproduce in a newspaper information relating to a crime given in confidence by a police officer to a reporter. It is also an offence to refuse on demand by a police officer not below the rank of inspector to disclose the source of information. This power of interrogation may, however, only be used with the permission of the Secretary of State and only in respect of espionage and similar serious offences. [4] The purpose of the Acts is to prevent the safety of the State being prejudiced by communication of secret information to potential enemies and the risk of abuse of powers is minimised by the requirement that the consent of the Attorney-General is required before a prosecution is brought under the Acts.

---

[1] *The King* v. *Aldred* (1909), 22 Cox 1; Dicey, *op. cit.*, p. 579.
[2] *The King* v. *Caunt* (1947), reported verbatim in *An Editor on Trial* (Morecambe Press, Ltd.).
[3] P. 368, *ante.*
[4] Official Secrets Act, 1920, s. 6, as amended by the Official Secrets Act, 1939, passed as the result of the decision in *Lewis* v. *Cattle*, [1938] 2 K.B. 454.

The Incitement to Mutiny Act, 1797, and the Incitement to Dis-   Seduction
affection Act, 1934, are aimed at preventing the seduction, by what-   from Duty.
ever means, of the armed forces from their duty or allegiance.[1]
Under the latter Act it is an offence for any person with intent to
commit or to aid, counsel or procure the offence of seducing a
member of the armed forces from his duty or allegiance, to have in
his possession or under his control any document of such a nature
that the dissemination of copies thereof among Her Majesty's Forces
would constitute the promotion of disaffection. The Act also goes
a long way to arming the Executive with power to restrict the
distribution of political propaganda and of pacifist literature in
particular, but no criticism can be based on the excessive use of
these powers, even during the Second World War when they were
temporarily increased by Defence Regulation.

Both Parliament and the courts have power to punish criticism   Contempt of
which they regard as unwarranted by committal for contempt.[2]   Court.
Criminal contempt of court takes two forms: (*a*) *conduct by strangers
or parties to a suit which scandalises the court.* A court of record may
fine or commit to prison for contempt any person who uses threatening words or abuses any judge of the court. It is, of course, permissible to discuss the merits of a judgment or sentence, but the court
has power to punish any criticism which it regards as mere invective
or as tending to bring into ridicule and contempt the administration
of justice; [3] (*b*) *conduct which is calculated to prejudice a pending
proceeding.* The offence is not confined to criminal proceedings, but
committal for this form of contempt of court is mainly used to prevent comments which might influence a jury about to try a criminal
offence. The applicant must show that something has been published
which is intended or calculated to prejudice a pending trial.[4] The
value of this protection is greatly diminished by the lawful practice
of publishing the proceedings before magistrates prior to committal
for trial. These proceedings, which are not a trial, but an enquiry to
find out if *prima facie* grounds exist for ordering a trial by judge and
jury, usually only disclose the case for the prosecution. It is customary
for the accused to reserve his defence until his trial. In Northern
Ireland, since 1953, the opening statement by the prosecution may not
be published and the court may prohibit the publication of evidence

---

[1] Publications calculated to cause disaffection among the police are prohibited by the Police Act, 1919, s. 3, which makes it an offence to cause disaffection among the police or to induce any member of a police force to commit
a breach of discipline.

[2] For committal for contempt by Parliament, see p. 125, *ante*.

[3] See *The King* v. *Editor of New Statesman* (1928), 44 T.L.R. 301; *Ambard*
v. *Attorney-General for Trinidad and Tobago*, [1936] A.C. 322; Dicey, *op. cit.*,
Appendix, Section II. (2) C.

[4] *The Queen* v. *Payne and Cooper*, [1896] 1 Q.B. 577.

which appears to the examining magistrate as prejudicial to the trial of the accused person.[1]

Freedom of Speech in Time of War. During the Second World War additional powers were taken by Defence Regulations to control propaganda. Defence Regulation 39B made it an offence to make use of any false statement, document or report to influence public opinion in a manner likely to be prejudicial to the defence of the realm or the efficient prosecution of the war. The regulation as originally made applied not only to false statements, but might also have been used to penalise honest criticisms of the Government. It was replaced early in the war and the new regulation was limited as a result of parliamentary criticism to penalising false statements. Defence Regulation 39A provided power to deal summarily with persons endeavouring to seduce from their duty or to cause disaffection likely to lead to a breach of duty among persons in His Majesty's service or employed by a public authority in connection with the public service or defence of the realm.

The Press. Defence Regulation 39B as originally made, also enabled a compulsory censorship of the Press to be established, but a few weeks later it was restricted to the control of the publication of matter prejudicial to our relations with foreign countries or relating to transactions in the course of negotiation between the Government and persons abroad. This concession left the Press free to use its own discretion as to the publication of other matter, subject to the risk of prosecution if it published matter prejudicial to security. Defence Regulation 2D, which was added to the code in 1940, gave power to suppress a newspaper without previous warning on the ground that it was systematically publishing matter calculated to foment opposition to the prosecution of the war. The regulation was used in 1941 to suspend *The Daily Worker*, and in 1942 *The Daily Mirror* was threatened with suspension as the result of the publication of a cartoon and other material calculated to cause unrest in the armed forces and the merchant navy.

Public Meeting. The right to hold a public meeting or procession is akin to, but separate from the right of free speech. There must be considered (*a*) the place where the meeting or procession is to be held, (*b*) the risk of disorder arising from it.[2]

The Public Highway. "The right of free speech is a perfectly separate thing from the question of the place where it is to be exercised." [3] In regard to use of the public highway a distinction must theoretically be drawn

---

[1] Summary Jurisdiction Act (Northern Ireland), 1953, s. 42.
[2] The law on this very complicated topic is fully discussed in Dicey, *op. cit.*, Appendix, Section II. (1). Here only a brief and dogmatic statement of the law is attempted.
[3] *McAra* v. *Magistrates of Edinburgh*, [1913] S.C. 1059, at p. 1073.

between meetings and processions.[1] The citizen's right to use the highway is a right of passing and re-passing,[2] not of standing still. A procession is *prima facie* lawful, but the use of the highway must be reasonable. A meeting on the highway is *prima facie* unlawful being a trespass against the body or person in whom the surface is vested, which in urban areas means the local authority. In practice there is little difference. It is an offence to obstruct the passage of any footway or other highway, nor is it a defence to show that the obstruction only affected part of the highway and left clear a right of passage; Highway Act, 1835, s. 72: *Homer* v. *Cadman* (1886), 16 Cox 51. A procession, just as a meeting, may cause an obstruction. Indeed, as has been pointed out,[3] it is difficult to imagine a procession which is not also an obstruction. So far, therefore, as the place of assembly is concerned, it would seem that a public meeting is only lawful in private premises with the consent of the owner or in a public open space or in a park where there is no right of way to be obstructed, and then only with the consent of the local authority in whom the open space or park is vested.[4]

The Public Order Act, 1936, s. 3, empowers a chief officer of police who has reasonable ground for apprehension that a procession may cause serious public disorder to give directions necessary for preserving public order and to prescribe the route to be taken and to prohibit the procession from entering any specified public place. Moreover the Commissioner of the Metropolitan Police (or of the City of London Police), with the consent of the Home Secretary, and in other urban areas the local authority on the application of the chief of police and with the consent of the Home Secretary, may prohibit for a period not exceeding three months the holding of any public procession in a police area or any part thereof.[5] *Power to Prohibit Processions.*

Apart from the question of the place of assembly there must be considered the risk of disorder arising from public meetings. Where those who take part in a meeting are themselves disorderly the law is comparatively simple. The position is difficult when otherwise lawful conduct excites or is likely to excite others to be disorderly. The common law relating to public meetings and processions reveals a conflict between two principles, (*a*) an act does not become unlawful because doing it may cause another to do an unlawful act, *e.g.* it is not unlawful for A to advocate birth control because B's dislike of it will cause B to assault A; cf. *Beatty* v. *Gillbanks* (1882), *Risk of Disorder.*

---

[1] See "Public Meetings and Processions," by A. L. Goodhart, 6 *C.L.J.* 161.
[2] *Harrison* v. *Duke of Rutland*, [1893] 1 Q.B. 142; *Hickman* v. *Maisey*, [1900] 1 Q.B. 752.
[3] Jennings, *The Law and the Constitution*, 4th ed., p. 258.
[4] *Ibid.*   [5] There is no power to prohibit meetings.

9 Q.B.D. 308; K. & L. 406 ; (*b*) a magistrate or police officer is under a duty to take any steps that are necessary to prevent a breach of the peace which he reasonably apprehends. The second principle appears to have prevailed,[1] so far as police power to prevent the holding of a meeting is concerned: *Duncan* v. *Jones*, [1936] 1 K.B. 218; K. & L. 411.[2]

> Mrs. Duncan, a woman speaker, was forbidden on her arrival by Jones, a police officer, to hold a meeting at a place opposite a training centre for the unemployed. Fourteen months previously Mrs. Duncan had held a meeting at the same spot which had been followed by a disturbance in the centre attributed by the superintendent of the centre to the meeting. Mrs. Duncan mounted a box to start the meeting but was taken into custody and charged under the Prevention of Crimes Acts, 1871 and 1885, with obstructing a police officer in the execution of his duty. There was no allegation of obstruction of the highway or of inciting or provoking any person to commit a breach of the peace. Quarter Sessions found (*a*) that Mrs. Duncan must have known of the probable consequences of her holding the meeting, viz. a disturbance and possibly a breach of the peace, and was not unwilling that such consequences should ensue, (*b*) that Jones reasonably apprehended a breach of the peace, (*c*) that in law it therefore became his duty to prevent the holding of the meeting, (*d*) that by attempting to hold the meeting Mrs. Duncan obstructed Jones when in the execution of his duty. On appeal to the Divisional Court it was held that Mrs. Duncan had been rightly convicted.

If this decision is correct, it would seem that the common law no longer protects the right of public meeting if a police witness is prepared to give evidence that he reasonably feared that a breach of the peace was likely.[3]

In *Thomas* v. *Sawkins*,[4] [1935] 2 K.B. 249, it was held that the police may attend a public meeting held in private premises if they reasonably suspect that a breach of the peace will occur or that seditious speeches will be made,[5] and need not withdraw at the request of the promoters of the meeting. Police may attend as members of the public and thus by their presence brand a meeting as one at which a breach of the peace is thought likely to occur. A magistrate too has a duty to preserve the peace and may disperse a meeting if he reasonably believes that only so can the peace be preserved: *O'Kelly* v. *Harvey* (1883), 14 L.R.Ir. 105.[6]

Binding Over.

Magistrates have a wide power to order any person to enter into a recognisance (undertaking) with or without sureties to keep the peace

---

[1] See, however, p. 400, *post*.
[2] For discussion of this case, see Dicey, *op. cit.*, pp. 557–60.
[3] Dicey, *op. cit.*, p. 559; K. & L. 401–5 for a criticism of this view.
[4] P. 366, *ante*.
[5] Or possibly that any offence will be committed.
[6] Cf. *Humphries* v. *Connor* (1864), 17 Ir. C.L.R. 1, where the removal of an emblem (a technical assault) was held justified in order to prevent a breach of the peace.

or to be of good behaviour (either in general or to a particular person): *Lansbury* v. *Riley*, [1914] 3 K.B. 229. On failure to comply with the order there may be imposed by a court of summary jurisdiction a sentence of six months' imprisonment: Magistrates' Courts Act, 1952, s. 91. The origin of this power is obscure; it may rest upon the Justices of the Peace Act, 1361, or may be inherent in the commission of the peace held by magistrates. It appears that it is not necessary to show that there has been anything done calculated to lead to violence: *The King* v. *Sandbach, ex parte Williams*, [1935] 2 K.B. 192, where the offender had despite warnings and previous convictions for obstructing the police repeatedly advised a street bookmaker of the approach of the police and so enabled him to avoid arrest. It was held that a magistrate may properly bind a man over whenever it is apprehended that he is likely to commit a breach of the peace or do something contrary to law. Since the making of an order to keep the peace does not constitute a conviction, there is no right of appeal open to the person bound over: *The King* v. *County of London Quarter Sessions Appeals Committee, ex parte Metropolitan Police Commissioner*, [1948] 1 K.B. 670, a case of binding over to be of good behaviour.

Hitherto consideration has been given primarily to the powers of magistrates and police officers to take steps to prevent disorder before it occurs. We must now consider the penalties for unlawful conduct at meetings. By section 5 of the Public Order Act, 1936, an Act which was primarily passed to prohibit the wearing of uniform for political purposes and the formation of societies of a military character, any person is guilty of an offence who in any public place or at any public meeting uses threatening, abusive or insulting words or behaviour with intent to provoke a breach of the peace or whereby a breach of the peace is likely to be occasioned. Disorderly behaviour for the purpose of preventing the transaction of business at a lawful public meeting is punishable under the Public Meetings Act, 1908, as amended by section 6 of the Public Order Act, 1936. Disorderly conduct at a meeting or procession in a public place is also in most urban areas an offence against the provisions of a local Act or by-law. The Metropolitan Police Act, 1839, ss. 52 and 54 and the Town Police Clauses Act, 1847, s. 28, are examples of general statutory provisions which punish obstruction and other forms of disorder. *Unlawful Conduct at Meetings.*

Those participating in a meeting may also be guilty of the common law misdemeanour of unlawful assembly. This offence is constituted by the meeting together of three or more persons for the accomplishment of some common design, lawful or unlawful, which is likely to involve violence or to produce in the minds of reasonable persons an apprehension of violence. The mere knowledge that opponents are likely to cause disorder does not, however, turn an *Unlawful Assembly.*

otherwise lawful assembly into an unlawful assembly: *Beatty* v. *Gillbanks, ante*. The promoters of a meeting may be guilty of the offence of obstructing the police in the execution of their duty; *Duncan* v. *Jones, ante*; and yet not necessarily be guilty of the offence of unlawful assembly. The distinction may be important. A civilian, and equally a soldier,[1] has a common law duty to take all necessary steps to disperse an unlawful assembly. He is not, however, obliged to take steps to disperse a meeting merely because a police officer has, in the exercise of his duty to prevent a breach of the peace, ordered the dispersal of the meeting.

The Seditious Meetings Act, 1817, s. 23, makes a meeting of more than fifty persons an unlawful assembly if held within one mile of Westminster Hall, when either House of Parliament is sitting.

Riot.

Riot at common law is a misdemeanour punishable with imprisonment. The elements essential to constitute a common law riot are five in number: (1) the presence of not less than three persons, (2) a common purpose, (3) execution or attempted execution of the common purpose, (4) an intent to help one another, by force if necessary, against anyone who may oppose them in the execution of the common purpose, (5) force or violence displayed in such manner as to alarm at least one person of reasonable firmness: *Field* v. *Receiver of the Metropolitan Police*, [1907] 2 K.B. 853. If the unlawful purpose upon which the rioters are engaged is itself felonious, *e.g.* arson, then the riot is a felony at common law. The distinction may be important because more force may be justified in order to suppress a felony than to suppress a misdemeanour.

Statutory Riot also a Felony.

A riot may also become felonious under the provisions of the Riot Act, 1714, quite apart from the actual commission of, or intention to commit, an independent felony which, as has been seen above, is sufficient to constitute the riot felonious. By the provisions of this Act a magistrate is empowered to order any twelve or more persons who are assembled together to the disturbance of the public peace to disperse within one hour after the reading of the proclamation in the Act. Failure to comply with the proclamation within the hour renders the rioters liable to be adjudged felons and punished with the maximum penalty of imprisonment for life.

Damage done by Rioters.

Formerly compensation for damage done to property by rioters was payable by the Hundred, an ancient division of a county. The Riot (Damages) Act, 1886, entitles property owners to recover compensation out of the county or borough funds (police expenses), thus throwing the burden on to the general body of the ratepayers. In a claim for compensation under this Act it was held that acts which constitute a riot when committed by civilians equally constitute a riot when committed by soldiers, notwithstanding that the acts may

[1] P. 420–21, *post*.

take place at a military camp in England during time of war: *Pitchers v. Surrey County Council*, [1923] 2 K.B. 57.

It is the duty of every citizen and the special duty of magistrates and police officers to suppress unlawful and disorderly assemblies: *Charge to the Bristol Grand Jury* (1832), 5 C. & P. 261; K. & L. 415. A magistrate or police officer must hit the exact line between excess and failure of duty and is guilty of criminal neglect if he fails to judge rightly: *The King* v. *Pinney* (1832), 5 C. & P. 254; K. & L. 418.[1] Soldiers have the same duty as other citizens to suppress riots, but it is desirable that they, like civilians, should act in subordination to a magistrate and that an officer in charge of troops should not order recourse to arms on his own initiative, unless the danger is pressing and immediate.[2]

Duty to Disperse Unlawful Assemblies and Riots.

[1] It is not the practice to prosecute a private citizen for failure to take action on his own initiative.

[2] See also p. 420–21, *post*.

PART IX.

THE ROYAL FORCES.
MILITARY AND MARTIAL LAW.

Manual of Military Law, 7th ed. Chapter IX. (Composition of the Forces).
Chapter II. (History of Military Law).

Law of the Constitution by A. V. Dicey, 9th ed., Part II., Chaps. VIII. and IX.
and Appendix, Section V.

CHAPTER 1.

THE FORCES OF THE CROWN.

Introductory.

In this Part there will be considered the composition and discipline of the armed forces, the nature of military law and the status of those who are subject to it. There will also be considered those special common law powers for the preservation of public order which may be exercised by the Executive and by military commanders in a time of major emergency. When an emergency arises or is foreseen, statutory powers are normally taken to enable the Executive to meet it, but the common law powers remain.[1] The common law imposes upon every citizen (and the soldier is no less a citizen because he is also a soldier) the duty to take all necessary steps to resist invasion and suppress insurrections. Those in command of troops are in the best position to deal with invasion or insurrection. In order to fulfil their duty it will be necessary for military commanders to interfere with the liberty of civilians. The imposition of the will of military commanders upon the civil population is often referred to —it is submitted unfortunately—as "martial law." It is convenient to discuss this topic in connection with the armed forces of the Crown.

A.

Composition and Discipline of the Army.

Feudal Levy.   In early times there were two distinct national forces, the Feudal Levy and the National (or Militia) Levy.[2] The Feudal Levy had,

---

[1] See *H. C. Deb.*, 5th Series, Vol. 363, col. 90 *et seq.*, and particularly the Attorney-General at col. 137.

[2] See *China Navigation Co.* v. *Attorney-General*, [1932] 2 K.B. 197, at pp. 225 ff.

since in the twelfth century actual service was commuted for a money payment (scutage), ceased to be of importance, though the payment of scutage constituted a burdensome incident of land tenure until it was remitted in 1385. The National Levy was a defensive force, organised by counties, with no liability, save in case of invasion, to serve outside the county. The force, which had its origin in pre-Norman days, was revived and reorganised after the Conquest, and at its head the Sheriff was replaced by the official now known as the Lord-Lieutenant. There was a general liability to military service in this force, though the actual forces of the Crown for war came to be raised by commissions of array, whereby each county supplied a compulsory quota for the King's Army. Strictly speaking, forces so raised could not, apart from invasion, be compelled to serve outside their own counties. These commissions were a frequent ground of complaint in the time of the three Edwards; by them and by other means the Crown strove to acquire a third force (a standing army), which could be employed, as the need for a permanent force began to be recognised, irrespective of the limitations as to time and place which attached to the Feudal and National Levies. The King provided himself with such an army either by voluntary enrolment, by impressment, or by contract, if he could afford to pay for it, or if Parliament granted him the necessary funds. How far such a force had a lawful basis in time of peace is doubtful. The Petition of Right, 1628, moreover, furnished a difficulty in maintaining army discipline, because no departure from the ordinary law was henceforth permissible, except on actual service. Commissions of martial law (the law of the Constable and Marshal) were thereby expressly declared illegal, though they were probably illegal apart from this declaration. *(National Levy.)*

(Standing Army.)

The National Levy, by this time known as the Militia, was reorganised after the Restoration by the Militia Act, 1661. This Act declared that: *(The Militia.)*

> the sole supreme government, command and disposition of the Militia and of all forces by sea and land is, and by the laws of England ever was, the undoubted right of the Crown.

The King was not, however, henceforth permitted to keep a standing army beyond "guards and garrisons" of unspecified numbers. On this footing, with constant disputes between King and Parliament, the matter continued until the Revolution of 1688. The Bill of Rights provided that:

> The raising or keeping of a standing army within the Kingdom in time of peace, unless it be with consent of Parliament, is against law.

This provision was due not so much to objection to military service as to the realisation that the army might be dangerous to the liberty of the subject in the hands of an unwise ruler.

Mutiny Acts.   Thus in the absence of enabling legislation a standing army within the realm in peace time was (1) unlawful; (2) its discipline could not be enforced by rules differing from the ordinary law; and (3) the supplies necessary for its maintenance were lacking, since the King had no private revenue to meet the expenditure. There was no doubt that a permanent army was required for national security and, even though an army could be raised in an emergency under the royal prerogative, it could not be maintained without the grant of supplies by Parliament. For a long while the first two legal objections were overcome by a succession of Mutiny Acts, the first of which was passed some time previous to the Bill of Rights in 1689. These Acts served the double purpose of legalising for a fixed period, by convention for one year only, the keeping of permanent land forces by the Crown and of providing a code of rules for enforcing discipline in their ranks. From 1713 to 1879 there was no break in these Acts.

Army Act, 1881, and the Army and Air Force (Annual) Act.   In 1879 military law was codified in a single enactment, subsequently replaced by the Army Act, 1881. The code was until 1955 continued in force from year to year by an annual Act, known formerly as the Army (Annual) Act and after 1917 as the Army and Air Force (Annual Act). The preamble to this annual Act expressly fixed the maximum numbers of the land forces and thus waived the prohibition contained in the Bill of Rights. A separate Air Force was constituted in 1917 by the Air Force (Constitution) Act of that year. The Army Act, 1881, with modifications governed the discipline of the Air Force.

Army Act, Air Force Act, 1955.   In 1955, following a series of reports of departmental committees and four reports[1] from a Select Committee of the House of Commons, which sat for three successive sessions and redrafted separate Bills to replace for the Army and for the Air Force the existing Acts, there were enacted the Army Act, 1955, and the Air Force Act, 1955. These Acts will be brought into force when the necessary changes required for their administration, such as re-writing parts of the Manual of Military Law, have been made. Meanwhile the old Acts will, with certain modifications be kept in force by the Revision of the Army and Air Force Acts (Transitional Provisions) Act, 1955. Not only are certain changes made in those Parts of the Acts which deal with disciplinary offences (some of these were called for by the presence of a high proportion of young national servicemen in the forces), but there was a departure from the old practice of requiring an Annual Act to continue the present legislation in force for another year. This practice ensured that each year amendments could be

[1] H.C. 244 (1952), 331 (1952), 289 (1953), 223 (1954).

considered to the law relating to the Army; but lawyers also regarded the Annual Act as necessary to meet the prohibition against a standing Army in the Bill of Rights. The official view, however, is that the prohibition is lifted by the Annual Appropriation Act which sanctions the votes for Army and Air Force pay and therefore by implication allows the forces who are in receipt of such pay to be maintained. The new Acts make two other changes; they extend a modified application of the disciplinary code to nine separate categories of civilians, including families of servicemen, being outside the United Kingdom, when not on active service; and the Army Act applies to the Royal Marines, though this force is at times also subject to the Naval Discipline Acts, *i.e.* when carried on the books of one of Her Majesty's Ships.

So far as the rank and file are concerned, members of all the forces were until 1939, except during part of the First World War, recruited by voluntary enlistment [1] for varying fixed periods of service, with liability to serve anywhere within or without the realm. Voluntary service on long term enlistment still provides a strong nucleus of the Army and Air Force and the great majority of the Royal Navy. Enlistment, which requires attestation before a recruiting officer, is in the nature of a contract between the soldier and the Crown. The Crown cannot vary the terms of enlistment without the soldier's consent, but like any other servant of the Crown a soldier is employed at the pleasure of the Crown; a member of the armed forces cannot sue for service pay or pension: *Leaman* v. *The King*, [1920] 3 K.B. 663.[2]

Terms of Service: (a) Rank and File.

Officers, in all branches of the forces, are appointed by the King's commission. They cannot resign or retire without leave, though they are usually in peace time permitted to retire at their own request: *The Queen* v. *Cuming, ex parte Hall* (1887), 19 Q.B.D. 13. They, too, are liable to be discharged at the pleasure of the Crown.

(b) Officers.

The National Service Act, 1948, as amended in 1950 fixed the period of whole-time service at twenty-four months, to be followed by three and a half years' service in one of the reserve forces. It requires compulsory service with one of the armed forces for all males between the ages of eighteen and twenty-six,[3] though those engaged in a few important occupations of national importance in time of war need not be called up. This provision converted the Territorial Army, which had hitherto been a volunteer force, into a force largely composed of men who have had a short period of regular army service, since the bulk of national service men are directed into the Army.

National Service.

[1] For compulsory service in war time, see p. 409, *post.*
[2] Part VII., Chap. 4.
[3] The age is extended to thirty-six in the case of British subjects resident abroad.

All ranks of the Regular Army, whilst actively employed, are subject to military law. This liability applies to the soldier whether he is serving at home or overseas.

Military Forces of the British Commonwealth.

Each of the other Member States of the British Commonwealth has its own military and air forces, and they may be classified as regular forces. Their permanent organisation is, broadly speaking, on a skeleton footing, providing for rapid expansion in time of war or other emergency. They are part of the forces of the Crown,[1] but their organisation, discipline and employment are exclusively under the control of their respective Governments. All legislation affecting them is enacted by their own Parliaments. There are also forces raised in certain colonies.

Visiting Forces.

The Visiting Forces (British Commonwealth) Act, 1933, empowered the military and naval authorities of a Dominion to exercise in the United Kingdom all the powers conferred by their own law in relation to the discipline and internal administration of a Dominion force visiting the country. The Act contained provisions enabling the authorities of this country to arrange for the arrest of alleged offenders at the request of the commander of a visiting force and to hand over deserters. During the Second World War similar rights were conferred by the Allied Forces Act, 1940, in respect of forces of allied States stationed in this country. The jurisdiction conferred by these Acts did not exclude the jurisdiction of the courts of this country in respect of offences committed by members of a visiting force, but by the United States of America (Visiting Forces) Act, 1942, exclusive jurisdiction was given to the American authorities in respect of criminal offences committed in this country by members of visiting American forces. This was a striking constitutional innovation made on grounds of political expediency. By the Allied Powers (Maritime Courts) Act, 1941, provision was made for the establishment during the war in the United Kingdom of maritime courts of allied States with jurisdiction over their merchant seamen; here the jurisdiction was not exclusive of that of our courts.

Visiting Forces Act, 1952.

In June, 1951, agreement was reached by the States which are parties to the North Atlantic Treaty on the legal status of the armed forces of one of the parties when stationed in the territory of another.[2] The United Kingdom and Canada are the only Commonwealth States who are parties to this Treaty. It thus became necessary to introduce in the United Kingdom Parliament, as in the Canadian Parliament, the necessary legislation to bring the agreement into force as part of the law of the United Kingdom. At the same time the Government of the United Kingdom agreed with all the Commonwealth Governments to amend the existing law relating to Common-

[1] Not in India since the adoption of a republican form of government.
[2] Cmd. 8279, (1951).

wealth Visiting Forces so as to bring it into line with the Agreement. Accordingly, the Visiting Forces Act, 1952, which repeals the Allied Forces Act and the United States of America (Visiting Forces) Act and the relevant part of the Visiting Forces (British Commonwealth) Act now provides a comprehensive statement of the law applicable to Visiting Forces both from all the States which are parties to the North Atlantic Treaty and from the principal States of the Commonwealth; the Act can be extended to other countries by Order in Council. As a result of this repeal the service courts of the United States no longer have an exclusive criminal jurisdiction over their armed forces while in the United Kingdom.

The principal provisions of the Act of 1952 may be summarised as follows:—[1]

(1) The service courts and authorities of Visiting Forces may exercise in the United Kingdom all the jurisdiction which is given to them by the law of their own country over all persons (including members of a civilian component) who may be subject to the law of that country governing their armed forces; the death penalty may not, however, be carried out in the United Kingdom unless under United Kingdom law the sentence of death could have been passed in similar cases.

(2) This jurisdiction is not exclusive of that of the criminal courts in the United Kingdom, but a member of a Visiting Force will not be liable to be tried for a criminal offence by a United Kindgom court if—

(a) the alleged offence arises out of and in the course of duty: or

(b) the alleged offence is one against the person of a member of the same or another Visiting Force; or

(c) the alleged offence is committed against the property of the Visiting Force or of a member thereof.

"An offence against the person" includes murder, manslaughter and all the more serious offences involving personal injury under the criminal law of England and of Scotland. It is only in the above cases that the jurisdiction of the criminal courts of the United Kingdom is excluded, unless the appropriate authority of the Visiting Force waives the jurisdiction. Thus a visiting soldier or airman will be tried for an offence against the Road Traffic Acts in the ordinary magistrates' courts or by a judge and jury.

3. A member of a Visiting Force who has been tried by his own service court cannot be put on trial in a United Kingdom court for the same offence.

4. From civil liability there is no immunity apart from the immunity afforded to a foreign State or its property by United Kingdom

[1] These provisions came into operation in 1954.

law.[1] Provision is however made for the satisfaction of civil claims in tort, but not in contract, by the Minister of Defence, whether or not the immunity can be claimed. In the event of the Minister declining to admit the claim the claimant is entitled to sue the member of the Visiting Force in the ordinary way. This provision applies where the defendant commits the tort while on duty or off duty; in the latter case any compensation paid on behalf of the Visiting Force is made without accepting liability.

5. The above provisions are in operation as the law of the United Kingdom irrespective of the provision of reciprocal facilities by the other countries to whose armed forces they apply in the United Kingdom.

Reserve and Auxiliary Forces: Army Reserve.

The reserve and auxiliary forces of the Crown consist as far as the Army is concerned of the various classes of the Army Reserve and the Territorial Army.[2] The Army Reserve consists of former regular soldiers who are liable for a fixed number of years after the expiry of their service to be called up for armed training or to assist the civil power in the preservation of order, and for general service in the regular army in the event of war. Officers are also liable to recall until they attain a given age which varies with their rank. One class of the Army Reserve (Section A) is liable to be called up at any time, but the main body of the Reserve can only be called out for general service when there exists a state of imminent national danger or grave emergency.

The Militia.

The old county force known as the Militia was disbanded in 1908, but from 1921 the term, Militia, was applied to the Special Reserve created by the Territorial and Reserve Forces Act, 1907. The Militia now forms part of the Army Reserve and is a body of reservists who have not served in the regular forces. Up to 1939 it was a force of comparatively small numbers.

Territorial Army.

The Territorial Army—the part-time citizen army—which superseded and absorbed the former Volunteers and Yeomanry, is a force which is administered and was formerly recruited exclusively on a voluntary basis by county associations which also administer the Air Force auxiliary units. As we have seen, the effect of the National Service Act, 1948, is to make its composition largely one of men who have completed their short-term compulsory regular service but the volunteers remain a vital element in all units. It was created by the Territorial and Reserve Forces Act, 1907, as part of the Army reforms associated with the name of Lord Haldane. After the calling out of the Army Reserve the Army Council can issue an order em-

---

[1] P. 208–12, *ante*.
[2] The statutes governing the Army Reserve and Territorial Army are permanent Acts. The legislation relating to the Territorial Army and Auxiliary Air Force was consolidated by the Auxiliary Forces Act, 1953.

bodying the Territorial Army, which thereupon is put on an active service footing of whole-time service at home or overseas. During armed training or on embodiment a member of the Territorial Army is subject to military law and receives the same pay and allowances of his rank as the regular army. Early in 1939 the Territorial Army was raised to a force of some half a million men and included also the newly raised Women Auxiliaries (A.T.S.). It thus provided at the outbreak of war a far larger defence force than the regular army. It was organised into field and anti-aircraft divisions. The latter were responsible for the whole of the air defence of Great Britain provided by the Anti-Aircraft Command. Its post-war role is:

(*a*) To form, with the Regular Army, a national army for service at home or overseas.

(*b*) To provide specific units required by the Regular Army to convert their force into a properly balanced organisation ready for battle.

The Home Guard raised, in May 1940, as the Local Defence Volunteers, was part of the armed forces of the Crown. It consisted at first of volunteers and later partly of those enrolled by directions under Defence Regulations. Its members were subject to military law with certain modifications as to discipline. Except when mustered to resist invasion, members of the Home Guard were not required to perform whole-time service or to live away from home, nor might they be required to enrol for a period exceeding the period of "the present emergency." The Force stood down at the end of 1944, but was formed again by the Home Guard Act, 1951. *Home Guard.*

In 1939 for the second time in twenty-five years the United Kingdom was forced to adopt a system of compulsory service. Conscription had long been regarded as an evil which should not befall a British subject in time of peace, though historically its abhorrence is based on the fear lest the King should be possessed of too powerful a weapon with which to coerce the people. On the outbreak of war the various reserve and auxiliary forces were absorbed into the regular forces and the statutory provisions relating to length of service, liability to serve overseas and terms of enlistment were all superseded by the introduction of compulsory military service. Earlier, in May, 1939 there had been passed the Military Training Act, 1939, which provided for the compulsory military training and enlistment as militiamen of male British subjects ordinarily resident in Great Britain between the ages of twenty and twenty-one. That Act too was superseded by the introduction of compulsory service for all males of military age after the outbreak of war. The Reserve and Auxiliary Forces Act, 1939, also passed *War-time Legislation and Compulsory Service.*

in May of that year, provided for calling out for service by Order in Council the members of any of the reserve or auxiliary forces, and under it the Naval Reserve, Army Reserve and Air Force Reserve were called out and the Territorial Army and Auxiliary Air Force were embodied. The Armed Forces (Conditions of Service) Act, 1939, permitted enlistment in the regular forces for the duration of "the present emergency," transfer to any corps without consent, the ordering abroad of any embodied part of the Territorial Army and of any part of the Auxiliary Air Force. The Military and Air Forces (Prolongation of Service) Act, 1939, provided that no member of the regular, reserve or auxiliary forces should be entitled to be discharged until the end of the emergency.[1] The National Service (Armed Forces) Act, 1939, introduced liability to compulsory military service for all males—subject to certain total or conditional exemptions for, in particular, conscientious objectors and regular ministers of any religious denomination—between the ages of eighteen and forty-one. The Act contained provisions for reinstatement in civil employment. The National Service Act, 1941, extended the liability to compulsory whole-time service to service in the Civil Defence Forces. Later in the same year the National Service (No. 2) Act, 1941, raised the age of liability to compulsory service in the forces to fifty-one and rendered women so liable as well as men. Women could be called up to serve in the Women's Royal Naval Service, the Auxiliary Territorial Service and the Women's Auxiliary Air Force. A woman could not, however, be required to use a lethal weapon without her written consent. This Act declared all persons of either sex to be liable to national service, whether under the Crown or not, and whether in the armed forces of the Crown, in civil defence, in industry, or otherwise. Liability to whole-time service in the forces remained restricted to those between the ages of eighteen and fifty-one, but any person might by Defence Regulations be directed to part-time service in the armed forces or civil defence forces or to whole or part-time service in any form of national service including civil defence employment. The Emergency Powers (Defence) Act, 1940, had made provision for Defence Regulations to compel persons to place themselves, their services and their property at the disposal of His Majesty, and these Defence Regulations were made under the authority of this Act which was intended to rally the nation to resist invasion. The Civil Defence Forces were the Police War Reserve, the Civil Defence Reserve, the National Fire Service, and the Kent County Civil Defence Mobile Reserves. The range of civil defence services was, however, wider and embraced service under the local authorities as air-raid wardens, rescue workers, ambulance drivers, mainly as part-time workers with a

[1] The Royal Marines were covered by separate legislation.

nucleus of whole-time salaried officers. The Allied Powers (War Service) Act, 1942, provided that the National Service Acts, 1939 to 1941, might apply to the nationals of allied States who were not serving in their own forces. Thus was rapidly built up by a series of elaborate statutory provisions, partly Acts of Parliament, partly Defence Regulations and orders and directions issued thereunder, the conception of national service for total war. So far as compulsory military service for males is concerned the liability to serve was governed by the National Service Acts, 1939–1942 until the end of 1948 when the National Service Act, 1947, was due to come into operation. The whole of the relevant statute law was meanwhile consolidated in the National Service Act, 1948.[1] The exemptions in favour of conscientious objectors and certain other classes are continued and there are provisions against persons being penalised as regards employment prior to as well as after service.

B.

Composition and Discipline of the Royal Marines, Navy and R.A.F.

The Royal Marines, a force of infantry and artillery, form part of the regular forces and are liable for general service on board ship and on shore. Although this force is raised and maintained by the Admiralty for naval service, its discipline and regulation is provided for by the Army Act. When on board one of Her Majesty's ships a marine also comes under the Naval Discipline Acts. There is also a Royal Marines Forces Volunteer Reserve. *Royal Marines.*

The Navy is the senior branch of the forces, but its constitutional interest is less. Unlike the Army, the Navy did not in former times come under the suspicion of Parliament. There is no reason to suppose that naval service was regarded as less burdensome than service in the Army, or that naval discipline could be enforced without interfering with the common law rights of the sailor as citizen. But the Navy had never been used by the King to coerce Parliament and so was not included in the prohibition in the Bill of Rights against a standing armed force. It has remained a prerogative force maintained on a permanent footing. So much is this so that the recruitment of the Navy by impressment has never been declared illegal, though the press-gang has, of course, long fallen into disuse. Enlistment is governed by the Naval Enlistment Acts, 1835 to 1884, and discipline by the Naval Discipline Act, 1866, as subsequently amended. Both types of enactment are permanent and do not come under annual review by Parliament for renewal. Conditions of service and regulations for discipline closely resemble those applicable *The Royal Navy.*

[1] P. 405, *ante.*

to the Army and Air Force and they do not call for separate discussion.[1] Despite its prerogative basis, the Navy comes under the control of Parliament, since its estimates are presented annually, as are those of the other services, to Parliament and the consequential votes in Committee of Supply afford full opportunity for discussion of naval administration and expenditure, which on account of constructional requirements is often controversial.

Naval Reserve. The Naval Reserve consists of two main divisions: the Royal Naval Reserve, recruited from members of the Merchant Navy; and the Royal Naval Volunteer Reserve which includes an Air Branch and provided the huge expansion in commissioned rank during the Second World War. A division of the Naval Reserve known as the Royal Fleet Reserve is recruited compulsorily from men who sign an engagement for seven years' active service and voluntarily from those who have done twelve years or from men who served on a temporary engagement for at least three years during the Second World War.

Dominion Navies. Naval forces, under the control of their own Parliaments and Governments for all purposes, including discipline,[2] except when serving with the Royal Navy,[3] are maintained by four of the Dominions, Canada, Australia, New Zealand and the Union of South Africa. India possesses, as does Pakistan, a comparatively small force largely for the purpose of replacing the Royal Indian Marine.

Royal Air Force. The Royal Air Force was constituted in 1917 as a force separate from both the Army and the Navy. The naval arm was transferred back to the Royal Navy before the Second World War as the Fleet Air Arm. and is now part of the Executive branch of the Navy. The Air Force does not call for separate notice from the point of view of constitutional law, as its position closely resembles that of the Army and its Reserve Forces.

C.

Women's Forces.

Women in the Post-War Armed Forces. The women's land, air and naval forces raised during the Second World War were not disbanded and have since become part of the regular and reserve forces under the titles of Women's Royal Army Corps, Women's Royal Air Force and Women's Royal Naval Service. The Army and Air Force (Women's Service) Act, 1948, gave power to raise and maintain the land and air forces, to grant

---

[1] A civilian on board a naval vessel may be tried by naval court-martial for seducing from their duty or allegiance members of the navy: Naval Discipline Act, 1866, s. 13; the maximum penalty for this offence is death.
[2] See Naval Discipline (Dominion Naval Forces) Act, 1911.
[3] See Colonial (Naval Defence) Act, 1931.

commissions to women officers and to make the necessary adaptations of the Army Act and the Air Force Act to bring women under military law. The naval service does not come under the Naval Discipline Acts, but maintains its discipline by expulsion and submission voluntarily to its code of service conduct. The National Service Act, 1948, excludes women from any form of compulsory service. Women's units are serving as regular arms of all three Services as well as in the Territorial Army and Air Force Reserve.

CHAPTER 2.

MILITARY LAW AND COURTS-MARTIAL.

A.

Military Law.

Nature of
Military
Law.

MILITARY LAW for the Army is contained in the Army Act, 1955, and the Acts relating to the auxiliary and reserve forces and is applied with modifications to the Royal Air Force by the Air Force Act, 1955. These Acts, which replace with important amendments the Army Act, 1881, and its application since 1917 to the Royal Air Force, are supplemented by rules of procedure, by Queen's Regulations and other regulations issued under the prerogative, by Royal Warrant, *e.g.* as to pay and promotion, and by Army Orders. Thus while the basic disciplinary code is statutory, other matters are dealt with by prerogative instruments. The Acts are limited in duration to twelve months, but for a period of five years, they may be continued in force from year to year without amendment by resolutions passed by both Houses of Parliament. No legislation is thus required until the end of five years from the coming into force of the Acts of 1955 unless the Government seeks to amend the Acts earlier. An army cannot be disciplined by the ordinary law applicable to civilians. Any association of individuals organised for the achievement of a particular object is bound to lay down certain rules by which the members agree to be bound on joining. In the case of a "members" club these rules are purely contractual and in no way conflict with the ordinary law of the land, to which all the members remain subject. In the case of the learned professions, particularly the law and medicine, the special rules are to some extent impressed with the authority of the State, being enforceable in some cases by statutory courts of discipline. With the armed forces of the Crown the sanction of Parliament is required for the more stringent provisions which are essential for preserving military discipline. The courts through the prerogative orders of certiorari and prohibition or by writ of habeas corpus are able to supervise, so far as excess of jurisdiction is concerned, the military tribunals (courts-martial) which are established by the Army Act for adjudication upon offences against military law. Prior to 1879 military law in time of peace consisted of those rules which were sanctioned each year by the Mutiny Act. From 1715 the

form of the statute was to implement the prerogative right, exercisable in time of war only, to make articles of war, by extending the
right to time of peace. By the provision of a code of rules governing
both peace and war by the Army Act, 1955, all important changes
are now brought under review by Parliament at least every five years
and annually, if need be. There is also power to make rules of
procedure for the administration of military law. These rules must
not conflict with the Army Act and must be laid before Parliament,
They are an important safeguard ensuring the conduct of a trial by
court-martial on the lines of a criminal trial in a civil court, but there
is no jury.

The offences created by the Army Act include desertion, absence Offences
without leave, fraudulent enlistment, and two offences which well under
illustrate the difference between military law and ordinary law. Army Act.
Section 64 of the Act provides that an officer who behaves in a
scandalous manner unbecoming to the character of an officer and a
gentleman shall, on conviction by court-martial, be cashiered.
Section 69 provides that any person who is guilty of any act,
conduct, disorder or neglect to the prejudice of good order and
military discipline shall be liable to be sentenced to two years'
imprisonment. Section 64 is rarely used as it lays down a minimum
punishment, but section 69 is largely used. This section gives a
wide discretion to a court-martial to treat any conduct as a criminal
offence, and it has been urged that military offences should be framed
with greater particularity.

The administration of military law by courts-martial composed of Administra-
serving officers is supervised by the Judge Advocate General of the tion of
Forces, whose functions until 1948 combined those of prosecutor, Military
judge and appellate tribunal as well as legal adviser to the Secre- Law
taries of State for War and for Air. The functions relating to prosecutions have been transferred to the separate departments of the
Army and Air Force Legal Services, each under a Director, who is
independent of the Judge Advocate General. In practice the separation had been secured before 1948, but the principle of combining
these functions with a judicial office was clearly inappropriate.

The Judge Advocate General, who is appointed by the Crown on
the recommendation of the Lord Chancellor to whom he is responsible, is thus now a judicial officer. He provides a judge advocate at all
trials by general court-martial held in the United Kingdom and at
the more serious cases tried by district court-martial as well as for
important trials abroad by general or field general court-martial.
The Judge Advocate attends the court in an advisory capacity. The
review of the proceedings of all courts-martial with a view to seeing
whether they have been regular and legal is undertaken by the
department of the Judge Advocate. Legal advice may be tendered on

confirmation or review or on petition. The Judge Advocate General has deputies and staffs with the major commands abroad as well as at home.

Military Courts. The Army Act regulates the constitution and proceedings of courts-martial for the enforcement of military law. Their jurisdiction is exclusively over persons subject to military law. They are convened by high military officers. The convening order details the officers who are to serve on the court, and, if qualified by length of service, all officers are liable to serve. There is a similarity between the constitutional procedure of civil and military courts. The lowest military court, apart from the summary and investigating powers of company and battery commanders, is the commanding officer, normally a lieutenant-colonel commanding a battalion or regiment. Non-commissioned officers and soldiers charged with military offences are brought before him on remand by the company commander, and his duty corresponds with that of a court of summary jurisdiction. After hearing the evidence he can either dismiss the charge or, if it is a minor charge against a soldier, he may deal with it summarily (his power of punishment is limited to twenty-eight days' detention) or order a summary of the evidence to be taken with a view to determining whether or not to send the accused for trial by court-martial. The accused has the right to trial by court-martial if the commanding officer proposes to order detention or forfeiture of pay: Army Act, 1955, s. 78. There is also a summary procedure for disposing of less serious charges against officers and warrant officers. A commanding officer can in the appropriate cases refer the charge for adjudication by a superior authority, *i.e.* an officer having power to convene courts-martial: s. 79.

Courts-Martial.[1] Should the commanding officer be of the opinion that a case cannot properly be dealt with summarily (and he may not punish an officer), he should send the offender for trial by court-martial. There are three forms of court-martial.[2]

A General Court-Martial, which must consist of at least five officers, can try any offence under the Army Act or Air Force Act, whether committed by an officer or a member of the rank and file.

A District Court-Martial cannot try an officer or award the punishments of death or more than two years' imprisonment; otherwise any offence under the Acts is within its jurisdiction. The court is constituted by at least three officers. These two courts correspond approximately with Assize Courts and Quarter Sessions.

---

[1] For a short history of the Court-Martial System and the Office of Judge Advocate General, see the Report of Army and Air Force Courts-Martial Committee, 1946, Cmd. 7608, 1949.

[2] The tribunals, also called courts-martial, for the trial by officers of members of the Royal Navy and of other persons subject to the Naval Discipline Acts do not call for separate treatment.

A Field General Court-Martial is for the trial of offences committed on active service, where a general or district court-martial cannot be convened without serious detriment to the public service.

A trial by court-martial is very much like a trial in an ordinary criminal court. If the offender so desires, a convening officer may appoint an officer to defend. A judge advocate may be (and in the case of a general court-martial must be) appointed to advise the court as to law and to summarise the facts, but he does not, as formerly, retire with the court when it is considering its findings. The same rules of evidence and presumption of innocence apply (as also before a commanding officer) as in a criminal court. Findings must be pronounced in open court at once and sentences announced as soon as determined. The main differences between a trial by court-martial and trial by a criminal court are:

(*a*) The court may arrive at its finding or sentence by a majority, whereas a jury must be unanimous.

(*b*) Members of the court fix the sentence subject to confirmation, whereas a jury has nothing to do with sentence.

(*c*) The probation system does not apply to military offenders, though there is power to suspend sentence.

A person sentenced by a court-martial may complain by petition to are viewing authority. Independently of petitions the proceedings of all courts-martial are reviewed in the office of the Judge Advocate General in order to detect any miscarriage of justice. Sentences must be confirmed by a competent higher military authority and may be modified by that authority. There is no power to increase the sentence awarded by the court. **Review of sentences.**

The Courts-Martial (Appeals) Act, 1951, established a Courts-Martial Appeal Court. The judges are the Lord Chief Justice and the puisne judges of the High Court (in practice the judges of the Queen's Bench Division) and the corresponding judges for Scotland and Northern Ireland, who may be nominated for the purpose, together with such other persons of legal experience as the Lord Chancellor may appoint. Like the Court of Criminal Appeal for England the Courts-Martial Appeal Court is constituted by an uneven number of judges, not less than three sitting; it may sit in divisions and may sit within or without the United Kingdom as the Lord Chief Justice may direct. Up to the end of 1954 it had sat only in London. Although the Court operates on similar lines to the Court of Criminal Appeal [1] leave to appeal can only be granted by the court itself and must be obtained even for an appeal on a question of law. But before application for leave can be made, a convicted **Courts-Martial Appeal Court.**

[1] P. 234, *ante.*; there is no appeal against sentence only.

person must await confirmation of the sentence by the convening authority and, unless he is under sentence of death, must petition the appropriate service authority, the Secretary of State for War or Air or the Board of Admiralty, for the quashing of his conviction and await the decision of that authority refusing the petition. An appeal lies to the House of Lords on a point of law certified by the Attorney-General to be of exceptional public importance.

Civil Courts in relation to Courts-Martial.

Courts-martial are limited to the powers conferred on them by statute. For an unlawful act done by such a court or by a military officer exercising his summary powers under the Army Act, the person injured has his remedy in the High Court. An excess of jurisdiction may be questioned by application to the Divisional Court of the Queen's Bench Division for the writ of habeas corpus or an order of certiorari or prohibition. There is no doubt that certiorari lies, at the discretion of the High Court, to control the limits of jurisdiction of a court-martial, just as it lies to control all inferior courts which are shown to have exceeded their jurisdiction. Civil tribunals may also be controlled when there is an abuse which may vitiate an otherwise lawful exercise of jurisdiction, as when the tribunal is shown to have acted maliciously or from corrupt motives. But the courts have shown a marked disinclination to interfere with the decisions of a court-martial or military court of enquiry, or even with the exercise by a commanding officer of his summary powers under the Army Act and the equivalent statutes, if the objection is based on malice or lack of reasonable and probable cause. The argument is that matters falling within the scope of military discipline should be subject to review only by higher military authority. In *Heddon* v. *Evans* (1919), 35 T.L.R. 642, McCardie, J., distinguished between liability for an act done in excess of, or without jurisdiction, by the military tribunal, which amounts to an assault, false imprisonment or other common law wrong, and one which, though within jurisdiction and in the course of military discipline, is alleged to have been done maliciously and without reasonable and probable cause. Only in the former case would the courts entertain proceedings against military officers. The distinction appears to lie in the fact that only when there is an excess of jurisdiction is any common law right of the complainant infringed. But this distinction, if upheld, would deprive a soldier of a civil remedy if the prosecution at the court martial was malicious.

It is still open to the House of Lords to review the whole issue of the powers of the civil courts over the exercise of disciplinary powers in the armed services and in particular to decide whether the dismissal of an officer or man from the service is open to review in a court of law: *Fraser* v. *Balfour* (1918), 87 L.J.K.B. 1116. This reluctance of the court to intervene in matters properly falling within the sphere of military affairs was also illustrated in an action for libel brought by a subordinate officer against his commanding officer. The action was based on letters written by the latter to the Adjutant-General in the course of military duty. The plaintiff's remedy lay through military channels as provided nowadays by Queen's Regulations: *Dawkins* v. *Paulet* (1869), L.R. 5 Q.B.D. 94; K. & L. 390. But if the military court has exceeded its jurisdiction by applying military law to persons not subject to that law, as in *Wolfe Tone's Case* (1798), 27 St. Tr. 614, or, in the case of persons so subject, misapplying military law by punishing without regular trial or inflicting a punishment in excess of its jurisdiction, the writ of habeas corpus or certiorari order afford a means of reviewing the case, and the officers concerned will be liable to an action for damages or criminal proceedings for assault, manslaughter or even murder. Thus in *The King* v. *Governor of Wormwood Scrubbs and the Secretary of State for War, ex parte Boydell*, [1948] 2 K.B. 193, a writ of habeas corpus was granted on the application of an officer, who had been arrested at his home a year after his release from the Army, tried and sentenced by court-martial in Germany for an offence committed while serving there and imprisoned in an English gaol to serve his sentence. Section 158 (1) of the Army Act, 1881 (which was amended in consequence of the case)[1] excluded liability to trial by court-martial of such a person at so long a period after he had ceased to be subject to military law.

B.

Status of Members of the Forces.

A person subject to the Army Act does not cease to be subject to the ordinary law and may be tried by any competent civil court for offences against the criminal law. The position of a member of the Royal Navy or Royal Air Force is similar. Except so far as the statutes creating military law provide, a soldier enjoys all the rights of the ordinary citizen and his obligations as a soldier imposed by the Army Act and Queen's Regulations are in addition to his duties as a citizen. In practice most criminal offences committed by members of the Army and Royal Air Force are dealt with in peace time by the civil courts, but an offence against the ordinary law committed by a person subject to military law is, at the discretion of the competent military authorities, triable by court-martial, with the exception of certain serious felonies, such as murder, which must, if committed in the United Kingdom, be tried by the competent civil court (the Assizes or the Central Criminal Court). The Jurisdiction in

Venue for trial of Offences.

[1] See now Army Act, 1955, ss. 131, 132.

Homicides Act, 1862, provides for the removal to the Central Criminal Court of the trial of a person subject to military law who is accused of murder or manslaughter in England and Wales of another person who is subject to military law. Application is made to the Queen's Bench Division by the Secretary of State (for War or Air), if he considers that in the interests of good order and military discipline the trial should be expedited by removal to London. Offences committed by persons subject to the Naval Discipline Acts out of the United Kingdom or if in the United Kingdom in any place within the jurisdiction of the Admiralty are triable under those Acts, but if an offence is committed by such a person in, *e.g.* a London street there is no naval jurisdiction.

Privileges. A person subject to military law enjoys the benefit of certain privileges and exemptions from the ordinary civil law and its processes. He is entitled to vote at parliamentary and local elections if necessary by appointing a proxy.[1] When on active service he can make a will in nuncupatory form without complying with the formalities of the Wills Act, 1837, even if he be a minor.

Dual Liability. A person subject to military law, though sentenced or acquitted by court-martial, may afterwards be tried by a civil court, if the offence is one triable under the ordinary law. The sentence of the court-martial must be taken into consideration by the civil court in awarding punishment. A person acquitted or convicted by a civil court is not liable to be tried by court-martial in respect of the same offence. Persons who have been released from the Army or the Royal Air Force may be tried by court-martial with the consent of the Attorney-General in respect of an offence committed outside the United Kingdom if the offence is one which would, when committed in England, be punishable under English law.[2] Offences committed by such persons in the United Kingdom are only triable by court-martial if the trial begins within three months of the release; but for the offences of mutiny, desertion and fraudulent enlistment there is no such time limit.

Conflict of Duty. It is sometimes alleged that obedience to military law may conflict with a soldier's duty as a citizen. Military law is, however, part of the law of the land and obedience to it cannot be unlawful. A soldier is only required to obey orders which are lawful (Army Act, 1955, s. 34) and an order which is contrary to the common law is not a lawful order. If an order involves a breach of the law, a soldier is not only under no obligation to carry it out, but is under an obligation not to carry it out. It may truly be said that this places the soldier in an awkward position. He has not time to weigh up the merits of an order; his training makes compliance instinctive. None

---

[1] P. 91, *ante.* [2] Army Act, 1955, s. 132.

the less unlawful injury inflicted as the result of compliance renders him liable to civil or criminal proceedings. The defence of obedience to the orders of a superior is not accepted by the civil courts. On the other hand, if a soldier disobeys an order on the ground that it is unlawful, a court-martial may hold that it was lawful. In practice, however, a tribunal, whether court-martial or a judge and jury, should take all the circumstances into consideration and it is probably better to leave the soldier in a position of difficulty than to place him outside the ordinary law. If a prosecution results from obedience to an order, there is some authority for saying that, if the order was not necessarily or manifestly illegal, the soldier who obeys it cannot be made criminally liable. In *Keighley* v. *Bell* (1866), 4 F. and F. 763, at p. 790, this opinion was expressed *obiter* by Willes, J., and it has been followed by a special tribunal in South Africa [1] which acquitted of murder a soldier who had shot a civilian in time of war in obedience to an unlawful order given to him by his officer. It would seem that for the defence to succeed the mistaken belief in the legality of the order must be reasonable.

In connection with the violation of the recognised rules of warfare by an enemy (war crimes) the defence of superior orders had for many years been recognised by the Manual of Military Law, which contains the official view on the laws and usages of war—matters of public international law. In 1944 the Manual was amended and it is no longer stated as a defence for a person accused of a war crime to plead that the orders of a superior confer upon him any immunity from punishment by the military courts of the injured belligerent State. The defence may put the plea in mitigation of punishment but in no circumstances can the plea deprive the act of its character as a war crime. This change in the official view may be regarded as a necessary corollary to the rule of English criminal law that members of the armed forces are only bound to obey lawful orders. But it is to be noticed that the defence that an unlawful superior order which was not necessarily or manifestly illegal could be pleaded was not laid down in the Articles of the Nuremberg Charter of 1945 under which the International Military Court tried persons accused of major war crimes.

[1] *The Queen* v. *Smith* (1900), 17 Cape of Good Hope Supreme Court Reports 561; K. & L. 396; see also Kenny, *op cit.*, p. 55.

CHAPTER 3.
MARTIAL LAW.

Meaning of
Martial Law.

THE term, martial law, means in international law the powers exercised by a military commander in occupation of foreign territory. The term, martial law, is also used to describe the action of the military when, in order to deal with an emergency amounting to a state of war, they impose restrictions and regulations upon civilians in their own country. It is this meaning of martial law that will be discussed in this Chapter. That the military may in a time of major emergency exercise such abnormal powers is recognised by common law: *Marais* v. *General Officer Commanding*, [1902] A.C. 109. The term, martial law, is, however, misleading. The powers of the military are different only in degree and not in kind from those of the ordinary citizen. Moreover they are part of the ordinary law of the land. Every citizen (and a soldier is a citizen) is under a duty to assist in the suppression of riotous assemblies and insurrections and in repelling invaders. The task of dispersing riotous assemblies in time of peace is best directed by the local civil authorities who have knowledge of local conditions. Normally an officer in command of troops will act only if called upon to do so by a magistrate. None the less he must exercise his own judgment whether to use force and, if so, how much force to use. The instructions of the civil authority will, however, rightly influence his judgment and will normally be followed.[1] In time of invasion or insurrection on a wide scale a reverse state of affairs arises. Both citizen and soldier have the same duty, but the military are in a state of war the best judges of the steps that should be taken. They are then entitled to give directions to and impose restrictions upon civilians in order to fulfil their duty to repel invaders or suppress rebels. This duty is a duty not only of the citizen but of the Executive. In time of war the Executive would normally act through military commanders. The duty is that of the Crown and its servants and of all citizens.

Interference
with
Civilians.

When the Government desires extraordinary powers for the military, emergency statutes are passed by Parliament, *e.g.* the Defence of the Realm Acts, 1914–15, and the Emergency Powers Act, 1939. Power may be taken to declare what is indistinguishable from a state of martial law as a common law power. For at common law there exist, apart from statute, powers to repel force by force and to

[1] See Evidence of Lord Haldane, then Secretary of State for War, before a Select Committee on Employment of Military in Cases of Disturbance (H. C. 236, 1908); *Manual of Military Law* (1929), p. 256.

take all necessary steps to preserve order. In the exercise of such powers the military may find it necessary to interfere with the actions, and even with the life and liberty of civilians. The relationship between the military and civilians known as a state of martial law has not arisen in this country since the Civil War of the seventeenth century. A state of martial law has, however, existed during the present century in South Africa, Southern Ireland, Palestine and parts of India. The degree to which the military may interfere with civilians will vary with the circumstances. The test is whether the interference is necessary in order to perform the duty of repelling force and restoring order. The military authorities would be justified in ordering civilians to quit their homes, to obey a curfew order, to dig trenches or to render services, provided such orders were necessary for the defence of the country. If a civilian refuses to comply with such an order, the military are justified in enforcing obedience.

In order to establish whether breaches of duty have been committed, the military may find it necessary to set up military tribunals to try civilians. Prompt punishment may be necessary as an example to others. In exceptional circumstances offenders may be condemned to death. It would on occasion be justifiable to shoot an offender without any trial at all, *e.g.* an officer in charge of troops might justifiably order his men to shoot anyone about to cut a telegraph wire with intent to assist the enemy. In every case the action taken must be judged by the test of necessity. Sometimes it would not be justifiable even to bring an offender before a military tribunal. It might be sufficient to detain him in custody until he could be brought before a civil court. The tribunals established by the military are not judicial bodies and must be distinguished from courts-martial set up to try persons subject to military law for offences under the Army or the Air Force Acts, 1955.[1] They are merely bodies set up to advise the military commander as to the action he should take in carrying out his duties: see *Re Clifford and O'Sullivan*, [1921] 2 A.C. 570; K. & L. 459.[2] It is, however, in regard to the establishment of these military tribunals that the most difficult problems regarding a so-called state of martial law arise. Before the establishment of military tribunals there will usually be a proclamation of a state of martial law, but it is not the proclamation which makes martial law, but the events which have created the emergency. Subjects have the right to question any act of the Executive or military in the courts which can decide whether or not a state of martial law exists. A proclamation may be evidence of such a

(marginal note: Military Tribunals.)

---

[1] P. 416, *ante*. In time of emergency additional statutory powers may be conferred upon courts-martial; see pp. 426–7, *post*.
[2] Pp. 425–6, *post*.

state being already in existence, but it cannot change existing conditions from a peace-time footing to one of war within the realm. The prerogative of declaring war does not enable the Crown to declare war on the people. But the Executive has a common law duty, which it shares with every subject and with the military to assist in the maintenance of order. If it is compelled in the exercise of this duty to hand over control to the military forces, it acts at its own risk as regards legal responsibility, and there is a state of martial law, which is not law in the sense of a code of rules, but a condition of affairs.

When does an Emergency amount to Martial Law. There can be no precise test to determine the state of emergency at which martial law exists. Clearly in any true emergency the authorities may have to act without regard to their strict legal powers, since perils to the public safety cannot always be suppressed by prosecuting under the criminal law or applying for an injunction in the civil courts. If the civil courts have on account of hostilities ceased to sit for the time being, the maintenance of order passes from the civil power to the military. The military can, it may be safely asserted, then take control. What is necessary in such a situation is primarily a matter of discretion for the commander-in-chief and his advisers. Even so, when the courts are again able to sit, the acts of the military may be shown to be illegal as having been in excess of what was necessary, unless confirmed or excused by an Act of Indemnity. Much has been written as to whether the test in such cases would be strict necessity or *bona fide* belief in the necessity of the action, and as to whether it would be for the defendant to show that the test had been complied with or for the complainant to show that it had not been complied with. There is no authority which makes it possible to answer these questions. Supposing that the courts have not ceased entirely to operate, as where the insurrection is confined to part of the country, military government may none the less be necessary. Martial law is thus a state of fact not to be decided by the simple test: Were the civil courts sitting at the time? The test would seem to be: Is the insurrection of such a kind that military rule is justified? It falls to the civil courts alone to determine this difficult question of fact.

Control of Military by Civil Courts. This leads to a further problem. In so far as the civil courts may be sitting, what control, if any, have they over the acts of the military? In *Marais* v. *General Officer Commanding*, [1902] A.C. 109; K. & L. 446, the Privy Council held that such acts are not at the time justiciable by the ordinary courts sitting in a martial law area where "war is still raging." The courts will determine for themselves whether or not war exists: *The King* v. *Strickland (Garde)*, [1921] 2 I.R. 317, at p. 329. Once a state of war is recognised by the courts, and such recognition in the nature of things must be *ex post facto*, the Executive, with the aid of its military forces, may conduct warlike operations with impunity. They may deal with the inhabitants of a martial law area on the same footing as with the population of hostile invaded territory in time of war, subject only, it may be presumed, to such rules of warfare as international law prescribes. It is difficult to say how far the military authorities could be called to account in the civil courts after hostilities, because an Act of Indemnity in the ordinary course would be passed by Parliament to protect them from legal proceedings.[1] Presumably such an Act would not indemnify them for acts done otherwise than in the course of *bona fide* operations for the suppression of the insurrection: *Wright* v. *Fitzgerald* (1798), 27 St. Tr. 765. But in the absence of such an enactment, it would seem that the acts of the military during war or rebellion could be challenged in the courts, though the action would not be tried so long as a state of hostilities continued: *Higgins* v. *Willis*, [1921] 2 I.R. 386.

The *Marais Case* was followed by the Irish courts in 1920–21. At that time the Restoration of Order in Ireland Act, 1920, was in force. That Act gave exceptional powers to the Executive, and the military were employed to execute those powers. In *The King* v. *Allen*, [1921] 2 I.R. 241; K. & L. 450, the King's Bench Division of Ireland accepted the statement of the military authority that the statutory powers were insufficient and declined to interfere with a sentence passed by a military tribunal, which was not a statutory court-martial, sitting in an area where the rebellion was raging. In one case the statutory powers were exceeded and the prisoner was released as the result of habeas corpus proceedings: *Egan* v. *Macready*, [1921] 1 I.R. 265. The decision of the Irish Chancery Division in the last-named case is difficult to reconcile with *The King* v. *Allen* and has been criticised on the ground that the exceptional statutory powers were not, like the statutory powers in the *De Keyser Case*,[2] exclusive of the common law powers, and that the common law gives the Executive the right to conduct operations without interference from the courts, if a state of war is raging. The better opinion is that inadequacy of statutory powers does not disable the military from taking whatever steps are deemed necessary in good faith to restore order.[3]

There is only one decision on martial law which can be regarded as binding on an English court. The House of Lords in *Re Clifford and O'Sullivan* (*ante*), (a case from Ireland before the establishment of the Irish Free State), discussed an application for a writ of

Cases from Ireland.

Prohibition.

---

[1] See *Tilonko* v. *Attorney-General of Natal*, [1907] A.C. 93, for an unsuccessful petition for leave to appeal from a judgment of a military court, the sentences of which had been subsequently declared lawful by the legislature of the Colony.
[2] P. 145, *ante*. [3] P. 422, *ante*.

prohibition to stay proceedings of a military tribunal set up after a proclamation of martial law. The decision turned upon the technical scope of the writ, which is only available against persons or bodies in the nature of inferior courts exercising a jurisdiction. It was held that the military tribunal in question was not such a body, but only an advisory committee of officers to assist the commander-in-chief, against which the writ could not lie. The House of Lords expressly refrained from discussing the merits of an application under a writ of habeas corpus or other process than prohibition.

Conclusion.   Thus the law, if it be correctly stated above, affords little protection to persons in a martial law area, at all events to those who have been convicted of capital offences under the military regime. If the courts are not sitting, they have no remedy. If the courts are in session, an order of prohibition, according to the decision in *Re Clifford and O'Sullivan* (*ante*) will not be granted, while the writ of habeas corpus is probably only available if the courts hold that war was not raging at the time of the commission of the offence (*The King* v. *Allen, ante*). On the other hand, it must be noted that neither *Marais*' nor *Allen's Cases* are binding on the English courts, which are, therefore, competent to say, should occasion arise, that even during a state of war the acts of the military are subject to the controlling jurisdiction exercisable by means of the writ of habeas corpus.

The United Kingdom: First World War.   Although the military obtained, under the Defence of the Realm Acts, 1914–15, a large measure of control in the United Kingdom and in Ireland, it cannot be claimed, apart from the Irish disturbances, that at any time between 1914 and 1918 a state of war was raging, despite hostilities by way of occasional enemy air-raids and bombardments from the sea. The control exercised during that period over the civilian population was strictly legal, while the courts were exercising, under certain statutory restrictions, their full functions. By the first of the Defence of the Realm Acts passed in 1914 trial by court-martial was authorised for the enforcement of regulations forbidding the sending of information to the enemy or for securing the means of communication, such as the railways and docks. Later there were added to the offences triable by court-martial rumour-mongering and offences against the Defence Regulations committed in areas where troops were being trained or concentrated. The Defence of the Realm (Admt.) Act, 1915, drastically curtailed the jurisdiction of courts-martial to try offences against the Regulations (except in case of invasion) and restored to British subjects the right to be tried by a jury in a civil court for those offences which had hitherto been punishable by courts-martial. Both civil and military authorities exceeded their legal powers from time to time, and there were many cases of the courts intervening at the instance of persons aggrieved. It is of interest to reproduce here the main operative section of the Indemnity Act, 1920, which, subject to certain provisos, expressly restricted the indemnity afforded to the authorities to acts done in good faith and in the public interest.

> No action or other legal proceeding whatsoever, whether civil or criminal, shall be instituted in any court of law for or on account of or in respect of any act, matter or thing done, whether within or without His Majesty's dominions, during the war before the passing of this Act, if done in good faith, and done or purported to be done in the execution of his duty or for the defence of the realm or the public safety, or for the enforcement of discipline, or otherwise in the public interest, by a person holding office under or employed in the service of the Crown in any capacity, whether naval, military, air force, or civil, or by any other person acting under the authority of a person so holding office or so employed; and, if any such proceeding has been instituted whether before or after the passing of this Act, it shall be discharged and made void. . . .

Indemnity Act, 1920, s. 1 (1).

In 1939 Parliament was not asked to supersede the jurisdiction of the ordinary courts by conferring on courts-martial the power to try persons not subject to military law. When in 1940 it became necessary to modernise the law of treason by creating the equivalent offence of treachery, the bar on trial by courts-martial was lifted, but only in respect of enemy aliens on the specific direction of the Attorney-General: Treachery Act, 1940. Trial by court-martial must be distinguished from trial by special civil courts. The Emergency Powers (Defence) (No. 2) Act, 1940, which was passed under the imminent threat of invasion, made it possible to substitute for a central system of administration of the criminal law a system of special war zone courts. These courts were only to exercise jurisdiction if the military situation was such, on account of actual or immediately apprehended military action, that criminal justice must be more speedily administered than it could be by the ordinary courts.[1] It was a condition precedent to the exercise of jurisdiction that the Minister of Home Security should first declare a particular area to be a war zone. The constitution of the war zone courts was essentially that of civil courts of record. They were never required to sit. These provisions only governed the procedure to be followed by the civil courts in the event of invasion. They did not in any way affect the common law powers of the military, but the fact that they were enacted on the eve of invasion shows the utter abhorrence of our people to any form of martial law, whatever be the academic

Second World War.

[1] The Administration of Justice (Emergency Provisions) Act, 1939, had made elastic provisions for the sittings of the ordinary courts "so that the Lord Chancellor could adapt the whole judicial system to the requirements of unforeseen crises." See Sir Cecil Carr, *Concerning English Administrative Law* (Cambridge University Press), p. 81.

doctrine with regard to the powers of the military to impose their will on civilians.

Contrast between First and Second World War.

In 1914 the range of offences triable by court-martial at first grew in number, but within seven months of the outbreak of war the right to trial by jury in a civil court had been restored to British subjects. In 1939 it was not intended to deprive the ordinary courts of jurisdiction, but the threat of invasion in the next year necessitated provision to guard against a breakdown in the ordinary administration of justice, and a solution was found which stopped short of substituting courts-martial for the ordinary courts. Thus within a few months of the outbreak of both wars trial in the ordinary courts was safeguarded except in the event of invasion. In 1915 courts-martial were to replace the civil courts in that event. In 1940 special civil courts were substituted, except that enemy aliens could for the most grave of all war-time offences be tried by court-martial.

PART X.

THE BRITISH COMMONWEALTH.

Constitutional Laws of the Commonwealth, Jennings and Young, Chapters I–III (Clarendon Press); a case book with introductory chapters.

Halsbury, *Laws of England*, 3rd edn., Vol. 5, Title *Commonwealth and Dependencies*, ed. S. A. de Smith and Olive M. Stone (Butterworths).

The Statute of Westminster and Dominion Status, by K. C. Wheare (Clarendon Press).

The Development of the Legislative Council, 1606–1945, by Martin Wight (Faber and Faber).

CHAPTER 1.

THE UNITED KINGDOM, CHANNEL ISLANDS AND ISLE OF MAN.

ENGLAND and Wales, Scotland and Northern Ireland form the United Kingdom of Great Britain and Northern Ireland. Though England and Wales and Scotland possess a common legislature,[1] and are united for most purposes of central government,[2] Scotland has her own system of law and her own courts,[3] and her own established Church.[4] The Parliament of the United Kingdom has functions in relation to colonial territories overseas, and, as such, exercises legislative supremacy over the Colonies and still has a special relationship with Canada on a few subjects of constitutional amendment.

Northern Ireland possesses her own Executive, a Governor-General and Cabinet, and a Legislature of two Houses, the Senate and House of Commons. It was originally intended that Ireland should be given a wide measure of Home Rule, while remaining part of the United Kingdom. Though abandoned as far as Southern Ireland was concerned, the constitution enacted with this intention by the Government of Ireland Act, 1920, came into force in Northern Ireland. Northern Ireland has retained representation in the United Kingdom Parliament and is subject to its legislative supremacy. Certain subjects, *e.g.* laws in respect of the Crown, treaties and foreign relations generally, defence, foreign trade and coinage are reserved for the United Kingdom Government and Parliament. From the courts of Northern Ireland appeal lies to the House of Lords. Constitutional issues may be referred for determination to the

Northern Ireland.

---

[1] Part III., Chap. 1.
[3] Part V., Chap. 1.
[2] Part IV., Chap. 5.
[4] Part XI.

Judicial Committee of the Privy Council.[1] In the event of a deadlock between the Senate and the House of Commons the Governor-General may, if a Bill is passed by the House of Commons in two successive sessions and is not agreed to by the Senate, convene a joint sitting of the two Houses. Any Bill passed by a majority at such a joint sitting becomes law. In the case of a financial Bill a joint sitting may be convened in the same session that the Bill is rejected.

The relationship thus established between the United Kingdom and Northern Ireland is not unlike a federal one with the important difference that the Parliament of the United Kingdom can legislate in amplification or in derogation of the powers of the Parliament of Northern Ireland. The Northern Ireland (Miscellaneous Provisions) Act, 1932, removed some of the causes of friction to which this relationship had given rise by giving the Parliament of Northern Ireland some additional powers, *e.g.* to enable the repeal and re-enactment of imperial legislation for purposes of consolidation. The Ireland Act, 1949, which recognised that Southern Ireland (Eire) ceased to be part of Her Majesty's dominions, affirmed that Northern Ireland remained part of the United Kingdom and that its status would not be altered without the consent of the Parliament of Northern Ireland.

Channel Islands.   The Channel Islands and the Isle of Man are included among the British Isles, but do not form part of the United Kingdom. Their citizens are entitled to be known as "of the United Kingdom, Islands and Colonies." [2] The laws of the Channel Islands are based on the ancient customs of the Duchy of Normandy, of which they formed part until 1204; this particularly applies to land law, inheritance and judicial procedure. The sovereignty of Her Majesty is, to the present day, only admitted in her right as successor to the Dukes of Normandy. The Channel Islands are subject to the legislative supremacy of the United Kingdom Parliament, which is exercised for them in relation to such subjects as nationality and defence. The legislative assemblies of Jersey and Guernsey, known as the States, have power to pass enactments which require the approval of the Queen in Council. The States of Guernsey legislate for the adjoining islands, Alderney, Sark, Herm and Jethou; the first two named have their own subordinate legislatures. Both Jersey and Guernsey possess their separate courts with unlimited civil and criminal jurisdiction. Alderney and Sark have courts with unlimited civil jurisdiction, but with limited powers in criminal causes. An appeal lies to the Judicial Committee of the Privy Council.[3] The Crown claims the right to

---

[1] Government of Ireland Act, 1920, s. 51.

[2] British Nationality Act, 1948, s. 33 (2).

[3] The Report of the Committee of the Privy Council (Cmd. 7074, 1947) recommended several changes which have been put into operation and proposed a joint court of appeal for Jersey and Guernsey which has not yet been set up.

legislate for the Islands by Order in Council, but it is doubtful how far such Orders in Council, which are registered in the Royal Courts of the Islands, are effectual until so registered.[1] The States and Royal Courts of Jersey and Guernsey are presided over by a Bailiff appointed by the Crown. Each Island has its own Law Officers (Attorney-General and Solicitor-General) similarly appointed by the Crown.

The Isle of Man has its own Parliament, known as the Tynwald Isle of Man. Court; it consists of the Governor and Council and the House of Keys. There is a general power to legislate subject to the approval of the Queen in Council. The Isle of Man also has its own courts, from which an appeal lies to the Judicial Committee of the Privy Council.

[1] The Royal Courts may request reconsideration of an Order in Council, but can in the last resort be compelle to register it: Halsbury, *Laws of England* (3rd. ed.), Vol. 5, p. 648.

CHAPTER 2.

THE COLONIES, PROTECTORATES AND TRUST TERRITORIES.

Classifica-
tion.

UNTIL recently the British Commonwealth overseas fell into two clearly distinguishable groups. Together with the United Kingdom as free and equal members of the British Commonwealth of nations were Canada, Australia, New Zealand, South Africa, India, Pakistan, Ceylon, and for most purposes Southern Rhodesia. The Colonial Empire on the other hand consisted of a large number of territories, all of which were subject to the legislative supremacy of the Parliament of the United Kingdom and to the right of the Crown to disallow on the advice of the Secretary of State for the Colonies the enactments of their legislatures. But the now generally accepted policy of self-government has resulted in a rapid advance in the case of some important colonial territories to a status of virtually complete internal independence. This has been effected by the introduction of constitutions granting a full or partial measure of ministerial responsibility to the local executive councils. In the result, although no colony has been added to full membership of the Commonwealth, a few, like the Gold Coast in particular, are no longer in practice subordinate to the United Kingdom Government and Parliament as regards internal government. The inhabitants of the colonial territories have the status of British subjects by virtue of a common citizenship with those of the United Kingdom, whereas such status in the Commonwealth is acquired by local citizenship laws.

All the overseas members of the Commonwealth have evolved out of colonies, except India and Pakistan, which, however, so far as they formed part of the old Indian Empire (as distinct from the Native States) were ruled through a Secretary of State who was responsible, as a member of the Cabinet, to the United Kingdom Parliament. A series of Government of India Acts reflected constitutional development in the Indian sub-continent. Some knowledge then of the constitutional status of a colony is needed for the study of the evolution of colonies to independence or, as the expression was until recently, to Dominion status. Most of the Protectorates and Trust Territories are governed under the prerogative as extended by the Foreign Jurisdiction Acts, 1890–1913, much as colonial territory is governed. Their inhabitants are not citizens of the United Kingdom and Colonies, though as British protected persons they are distinguishable from aliens and have limited privileges as regards acquiring citizenship by naturalisation.

The inhabitants of the colonial territories are mainly non-European, those of the older States in the Commonwealth are European in origin except in South Africa where the ruling Europeans are heavily outnumbered; in India, Pakistan and Ceylon the population is Asiatic, but cabinet government on United Kingdom lines has been accepted as the basis of their constitutions. While the ultimate goal of all territories is self-government, its attainment may be remote in some of the smaller or more backward territories. For some of these federation may be the solution; for a few the kind of autonomy enjoyed by the Channel Islands may be sought.

Variety and individuality have long been features of the British colonial system. Colonial constitutions are not of a standard pattern. Variety extends to the franchise and to methods of election to legislative councils where these exist. Colonial constitutions are mainly enacted (1) by letters patent issued by the Queen in Council constituting the office of Governor and providing for the government of the colony (including, if necessary by separate letters patent, provision for a legislative council) and (2) by formal instructions to the Governor issued by the Queen under the royal sign manual. The appointment of a Governor is by commission under the royal sign manual countersigned by the Secretary of State for the Colonies.[1]

The Colonial System.

It is, of course, competent for the Parliament of the United Kingdom to enact a colonial constitution. In the past this was done to give settlers from Great Britain and Ireland representative legislatures or to give legal force to a constitution Bill promoted by a colonial legislature before the enactment of the Colonial Laws Validity Act, 1865 [2]; see, for example, the Victoria Constitution Act, 1855. Nowadays even where statutory authority is required, as with legislative councils constituted under the British Settlements Act, 1887,[3] or in the case of protectorates, the Foreign Jurisdiction Act, 1890,[4] or by separate Act, such as the British Guiana Act, 1928, Parliament authorises the Crown to grant a constitution as a whole or constitutional amendment by Order in Council.

When settlers annexed for the Crown territory which had no civilised system of law, the law of the colony was the common law of England and, in so far as it was applicable, the statute law existing at the time of the settlement. The Crown could grant institutions, but could not take away rights; it had no powers of legislation; nor could it impose a tax. It followed that in such colonies changes in the constitution, like all changes of law, could only be effected by Act of the United Kingdom Parliament. But in 1887 general powers

Distinction between Settled Colonies and those acquired by Conquest or Cession.

---

[1] See "The Making of a Colonial Constitution" (Singapore), by O. Hood-Phillips, 71 L.Q.R. 51, for an interesting account of the negotiations and stages in the enactment of a new colonial constitution.

[2] P. 448, *post*.   [3] P. 434, *post*.   [4] P. 443, *post*.

to alter the constitutions of settled colonies were granted to the Crown (acting by delegation if desired) by the British Settlements Act.[1] The Act applied to any settled colonies which were not at that time within the jurisdiction of a colonial legislature, *e.g.* the Falkland Islands, the Gold Coast. Thus for constitutional purposes henceforth there was no difference between such colonies and those which had been acquired by conquest or cession. For in the latter case it always had been, and still is, competent for the Crown to legislate by prerogative. But in colonies so acquired there was no automatic application of English law, the law in force at the time of the conquest or cession remaining in force until altered. Illustrations of this are to be found to-day in the Union of South Africa and in Ceylon, where the basic law is Roman-Dutch, and in Quebec where the pre-Napoleonic French law still provides the common law of the Province.

Rule in
Campbell v.
Hall.

So far as the form of government is concerned it rests with the Crown to grant or withhold a constitution as a matter of prerogative right in the case of territory which has been ceded to it or conquered. But once a grant of a representative legislature has been made to such a colony, the power to legislate or to raise taxes by prerogative is irrevocably abandoned, so long as the legislature continues in existence. This was laid down in the great case of *Campbell* v. *Hall* in 1774 in relation to the Island of Granada. But there may be expressly reserved by the instrument creating the legislature, or by a subsequent Act of the Parliament of the United Kingdom, a power of concurrent legislation by prerogative.[2] The definition of representative legislature given by section 5 of the Colonial Laws Validity Act, 1865,[3] is limited to that Act. When *Campbell* v. *Hall* was decided such a legislature meant any assembly of the inhabitants summoned by the Crown. In the days of the old Colonial Empire, which came to an end with the revolt of the North American Colonies, elected majorities sat in most legislative councils along with the Governor and his Executive Council, but with the advent of colonies with an overwhelming preponderance of native inhabitants the acquisition of a representative legislature only comes as a stage in the process of acquiring self-governing powers. In practice in most letters patent creating colonial constitutions with representative legislatures power is expressly reserved to revoke the grant. Where the Crown, as in Ceylon, originally a conquered and ceded colony, had reserved the

---

[1] British Settlements Act, 1945, removed the requirement that delegation must be to three or more persons.
[2] *Campbell* v. *Hall* (1774), Lofft. 655; K. & L. 487; J. & Y. 57; as interpreted in *Sammut* v. *Strickland*, [1938] A.C. 678, especially at p. 704, which makes it clear that the continued existence of the legislature is requisite. If the legislature is surrendered, the prerogative is revived.
[3] P. 448, *post*.

power to revoke, alter or amend the constitution, the power could be exercised retrospectively and this is the position to-day in the case of such colonies. *In Abeyesekera* v. *Jayatilake*, [1932] A.C. 260, the respondent had rendered himself liable to penalties for sitting and voting in the Ceylon Legislative Council by reason of disqualification under an Order in Council of 1923; it was held that a later Order of 1928 had retrospectively removed the disqualification. Where power to legislate is not reserved, an Act of the Imperial Parliament is necessary to authorise constitutional amendment by Order in Council.[1] Many colonies which in early colonial days received grants of representative legislatures subsequently surrendered their constitutions and received in exchange constitutions which reserved the right of the Crown to legislate by Order in Council. Thus to the greater number of colonies the rule in *Campbell* v. *Hall* has no application. The intervention of Parliament is not required to make changes in the constitution. These can be effected by Order in Council or Letters Patent on the advice of the Secretary of State for the Colonies after consultation with the Governor.

Where annexation was the result of a treaty of cession with a native ruler, the treaty might contain provisions preserving or modifying private or community rights.[2] The annexation of territory is, however, an act of State[3] and an obligation undertaken upon annexation to protect private property, though in accordance with international law, is not enforceable by a municipal tribunal, unless the terms of the treaty of cession have been made part of municipal law.[4] An act of State must be accepted as effective,[5] and no special formality is required for annexation.[6]

Annexation.

The great legal landmark in colonial constitutional law, the Colonial Laws Validity Act, 1865, will be discussed in the next chapter as part of the evolution to self-government and Commonwealth status. Here it is sufficient to remark that it made colonial legislatures supreme in their own spheres and therefore able to change the common law of England or whatever system prevailed in the colony; but so long as they remain subject to the Parliament at

Powers of Colonial Legislature.

---

[1] There is no justification for the suggestion made in *North Charterland Exploration Co.* v. *The King*, [1931] 1 Ch. 169, that the rule in *Campbell* v. *Hall* has no effect since the passing of the Foreign Jurisdiction Acts, 1890–1913. These Acts, which regulate the exercise by the Crown of jurisdiction in foreign territory, have no application to British territory, and the rule is still of authority; see *Abeyesekera* v. *Jayatilake* (*ante*).

[2] *Amodu Tijani* v. *Secretary, Southern Nigeria*, [1921] 2 A.C. 399.

[3] Part IV., Chap. 10, A.

[4] *Cook* v. *Sprigg*, [1899] A.C. 572; *Hoani Te Heuheu Tukino* v. *Aotea District Maori Land Board*, [1941] A.C. 308; *Secretary of State for India* v. *Sardar Rustam Khan*, [1941] A.C. 356.

[5] *Salaman* v. *Secretary of State for India*, [1906] 1 K.B. 613; K. & L. 104.

[6] *In re Southern Rhodesia*, [1919] A.C. 211, at p. 238.

Westminster, they cannot change statute law contained in such Acts of Parliament as apply to the colonies, *e.g.* the British Nationality Act, 1948. Moreover in a colony that possesses a representative legislature (a legislative body of which at least one-half the members of one house are elected by inhabitants of the colony) the legislature may amend its constitution freely, provided that such amendments do not conflict with either imperial or local legislation, which prescribes any particular procedure for constitutional amendment. The power of amendment will not, however, extend to a complete abdication of its functions by a legislature which attempts to create and endow with its own capacity a new legislative body not created by the Act to which it owes its own existence: *In re the Initiative and Referendum Act*, [1919] A.C. 935. Non-representative legislatures are not given power to amend the constitution.

Governors.   The Governor of a colony is both in form and in fact the executive. There are some fifty dependencies which are thus subject to the direct rule of the Governor. In most cases he is assisted by an executive council which he must consult, though he is only required to follow its advice so far as responsibility for certain subjects is under the constitution entrusted to members chosen from the legislative council to act as Ministers. Formerly this was never the case and the personal rule of the Governor could prevail over the advice of his executive council, if need be. There are still a few territories where there is no executive council at all, and several others without a legislative council. In some thirty-five colonies there are both executive and legislative councils, usually uni-cameral bodies of elected members, together with the chief officials and a number of unofficial members appointed by the Governor. Most councils are thus semi-representative; in some the representative element predominates, but the Governor cannot be held responsible to the legislature and therefore cabinet government with the executive responsible to the legislature does not prevail. That stage of constitutional development is only reached when the Governor receives instructions which require him to select his executive council from members of the legislative council who can command a majority in that body. Then self-government is attained, though it may be applied, as in the Gold Coast and Malta, with reservations as to special topics, such as defence and foreign affairs. The Governor is appointed by the Crown, represents the Crown, and is responsible to the Crown. He must obey any instructions that he receives from the Secretary of State for the Colonies through the Colonial Office. The chief officer under the Governor of a colony which has not attained to responsible government is the Colonial Secretary. The daily work of administration is performed by district officers who under varying names and forms appear in almost all the colonial territories. As the advance to responsible government progresses, usually by relatively rapid stages, the more senior posts in the administration are filled by a higher proportion of officers who have been recruited locally, in place of expatriate (European) members of the Overseas Civil Service. A Governor is appointed to hold office during Her Majesty's pleasure, but does not normally hold office for more than six years. He derives his authority from his commission. He does not by virtue of his office enjoy the full immunities or prerogatives of the Queen, but only such as are expressly or impliedly conferred upon him by statute or by his commission.[1] The commission does not enumerate specific powers, but refers to the letters patent constituting the office of Governor and providing for the government of the colony and to the instructions to the Governor of the colony. These two documents form the constitution of a colony. The former lays down the constitutional framework, *e.g.* it provides for the establishment of an executive council. The latter sets out the Governor's duties, *e.g.* it provides for the Governor's obligation to consult his executive council.

A Governor, as such, does not enjoy any immunities from criminal or civil liability. It is, however, a defence if he can prove that an act which is otherwise tortious was done by him within the authority of the Crown and that his commission gives him power to exercise that authority. Thus it is unlikely that a colonial civil servant could successfully sue the Governor of his colony in respect of damages alleged to have been suffered from disciplinary action taken against him in his official work. But in *Musgrave* v. *Pulido* (1879), 5 App. Cas. 102, where an action for trespass was brought against the Governor for the seizure and detention of a ship at Kingston in Jamaica, the Judicial Committee rejected the defences based on privilege and on act of State. A Governor is liable in contract in respect of his obligations entered into in a private capacity, *e.g.* for household goods; but he is not personally liable in damages for breach of a contract entered into on behalf of the government service.[2] A Governor may be sued in respect of civil liability (contract or tort) either in the courts of his colony[3] or in England,[4] but if

Legal Liabilities of Governor.

---

[1] This applies also, as does the method of appointment, to a Governor-General of a Commonwealth State; see, however, p. 473, *post.*

[2] *Macbeath* v. *Haldimand* (1786), 1 T.R. 172. The proper remedy was formerly by Petition of Right; under the Crown Proceedings Act, 1947, which only applies to proceedings brought in a court in the United Kingdom, it would appear to be an action against the Secretary of State for the Colonies or the Attorney General if the action was in respect of a contract which could be enforced in the United Kingdom. In some cases the law of the colony makes express provision for suits being brought against the local Attorney-General, acting for the colonial government.

[3] *Hill* v. *Bigge* (1841), 3 Moo. P.C. 465.

[4] *Mostyn* v. *Fabrigas* (1774), 1 Cowp. 161; *Phillips* v. *Eyre* (1870), L.R. 6 Q.B. 1; K. & L. 492.

the action is brought in England the injury complained of must be tortious both under English law and the law of the colony and the action can therefore be barred if the colonial legislature has passed an Act of Indemnity.[1] It is possible that a Governor may be prosecuted in the courts of his colony for a criminal offence, but such a contingency is unlikely; moreover the Governor has delegated to him the prerogative of pardon. In practice proceedings in respect of crimes alleged against a Governor would be tried in England at a court of assize.[2] The question of the prosecution of a colonial Governor is hardly likely to arise nowadays, but the matter is one of some obscurity.

Colonial Constitutions.

It is not proposed to attempt any classification of colonial constitutions, nor to describe the detailed constitutions of any colony. Professor Martin Wight in his study, *The Development of the Legislative Council, 1606–1945*, has shown the considerable difficulties of any generalised narrative. He gives[3] a classification as in 1945 under nine headings, but since then there have been many changes which call for modification of the list. Suffice it to say here that there are a few dependencies where the Governor rules without even an executive council; that some lack as yet legislative councils; that in others the legislative council is wholly nominated, though containing both official and unofficial members; or contains only a minority of elected members; that other legislative councils are without an official majority, but only a minority of the unofficial members are elected as distinct from being nominated; that finally there are an increasing number of colonies where a majority of elected members compose the legislature, with an executive council responsible to that majority, at all events for most subjects of internal government. In these colonies the executive council rather than the Governor is the principal instrument for determining policy. Surviving from the old representative system of the first Empire are the constitutions of the Bahamas, Barbados and Bermuda where the bi-cameral system obtains, the legislative council (the upper house) being nominated and the assembly wholly elected. There are great variations in the franchise. Some colonies have universal adult suffrage; elsewhere property, linguistic and other qualifications are required.

The Official Element.

The official element is composed of those who sit in the legislative council by virtue of their office in the colonial executive. In addition to the Governor who presides, members of the executive

---

[1] *Phillips* v. *Eyre* (ante).

[2] 11 Wm. 3, c. 12 (The Governors Act) and 42 Geo. 3, c. 85, as amended by the Criminal Justice Act, 1948, 10th Schedule. These Acts do not extend to felonies: *The King* v. *Shawe* (1816), 5 M. & S. 403, but any British subject can be tried in England for certain crimes wherever committed, *e.g.* murder, manslaughter, bigamy.

[3] *Op. cit.*, App. 8.

council such as the Colonial Secretary, the Attorney-General, the Financial Secretary, the Director of Medical Services, the Secretary for Native Affairs will sit along with other directors of departments who are not members of the executive council. Thus there is assured a body of homogeneous opinion which assures the executive council of support from the legislature.

A few years ago it was possible to make the generalisation that the official majority was the very kernel and essence of Crown colony government.[1] It is still the characteristic institution in the smaller or less developed colonies. Since the consent to legislation and to the annual estimates is assured where the official element forms a majority, it may well be asked whether a legislative council is really legislative in its function as the capacity of unofficial members is advisory only. But it does secure a full and public discussion of legislative proposals, even if it fails to create effective political authority in the unofficial element, whether nominated or elected. Moreover it affords a platform for the discussion of grievances arising from the administrative services in just the same way as the Opposition in the House of Commons can ventilate such grievances on Supply Days.[2]

The powers of colonial legislatures are fixed by the instrument, prerogative or statutory, which grants the constitution. Power is given to legislate for the peace, order and good government of the colony. Any limitations or reservations are contained in the Governor's powers or those of the Government of the United Kingdom, *i.e.* (1) the veto of the Governor or of the Crown on the advice of the Secretary of State, (2) the Crown's power of disallowance which, where the power exists, may override the Governor's assent, (3) the power of the Crown itself to enact overriding legislation, a power which is in practice only used for constitutional changes, and (4) the power of Parliament to pass legislation applying to the colony. The extent to which in practice these powers are made use of depends on the stage of constitutional development which a colony has reached.

Powers of Colonial Legislatures.

Within its territorial limits and subject to the rule enacted in the Colonial Laws Validity Act, 1865, s. 2, that any colonial law repugnant to an Act of the Imperial Parliament extending to the colony (or any order or regulation made under such Act) shall to the extent of such repugnancy be void and inoperative, a colonial legislature has full power and is not the delegate of the Imperial Parliament. It can, therefore, itself delegate the power to legislate by regulation to the executive officials of the colony: *Hodge* v. *The Queen* (1883),

[1] Sir Anton Bertram, *The Colonial Service* (Cambridge University Press), p. 168; Wight, *op. cit.*, pp. 73, 100–1.
[2] Part III, chap. 3.

9 App. Cas. 117; *Powell* v. *Apollo Candle Co.* (1885), 10 App. Cas. 282; J. & Y. 65. In some cases power to legislate with extra-territorial operation has been conferred by Acts of the Imperial Parliament; Merchant Shipping Act, 1894, ss. 735, 736; Emergency Powers (Defence) Act, 1939, s. 5.

Reservation and Disallowance.
All colonial legislation requires the assent of the Governor. The Governor may either refuse his assent at once, or may reserve a Bill until the pleasure of the Crown, which means the pleasure of the Imperial Government, is known. A Governor's instructions contain provisions requiring the reservation of specific classes of legislation, and similarly where the constitution is contained in a statute, the statute usually makes specific provision for the reservation of special classes of measures. Apart from his instructions a Governor may on his own initiative reserve a Bill. Frequently a Bill itself contains a clause providing for reservation. Even when the Governor's assent has been given, the Crown may disallow colonial legislation. The various constitutions provide for the period, usually one or two years, within which the power to disallow may be exercised. Where there is a non-official majority in a colonial legislature but fully responsible government has not been granted, the constitution usually provides that the Governor may, when essential for law and order, pass legislation without the consent of the legislature.

Courts in the Colonies.
In every colonial territory there is a court of unlimited jurisdiction established by Order in Council or local statute. The judges are appointed by the Governor, on the instructions of the Queen which are given through the Secretary of State for the Colonies, as the responsible Minister. They hold office at the pleasure of the Crown, but it has been the practice since 1870 that the dismissal of a colonial judge of a superior court should be subject to a reference to the Judicial Committee of the Privy Council.[1] The chief court in each colony is styled the Supreme Court. Certain colonies are grouped together to constitute an appellate court, *e.g.* the East African and West Indian Courts of Appeal. Appeals lie from the highest court in any colony[2] to the Judicial Committee of the Privy Council.[3] A writ of habeas corpus may not issue out of England to any colony which has a court with authority to issue the writ, but where there is no such court in a colony, an English court will grant the writ: Habeas Corpus Act, 1862; cf. *Sprigg* v. *Sigcau*, [1897] A.C. 238.

[1] See Note in [1954] C.L.J. 2–7; and *Terrell* v. *Secretary of State for the Colonies*, [1953] 2 Q.B. 482.
[2] Where colonies are grouped for the purpose of appeals, there is sometimes a right of appeal to the Privy Council from the appellate court only; sometimes both from the appellate court and also direct from the colonial Supreme Court.
[3] Chap. 4, *post*.

Below the level of the Supreme Court (the Chief Justice and Puisne Judges) embodying the independence of the judiciary in all its relations with the executive, there is a great variety of judicial institutions adapted to local conditions. The place of the lay justice of the peace in England is taken by the district magistrate who exercises summary powers as well as investigating in the first instance more serious cases before trial. Often he has limited jurisdiction in civil cases. In Africa in particular his work is discharged by local administrative officers except in a few urban areas. In the smallest colony it may suffice to have a Chief Justice and a single magistrate. Elsewhere there may be an intermediate judiciary working on a centralised system or organised district by district. The jury system in criminal cases prevails in many colonies; in others the trial is by a judge with two or more assessors.

It is not the purpose of this chapter to discuss colonial policy, but the bare bones of colonial constitutions are of little interest unless studied in their proper setting in which racial and economic matters must predominate. Thus the Colonial Development and Welfare Act, 1945, which made available over a ten-year period substantial financial assistance, and the establishment in 1946 of the Colonial Economic and Development Council are steps which are having more far-reaching effects than the constitutional measures, numerous though they are.[1] *Constitutional Developments.*

During the past ten years constitutional changes have been numerous as a direct result of the adoption of the policy of granting a liberal measure of internal self-government in the case of the larger colonies where its introduction is practicable. Nor have constitutional developments been lacking in the smaller territories which may seek autonomy without having the necessary strength to become independent States. One of the more significant developments has taken place in the Gold Coast where a measure of African self-government through an Executive modelled on the Cabinet system has been in operation since 1951. The Governor, however, remains the President of the Cabinet and retains a few important reserved powers in relation to legislation and public services. Nigeria also, which is by far the largest in population of the colonial territories, has made considerable progress towards self-government. Its territory is divided into three principally autonomous regions, but there is a Central Legislature and Council of Ministers whose constitution had to be modified in 1953 in order to implement the need for greater regional autonomy. Further developments have been forecasted for 1956.

[1] The Colonial Empire (1939–47), Cmd. 7167; and the Colonial Territories (1948–49), Cmd. 7715 and the subsequent annual volumes may be consulted on these matters.

Where neighbouring colonies have common interests there is a tendency to develop machinery for consultation. Federation of the West Indian colonies which have common economic and defence problems is nearing attainment.[1] The Windward Islands have a common Governor, so have the Leeward Islands. The federation of Malaya, which is basically a group of protected States, was achieved in 1947.[2] The aim of British policy is the development of federation at such time as the balance of opinion in the various colonies is in favour of a change. Services which are suggested for centralised administration in the case of groups of colonies, as in particular in the West Indies, are defence, customs, income tax, penal administration, communications, research and planning; administrative, medical, legal and police services could be unified and administered by a central authority. In East Africa there is a High Commission which is responsible for certain common services such as railways, customs, posts and telegraphs for Kenya, the protectorates of Uganda and Zanzibar, and the trust territory of Tanganyika. The Commission has a permanent secretariat and a central assembly has been established. During the Second World War common supply and production boards were established for the four territories. In West Africa the necessities of defence led in 1942 to the appointment of a Minister Resident to preside over regular conferences of the Governors of the West African colonies and protectorates, but this was a war-time measure only.

Bases have been leased to the United States for ninety-nine years on several West Indian Islands, the Bahamas and British Guiana, and a joint Anglo-American Caribbean Commission was established in 1942 to effect collaboration in that area. The Commission inaugurated a regular system of West Indian Conferences with a continuing existence and a central secretariat. There are four British members of the Commission, two of whom are elected by the colonial legislatures.

B.
Protectorates and Trust Territories.

Foreign Jurisdiction Acts, 1890–1913.

There is little difference between the administration of some of the colonies and that of some other territories (protectorates) which have come under the control of the Government of the United

---

[1] *Report of West Indian Conference held in Barbados*, 1944, Colonial Office, No. 187, and *Closer Association of the British West Indian Colonies*, 1947 (Cmd. 7120). A Standing Committee was set up in 1947 to work out proposals for federation. See for the scheme proposed Report by the Conference on West Indian Federation, 1953, (Cmd. 8837) and *Plan for a British Caribbean Federation* (Cmd. 8895, 1953).

[2] *Federation of Malaya*, 1947 (Cmd. 7171).

Kingdom. The legal distinction is that, while a colony is part of Her Majesty's dominions, the other territories are not. But for constitutional purposes the Foreign Jurisdiction Acts, 1890–1913, authorise the Crown to exercise jurisdiction in the same and in as ample a measure as if the territory had been acquired by conquest or cession. The territories in question are described in the Act of 1890 as those where the Crown has secured the right of government "by treaty, capitulation, grant, usage, sufferance and other lawful means." The Crown legislates for colonial protectorates by Order in Council under the Foreign Jurisdiction Acts. These Acts were originally intended to provide for the exercise by the Crown of jurisdiction over British subjects in foreign countries, where such jurisdiction was acquired by treaty or grant, *e.g.* where British subjects had extra-territorial rights and jurisdiction was exercised by consular and other similar courts. They have, however, been also applied to the exercise of jurisdiction in protectorates over both British protected persons and foreigners: *The King* v. *Crewe, ex parte Sekgome*, [1910] 2 K.B. 576. The issue of an Order in Council under the Foreign Jurisdiction Acts is a legislative act: *North Charterland Exploration Company* v. *The King*, [1931] 1 Ch. 169, and the Crown cannot, except by statute, fetter the subsequent exercise of its right to legislate: *Sobhuza II.* v. *Miller*, [1926] A.C. 518; J. & Y. 26.

But not all such territories are governed as colonies and given constitutions. It may be more convenient to administer a backward area as a protectorate rather than as a colony. This is so in those parts of Africa, particularly the hinterland of colonies, where there is in force the system of indirect rule, which means government by native chiefs who are advised by European officials, members of the colonial administrative service. Other protectorates, usually called protected States as distinct from colonial protectorates, are internally autonomous, only their foreign relations being controlled by the United Kingdom.

An act of the Crown in a protectorate in relation to a native inhabitant is an act of State [1] and cannot be questioned in a British court. In *The King* v. *Crewe, ex parte Sekgome* (*ante*) there was refused an application for a writ of habeas corpus by the chief of a native tribe in Bechuanaland; and Vaughan Williams, L.J., said: "The idea that there may be an established system of law to which a man owes obedience, and that at any moment he may be deprived of the protection of that law, is an idea not easily accepted by English lawyers. It is made less difficult if one remembers that the protectorate is over a country in which a few dominant civilised men have to control a great multitude of the semi-barbarous."

Authority of Crown not Challengeable.

---

[1] Part IV., Chap. 10, A. It is not so in colonies after annexation. For habeas corpus in colonies, see pp. 375 and 440, *ante*.

The Crown is not bound even by the treaty by which the jurisdiction is first acquired; *Sobhuza II.* v. *Miller (ante).* Thus the question is considered as one of English constitutional law and not by reference to the powers which by international law a State may exercise within the territory of another.

Status of Native Inhabitants. All protectorates are treated as foreign territory; their inhabitants are not British subjects and they are not, as such, qualified for citizenship of the United Kingdom and Colonies. They are classified as British protected persons and, as such, enjoy certain advantages as regards qualifying for naturalisation. Strictly speaking they do not owe allegiance to the Crown, but as an equivalent for its protection the duty of obedience may be implied to a practically unlimited extent, as it is in the case of colonial protectorates: *The King* v. *Crewe, ex parte Sekgome,* [1910] 2 K.B. 576, at p. 620, *per* Kennedy, L.J.

The Mandated Territories. After the First World War certain territories formerly administered by Germany and Turkey were by the provisions of the Treaty of Versailles placed under the Crown by the League of Nations. A Permanent Mandates Commission was created by the League to supervise the carrying out of each mandate by the mandatory State. Mandated territories were divided into three classes: Class A, future independent States to which the mandatory must give advice and assistance; Palestine was the principal territory held by the United Kingdom in this class of mandate. The Palestine Act, 1948, determined all jurisdiction of His Majesty in Palestine from May 15, 1948. Class B, *e.g.* Tanganyika, in which the mandatory was responsible for internal administration, but had to provide equal opportunities for trade and commerce to other members of the League of Nations; Class C, *e.g.* the Cameroons, which, subject to certain obligations, might be administered as an integral part of the mandatory's own territory. Mandates of this type were also entrusted to the Dominions, *e.g.* Samoa to New Zealand. The Crown legislated under the Foreign Jurisdiction Acts for mandated territories entrusted to the United Kingdom Government.[1]

Trusteeship Territories. At the end of the Second World War the mandates system was replaced by the trusteeship system.[2] The primary purpose of the system is to promote the political, economic, social and educational advancement of the inhabitants of trust territories. There is an obligation to safeguard the interests of the inhabitants and this is a limitation even upon the duty of ensuring equal treatment in social and economic matters for nationals of all members of the United Nations. The charter recognises as one of the objectives progressive

[1] For the legal basis of Dominion legislation for mandated territories, see *The British Dominions as Mandatories,* by H. V. Evatt (Melbourne University Press).
[2] See Oppenheim, *International Law,* 8th ed., Lauterpacht; Part I Chap. I, section IX,A, for a full account of the new system; section IX. for the mandate system.

development towards self-government or independence. Supervision of the new system is entrusted to the Trusteeship Council, one of the six principal organs of the United Nations. Territories are placed by trusteeship agreements into the following categories; (*a*) territories previously held under a mandate; (*b*) territories detached from defeated States as a result of the Second World War; (*c*) other territories voluntarily placed under the trusteeship system by States hitherto exercising exclusive sovereignty over them. With regard to category (*a*) the United Kingdom, Australia and New Zealand have placed their mandated territory under the new system.[1] The Union of South Africa, which held the mandate for the former German South-West Africa, sought (and is still seeking) to incorporate the territory into the Union. There are not yet any examples of territories falling within categories (*b*) and (*c*).

Responsibility for the administration of trust territories under the United Kingdom Government lies with the Secretary of State for the Colonies and legislation is by Order in Council or other prerogative instrument under the Foreign Jurisdiction Acts.

The inhabitants of a mandated territory owed, in return for the protection afforded, allegiance to the mandatory power. Thus in *The King* v. *Christian*, [1924] A.D. 101, the Supreme Court of South Africa decided that the Union as mandatory power had sufficient internal sovereignty over the South West African territory held under mandate to permit the conviction of an inhabitant for treason. But the inhabitants of a mandated territory retained their original nationality: *The King* v. *Ketter*, [1939] 1 All E. R. 729. The substitution of trusteeship for mandates has made no difference; the inhabitants of trust territory administered by the United Kingdom Government are British protected persons within the definition given in the British Nationality Act, 1948. The British Protectorates, Protected States and Protected Persons Order in Council (S.I., 1949, No. 140), made under the British Nationality Act, 1948, names the territories to which, as colonial protectorates, protected states or trust territories, the Act applies and defines who are to be British protected persons for the purposes of the Act.

Allegiance.

[1] For the United Kingdom, see Mandated and Trust Territories Act, 1947, which applies with modifications the operation of enactments appropriate to mandated territories to trust territories.

CHAPTER 3.

COMMONWEALTH CONSTITUTIONAL RELATIONS.

A.

Introductory.

THE member States of the British Commonwealth are the United
Kingdom, the Dominion of Canada, the Commonwealth of Australia, the Union of South Africa, New Zealand, India, Pakistan and
Ceylon.[1] India is an independent sovereign republic, but has chosen
to remain a member of the Commonwealth. All the other States
proclaimed the accession of the Queen in 1952. Pakistan has since
announced the intention of becoming an Islamic Republic, but of
remaining, like India, within the Commonwealth. The Union of
South Africa and Ceylon, according to their present Governments,
aim at republican status in the near future. In these circumstances
allegiance to the Crown, the legal tie, can scarcely be regarded as a
necessary requirement of membership of the Commonwealth. The
Republic of Ireland and Newfoundland, now a Province of the
Dominion of Canada, are former member States of the Commonwealth. Apart from India and Pakistan which have evolved out of the
Indian Empire and the Native States, the other members have advanced from colonial status in subordination to the United Kingdom
Government to dominion status, as it was until recently called.
Members of the Commonwealth are "equal in status, in no way subordinate one to another in any aspect of their domestic or external
affairs, though united by common allegiance to the Crown and freely
associated as members of the British Commonwealth of Nations." [2]
These words which the Imperial Conference of 1926 accepted from
a committee over which Lord Balfour presided are, so far as they
postulated common allegiance, no longer apt to describe the status
even of the older members. By substituting for a common nationality
law enactments of varying content to determine local citizenship
which, as we have seen,[3] is accepted as the qualification as Commonwealth citizen (a term of law alternative to British subject), the legal
bond depends upon a different law in each State.

We will first discuss the meaning which was given to dominion
status. For, although the advent of the Dominions of Asia has

---

[1] Southern Rhodesia has attended inter-Commmonwealth deliberations; no
doubt the Central African Federation will in future be represented as in 1955.
[2] Imperial Conference, Summary of Proceedings, 1926, Cmd. 2768.
[3] Part IV., Chap. 9.

resulted in the substitution of the term, Commonwealth status, the former term was in universal use in the critical deliberations between the World Wars which resulted in the 1926 formula and the subsequent enactment in 1931 of the Statute of Westminster. In what follows we are primarily concerned with the older member States of the Commonwealth, leaving for separate treatment the advent of the three Asiatic States. It should be remembered that there was no precedent for the evolution of a colony into an autonomous State which nevertheless retained common allegiance to the head of the colonial power to which it was formerly in subjection. This explains why the attainment of independence has been by a process of trial and error in which conventions have been all the time ahead of the rules of constitutional law. Thus when the Imperial Conference (a term now obsolete to describe the periodic meetings of Commonwealth Prime Ministers) in 1926 affirmed that equality of status was the root principle governing the relations of members with one another, it was careful to state: "But the principles of equality and similarity appropriate to status do not universally extend to function. Here we require something more than immutable dogmas." [1] There are now few matters where equality of function has not been attained and in law it is now attainable in all. But at the earlier date the supremacy of the Parliament of the United Kingdom survived and was actively in operation in a few spheres of law, such as nationality, merchant shipping and the royal title.[2] It is in Acts passed at Westminster or in Letters Patent issued by the King in Council in London that are to be found the present constitutions of all the older States and of Ceylon. India has made and Pakistan is in the process of making a constitution; elsewhere amendments, except in Canada, have been made independently within the State affected. Even now Canada on account of dominion-provincial relationship is hesitating before seeking to acquire full constitution-making powers which will no longer require to be enacted at Westminster. But British North America Bills can be sent across the Atlantic with the knowledge that not a comma of the Canadian draftsmen's work will be changed.[3]

All the States have, like the United Kingdom, responsible government, that is, government by an executive which is responsible to, and must normally command a majority in an elected legislature, which alone can impose taxes and without whose authority laws cannot be made. The grant of representative institutions and the establishment of an independent judiciary in a colony have usually been stages on the road to responsible government. An irresponsible

Responsible Government.

---

[1] Imperial Conference, Summary of Proceedings, 1926, Cmd. 2768.

[2] See C., *post*, for amendment of Canadian and New Zealand constitutions. An Act of the United Kingdom Parliament is still required to amend the constitutions of the Australian States.

[3] Pp. 453–4, *post*.

executive cannot for long work in harmony with an elected legislature, and with three exceptions, the Bahamas, Barbados and
Bermuda, those colonies that attained representative institutions
have either advanced to responsible government or abandoned the
institution. Responsible government in the Dominions was inspired
by the Durham Report of 1839. Instructions were first sent to the
Governor of Nova Scotia and to Lord Elgin in Canada in 1848 that
they should act on the advice of Ministers acceptable to the representative legislatures. There followed the grant of responsible
government to Newfoundland, the other colonies of British North
America, and the Australian and South African colonies. In each
case a relaxation of imperial control followed the grant of responsible
government, although, just as responsible government was granted
without being expressly embodied in the several constitutions, so the
formal legal supremacy of the Imperial Parliament was not limited
until the Statute of Westminster, 1931; but for long all these have
exercised complete internal sovereignty and have been free from all
control by the Parliament and Government of the United Kingdom.

Colonial
Laws
Validity
Act, 1865

The first great legal landmark after the granting of responsible
government was the passing of the Colonial Laws Validity Act,
1865. The courts of South Australia, in a series of judgments delivered by Mr. Justice Boothby in the middle of the nineteenth
century, cast doubts upon the validity of colonial legislation that
conflicted with English law. This application of a doubtful common
law rule that legislation by a colonial legislature was void if repugnant to the law of England, whether common law or statute
law, would have stultified the recent grants of responsible government by disabling the legislature over a wide field of legislation.
Accordingly the Act was passed in order to make it plain that within
its own sphere a colonial legislature was sovereign and was subordinate only to the Imperial Parliament. By this Act, "An Act to
remove doubts as to the validity of colonial laws," a legislature is
defined as the authority, other than the imperial Parliament or the
Queen in Council, competent to make laws for the colony and a representative legislature is defined as a legislature comprising a legislative
body of which one-half are elected by the inhabitants of the colony.
The provisions of the Act relate only to colonies possessing legislatures. It was enacted—

(a) that colonial laws which are in any respect repugnant to an
Act of the Imperial Parliament extending to such colony shall
be read subject to such Act and to the extent of such
repugnancy shall be void and inoperative;

(b) that no colonial law shall be void by reason only of repugnancy to the law of England, *i.e.* the common law as opposed
to statute law applicable to the colony;

(c) that no colonial law shall be void by reason of any instructions given to the Governor other than the formal letters patent which authorise the Governor to assent to Bills;

(d) that every colonial legislature shall have power to establish courts of judicature and every colonial representative legislature shall have power to make laws respecting the constitution, powers and procedure of its own body, provided that such laws are passed in such manner and form as may from time to time be required by any Act of Parliament, letters patent, Order in Council, or colonial law for the time being in force in the said colony.

Thus, while the supremacy of the United Kingdom Parliament remained unchallenged, henceforth a colonial legislature could depart from the rules of the common law without fear of challenge in the courts. Nor can the Governor be ordered to revoke his assent to a particular enactment, but must rely upon the provisions as to veto or reservation contained in the constitution of his colony. The provision enabling colonial legislatures to establish courts of justice was essential for the extension to the colony of the independence of the judiciary, a matter which was treated by the United Kingdom Government as a condition precedent to the grant of responsible government.

The final provision may be illustrated by the following case. **Powers of** The Privy Council, affirming a decision of the High Court of **Constitu-** Australia, held invalid a Bill to abolish the Legislative Council of **tional Amendment.** New South Wales which was not passed in accordance with a colonial Act requiring the approval of the electorate to be given to such a measure.[1] The Colonial Laws Validity Act, 1865, required that a law respecting the constitution should be passed in the manner and form provided by existing legislation. The Privy Council rejected the argument that the colonial Act requiring the approval of the electorate was invalid as fettering the freedom of a future legislature, but was not called upon to decide whether the Supreme Court of New South Wales had been right in granting an injunction to restrain the officers of the legislature from presenting the Bill for assent.

During the latter half of the nineteenth century the Dominions **Imperial** attained nationhood rapidly. Since 1887 there had been periodic **Conferences.** conferences for the purpose of consultation between the Governments of the Commonwealth. They were conferences of Governments, meeting under the chairmanship of the Prime Minister of the United Kingdom, not of delegates with power to commit

---

[1] *Attorney-General for New South Wales* v. *Trethowan,* [1932] A.C. 526; J. & Y. 76.

their respective Parliaments. These conferences were first named Imperial Conferences in 1907, when the term, Dominion, was first used in the sense of being contrasted with the term, colony. At the Imperial Conference of 1926 it was realised that political reality had outgrown legal status. The Dominions had obtained, as a result of the Imperial Conference, 1923, the right to make separate treaties with foreign powers in the name of the Crown without the participation of the Imperial Government or Parliament, except that a United Kingdom Secretary of State had to take part in the affixing of the Great Seal to the formal instruments for the grant of full powers and of ratification. The right of separate diplomatic representation had been conceded. The Dominions had complete internal freedom from interference; they were (with the exception of Newfoundland) separate members of the League of Nations; and they had taken their place as equals at the Congress of Versailles held at the close of the First World War, in which they had participated. A conference mainly of experts which reported to the Imperial Conference, 1930, was called to consider how far legal powers should be changed, and brought into line with existing facts. Before considering the recommendations of that conference [1] which resulted in the passing of the Statute of Westminster, 1931, it is convenient to examine the legal limitations upon Dominion autonomy which existed before the passing of that statute, but these limitations cannot properly be appreciated without some outline of the separate constitutions of the older Dominions where government was and is in the hands of a population attuned to the British conception of a parliamentary democracy. Here we may note that the last formal Imperial Conference met in 1937. During the Second World War the Dominions were represented at periodic meetings of the War Cabinet by visiting Ministers or their High Commissioners, but it was not until 1944 that a meeting of Prime Ministers took place in London.[2] Since that date they have been held at intervals for the discussion of common political problems.

B.

Constitutions in the Commonwealth.

Dominion of Canada.

The Dominion of Canada [3] is a federation of ten Provinces. The constitution is based upon the British North America Act, 1867,

---

[1] *Report of the Conference on the Operation of Dominion Legislation and Merchant Shipping Legislation*, 1929 (Cmd. 3479).

[2] For post-war consultation, see p. 475, *post*.

[3] For the Canadian Constitution, see W. P. M. Kennedy, *The Constitution of Canada* (Clarendon Press); R. M. Dawson, *The Government of Canada* (University of Toronto Press).

as amended by subsequent Acts of the Imperial Parliament, of which the latest is the British North America Act, 1951. The Act formed a federation of the self-governing colonies of Canada (Ontario and Quebec), Nova Scotia and New Brunswick. Other Provinces were added later in accordance with the provisions of the British North America Act, 1867. Newfoundland entered the federation on agreed terms of union which were confirmed by the British North America (No. 1) Act, 1949.

Federation pre-supposes a desire for some form of union among independent States, which, though they desire union for certain purposes, nevertheless wish to preserve their identity and some measure of independence. It follows that a federal constitution must be to a large degree a rigid constitution. There must be a distribution of powers between the federal government and the governments of several States forming the federation. If constitutional amendments could be made without the consent of the federating States, there would be no safeguard for the preservation of State rights. Thus the legislature of a federation cannot be supreme in the sense that the Parliament of the United Kingdom possesses supremacy.[1] There must be special machinery for constitutional changes, and there must be some authority, normally the courts of law, which can prevent the federal and state governments from encroaching upon each other's powers, and can declare legislation void on the ground of excess of powers. *(margin: Federation.)*

Just as the Supreme Court is the great safeguard of the constitution in the United States, so the Supreme Court safeguards federalism in Canada. There has been in Canada a further safeguard in the appeal, which was abolished in 1949, from the Canadian courts to the Judicial Committee of the Privy Council,[2] whose decisions have been authoritative in interpreting the provisions of the constitution relating to the respective powers of the Dominion and the Provinces. Further, the Canadian constitution has been based upon Acts of the Imperial Parliament and could only be amended by that legislature, so that any *ultra vires* legislation by either the Dominion or the Provinces would be held by the courts to be invalid as conflicting with Acts of the Imperial Parliament.[3] Such external safeguards are not, however, necessary to federation. In the Commonwealth of Australia they do not exist. The Commonwealth constitution can be amended without any intervention on the part of the Imperial Parliament,[4] *(margin: Safeguards of Federation.)*

[1] Part II., Chap. 2.   [2] Chap. 4, *post.*   [3] P. 449, *ante.*
[4] For an amendment tending towards centralisation, see *New South Wales v. The Commonwealth* (1932), 46 C.L.R. 185, and 49, *L.Q.R.* 329. The amendment, enacted by the Commonwealth Parliament in 1929 (section 105A of the Commonwealth Act, 1900), empowered the Commonwealth to make agreements with the States with respect to the public debts of the States, and authorised that Parliament to make laws for the carrying out by the parties (whether the Commonwealth or the States) of any such agreement.

nor on certain constitutional matters is there an appeal from the High Court of Australia to the Judicial Committee of the Privy Council, except by leave of the High Court itself.

Canada; Dominion Executive and Legislature.

Executive power in the Dominion of Canada is vested in the Governor-General as the Queen's representative, advised by a Privy Council. In Canada, as in all the older Dominions, responsible government rests almost wholly upon convention. The Governor-General acts on the advice of those members of the Privy Council who form the Cabinet and enjoy the confidence of the House of Commons. The Canadian constitution reconciles federalism with cabinet government. It is the practice to divide cabinet posts amongst representatives of the different Provinces. Legislative power is vested in the Governor-General, a Senate of members nominated for life by the Governor-General (on the advice of the Cabinet), and an elected House of Commons. In the Senate there are twenty-four members for each of four territorial divisions, Ontario, Quebec, the Maritime Provinces and Prince Edward Island, and the Western Provinces. There is no provision for avoiding a deadlock between the two chambers, except that the Governor-General may add to the Senate four or eight members representing equally the above four territorial divisions. Such provision should be contrasted with the royal prerogative to create an unlimited number of new peers in the United Kingdom.[1] The House of Commons is composed of members elected for each Province in accordance with its population, the number of seats (255 in 1946) being based on a formula which secures the same proportion of members to population in each Province. Representation is adjusted after each decennial census. Redistribution of seats in the House of Commons is effected by Bill after each census and is governed by fixed rules to secure equality of representation on the basis of the total population.

The Provinces.

The ten Provinces all enjoy responsible government. Executive power is vested in a Lieutenant-Governor, who is appointed by the Governor-General of Canada on the advice of the Dominion Government and is dismissible by the Governor-General, and an Executive Council. The Lieutenant-Governor represents the Crown, and exercises prerogative powers in relation to the Province: *Liquidators of Maritime Bank of Canada* v. *Receiver-General of New Brunswick*, [1892] A.C. 437; J. & Y. 194. Provincial legislatures have the power of constitutional amendment, save that such amendment must not affect the office of Lieutenant-Governor. The Governor-General of the Dominion has the right to disallow provincial legislation, acting on the advice of the Dominion Government. The main reason for disallowance is that a Province has

---

[1] P. 77, *ante*.

clearly exceeded its powers. This is more properly a matter for judicial decision and there tends to be a lessening use of the power to disallow. A provincial statute may also be disallowed on grounds of inequality and injustice.[1] The power is, however, not subject to any legal limitations or restrictions, save that it shall be exercised within a year of the receipt of the Provincial Act by the Governor-General.[2] A provincial legislature is not a delegate either of the Imperial or the Dominion Parliament, but is supreme in its own sphere: *Hodge* v. *The Queen* (1883), 9 App. Cas. 117. Since the passing of the Statute of Westminster, 1931, provincial legislation is not subject to the provisions of the Colonial Laws Validity Act, 1865.

Certain specific powers are by section 92 of the British North America Act, 1867, assigned exclusively to the Provinces. The Dominion has by section 91 a general authority to legislate on all matters not exclusively assigned to the Provinces, and in particular exclusive authority over certain enumerated subjects. The making of criminal law and the regulation of criminal procedure are assigned to the Dominion, but to the Provinces are assigned the constitution and organisation of provincial courts, both civil and criminal, which administer both dominion and provincial law. Appeals from provincial courts lie to the Supreme Court of Canada.[3] The Governor-General may obtain an opinion of law or fact from the Supreme Court. *Distribution of Powers.*

Formerly the constitution of the Dominion, being contained in an Act of the Parliament of the United Kingdom which contained no provisions for amendment, could only be amended by an Act of that Parliament. Such an Act was always passed at the request of both Houses of the Dominion Parliament,[4] *e.g.* when during the First World War the Dominion Government wished to prolong the duration of Parliament, there was passed the British North America Act, 1916; and the British North America Act, 1930, restored their natural resources to the Western Provinces. The British North America Act, 1940, gave to the Dominion power to regulate unemployment insurance;[5] the British North America Act, 1946, provided *Constitutional Amendment.*

[1] *Report of Royal Commission on Dominion and Provincial Relations* (Ottawa, 1940), Book I., p. 254.

[2] *Reference re Power to disallow Provincial Legislation*, [1938] S.C.R. 71.

[3] Supreme Court Act, 1949, s. 3 (R.S.C.) which abolishes all Canadian appeals to the Judicial Committee of the Privy Council.

[4] Such a request should in practice have the concurrence of the Provinces if any change in their legislative powers were proposed; see Imperial Conference, 1930, *Summary of Proceedings*, Cmd. 3717, p. 18, and Canada, *House of Commons Debates*, June 30, 1931. See, however, *The Statute of Westminster and Dominion Status*, by K. C. Wheare, pp. 179 ff. and Dawson, *op. cit.*, pp. 142–9.

[5] Passed on the recommendation of a Royal Commission on dominion-provincial relations which was appointed by the Dominion Government in 1937 and reported in 1940.

for the readjustment of representation in the House of Commons on the basis of the population of Canada.

The British North America (No. 2) Act, 1949, gave legislative authority to the Parliament of Canada to amend the constitution. The enabling provision adds the subject of constitutional amendment to section 91 of the British North America Act, 1867, which enumerates the subjects within the exclusive authority of that Parliament. There are excluded from the new power matters which are by section 92 of the Act of 1867 exclusively assigned to the provincial legislatures, the statutory rights and privileges of those legislatures and governments, matters affecting schools and the use of the English or the French language and the existing requirements of annual sessions and maximum duration of the life of a Parliament of Canada (except in an emergency). Thus the position of the Provinces is still safeguarded by the necessity of amendment of the relevant provisions of the British North America Acts by the Parliament of the United Kingdom. Although the request for amending legislation by custom emanates from the Government of the Dominion in the form of forwarding addresses from both Houses of the ·Dominion Parliament, prior consultation has been customary when proposed legislation has affected the rights of a particular province, but not always when all have been affected.

Commonwealth of Australia. The Commonwealth of Australia is a federation of six self-governing States formed by the Commonwealth of Australia Constitution Act, 1900. Executive power is vested in a Governor-General advised by an Executive Council. In fact, the Cabinet constitutes the Executive Council; there is not as in the United Kingdom and Canada a formal Privy Council distinct from the Cabinet. Legislative power is vested in a Senate with an equal number of members for each State and a House of Representatives. The Senate consists of sixty members, ten being elected by the electors of each State. The House of Representatives is elected on a population basis; the number of representatives chosen by the electors of each State depends upon the population of the State. Voting and registration are compulsory. Thus the Senate, as in the United States, represents State rights, a State with a small population having equal membership with a State with a large population. In the event of a deadlock between the two Houses, the Governor-General may, if the House of Representatives again passes the proposed law after an interval of three months, simultaneously dissolve both Houses, and, if after dissolution a similar deadlock occurs, may convene a joint sitting, at which a law may be passed by an absolute majority.

The States. The States all enjoy responsible government. Their constitutions, unlike those of the Canadian Provinces, were not remodelled at the time of federation. Executive power is vested in Governors advised by Councils. In contrast to Lieutenant-Governors in Canada, State Governors are appointed by the Crown and are still appointed on the advice of the Government of the United Kingdom after consultation with the State concerned. In similar contrast there are direct relations between the States and that Government in relation to the disallowance and reservation of legislation, the terms of which are contained in the Instructions to the Governors. If the dismissal of Mr. Lang, the State Premier, by the Governor of New South Wales in 1932 was constitutional, it would appear that a State Governor has wider constitutional powers than those of a Governor-General of a Dominion. Mr. Lang's Ministry commanded a majority in the Lower House, but was dismissed on the grounds that it was instructing officials to break the law. The States are subject to the provisions of the Colonial Laws Validity Act, 1865.[1]

The States possess all the powers that they possessed at the time of federation, except those exclusively assigned to the Commonwealth. State powers cover most matters which concern the ordinary well-being of the citizen.[2] The Commonwealth possesses only those powers assigned to it by the constitution. Some of the assigned subjects were not within the powers of the States at the time of federation, but where the States had power, that power remains concurrent with that of the Commonwealth, unless the subject of the power is expressed to be exclusively assigned to the Commonwealth. Where, however, on a subject of concurrent powers, a State law is inconsistent with a Commonwealth law, the latter prevails. The State courts exercise both federal and State jurisdiction, except that State Supreme Courts have no jurisdiction over disputes as to the limits *inter se* of the constitutional powers of the Commonwealth and those of any State or States, or as to the limits *inter se* of the constitutional powers of any two or more States.[3] An appeal lies from the State Supreme Courts either to the High Court of Australia or to the Judicial Committee of the Privy Council.[4] The High Court of Australia possesses appellate jurisdiction and also an original federal jurisdiction. {.margin-note: Distribution of Powers.}

The constitution of the Commonwealth is contained in the Schedule to the Commonwealth of Australia Constitution Act, 1900, and may be amended by a law which has received the approval on a referendum of a majority of all the voters in the Commonwealth {.margin-note: Constitutional Amendment.}

---

[1] P. 448, *ante.*
[2] H. V. Evatt. "Constitutional Interpretation in Australia," 3 *Toronto Law Journal* 1.
[3] This limitation does not exclude jurisdiction over a dispute as to the powers of a particular State on a subject over which neither Commonwealth nor States have power, or over which the jurisdiction of the Commonwealth is undisputed and only the State's power is in question: *James* v. *Cowan,* [1932] A.C. 542.
[4] Chap. 4, *post.*

and a majority of electors in a majority of the States (s. 128). It will be seen that by this procedure the constitution may be altered to the disadvantage of a State without the consent of that State, but no alteration may be made affecting the proportionate representation of a State in either House of Parliament, or altering the boundaries of a State, without the consent of a majority of the electors in that State. The constitution itself contains many provisions which can be altered without invoking the machinery for constitutional change; there are some thirty powers which are expressed to be exercisable until the Parliament of Australia otherwise determines. There is no provision enabling the amendment of sections 1 to 8 of the Constitution Act which establish the federation, and therefore without an Act of the Imperial Parliament it would be impossible legally to abolish the federation.[1] While the constitution, and even the machinery for amendment of the constitution, may be altered by the provisions of the constitution, the federal basis must be observed.[2]

Interpreta-
tion of Con-
stitution;
Australia.

When a conflict arises between a federal government and one of the States composing the federation in regard to the exercise of a power, it must be decided whether or not the power claimed has been granted by the constitution. The established courts of justice must of necessity determine that question; and the only way in which they can properly do so is by looking to the terms of the instrument by which affirmatively the legislative powers were created, and by which negatively they are restricted. If what has been done is within the general scope of the affirmative words which give the power, and if it violates no express condition or restriction by which that power is limited, it is not for any court of justice to enquire further or to enlarge constructively those conditions and restrictions: *James* v. *Commonwealth of Australia*, [1936] A.C. 578; J. & Y. 317, in which the Privy Council held that the Dried Fruits Act, 1928–35, of the Commonwealth Parliament was invalid as contravening section 92 of the Australian Constitution. This section declares that trade, commerce and intercourse among the States shall be absolutely free and thus the Commonwealth is bound equally with the States not to impose restrictions by legislation or executive action.[3] In *Commonwealth of Australia* v. *Bank of New South Wales*, [1950] A.C. 235 a provision which prohibited private banking in the Commonwealth was similarly held by the Privy Council to be invalid on the ground that it necessarily restricted the inter-State business of banking. At one time the High Court of Australia adopted

---

[1] A contrary view is taken by W. Anstey Wynes, *Legislative and Executive Powers in Australia* (Law Book Co. of Australasia), at p. 364.

[2] P. 468 and 447, *post*.

[3] See, however, *Section 92—a Problem Piece*, by Lord Wright, 1 *Sydney Law Review* 145, esp. at p. 151. The author's view is that S. 92 should be limited to fiscal matters.

principles of interpretation which were formerly held in the United States and was prepared to reject as unconstitutional laws which were valid if the constitution was interpreted in accordance with ordinary principles of statutory interpretation. This method of interpretation was, however, disapproved in the famous Engineers' Case, *Amalgamated Society of Engineers* v. *Adelaide Steamship Company Ltd.* (1920), 28 C.L.R. 129; J. & Y. 305,[1] in which the High Court rejected the doctrine of the immunity of the Commonwealth and of the States from undue interference on the part of the other, and held that the power of the Commonwealth as to industrial disputes included in the natural meanings of the words disputes to which the Government of a State was party.

The strict statutory interpretation of federal constitutions has, Canada. especially in Canada, rendered it difficult for the federal Government to secure the enactment of national legislation required by the needs of a great nation under modern conditions. Thus the Privy Council has been compelled to hold that without provincial concurrence the Dominion Parliament has no power to pass the necessary legislation to implement an international convention regulating hours of work,[2] or to establish a nation wide scheme of social insurance.[3] The decisions aroused criticism of the former right of appeal from the Supreme Court of Canada to the Judicial Committee. It is unfortunate that, though the decisions just mentioned may be legally correct, it is easy to point to inconsistency of principle in the numerous decisions of the Judicial Committee on the respective powers of the dominion and provincial legislatures.[4]

The problem of interpretation is easier in Australia, for, whereas Contrast of in Canada the problem is one of classifying disputed legislation interpretation. under two stated heads of power,[5] in Australia the task is essentially different.[6] There is no precise division of functions, but concurrent powers are, as far as possible, given to the Commonwealth and the States. The question is still one of construction; but it is the construction of one of forty concurrent powers conferred

[1] See W. A. Holman, "Constitutional Relations in Australia," 46 *L.Q.R.* 502; W. A. Wynes, *op. cit.*; H. V. Evatt, "Constitutional Interpretation in Australia," 3 *Toronto Law Journal* 1.

[2] *Attorney-General for Canada* v. *Attorney-General for Ontario*, [1937] A.C. 326 (No. 1); J & Y. 256.

[3] *Attorney-General for Canada* v. *Attorney-General for Ontario*, [1937] A.C. 355 (No. 2). This decision was in effect reversed by the British North America Act, 1940; see p. 453, *ante*.

[4] See special Constitutional Number, 15 *Canadian Bar Review*, No. 6, June 1937; Sir Ivor Jennings, "Constitutional Interpretation—the Experience of Canada," 51 *Harvard Law Review* 1; Vincent C. MacDonald, "Judicial Interpretation of the Canadian Constitution," 1 *Toronto Law Journal* 284; W. P. M. Kennedy, "The Interpretation of the British North America Act," 8 C.L.J. 146.

[5] P. 453, *ante*.

[6] P. 455, *ante*.

upon the Commonwealth by section 51 of the constitution and, so long as its legislation is truly referable to any one of those powers, the fact that it is also referable to subject-matters not therein included is irrelevant; nor is the fact that legislation or executive power of a State may be affected.[1] The onus is upon the Commonwealth to point to a grant of power in the constitution which will support an enactment.[2] It follows as a corollary that those who impugn the enactment must point to some express limitation upon the power established. The legislative powers of the States are only exclusive in respect of matters not covered by the specific enumeration of powers of the Commonwealth, while the exclusive powers of the Commonwealth are limited to six topics which include the armed forces, customs and coinage; sections 52, 90, 114, 115, and 128.

Common-
wealth and
external
affairs.

In the Commonwealth the legislative power over external affairs is interpreted as extending to agreements entered into by Australia on its own international responsibility, whether imperial, inter-dominion or foreign: *The King* v. *Burgess* (1936), 55 C.L.R. 608, where the validity of the Air Navigation Act, 1920, which carried into effect an international convention, was upheld, despite the effect it might have upon the right of a State to control transport within its borders. This right of control is unimpaired in relation to civil aviation in general.[3]

Common-
wealth and
taxation.

During the Second World War the Commonwealth passed four laws which in effect made it impossible for the States to continue to levy income tax. It was held by the High Court that the Commonwealth has power to make commonwealth taxation effective by giving priority to the liability to pay such taxation over the liability to pay State taxation. Moreover, the Commonwealth in the exercise of its power to make laws with regard to the naval and military defence of the Commonwealth could for the duration of the war take over from the States their officers, equipment and premises concerned with the collection of taxes. It was further legal for the Commonwealth to make grants dependent upon abstention by the States from collecting income tax.[4]

Extension of
Common-
wealth
Powers.

During the war too an attempt was made to secure very wide powers for the Commonwealth with a view to post-war reconstruction. After prolonged negotiations with the States which started in October 1942 and the holding of a constitutional convention, at which there were represented the Governments and the opposition parties of both Commonwealth and States, a Bill was in 1944 submitted to the electors on a referendum,[5] but was rejected.

[1] *Huddart Parker* v. *The Commonwealth* (1931), 44 C.L.R. 492.
[2] W. Anstey Wynes, *op. cit.*, p. 26.
[3] Evatt, *op. cit.*, 3 *Toronto Law Journal* 12–13.
[4] *South Australia* v. *The Commonwealth* (1942), 65 C.L.R. 673.
[5] P. 455, *ante*.

The Bill would have conferred upon the Commonwealth full powers over fourteen diverse subjects, including employment, agricultural marketing trusts, national works, overseas exchange, social security, air transport and national health. The new powers would have been conferred for a period of five years after the conclusion of hostilities when it was intended that a new constitutional convention should be held.

The Union of South Africa has a unitary constitution.[1] Executive power is vested in a Governor-General advised by an Executive Council. Legislative power is vested in the Senate and the House of Assembly. Eight senators are elected for each Province by the members representing the Province in the South African House of Assembly in joint session with the members of the Provincial Council of the Provinces, and the Governor-General in Council appoints eight senators, half of whom are selected on the ground mainly of their thorough acquaintance, by reason of their official experience or otherwise, with the reasonable wants and wishes of the coloured races in South Africa. The House of Assembly is chosen by direct election of the electors of the Union. In the event of a deadlock between the two Houses a joint sitting may during the second session, or in relation to an appropriation Bill during the same session, be convened by the Governor-General and pass a Bill by a simple majority of both Houses. Provision is made for the simultaneous dissolution of the Senate and House of Assembly, as well as for the dissolution of the House of Assembly alone; in the latter event the dissolution of the Senate may follow within 120 days. The exercise of these powers by the Governor-General is governed by conventions similar to those in force in the United Kingdom.

Union of South Africa.

Each Province has a chief executive officer styled an Administrator, and each Province has a provincial council. Each provincial council elects an executive committee. Certain distinct heads of legislative power are granted to the provincial councils and further powers may be specially delegated to them by the Union Parliament. Provincial powers within the limits of provincial jurisdiction are plenary and absolute. Provincial ordinances require, however, the assent of the Governor-General in Council; and any provincial ordinance is void if repugnant to an Act of the Union Parliament. Under the South Africa Act Amendment Act, 1934 of the Union Parliament, Parliament shall not abolish any provincial council or abridge the powers conferred on provincial councils under the South Africa Act, 1909, except by petition to Parliament by the provincial council concerned. This Act could itself be repealed at any time by the Union Parliament.

Provinces.

[1] South Africa Act, 1909. See H. J. May, *The South African Constitution* (Juta & Co.), 1949.

"Entrenched" Provisions.

By the South Africa Act, 1909, the Union of South Africa possesses full powers of constitutional amendment, though for certain amendments (official language, franchise) the special procedure of a two-thirds majority at a special sitting of both Houses of the legislature is necessary: South Africa Act, 1909, s. 152. The provisions of the constitution which require special machinery for amendment are known as the entrenched provisions and the section cannot be repealed without the employment of the special machinery. The Statute of Westminster, 1931, did not expressly or by implication affect this provision. Accordingly, as a matter of law, it would seem that the Parliament of the Union has full power to amend the Union of South Africa Act, though the special procedure must be followed to secure the amendment of section 152 as well as the other entrenched provisions.[1]

Sovereignty of Union Parliament.

Under the Status of the Union Act, 1934, passed by the Union Parliament to implement the Statute of Westminster, legislative sovereignty is declared to be vested in the Union Parliament alone. Section 2 of the Act provides that no Act of the United Kingdom Parliament passed after December 11, 1931, shall extend to the Union as part of the law of the Union, unless extended thereto by an Act of the Union Parliament. The Royal Executive Functions and Seals Act, 1934, also a Union Act, accords to the Governor-General the power to exercise any royal function in respect of both internal and external affairs on the advice of the Ministry without royal approval. Provision is made by section 151 of the South Africa Act, 1909, for the transfer to South Africa with the consent of the King in Council of Bechuanaland, Basutoland and Swaziland. It is agreed by South Africa that such a transfer still requires the consent of the United Kingdom Government.

New Zealand.

By the New Zealand Constitution Act, 1852, of the United Kingdom Parliament New Zealand has a unitary constitution with (since 1950 when the Upper House was abolished) a unicameral legislature, the House of Representatives. The Executive Council responsible to the legislature consists of members of the Cabinet. Full powers of constitutional amendment were conferred by the New Zealand Constitution (Amendment) Act, 1947, after the adoption by the Dominion of the Statute of Westminster, which did not confer any new power to amend the constitution.[2] These powers were used to abolish the upper house, which was a nominated Legislative Council.

Central African Federation.

The Central African Federation was constituted by Order in

[1] *Minister of the Interior* v. *Harris*, [1952] (4) S.A. 769. A.D. where the Appellate Court held invalid an attempt to create a new constitutional court by a bi-cameral Act which infringed Section 152.

[2] P. 468, *post.*

Council [1] which was made under the Rhodesia and Nyasaland Federation Act, 1953. It is composed of the colony of Southern Rhodesia, which has been virtually self-governing since 1923 and of the two Protectorates of Northern Rhodesia and Nyasaland; the latter is in the early stages of constitutional development having a nominated legislative council. The Protectorates continue to be governed as colonies except as regard the powers which are entrusted to the Federation; similarly Southern Rhodesia retains its own form of responsible government for non-federal subjects.

Under the federal constitution the Governor-General exercises a few powers in his individual discretion but in general he is required to act on the advice of the Executive Council (the Cabinet) which is responsible to the Assembly. This is a Legislature of thirty-five members of whom twenty-six are directly elected, three are European members who are responsible for African interests and six are Africans, two of these being elected for each of the three territories. There is also a Federal Supreme Court and an African Affairs Board. The status of the latter is that of a Standing Committee of the Assembly; it is specifically charged with watching in an advisory capacity the interests of Africans; it consists of the three European members with African responsibilities in the National Assembly and one of the elected African members from each territory.

The Irish Free State came into being as the result of "Articles of Agreement for a Treaty between Great Britain and Ireland" in 1921. Up to that date Ireland had been since the Act of Union of 1800 part of the United Kingdom. The Articles of Agreement received statutory effect in the Irish Free State (Agreement) Act, 1922, and the resulting Constitution was enacted by the Irish Free State (Constitution) Act, 1922, of the Parliament of the United Kingdom and the Constitution of the Irish Free State (Saorstát Eireànn) Act, 1922, passed by the Irish Free State Assembly. The treaty provided that, subject to its express terms, the position of the Irish Free State in relation to the Imperial Parliament and Government, and otherwise, should be that of the Dominion of Canada and that the law, practice and constitutional usage governing the relationship of the Crown, or the representative of the Crown, and of the Imperial Parliament to the Dominion of Canada should govern their relationship to the Irish Free State. It further provided for the grant of certain facilities in Ireland to the naval and military forces of the United Kingdom. These facilities were abandoned by agreement confirmed by an imperial Act: Eire (Confirmation of Agreements) Act, 1938. The requirement of the taking of an oath of allegiance by members of the Legislature was abolished in 1933. The constitution was to be construed with reference to the treaty, and in the event of

The Irish Free State: the Irish Treaty.

---

[1] S. 1, 1953, No. 1199.

inconsistency the treaty was to prevail. This provision was also repealed in 1933.

Republic of
Ireland.

Since 1949 Southern Ireland, styled successively the Irish Free State, Eire and the Republic of Ireland has ceased to be a member State of the Commonwealth. The present constitution came into operation in December, 1937, and from the brief description which follows it can be seen that it reflected the desire to be dissociated from the King as Head of the British Commonwealth. That separation was made legal by local enactment which came into operation in April, 1949, and was subsequently recognised by the Ireland Act, 1949, passed at Westminster. By this Act a citizen of the new Republic still enjoys when resident in the United Kingdom privileges such as the franchise, qualification for office (including ministerial office and membership of Parliament) which attach to citizenship of the United Kingdom.

The main provisions of the constitution are:—the President is elected by direct popular vote by proportional representation and holds office for seven years. Legislative power is vested in a National Parliament known as the Oireachtas consisting of two Houses, a Senate (Seanad Eireànn) and a House of Representatives (Dail Eireànn). The Senate has a very limited suspensory veto only. Executive power is vested in the Government at the head of which is the Prime Minister who is chosen by Dail Eireànn. The Government is expressly made responsible to the Dail by the constitution. There is a Council of State which consists of certain high officers and ex-officers of State to advise the President in the exercise of his functions. Executive authority in regard to external affairs is to be exercised by or on the authority of the Government.

C.
The Statute of Westminster, 1931.

Limitations
upon
Dominion
Autonomy.

There were, before the passing of the Statute of Westminster, 1931, the following limitations upon the legislative autonomy of the Dominions which were considered and reported upon by the Conference on the Operation of Dominion Legislation and Merchant Shipping Legislation, 1929.[1] It is important to remember that the Statute of Westminster is concerned only with legislative powers. Changes in, for example, the exercise of functions and the status of Governors-General, were made by executive action following declarations of policy made at Imperial Conferences.

---

[1] 1930, Cmd. 3479; p. 450, *ante*.

(*a*) There still existed the power of disallowance, but this power Dis- had become obsolete. It had not been exercised in relation to allowance. Australian legislation since 1862 or Canadian legislation since 1873, and never in relation to South Africa or New Zealand. But admission to the list of trustee securities in the United Kingdom is, under the Colonial Stock Act, 1900, given to dominion securities provided that the Dominion concerned consents to the disallowance of any legislation affecting such admitted stocks. The Conference for this reason did not recommend the abolition by imperial legislation of the power of disallowance, but suggested that it should be left to the Dominions either to abolish the power by constitutional amendment, or, where an imperial Act is required for such amendment, as in the case of Canada, to request the passing of such Act. South Africa abolished the power of disallowance in 1934. The other Dominions concerned have taken no steps. By the Colonial Stock Act, 1934, of the Imperial Parliament there may be substituted an undertaking by a Dominion Government that legislation affecting the existing rights of stockholders shall not be submitted for the royal assent except by agreement with the Government of the United Kingdom. This safeguards the rights of investors in lieu of the protection afforded by the power of disallowance.

(*b*) There still existed the Governor-General's discretionary Reservation. power to reserve Bills which had only been exercised on one or two occasions in the twentieth century, and also constitutional provisions requiring the reservation of Bills dealing with particular subjects and provisions requiring reservation in certain imperial statutes, *e.g.* the Merchant Shipping Acts.[1] The Imperial Conference of 1926 [2] had placed it upon record that it is recognised that it is the right of the Government of each Dominion to advise the Crown in all matters relating to its own affairs, and that consequently it would not be constitutional for the Government of the United Kingdom to advise the King upon any matter relating to a Dominion against the views of the Government of that Dominion. It was, therefore, recommended that, as in the case of disallowance, it should be left to each Dominion to take such steps as it should desire to abolish both discretionary and compulsory reservation. The Irish Free State consequently abolished reservation by the Constitution (Amendment No. 21) Act, 1933. In regard to South Africa the Status of the Union Act, 1934, abolished discretionary reservation. Compulsory reservation was retained in respect of Bills limiting the right to request special leave to appeal to the Privy Council [3] and Bills altering the terms of the Schedule to the South Africa Act, 1909, in regard

---

[1] See *Report of Conference on the Operation of Dominion Legislation*, p. 13.
[2] *Summary of Proceedings*, p. 17.
[3] Such appeals were abolished in 1950.

to the transfer of native territory to the Union. Assent to such Bills would be given or withheld on the advice of South African Ministers.

Repugnancy.   (c) Under the provisions of the Colonial Laws Validity Act, 1865,[1] dominion legislation would be held void if repugnant to an Act of the Imperial Parliament applying to such Dominion.[2] The Conference recommended that this Act should cease to apply to the Dominions which would thus secure the power to amend any such Acts. Examples of such Acts were Acts of the Imperial Parliament relating to fugitive offenders, extradition, foreign enlistment, *e.g.* Extradition Act, 1870, and Fugitive Offenders Act, 1881.

Extra-Territorial Legislation.   (d) The Dominions had no general power to pass legislation taking effect outside their own territories, *e.g.* to punish crimes committed abroad.[3] The extent of this limitation was difficult to define,[4] but it was of grave inconvenience in relation not only to criminal law, but, *e.g.* to the control of dominion forces abroad. The Conference recommended the abolition of this limitation. A Dominion and probably also a Colony may—apart from the Statute of Westminster—pass legislation having extra-territorial operation where such is necessary to give effect to enactments which are within the competence of the Dominion as being for the peace, order and good government of the Dominion: *Croft* v. *Dunphy*, [1933] A.C. 156; J. & Y. 104, though it has been doubted whether the authority of this case extends beyond customs law. It has been suggested—and the point is still of importance in regard to the Australian States since the abolition of the limitation by the Statute does not operate there—that the test is whether the law in question does not, in some aspects and relations, bear upon the peace, order and good government of the Dominion either generally or in respect to specific subjects: *Trustee Executors and Agency Co. Ltd.* v. *Federal Commissioner of Taxation* (1933), 49 C.L.R. 220; J. & Y. 107.

Power of Imperial Parliament to legislate for Dominions.   (e) The Imperial Parliament still had legal power to legislate for the Dominions. In fact, this power was by constitutional usage only exercised at the request and with the consent of the Dominions, and the Conference recommended that the constitutional convention should receive legislative recognition.

Limitations upon Constitutional Amendment.   (f) The Constitution of Canada could, as we have seen, only be amended by an Act of the Imperial Parliament, and an Act of the Imperial Parliament was also necessary for the amendment of sections 1 to 8 of the Commonwealth of Australia Constitution Act, 1900. Any enlargement of the powers of Canada or Australia in this respect would have affected both the Provinces and States

---

[1] P. 448, *ante*.
[2] *Nadan* v. *The King*, [1926] A.C. 482; J. & Y. 111.
[3] *In re Criminal Code Bigamy Sections, Canada* (1897), 27 S.C.R. 461.
[4] See J. & Y., *op. cit.*, pp. 51–2.

as well as the Dominion and Commonwealth, and the Conference made no positive recommendations upon this matter.

The recommendations of the Conference were with minor modi- The Statute of fications adopted by the Imperial Conference of 1930,[1] and they Westminster, were given legal effect by the passing of the Statute of Westminster, 1931. 1931, by the Imperial Parliament on December 11, 1931.[2]

The preamble to the Statute affirms the free association of the Preamble; members of the British Commonwealth of Nations united by a Succession. common allegiance to the Crown, and records that it would be in accord with the established constitutional position that any alteration in the law touching the succession to the throne or the royal style and titles should hereafter require the assent as well of the Parliaments of all the Dominions as of the Parliament of the United Kingdom.[3] The preamble further sets out, in addition to a similar provision made in section 4 of the Statute itself, that it is in accord with the established constitutional position that no law hereafter made by the Parliament of the United Kingdom shall extend to any of the Dominions otherwise than at the request and with the consent of that Dominion. Section 4 requires an express declaration in the Imperial Act that the Dominion has requested and consented to the enactment thereof. On the abdication of Edward VIII. in 1936 the request and consent of Canada were recited in the preamble to His Majesty's Declaration of Abdication Act, 1936, passed on December 11, 1936, and the assent of the Dominion Parliament was signified when Parliament re-assembled early in 1937 by the passing of an Act of Assent. Australia had not at that date adopted the Statute of Westminster, so convention only, not strict law, had to be considered. A resolution of the Commonwealth Parliament was passed on the same day and before the Imperial Act was passed, and the assent of the Commonwealth of Australia and of New Zealand and South Africa was referred to in the Imperial Act. The Government of New Zealand requested the passing of the Imperial Act and the assent of the New Zealand Parliament was subsequently given. The South African Government took the view that the throne was vacated by Edward VIII. immediately he signed the Instrument of Abdication on December 10, and therefore George VI. was King in South Africa before the passing of the United Kingdom Abdication Act on December 11. The Status of the Union Act, 1934, provided (section 5) that the heirs and successors of the Crown mean His Majesty's heirs and successors in the sovereignty of the United Kingdom as determined by the laws relating to the succession of the Crown of the United Kingdom. By His

[1] *Summary of Proceedings*, pp. 17–21, 1930, Cmd. 3717.
[2] For text, see K. & L. 503–6.
[3] P. 131, *ante*.

Majesty King Edward the Eighth's Abdication Act, 1937, the Union Parliament recorded its assent to the alterations in the law touching the succession to the throne and reaffirmed that George VI. had been King since December 10, 1936.[1] The Irish Free State by the Executive Authority (External Relations) Act, 1936, passed on December 12, provided that King Edward's abdication should take effect immediately upon the passing of the Act. The Irish Free State had thus, like South Africa, for the space of part at least of one day, a different sovereign from the rest of the British Commonwealth.

In the operative part of the Statute of Westminster it was enacted:

Colonial Laws Validity Act, 1865. Statute of Westminster, 1931, s. 2.

(a) That the Colonial Laws Validity Act, 1865, should cease to apply to the Dominions or to the Provinces of Canada; that the Dominions and the Provinces of Canada should have power to repeal or amend Acts of the Imperial Parliament in so far as they form part of the law of that Dominion; and that no law of either a Dominion or a Province of Canada should be void on the ground of repugnancy to an Act of the Imperial Parliament or to the law of England. Canada by statute gave extra-territorial operation to all statutes passed before December 11, 1931, which by their terms or by necessary implication were intended to have such operation. It was argued [2] that section 2 of the Statute of Westminster did not enable a Dominion to exercise powers, *e.g.* of constitutional amendment, which it could not exercise under the original Act which enacted its powers. It was suggested that section 2 merely removed the restriction of repugnancy to an Act of the Imperial Parliament and did not enlarge the ambit of the powers of a Dominion Parliament. The Privy Council, however, held [3] that by section 2 a Dominion Parliament was given full legislative powers, save in so far as such powers were restricted by subsequent sections of the Statute of Westminster itself. The Statute can be amended by a Dominion Parliament so far as it is part of its own statute law.

Royal Prerogative.

It was argued [4] that in the absence of express words the Statute of Westminster did not enable a Dominion to legislate so as to affect the royal prerogative. Though the decision was based also on other grounds, the Privy Council held that a Dominion may now legislate so as to affect the prerogative in regard to the Dominion: *British Coal Corporation* v. *The King*, [1935] A.C. 500, at p. 518; J. & Y. 159. In *Attorney-General for Ontario* v. *Attorney-General for Canada*, [1947] A.C. 127; J. & Y. 169, it was held on a reference to the Judicial

[1] For a very full study of this complicated subject, see "The Abdication Legislation in the United Kingdom and in the Dominions," by K. H. Bailey, *Politica*, Vol. III., pp. 1–26, 97–117.
[2] K. C. Wheare, *op. cit.*, at pp. 180 ff.
[3] *Moore* v. *Attorney-General of Irish Free State*, [1935] A.C. 484; J. & Y. 150.
[4] W. Anstey Wynes, *op. cit.*, p. 365.

Committee that it would be *intra vires* the Parliament of the Dominion to enact legislation to abolish all appeals from all Canadian Courts Dominion and Provincial, civil and criminal, to the Privy Council, including special leave to appeal granted under the prerogative. The Bill to enact this was not proceeded with at the time, but the Supreme Court Act, 1949 (R.S.C.) abolished all such appeals.

(*b*) That the Dominion Parliaments shall have full power to make laws having extra-territorial operation.[1]

Extra-Territorial Legislation. Statute of Westminster, 1931, s. 3.

There still remains a difficulty in that no such power is given to the Provinces of Canada or States of Australia, although criminal law is in general within the powers of the States and accordingly there is difficulty in providing for the punishment of offenders who have committed offences outside a State's jurisdiction.[2]

(*c*) That no Act of Parliament of the United Kingdom passed after the commencement of the Statute of Westminster shall extend to a Dominion as part of the law of that Dominion, unless it is expressly declared that that Dominion has requested, and consented to, the enactment thereof. It is not clear how far the word, Dominion, should here be interpreted territorially, *i.e.* whether the Imperial Parliament could no longer pass legislation for the Provinces of Canada on matters within the provincial sphere. It is probable that the power no longer exists, and it is noticeable that it is expressly stated in the Statute that the power of the Imperial Parliament to legislate for the States of Australia remains (section 9), and that the exercise of such power shall not require the concurrence of the Commonwealth where before the Statute such consent would not have been required by constitutional practice. It is expressly provided by section 9 (3) of the Statute that in regard to the Commonwealth of Australia the request and consent referred to in section 4 shall mean the request and consent of both the Parliament and Government of the Commonwealth.[3] Lord Sankey, L.C., stated in *British Coal Corporation* v. *The King, ante,* "it is doubtless true that the power of the Imperial Parliament to pass on its own initiative any legislation that it thought fit extending to Canada remains unimpaired. Indeed, the Imperial Parliament could, as a matter of abstract law, repeal or disregard section 4 of the Statute. But that is theory and has no relation to realities." A contrary view was expressed by an eminent Australian constitutional lawyer who has said of section 4 that it "is a restriction upon British parliamentary

Legislation by the Imperial Parliament. Statute of Westminster, 1931, s. 4.

---

[1] In *Croft* v. *Dunphy, ante,* the Judicial Committee refused to decide whether this provision was retrospective. See J. & Y., pp. 51–2, for a discussion of the restriction on such legislation, a question which is still important to the Colonies.

[2] Cf. *Macleod* v. *Attorney-General of New South Wales,* [1891] A.C. 455; J. & Y. 97.

[3] *E.g.* Cocos Islands Act, 1955, enabling the Islands to be placed by the Queen under the authority of the Commonwealth. This is one of the very few examples of the United Kingdom Parliament legislating under s. 4.

supremacy of the law." [1] The same view has been expressed by the Supreme Court of South Africa—"freedom once conferred cannot be revoked." [2]

Status of the Union Act, 1934.

The Status of the Union Act, 1934, went even further than section 4 and by it the Union Parliament enacted that no Act of the United Kingdom Parliament passed after December 11, 1931, shall extend or be deemed to extend to the Union as part of the law of the Union, unless extended thereto by an Act of the Union Parliament. The Statute of Westminster itself has been scheduled to the Status of the Union Act, 1934, thus giving it the force of a statute of the Union Parliament.

Safeguards for State and Provincial Rights. Statute of Westminster, 1931, ss. 7, 8 and 9.

It has been shown that the giving of further powers of constitutional amendment to Canada and Australia would have involved the removal of the safeguard to provincial and state rights which was afforded by the necessity of legislation by the Imperial Parliament in order to amend the Constitution of Canada or sections 1 to 8 of the Commonwealth of Australia Constitution Act, 1900. Such additional powers would at once be given, should the Provinces or States concur in requesting them, but in the meantime the existing position was preserved.[3] It is enacted expressly (section 7) that nothing in the Statute shall extend to the repeal, amendment or alteration of the British North America Acts, 1867 to 1930, and that the new powers conferred upon the Dominion Parliament and the provincial legislatures of Canada shall be restricted to enacting laws within their respective spheres of competence. It is further enacted (section 8) that nothing in the Statute gives any new power to alter the constitutions of the Commonwealth of Australia or New Zealand, and (section 9) that the Commonwealth is given no new power to legislate on any matter not within its authority, but within the authority of the States.

Adoption of Statute of Westminster.

The substantive sections of the Statute, sections 2, 3, 4, discussed above together with section 5 (Merchant Shipping), and section 6 (Courts of Admiralty) did not apply to Australia or to New Zealand until adopted by the Parliaments of those Dominions. The Commonwealth Parliament by the Statute of Westminster Adoption Act, 1942, adopted the sections in question with effect from September 3, 1939. Similarly the Parliament of New Zealand adopted sections 2–6 in 1947 and thereupon requested and consented to the enactment at

---

[1] "The Law and the Constitution," 51 *L.Q.R.* 611, by Mr. Justice Dixon; see H. V. Evatt, *The King and His Dominion Governors* (Clarendon Press), Appendix.

[2] *Ndlwana* v. *Hofmeyr*, [1937] A.D. 229, at p. 237; although this decision was overruled by *Harris* v. *Minister of the Interior*, [1952] (2) S.A. 428 A.D., the sovereignty of the Union Parliament was expressly confirmed. For a critical discussion of the constitutional issues involved in the latter case, see "Legislature and Judiciary," by D. V. Cowen, 15 M.L.R. 282, 16 M.L.R. 273.

[3] See British North America (No. 2) Act, 1949, at p. 454, *ante*.

Westminster of the New Zealand Constitution (Amendment) Act, 1947, which removed all restrictions upon the power of constitutional amendment by the Parliament of that Dominion. Thus section 8 of the Statute of Westminster has been by implication repealed in its application to New Zealand.[1]

D.

The Commonwealth in Asia.

The Indian Independence Act, 1947, declared that as from the 15th day of August, 1947, two independent Dominions should be set up in India, to be known respectively as India and Pakistan. Prior to 1947 India was divided politically into British India consisting of Governors' Provinces and the Indian Native States. The Provinces of British India were divided between the new Dominions in accordance with the terms of the Act; in one case a referendum was required and in others boundaries were fixed by commissioners. The Native States were left to join either Dominion or to retain their independence. These States were not British territory and were ruled by hereditary Indian Princes. The relationship of the Crown was known as paramountcy and in effect meant that the Crown had a general right of interference in the interests of India as a whole. It included the right to intervene in cases of gross mis-government by the Princes. Acts of the Crown in the exercise of paramountcy were acts of State and were not subject to challenge in any court.[2] With the enactment of the Act of 1947 paramountcy lapsed and the Indian princes were left to make the best terms they could with regard to joining India or Pakistan, whether as units in a federal system in the case of the largest, or by merger into an existing province.

India and Pakistan Created.

The power to provide for its new constitution was made exercisable by a constituent assembly in both cases. The constitution of the Union of India came into force in January, 1950. Pakistan has not yet adopted her new constitution which, it has been officially stated, will be that of a republic. The Colonial Laws Validity Act, 1865, never applied to British India, which was not part of the Colonial Empire, but the Act of 1947 repeated the substance of section 2 (2) of the Statute of Westminster, lest the issue of repugnancy to English law should be raised.[3] The Government of India Act, 1935, had provided for a federal constitution for all India and the constituent assembly was empowered to exercise the powers of the Federal

Constituent Assembly.

---

[1] Wheare, *op. cit.*, pp. 231 ff. and App. VI.
[2] Part IV., Chap. 10A.   [3] Pp. 448 and 464, *ante.*

Legislature under that Act pending the adoption of its new constitution. Although India never had a Federal Government under the 1935 Act, the Indian Legislature exercised the exclusive and concurrent powers of the proposed Federal Legislature in relation to the Provincial Legislatures at the time of the coming into operation of the Indian Independence Act. Responsible government under the terms of the Act of 1935 was introduced in the Provinces in 1937.

The Federation of India, 1950.

The constitution of the Federal Union of India was enacted by the Constitutional Assembly and came into force early in 1950. It established a Federal Union of States (of which there were constituted three different categories) with a parliamentary executive, on the British Cabinet model, which is responsible to the House of the People, the directly elected Chamber of the bi-cameral Parliament. The second House, the Council of States, is constituted by the representatives of the member States, the seats being allocated unequally between the States. The executive power is vested in the President who is chosen by an Electoral College which consists of the elected members of both Houses of Parliament and of the Legislative Assemblies of the States. The President appoints the Federal Prime Minister and, on his advice, the other Ministers forming the Council of Ministers; they hold office at the President's pleasure.

The constitution of the Federal Union is that of a republic, but it follows the general lines of the Government of India Act, 1935, in the distribution of legislative powers which allows for a category of concurrent subjects in addition to those exclusive to the Federal and State legislatures respectively. In the definition of the obligations both of the citizen and of the State the constitution departs from the British constitutional pattern and not only contains an elaborate definition of human rights, but provides machinery whereby the individual citizen can take action in the Supreme Court to safeguard those rights. Principles which the Governments and Parliaments should follow in framing legislation are enacted, but without legal sanction to secure enforcement. Cabinet government prevails both in the Union and in the member States and the position of the Prime Minister in both follows the British model. It was, however, necessary to vest wide powers in the President as Head of the State, since these powers were no longer vested in the Crown, who remains the symbol of India's membership of the British Commonwealth, but without prerogative or statutory powers as such.

The India (Consequential Provisions) Act, 1949, enacted by the United Kingdom Parliament followed immediately upon the adoption of the Constitution by the Indian Constituent Assembly in November, 1949, and before it was brought into force in January,

1950. This Act secured that all rules of the common law and all statutory rules, so far as they were part of the law of the United Kingdom, colonies, protectorates and trust territories on the date of India becoming a republic should continue to have the same operation in relation to India, subject to any modifications of the law (to be made by Order in Council) which were deemed necessary or expedient in view of India's status of being a republic, while remaining a member of the Commonwealth. There was no time limit imposed to this wide delegation of legislative power, but it may be justified perhaps by the nature of a legal problem for which there was no precedent; on the other hand it enabled amendment of a very wide range of statutes without previous consideration by Parliament, as for example the British Nationality Act, 1948.

In February, 1948, Ceylon[1] attained "fully responsible status within the British Commonwealth of Nations," a description which replaces the term, dominion status.[2] The Ceylon Independence Act, 1947, expressly released the Government of the United Kingdom from responsibility for the Government of Ceylon which had since 1931 been governed under a constitution which found its inspiration in the pattern of the English county council. It was an attempt to avoid the divorce of power from responsibility, which is a common feature of colonial constitutions, without adopting responsible Government; the State Council, to which was entrusted the ordinary business of government, foreign affairs, finance and justice being excepted, was divided into committees, the chairman of each being equivalent to a departmental Minister. The Council was thus both an executive and legislative body, but the excepted subjects were the direct responsibility of the principal officials and the Governor had paramount powers in an emergency to override the State Council.

This constitution could at best be a bridge to assist the transition to full responsibility and it could be amended or revoked by Order in Council. The impact of war upon the island resulted in a promise made in 1943 to review the position and after protracted negotiations which included a visit to Ceylon by a Royal Commission the Independence Act was enacted at Westminster in 1947. The Act did not contain a new constitution. It extended to Ceylon the main provisions of the Statute of Westminster by repeating the provisions of sections 2–6 of that Act and declaring that from the appointed day the United Kingdom Government should have no responsibility for the government of Ceylon. The new constitution, which substantially adopted a draft which was discussed with the Royal Commission, is contained in the Ceylon (Constitution) Order in Council, 1946, as

Ceylon.

[1] Sir Ivor Jennings, *The Constitution of Ceylon* (3rd. edn.) (Oxford University Press).
[2] See F. R. Scott, *End of Dominion Status*, 23 C.B.R. 725.

amended in 1947, so as to confer fully responsible status, *i.e.* by replacing the Governor by a Governor-General who in the exercise of his powers and functions acts in accordance with the constitutional conventions applicable to the exercise of similar powers and functions in the United Kingdom by the King. Defence, external affairs and constitutional amendment ceased to be reserved subjects and the reservation of Bills for His Majesty's pleasure was abolished.[1]

E.

The Present Position of the Commonwealth.

Legislative Autonomy.

Inasmuch as the status of the Commonwealth is without precedent, it is difficult to describe it accurately. The legal supremacy of the Parliament of the United Kingdom has not been abolished in relation to other members of the Commonwealth, but it remains only to be exercised at their request and with their consent.[2] The limitations that remain since 1931 upon constitutional amendment are preserved only so long as the people of Canada and Australia desire their preservation as machinery for maintaining the federal basis of their constitutions.

The Crown.

Little is left of the formal unity of the Commonwealth in which the Crown played the predominant part. Common allegiance to the Crown has ceased to be the one legal link which joins members of the Commonwealth. The position of the Crown involves difficulties that can only be solved by co-operation and adjustment. It is agreed that the Crown will only be advised upon matters relating to a Commonwealth State overseas by the Ministers of that State. It might be that the Ministers of one State would advise a course of action hostile to another State. It is no answer to this difficulty to say that the powers of the Crown will only be exercised by the Governor-General, and that the Queen herself will not receive conflicting advice. The prerogatives of declaring war and making peace have not been delegated to Governors-General.[3] There are occasions where the interests of two Commonwealth States might be vitally concerned, where the assent of the Crown would be necessary, and where conflicting advice might be given. These are not problems that lawyers can solve.

[1] See "The Making of a Dominion Constitution," by Sir Ivor Jennings, 65 *L.Q.R.* 456.
[2] See *e.g.* the Cocos Islands Act, 1955, which was enacted at Westminster; the Act recites the request and consent to its enactment made by the Parliament and Government of the Commonwealth of Australia. The Act enabled the Queen to place the Islands under the Commonwealth of Australia.
[3] But as to Union of South Africa, see Status of the Union Act and Royal Executive Functions and Seals Act, passed by the Union Parliament in 1934; see pp. 41 and 460, *ante.* In Canada full prerogative powers were delegated in 1937. (See p. 474 *post.*)

It is true, however, to say that ordinary difficulties can be avoided by the fact that the powers of the Crown are exercised by the Governors-General, who no longer in any way represent the Government of the United Kingdom. The appointment of a Governor-General is now made on the advice of the Government concerned. This change of practice first received recognition in the formal instruments when the Governor-General of Canada was appointed in 1931. It is for each State to decide whether or not to appoint distinguished citizens from the United Kingdom. Citizens of the State concerned have been appointed on occasions in every member State. In South Africa, as in Ceylon, it is unlikely that any future appointment will deviate from this practice. Although Ceylon asked for an English peer as her first Governor-General, she appointed as his successor one of her own citizens. India, where the Queen has since been replaced by the President, and Pakistan appointed their own nationals after the departure of the last Viceroy of India who for a while was Governor-General of India, but not of Pakistan.

Governors-General.

It was for a long time debated how far a Governor-General could constitutionally reject the advice of his Ministers. In 1926 Lord Byng refused a dissolution to the Prime Minister of Canada, and then granted one to his successor. The refusal took place during the progress of a motion of censure on the Government and followed closely a previous dissolution, as a result of which the Government had failed to obtain a clear majority. The new Prime Minister was unable to avoid defeat in the Commons. This action aroused acute controversy, and as a result the position of a Governor-General was defined by the Imperial Conference of 1926. It was laid down "that it was an essential consequence of the equality of status existing among the members of the British Commonwealth that the Governor-General of a Dominion is the representative of the Crown, holding in all respects the same position in relation to the administration of public affairs in the Dominion as is held by His Majesty the King in Great Britain, and that he is not the representative or agent of His Majesty's Government in Great Britain." [1] The conventions, however, which regulate the constitutional duty of the Sovereign in relation to such questions as the granting of a dissolution are not entirely clear. [2] No step has ever been taken to free a Governor-General from the legal liabilities of a colonial Governor; in practice no question is likely to arise, as any liabilities would be those of the responsible Minister (apart from personal affairs). [3]

Exercise of Prerogative of Dissolution.

[1] *Summary of Proceedings,* 1926, Cmd. 2768, p. 7.
[2] H. V. Evatt, *op. cit.*
[3] P. 437, *ante.* See "The Imperial Conferences, 1926–1930 and the Statute of Westminster," by Professor W. P. M. Kennedy, 48 *L.Q.R.* 191; and *J.C.L.,* Vol. XIV., pp. 262–63.

Delegation
of
Prerogative.

It has been seen that the vital external prerogatives of declaring war and making peace and of accrediting diplomatic representatives have not been delegated to the Governor-General. Specific delegation from the Crown is required for each case, except for South Africa where the Royal Executive Functions and Seals Act, 1934, empowered the Governor-General to act on the advice of his Ministers without royal approval.[1] The Governor-General of Australia in 1941 declared war against Japan under a power specially assigned to him by the King on the exclusive advice of his Australian Ministers.[2] It may be assumed that since the Statute of Westminster, 1931, there are implicit in the office of Governor-General all such prerogatives as are necessary for the government of the State concerned, while it must be left to convention to determine what prerogatives the Queen will still exercise in person, such as opening a session of Parliament and conferring honours when present in person during a visit. In the case of Canada, however, letters-patent issued in 1937 gave the Governor-General authority to exercise on the advice of Canadian Ministers all the royal powers and prerogatives in respect of Canada. This made the exercise of all prerogative acts possible without reference to the Sovereign; previously the authority to enter into treaties and to appoint ambassadors to represent Canada had not been vested in the Governor-General.

Communications with the United Kingdom.

The Secretary of State for Commonwealth Relations is the member of the United Kingdom Cabinet who is responsible for inter-commonwealth relations. In the nature of things, since the United Kingdom is the only one of the Great Powers within the Commonwealth, much business with which the Foreign Office in particular deals, is unknown to the other Governments of the Commonwealth unless and until it is communicated to them. The normal channel is the Secretary of State and through his office there is a constant interchange of information between the Governments of the Commonwealth, but this does not exclude direct communications between the Prime Ministers, Foreign Ministers or Finance Ministers on important occasions.

Not only is it important to hold periodic conferences of Ministers, but provision must be made for regular representation of each Government at other capital cities in the Commonwealth. The representation is by High Commissioners who are equal in rank and status to ambassadors representing foreign States. The High Commissioner for the United Kingdom in the Union of South Africa also holds the separate office of High Commissioner for Basutoland, Bechuanaland Protectorate and Swaziland. For a time, in 1932 and

---

[1] P. 460, *ante*. The authority of the Crown has ceased in regard to India.
[2] P. 477, *post*.

1933, Mr. S. M. Bruce, a former Commonwealth Prime Minister, combined membership of the Commonwealth Cabinet with the task of representing the Commonwealth in London, thus giving the Australian Cabinet the opportunity of direct audience whenever desired with the King through one of its members.[1]

Formerly Imperial Conferences were held periodically and representatives of the Dominions attended the old Committee of Imperial Defence.[2] During the Second World War the Prime Minister of the United Kingdom was in direct communication with the other Commonwealth Prime Ministers. There was also a daily stream of telegrams through the Dominions Office (as it then was named). Daily meetings of High Commissioners in London were presided over by the Secretary of State for Dominion Affairs and attended by a representative of the Foreign Office. Dominion Prime Ministers and other Ministers visited London from time to time, and Mr. Churchill visited Canada. On the occasion of his second visit in 1943 there was held a joint meeting of the Canadian War Cabinet Committee and the British War Cabinet. The Australian High Commissioner in London was given the right to attend meetings of the United Kingdom War Cabinet whenever matters of direct and immediate concern to Australia were under consideration. In 1944 there was held in London a meeting of Prime Ministers attended by the Prime Ministers of the United Kingdom, Canada, Australia, New Zealand, South Africa and Southern Rhodesia and representatives of India. To meet the special needs of the Pacific there were set up Pacific War Councils in both Washington and London, Canada, Australia and New Zealand were represented on both bodies, Subsequent meetings of Prime Ministers have taken place in 1946, 1948, 1949, 1953 and 1955. Such meetings are much less formal than were the Imperial Conference and, in particular, brief and uninformative communiques have replaced the detailed reports which in the years between the wars contained much of interest on the constitutional developments of the period. On the other hand the new methods are much more flexible and, with constitutional issues largely settled, the volume of exchange of information has greatly increased as the political problems have increased in number and complexity.

Changes since 1939.

As was stated by the Imperial Conference of 1926 equality of status does not necessarily involve equality of function. All the member States have the right to separate diplomatic and consular representation in foreign countries. But a State may request the United Kingdom representative to act on its behalf where it has not appointed its own representative. All members, while maintaining their own defence forces, must rely upon the armed forces of the

Foreign Affairs.

---

[1] In 1950 the Commonwealth Minister of Defence was resident in London.
[2] P. 158, *ante*.

United Kingdom for defence against aggression. The Canadian Navy with its air arm was, however, increased during the Second World War so as to enable it to play a vital and substantial part in the Battle of the Atlantic as a separate fleet, and the Australian Navy played a vital part in the Pacific. The Queen's Ministers, say in, Australia, may advise the Crown to exercise the prerogative power of treaty making, and thus the Commonwealth of Australia may make a treaty without the consent of the United Kingdom Government. Where a treaty is made in the name of the Crown to which several Commonwealth States are parties,[2] a United Kingdom plenipotentiary signs on behalf of Great Britain and Northern Ireland and all territories overseas which are not separate members of the United Nations; separate plenipotentiaries sign for each of the other member States. Unless a State has, as have the Dominion of Canada and the Union of South Africa, its own Great Seal, the formal concurrence of a United Kingdom Minister is necessary in the issuing of formal powers under the Great Seal, but it would be unconstitutional for such Minister to tender advice contrary to that given by the State concerned.

The Commonwealth in International Law.

Inter-Imperial declarations and changes of practice do not in themselves alter international law, and cannot in themselves bind foreign States. The position in international law is still not entirely clear. Each member State, except Ceylon,[3] has a separate membership of the United Nations and the older Dominions were members of the League of Nations; they have given separate adherence to the International Court of Justice. These factors go a long way towards establishing the recognition of the independent status of members by foreign States. But the conception of the Commonwealth as an entity recognised in international law has not been raised. As between the members of the British Commonwealth it is recognised that a State is not bound by a treaty made in the name of the Crown to which it has not assented and which it has not ratified. Similarly no State would be regarded as under any obligation to assist in a war declared without its consent. These are matters, not of international law, but of inter-imperial relations. The Crown, however, is the formal head of the Commonwealth, though in the case of India and Pakistan the Queen is only accepted as the symbol of free association between independent States and allegiance is not owed to her.

Declaration of War.

The question whether the Crown can be both at war and at peace has not yet been answered by any formal pronouncement. The

---

[1] Part IV, Chap. 10.

[2] Imperial Conferences, 1926 and 1930, Summaries of Proceedings. (Cmd. 2768 and 3717).

[3] Owing to the veto of the U.S.S.R. on the election of new members, Ceylon is not yet a member of the United Nations.

position of Eire during the Second World War may be regarded as a precedent, but by that date the link with the Crown had already been severed to all purposes. Eire remained neutral throughout the war. It was, however, the fact that on the outbreak of war formal declarations of war were made on different dates by members of the Commonwealth. Canada did not formally declare war on Germany until seven days after the United Kingdom. On September 10, 1939, a separate formal declaration of war on Germany was made by the King on the advice of his Canadian Ministers following the acceptance by the Canadian Parliament of an address from the Throne. On September 3, 1939, Australian Ministers met in Melbourne and the Cabinet approved a notification that a state of war existed with Germany. A different procedure was followed by Australia in 1941 in declaring war against Japan. War was declared by the Governor-General under powers specially assigned to him by the King acting on the exclusive advice of the Australian Government. On September 6, 1939, the Governor-General of South Africa issued a proclamation notifying a state of war with Germany. It is thus difficult to contend that a declaration of war by the Government of the United Kingdom would bind the other members of the Commonwealth without their governments making separate declarations. Such declarations, being by the Crown, could not extend to India or Pakistan.

A Member of the Commonwealth can make a declaration of inde- Secession. pendence which for international validity requires a treaty or some form of recognition. When Burma was granted independence by the decision of the United Kingdom Government in 1947, she elected not to remain within the Commonwealth and section 1 of the Burma Independence Act, 1947, gave effect to this choice. Burma's relationship with the members of the Commonwealth is therefore limited to treaty obligations. In the case of Eire's decision in 1949 to sever all ties with the United Kingdom which she effected by statute in her Parliament, the new status was expressly recognised by the subsequent enactment of the Ireland Act, 1949, by the Parliament of the United Kingdom. In a more limited sphere the question of the right of Western Australia to secede from the Commonwealth of Australia and resume its position as a unitary Dominion was considered in 1934. As the law stands, this secession could only be effected by an Act of the Imperial Parliament, even since the Commonwealth has adopted the Statute of Westminster.[1] The Imperial Parliament took the view that such a matter could only be considered on the initiative of the Commonwealth. In effect the State was told that its constitutional rights were as a matter of constitutional practice limited by the federal system.

[1] P. 468, *ante.*

The Declaration of London,1949.
The following is the text of a communique issued at the conclusion of a meeting of the Prime Ministers of the Commonwealth in April, 1949.

The Governments of the United Kingdom, Canada, Australia, New Zealand, South Africa, India, Pakistan and Ceylon, whose countries are united as Members of the British Commonwealth of Nations and owe a common allegiance to the Crown, which is also a symbol of their free association, have considered the impending constitutional changes in India.

The Government of India have informed the other Governments of the Commonwealth of the intention of the Indian people that under the new constitution which is about to be adopted India shall become a sovereign independent republic. The Government of India have, however, declared and affirmed India's desire to continue her full membership of the Commonwealth of Nations and her acceptance of The King as the symbol of the free association of its independent member nations and as such the Head of the Commonwealth.

The Governments of the other countries of the Commonwealth, the basis of whose membership of the Commonwealth is not hereby changed, accept and recognise India's continuing membership in accordance with the terms of this declaration.

Accordingly the United Kingdom, Canada, Australia, New Zealand, South Africa, India, Pakistan and Ceylon hereby declare that they remain united as free and equal members of the Commonwealth of Nations, freely co-operating in the pursuit of peace, liberty, and progress.

The effect of this important pronouncement has not yet been clarified. The lawyer will note that, since India ceased to owe allegiance to the Crown on becoming a republic, the King did not become the Head of the new State and ceased to be represented by a Governor-General appointed by himself. He thus had no constitutional functions to perform in the Republic which acclaimed him as the symbol of its membership of the Commonwealth. But the document shows that there was a unanimous wish that India should remain a full member.

A similar communique was issued in February, 1955, in relation to the declared intention of Pakistan to become a republic within the Commonwealth. The occasion was another meeting of the Prime Ministers of the Commonwealth.

CHAPTER 4.

THE JUDICIAL COMMITTEE OF THE PRIVY COUNCIL.

THE Judicial Committee of the Privy Council exercises in respect of Jurisdiction. appeals from the courts of all colonies and also from the courts set up by the Crown in protectorates and trust territories [1] the ancient jurisdiction of the King in Council which has been confirmed by statute [2] to hear appeals from the Overseas Dependencies. In respect of appeals from the courts of certain member States of the Commonwealth this jurisdiction of the Judicial Committee has been limited according to the wish of the particular member State concerned.[3] The Judicial Committee is also the final Court of Appeal from the Ecclesiastical Courts of England, from the Channel Islands and the Isle of Man, and from Prize Courts in the United Kingdom and Colonies. An appeal lies to the Committee against a decision by the Disciplinary Committee of the General Medical Council to strike a practitioner off the Medical Register.[4] In addition to its appellate jurisdiction the Judicial Committee has jurisdiction also confirmed by statute [5] to determine by its advice references made to it by the Crown. The Committee has no power to place any limit as to the matters which may be so referred; they may be matters of original jurisdiction, as in the dispute between the Dominion of Canada and Newfoundland as to the Labrador territory: *In re Labrador Boundary* (1927), 34 T.L.R. 289. The Committee also hears references under certain statutes, *e.g.* with relation to the review of ecclesiastical benefices under the Union of Benefices Measures, 1923–36.

The appellate jurisdiction of the Privy Council is based on "the Basis of Appellate Jurisdiction. inherent prerogative right, and on all proper occasions, the duty of the King in Council to exercise an appellate jurisdiction, with a view not only to ensure, as far as may be, the due administration of justice in the individual case, but also to preserve the due course of procedure generally." An appeal may be entertained in any matter, whether civil or criminal, by whichever party to the proceedings the appeal is brought, unless the right has been expressly renounced.[6]

---

[1] *Jerusalem and Jaffa District Governor* v. *Suleiman Murra*, [1926] A.C. 321; J. & Y. 30; Chap. 2 B., *ante.*
[2] Judicial Committee Acts, 1833 and 1844.   [3] P. 481, *post.*
[4] Medical Act, 1950, s. 20.   [5] Judicial Committee Act, 1833, s. 4.
[6] *The Queen* v. *Bertrand* (1867), L.R. 1 P.C. 520; *Attorney-General of Ceylon* v. *Perera*, [1953] A.C. 200, where an order for a new trial made by the Court of Criminal Appeal in Ceylon was set aside and the conviction restored.

The ancient jurisdiction of the King in Council to hear appeals from overseas, which was in practice exercised by the legal members of the Council, was made statutory by the Judicial Committee Act, 1833 (as amended by the Judicial Committee Act, 1844, and subsequent Acts) which set up a Judicial Committee to hear appeals either under the Act itself or under the customary jurisdiction of the Privy Council. The Judicial Committee does not in theory deliver judgment. It advises the Sovereign who acts on its report and issues an Order in Council to give effect thereto.[1] Only the view of the majority of the members sitting is expressed. The constitutional nature of the Committee's functions was well expressed by Viscount Haldane at the time of the hearing of the first appeals to the Judicial Committee from the Irish Free State:[2]—

> We are not Ministers in any sense; we are a Committee of Privy Councillors who are acting in the capacity of judges, but the peculiarity of the situation is this: it is a long-standing constitutional anomaly that we are really a Committee of the Privy Council giving advice to His Majesty, but in a judicial spirit. We have nothing to do with policies, or party considerations; we are really judges, but in form and in name we are the Committee of the Privy Council. The Sovereign gives the judgment himself, and always acts upon the report which we make. Our report is made public before it is sent up to the Sovereign in Council. It is delivered here in a printed form. It is a report as to what is proper to be done on the principles of justice; and it is acted on by the Sovereign in full Privy Council; so that you see, in substance, what takes place is a strictly judicial proceeding.

The Judicial Committee is not "an English body in any exclusive sense." There may sit among its members Privy Councillors from the other member States of the Commonwealth. It has in the past been described as an "Imperial Court which represents the Empire and not any particular part of it." [3]

Composition of Committee.

The Judicial Committee is composed of the Lord Chancellor, the Lord President of the Council, and former Lords President and such members of the Privy Council as hold or have held high judicial office (including the nine Lords of Appeal in Ordinary [4]); judges or ex-judges of the superior Courts of the Dominions (or of any Colony that may be determined by Order in Council) who are Privy Councillors.[5] The Queen may also appoint two other Privy Councillors with no restrictions as to their qualifications. Any judge of a Superior Court of a Dominion (or of any Colony that may be determined by Order in Council) from which an appeal is being may heard be summoned to sit as an assessor, as also may such archbishops and bishops

---

[1] P. 503, *post*, for an example of a Judicial Order in Council.
[2] *Hull* v. *M'Kenna and Others*, [1926] I.R. 402.
[3] *Hull* v. *M'Kenna, ante.*
[4] Part V, Chap. 1.
[5] The former limitation of this class of members to seven was repealed by the Administration of Justice Act, 1928, s. 13.

as are Privy Councillors at the hearing of an ecclesiastical cause. Appeals are heard by three or more members; usually five constitute the Board, as sittings are called.

Appeals are either without the special leave of the Privy Council or with special leave. Appeals without special leave are regulated by Order in Council or local Acts or in some cases by an Act of the United Kingdom Parliament. Under such Orders or Acts the right to appeal is regulated according to the amount at stake in the suit, and in addition the local court may give leave to appeal in other cases. Where appeals lie as of right, application must first be made to the court from which the appeal comes for a decision whether there is a right under the statutory provisions applicable. The Judicial Committee will itself interpret local legislation regulating the right of appeal.[1] The Judicial Committee may always give special leave to appeal where any point of importance is involved, except when prevented from so doing by Act of Parliament or a statute made under the authority of such an Act. Right of Appeal in Civil Cases.

Appeals without special leave lie from the Supreme Courts of New Zealand, Ceylon and the six Australian States. From the Supreme Court of Canada appeal formerly lay by special leave of the Privy Council. It was restricted in 1933 to civil causes. The Canadian Parliament abolished this jurisdiction in 1949. From the High Court of the Commonwealth of Australia there is an appeal only by special leave of the Privy Council, and such leave may not be given where there are involved questions relating to the limits *inter se* of the constitutional powers of the Commonwealth and those of any State or States, or as to the limits *inter se* of the constitutional powers of any two or more States.[2] In such cases an appeal only lies where the High Court itself gives its certificate. The Commonwealth of Australia has by the express terms of the constitution (s. 74) power to impose limitations as to the right to appeal from a decision of the High Court of Australia. The Union of South Africa in 1950 abolished appeals which formerly only lay by special leave given by the Judicial Committee. Eire, before her secession, abolished appeals by special leave. No appeal lies from the courts of the Union of India or its States, or from the Pakistan Federation or States.

Appeals are not allowed in criminal matters, unless there has been a disregard of the forms of legal process, or as the result of some violation of the principles of natural justice, or otherwise, substantial and grave injustice has been done.[3] In *Knowles* v. *The King*, [1930] A.C. 366, an appeal was allowed from the decision of a judge in Ashanti, who, sitting without a jury, convicted and sentenced a man Criminal Appeals.

[1] *Davis* v. *Shaughnessy*, [1932] A.C. 106.
[2] P. 455, *ante*, text and note 3.
[3] *In re Dillett* (1887), 12 App. Cas. 459.

R

to death for murder without considering the possibility of manslaughter. In *Ras Behari Lal* v. *The King Emperor* (1933), 102 L.J. (P.C.) 144, the appeal succeeded on disclosure that a member of the jury did not understand the language in which the trial was conducted; cf. *King* v. *Thomas*, [1933] 2 K.B. 489. In *Mahlikilile Dhalamini* v. *The King*, [1942] A.C. 583, an appeal succeeded where there had been a failure to hold in public the whole of the proceedings in a murder trial.

Common-
wealth
Appeals.

While the Privy Council retains, unless and until modified or abolished by or at the wish of the member State concerned, the right to grant special leave to appeal from courts of other States in the Commonwealth, it has long been recognised that in deciding whether or not to grant special leave regard should be paid primarily to the wishes of the State concerned.[1] Until the passing of the Statute of Westminster the appeal by special leave could only be abolished by an Act of the Parliament at Westminster. In *Nadan* v. *The King*, [1926] A.C. 482; J. & Y. 111, the Judicial Committee held invalid a section of a Canadian statute abolishing appeals to the Privy Council in criminal cases. The section was repugnant to the provisions of the Judicial Committee Acts of 1833 and 1844 and was therefore void under the Colonial Laws Validity Act, 1865.[2] Furthermore the section could only be effective if construed as having extra-territorial operation, whereas according to the law at that time a Dominion Statute could not in general have extra-territorial operation.[3] A similar section was enacted in 1933 and challenged before the Privy Council, *British Coal Corporation* v. *The King*, [1935] A.C. 500; J. & Y. 159. It was argued that, though under section 2 of the Statute of Westminster Canada could enact legislation repugnant to the terms of the Judicial Committee Acts of 1833 and 1844, yet the power of the Crown to grant special leave to appeal to the Privy Council was an essential part of the royal prerogative which could only be restricted under the express authority of an Act of the Imperial Parliament. The argument was rejected. By section 91 of the British North America Act, 1867, the Dominion Parliament had power to make laws for the peace, order and good government of Canada in relation to (*inter alia*) criminal law including criminal procedure. The appeal by special leave was but one element in the general system of appeals in the Dominion. By necessary intendment section 91 of the British North America Act gave to the Dominion of Canada power to prohibit in cases within its jurisdiction the appeal to the King in Council.

---

[1] "It becomes with the Dominions more and more or less and less as they please "—Viscount Haldane in *Hull* v. *M'Kenna, supra*.
[2] P. 448, *ante*.   [3] P. 464, *ante*.

Despite certain wide statements as to Canadian sovereignty the decision in the *British Coal Corporation* case applied only to criminal appeals. It was still doubtful whether special leave to appeal in civil cases could be restricted by a Dominion Act. The chief function of the Privy Council in regard to Canadian appeals had been for many years the determination of disputes between the Dominion and the Provinces as to their respective powers under the federal constitution established by the British North America Act, 1867. The view was widely held in Canada that the Privy Council had been unduly restrictive in its construction of Dominion powers. By Bill 9 introduced into the Canadian Parliament in 1939 it was provided that the Supreme Court of Canada should exercise final and exclusive ultimate appellate civil and criminal jurisdiction within and for Canada. Appeals by special leave in civil and criminal cases would be abolished. The Bill applied to both Dominion and Provincial courts. On a reference by the Governor-General in Council the Supreme Court of Canada upheld the validity of the Bill.[1] The Judicial Committee has upheld the view of the Supreme Court of Canada in the case of *Attorney-General for Ontario* v. *Attorney-General for Canada*, [1947] A.C. 127; J. & Y. 169. Section 101 of the British North America Act, 1867, authorised the Dominion Parliament to establish a general court of appeal for Canada. The section vested in the Dominion Parliament plenary authority to legislate in regard to appellate jurisdiction. This authority was qualified only by that which lay outside the Act, namely the sovereign power of the Imperial Parliament. Since the passing of the Statute of Westminster the authority stood unqualified and absolute. Viewing the matter from a wider point of view it is not consistent with the political conception which is embodied in the British Commonwealth of Nations that one member of the Commonwealth should be precluded from setting up a supreme court of appeal having a jurisdiction both ultimate and exclusive of any other member.[2] It is now clear beyond doubt that any State may abolish the right of appeal to the Privy Council which, as stated above, now survives only in Australia, Ceylon and New Zealand.

The British Commonwealth has now reached the stage at which the link through the provision of appeals to the Judicial Committee sitting in London has worn thin. Whatever jurisdiction may remain, it will no longer fall to the Committee to act as the final interpreter of federal constitutions, in which task it has been the counterpart of the Supreme Court of the United States, in exercising jurisdiction on appeal from the Supreme Court of Canada and up to a point from Australian and Indian courts. The results have been on occasions

Future Jurisdiction.

---

[1] [1940] S.C.R. (Can.) 49.
[2] *Per* Lord Jowitt, L.C., [1947] A.C., at p. 153.

freely criticised, especially on account of the composition of the Committee on which judges of the United Kingdom unversed in the complexities of federal organisation have normally been the main, if not the exclusive, element. Yet there can be little doubt that the Committee has made great contributions towards moulding the constitutions of the older member States of the Commonwealth remote from the local political background.

Wherever the common law has been planted, outside the United States, the Judicial Committee has been the unifying agency; it has enjoyed prestige in this respect from the knowledge that most of its members are engaged in the judicial work of the House of Lords. It is apparent that far greater diversity would have developed in the common law countries without its guidance. The amount of uniformity in legal principles which was introduced by the appellate jurisdiction of the Council in the seventeenth and eighteenth centuries helped to root those principles so firmly across the Atlantic in the first British Empire that they survived the War of Independence.[1] In criminal cases the Judicial Committee has been the means of avoiding grave miscarriages of justice in colonial territories, even in recent years. Much of its jurisdiction has been outside the common law in hearing appeals from countries where Hindu or Mohammedan or Roman-Dutch law is in force. For the future its jurisdiction will mainly be restricted to appeals from colonial territories. If so, the main chapter of its history can now be written. The task may well be entrusted to lawyers who have travelled from Canada, from Australia and from India to plead before it.

[1] *H.E.L.*, Vol. X., 101.

PART XI.

CHURCH AND STATE.

Establishment in England, by Sir L. T. Dibdin (Macmillans).
Church and State in England, by Dr. Cyril Garbett (Hodder and Stoughton).
The Ecclesiastical Courts, Chaps. I–III; the Report of Archbishops' Commission, 1951–4 (S.P.C.K.).

A.

Religious Bodies.

THERE are no restrictions upon freedom of worship and with but few exceptions there are to-day no disabilities attached to membership of any particular religious community. The Church of England, however, has a special status as an established church and its consequent connection with the State will require examination. Under the provisions of the Act of Settlement the Sovereign must join in communion with the Church of England, and Roman Catholics and those who marry Roman Catholics are expressly excluded from the Throne. It is probable that a Roman Catholic may not hold the office of Lord Chancellor or High Commissioner of the Church of Scotland.[1] Religious Freedom.

The recognition by the State of religious bodies necessarily involves relationship between these bodies and the State. The position of the Church of England as an established church is special and requires separate treatment, but all other religious bodies in England can be regarded as being upon the same footing as far as their relations with the State are concerned. The Roman Catholic Church, though an international organisation, is to the constitutional lawyer in this country a non-conformist religious body distinguished from other non-conformist bodies only because Roman Catholics remain under certain statutory disabilities. Religious bodies may hold property, in relation to which the courts administer the ordinary law of charitable trusts. The courts, too, may be required to enforce and pronounce upon the validity of the rules by which religious communities are governed. Members of a religious body may bind themselves to observe rules, and tribunals may be created to enforce such laws. Such tribunals, like other domestic tribunals, may be restrained by the courts from violating their own rules or the rules of natural justice. It may be necessary for the Effects of Recognition.

---

[1] See speech of Viscount Simon, L.C.: *H.L. Deb.*, 5th Series, Vol. 127, col. 463.

courts to determine as a question of fact the nature of the doctrines of a religious community. Thus, in the famous case of *Free Church of Scotland* v. *Lord Overtoun*, [1904] A.C. 515, the House of Lords held that a majority of the members of a religious community might not, without committing a breach of trust disentitling them to hold the property of their community, change the doctrines on which the identity of the community was based.

Church of Scotland.

The Established Church of Scotland is a Presbyterian Church with only a limited connection with the State. Its preservation was an essential term of the Act of Union between England and Scotland. Church Government in Scotland is based upon the presbytery, or assembly of ministers of a district and of representative laymen, called elders. The supreme legislative and judicial body of the Scottish Church is the General Assembly. Though presided over by the Moderator—an officer of the Church—there is present at its meetings the High Commissioner, appointed by the Crown, who takes no part in discussions, but represents the connection between Church and State.

Welsh Church.

In Ireland and Wales there are now no established churches, but the Church in Wales retains in relation to marriage laws the privileges of the Established Church in England.

B.

The Church of England.

The Establishment and Patronage.

As the result of the Reformation Settlement of the sixteenth century the Church of England became a separate national church independent of the Pope. As an established church its acts and decrees are given legal sanction. The Sovereign is the Supreme Governor of the realm in all spiritual and ecclesiastical causes as well as temporal.[1] The Royal Supremacy is exercised on the advice of Ministers who are responsible to Parliament and has been subject since 1689 to parliamentary control. The Church has special privileges in relation to, *e.g.* marriage laws, the Coronation, and since 1919 legislation. Its laws are enforced by its own ecclesiastical courts. Its chief officers, the archbishops and bishops, who to the number of twenty-six sit in the House of Lords as spiritual peers [2] are appointed by the Crown, on the recommendation of the Prime Minister who is understood to consult the Archbishop of Canterbury. The Crown sends to the Dean and Chapter a *congé d'élire* with letters missive containing the name of the person who is to be elected as bishop. This permission to elect is a form only. If the election were not made, the Crown would appoint by letters patent.

---

[1] Act of Supremacy, 1558.   [2] Part III., Chap. 1.

So long as the Church of England is established, the law of the Church is part of the law of the land. Jurisdiction to enforce ecclesiastical law is divided between the ecclesiastical courts and the temporal courts.[1] Matters concerning the Church of England may be declared some in ecclesiastical courts and others in temporal courts; in the former the temporal remedies of imprisonment and money damages have no place. It is probably better to limit the term, ecclesiastical law to those subjects concerning which the law is declared exclusively by the ecclesiastical courts. Discipline of the clergy and such administrative matters as the grant of faculties and licences for marriage according to the rites of the Church of England are clear examples. But there are other subjects, such as consecration, registration, dilapidations when the temporal courts give effect to the law which can only be declared by the ecclesiastical courts. On the other hand the law of the Church administered in the temporal courts includes such matters as advowsons[2] and church property and here the ecclesiastical courts have no jurisdiction.[3]

The Church of England is divided into two provinces, the province of Canterbury and the province of York. Each province is governed by an archbishop. The Archbishop of Canterbury is not only the ruler of his own diocese and province, but is also Primate of All England and the President of the Church Assembly. Each province is divided into dioceses governed by bishops. Dioceses are divided into archdeaconries, and archdeaconries into rural deaneries. A rural deanery is composed of parishes, each with its church and parish priest. Ecclesiastical parishes do not necessarily coincide with civil parishes.[4] Parishioners, *i.e.* all who reside in a parish, have, as such, rights in relation to their parish church, *e.g.* to receive the ministrations of the clergy.

The Church may legislate for itself, but its legislation requires the consent of the State. Its forms of worship cannot be altered without the consent of Parliament.

The ancient legislative assemblies of the Church are the Con- vocations of the two provinces of Canterbury and York. In each Convocation the bishops of the province form the Upper House, and the representatives of the clergy form the Lower House. Convocation can meet only when summoned by the Crown. Its legislation takes the form of canons, which are of no effect without the

---

[1] *Attorney-General* v. *Dean and Chapter of Ripon Cathedral*, [1945] Ch. 239, at p. 245.

[2] P. 492, *post.*

[3] See *The Meaning of Ecclesiastical Law*, article by Sir Alfred Denning in 60 L.Q.R. 235 and *Attorney-General* v. *Dean and Chapter of Ripon Cathedral*, (*ante*), which decided that the statutes relating to the internal regulation of a cathedral and its services were matters for the ecclesiastical courts.

[4] Part VI., Chap. 2, C.

royal assent. Unless they subsequently receive the authorisation of Parliament or merely declare ancient custom, such canons bind only the clergy and laymen holding ecclesiastical office, *e.g.* church-wardens.

National Assembly of the Church of England.

The difficulty of obtaining proper discussion in Parliament of proposals for legislation affecting the Church and the pressure of ordinary business upon parliamentary time led in 1919 to the passing of the Church of England Assembly (Powers) Act and the setting up of a new legislative assembly for the Church under the name of the National Assembly of the Church of England. The Assembly comprises three Houses. The House of Bishops and the House of Clergy consist respectively of the members for the time being of the Upper and Lower Houses of the Convocations of Canterbury and York. The House of Laity consists of representatives elected by a system of indirect representation, the foundation of which is the parochial church council elected by parishioners on the electoral roll of each parish at the annual parochial church meeting.[1] The House may co-opt not more than ten additional members. The Assembly may pass measures to be submitted by its Legislative Committee to the Ecclesiastical Committee of Parliament, which consists of fifteen members of the House of Lords and fifteen members of the House of Commons, nominated at the beginning of each Parliament by the Lord Chancellor and the Speaker. The Ecclesiastical Committee reports to Parliament upon the expediency of measures submitted to it, especially with relation to the constitutional rights of Her Majesty's subjects. Before reporting to Parliament the Ecclesiastical Committee submits its report to the Legislative Committee of the Church Assembly and does not present the report to Parliament, unless the Legislative Committee desires it. If the report is not presented, the measure is dropped. The report and the proposed measure are laid before both Houses of Parliament, and, upon the passing by both Houses of simple resolutions to that effect, the measure is presented for the royal assent. There is no power to amend a measure. On the receipt of such assent a measure has all the force and effect of an Act of Parliament and is published in the annual volume of the statutes. This procedure preserves the control of the State, while enabling the Church to prepare its own measures with full deliberation. The formation of the Church Assembly gave to the laity for the first time an official voice in the counsels of the Church. The National Assembly is a deliberative, and not a judicial, body, and prohibition does not lie to it from the High Court: [2] *The King* v. *The Legislative Committee of the Church Assembly, ex parte Haynes-Smith*, [1928] 1 K.B. 411. The power of Parliament to legislate for

---

[1] Any member of the Church of England is entitled to be placed on the electoral roll. Those elected must be communicants.

[2] P. 319, *ante.*

the Church in the ordinary way remains unfettered, but in practice has not, since 1921, been exercised. The procedure which regulates the relationship between Parliament and the Church Assembly may form a model to be followed, should parliamentary powers ever be devolved on regional legislatures for, *e.g.* Scotland and Wales.[1]

Many churchmen consider that the House of Commons, comprising not only many non-churchmen, but even professed non-Christians, is not a fit body to legislate for the spiritual needs of the Church of England. The forms of worship of the Church of England, though not a result of parliamentary authorship, are sanctioned by parliamentary authorisation, and without such authorisation cannot be changed. The Prayer Book of the Church was given statutory force by the Act of Uniformity of 1558, and subsequent changes were authorised by Parliament in 1662 and again in 1872. The need of the sanction of King and Parliament for an alteration to the services of the Church is an essential part of the Royal Supremacy and the Establishment as regulated by the Elizabethan settlement. The dissatisfaction felt with the existing position is due to the change in conditions since the sixteenth century. In Elizabethan England there was no antithesis between Church and State. Every member of the State was a member of the Church. A conflict between Church and State meant only a conflict between the laity of the Church and Clergy. "The amalgamation of Church and State had been brought about less by the Act of Supremacy than by the admission of the laity to the churchman's privileges and of the clergy to the layman's."[2] It was expected by many that the creation of the National Assembly would avert any conflict between the Church and the State; that the House of Commons would not resist the demands of a body representing the lay as well as the clerical element in the Church of England; that spiritual freedom could thus be obtained without the need of disestablishment. These expectations were not fulfilled when there was rejected in 1927, and again in 1928, a revised Prayer Book which had been carried by a large majority in both Convocations and in the National Assembly. This rejection led to a movement for the disestablishment of the Church of England. A large body in the Church insists upon the need of complete freedom to legislate upon spiritual matters, while the fear of "Romish" tendencies in a section of the Church, combined with the ancient non-conformist hostility to Church privileges, makes it unlikely that Parliament will consent to the maintenance of the privileges of the Establishment, together with the abandonment of State control.

The law of the Church consists of (*a*) statute law, *i.e.* Acts of Parliament and, since 1921, Measures of the National Assembly,

Church and State.

The Law of the Church.

---

[1] P. 44, *ante.*
[2] A. F. Pollard, *Political History of England*, Vol. VI. (Longmans).

R*

(*b*) such canons and ancient customs as were in force in England before the Reformation and have been continuously acted upon since, and are not in conflict with the laws of the land, and (*c*) post-Reformation canons which have received the royal assent. As regards statute law, from the time of Elizabeth to the creation of the National Assembly numerous statutes have regulated Church affairs, *e.g.* Acts disestablishing the Church of Ireland (1869) and the Church of England in Wales (1914), Acts founding new dioceses, authorising the creation of new parishes, establishing the Ecclesiastical Commissioners to administer church property and providing for clerical discipline. Such matters are now dealt with by Ecclesiastical Measures in the National Assembly.

The Ecclesiastical Courts.

The ecclesiastical courts constitute a graduated hierarchy, and consist of the Court of the Archdeacon, the Consistory Court of the Bishop of each diocese, and the Provincial Court of the Archbishop of each of the two provinces. They are courts in the full sense, coordinate with the courts of common law, but administering a different system of law. An order for certiorari does not lie from the Queen's Bench Division to review their decisions; *The King* v. *Chancellor of St. Edmundsbury and Ipswich Diocese, ex parte White*, [1948] 1 K.B. 195. Prohibition lies to the ecclesiastical courts from the Queen's Bench Division when they act without jurisdiction or contrary to the rules of natural justice: *The King* v. *North, ex parte Oakey*, [1927] 1 K.B. 491. The Archdeacon's Court is to-day practically obsolete, though the Archdeacon still possesses minor rights of jurisdiction. The judge of the Consistory Court is the Chancellor of the Diocese, usually a barrister, appointed by the Bishop, from whom he derives his authority. In appointing the Chancellor the Bishop may reserve the right to exercise jurisdiction himself in matters where statutes do not prescribe a lay judge. Since the transfer in 1857 of the testamentary and matrimonial jurisdiction of the Ecclesiastical Courts to the Probate and Divorce Courts, the Consistory Courts deal mainly with moral offences by the clergy and applications for faculties for additions to and alterations in consecrated buildings. In exercising faculty jurisdiction the Chancellor is assisted by an advisory committee. The Clergy Discipline Act, 1892, provided for the assistance of the Chancellor by five assessors in the case of moral offences. An appeal always lies from the Consistory Court to the Provincial Court, in the province of Canterbury the Court of Arches, in the province of York the Chancery Court of York. The Dean of Arches is judge of both these courts.

The authority of diocesan courts has been weakened by statutes establishing special tribunals and procedure for special classes of offences. Thus doctrinal and other offences, except those involving immorality, committed by clergy against ecclesiastical law are heard, under the provisions of the Church Discipline Act, 1840, not in the Consistory Court, but by Commissioners appointed by the Bishop, of whom the Chancellor may or may not be one. Offences in respect of ritual and ceremony under the Public Worship Regulations Act, 1874, are either sent direct to the Provincial Court by letters of request from the Bishop, or are heard by consent by the Bishop himself. The Incumbents (Discipline) Measure, 1947, and the Church Dignitaries Retirement Measure, 1949, enlarge the liability of beneficed clergy and ecclesiastical dignitaries respectively for neglect of duty, including criminal conduct and immorality such as to constitute an ecclesiastical offence under the Clergy Discipline Act, 1892, which expressly excludes matters of doctrine and ritual. These Measures provide a carefully constructed judicial procedure for the assistance of the diocesan Bishop who may, however, personally investigate and deal with a complaint. There is a right of appeal to the Provincial Court against the findings of the Special Court consisting of five members presided over by the Judge of the Consistory Court which may be directed by the Bishop to hear the charges, as also against the exercise by the Bishop of his powers of censure, inhibition and declaration of a vacancy in the benefice.

The Royal Supremacy involves the right of appeal to the Crown from the Provincial Courts, unless it is excluded by statute. In 1832 the hearing of ecclesiastical appeals was transferred from the Court of Delegates to the Judicial Committee of the Privy Council [1] sitting with ecclesiastical assessors. Much dissatisfaction has been expressed with the Judicial Committee as a final court of appeal for the Church, and it has been said that disobedience and disregard of the authority of the ecclesiastical courts has been due to the fact that a lay court has been the supreme tribunal for declaring the doctrines of the Church. The system entrusts the interpretation of the formularies, the exposition of the traditions and the infliction of the spiritual censures of the Church to persons of no theological education; it grants no representation to the voice of the Church except in the utterances (which may be totally disregarded by the lay tribunal) of episcopal assessors who are alone acquainted with their purport. [2] These criticisms are considered by many to be based upon a misconception. The decision as to whether or not a given opinion is in accordance with the received doctrines of the Church involves no claim to make or unmake these doctrines. It is, however, widely felt that the supreme tribunal of the Church should have some spiritual authority, and that pronouncements as to doctrine should be made by the Church and not by a lay court. It has been suggested that in all cases in which it is necessary to determine what is the doctrine of the

Appeals to the Crown.

[1] Part X., Chap. 4.
[2] *Report of Ecclesiastical Courts Commission*, 1883.

Church of England such question should be referred to an Assembly of the Archbishops and Bishops of both provinces.

The Clergy.   The clergy, like members of the armed forces, are subject not only to special laws, but also to the ordinary laws of the land. They have certain privileges (*e.g.* exemption from jury service and compulsory national service) and also certain disabilities. The most important legal disability is that no clergyman of the Established Church of England, the Church of Ireland,[1] or the Church of Scotland can be elected to the House of Commons.[2] It has been seen that the clergy are still summoned to Parliament by the *praemunientes* clause.[3]

Property.   The Church of England is not a corporate body, and church property is the property of various corporations, sole and aggregate, which exist within the Church, *e.g.* the dean and chapter of a cathedral or the rector or vicar of a parish. There must be specially mentioned the ancient liability on all landowners to pay tithe for the benefit of the Church, mainly for the support of the parochial clergy. Tithe, originally a tenth of the fruits of the land, was commuted in 1836 for a charge upon land varying with the price of corn. The Tithe Act, 1925, stabilised tithe rent charges and provided for their payment in trust for tithe owners to Queen Anne's Bounty, a corporation originally set up to administer property restored to the Church in the reign of Queen Anne. By the Tithe Act, 1936, tithe rent charges were extinguished. Tithe owners received stock in lieu of tithe rent charges, and land subject to a tithe rent charge was made subject to the payment of a redemption annuity for a period of sixty years.

Ecclesiastical Commissioners.   The largest holders of Church property were the Ecclesiastical Commissioners. In the reign of William IV. there was a redistribution and fixing of the incomes of many bishops and cathedral chapters. The surplus income was handed over to the Ecclesiastical Commissioners, a corporation appointed by Act of Parliament, to be administered for the general benefit of the Church. In 1948 the Commissioners and those for Queen Anne's Bounty were merged in a single body, the Church Commissioners for England, by the Church Commissioners Measure, 1947. The properties of the Commission are administered by an Estates and Finance Committee consisting of three Church Estates Commissioners of whom two are appointed by the Crown and not more than four of the Church Commissioners. The Second Church Estates Commissioner is usually a member of Parliament who, though not a Minister of the Crown, replies to parliamentary questions on the Commission's affairs.

Advowsons.   An advowson is the right to present a clergyman to a benefice.

[1] P. 83, *ante.*
[2] Priests of the Roman Catholic Church also disqualified by law.
[3] P. 78, *ante.*

Advowsons are a species of property. The right to present can since 1931 only be exercised after consultation with the parochial church council. In the event of disagreement between a patron and a church council the patron may only present if he obtains the approval of the bishop of the diocese. If the bishop refuses to approve the patron's nominee, the patron may submit the bishop's decision to the archbishop of the province for review. Advowsons may be transferred, but may not be sold or transferred for valuable consideration separately from the land to which they are appendant after two vacancies have occurred subsequent to July 14, 1924.[1] Advowsons are held by laymen as well as by bishops, chapters, clerical trusts, and colleges in the older universities. Many benefices are in the patronage of the Crown, who is not bound by the provisions set out above in regard to consultation with parochial church councils.

[1] Benefices Act, 1898 (Amendment) Measure, 1923.

INDEX TO APPENDICES.

APPENDIX A. LEGISLATIVE FORMS.

APPENDIX B.   NOTE ON DOCUMENTS ISSUED BY THE CROWN

APPENDIX C.   FORMS OF PREROGATIVE AND STATUTORY INSTRUMENTS.

APPENDIX A.

Legislative Forms.[1]

TREATY OF PEACE ACT, 1919.

CHAPTER 33.

Short title.

AN Act for carrying into effect the Treaty of Peace between His Majesty and certain other Powers.

[31*st July*, 1919]

Long title.

Date of Royal Assent.

WHEREAS at Versailles, on the twenty-eighth day of June, nineteen hundred and nineteen, a Treaty of Peace (including a protocol annexed thereto), a copy of which has been laid before each House of Parliament, was signed on behalf of His Majesty, and it is expedient that His Majesty should have power to do all things as may be proper and expedient for giving effect to the said Treaty :

Preamble.

BE it enacted by the King's most Excellent Majesty, by and with the advice and consent of the Lords Spiritual and Temporal, and Commons, in this present Parliament assembled, and by the authority of the same as follows :

Enacting Clause.

1. (1) His Majesty may make such appointments, establish such offices, make such Orders in Council, and do such things as appear to him to be necessary for carrying out the said Treaty, and for giving effect to any of the provisions of the said Treaty.

Delegated Powers.

(2) Any Order in Council made under this Act may provide for the imposition, by summary process or otherwise, of penalties in respect of breaches of the provisions thereof, and shall be laid before Parliament as soon as may be after it is made, and shall have effect as if enacted in this Act, but may be varied or revoked by a subsequent Order in Council and shall not be deemed to be a statutory rule within the meaning of section one of the Rules Publication Act, 1893:

Provided that, if an address is presented to His Majesty by either House of Parliament within the next twenty-one days on which that House has sat after any Order in Council made under this Act has been laid before it praying that the Order or any part thereof may be annulled, His Majesty in Council may annul the Order or such part thereof, and it shall thenceforth be void, but without prejudice to the validity of anything previously done thereunder.

Method of Parliamentary Control of Delegated Power.

(3) Any expenses incurred in carrying out the said Treaty shall be defrayed out of moneys provided by Parliament.

2. This Act may be cited as the Treaty of Peace Act, 1919.

Citation.

[1] Excluding Statutory Instruments.

ENACTING CLAUSE (SUPPLY BILL).

MOST GRACIOUS SOVEREIGN,

We, Your Majesty's most dutiful and loyal subjects, the Commons of the United Kingdom in Parliament assembled, towards raising the necessary supplies to defray Your Majesty's public expenses, and making an addition to the public revenue, have freely and voluntarily resolved to give and grant unto Your Majesty the several duties hereinafter mentioned: and do therefore most humbly beseech Your Majesty that it may be enacted, and be it enacted by the Queen's most Excellent Majesty, by and with the advice and consent of the Lords Spiritual and Temporal, and Commons, in this present Parliament assembled, and by the authority of the same, as follows:

VOTE FOR SUPPLY SERVICES.

APPROPRIATION ACT, 1948.

Schedule (B), Part 12.

Civil—Class II.

Schedule of sums granted and of the sums which may be applied as appropriations in aid in addition thereto, to defray the charges of the several Civil Services herein particularly mentioned, which will come in course of payment during the year ending on the 31st day of March, 1949, viz.:

	Sums not Exceeding	
	Supply Grants.	Appropriation in Aid.
Vote.		
1. For the salaries and expenses of the Department of His Majesty's Secretary of State for Foreign Affairs and the salary of a Minister of State .	3,171,221	312,000
2. For the expenses in connection with His Majesty's Embassies, Missions and Consular Establishments Abroad; certain special grants and payments, including grants in aid; and sundry other services (including a supplementary sum of £350,000)	12,212,247	420,000
3. For a grant in aid of the British Council . .	2,570,000	—
4. For a contribution towards the expenses of the United Nations	915,500	—
Carried forward	18,868,968	732,000

	Sums not Exceeding	
	Supply Grants.	Appropriation in Aid.
Brought forward	18,868,968	732,000

Vote.
5. For a contribution towards the expenses of the International Refugee Organisation . . — 5,665,625 | —
6. For the salaries and expenses of the Department of His Majesty's Secretary of State for Commonwealth Relations . . . . . — 182,460 | 1,105
7. For sundry Commonwealth services, including ing certain grants in aid; for the salaries and expenses of Pensions Appeal Tribunals in Eire; for expenditure in connection with ex-service men and women in Eire; and for a grant in aid to Eire in respect of compensation to transferred officers . . . . . . — 729,785 | 1,100

8. For the salaries and expenses of the India and Pakistan Division of the Department of His Majesty's Secretary of State for Commonwealth Relations; for sundry India and Pakistan services, including a grant in aid; and for certain remanet expenditure in connection with former Burma Services (including a Supplementary sum of £401,600) . . . — 2,075,558 | 239,800
9. For the expenses connected with Oversea Settlement . . . . — 282,960 | 13,140
10. For the salaries and expenses of the Department of His Majesty's Secretary of State for the Colonies and the salary of the Minister of State for Colonial Affairs . . . . . — 789,591 | 264,375

11. For sundry Colonial and Middle Eastern Services under His Majesty's Secretary of State for the Colonies, including certain non-effective services and grants in aid . . . . — 3,287,896 | 6,200
12. For the salaries and expenses of the West African Produce Control Board, including the cost of trading services; and for a grant in aid of a sum equivalent to accumulated profits realised under the West African cocoa control scheme for allocation to the Governments of the Gold coast, Nigeria and Sierra Leone . . . — 2,044,510 | —

13. For the development of the resources of colonies, protectorates, protected states and mandated territories, and the welfare of their peoples . — 4,310,000 | —
14. For the development of the resources of the South African High Commission Territories and the welfare of their peoples . . . . — 283,000 | —
15. For certain expenses of the Imperial War Graves Commission, including purchase of land in the United Kingdom and a grant in aid . . — 690,678 | —

| Total, Civil, Class II. . . £ | 39,211,031 | 1,257,720 |

TITLE OF MEASURE OF NATIONAL ASSEMBLY.

MEASURES (20 GEO. 5)—No. 1.

A Measure passed by the National Assembly of the Church of England. To consolidate and amend the Law relating to the sale, purchase and improvement of Parsonage Houses.

[*20th March*, 1930]

TITLE OF PROVISIONAL ORDER CONFIRMATION ACT.

25 and 26 GEO. 5. c. XLV.

An Act to confirm a Provisional Order of the Minister of Transport under the Portsmouth Corporation Act, 1930, relating to Portsmouth Corporation Trolley Vehicles.

APPENDIX B.

Note on Documents issued by the Crown.[1]

SOME appreciation of the wide activities of government may best be gathered from a consideration of documents issued by the Crown and Ministers. These fall into two main classes: (1) instruments executed by, or in the name of the Queen, many of which bear Her Majesty's signature, and (2) departmental instruments. The latter category is so vast that, beyond a reproduction in Appendix C of some specimen orders, no attempt can be made to enumerate the documents which issue from the departments in the course of their administrative activities. Some figures of Statutory Instruments published in recent years, which include the more important documents of this class, have been given elsewhere.[2]

Royal instruments fall under three heads:

(1) Orders in Council.

(2) Warrants, Commissions, Instructions to Colonial Governors and Orders under the Sign Manual.

(3) Proclamations, Writs, Letters Patent, Charters, Grants and other documents under the Great Seal.

(1) By means of Orders made by the Sovereign, by and with the advice of the Privy Council, are exercised the prerogative and statutory powers of the Crown. As an example of a prerogative Order in Council may be cited colonial legislation, such as the Mauritius (Legislative Council) Order in Council, 1947, reconstituting the Legislative Council of the Colony, or the Order in Council commanding the issues of writs for the calling of a new Parliament, which accompanies the Proclamation dissolving Parliament. The statutory powers of the Crown are normally exercised by Order in Council, if they are conferred upon the Crown, as under the Foreign Jurisdiction Act, 1890, and not upon a specified Minister. The results attendant on appeals to the Judicial Committee are promulgated in this manner, the Queen in Council making an Order on the advice tendered by the Committee. While legal responsibility for Orders in Council rests upon the members of the Privy Council in attendance at the meeting (usually not more than four or five), other than the Sovereign, if present, political responsibility rests with the Minister, in whose department the draft Order is framed. *(Orders in Council.)*

(2) Documents under the Sign Manual relate both to prerogative and statutory powers. They are used to authorise administrative acts and to make appointments to office or to commissioned ranks in the Forces. *(Warrants, Commissions and Orders under the Sign Manual.)*

[1] Halsbury, *Laws of England* (3rd ed.), Vol. 7., pp. 331 ff., should be consulted on this subject. See also, Anson *Law and Custom of the Constitution*, 4th ed., Vol. 2, Part I., pp. 62–72.

[2] P. 352, *ante.*

Instructions to Colonial Governors, as well as their Commissions of Appointment, are examples of documents so executed. The term, Sign Manual, is applied to the execution by signature of instruments which require the Queen's own hand. Either the Seal of the Secretary of State concerned or the counter-signature of such Secretary or other responsible Minister is required.

The Great Seal.

(3) The Great Seal is employed for the issue of writs for parliamentary elections and to summon peers to sit in Parliament, for treaties, for Letters Patent constituting the office of Governor of a Colony and making provision for the Government thereof and for all public instruments and orders of State which relate to the whole Kingdom. It is brought into use by a Warrant under the Sign Manual, signed by the Queen's own hand and counter-signed either by the Lord Chancellor, a Secretary of State, or two Lords Commissioners of the Treasury, but in some cases it may be employed by order of the Lord Chancellor without previous authorisation by Sign Manual Warrant: Great Seal Act, 1884. Proclamations may only be issued by authority of the Crown under the Great Seal; no private person may issue a proclamation. Proclamations are valid in law on publication in the *London Gazette*; they receive judicial notice and are of the same validity as Acts of Parliament, though their lawful use is restricted to prerogative acts and calling attention to provisions of existing law: *Case of Proclamations* (1611).[1]

Letters Patent are used (*inter alia*) to constitute an office, to confer a title, to appoint a Royal Commission enquiring into an important problem of the day and to provide for the government of a colony. They must be distinguished from a Patent conferred by statutory authority under the seal of the Patent Office, granting a monopoly of making, using and selling an article of manufacture new within the realm to the first and true inventor, a purely departmental matter under the Board of Trade.

Grants and Charters confer franchises, create corporations and grant prerogative privileges, many of which are now regulated by statute.

APPOINTMENTS TO OFFICE.

The following are a few examples of the various ways in which appointments to office are effected:

Office.	*Mode of Appointment.*
Most appointments to office as Ministers of Cabinet Rank.	Delivery of Seals of Office.
Colonial Governor.	Commission under Sign Manual and Signet.
Lord President of the Council.	Declaration by the Sovereign.
Army Officer.	Commission from the Sovereign.
Naval Officer.	Commission from Lords Commissioners of the Admiralty.
Civil Service Commissioners.	Order in Council.

[1] Pp. 33–4, *ante.*

APPENDIX C.

Forms of Prerogative and Statutory Instruments.

THE object of this Appendix is to present the reader with specimens of some of the executive documents to which reference has been made from time to time. Both documents issued in the name of the Queen and specimens of departmental statutory instruments, which are a leading feature of present-day administration, are included. The authors desire to acknowledge the assistance of the Departments of State in facilitating the reproduction of certain documents and the courtesy of the Comptroller of H.M. Stationery Office in allowing the reproduction in an unofficial work of documents, the copyright of which is vested in the Crown. For the accuracy of reproduction the authors alone are responsible.

BY THE KING.

A PROCLAMATION.

Royal Proclamation.

For Dissolving the Present Parliament, and Declaring the Calling of another.
   GEORGE R.I.[1]

WHEREAS We have thought fit, by and with the advice of Our Privy Council, to dissolve this present Parliament which stands prorogued to Friday, the Twenty-fourth day of May instant; We do, for that End, publish this Our Royal Proclamation, and do hereby dissolve the said Parliament accordingly: And the Lords Spiritual and Temporal, and the Knights, Citizens, and Burgesses, and the Commissioners for Shires and Burghs, of the House of Commons, are discharged from their Meeting and Attendance on the said Friday, the Twenty-fourth day of May instant: And We being desirous and resolved, as soon as may be, to meet Our People, and to have their Advice in Parliament, do hereby make known to all Our loving Subjects Our Royal Will and Pleasure to call a new Parliament: And do hereby further declare, that, by and with the advice of Our Privy Council, We have given Order that Our Chancellor of Great Britain and Our Governor of Northern Ireland do respectively, upon Notice thereof, forthwith issue out Writs, in due Form and according to Law, for calling a new Parliament: And We do hereby also, by this Our Royal Proclamation under Our Great Seal of Our Realm, require Writs forthwith to be issued accordingly by Our said Chancellor and Governor respectively, for causing the Lords Spiritual and Temporal and Commons who are to serve in the said Parliament to be duly returned to, and give their

[1] Until 1947 the King's Title included Emperor (Imperator) of India.

Attendance in, Our said Parliament on Tuesday, the Twenty-fifth day of June next, which Writs are to be returnable in due course of Law.

> Given at Our Court of Saint James, this Tenth day of May, in the year of Our Lord One thousand nine hundred and Twenty-nine, and in the Twentieth year of Our Reign.

GOD SAVE THE KING.

A Proclamation followed commanding all the peers of Scotland to meet at the Palace of Holyroodhouse, Edinburgh, at noon on Friday, May 31, to choose the 16 peers to sit and vote in the House of Lords in the next Parliament.

Orders in Council were also gazetted as follows:

The Lord High Chancellor of Great Britain and the Governor of Northern Ireland were ordered forthwith to cause writs to be issued for the calling of a new Parliament, to meet on Tuesday, June 25.

The Convocations of Canterbury and York were forthwith dissolved, and the Lord Chancellor was to cause writs to be issued for electing new members of the Convocations. The writs were to be returnable on Wednesday, July 10.

Orders in Council.
(1) Prerogative Legislation.[1]

KENYA.

THE KENYA (ANNEXATION) ORDER IN COUNCIL, 1920.

1920, No. 2342.

At the Court at Buckingham Palace, the 11th day of June, 1920.

PRESENT,

The King's Most Excellent Majesty in Council.

WHEREAS the territories in East Africa situate within the limits of this Order and forming part of the Protectorate known as the East Africa Protectorate, are under the Protection of His Majesty the King:

And whereas British subjects have settled in large numbers in the said territories, and it is expedient, with a view to the further development and more convenient administration of the said territories, that they should be annexed to and should henceforth form part of His Majesty's Dominions:

Now, therefore, His Majesty is pleased, by and with the advice of His Privy Council, to order, and it is hereby ordered, as follows:—

I. This Order may be cited as the Kenya (Annexation) Order in Council, 1920.

II. Until further provision shall be made in respect thereof, the limits of this Order are the territories comprised in the East Africa Protectorate as specified in the East Africa Order in Council, 1902, save and excepting only such territories therein included as form part of the Dominions of His Highness the Sultan of Zanzibar.

[1] The form of an Order in Council made under statutory powers is similar.

III. From and after the coming into operation of this Order the said territories shall be annexed to and form part of His Majesty's Dominions and shall be known as the Colony of Kenya, hereinafter called the Colony.

IV. Nothing in this Order shall affect the validity of any Commission or Instructions issued by His Majesty under the Royal Sign Manual and Signet to the Governor and Commander-in-Chief of the territories now included within the limits of this Order, or of any Order in Council affecting the said territories, or of any Ordinances, Proclamation or Regulations passed or issued under any such Instructions or Order, or of any act or thing done under such Instructions, Order, Ordinance, Proclamation or Regulations, save in so far as any provision of any such Order in Council, Ordinance, Proclamation or Regulations may be repugnant to the provisions of any Act of Parliament which may, by reason of the annexation hereby declared, become extended to the Colony, or to any Order or regulation made under the authority of any such Act, or having in the Colony the force and effect of any such Act.

V. This Order shall be published in the Official Gazette of the East Africa Protectorate, and shall thereupon commence and come into operation, and the Governor shall give directions for the publication of this Order at such places and in such manner, and for such time or times, as he thinks proper for giving publicity thereto within the Colony.

VI. His Majesty may from time to time revoke, alter, add to, or amend this Order.

And the Right Honourable Viscount Milner, G.C.B., G.C.M.G., one of His Majesty's Principal Secretaries of State, is to give the necessary directions herein accordingly.

ALMERIC FITZROY.

JUDICIAL ORDER IN COUNCIL.

At the Court at Buckingham Palace, the 26th day of June, 1930.

PRESENT,

The King's Most Excellent Majesty.

Lord President.	Lord Colebrooke.
Lord Passfield.	Lord Blanesburgh.

Orders in Council. (2) Order on Report of Judicial Committee of Privy Council.

WHEREAS there was this day read at the Board a Report from the Judicial Committee of the Privy Council dated the 23rd day of June, 1930, in the words following, viz.:

WHEREAS by virtue of His late Majesty King Edward the Seventh's Order in Council of the 18th day of October 1909 there was referred unto this Committee the matter of an Appeal from the Supreme Court of Canada between the Trustees of St. Luke's Presbyterian Congregation of Saltsprings a body Corporate Alex. C. Macdonald William Fraser William H. Mackay D. Hedley Ross Munro Gunn Robert A. Robertson George Gray Roderick Mackay and John R. Young Appellants and Alexander Cameron Gordon Proudfoot C. A. Maxwell K. A. Murray John Bishop W. C. Proudfoot Robert Johnston John McN. Campbell and Alexander Halliday Respondents (Privy Council Appeal No. 98 of 1929) and likewise a humble Petition of the Appellants setting forth that on the 1st September 1925 the Respondents brought an Action in the Supreme Court of Nova Scotia alleging that in accordance with the United Church of Canada Act (Statutes of Canada 14-15 Geo. 5, c. 100) the St. Luke's Presbyterian Congregation of Saltsprings at a meeting regularly called and held decided by a majority of votes not to enter the Union of Churches provided for by the Act; that under the Act and the Nova Scotia Act c. 122 of the Acts of 1924 the congregation became and was a non-concurring congregation and that an alleged subsequent meeting of the congregation held on or about the 27th July 1925 and all proceedings thereat were null and void and of no effect and the Respondents claimed declarations injunctions and other relief: that on the 2nd February 1926 the Supreme Court delivered judgment dismissing the Respondents' Action: that the Respondents having appealed to the Supreme Court of Nova Scotia *in banco* the Court by a majority (Mellish J. dissenting) on the 9th April 1927 delivered judgment allowing the Appeal: that the Appellants having appealed and the Respondents having cross-appealed to the Supreme Court of Canada the Court on the 5th February 1929 delivered Judgment by a majority (Duff J. dissenting) varying the Judgment of the Supreme Court of Nova Scotia *in banco* by striking out the fourth paragraph thereof containing the declaration that the congregation might still enter the Union and suspending the enforcement of the Judgment and subject to such variation affirming the Judgment: that by Your Majesty's Order in Council dated the 15th August 1929 the Appellants were granted special leave to appeal upon depositing in the Registry of the Privy Council the sum of £400 as security for costs which condition has since been complied with; And humbly praying Your Majesty in Council to take their Appeal into consideration and that the Judgment of the Supreme Court of Canada dated the 5th February 1929 may be reversed altered or varied or for further or other relief:

THE LORDS OF THE COMMITTEE in obedience to His late Majesty's said Order in Council have taken the appeal and humble Petition into consideration and having heard Counsel on behalf of the parties on both sides Their Lordships do this day agree humbly to report to Your Majesty as their opinion (1) that the Judgment of the Supreme Court of Nova Scotia *in banco* dated the 9th day of April 1927 as varied by the Judgment of the Supreme Court of Canada dated the 5th day of February 1929 ought to be further varied by deleting from the second paragraph thereof sub-paragraph "(2) that the Reverend Robert Johnston was at all material times and is Moderator *pro tempore* or *interim* Moderator of the said congregation" and also by deleting from the third paragraph thereof the following words with which that paragraph concludes: "and from interfering with the exercise by the Plaintiff Robert Johnston of the rights powers and privileges of the office of Moderator *pro tempore* or *interim* Moderator of the said congregation"; (2) that in all other respects this Appeal ought to be dismissed and the Judgment of the Supreme Court of Canada dated the 5th day of February 1929 affirmed; and (3) that there ought to be paid by the Appellants to the Respondents their costs of this

Appeal incurred in the Supreme Court of Canada and that out of the said sum of £400 so deposited as aforesaid the Registrar of the Privy Council ought to be directed to pay out to the Solicitors for the Respondents in England the sum of £361 12s. 10d. (being the amount of the Respondents' taxed costs of this Appeal incurred in England) and to repay to the Solicitors for the Appellants in England the sum of £38 7s. 2d. (being the balance of the said sum of £400 after payment thereout of the said taxed costs of the Respondents).

His Majesty having taken the said Report into consideration was pleased by and with the advice of His Privy Council to approve thereof and to order as it is hereby ordered that the same be punctually observed obeyed and carried into execution.

Whereof the Governor-General or Officer Administering the Government of the Dominion of Canada for the time being and all other persons whom it may concern are to take notice and govern themselves accordingly.

M. P. A. Hankey.

STATUTORY RULES AND ORDERS,[1] 1942, No. 2072.

EMERGENCY POWERS (DEFENCE).

Location of Industry (Restriction).

(1) Order made under a Defence (statutory) Regulation.

The Location of Industry (Restriction) Order, 1942, dated October 6, 1942, made by the Board of Trade under Regulation 55A of the Defence (General) Regulations, 1939.

The Board of Trade in pursuance of the powers conferred upon them by Regulation 55A of the Defence (General) Regulations, 1939, hereby order as follows:—

1. No person shall, except under the authority of a licence granted by the Board of Trade and in accordance with conditions attached thereto, carry on at any premises situated in Great Britain.

(a) (being premises which on the 26th July, 1941, had been, or were being used, otherwise than as a factory or a warehouse), any trade or business which would cause those premises to be either a factory or a warehouse; or

(b) (being premises which on the 26th July, 1941, had been, or were being used, as a factory or warehouse) any trade or business which was not being carried on to a substantial extent by that person at those premises on that date.

2. This Order shall not apply to a local authority.

3. For the purposes of this Order:—

(a) the expression "factory" has the meaning assigned in Section 151 of the Factories Act, 1937.

(b) the expression "local authority" has the meaning assigned in Regulation 100 of the Defence (General) Regulations, 1939.

(c) the expression "warehouse" means any premises used for the purposes of storing articles of any description, not being vehicles

[1] From 1948 called Statutory Instruments.

(other than motor vehicles or pedal cycles, carrier cycles and tricycles) or vessels.

4.—(1) The Location of Industry (Restriction) Order, 1941 **(b)**, is hereby revoked.

(2) Any licence granted by the Board of Trade under the Order hereby revoked which was in force immediately before the coming into operation of this Order shall continue in force, and shall have effect as if it had been issued hereunder.

(3) Nothing in this Order shall prohibit any person from continuing to carry on any trade or business which he could lawfully have continued to carry on if the Order hereby revoked had remained in force.

5. This Order may be cited as the Location of Industry (Restriction) Order, 1942, and shall come into operation on the 12th day of October, 1942.

Dated this sixth day of October, 1942.

R. J. W. STACY,
An Assistant Secretary
of the Board of Trade.

(b) S.R. & O. 1941 (No. 1100) II, p. 1370.

EXPLANATORY NOTE.[1]

By this Order, the obligation to obtain a licence from the Regional Offices of the Control of Factory and Storage Premises before changing the use to which a factory or warehouse of 3,000 square feet or over is put, or using any premises of that size for production or storage purposes, is now extended to premises below 3,000 square feet.

This Order replaces the earlier Order, but existing licences are not affected, nor does the Order impose any obligation to apply for a licence in order to continue to carry on business in premises which were exempt under the earlier Order.

The General Storage Licence issued under the earlier Order remains in force. This General Licence permits goods to be stored temporarily for 28 days without a licence.

(2) Demolition Order, Form of, under Housing Act, 1936, s. 11. Schedule to Housing Act (Form of Orders and Notices) Regulations, 1937.	<div align="center">**ORDER FOR DEMOLITION OF A HOUSE.**</div> Whereas the [Council of　　　　　　] (hereinafter referred to as "the Council") are satisfied that the house　　　　which is occupied, or of a type suitable for occupation, by persons of the working classes, is unfit for human habitation, and is not capable at a reasonable expense of being rendered so fit; and Whereas in accordance with the requirements of section 11 of the Housing Act, 1936, notices of the time and place fixed for the consideration of the condition of the above-mentioned house and any offer with respect to the carrying out of works or the future user of the house have been duly

[1] An explanatory note is not an operative part of a statutory instrument and may not, therefore, be used to assist interpretation of the instrument by a court of law.

served upon all persons upon whom such notices are required to be served;

and Whereas the Council after such consideration have not accepted an undertaking from an owner or mortgagee with respect to the carrying out of such works or the future user of the house:

Now Therefore the Council in pursuance of sub-section (4) of section 11 of the Housing Act, 1936, hereby order as follows:—

(1) that the said house be vacated within   days from the date on which this Order becomes operative:

(2) the said dwelling-house be demolished within six weeks after the expiration of the last-mentioned period, or if the house is not vacated before the expiration of that period, within six weeks after the date on which it is vacated.

Dated this   day of   19 .

(To be sealed with the Common Seal of the Local Authority and signed by their clerk.)

NOTE.

Any person aggrieved by a demolition order .... may within 21 days after the date of the service of the Order appeal to the County Court.................. No proceedings may be taken by the local authority to enforce any order against which an appeal is brought, before the appeal has been finally determined...................

PATENT FOR CREATION OF A PEER.

ELIZABETH THE SECOND by the Grace of God of the United Kingdom of Great Britain and Northern Ireland and of her other realms and territories. Queen, Head of the Commonwealth, Defender of the Faith, To all Lords Spiritual and Temporal and all other Our Subjects whatsoever to whom these Presents shall come Greeting Know Ye that We of Our especial grace certain knowledge and mere motion do by these Presents advance create and prefer Our   to the state degree style dignity title and honour of Baron   of in Our County of   And for Us Our heirs and successors do appoint give and grant unto him the said name state degree style dignity title and honour of Baron   to have and to hold unto him and the heirs male of his body lawfully begotten and to be begotten Willing and by these Presents granting for Us Our heirs and successors that he and his heirs male aforesaid and every of them successively may have hold and possess a seat place and voice in the Parliaments and Public Assemblies and Councils of Us Our heirs and successors within Our United Kingdom amongst other Barons And also that he and his heirs male aforesaid successively may enjoy and use all the rights privileges pre-eminences immunities and advantages to the degree of a Baron duly and of right belonging which other Barons of Our United Kingdom have heretofore used and enjoyed or as they do at present use nd enjoy.

In Witness, &c.

Letters Patent. Form for creation of Baron.

APPOINTMENT OF AMBASSADOR.

ELIZABETH R.

ELIZABETH, by the Grace of God, of the United Kingdom of Great Britain and Northern Ireland, and of her other realms and territories Queen, Head of the Commonwealth, Defender of the Faith

To All and Singular to whom these Presents shall come, Greeting!

Whereas it appears to Us expedient to nominate some Person of approved Wisdom, Loyalty, Diligence, and Circumspection to represent Us in the character of Our Ambassador Extraordinary and Plenipotentiary to

Now Know Ye that We, reposing especial trust and confidence in the discretion and faithfulness of Our (Right) Trusty and Well-beloved (Counsellor) (Sir).. have nominated, constituted and appointed, as We do by these Presents nominate, constitute and appoint him the said

to be Our Ambassador Extraordinary and Plenipotentiary to

as aforesaid. Giving and Granting to him in that character

all Power and Authority to do and perform all proper acts, matters and things which may be desirable or necessary for the promotion of relations of friendship, good understanding and harmonious intercourse between our Realm and

and for the protection and furtherance of the interests confided to his care; by the diligent and discreet accomplishment of which acts, matters and things aforementioned he shall gain Our approval and show himself worthy of Our high confidence.

And We therefore request all those whom it may concern to receive and acknowledge Our said

as such Ambassador Extraordinary and Plenipotentiary as aforesaid and freely to communicate with him upon all matters which may appertain to the objects of the high Mission whereto he is hereby appointed.

Given at Our Court of Saint James, the   day of
in the year of Our Lord One Thousand Nine Hundred and
and in the   Year of Our Reign.

By Her Majesty's Command.

(Countersigned by One of Her Majesty's Principal Secretaries of State.)

FREE PARDON.

ELIZABETH THE SECOND, by the Grace of God, of the United Kingdom of Great Britain, and Northern Ireland and of her other realms and territories Queen, Head of the Commonwealth, Defender of the Faith. To all to whom these Presents shall come, Greeting!

WHEREAS A.B.   was convicted of
            and was thereupon sentenced to

Now KNOW YE that We in consideration of some circumstances humbly represented to Us are graciously pleased to extend Our Grace and Mercy to the said A.B.   and to grant him Our Free Pardon in respect of the said conviction, thereby pardoning, remitting and releasing unto him all pains penalties and punishments whatsoever that from the said conviction may ensue; and We do hereby command the Judges, Justices and others whom it may concern that they take due notice hereof; and We do require and direct our Prison Commissioners and the Governor of any Prison in which the said A.B.
            may be detained in respect of the said conviction to cause him to be forthwith discharged therefrom;
    And for so doing this shall be a sufficient Warrant.
    Given at Our Court at St. James's the   day of
19   in the   year of Our reign.

    By Her Majesty's Command.

    (Countersigned by One of Her Majesty's Principal Secretaries of State.)

GENERAL INDEX.

Note.—Where two or more references are given to the same subject, the principal references (if any) are shown in thicker type.

A

s